ECOLOGY AND POWER IN THE AGE OF EMPIRE

Ecology and Power in the Age of Empire

Europe and the Transformation of the Tropical World

COREY ROSS

OXFORD
UNIVERSITY PRESS

OXFORD

UNIVERSITY PRESS

Great Clarendon Street, Oxford, OX2 6DP,
United Kingdom

Oxford University Press is a department of the University of Oxford.
It furthers the University's objective of excellence in research, scholarship,
and education by publishing worldwide. Oxford is a registered trade mark of
Oxford University Press in the UK and in certain other countries

© Corey Ross 2017

The moral rights of the author have been asserted

First edition published 2017

Published in the United States of America by Oxford University Press
198 Madison Avenue, New York, NY 10016, United States of America

British Library Cataloguing in Publication Data
Data available

Library of Congress Control Number: 2016956622

ISBN 978-0-19-959041-4

Cover images: (Front): TM-10028392: Cleared terrain on a rubber plantation
overlooking Wijnkoopsbaai (now Pelabuhan Ratu Bay), Sukabumi Regency, western
Java, 1929. By permission of the Nationaal Museum van Wereldculturen, coll. N.
10028392; (Back): TM-60044579: Drill site of the Bataafsche Petroleum Maatschappij,
Tarakan Island, off north-eastrn Borneo, 1915-24. By permission of the Nationaal
Museum van Wereldculturen, coll. no. 60044579.

Preface

This book has been quite some time in the making. In some ways its origins reach back over a quarter-century, when I was torn between undergraduate degrees in Biology and History, and ended up studying both. Against the odds, it was History that eventually gained the upper hand, though I always retained a keen interest in environmental issues that was first kindled in my childhood and was strongly reinforced while I was a student. Looking back, it seems almost inevitable that these two interests would eventually merge. Around eight years ago, when I was pondering what to do next after completing my last project, the decision to move into environmental history was an easy one—far easier, as I found out, than the actual work that it required. Here, at long last, is the result.

One of the best, and simultaneously worst, aspects of moving into a new subfield of history is the steep learning curve that goes along with it. In my case, climbing the curve would have been far more difficult were it not for the generous advice and encouragement of numerous colleagues and friends. A special word of thanks goes to Frank Uekötter, who has not only read and critiqued the entire manuscript, but who has also been an invaluable and almost frighteningly knowledgeable conversation partner on nearly all matters relating to environmental history. He, Max Bolt, Francesca Carnevali, Reginald Cline-Cole, Peter Coates, Matthew Hilton, Simon Jackson, Sabine Lee, Su Lin Lewis, and Tom McCaskie all read parts of the manuscript in some form or other, and are likewise owed a big favour for their help. I wish that I could repay my debt to Francesca, for this and for many other things; it is now more than three years since she died, and her absence is still keenly felt by all of us who had the privilege of her friendship.

There were many others who (knowingly or unknowingly) helped my thinking along the way, among them Gareth Austin, Paul Betts, William Gervase Clarence-Smith, Geoff Eley, Bernhard Gißibl, Hugh Gorman, Tait Keller, Miles Larmer, Tim LeCain, John MacKenzie, Stuart McCook, John McNeill, Jean-François Mouhot, Simon Pooley, Julia Adeney Thomas, Richard Tucker, and Kim Wagner. My thanks to all of you, and to my colleagues in the History Department and the College of Arts and Law at Birmingham for providing such a stimulating place to work. Of course, historians cannot live on advice alone, so I would also like to express my gratitude to the British Academy for its generous financial support for the project. In addition, some of the ideas and arguments were presented at various forums in Oxford, London, Munich, Turku, Guimarães, Geneva, Paris, and Versailles, and I am grateful for the suggestions that I received there.

I would also like to thank the editors of the *Journal of Global History* for permission to reproduce sections of 'The Plantation Paradigm: Colonial Agronomy, African Farmers and the Global Cocoa Boom, 1870s–1940s', *Journal of Global History* vol. 9, no. 1 (Mar. 2014), 49–71; the editors of *Environmental History* for allowing me to reproduce parts of 'The Tin Frontier: Mining, Empire and

Environment in Southeast Asia, 1870s–1930s', *Environmental History* vol. 19 (2014), 454–79; and the editors of *Past & Present* for permission to reproduce sections of 'Tropical Nature as Global *Patrimoine*: Imperialism and International Nature Protection in the Early Twentieth Century', in: Paul Betts, Corey Ross (eds), *Heritage in the Modern World: Historical Preservation in Global Perspective* (supplement of the journal *Past & Present*, 2015), 214–39. All of this material is acknowledged in the chapters where it appears. Illustrations are reproduced with the permission of the Nationaal Museum van Wereldculturen, the National Archives Image Library, and Oxford University Press. For those illustrations where no credit is indicated, every reasonable effort has been made to contact all copyright holders, and any omissions will be rectified in subsequent printings if notice is given to the publishers.

My final thanks go to my parents, Charles and Charlotte, for first instilling in me a curiosity about the natural world and our place within it, and to Deborah, Alex, and Tessa for cheerfully (most of the time, anyway) indulging my interest in talking about such things.

Corey Ross

Birmingham
July 2016

Contents

List of Illustrations

Introduction
Ecology, Power, and Imperialism

Since the turn of the twenty-first century, the world has been witnessing what most commentators have called a 'global land grab'—that is, a wave of large-scale land acquisitions, primarily in the global South, by corporations and by states eager to gain control over resources beyond their own borders. Just how much land has changed hands is difficult to pin down due to the dearth of firm data, uncertainty about ownership status, and ambiguity surrounding the types of transactions that are counted. But in any event, it is clear that the area involved is huge. Since 2000, the Land Matrix (an independent monitoring coalition of NGOs, academics, and sponsoring agencies) has recorded over 1,230 separate land deals covering nearly 44 million hectares worldwide.[1] This equates to an area approximately the size of Sweden, but observers are in no doubt that it represents only the tip of the iceberg. Other estimates, for what they are worth, suggest that the tally might well exceed 200 million hectares, which is roughly equivalent to the surface of Western Europe. Although most of the purchases have taken place in sub-Saharan Africa, large areas of Southeast Asia and Latin America have also been bought up by foreign governments and investors. And although the global food insecurities that stimulated many of these acquisitions have somewhat subsided since the acute food crisis of 2007/8, on current trends the transactions are not likely to slow down any time soon.[2]

It is clear what has been driving this process: above all the spectre of worldwide food shortages, growing water shortages, and international commitments to raise the proportion of plant-based biofuels, with further acquisitions arising from mining interests, tourism, and even conservation initiatives (so-called 'green grabbing'[3]).

---

[1] Estimate as of July 2016: <http://www.landmatrix.org/en/>.

[2] There has been a huge outpouring of literature on the subject. For recent overviews, see Mayke Kaag and Annelies Zoomers (eds), *The Global Land Grab: Beyond the Hype* (London: Zed, 2014); Marc Edelman, Carlos Oya, and Saturnino M. Borras Jr (eds), *Global Land Grabs*, special issue of *Third World Quarterly*, vol. 34 no. 9 (2013); Alexander Reid Ross (ed.), *Grabbing Back: Essays Against the Global Land Grab* (Oakland, Calif.: AK Press, 2013); Lorenzo Cotula, *The Great African Land Grab? Agricultural Investment and the Global Food System* (London: Zed, 2013); Wendy Wolford, Saturnino M. Borras, Jr, Ruth Hall, Ian Scoones, and Ben White (eds), *Governing Global Land Deals: The Role of the State in the Rush for Land* (Chichester: Wiley, 2013).

[3] James Fairhead, Melissa Leach, and Ian Scoones, 'Green Grabbing: A New Appropriation of Nature?', *Journal of Peasant Studies*, vol. 39 no. 2 (2012), 237–61; Benjamin Gardner, 'Tourism and the Politics of the Global Land Grab in Tanzania: Markets, Appropriation and Recognition', *Journal of Peasant Studies*, vol. 39 no. 2 (2012), 377–402.

It is likewise fairly clear who has been driving it: chiefly international agribusinesses, investment banks, sovereign wealth funds, and forestry corporations hungry for land. And it is abundantly clear that, despite all the assurances of economic benefits and corporate social responsibility, many deals are done secretly, local groups are often not consulted, compensation is frequently lacking or less than what had originally been promised, and people are losing land as a result.

By no means is this all a matter of 'North–South' exploitation. China, India, various Gulf States, and 'Asian Tigers' also number among the main investor countries alongside Europe and the United States, which reflects the increasingly multipolar framework of the global economy. Nor is it simply a case of external versus internal interests, since many of the resources that are changing hands have long been the subject of competing local claims. Throughout the developing world, political and economic elites keen to attract outside investment in order to 'modernize' their rural economies argue that the land in question is underused, idle, or uninhabited, which is very often not the case. Since the purchases generally involve relatively fertile tracts with adequate water availability and transport connections, the impact on local livelihoods is disproportionately large. In a curious twist of the concept of 'economic development', vast territories in countries receiving food aid are now used to grow crops (both food and non-food) destined solely for export to wealthier countries. Furthermore, since the acquired tracts are generally earmarked for intensive production, they commonly end up being degraded by the familiar problems of deforestation, mono-cropping, and agrochemical usage.[4]

In short, the world has been witnessing a process of ecological imperialism in which powerful countries and organizations have tapped huge resource subsidies in other parts of the world as a means of overcoming the ecological limits that their own territories place on economic growth and commercial activity. Political and economic power has remade global ecology, and ecological constraints have profoundly shaped global politics and economic arrangements. It is a worldwide lesson in the subject of 'political ecology'—that is, the study of how wealth and power are produced and distributed (the focus of classical political economy) and how ecosystems constitute the ultimate source of both.[5] Seen from this perspective, wealth and power are based not only on the social construction of human productive activity, but also on the ability to modify the rest of the biosphere and harness its productivity for human purposes. Whenever this power is used to establish, maintain, or assist a regime in which foreign actors control, exploit, and seek to benefit from the natural assets of other, less powerful territories, there is good reason to regard it as a form of imperialism.[6]

---

[4] Kaag and Zoomers (eds), *The Global Land Grab*, 201–16 and *passim*.

[5] Richard Peet, Paul Robbins, and Michael Watts (eds), *Global Political Ecology* (London: Routledge, 2011); Paul Robbins, *Political Ecology: A Critical Introduction* (Chichester: Wiley, 2012); Philip Stott and Sian Sullivan (eds), *Political Ecology: Science, Myth and Power* (London: Arnold, 2000).

[6] For our purposes, 'imperialism' can be elementally defined as a form of domination imposed by one society over another in which the two are incorporated in a differentiated hierarchy that works to the advantage of the dominant party.

Despite the peculiarities of the twenty-first-century 'global land grab', in many respects it is not entirely new. Far from it: defining other people's land as underused, alienating it for purportedly more productive purposes, forging alliances between external and internal interests in order to exploit a territory's resources, and presenting it all as a contribution to human progress have an extremely long historical pedigree.

Our concern in the pages that follow is to explore the relationship between ecology and imperial power in the past, and to consider how earlier changes have come to shape the global biosphere today. This is a topic that could take us to many different times and places; empires are, after all, among the most persistent features of human history, and contests over natural resources are more pervasive still. But when seeking to understand the world in which we currently live, it makes sense to start with the last great imperial expansion in human history, indeed the largest one ever seen, when a handful of European powers extended the territory under their control by no less than 23 million km²—around one-fifth of the entire world land surface—during the late nineteenth and early twentieth centuries. Together, these empires connected disparate peoples over vast areas; they redrew political maps on a global scale; they crafted much of the architecture of worldwide trade; and, in the process, they helped create and amplify inequalities of wealth and power that are still visible today. Without a doubt, European imperialism was a central feature of modern world history. Few aspects of the contemporary world are untouched by its legacies.

At the same time, the spread of European power was also a central feature of global environmental history.[7] The unprecedented appetite for raw materials in the industrial metropoles generated enormous demands on natural resources in the rest of the world, from croplands and forests to mineral and energy deposits. It spawned a range of different methods for extracting wealth from nature, from plantations and mining complexes to new forms of agriculture and 'rational' land management systems. It stimulated a huge increase in the traffic of living organisms around the globe. At the heart of European imperialism was an attempt to transform forests, savannahs, rivers, coastal plains, and deserts into productive and legible spaces, all of which brought hefty environmental consequences: deforestation, erosion, siltation, pollution, disease, and habitat destruction. Eventually these consequences encouraged the formation of extensive counter-attempts to conserve soil, woodlands, game, and other resources. European imperialism thus engendered not only new ways to exploit the physical environment, but also new anxieties about the human impact on the rest of nature.

Reordering environmental relationships and altering ecosystems was an integral part of modern imperialism, and the basic aim of this book is to examine how this process unfolded during the late nineteenth and twentieth centuries. It considers the efforts of colonizers to transform nature for human purposes, as well as the constraints that moulded this endeavour and the unintended consequences that

---

[7] On the relationship between global and world history (as well as other types of history), see Diego Adrián Olstein, *Thinking History Globally* (Basingstoke: Palgrave, 2015).

often resulted. It not only focuses on intensive exploitation by rapacious entrepreneurs and revenue-hungry political elites (though there is plenty of this), but also investigates the ambivalent motivations of colonial conservation efforts and the outcomes of attempts to place production regimes on a more sustainable footing. Despite the huge and often destructive environmental transformations that it charts, it does not provide a narrative of inexorable degradation at the hands of European imperialists, since Europeans were by no means the sole agents of change, and not all change can be regarded as despoliation in any event. The story therefore features a range of different groups, motives, and interests, from international corporations to indigenous smallholders and from plantation owners to conservation advocates. Most importantly, perhaps, it is not just about people but about their relationship with the ecosystems in which they were themselves embedded: the soil, water, plants, and animals that were likewise a part of Europe's empire.[8]

ECOLOGY AND IMPERIAL HISTORY

Such ecological entwinements were a fundamental feature of the imperial past—so elemental, it would seem, as to be easily overlooked. Despite the pervasive presence of ecological dynamics in the history of empire, the physical environment has often gone unheeded or been relegated to the role of raw materials, climatic events, or the incentive for new forms of bio-political governance. But human activity always has an ecological dimension, regardless of whether historians choose to focus on it. Given the manifold biophysical interconnections that were involved in the global spread of European power, it is useful to conceive of colonialism not so much as a social project with ecological consequences, but as a socio-ecological project (or better: series of projects) in and of itself. In essence it was a process of modification and subjugation that sought to reorder nature–society arrangements across large parts of the globe.[9] How this process unfolded throughout the colonial world, and the transformations that it entailed, are the central concern of this book.

Although ecology rarely occupies centre stage in histories of empire, the role of imperialism in reshaping the biosphere is hardly unknown territory. Ever since the appearance of Alfred Crosby's *Columbian Exchange* (1972) and *Ecological Imperialism* (1986), it has been widely recognized that Europe's overseas expansion powerfully reordered global ecology since the early modern period, just as environmental factors played a central role in the process of European conquest.[10] There

---

[8] On Europe and the colonial encounter generally: Dipesh Chakrabarty, *Provincializing Europe: Postcolonial Thought and Historical Difference* (Princeton: Princeton University Press, 2000); Jane Burbank and Frederick Cooper, *Empires in World History: Power and the Politics of Difference* (Princeton: Princeton University Press, 2010).

[9] I draw here on Jason W. Moore, "'Amsterdam is Standing on Norway' Part II: The Global North Atlantic in the Ecological Revolution of the Long Seventeenth Century', *Journal of Agrarian Change*, vol. 10 (2010), 188–227.

[10] Alfred Crosby, *The Columbian Exchange: Biological and Cultural Consequences of 1492* (Westport, Conn.: Greenwood, 1972); Alfred Crosby, *Ecological Imperialism: The Biological Expansion of Europe, 900–1900* (Cambridge: Cambridge University Press, 1986).

is an excellent though hardly copious literature that surveys the manifold environmental ramifications of Europe's maritime empires, including the inter-continental transfer of plants, animals, and microbes; the imperial origins of conservationist thought; as well as the rise of scientific networks and 'imperial improvement' efforts in the eighteenth and nineteenth centuries.[11] By comparison, the relationship between imperialism and environmental change during the late nineteenth and twentieth centuries has been studied in a more piecemeal fashion, despite the fact that this period marked the apogee of Europe's global dominance, and despite the important role played by environmental factors—climate, disease, flora, fauna, natural resources—in shaping the geography of European empire.

This is all the more striking when one considers the changes that were under way at the time. The final third of the nineteenth century saw the convergence of four interrelated developments that together unleashed an unprecedented transformation of the global environment. Innovations in transportation and communications (submarine telegraph cables from the 1860s, the Suez Canal in 1869, the huge proliferation of steamships thereafter) laid the foundations for an explosive growth in worldwide trade and commodity production.[12] The key engine behind this growth was the spread of industrialization and new technologies in Europe (the so-called 'second industrial revolution'), which created an enormous demand for plant and mineral resources, many of them from overseas. In turn, lower shipping and production costs led to higher living standards and a sharp rise in European consumer demand, including for many 'exotic' goods previously regarded as luxuries. At the same time, a string of military and medical advances— the so-called 'tools of empire'[13]—were making the tropics a far safer place for Europeans to operate. Together, this bundle of interrelated factors, in the context of intense rivalry between European states, helped propel the rush for overseas territories during the late nineteenth century—above all in sub-Saharan Africa and Southeast Asia—and ushered in a new phase of global political and economic reorganization under European aegis.

Many aspects of this story have been told before, from the economic penetration of hitherto remote areas to the rise of indigenous resistance movements to the cultural (re)orientations that fuelled, moulded, and emerged out of Europe's

---

[11] Richard Drayton, *Nature's Government: Science, Imperial Britain, and the 'Improvement' of the World* (New Haven: Yale University Press, 2000); John R. McNeill, *Mosquito Empires: Ecology and War in the Greater Caribbean, 1620–1914* (Cambridge: Cambridge University Press, 2010); Richard H. Grove, *Green Imperialism: Colonial Expansion, Tropical Island Edens and the Origins of Environmentalism, 1600–1860* (Cambridge: Cambridge University Press, 1995); Lucile H. Brockway, *Science and Colonial Expansion: The Role of the British Royal Botanic Gardens* (New York: Academic Press, 1979); Alan Mikhail, *Nature and Empire in Ottoman Egypt: An Environmental History* (Cambridge: Cambridge University Press, 2011).

[12] Valeska Huber, *Channelling Mobilities: Migration and Globalisation in the Suez Canal Region and Beyond, 1869–1914* (Cambridge: Cambridge University Press, 2013); Daniel R. Headrick, *The Invisible Weapon: Telecommunications and International Politics, 1851–1945* (Oxford: Oxford University Press, 1992).

[13] Daniel R. Headrick, *The Tools of Empire: Technology and European Imperialism in the Nineteenth Century* (Oxford: Oxford University Press, 1981); Daniel R. Headrick, *The Tentacles of Progress: Technology Transfer in the Age of Imperialism, 1850–1940* (Oxford: Oxford University Press, 1988).

imperial projects. Yet amidst the vast literature on modern empire one still finds relatively little about the far-reaching ecological transformation of the tropical world and how it both shaped and was shaped by these other developments. To be sure, there are many excellent studies of the environmental history of particular areas and topics, and the following pages draw on them extensively and apprecia-tively. But this specialist literature is, for one thing, remarkably uneven, with some themes and regions (such as forestry in India) receiving vastly more attention than others (such as mining in Southeast Asia). Furthermore, there has so far been little attempt to draw together these disparate strands and to situate them within the wider context of global environmental change. This book accordingly follows a twofold rationale: to deepen our understanding of some of the less-familiar sides of the story, and to integrate them into a broader synthetic framework.

Both of these aims require us to transcend the confines of individual empires, and in particular to look beyond the dominant imperial power of the period. Like so many aspects of the history of modern imperialism—and probably more than most—research on its environmental dimensions has centred overwhelmingly on the British experience. To some extent this mirrors the sheer size and significance of the British Empire, but it also partly reflects the inevitable boundaries of linguistic and regional expertise. To date, the only wide-ranging overview is William Beinart and Lotte Hughes's *Environment and Empire*, which surveys a broad array of topics over several centuries but is solely devoted to the British Empire.[14] Much the same applies to the bulk of edited collections on the subject.[15] By contrast, this study expressly includes the other major European empires—above all those of France, Germany, the Netherlands, and Belgium (with Portugal, Spain, and Italy featuring more on the margins)—whose environmental histories have attracted far less scholarly attention to date. It draws on the literature available in English, German, French, and Dutch, and makes extensive use of contemporary material from a range of different sources. Its focus on the colonies of Western European states is not to deny the importance of other imperial projects, whether Russian, Ottoman, Japanese, or American (all of which feature below), but is simply intended to reflect their predominant collective reach during the nineteenth and early twentieth centuries.[16]

[14] William Beinart and Lotte Hughes, *Environment and Empire* (Oxford: Oxford University Press, 2007).

[15] James Beattie, Edward Melillo, and Emily O'Gorman (eds), *Eco-Cultural Networks and the British Empire: New Views on Environmental History* (London: Bloomsbury, 2015); Deepak Kumar, Vinita Damodaran, and Rohan D'Souza (eds), *The British Empire and the Natural World: Environmental Encounters in South Asia* (New Delhi: Oxford University Press, 2011); John M. MacKenzie (ed.), *Imperialism and the Natural World* (Manchester: Manchester University Press, 1990); Richard H. Grove, Vinita Damodaran, and Satpal Sangwan (eds), *Nature and the Orient: The Environmental History of South and Southeast Asia* (Delhi: Oxford University Press, 1998); Tom Griffiths and Libby Robin (eds), *Ecology and Empire: Environmental History of Settler Societies* (Edinburgh: Keele University Press, 1997); an exception is Christina Folke Ax, Niels Brimnes, Niklas Thode Jensen, and Karen Oslund (eds), *Cultivating the Colonies: Colonial States and their Environmental Legacies* (Athens, Oh.: Ohio University Press, 2011).

[16] See also Robin Butlin, *Geographies of Empire: European Empires and Colonies c.1880–1960* (Cambridge: Cambridge University Press, 2009); for an interesting critique, Jordan Sand, 'Subaltern Imperialists: The New Historiography of the Japanese Empire', *Past & Present*, vol. 225, issue 1 (2014), 273–88.

Such a multi-empire approach has a number of advantages, quite apart from helping us explore areas of relative neglect. One is that it allows for comparisons.[17] Just as individual empires tended to structure their colonial polities somewhat differently (with varying degrees and forms of centralization) and sought to mobilize subject labour somewhat differently (with varying degrees and forms of coercion), there were also diverse patterns of resource exploitation and land management. A more important benefit is that it enables us to trace linkages, shared assumptions, aspirations, and consequences among different empires and colonies. Biophysical processes and ecological interrelationships showed little respect for political or linguistic boundaries, and nor could imperial frontiers contain the effects of commodity booms, exotic species introductions, or population pressures. Like their predecessors in the early modern period, Europe's nineteenth- and twentieth-century empires are best understood not on their own terms but in connection with one another. For all the rivalry between them, these empires were fundamentally interactive entities whose commonalities constantly opened up spaces for cross-border coordination.[18] Colonial authorities faced many similar problems in their bid to capitalize on the resources of subject territories, and ideas about how to manage productive environments and safeguard natural assets were among the key realms of such trans-imperial overlap.

Our main focus will be on what is commonly called the era of 'high imperialism' or 'modern colonialism', from around the 1860s/70s to the process of decolonization between the 1940s and early 1960s. These temporal parameters will be handled flexibly and will vary according to the subject in question, since many of the changes can only be understood by placing them within a longer chronological context. Given the enormous ecological repercussions of imperial trade structures and resource management practices, we will also explicitly reflect on the environmental legacies of colonialism for the half-century or so that followed formal decolonization. One can, of course, imagine different chronological possibilities, perhaps especially for the beginning of the story. The question of whether the late nineteenth century marked the advent of a genuinely 'new' form of imperialism is as old as the events themselves. Clearly there were many continuities—political, cultural, economic—with older imperial formations, and recent research has emphasized the multiple parallels with processes of empire-building in other times and places.[19] Yet there were nonetheless a number of factors that gave the imperial politics of the period a peculiar dynamic.

---

[17] On comparing empires: Pierre Singaravélou (ed.), *Les Empires coloniaux xixᵉ–xxᵉ siècle* (Paris: éditions Points, 2013); Miguel Bandeira Jerónimo and António Costa Pinto (eds), *The Ends of European Colonial Empires: Cases and Comparisons* (Basingstoke: Palgrave, 2015).

[18] See, generally, Volker Barth and Roland Cvetkovski (eds), *Imperial Co-operation and Transfer, 1870–1930: Empires and Encounters* (London: Bloomsbury, 2015); Jeremy Adelman, 'Mimesis and Rivalry: European Empires and Global Regimes', *Journal of Global History*, vol. 10, issue 1 (March 2015), 77–98.

[19] For an overview, see Burbank and Cooper, *Empires*, 1–22, 287–329.

To begin with, the sheer scale of these empires was extraordinary. By the turn of the century, a handful of Western European states governed (however unevenly)[20] more than half of the land surface of the entire globe, with the British Empire alone accounting for around a quarter of the world's population. Moreover, in the wake of the 'Great Divergence' of economic growth between the West and the rest of the world after 1800, the vast wealth of the European powers also meant that they had more resources than their imperial predecessors for the purpose of dominating subject landscapes and populations.[21] This was, in turn, closely related to the unprecedented technological differential that had opened up during the nineteenth century, which enabled Europeans for the first time to control large swathes of Africa and Asia beyond the coastal enclaves to which they had largely been confined in the past. Although the ensuing encounters were never quite as one-sided as some historians have suggested, the fundamental disparity was tersely captured by Hilaire Belloc's oft-quoted couplet from *The Modern Traveller* (1898): 'Whatever happens, we have got | the Maxim gun, and they have not.' Furthermore, new technologies not only allowed the penetration of regions previously beyond grasp, they also encouraged the application of European capital, knowledge, and management techniques as a means of utilizing the natural wealth of conquered lands for human ends. If the shift from trade-based imperialism towards a more territorial form of domination was made possible by technology, it was also motivated by a desire to secure important resource flows and to ensure that no rival power monopolized control over them.

For what it is worth, many contemporaries certainly believed that they were witnessing a new age of empire-building. Imperialist advocates such as the economist Paul Leroy-Beaulieu, the sociologist Benjamin Kidd, or the theologian-publicist Friedrich Fabri were all, in their different ways, firmly convinced of the superiority of European civilization over the supposedly backward societies of the colonial world, and propounded the idea of an enlightened modern colonialism in which soldiers would be replaced by engineers and scientists, and where brute force and exploitation would give way to mutual benefit and civilizational uplift.[22] As things turned out, the actual outcomes fell far short of the rhetoric. While entrepreneurs raced to extract resources, colonial territories received only a fraction of the foreign investment that poured out of Europe.[23] Instead of introducing resolutely progressive forms of government, colonial states were generally under-resourced and heavily

[20] Lauren Benton, *Law and Colonial Cultures: Legal Regimes and World History, 1400–1900* (Cambridge: Cambridge University Press, 2002).

[21] Kenneth Pomeranz, *The Great Divergence: China, Europe, and the Making of the Modern World Economy* (Princeton: Princeton University Press, 2000); Jürgen Osterhammel, *Die Verwandlung der Welt. Eine Geschichte des 19. Jahrhunderts* (Munich: Beck, 2009); Eric Jones, *The European Miracle: Environments, Economies and Geopolitics in the History of Europe and Asia*, 3rd edn (Cambridge: Cambridge University Press, 2003); Prasannan Parthasarathi, *Why Europe Grew Rich and Asia Did Not: Global Economic Divergence, 1600–1850* (Cambridge: Cambridge University Press, 2011).

[22] Paul Leroy-Beaulieu, *De la colonisation chez les peuples modernes* (Paris: Guillaumin, 1874); Benjamin Kidd, *The Control of the Tropics* (London: Macmillan, 1898); Friedrich Fabri, *Bedarf Deutschland der Colonien? Eine politisch-ökonomische Betrachtung* (Gotha: Perthes, 1879).

[23] George Kenwood, *The Growth of the International Economy, 1820–2000* (London: Routledge, 1999), 27–30.

reliant on indigenous elites to help govern colonial territories, which dampened their enthusiasm for social reform. New technologies did not automatically lead to more rational forms of colonial rule, and in the worst cases they simply provided more efficient means of plundering and subordinating conquered lands and peoples. In practice, modern colonial regimes drew on a host of older methods, habits, and frames of mind from the long history of overseas expansion, and individual states deployed a variety of different strategies—formal versus informal authority, cultural assimilation or the maintenance of indigenous 'customs', direct or indirect mechanisms of rule—as part of the 'imperial repertoire' of modern European colonialism.[24]

In many respects, the conceit of bringing civilization to supposedly benighted peoples and underused wastelands was therefore hardly new in the late nineteenth and twentieth centuries, but instead grafted onto much older discourses of imperial providence and 'improvement'. Nonetheless, an important difference was the decidedly technocratic ethos that animated the process of empire-building during this period. If the conquistadores were convinced that they had God on their side, modern imperialists believed they had unlocked many of his secrets.

By the end of the nineteenth century, the extraordinary accomplishments of European science and industry had spawned a widespread sense that these societies were extricating themselves from 'nature'. Modern civilization, it seemed, was capable of liberating humankind from the tyranny of material constraints that had previously restricted its endeavours. The European claim to mastery over nature was a central legitimatory prop of modern imperialism—one that not only resonated with contemporary notions of racial hierarchy and societal evolution, but that also nourished a belief in the right, even duty, of Europeans to govern those who were less capable of controlling the world around them.[25] 'It is neither natural nor just that Western civilized peoples amass indefinitely and suffocate within the limited spaces that were their initial home, that they accumulate the marvels of science, art and civilization...and leave perhaps half of the world to ignorant and powerless groups of people', remarked Leroy-Beaulieu in 1891. Civilization, in this view, essentially meant 'the domination of Man over himself and over matter', colonization 'the methodical effect of an organized people on another people whose organization is defective'.[26]

Ideally, at least, the task of the modern colonial power was not simply to govern and tax the economies of such 'defective' areas, but to develop them through the application of scientific knowledge and technology. During the first half of the twentieth century such notions gave rise to a distinctly interventionist form of

---

[24] Burbank and Cooper, *Empires*, 3–8, 287–90; also Boris Barth and Jürgen Osterhammel (eds), *Zivilisierungsmissionen. Imperiale Weltverbesserung seit dem 18. Jahrhundert* (Konstanz: UVK, 2005).
[25] Michael Adas, *Machines as the Measure of Men: Science, Technology, and Ideologies of Western Dominance* (Ithaca, NY: Cornell University Press, 1989).
[26] Leroy-Beaulieu, *De la colonisation*, 4th edn (Paris: Guillaumin, 1891), 842, 845; such sentiments remained widespread over the following decades, finding clear expression in, for instance, the works of Albert Sarraut, *La Mise en valeur des colonies françaises* (Paris: Payot, 1923); *Grandeur et servitude coloniales* (Paris: Éditions du Sagittaire, 1931).

colonialism that spanned the realms of agriculture, forestry, resource extraction, conservation, and public hygiene.[27] In practice, such interventions resulted more from short-term improvisation than from any master plan, and were in any event tightly circumscribed by the pressure to cover their costs. But if the actual commitment to this development agenda only occasionally lived up to its billing, it nonetheless became a vital centrepiece of colonial policy after the First World War, and played a crucial role in both the maintenance and eventual decline of imperial power after the Second. Indeed, it continued to be the core aim of independent governments long after decolonization. Throughout the colonial period and beyond, the central thrust of development efforts was to raise economic production through the more effective domestication of the biophysical environment.

There was, in other words, an important ecological dimension to the rise, legitimization, and operation of modern colonialism, one that was tightly interwoven with the political, cultural, and economic aspects of imperial power. Understanding these socio-environmental dynamics is therefore crucial for understanding the history of colonialism itself.

EMPIRE, INDUSTRY, AND THE GLOBAL ENVIRONMENT

One of the central issues facing any history of European imperialism is how to situate it within longer patterns of historical change. Towards this end, the book makes three basic propositions: that modern imperialism marked a seminal period for the ecosystems of the colonial world, that the transformations of the colonial era commonly built on longer histories of escalating human intervention, and that the overall balance of change was—for all the socio-ecological hybridity of even the most 'natural' looking landscapes—one of considerable harm to the biophysical environment. In some respects these are fairly uncontroversial arguments, and in other respects less so. Although historians generally agree that the wave of formal empire-building during the late nineteenth and early twentieth centuries reshaped economic, political, and ecological relationships across large parts of the globe, the nature and scale of the changes have nonetheless been interpreted quite differently.

Many scholars have regarded the spread of European imperialism as a singular milestone for the environments it colonized, a clear watershed in their natural history. This was certainly the view of an older imperialist historiography that celebrated the European conquest of tropical nature. Oddly enough, it also has its mirror image in diametrically opposed radical and subaltern-studies accounts of imperialism, which have often painted an apocalyptic picture of colonial-era devastation

---

[27] On interventionist colonialism and development: Frederick Cooper and Randall Packard, 'Introduction', in Frederick Cooper and Randall Packard (eds), *International Development and the Social Sciences: Essays on the History and Politics of Knowledge* (Berkeley: University of California Press, 1997), 6–9; for an excellent recent overview of international development, Joseph M. Hodge, 'Writing the History of Development', Parts 1 and 2, *Humanity*, vol. 6 no. 3 (Winter 2015), 429–63, and vol. 7 no. 1 (Spring 2016), 125–74.

and occasionally traced the origins of today's ecological woes to the interferences of European rule. The shift from communal landownership to private property, the enclosure of resources that were once freely available, the alienation of land to concessionary companies or European settlers, the suppression of itinerant modes of agriculture, the commodification of natural resources, and the industrial scale of exploitation—all of these imperial incursions overturned older socio-ecological arrangements that were purportedly (and sometimes undoubtedly) more sustainable than what replaced them. Such accounts have provided an important critical perspective on colonial-era impacts. They are, however, less useful for gauging the overall extent of change insofar as pre-colonial arrangements are often taken for granted and occasionally appear, at least in the rosiest variations on this theme, as an implausibly harmonious state of equilibrium between locals and their natural surroundings, a kind of Edenic myth that most environmental historians have long since abandoned.[28]

By contrast, some accounts have emphasized instead the brevity and tenuousness of European rule across large swathes of nominally colonized territory, and accordingly treat the era of modern colonialism as a mere episode within much longer patterns of social and environmental change. In sub-Saharan Africa in particular, the fact that colonial rule lasted barely seventy years makes the environmental impact of imperial conquest appear less decisive than is often assumed.[29] The same point can also be made, somewhat differently, about colonial Asia. Although the European presence in many Asian territories was longer and stronger than in Africa, the existence of dense agrarian populations and powerful states made a deep imprint on the landscape long before the onset of colonial rule.[30] By relativizing the impact of imperial incursions, such perspectives provide a valuable corrective to overblown notions of a sudden ecological calamity and to Euro-centric narratives in which the colonizers are the sole or dominant agents of environmental transformation. Yet approaching the colonial era as merely a stage within longer cycles

---

[28] Seminal interpretations in this vein include: for Africa, Helge Kjekshus, *Ecology Control and Economic Development in East African History: The Case of Tanganyika, 1850–1950* (London: Heinemann, 1977); for India, Madhav Gadgil and Ramachandra Guha, *This Fissured Land: An Ecological History of India* (Berkeley: University of California Press, 1992); more generally Mike Davis, *Late Victorian Holocausts: El Niño Famines and the Making of the Third World* (London: Verso, 2001). Cf. the critical comments in Mahesh Rangarajan, 'Environmental Histories of India: Of States, Landscapes, and Ecologies', in Edmund Burke III and Kenneth Pomeranz (eds), *The Environment and World History* (Berkeley: University of California Press, 2009), 229–54, here 231–2; on the parallel North American context, Shepard Krech III, *The Ecological Indian: Myth and History* (New York: Norton, 1999). On 'apocalyptic' and other schools of thought: John M. MacKenzie, 'Empire and the Ecological Apocalypse: The Historiography of the Imperial Environment', in Griffiths and Robin (eds), *Ecology*, 215–28.

[29] See John Iliffe, *Africans: The History of a Continent* (Cambridge: Cambridge University Press, 1995); Andrew Roberts, *The Colonial Moment in Africa: Essays on the Movement of Minds and Materials, 1900–1940* (Cambridge: Cambridge University Press, 1990); also William Beinart, 'Beyond the Colonial Paradigm: African History and Environmental History in Large-Scale Perspective', in Burke and Pomeranz (eds), *The Environment*, 211–28, esp. 218; Burbank and Cooper, *Empires*, 21.

[30] See, generally, Victor Lieberman, *Strange Parallels: Southeast Asia in Global Context c.800–1830*, 2 vols (Cambridge: Cambridge University Press, 2003, 2009); John F. Richards, *The Mughal Empire* (Cambridge: Cambridge University Press, 1993); C. A. Bayly, *Indian Society and the Making of the British Empire* (Cambridge: Cambridge University Press, 1988).

of environmental variation runs the risk of downplaying the exceptional scale and far-reaching consequences of the alterations that occurred.

Cutting across these two viewpoints is a more recent emphasis on the widely shared 'developmentalist project' since around the sixteenth century, one just as evident in Mughal India, Qing China, or Asante-ruled West Africa as in Europe. Broadly speaking, what this refers to is a deliberate process of state-building, the expansion of settlement frontiers, the sedentarization of itinerant groups, and the intensification of revenue and resource extraction, all of which entailed significant and long-lasting socio-ecological changes across many parts of the world.[31] Since the early 2000s this perspective has become particularly influential among historians working on a global scale, whose research has increasingly questioned the idea that there was much that was specifically 'colonial' (or even European) about the way in which nineteenth- and twentieth-century colonial states approached the biophysical world. Rather, colonial regimes regularly built upon existing strategies for mobilizing resources and organizing landscapes, and their fundamental aims often coincided more closely with those of their predecessors, as well as many of their subjects, than either contemporaries or some historians have imagined.[32]

This book broadly endorses this approach, albeit with certain qualifications. Clearly, it works much better for some parts of the world than others: better, for instance, in the intensively farmed rice paddies of Tonkin than in the sparsely inhabited forests of Borneo. Equally clearly, it is important not to lose sight of the racial and social specificities of European colonialism, as well as the fact that some groups bitterly opposed the upheavals that it brought to their lives and to the lands they inhabited. Yet on balance the notion of a shared 'developmentalist project' is highly useful for placing colonial-era changes within a longer chronological context and a broader global framework of environmental transformation. In addition, by transcending visions of a colonial fall of Man, it also captures a broader spectrum of human agency and thus helps to avoid the Euro-centric implications of an apocalyptic imperial intrusion. Instead of viewing colonial-era changes in strict isolation from preceding socio-ecological modifications, it situates them as part of the wider expansion of managed landscapes over natural ecosystems in many parts of the world. This was, after all, a process that transcended European colonialism both spatially and temporally, and that eventually reached a crescendo only after the Second World War.

Seen in this light, the era of 'high imperialism' appears less as a fundamental shift of direction than as an acceleration of overarching trends. The huge extension of European political, economic, and military power contributed mightily to the ongoing project of domestication in the colonial world, both during and after its

---

[31] Kenneth Pomeranz, 'Introduction: World History and Environmental History', in Burke and Pomeranz (eds), *The Environment*, 3–32, esp. 7–14; John F. Richards, *The Unending Frontier: An Environmental History of the Early Modern World* (Berkeley: University of California Press, 2003), 17–24. See also Frederick Cooper, *Africa in the World: Capitalism, Empire, Nation-State* (Cambridge, Mass.: Harvard University Press, 2014), esp. ch. 2.

[32] A point that applies even in relatively unexpected parts of the world: see e.g. Pekka Hämäläinen, *The Comanche Empire* (New Haven: Yale University Press, 2008).

heyday. When placed in this wider context, what made modern colonialism distinctive was more the quantity than the quality of change that it wrought.

Above a certain point, however, quantity has a quality all its own, and it is at this point that the idea of an ongoing 'developmentalist project' no longer fully captures the dynamics at work. Despite the continuities with earlier modes of extraction and frontier expansion, when one considers the extent of human-induced environmental change since the nineteenth century it is difficult to escape the conclusion that modern imperialism marked a decisive and largely negative milestone for the ecosystems of the colonial world. To understand why this was so, it is necessary to relate the changes in the colonies to the momentous socio-ecological shifts that were concurrently taking place in Europe itself.

Among many other things, imperialism was, to borrow from Richard Drayton, a 'campaign to extend an ecological regime: a way of living in Nature'.[33] A crucial point to recognize is that, over the course of the nineteenth century, societies in Western Europe had developed a very peculiar way of living in Nature, one that, for the first time in human history, transcended the constraints of what Braudel famously called the 'biological old regime'.[34] Briefly, what this term denotes is a system of production that draws its essential energy needs from the sun, or more precisely from the process of photosynthesis: that is, wood serving as the principal fuel, and mechanical power deriving mainly from human or animal muscles that acquired their energy, either directly or indirectly, through the ingestion of plant matter. Because solar energy is diffusely distributed, and because harnessing it in the form of fuel, food, and fodder places competing demands on land resources, the operation of this regime imposed tight limits on population sizes and economic growth, which for most of human history rose slowly and erratically if at all. Over the centuries, agriculturists made many refinements to this system in order to maximize their energy harvest, but moving beyond its outer limits could only happen by tapping subsidies from elsewhere, either from other places (importing raw materials) or from another time (using fossil fuels).[35]

Before the nineteenth century, European societies tapped some of both, but eventually it was the time subsidy that really changed things. The momentous implications of the shift towards fossil fuels are why environmental historians, perhaps more than any other subset within the discipline, tend to see industrialization as a crucial watershed in human history. The massive use of fossilized energy, buttressed by the growing trade subsidies from 'ghost acres' abroad, signalled a

---

[33] Drayton, *Nature's Government*, 229.

[34] Fernand Braudel, *The Structures of Everyday Life: The Limits of the Possible* (London: Collins, 1981), 70–92; Robert Marks, *The Origins of the Modern World* (Lanham, Md: Rowman & Littlefield, 2007), 22–32, 101–8.

[35] See esp. E. A. Wrigley, *Energy and the English Industrial Revolution* (Cambridge: Cambridge University Press, 2010); Rolf Peter Sieferle, *The Subterranean Forest: Energy Systems and the Industrial Revolution* (Cambridge: White Horse Press, 2001); Paul Warde, *Energy Consumption in England and Wales, 1560–2000* (Rome: Instituto di Studio sulle Società del Mediterraneo, 2007); also Robert C. Allen, *The British Industrial Revolution in Global Perspective* (Cambridge: Cambridge University Press, 2009); on refinements to pre-modern agriculture: Peter M. Jones, *Agricultural Enlightenment: Knowledge, Technology, and Nature, 1750–1840* (Oxford: Oxford University Press, 2016).

fundamental alteration of existing socio-ecological relationships on both a material level (by vastly accelerating the rate of economic activity) as well as a cultural level (by removing older caps on behaviour and expectations).[36] This is why most historians, and by no means just those who specialize on Europe, opt for early industrialization as the starting point of the so-called Anthropocene, the era of Earth's history shaped primarily by human activity.[37]

To be clear, the thoroughgoing industrialization of Europe was not a prerequisite for imperial expansion. Even the conquest of India during the late eighteenth and early nineteenth centuries had little to do with any far-reaching modification of energy regime, however important specific metallurgical and weaponry innovations undoubtedly were. Nor did it make imperial expansion in any way inevitable or 'natural'. As Greg Cushman has rightly emphasized, the deliberate efforts of European states and entrepreneurs to exploit the labour and natural resources of overseas territories were a crucial force behind modern imperialism and the global asymmetries that it helped to create, which no amount of biological or geographic advantages can adequately explain.[38] But once industrialization gathered pace, it radically changed Europe's capacity to project its influence and to transform the areas that it conquered. By the late nineteenth century, the power it conferred on those societies that made the shift was what enabled them to extend their global authority in the first place. It furnished the new 'tools of empire'.[39] Even more important from an environmental perspective, the spread of Europe's imperial reach also extended its new ecological regime to much of the rest of the world—not in the sense that subordinate territories made this transition themselves (indeed, many former colonies still have scarcely done so) but rather that they became more firmly enmeshed than ever before into an increasingly worldwide economic web that was based upon the needs and rhythms of the new industrial metabolism.

Put somewhat differently, Europe's expanding power also created an empire of new tools, new ways of bending nature to human designs (especially, but not exclusively, metropolitan ones) on a vastly greater scale than ever before.[40] This is emphatically not to suggest that Europeans introduced a measure of their own

---

[36] John R. McNeill, *Something New Under the Sun: An Environmental History of the Twentieth Century* (London: Penguin, 2000), 10–17; Marks, *Origins*, 95–121; 'ghost acres' from Pomeranz, *Great Divergence*.

[37] See Gareth Austin (ed.), *Economic Development and Environmental History in the Anthropocene: Perspectives on Asia and Africa* (London: Bloomsbury, 2017); Christophe Bonneuil and Jean-Baptiste Fressoz, *L'Événement Anthropocène* (Paris: Seuil, 2013); Jens Kersten, *Das Anthropozän-Konzept. Kontrakt, Komposition, Konflikt* (Baden-Baden: Nomos, 2014); Fredrik Albritton Jonsson, 'The Industrial Revolution in the Anthropocene', *Journal of Modern History*, vol. 84 no. 3 (Sept. 2012), 679–96; for an interdisciplinary overview, Will Steffen, Jacques Grinevald, Paul Crutzen, and John McNeill, 'The Anthropocene: Conceptual and Historical Perspectives', *Philosophical Transactions of the Royal Society A*, vol. 369 no. 1938 (Mar. 2011), 842–67.

[38] Gregory T. Cushman, *Guano and the Opening of the Pacific World: A Global Ecological History* (Cambridge: Cambridge University Press, 2013), 236–8, 342–3, critiquing Crosby, *Ecological Imperialism*, and Jared Diamond, *Guns, Germs, and Steel: The Fates of Human Societies* (London: Jonathan Cape, 1997).

[39] Headrick, *Tools of Empire*.

[40] On the appropriation of these technological tools, see esp. James L. Gelvin and Nile Green (eds), *Global Muslims in the Age of Steam and Print* (Berkeley: University of California Press, 2014); Headrick, *Tentacles*.

dynamism to supposedly stagnant societies that were still subservient to nature, as many contemporaries liked to think. The point is rather that modern imperialism both fed the 'new ecological regime' and spread it, extending its footprint around the globe to tap even greater subsidies destined for even more consumers who were even further removed from the environmental and social consequences of production. The resulting connections soon generated a host of socio-ecological tensions. The pace and rhythms of Europe's industrializing economies were very different from those of the 'organic economies' that still prevailed in the rest of the world, and often drew in resources faster than they could be replenished. The new fossil-fuelled ecological regime may have released much of Europe's land surface from the requirements of energy production, but feeding its rapid metabolism still required far more land and resources from elsewhere.[41] For all of these reasons, the colonial period was—despite the continuities with earlier developmentalist practices—a pivotal phase for the ecosystems of the tropical world. By simultaneously provisioning and propagating Europe's new way of living in Nature, imperialism was as significant as industrialization for transforming the global environment.

Accordingly, some of the most important environmental consequences of imperialism stemmed not so much from the transformation of particular spaces as from the compression of space itself. European imperialists certainly did not invent long-distance trade and exchange networks in the regions they conquered, but they did reshape and expand them. In many respects, the 'imperial' helped forge the 'global' during this period—not in the sense that it stretched across the entire world or fully penetrated subject societies, let alone that its impact was always or consistently 'globalizing' (as ongoing rivalries and occasional autarkic tendencies attest), but rather that it operated on an increasingly global scale that directly or indirectly influenced economic and social developments nearly everywhere.[42] Europe's empires created institutions and forms of governance that were specifically designed to travel. They applied technical and scientific knowledge that claimed universal validity. Perhaps most importantly from an environmental perspective, they assembled markets and transport networks that spanned oceans and continents. The years from 1870 to 1914 are commonly regarded as the 'first era of trade globalization', a period in which trade growth averaged around 4 per cent annually and in which foreign investment, the vast bulk of it from Western Europe, rose more than sevenfold. Trade links were the vital sinews of European empire, and from 1870 to 1940 world trade more than quadrupled.[43]

---

[41] On 'organic economies', Wrigley, *Energy*, 9–24; on the need for distant resources, Timothy Mitchell, *Carbon Democracy: Political Power in the Age of Oil* (London: Verso, 2011), 16–17.

[42] On the potential and limits of this perspective, see Tony Ballantyne and Antoinette Burton, 'Empires and the Reach of the Global', in Emily S. Rosenberg (ed.), *A World Connecting, 1870–1945* (Cambridge, Mass.: Belknap, 2012), 285–431; Frederick Cooper, *Colonialism in Question: Theory, Knowledge, History* (Berkeley: University of California Press, 2005), 91–112; Jürgen Osterhammel, *Geschichte der Globalisierung. Dimensionen, Prozesse, Epochen* (Munich: Beck, 2003); C. A. Bayly, *The Birth of the Modern World, 1780–1914: Global Connections and Comparisons* (Oxford: Blackwell, 2004), *passim*.

[43] Kenwood, *Growth*, 24; Steven C. Topik and Allen Wells, 'Commodity Chains in a Global Economy', in Rosenberg (ed.), *World Connecting*, 593, 618–19.

The overall result was a multitude of material teleconnections, and these connections had profound ecological implications. First of all, long-distance trade helped detach production from consumption, and consumption from its costs. This is important because the manner in which land is treated depends very much on whether those in control of it have to live with the consequences. Another upshot of far-flung markets is that they concentrated a spatially diffuse demand for particular goods onto spatially bounded supply areas that were best placed to produce those goods. Like sunlight through a magnifying lens, the effects were often intense. At the same time, the benefits of such changes were also concentrated through the mechanisms of unequal exchange, which functioned on an ecological as well as an economic level. By and large, the net flow of resources (energy, minerals, nutrients, fertility) worked very much in favour of the metropoles over their colonial suppliers.[44] Finally, imperial trade and investment reshuffled biota—cultivars, livestock, microbes, people—across vast distances, remaking entire ecosystems in the process. Like the new cultural amalgams in colonial port cities or the shifting traditions of diasporic merchant and labourer communities,[45] imperial exchange circuits also created new hybrid ecologies, new combinations of living organisms brought together from different regions and continents, that reflected the immense scope and variety of the environments connected by empire.

COVERAGE, THEMES, ORGANIZATION

Clearly it is impossible to survey the full spectrum of this variety here. Our main focus is on what can loosely be called the 'tropics', and principally on those territories that lay under formal European control during the late nineteenth and early twentieth centuries. I use the term 'tropical' broadly yet cautiously: broadly for its capacity to link together disparate regions and to look across empires, and cautiously because of its ambiguity and historical baggage. It is not intended to denote a singular climatic zone, less still a rigidly defined geographic or cartographic space,

[44] Alf Hornborg, 'Ecosystems and World-Systems: Accumulation as an Ecological Process', in Christopher Chase-Dunn and Salvatore J. Babones (eds), *Global Social Change: Historical and Comparative Perspectives* (Baltimore: Johns Hopkins University Press, 2006), 161–75; Alf Hornborg, 'Introduction: Environmental History as Political Ecology', in Alf Hornborg, John R. McNeill, and Joan Martinez-Alier (eds), *Rethinking Environmental History: World-System History and Global Environmental Change* (Lanham, Md: AltaMira, 2007), 1–24; John Bellamy Foster and Hannah Holleman, 'The Theory of Unequal Ecological Exchange: A Marx-Odum Dialectic', *Journal of Peasant Studies*, vol. 41 no. 2 (2014), 199–233.

[45] This has been the focus of some of the most innovative recent work on the history of empire: e.g. Sunil S. Amrith, *Migration and Diaspora in Modern Asia* (Cambridge: Cambridge University Press, 2011); Andrew Arsan, *Interlopers of Empire: The Lebanese Diaspora in Colonial French West Africa* (Oxford: Oxford University Press, 2014); Sugata Bose, *A Hundred Horizons: The Indian Ocean in the Age of Global Empire* (Cambridge, Mass.: Harvard University Press, 2006); Thomas R. Metcalf, *Imperial Connections: India in the Indian Ocean Arena, 1860–1920* (Berkeley: University of California Press, 2007); Tony Ballantyne, *Between Colonialism and Diaspora: Sikh Cultural Formations in an Imperial World* (Durham, NC: Duke University Press, 2006); Claude Markovits, *The Global World of Indian Merchants, 1750–1947: Traders of Sind from Bukhara to Panama* (Cambridge: Cambridge University Press, 2000).

since many of the stories take us into areas that were technically in 'subtropical' latitudes (e.g. northern India, the Middle East, South Africa, the Maghreb). It certainly does not seek to evoke colonial-era connotations of tropical luxuriance and lazy natives, let alone of green hells and irretrievable barbarism.[46] I use it merely as a convenient shorthand for referring to those non-temperate parts of the world that were controlled by Europe during this period and that were, for the most part, not sites of large-scale European settlement (with some important exceptions, especially in Africa).

The term 'tropics' is employed here essentially as a socio-political concept in the sense that 'global South' is used nowadays. Common to all of the areas we will examine was the European attempt to control overseas lands and peoples and to harness their productivity for imperial purposes. While most of the tropical regions at the core of this book only came under European rule after 1870, some had been colonized for much longer (India, Java, the Caribbean). And while the main focus will be on formal colonies, we will also examine areas under various forms of protectorate and semi-autonomous status. Since most of the American tropics (apart from the Caribbean) fall under none of these categories, they will not be a central concern, despite the many trade and investment links to Europe. This is partly a matter of sheer practicality given how much ground we will already be covering, but it also has a certain historiographical rationale. From the 1890s the United States increasingly became the main 'imperial' power throughout much of Central and South America, and over the last two decades a number of fine studies have charted the ecological effects of US businesses, consumers, scientists, and engineers in the region.[47] In a sense, this book complements this literature by tracing the concurrent expansion of other imperial powers in other parts of the tropical world.

The fields of environmental history and imperial history have long shared points of overlap, and one of the aims of this study is to integrate them still further. The book offers a kind of two-way lens for examining how empires shaped

---

[46] On notions of 'tropicality': David Arnold, *The Problem of Nature: Environment, Culture and European Expansion* (Oxford: Blackwell, 1996), 141–68; David Arnold, *The Tropics and the Travelling Gaze: India, Landscape, and Science, 1800–1856* (Seattle: University of Washington Press, 2006); Paul S. Sutter, 'The Tropics: A Brief History of an Environmental Imaginary', in Andrew C. Isenberg (ed.), *The Oxford Handbook of Environmental History* (Oxford: Oxford University Press, 2014), 178–204; Nancy Leys Stepan, *Picturing Tropical Nature* (Ithaca, NY: Cornell University Press, 2001); Felix Driver and Luciana Martins (eds), *Tropical Visions in an Age of Empire* (Chicago: University of Chicago Press, 2005).

[47] e.g. Richard Tucker, *Insatiable Appetite: The United States and the Ecological Degradation of the Tropical World* (Berkeley: University of California Press, 2000); John Soluri, *Banana Cultures: Agriculture, Consumption and Environmental Change in Honduras and the United States* (Austin, Tex.: University of Texas Press, 2005); Steve Striffler, *In the Shadows of State and Capital: The United Fruit Company, Popular Struggle, and Agrarian Restructuring in Ecuador, 1900–1995* (Durham, NC: Duke University Press, 2002); Paul S. Sutter, 'Nature's Agents or Agents of Empire? Entomological Workers and Environmental Change during the Construction of the Panama Canal', *Isis*, vol. 98 no. 4 (Dec. 2007), 724–54; Greg Grandin, *Fordlandia: The Rise and Fall of Henry Ford's Forgotten Jungle City* (London: Icon, 2010); Sterling Evans, *Bound in Twine: The History and Ecology of the Henequen-Wheat Complex for Mexico and the American and Canadian Plains, 1880–1950* (College Station, Tex.: Texas A&M University Press, 2007); in a partially related vein: Edward Melillo, *Strangers on Familiar Soil: Rediscovering the Chile–California Connection* (New Haven: Yale University Press, 2015).

the biophysical environment and how environmental factors influenced the development of empires. On the one hand, it argues for the central importance of nineteenth- and twentieth-century imperialism in remaking ecosystems on a global scale. As historians try to chart the material constitution of the world in which we currently live, imperialism must be regarded as a key process alongside industrialization, the explosion of world trade, and the rise of mass consumption. On the other hand, it also highlights the importance of socio-environmental interactions in the maintenance and eventual decline of imperial power. Tropical environments were by no means merely a picturesque stage on which human action took place, but were an essential part of the story, powerfully shaping and being shaped by the entire enterprise of modern empire.

Integrating these stories forces us to think about the inseparable interrelationships between cultural, social, and material factors in human history: how the biophysical environment set outer parameters within which human action could take place, and how human action, refracted as always through different social habits and cultural expectations, could nonetheless produce a wide range of outcomes. Time and again, people's physical surroundings opened certain opportunities while impeding or discouraging others, and as people pursued these opportunities for the sake of wealth, power, or convenience, they further transformed their surroundings in a mutual process of co-evolution. Such 'new materialist' visions of reciprocal entanglement raise some fundamental questions about our understandings of causality and non-human agency.[48] Although the ontological debates over these issues do not concern us here, instances of material agency will periodically crop up in this book—for instance, when considering how the different biological needs of particular cultivars or the specific physical characteristics of certain mineral deposits influenced the ways in which people took advantage of them as well as the social, economic, and ecological effects. Far from propagating a European 'mastery of nature', what imperialism effectively did was enlarge the spatial scale of such entanglements and broaden the cast of actors—or 'actants' in Bruno Latour's terminology—that were involved.[49]

Imperialism was, in this sense, a multi-polar enterprise, and this was true in other respects as well. In recent years it has become axiomatic to view empires less in terms of centralized hubs and spokes than as complex webs of interconnection and mutual influence, both within individual empires and across imperial boundaries. In place of an older diffusionist model of centres and peripheries, scholars have mapped out a much more complex geography of ideas and practices circulating

---

[48] See esp. Bruno Latour, *Politics of Nature: How to Bring the Sciences into Democracy* (Cambridge, Mass.: Harvard University Press, 2004); Tony Bennett and Patrick Joyce (eds), *Material Powers: Cultural Studies, History and the Material Turn* (London: Routledge, 2010); Hans Schouwenberg, 'Back to the Future? History, Material Culture and New Materialism', *International Journal for History, Culture and Modernity*, vol. 3 no. 1 (Apr. 2015), 59–72; Timothy J. LeCain, 'Against the Anthropocene: A Neo-Materialist Perspective', *International Journal for History, Culture and Modernity*, vol. 3 no. 1 (Apr. 2015), 1–28.

[49] Bruno Latour, *Reassembling the Social: An Introduction to Actor-Network-Theory* (Oxford: Oxford University Press, 2005).

between metropoles, colonies, and various sub-imperial formations.[50] From this perspective, empire-building was not simply a matter of imposing external power over subject societies. Such a view is more a reflection of contemporary imperialist fantasies—the dream of remaking the world in Europe's image—than of the pragmatic compromises necessary for colonial rule to function on the ground. As Frederick Cooper has deftly put it, empire-states had 'long arms' but 'weak fingers'.[51] For all the power differentials and conflicts that were involved, imperial rule could only work by giving subject peoples, and especially indigenous elites, some kind of a stake in it. Modern colonialism was a system that bound lands and peoples together and that opened new prospects and incentives for non-Europeans too, including new possibilities for opposition.[52] As this book shows, this certainly applies to processes of ecological transformation, which were frequently—and in some cases predominantly—driven by indigenous producers or third-party groups (so-called 'foreign natives') rather than European colonialists, and that sometimes ran counter to colonial designs. Furthermore, although we can only touch on the reciprocal impact of imperialism on metropolitan environments, the resources that flowed in from around the world powerfully shaped rural and urban landscapes throughout Europe as well.

Given the vast range of issues and spaces that we could cover, the book necessarily adopts an illustrative rather than a comprehensive approach. It is divided into three main parts that loosely blend a chronological and thematic format. The first and largest part will focus on the environmental impacts of imperial trade networks, and in particular on the colonial-era boom in commodity production as a key motor of environmental change. Throughout the period under discussion, a combination of infrastructural investment, administrative systematization, scientific research, and private initiative (in many cases indigenous initiative) was jointly geared towards boosting exports of colonial goods that were either coveted on world markets or deemed strategically and militarily important by metropolitan governments. Reconstructing these processes through the stories of particular commodities—rather than, say, by surveying the output from different geographic regions—brings a number of analytical advantages, above all the ability to explore changes at a local level while also shedding light on the many linkages between different producer areas as well as their connections with other parts of the world. The six chapters in this part examine six different commodities (three vegetal, three mineral) that collectively demonstrate the broad range of socio-environmental transformation wrought by burgeoning trade and consumption, but that individually highlight quite different themes—about smallholders versus plantations, about the interpenetration of labour systems and ecosystems, about the associations between race and technology, about indigenous and colonial agency—in the environmental history of empire. If the overall upsurge of imperial extraction brought huge ecological

---

[50] For a recent overview of the field: Heather Streets-Salter and Trevor Getz, *Empires and Colonies in the Modern World: A Global Perspective* (Oxford: Oxford University Press, 2016).

[51] Cooper, *Colonialism in Question*, 153–203, quote p. 197.

[52] On the intricacies of subject status and subjectivity, see Partha Chatterjee, *Nationalist Thought in the Colonial World: A Derivative Discourse?* (London: Zed, 1986).

consequences, the stories were remarkably diverse and the effects were neither predictable nor inevitable.

The second part then investigates how colonial authorities tried to deal with
these changes and manage colonial environments more 'rationally'. The two basic
elements of this programme were to conserve resources and ecosystems, and to
improve their productivity. Although both processes began long before the First
World War, they quickly gathered momentum during the 1920s and 1930s amidst
mounting fears of overexploitation and environmental crisis. What Adam Rome
has called the 'environmental management state' in the United States had its counterparts (and in some respects its antecedents) in Europe's tropical colonies, where
conservationists eagerly brandished the authority of state-based technical expertise
in their campaigns to ensure the 'wise use' of nature's assets.[53] We examine three
different aspects of this process in three interrelated chapters. The first will focus on
efforts to preserve tropical 'nature' (especially wildlife), the second on the rise of
colonial forest conservation, and the third on attempts to improve tropical agriculture. In all of these areas, colonial governments and officials frequently dictated
environmental policy with scant regard for the needs and interests of the people
directly affected. As a result, there has been much criticism of conservation *qua*
'colonial science' as fundamentally authoritarian and often startlingly myopic. But
as this part shows, there was also a growing recognition of the bewildering ecological and social complexity in the colonial world, and conservation initiatives
could sometimes act as an important brake against the unbridled exploitation of
colonized environments and peoples.[54]

Part III focuses on the rapid acceleration of all these trends after the Second
World War, an era of unprecedented socio-economic and ecological transformation
throughout the tropics. Chapter 10 examines the environmental dimensions of the
'development' drives of the 1940s and 1950s, which in many respects marked the
high point of colonial ecological intervention. Chapter 11 then explores the longer-
term legacies of colonial rule by considering how the institutional arrangements,
resource management practices, and trade patterns that emerged or expanded under

---

[53] Adam Rome, 'What Really Matters in History: Environmental Perspectives on Modern
America', *Environmental History*, vol. 7 no. 2 (Apr. 2002), 303–18, here 304; also Paul S. Sutter, 'The
World with Us: The State of American Environmental History', *Journal of American History*, vol. 100
no. 1 (June 2013), 94–119, here 100–5.

[54] On science and colonialism, see the special issue of *Isis*, vol. 96 no. 1 (Mar. 2005); Roy MacLeod
(ed.), *Nature and Empire: Science and the Colonial Enterprise*, *Osiris*, vol. 15 (Chicago: University of
Chicago Press, 2000); Brett M. Bennett and Joseph M. Hodge (eds), *Science and Empire: Knowledge
and Networks of Science across the British Empire, 1800–1970* (Houndmills: Palgrave, 2011); for
insightful reconsiderations of the issues involved, see William Beinart, Karen Brown, and Daniel
Gilfoyle, 'Experts and Expertise in Colonial Africa Reconsidered: Science and the Interpenetration of
Knowledge', *African Affairs*, vol. 108 no. 432 (May 2009), 413–33; Helen Tilley, *Africa as a Living
Laboratory: Empire, Development, and the Problem of Scientific Knowledge, 1870–1950* (Chicago:
University of Chicago Press, 2011), 1–30, esp. 10–11; Pierre Singaravélou, *Professer l'Empire: les 'sci-
ences coloniales' en France sous la IIIe République* (Paris: Publications de la Sorbonne, 2011); Marc
Poncelet, *L'Invention des sciences coloniales belges* (Paris: Éditions Karthala, 2008); Jens Ruppenthal,
Kolonialismus als 'Wissenschaft und Technik'. Das Hamburger Kolonialinstitut 1908 bis 1919 (Stuttgart:
Steiner, 2007); Peter Boomgaard (ed.), *Empire and Science in the Making: Dutch Colonial Scholarship
in Comparative Global Perspective, 1760–1830* (Basingstoke: Palgrave, 2013).

colonialism continued to shape the relationships of human societies with tropical environments during the decades following formal decolonization. To an extent, the concluding part contextualizes the history of late colonialism and its after-effects within the so-called 'Great Acceleration', the most recent phase of the Anthropocene during which nearly all of the measures of human impact on the global environment—fossil fuel consumption, greenhouse emissions, waste nitrogen, water consumption, land conversion, species extinction, etc.—escalated rapidly, and in which we still, despite attempts at deceleration, find ourselves firmly fixed.[55]

Highlighting these links between the past and the present is important in view of the indelible mark that imperialism has left on the world in which we live. When we consider the rise of new modes of extraction and exploitation; the uneven structure of worldwide resource flows; the circulation of people, crops, microbes, livestock, and pests across oceans and continents; the advent of new understandings of the biophysical world; even the continual growth of anxieties about the impact that humans have had on it; we see the traces of empire all around us. By relating the story of Europe's imperial power to the momentous ecological shifts that it entailed, this book ultimately seeks to provide a historical perspective on the vital nexus of social, political, and environmental issues that we currently face. Clearly, historians cannot offer any ready answers to such questions, but if this book helps improve our understanding of how they have become so urgent, that will more than suffice.

---

[55] On the 'Great Acceleration': Steffen, Grinevald, Crutzen, and McNeill, 'The Anthropocene', 849–53; Will Steffen, Wendy Broadgate, Lisa Deutsch, Owen Gaffney, and Cornelia Ludwig, 'The Trajectory of the Anthropocene: The Great Acceleration', *Anthropocene Review*, vol. 2 no. 1 (Apr. 2015), 81–98.

PART I

A WORLD OF GOODS

The Ecology of Colonial Extraction

1

The Ecology of Cotton
Environment, Labour, and Empire

Among the many drivers of global environmental change in the nineteenth century, historians often single out three in particular: industrialization, imperialism, and the expansion of capitalist production and trade. There are good reasons for doing so. These processes were not only important in their own right, they also formed an interconnected trio. Industrial capitalism brought enormous power to the societies that pioneered it, enabling them to control and extract resources in other parts of the world, which further fuelled the expansion of their economies and imperial trading networks. Of all the materials that helped link them together, perhaps none were more central than cotton.

The key role of cotton in Europe's industrialization is axiomatic. For all the debates about the roots of the industrial revolution, scholars generally agree that cotton was one of the sectors in which the new modes of manufacturing first developed. Technological innovations for spinning and weaving were transformative milestones in the rise of the machine age. The modern factory system, along with the wrenching social dislocations it caused, was likewise pioneered by the cotton industry, which soon came to dominate manufacturing in Europe and North America. Cotton accordingly became one of the chief commodities of global exchange over the course of the nineteenth century, far surpassing all other crops in both the value and volume of trade. As raw cotton streamed into Europe from overseas, millions of workers processed it into products that were subsequently sold in nearly every corner of the earth. By the end of the century the global business of cultivating, transporting, and manufacturing cotton involved around 1.5 per cent of the entire human population. Little wonder that contemporary observers viewed cotton as nothing less than a 'world power'.[1]

The European cotton industry was not made from whole cloth (forgive the pun), but rather built on centuries of manufacturing and commercial development elsewhere in the world. By the early nineteenth century cotton had been among the world's leading industries for at least a millennium, spanning large parts of South, East, and Central Asia, the Americas, and Africa. Europe played a marginal role for most of this period, and its transition from the fringes to the centre of the

---

[1] James A. B. Scherer, *Cotton as a World Power: A Study in the Economic Interpretation of History* (New York: Stokes, 1916). The figure of 1.5 per cent of world population is from Sven Beckert, *Empire of Cotton: A New History of Global Capitalism* (London: Allen Lane, 2014), xix.

global cotton trade reflected a long-term acquisition of skills, materials, and tastes from earlier heartlands of production, above all India.[2]

Yet despite these deep roots, the Europe-led cotton economy was quite different from the Asian-centred system that preceded it. The most obvious dissimilarity was the deployment of machinery driven by fossil energy, but an equally fundamental difference was the huge spatial detachment of cotton manufacturing from its sources of raw material. Whereas most producer regions had previously engaged in both cotton cultivation and fabrication, the deepening international division of labour in the nineteenth century led to a tight concentration of profits and technical know-how at the centre of industrial manufacture.[3] In place of a diffuse global web of exchange in which techniques and resources were broadly shared, industrialization in Europe created a more centralized and exploitative 'empire of cotton'.[4]

As this commercial empire grew, it also played an important role in the spread of more formal structures of imperial control. European mill owners were never able to acquire adequate supplies of raw cotton solely through the mechanisms of free trade. As a general rule, rural populations were wary of devoting more than a small proportion of their land and labour to export crops, preferring instead to place their own needs for food and fibre above the demands of markets. This is why, during the first half of the nineteenth century, European manufacturers depended mainly on cotton produced by slaves or indentured labourers who had no control over what they grew. By the 1860s, however, they increasingly had to rely on other methods for compelling agrarian populations to tailor their land use to the needs of industrial production, partly through the development of new labour and tenure relations in the post-slavery American South, but also through the extension of European state power over tropical and subtropical areas that could supply the ever-growing quantities of raw materials they required. This shift towards a 'neo-mercantilist' mode of resource procurement not only signalled a closer relationship between state power and capital, it also helped propel the surge of colonial expansion that swept through much of Africa and tropical Asia during the late nineteenth and early twentieth centuries. Cotton, more than any other agricultural good, was central to the emergence of these new forms of imperialism, and remained a preoccupation of many colonial states for decades to come.[5]

The close interconnections between cotton, industrialization, and colonialism have long been recognized by historians, as have the myriad social, economic, and technological changes associated with the cotton industry. Only recently, however, have scholars begun to appreciate the environmental and biological dimensions of

---

[2] Giorgio Riello, *Cotton: The Fabric that Made the Modern World* (Cambridge: Cambridge University Press, 2013), parts 1 and 2.

[3] Riello, *Cotton*, 264–87.   [4] See the excellent study by Beckert, *Empire*.

[5] Beckert, *Empire*, 274–311; Sven Beckert, 'Emancipation and Empire: Reconstructing the Worldwide Web of Cotton Production in the Age of the American Civil War', *American Historical Review*, vol. 109 no. 5 (Dec. 2004), 1405–38.

this story.[6] At the most basic level, cotton cultivation brought a massive wave of land conversion. It is estimated that from 1800 to 1914 world cotton production rose by a factor of twenty-five, from around 500 million lb (227 million kg) per year to over 12.6 billion lb (5.72 billion kg).[7] Global cotton acreage in this period is anyone's guess, since there were vast areas known to grow cotton that escaped any statistical capture.[8] But even confining oneself to the known crop, and generously assuming an average yield of 200 lb per acre (224 kg/ha, the norm for US production around 1900), cotton must have covered at least 255,000 km²—an area greater than the entire United Kingdom—of the planet's surface by the early twentieth century, and probably closer to twice this figure, making cotton by far the world's leading non-food crop in terms of acreage.

The vast surface area devoted to cotton vividly illustrates the ways in which industrialization, far from liberating human activity from the constraints of nature, remained deeply embedded in wider ecological processes. Although we tend to associate the rise of industrial civilization with the growth of coal-fired cities in Europe and North America, it also relied on a far-reaching transformation of rural ecosystems and communities across large areas of the globe. The development of intensive, mechanized production in some parts of the world brought a parallel increase in extensive, organic forms of production in many others. The cotton mills that spearheaded the industrial transition could only put their huge concentrations of fossilized energy to work by processing commensurately large quantities of a raw material that was still based on diffuse flows of solar energy, nutrients, and moisture (namely, through photosynthesis and muscle power).[9] As the cotton industry grew, capturing these flows required the control of ever-greater amounts of land and human labour, most of it outside of Europe. It was a messy and disruptive process for the areas that were involved, for the pace and rhythms of these different production systems—the industrial and the organic—were very different. From an ecological perspective, the huge expansion of cotton acreage represented an attempt to overcome the temporal dissonance between the two systems, though the wild fluctuation of markets and prices testified to the perennial difficulty of harmonizing them.

The biological characteristics of the cotton plant itself were equally significant, for in several ways it was particularly well suited to the needs of large-scale mechanized production. As Giorgio Riello has emphasized, cotton had an exceptionally high 'ecological potential' as a source of raw fibre. Because of the energy loss

---

[6] See esp. Edmund Russell, *Evolutionary History: Uniting History and Biology to Understand Life on Earth* (Cambridge: Cambridge University Press, 2011), 103–31; Alan L. Olmstead and Paul W. Rhode, *Creating Abundance: Biological Innovation and American Agricultural Development* (Cambridge: Cambridge University Press, 2008), 98–198; Alf Hornborg, 'Footprints in the Cotton Fields: The Industrial Revolution as Time-Space Appropriation and Environmental Load Displacement', in Hornborg, McNeill, and Martinez-Alier (eds), *Rethinking*, 259–72.

[7] See Douglas Farnie, 'Cotton, 1780–1914', in David Jenkins (ed.), *The Cambridge History of Western Textiles* (Cambridge: Cambridge University Press, 2003), 721–60, here 744; also John A. Todd, *The World's Cotton Crops* (London: Black, 1915), 395.

[8] Scherer, *Cotton*, 339.

[9] See Mitchell, *Carbon Democracy*, 16–17; also Beckert, *Empire*, xviii.

associated with the conversion of grass into animal hair, wool required around twelve times more land than cotton to produce the same amount of fibre.[10] Moreover, the fibre quality of certain cotton varieties was also crucial. Over thousands of years of human domestication, four species of the *Gossypium* genus evolved to produce not only larger bolls but also longer fibres than their wild ancestors. Two of these species (*G. herbaceum* and *G. arboreum*) evolved in Asia and Africa, and formed the basis of the cotton economies there. The two others (*G. barbadense* and *G. hirsutum*) developed in the Americas, the latter becoming the fabled 'king' of the US cotton belt. These New World species, which were quickly disseminated to other parts of the world, boasted longer fibres than their Old World cousins and therefore allowed the production of stronger, finer thread that was far less likely to break under the strain of mechanized spinning. According to Edmund Russell, the anthropogenic evolution of the cotton plant ultimately made the industrial revolution possible by providing fibre of the right quality and quantity to trigger the path-breaking inventions of Britain's cotton industry.[11]

Finally, the cultivation needs of the cotton plant also had important historical consequences. Compared to most cultivars, it was a time-consuming crop that demanded large and frequent labour inputs far beyond planting and harvest time. In many parts of the tropical and subtropical world, its life-cycle, water, and maintenance requirements clashed with the working timetable of other crops. In addition, the creation of high-yielding long-staple varieties that were suitable for different soil and climatic conditions involved the painstaking manipulation of the plant as well as the careful management of growing conditions, seed distribution, and fieldwork. As a result, large-scale cotton production often brought a major shift in the relationship between the land and the people who worked it, diverting manpower from subsistence activities, modifying long-established cropping and rotation patterns, and altering structures of ownership and labour control. What the story of cotton highlights above all else is the fundamental intersection of work systems and agro-ecosystems.

For all of these reasons, the production of cheap, machine-friendly cotton involved a rigorous framework of biological and social control.[12] The purpose of this chapter is to explore the workings and effects of this regime in the main producer regions of Europe's colonial empire. It begins by surveying the fallout of the 1860s 'cotton famine' and the rapid growth of cotton cultivation in India and Egypt, the world's second and third largest producers (behind the USA) in the late nineteenth and early twentieth centuries. It then shifts the focus to Africa and the series of colonial cotton campaigns that sought to mobilize the supposedly latent agricultural reserves of the continent. In all three areas, the story of colonial cotton

---

[10] Riello, *Cotton*, 239–46. The main difference between cotton and flax, another plant fibre, was the much higher labour inputs required to process the latter.

[11] Russell, *Evolutionary History*, 108–21; see also Olmstead and Rhode, *Creating Abundance*, 98–133.

[12] As argued by Andrew Zimmerman, *Alabama in Africa: Booker T. Washington, the German Empire, and the Globalization of the New South* (Princeton: Princeton University Press, 2010), 17–18, 148–53.

is one in which the exploitation of land, labour, and plant resources were inextricably intertwined. In this new ecology of cotton, changes to one element entailed modifications for all the rest.

THE COTTON CRISIS AND THE EXPANSION OF COLONIAL CULTIVATION

By the middle of the nineteenth century cotton textile production was the largest manufacturing industry in the world, employing more people, directly or indirectly, than any other. It was the lifeblood of mill towns from Lancashire to Rouen and from Saxony to New England. In north-west England alone there were over 2,600 factories with around half a million employees.[13] Most of the cotton they processed came from the southern USA, which accounted for around three-quarters of world production.[14] By the 1850s the southern states were annually exporting over 2 million bales (each 500 lb, or 227 kg) of raw cotton to Europe, roughly five times more than all the cotton imported from India, Brazil, and the West Indies combined. On average, US imports represented over three-quarters of British cotton supplies, around two-thirds for the German *Zollverein*, and 90 per cent for France, making the plantations of the American South—and the 4 million slaves who worked them—an essential part of Europe's cotton empire.[15]

When the outbreak of the Civil War and the Union blockade of Confederate ports severed this vital supply chain, it sent shockwaves through European markets. Between 1859/60 (a bumper year for Southern producers) and 1861/2, exports dropped from 3.5 million bales to a mere 10,000. As European stockpiles dwindled, mills worked on short time or closed altogether, causing huge losses for manufacturers, throwing hundreds of thousands out of work, and touching off a series of violent disturbances in several of Europe's textile centres. Fearful of the consequences for public order, French authorities worried that 'too long a stoppage in the production of sufficient cotton would constitute a veritable *social* hazard in the country'.[16] As *The Times* of London put it, 'No crisis in modern times has been so anxiously watched, nor has any European war or revolution so seriously threatened the interests of England.'[17]

---

[13] Cotton manufacture supported at least one-fifth of England's population at the time: W. O. Henderson, *The Lancashire Cotton Famine, 1861–1865* (Manchester: Manchester University Press, 1934), 1.

[14] Scherer, *Cotton*, 263–4.

[15] David Christy, *Cotton is King: Or, The Culture of Cotton, and its Relation to Agriculture, Manufactures and Commerce* (Cincinnati: Moore, Wilstach, Keys, 1855), 206; Beckert, 'Emancipation', 1409; Henderson, *Lancashire*, 5.

[16] Céleste Duval, *Question cotonnière: la France peut s'emparer du monopole du coton par l'Afrique; elle peut rendre l'Angleterre, l'Europe, ses tributaires; l'Afrique est le vrai pays du coton* (Paris: Cosson, 1864), 15, italics in the original; see also Claude Fohlen, *L'Industrie textile au temps du Second Empire* (Paris: Librairie Plon, 1956), 257–68; Hubert Galle, *La 'Famine du coton', 1861–1865: effets de la guerre de sécession sur l'industrie cotonnière gantoise* (Brussels: Université libre de Bruxelles, 1967).

[17] Scherer, *Cotton*, 264–8, 420; Henderson, *Lancashire*, 108–17; R. Arthur Arnold, *The History of the Cotton Famine, from the Fall of Sumter to the Passing of the Public Works Act (1864)* (London: Saunders, Otley & Co., 1865).

The overwhelming reliance on American cotton and the potentially dire effects of a prolonged shortage made the 'cotton famine' a matter of the utmost strategic importance. While some European merchants and politicians called for military intervention to break the Union blockade, most pinned their hopes on stimulating production—via administrative, fiscal, or more forcible means—in overseas lands that already lay under their formal or informal influence.

India was in many respects the prime candidate, since it was already a major cotton producer in its own right. For centuries, South Asian farmers had grown cotton alongside a range of other crops, selling most of it to the thriving domestic handloom industry that had long led the world in the production of fine cotton cloth.[18] Although the industry had declined precipitously in the early 1800s under the impact of British cloth imports, raw cotton was still an important cash crop across large parts of the subcontinent, above all in the 'black soil' regions of the Bombay Presidency, North-Western Provinces, Madras, and Berar, where it was generally sown with the early rains and harvested after the monsoons.[19] Bombay was the chief conduit through which Indian cotton was shipped to China, Britain, and continental Europe. Even before the advent of the railways, exports rose from 27 million kg in the mid-1820s to over 61 million kg in 1847–8 (Fig. 1.1).[20]

The potential for India to reduce Britain's dependence on US cotton imports had long attracted the attention of officials and traders. Over the first half of the mid-nineteenth century the East India Company launched dozens of initiatives to improve Indian cotton production, though little came of such efforts due to the dominance of US output and the continued transport and quality problems of the Indian crop.[21] Before the 1860s, most metropolitan manufacturers regarded Indian cotton as an emergency buffer against unexpected price increases for the American long-staple product that they strongly preferred. As a result, demand for Indian cotton was highly volatile. Annual prices fluctuated by as much as 70 per cent, and this unpredictability made Indian farmers all the more hesitant to increase their cotton acreage for sale to European merchants who might or might not want their produce.[22]

---

[18] See Giorgio Riello and Tirthankar Roy (eds), *How India Clothed the World: The World of South Asian Textiles, 1500–1850* (Leiden: Brill, 2009).

[19] Generally, Peter Harnetty, '"Deindustrialization" Revisited: The Handloom Weavers of the Central Provinces of India, c.1800–1947', *Modern Asian Studies*, vol. 25 no. 3 (1991), 455–510; Albert Howard, *Crop Production in India: A Critical Survey of its Problems* (Oxford: Oxford University Press, 1924), 88–96.

[20] J. F. Richards and Michelle B. McAlpin, 'Cotton Cultivating and Land Clearing in the Bombay Deccan and Karnatak: 1818–1920', in Richard P. Tucker and J. F. Richards (eds), *Global Deforestation and the Nineteenth-Century World Economy* (Durham, NC: Duke University Press, 1983), 68–94, here 81.

[21] J. Forbes Royle, *On the Culture and Commerce of Cotton in India and Elsewhere: With an Account of the Experiments Made by the Hon. East India Company up to the Present Time* (London: Smith, Elder & Co., 1851), esp. 82–116; Walter R. Cassels, *Cotton: An Account of its Culture in the Bombay Presidency* (Bombay, 1862), 8–30; Peter Harnetty, 'The Cotton Improvement Program in India 1865–1875', *Agricultural History*, vol. 44, no. 4 (Oct. 1970), 379–92.

[22] Neil Charlesworth, *Peasants and Imperial Rule: Agriculture and Agrarian Society in the Bombay Presidency, 1850–1935* (Cambridge: Cambridge University Press, 1985), 81.

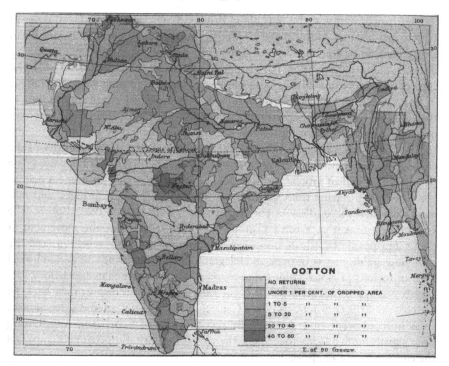

Fig. 1.1. Map of cotton regions in colonial India: *The Imperial Gazetteer of India*, vol. 26, Atlas edited by J. G. Bartholomew (Oxford: Clarendon, 1909), Map 18. By permission of Oxford University Press.

All of this changed abruptly with the onset of the 'cotton famine'. As prices for Indian cotton surged—nearly quintupling 1861–4—cultivators responded by clearing new land and planting cotton in fields that had previously been used for subsistence crops. From 1860/1 to 1864/5 the total cotton surface in India's main producer provinces rose by 75 per cent, from 1.8 million to 3.16 million hectares. Overall production grew accordingly from an estimated 273 million kg before the crisis to 409 million kg afterwards (the slight lag behind acreage growth probably reflected an expansion onto more marginal lands). Most of the increase went into exports, which rose from 179 million kg in 1861–2 to 406 million kg in 1865–6. Despite the quality problems that Indian cotton posed for European mills, it none-theless helped keep them running throughout the early 1860s. Whereas India accounted for only 15 per cent of British cotton imports in 1860, by 1862 its share leapt to 75 per cent. In France, too, India supplied as much as 70 per cent of cotton imports during the American Civil War.[23]

---

[23] Figures from Peter Harnetty, 'Cotton Exports and Indian Agriculture, 1861–1870', *Economic History Review*, vol. 24 no. 3 (Aug. 1971), 414–29, here 414–16; Peter Harnetty, *Imperialism and Free Trade: Lancashire and India in the Mid-Nineteenth Century* (Vancouver: University of British Columbia Press, 1972), 83, 92–3; Beckert, 'Emancipation', 1413.

High prices were not the only thing driving these changes. In the summer of 1861 a coalition of cotton magnates and colonial officials expanded experiment farms, distributed seeds to farmers, dispatched cotton gins into the main growing districts, and even offered a 10,000-rupee award to whoever delivered the largest consignment of cotton from a 30-acre plot.[24] Over the coming years, the impact of improved communications, amendments to contract law, and innovations in the credit system were the most important factors. As soon as prices began to rise, indigenous moneylenders and cotton dealers (often backed by European trading firms) offered advances to farmers for the purchase of seed on the security of the crop to be harvested. To assist the inflow of capital, colonial legislators passed new lien laws designed to protect investors for the entire value of the advances paid to growers.[25] At the same time, government investment in roads, bridges, and railways expedited the outflow of cotton from inland districts to coastal ports. The Crown government of Viceroy Canning was keen to facilitate the movement of goods and people (not least troops) in the wake of the 1857 rebellion, and the thousands of kilometres of track and telegraph lines built during this period linked interior regions to global commodity markets more directly than ever before. The Bombay–Nagpur Line, completed in the early 1860s, cut transport time between the coast and the cotton tracts of the Central Provinces from around three months to as little as twenty-four hours.[26] By reducing carrying costs and transmitting price signals more quickly to farmers, the new communication channels amplified the effect of boom-era prices.

Meanwhile, some 5,000 kilometres to the west, the convulsions of the world cotton market unleashed a similar dynamic in Egypt. Here, too, cotton was already an important export crop. In 1861 it covered around a quarter million feddans (*c.*105,000 ha) of land, which together yielded between half a million and 600,000 cantars (*c.*27 million kg) of raw cotton per year.[27] By 1865 Egyptian cotton production had risen fourfold and acreage nearly fivefold, covering around 40 per cent of the entire cultivable area of Lower Egypt. Exports to Europe roughly trebled over the same period, the bulk of it going to Britain with the balance mainly shipped to Marseille and Trieste.[28] The cotton famine of the 1860s marked a fundamental turning point for Egypt by cementing cotton's status as its dominant commercial export. As Timothy Mitchell has remarked, 'No other place in the world in the nineteenth century was transformed on a greater scale to serve the production of a single industry.'[29] As one contemporary put it, by the turn of the century it was 'not exaggerated to say that Egypt has become a land of monoculture'.[30]

24 Cassels, *Cotton*, 343; Harnetty, *Imperialism*, 78–80.
25 See Beckert, 'Emancipation', 1411–13; Harnetty, *Imperialism*, 74–5.
26 Richards and McAlpin, 'Cotton Cultivating', 82; Harnetty, 'Cotton Exports', 416.
27 The conversion rates are: 1 feddan = 1.038 acres = 0.42 ha; 1 cantar = 99 lb = 45 kg.
28 Figures from Todd, *World's Cotton*, 421; Roger Owen, *Cotton and the Egyptian Economy, 1820–1914: A Study in Trade and Development* (Oxford: Clarendon, 1969), 89–90, 92–5, 103, 161–6; Alan Richards, *Egypt's Agricultural Development, 1800–1980: Technical and Social Change* (Boulder, Colo.: Westview, 1982), xiii.
29 Timothy Mitchell, *Colonising Egypt* (Cambridge: Cambridge University Press, 1988), 16.
30 François Charles-Roux, *La Production du coton en Égypte* (Paris: A. Colin, 1908), 329.

The seeds for this transformation were sown several decades earlier under the arch-modernizer Muhammad 'Ali. After seizing power in 1805 and crushing his Mamluk opponents in 1811, 'Ali's principal goal was to strengthen the Egyptian army in a bid for independence from Ottoman rule. This required more revenue, but since most of Egypt's commerce was with the Ottoman Empire, the key to achieving his goal was to reorient trade towards Europe. Cotton was by far the most promising means for doing so, and soon became the chief moneymaker behind 'Ali's modernization strategy. The first step was the propagation and dissemination of long-stapled 'Jumel' cotton (a perennial tree variety named after a Frenchman working for 'Ali) after the 1820s. Over the longer term it involved the construction of hundreds of kilometres of new irrigation canals, the deepening of existing water channels, and the building of countless *saqiyas* and *shadufs* to lift the low summer waters into the fields. In the 1840s work began on the massive Delta Barrage about 30 kilometres below Cairo (though construction faults delayed its use for several decades), and after 'Ali's death in 1848 his successors continued to expand the network of canals, barrages, railways, and port facilities for the express purpose of boosting cotton exports.[31]

The cotton famine of the 1860s triggered a huge acceleration of these ongoing efforts. Just as in India, the bull market brought a rapid expansion of communications, ginning, and credit facilities, mostly underpinned by European capital. After the completion of the Alexandria–Cairo and Cairo–Suez railways in the 1850s, numerous branch-lines were built into the Delta. Large cash injections were also needed to purchase additional seed and foodstuffs as more and more growers increased their cotton acreage. Whereas wealthy landowners could obtain the necessary advances from banks, ordinary fellaheen (smallholders) usually turned to the swelling number of usurers plying the countryside, many of them tied to foreign merchants in Alexandria who were eager to secure as much cotton as possible for transhipment to Europe. Irrigation efforts similarly intensified as a result of the crisis; under the reign of Isma'il (1863–79) some 13,500 kilometres of new canals were dug.[32]

In many respects Egypt was even better placed than India to offset Europe's reliance on US cotton. Lower transport costs were one advantage—all the more so before the opening of the Suez Canal in 1869—but higher quality was just as important. In stark contrast to the short, brittle fibres that characterized most South Asian cotton varieties, Egyptian Jumel boasted a fine, long, and sturdy staple that commanded a premium on world markets. Even better was the Ashmouni variety (a cross between local stocks and imported American Sea Island) that spread

---

[31] Owen, *Cotton*, 50; Robert Hanbury Brown, *History of the Barrage at the Head of the Delta of Egypt* (Cairo: E. Diemer, 1896); M. A. Hollings (ed.), *The Life of Sir Colin C. Scott-Moncrieff* (London: John Murray, 1917), 200–5; Richards, *Egypt's Agricultural Development*, 20–30; Thomas K. Fowler, *Report on the Cultivation of Cotton in Egypt: Its Origin, Progress, and Extent at the Present Day; The Obstacles which Prevent its Extension; Suggestions for Effectually Removing them, etc.* (Manchester, 1861).

[32] Owen, *Cotton*, 105–6; Richards, *Egypt's Agricultural Development*, 29–30.

throughout Egypt's fields after the 1860s.[33] To make the most of this botanical advantage, Egyptian authorities established a strict system of quality control. In contrast to India, where the long chain of middlemen often obscured responsibility for dirty or substandard cotton, the major Alexandria merchants bought directly at central collection points and paid growers according to grade. All of this was made easier by the fact that much of Egypt's cotton was grown not on smallholdings but on the estates of rich landlords who were eager to deploy the latest techniques and to set quality standards for smallholders to follow. Isma'il himself, who seized vast areas of land for his family and supporters, took considerable pride in his role as a 'model farmer'.[34]

The rapid expansion of cotton in Egypt and India was extraordinary, but it was not wholly unique. The collapse of American exports and the record prices of the early 1860s prompted a rash of planting in many other parts of the world, from Brazil to Turkey and from Argentina to West Africa.[35] Yet none of them—with the partial exception of Brazil—were more than marginal players compared to India and Egypt. In these two new centres of world cotton production, the upheavals caused by the American Civil War triggered a burst of land conversion and agricultural commercialization whose effects reverberated for many decades to come.

COLONIAL COTTON AND ENVIRONMENTAL CHANGE IN INDIA AND EGYPT

As soon as reports of the Confederate surrender in April 1865 were telegraphed around the globe, cotton markets plunged. Although it was a disastrous blow for many growers and merchants, for some observers it was decidedly welcome news. Sir Alfred Comyn Lyall, then a district officer at Hoshungabad in India's Central Provinces (later Home Secretary and Foreign Secretary to the Government of India), remarked that 'I hope it will never rise again, for the government wearied the life out of us district officers by making us turn cotton fanciers. . . . I am terribly sick of the name of cotton, and I am very glad to see the honest rustics of Hoshungabad returning to wheat crops.'[36]

As things turned out, the swift return of the United States as the world's leading exporter brought only a temporary halt to colonial cotton expansion. Indian exports, despite falling by over half between 1865/6 (406 million kg) and 1866/7 (194 million kg), were still significantly higher than before the 1860s, and eventually climbed to 545 million kg by the First World War, most of it going to continental

[33] W. Lawrence Balls, *The Cotton Plant in Egypt: Studies in Physiology and Genetics* (London: Macmillan, 1919), 2–4; Todd, *World's Cotton*, 236–8.

[34] Owen, *Cotton*, 75–6, 93, 98. By 1863, estates already accounted for over one-seventh of the cultivated surface: Timothy Mitchell: *Rule of Experts: Egypt, Techno-politics, Modernity* (Berkeley: University of California Press, 2002), 71.

[35] Beckert, *Empire*, 242–73.

[36] Sir Mortimer Durand, *Life of the Right Hon. Sir Alfred Comyn Lyall* (Edinburgh: Blackwood, 1913), 122. I thank John M. MacKenzie for kindly bringing this quote to my attention.

Europe and Japan.[37] Egyptian output recovered even more quickly. After suffering a short-term collapse, exports surpassed their 1865 peak in the early 1870s and proceeded to grow to around 340 million kg by 1914, the bulk of it destined for Britain.[38] Well into the twentieth century, Europe's textile industries continued to draw heavily on the soil, water, and labour resources of India and the Nile valley.

Extracting these assets required a major transformation of the landscape. In the central and western provinces of India, huge tracts of acacia bush and dry monsoon forest were cleared for cultivation. Although cotton was only one of many crops on the rise during the late nineteenth century, it nonetheless accounted for a disproportionate share of land clearance in these regions, and served as an important catalyst for agricultural commercialization more generally. In the Bombay Deccan and Karnatak, cotton acreage roughly doubled from the early 1860s to the 1910s, growing around twice as fast as the overall cultivated area.[39] In newly established cotton belts such as the Khandesh district in the northern Deccan, a sixfold rise in cotton acreage covered around one-third of all the land farmed there. As the *Khandesh Gazeteer* commented in 1878, whereas 'a vast belt of good soil, covered with a tangled growth of *babhul* or *palas* trees, stretched for miles from the Satpuda Hills south towards the Tapti (River)' before the 1860s, less than two decades later 'no tracts of good land lie waste. Scrub jungle there still is, but this is confined to rocky lines of hill or rolling stony ground that will yield no crop save grass.'[40]

Trees were by no means the only things that disappeared. As the forests made way, so too did most of the animals living in them, whether through the creeping process of habitat destruction or deliberate culling campaigns. In Berar, for instance, authorities paid bounties of 20 rupees per tiger, 15 rupees per panther, 7 for wolves, and 5 for bears and hyenas.[41] Springs and perennial streams also dried up as woodlands vanished. By the 1870s officials in the cotton tracts of Hyderabad complained that 'the influences which help to conserve moisture have been removed. Not only is it that the rainfall drains off more rapidly, but the face of the soil is exposed to evaporate influences to a far greater extent than formerly.'[42] Local farmers likewise worried that forest clearance was lowering regional rainfall, which in fact declined significantly in some regions in the latter nineteenth century. In the rain-fed cotton tracts of central and western India, the

[37] By 1914, the bulk of Indian output went to continental Europe and Japan rather than Britain: Todd, *World's Cotton*, 19, 45; Harnetty, 'Cotton Exports', 414; Beckert, 'Emancipation', 1421–3.

[38] Todd, *World's Cotton*, 421–6; Richards, *Egypt's Agricultural Development*, 32–3.

[39] Richards and McAlpin, 'Cotton Cultivating', 79–80.

[40] Quoted from Richards and McAlpin, 'Cotton Cultivating', 89.

[41] Laxman D. Satya, *Cotton and Famine in Berar 1850–1900* (New Delhi: Manohar, 1997), 57.

[42] Sir A. C. Lyall, 1870, *Gazetteer of the Haidarabad Assigned Districts, Commonly called Berar* (1870), 45, quoted from Satya, *Cotton and Famine*, 194; see also Allan Octavian Hume, *Agricultural Reform in India* (London: W. H. Allen, 1879), 58–9; Richards and McAlpin, 'Cotton Cultivating', 84–6; on 'desiccation' more generally, Richard H. Grove, 'A Historical Review of Institutional and Conservationist Responses to Fears of Artificially Induced Global Climate Change: The Deforestation–Desiccation Discourse in Europe and the Colonial Context, 1500–1940', in Yvon Chatelin and Christophe Bonneuil (eds), *Nature et environnement* (Paris: Orstom Éditions, 1995), 155–74.

removal of forest cover thus threatened to undermine the yield of the very crops that replaced it.[43]

In the densely populated Nile valley, much of which had been cultivated for millennia, the main ecological consequences came not in the form of forest loss but rather in the alteration of long-established methods of land use and water control. Much of the acreage that was planted with cotton had previously been used as pasture, and the state-sponsored push to convert such land—much of it seized by large estates—to more commercially profitable uses was especially hard on nomadic groups whose transhumant grazing patterns were forcibly suppressed by a tax-hungry khedive bent on sedentarizing them.[44] But even on plots that had been cultivated for generations, the expansion of cotton brought major changes.

For thousands of years, farmers in Egypt employed an ingenious system of basin irrigation designed to capitalize on the annual ebb and flow of the Nile's waters, which flooded from August to October and were at their lowest in the early summer months. The basic technique was to construct low dykes around fields and then excavate canals through the river banks to allow the seasonal floods to inundate the basins, where they deposited a layer of rich volcanic silt carried downstream from the Ethiopian highlands. After standing on the fields for around forty days, the water was released back into the river or into an adjacent basin. The system was generally maintained by the fellaheen who directly benefited from it, and it boasted many virtues. It demanded little fertilization beyond the annual silt subsidy; it minimized labour inputs by allowing planters to sow crops on soft, moist fields; it avoided the build-up of salts in the soil through the annual flushing of the basins; and it aided soil aeration by allowing the soil to heat and crack during the hot summer months just before the flood.

According to the renowned British engineer William Willcocks, basin irrigation was 'the most efficacious method of utilising existing means of irrigation which the world has witnessed'.[45] The problem was that it was ill suited to raising summer crops, especially cotton, whose growing season from February to October mapped awkwardly onto the rhythms of the Nile. Because cotton was harvested after the floodwaters began to rise, it had to be planted on high ground to avoid being destroyed. Yet during its main growing season from early spring to summer it also needed copious amounts of water—around one vertical metre per crop—precisely when the river was at its lowest ebb.[46] It was a prime example of a systemic temporal disjunction, for the needs of large-scale cotton cultivation and the cadences of the Nile simply did not match. For cotton to become a major export crop in Egypt, year-round irrigation was a must.

The advent of perennial irrigation was an epoch-making watershed for the anthropogenic ecosystems of the Nile valley. Fields that had been cultivated for

---

[43] Sandip Hazareesingh, 'Cotton, Climate and Colonialism in Dharwar, Western India, 1840–1880', *Journal of Historical Geography*, vol. 38 no. 1 (2012), 1–17; Satya, *Cotton and Famine*, 81, 195.

[44] Mitchell, *Rule of Experts*, 61–2.

[45] Sir W. Willcocks and J. I. Craig, *Egyptian Irrigation*, vol. 1, 3rd edn (London: Spon, 1913), 299.

[46] Willcocks and Craig, *Egyptian Irrigation*, vol. 2, 768–73; Richards, *Egypt's Agricultural Development*, 15–19.

millennia according to the rhythm of the annual floodwaters could now grow crops year-round. Intensifying the use of Egypt's fertile alluvial soils had been the basic aim of irrigation modernizers ever since Muhammad 'Ali's day, and the British, for their part, took the endeavour to new lengths after occupying Egypt in 1882. In Lower Egypt, the completion of the Delta Barrage in 1891 raised summer water levels and extended cotton cultivation across the entire Delta. Further upstream, the Assiut Barrage (1903) and the first Aswan Dam (1902) extended year-round water supplies to much of Middle and Upper Egypt.[47] By the eve of the First World War over 1.6 million hectares had been converted to perennial irrigation, leaving only 522,000 hectares under traditional basin irrigation.[48] Cotton was not, of course, the only cultivar grown on these lands: maize, sugar cane, and rice also became important summer crops. But it was very much the driving force behind the changes, and accounted for over three-quarters of the total summer acreage in the early 1900s.[49] It was less a matter of irrigation promoting cotton cultivation than the other way around. As contemporaries clearly recognized, 'the increasingly important role of cotton in Egyptian agriculture is the cause of the unremitting advance of irrigation'.[50]

All of these changes in Egypt and India were part of a broader reordering of relations between those living on the land and the resources on which they depended. Broadly speaking, the attempt to intensify the use of soil and water resources often had the effect of distancing them from local communities, which meant that the environmental and social consequences of cotton expansion were inextricably intertwined. For millions of Egyptian farmers, the shift from seasonal basin irrigation towards a more centralized perennial irrigation system brought a reduction of control over both local water supplies as well as their own labour. Ever since the reign of Muhammad 'Ali, the vast amounts of manpower needed to build new canals, to lower the beds of existing channels, or to construct dams and *saqiyas* was obtained via a *corvée* system that was larger than anything seen since the days of the pharaohs.[51] Nor did these labour exactions cease upon the completion of the canals, which regularly had to be cleared after the annual floods to maintain their flow. Moreover, commercial cotton production often involved gambling with one's rights over the land itself. In India and Egypt alike, the debts that farmers took on to buy seed, tools, and food for the growing season were generally secured against their land or their cotton crops, thus enmeshing them in a web of credit and market dynamics over which they had no control. It was a riskier mode of life all around, one that traded communal forms of tenure for

[47] Sir W. Willcocks, *The Assuan Reservoir and Lake Moeris* (London: Spon, 1904), 5–9; Richards, *Egypt's Agricultural Development*, 69; more generally on changes to the Nile, Terje Tvedt, *The River Nile in the Age of the British: Political Ecology and the Quest for Economic Power* (London: Tauris, 2004).

[48] Willcocks and Craig, *Egyptian Irrigation*, vol. 1, 303, 366.

[49] Willcocks and Craig, *Egyptian Irrigation*, vol. 2, 770: cotton covered 1.64 million out of 2.18 million acres.

[50] Charles-Roux, *La Production*, 210.

[51] Willcocks and Craig, *Egyptian Irrigation*, vol. 1, 371; Hollings (ed.), *Scott-Moncrieff*, 208–11; Todd, *World's Cotton*, 242–3; Owen, *Cotton*, 47–8; Richards, *Egypt's Agricultural Development*, 19.

individual titles and loans, and that swapped the relative security of food crops for higher rates of return.[52]

As long as prices and yields were good, the implicit drawbacks of this modus operandi were less apparent than the attendant benefits. During the boom of the early 1860s, incomes for cotton cultivators rose considerably in spite of the margins creamed off by moneylenders and tax collectors. Windfall profits enabled many Egyptian fellaheen to build houses or purchase valuables such as jewellery or furniture. From Gujarat to Berar, high cotton returns provided ryots with a welcome, albeit temporary, respite from their persistent dependence on moneylenders.[53] In the short term, the main threats to food security stemmed more from exogenous factors—the Nile floods and cattle plague of 1863, or the regional monsoon failures of the mid-1860s—than from the conversion to cotton per se. In western India the profits gained from cotton actually helped see some cultivators through these periods of food shortage.[54]

Yet as prices fell sharply during the late 1860s–70s, millions of peasant households found themselves hopelessly overextended. Some of the worst effects were felt in the Nile Delta, where the price drop coincided with hefty land tax hikes designed to service the government's ballooning debt to British and French creditors.[55] Faced with unpayable tax burdens, some fellaheen simply abandoned their land to escape the levies. Many who remained went bankrupt, setting off a wave of foreclosures that further polarized social relations in the Egyptian countryside. As land passed increasingly into the hands of moneylenders, pashas, and village sheikhs, a growing army of landless labourers—estimated to comprise around one-third of the rural population in the early 1870s—ended up working for wages on the large estates or migrating to the cities.[56] Against this backdrop it is hardly surprising that so many fellaheen joined the 'Urabi rebellion of 1882 in a bid to cancel peasant debt and 'banish the usurers'. This basic trend continued more or less unchanged after the suppression of the rebellion and the establishment of the British protectorate. In 1888, six years after the British occupation, the top 1 per cent of Egyptian landowners owned over two-fifths of the land, while the bottom 80 per cent held only one-fifth.[57] During the 1870s and 1880s a broadly similar story unfolded in the cotton tracts of India. Although peasant indebtedness was an enduring feature of life in much of the central and western subcontinent, the unprecedented levels of borrowing during the boom years of the early 1860s made it impossible for many farmers to repay their loans. To make matters worse, many of the lenders were no longer local elites with an awareness of traditional land-use rights, but were instead distant outsiders armed with new colonial lien laws that

[52] Owen, *Cotton*, 106–7, 147–8.

[53] Hume, *Agricultural Reform*, 63–4; Harnetty, 'Cotton Exports', 414–29; Owen, *Cotton*, 107; Charlesworth, *Peasants*, 135–7.

[54] Harnetty, 'Cotton Exports', 420; Owen, *Cotton*, 98–102.

[55] For background: David S. Landes, *Bankers and Pashas: International Finance and Economic Imperialism in Egypt* (Cambridge, Mass.: Harvard University Press, 1958), 224–318.

[56] Owen, *Cotton*, 147–8.

[57] Richards, *Egypt's Agricultural Development*, 37–44, quote from p. 42.

gave them effective control over the land and labour of their debtors. In some of the poorest districts of Maharashtra the resulting displacement and desperation eventually exploded in the Deccan Riots of 1875, which specifically targeted 'foreign' moneylenders and merchants.[58]

This reorganization of the countryside left millions in a more precarious situation than before, estranged from the land and dependent on the cash economy for survival. But if the transformation was often subtle, the consequences could be catastrophic. In the late 1870s, and once more in the late 1890s, millions of people in central and western India died of starvation as falling cotton prices and rising grain costs made food unobtainable for the poorest growers. Food crises were certainly not new to these regions, and nor were they confined to cotton-growing centres, but there is little doubt that the famines of the late nineteenth century were tied to cotton cultivation in several ways.[59] Mortality rates were particularly high in Berar, India's leading cotton-producing region, where the famines of the 1890s killed around 10 per cent of the entire population. By the 1870s cotton covered a far higher proportion of land in Berar (around a third) than in any other province, prompting Sir Allan Octavian Hume, then a secretary in the Department of Revenue, Agriculture, and Commerce, to warn that 'the more the area of food stocks is diminished in favour of fibres, the greater the danger from any failure of the monsoon becomes'.[60] In the event, the high death tolls in Berar resulted not from a lack of food—on average, the region exported around a quarter of its food grains throughout the entire period 1879–1903, shipping out food in each of these years[61]—but rather, as colonial officials themselves came to acknowledge, from an inability of the poorest groups to purchase the food they needed. Worst affected were small landholders, landless labourers, and especially women, whose wages were generally lower than men's. In this sense, the heavy reliance on cotton rendered regions such as Berar more susceptible to famine by enmeshing poor growers into a cash economy that exposed them to high food prices in times of shortage.[62]

The growth of colonial cotton thus illustrates a fundamental point: in agrarian societies operating close to subsistence levels, any alteration in the choice of crops or land-use practices carries profound social implications. For farming communities across the world, the essential unity of the human economy and nature's economy is clear and immediate. It is well understood that the relationships binding them together are fundamentally reciprocal. Indeed, this reciprocity is so powerful as to

[58] Neil Charlesworth, 'The Myth of the Deccan Riots of 1875', *Modern Asian Studies*, vol. 6 no. 4 (1972), pp. 401–21, esp. 413–16. For a detailed regional study: Maurus Staubli, *Reich und arm mit Baumwolle. Exportorientierte Landwirtschaft und soziale Stratifikation am Beispiel des Baumwollanbaus im indischen Distrikt Khandesh (Dekkan) 1850–1914* (Stuttgart: Steiner, 1994).

[59] Satya, *Cotton and Famine*, 281–96; Hazareesingh, 'Cotton', 13, 16.

[60] *Report of the Cotton Trading Season of Central Provinces and Berar*, in *Proceedings of the Dept. of Revenue, Agriculture and Commerce* (Fibre and Silk Branches), quoted from Satya, *Cotton and Famine*, 196.

[61] Mortality and export figures from Satya, *Cotton and Famine*, 184–5, 284–6.

[62] More generally on famine and the cash economy, Davis, *Late Victorian Holocausts*; Amartya Sen, *Poverty and Famines: An Essay on Entitlement and Deprivation* (Oxford: Clarendon, 1981).

render the same point equally true in reverse: wherever the bulk of people live directly from the land, any changes in the social fabric have important environmental consequences. For this reason, the social dislocations caused by new systems of land tenure, credit, and market integration were mirrored in a corresponding set of biophysical changes in the main colonial cotton-growing areas.

One of the chief casualties was the soil, or more specifically the various fallow systems that had long been employed to maintain fertility. Wherever cotton had been grown over many generations it was generally cultivated alongside other crops in systems of long-term rotation. Most Indian smallholders, for instance, traditionally grew it no more than every three or four years, and even in the 1910s it was still widely planted as a mixed crop.[63] But as economic pressures encouraged cotton growers to extract more revenue from the soil—whether to capitalize on high prices while they could, or to meet tax and credit burdens when markets were low—such traditional safeguards were increasingly ignored. In the wake of the famines of the 1870s, an official in Berar noted that 'the rapid succession on which crop succeeds crop in the present was not known in the bygone period of reference, and field land has therefore undergone an exhaustion of its fertile elements'. Whereas cultivators 'used to take for their use as much land as they pleased for a nominal rent, thus enabling themselves to allow rest alternately to portions of the land', the colonial system of individual title and taxation meant that farmers 'cannot now take an inch more than is allotted to them, and try to realize out of it as much crop as they can to defray Government demand, as also to satisfy their avarice, which has considerably increased on account of high prices'.[64]

While the curtailment of fallows took its toll on the fields, soil fertility was further compromised by the encroachment of cotton on to forest and scrub. The clearance and cultivation of former 'wastelands' meant that there was less opportunity to graze livestock, and with fewer livestock came a growing shortage of manure. In the black-soil tracts of central India, where peasants were understandably reluctant to set aside arable land for pasturage and shrank their herds accordingly, the supply of manure became 'so reduced as to be altogether insufficient to meet the demands of the soil for nourishment'.[65] To make matters worse, the concurrent clearing or government enclosure of wooded areas (see Chapter 8) also forced many peasants to burn crop stalks or dung for fuel, further depriving the soil of nutrients.[66] By the early twentieth century the shortage of manure was regarded as one of the chief factors behind the stagnation of cotton yields in India, which remained only half of those in the United States and a quarter of yields in Egypt.[67] This 'mining' of soil

[63] Cassels, *Cotton*, 202, 246; Todd, *World's Cotton*, 19.

[64] *Famine Commission Report* (1881), 299, quoted from Satya, *Cotton and Famine*, 77–8.

[65] *Famine Commission Report* (1881), 299, from Satya, *Cotton and Famine*, 79.

[66] See John Augustus Voelcker, *Report on the Improvement of Indian Agriculture* (London: Eyre & Spottiswoode, 1893), 407–8, who sharply criticized the Agricultural Department for its fixation on cotton hybrids and ploughing at the expense of such wider issues.

[67] Sir George Watt, *The Wild and Cultivated Cotton Plants of the World: A Revision of the Genus Gossypium* (London: Longmans, Green, 1907), 99–100, 198–200; Howard, *Crop Production*, 89; Todd, *World's Cotton*, 19; Voelcker, *Report*, 255–6; Harnetty, *Imperialism*, 86–7.

and forest resources diminished the ecological reserves that sustained overall crop production, including cotton itself.[68]

In Egypt, too, there was a strong connection between the privation of cultivators and the impoverishment of the soil. After the boom of the early 1860s, the combination of collapsing cotton prices and rapid tax increases not only forced farmers to boost production, it also reduced the value of their land, in some cases to the point of making it a financial liability. These twin pressures of sinking incomes and rising costs—which were further compounded by levies for *corvée* or military service—furnished an overwhelming incentive to generate cash from the land as quickly as possible. Instead of growing cotton every four years, many cultivators began to plant it every three or even two years, with maize or fodder crops often following the harvest instead of a period of fallow. By 1908, over half of the Delta was on two-year rotations, including the bulk of land in the cotton districts of Daqahliyah, Buhaira, Sharqiya, and Gharbiya.[69] In the short term this shortening of fallows—along with the introduction of the pest-resistant Mit Afifi strain in the late 1880s—achieved impressive yields, which increased from around 3.5 to nearly 5.5 cantars per feddan during the 1890s alone. But over the longer term it damaged soil fertility by depleting nutrients and eliminating any period during which the ground could heat up and crack, which was important not only for soil aeration but also, as agronomists later discovered, for killing off protozoa that competed with beneficial nitrifying bacteria.[70] In other words, the spike in productivity that was achieved during the 1890s was largely based on the extraction of fertility reserves that had previously been maintained by less intensive forms of cropping. And it was not long before these reserves were depleted. Yields soon stagnated after the turn of the century, and eventually fell back to 1880s levels by the latter 1910s.

After decades of steady growth in Egypt, this productivity slump caused widespread consternation. The ensuing debate about its causes and potential remedies repays closer attention, for it highlights how the inertia of political and economic habits shapes understandings of, and responses to, environmental change.

Broadly speaking, there were four main explanations for the problem: the deterioration of the Mit Afifi variety through unwanted hybridization, attack by pests (especially boll worm and cotton worm), over-cropping, and the effects of rising groundwater levels.[71] Separating these factors was problematic, for there were 'so many influences affecting the yield of cotton that it is difficult to decide which has predominated in any particular year'.[72] After extensive debate, scientists eventually

---

[68] Richards and McAlpin, 'Cotton Cultivating', 93–4. Generations of Southern planters had learned this lesson the hard way in the form of barren fields and acute erosion problems—lessons that eventually played a central role in the formation of the US Soil Conservation Service: Paul Sutter, 'What Gullies Mean: Georgia's "Little Grand Canyon" and Southern Environmental History', *Journal of Southern History*, vol. 76 no. 3 (Aug. 2010), 579–616.

[69] Owen, *Cotton*, 149, 186.

[70] Richards, *Egypt's Agricultural Development*, 70–6; Moritz Schanz, *Cotton in Egypt and the Anglo-Egyptian Sudan* (Manchester: Taylor, Garnett, Evans, 1913), 25–6.

[71] Charles-Roux, *La Production*, 270–2; Schanz, *Cotton in Egypt*, 75–7; Todd, *World's Cotton*, 258; Owen, *Cotton*, 194.

[72] Hanbury Brown, 'Introduction', in Willcocks and Craig, *Egyptian Irrigation*, vol. 1, xxii.

singled out waterlogging as the primary culprit. Careful measurements established that water tables in the middle Delta had risen from between 6 and 8 metres below the surface in the early nineteenth century to around 3 to 4 metres in the mid-1880s, to only 1 metre by 1908.[73] The rise in groundwater levels not only asphyxiated plant roots, it also encouraged salinization by drawing subsoil salts up to the surface through capillary action. In the case of a thirsty summer crop like cotton, the problem of salinization was amplified by high evaporation rates, which significantly raised the salinity levels of summer irrigation water. At the same time, the presence of so much water promoted pest infestation, as did the more intensive cropping systems, which guaranteed a steady supply of host plants for harmful fungi and insects to feed on (a classic problem of monocultures).[74]

The fact that nearly all of these problems were linked to perennial irrigation did not escape notice, but for most contemporaries the idea that constant water supplies could be detrimental to yields was counter-intuitive. After all, irrigation was long seen as 'the source of everything in Egypt', where average annual rainfall is less than 80 mm.[75] Since nearly all of this precipitation falls in the winter months, irrigation was particularly vital for summer crops such as cotton. Ever since the days of Muhammad 'Ali, perennial irrigation was the basis of what seemed a winning 'package', one that raised the amount of labour per unit of land, increased the ratio of cropped area to cultivated area, and enabled farmers to keep a higher proportion of their fields under cotton. The issue came to a head in 1908–9 with a pair of unusually high and early Nile floods. Many assumed that these would be bumper years on the principle of 'the more water the better'. Instead, the result was a disastrously meagre crop of only 5 million cantars, mainly because the higher floodwaters increased the problem of waterlogging. Whereas before 1909 'the idea that too much water was possible would have been laughed to scorn', it soon became widely accepted.[76]

To a large extent, the slumping cotton yields after 1900 were the result of a decades-long overemphasis on water supply at the expense of adequate drainage. And as is so often the case when major environmental interventions go wrong, it stemmed not so much from a lack of knowledge as from a habit of ignoring unwelcome warning signs. By the early 1890s none other than the chief British engineer in the Irrigation Department, Sir Colin Scott-Moncrieff, cautioned that 'as irrigation without drainage always tends to injure the soil, and as drainage had been quite neglected, it had to be taken in hand'.[77] Like most irrigation officers in the Egypt, Scott-Moncrieff had first-hand experience of such problems in India and sought to avoid a recurrence. William Willcocks was even more critical of British efforts in Egypt, and advocated a wholesale return to traditional basin and

[73] H. T. Ferrar, *Preliminary Note on the Subsoil Water in Lower Egypt and its Bearing on the Reported Deterioration of the Cotton Crop* (Cairo: National Printing Dept, 1910), 9–15.

[74] Charles-Roux, *La Production*, 270–2; Schanz, *Cotton in Egypt*, 76–7; Balls, *Cotton Plant*, 176–8; Richards, *Egypt's Agricultural Development*, 72–6; Owen, *Cotton*, 190–4.

[75] Quote from the *Pall Mall Gazette*, 23 Mar. 1888, from Hollings, *Scott-Moncrieff*, 210.

[76] Todd, *World's Cotton*, 255–7, quote 257; Schanz, *Cotton in Egypt*, 25–6.

[77] Hollings, *Scott-Moncrieff*, 205.

lift irrigation. Although few other observers went this far, it was generally accepted after 1910 that better drainage was necessary to protect yields.[78]

What was missing was not an awareness of the problem but a sufficient incentive to deal with it. Unlike the expansion of the water supply, drainage did not quickly amortize its costs. This posed a dilemma, for the desire to ensure the repayment of Egypt's loans to European creditors was among the mix of factors that prompted the British decision to occupy the country in the first place. The French government, for its part, was opposed to any diversion of Egyptian revenues from the Caisse de la Dette Publique into works that would not quickly pay for themselves. The British authorities in Cairo likewise had little appetite to drum up the necessary funds since subventions from London would have contradicted the policy of financial self-sufficiency, and higher domestic taxes within Egypt would have undermined their ability to reduce land levies as a means of 'pacification'. The result, as one commentator summed it up, was that millions were annually spent on irrigation, and only thousands on drainage.[79]

It was only after Egypt achieved independence in 1922 that a large-scale drainage programme was finally carried out, but this hardly put an end to the problems of perennial irrigation. By the 1920s soil salinization in the provinces around Cairo had become so severe as to turn large areas into 'veritable man-made salt wastes'. In some districts cotton yields sank by as much as 75 per cent, mostly because of the previous failure, as one soil scientist put it, to 'consider these entirely self-evident pedological consequences in the quest for large profits'.[80] The barrages feeding the irrigation systems further compounded the effects of salinization. The first Aswan Dam, completed in 1902 to increase the supply of summer water, accelerated the decline in soil fertility by reducing the amount of silt deposited by the annual floods. Over the following years, and especially after the High Dam stopped the flow of silt altogether after 1970, only vast doses of artificial fertilizer could stabilize yields on the depleted soils of the Delta.[81] More alarming still was the gradual shrinkage of the Delta itself, whose millennia-long advance into the Mediterranean was initially halted and eventually reversed with the decline of silt deliveries. By the second half of the twentieth century, the falling nutrient subsidy from the Nile was also adversely affecting the fisheries of the south-eastern Mediterranean.[82] Another unwanted by-product was a swift rise in water-borne diseases, including malaria and especially bilharzia. Although the schistosome parasites that cause bilharzia had always existed in Egypt, the expansion of perennial irrigation created an ideal habitat for their snail hosts and quickly turned it into the country's foremost health problem after the turn of the century. As one

---

[78] Willcocks, Craig, *Egyptian Irrigation*, vol. 1, 410–11; Balls, *Cotton Plant*, 176–8; Todd, *World's Cotton*, 259–64.

[79] Todd, *World's Cotton*, 255.

[80] Quotes from Paul Vageler, *Koloniale Bodenkunde und Wirtschaftsplanung* (Berlin: Parey, 1941), 10–11.

[81] Richards, *Egypt's Agricultural Development*, 120–8.

[82] Daniel Jean Stanley and Andrew G. Warne, 'Nile Delta in its Destruction Phase', *Journal of Coastal Research*, vol. 14 no. 3 (Summer 1998), 794–825; Daniel Jean Stanley, 'Degradation of the Nile Delta', *Environmental Review*, vol. 4 (1997), 1–7; McNeill, *Something New*, 171–3.

historian has put it, 'cotton first tied bilharzia and Egypt together in a knot that has yet to be untangled'.[83]

Feeding Europe's cotton mills thus entailed a lasting withdrawal on nature's capital, one whose social costs were mostly borne by ordinary farmers, past, present, and future. As forests were cleared, rivers harnessed, and soils depleted, millions who planted cotton in an attempt to boost their incomes and improve their lives eventually found themselves working harder to survive and paying for things that used to be freely available. But resource exhaustion and stagnating yields were a problem not only for colonial cotton growers. By the turn of the century the threat of another cotton shortage also began to worry those at the very heart of imperial power. The difference, of course, was that European merchants and mill owners, unlike cultivators in the colonies, had the opportunity to escape such problems by drawing on hitherto untapped resources in other parts of the world. As European power swept across sub-Saharan Africa, the scope for doing so grew enormously.

NEW FRONTIERS: PEASANTS, PLANTATIONS, AND THE AFRICAN COTTON CAMPAIGN

At the close of the nineteenth century, the state of global cotton supplies once again provoked widespread anxiety in Europe. A marked rise in cotton prices—the first in a generation—sharpened concerns about the expanding textile industries in Japan and especially the United States, whose growing domestic market threatened to reduce the amount of cotton that it could ship overseas.[84] At the same time, the ravages of the boll weevil, which first entered Texas from Mexico in 1892 and quickly spread throughout the Cotton Belt, also posed a danger to US output.[85] Market volatility, punctuated by a temporary cornering of the US market by a group of American speculators in 1903–4, further stoked fears of higher prices for European manufacturers, who still relied overwhelmingly on the United States for raw cotton. Despite decades of effort to develop alternative supply regions, US market share actually peaked in 1897–8, accounting for 86 per cent of world cotton exports and three-quarters of global mill consumption.[86] Altogether, the situation had the makings of a major resource crisis.

[83] John Farley, *Bilharzia: A History of Imperial Tropical Medicine* (Cambridge: Cambridge University Press, 1991), 298; also Nancy E. Gallagher, *Egypt's Other Wars: Epidemics and the Politics of Public Health* (Syracuse, NY: Syracuse University Press, 1990).

[84] From 1877 to 1907, the number of spindles in the United States more than doubled from 10.6 to 23.2 million: Farnie and Jeremy (eds), *The Fibre*, 130. The UK still dominated textile production with 52.8 million spindles.

[85] James C. Giesen, *Boll Weevil Blues: Cotton, Myth, and Power in the American South* (Chicago: University of Chicago Press, 2011).

[86] Farnie and Jeremy (eds), *The Fibre*, 21.

Haunted by memories of the 1860s cotton famine, industrialists and policy-makers moved swiftly in search of new sources of supply. From a strategic standpoint, the ideal solution was to acquire larger quantities of cotton from territories already under European control. Previous Russian achievements in Central Asia—which made it one of the world's leading cotton producers by the early twentieth century—showed what could be accomplished through close cooperation between private capital and an expanding imperial state. Japanese efforts at state-based cotton expansion in Korea pointed in much the same direction.[87] 'The opening of new sources of cotton', remarked a German commentator, 'is one of the most pressing questions of economic survival, whose satisfactory solution is of equal interest to nearly all industrialized countries.'[88]

Much of the attention fell on the recently acquired colonies of sub-Saharan Africa, which seemed to possess vast areas of open land suitable for cotton. The idea of boosting African cotton production was in itself nothing new at the turn of the century. French officials had tried to stimulate cotton exports from Senegal as early as 1817, followed by Portuguese efforts in Angola.[89] During the American Civil War there was a chorus of calls to increase output in West Africa, Mozambique, and Madagascar, though dreams of transforming Africa into 'the true land of cotton' vanished as soon as US exports resumed.[90]

Before the 1890s there was little that European merchants or officials could do to influence African cotton production, confined as they were to coastal districts and unable to control inland trading networks. With the acquisition of formal colonies, a whole new range of possibilities opened up. Territorial states could facilitate the exploitation of resources in ways that private traders could not: through the construction of infrastructure, the alteration of land rights, new forms of taxation, or the mobilization of labour. At the same time, metropolitan cotton interests also became better organized to influence colonial policy from within. British cotton manufacturers, already well versed at lobbying government, stepped up their efforts through the creation of the British Cotton Growers' Association (BCGA) in 1902, which was followed a year later by the founding of the French Association Cotonnière Coloniale. Interest in African cotton was equally intense among the imperial newcomers. In Germany, the Kolonial-Wirtschaftliches Komitee was established in 1896 largely as a vehicle for promoting colonial cotton production, and German cotton magnates also formed a powerful bloc within the Kolonialgesellschaft. Similar associations sprang up in Italy, Belgium, and Portugal, and as fears of a supply crisis mounted, these organizations spearheaded European

---

[87] Beckert, *Empire*, 341–8.

[88] Moritz Schanz, 'Der koloniale Baumwollenbau', in *Verhandlungen des deutschen Kolonialkongresses 1910* (Berlin: Reimer, 1910), 817–41, here 819.

[89] Richard L. Roberts, *Two Worlds of Cotton: Colonialism and the Regional Economy in the French Soudan, 1800–1946* (Stanford, Calif.: Stanford University Press, 1996), 60–5; M. Anne Pitcher, 'Sowing the Seeds of Failure: Early Portuguese Cotton Cultivation in Angola and Mozambique, 1820–1926', *Journal of Southern African Studies*, vol. 17 no. 1 (Mar. 1991), 43–70.

[90] Céleste Duval, *Question cotonnière*.

efforts to boost African cotton exports.[91] Although cotton was not a motivating factor behind the initial 'scramble for Africa', it soon became a focal point for colonial states across much of the continent.

For a variety of reasons that we will examine below—social, economic, and environmental—the results of all this effort fell far short of expectations. Throughout the colonial era, Egypt alone produced more cotton than all of sub-Saharan Africa combined, accounting for over 95 per cent of African exports before 1914 and over three-quarters at the end of the 1920s.[92] The trickle of exports from sub-Saharan Africa never covered more than a tiny fraction of metropolitan cotton needs, and with no more than about 1 per cent of the global cotton trade, these colonies have often been relegated to a footnote in the wider history of the cotton industry.[93]

Yet in many respects this commercial perspective misses the point. African cotton may not have had a major impact on global or even European markets, but it nonetheless had profound consequences for African societies and environments.[94] The desire to secure cotton supplies was one of the principal drivers behind the intensification of colonial rule during the early twentieth century. No other crop elicited the same level of attention or was pushed as vigorously by the colonial powers. As one historian has aptly put it, 'the language of cotton became inextricably intertwined with the language of colonialism', most notably in the twin tropes of idle land and untapped labour.[95] Across large parts of the continent, converting these 'reserves' into white gold formed a centrepiece of colonial policy.

The attempt to do so rested on two interrelated sets of assumptions, one about Africa and the other about cotton. As far as Africa was concerned, the basic idea was that the right combination of market stimuli and infrastructure would unlock the latent productivity of its vast land and labour reserves—a kind of prototype of what later became the 'vent for surplus' theory.[96] Against the backdrop of West African palm oil and cocoa exports (see Chapter 2), the high hopes for cotton

---

[91] This paragraph is drawn from Beckert, *Empire*, 347–50; Galle, *La 'Famine du coton'*, 9; Thaddeus Sunseri, 'The *Baumwollfrage*: Cotton Colonialism in German East Africa', *Central European History*, vol. 34 no. 1 (Mar. 2001), 31–51; Steve Onyeiwu, 'Deceived by African Cotton: The British Cotton Growing Association and the Demise of the Lancashire Textile Industry', *African Economic History*, no. 28 (2000), 89–121; Jonathan Robins, 'Lancashire and the "Undeveloped Estates": The British Cotton Growing Association Fund-Raising Campaign, 1902–1914', *Journal of British Studies*, vol. 54 no. 4 (2015), 869–97, which emphasizes the widespread reluctance in Britain to fund empire cotton.

[92] Egyptian cotton yields were more than double those of any other African producer: League of Nations, Economic Intelligence Service, *Statistical Year-book of the League of Nations, 1929* (Geneva: League of Nations, Economic and Financial Section), 94; League of Nations, Economic Intelligence Service, *Statistical Year-book of the League of Nations, 1926*, 72.

[93] Africa scarcely figures in the recent survey by Farnie and Jeremy (eds), *The Fibre*; it is covered more generously in Beckert, *Empire*, 363–75.

[94] The best overview remains Allen Isaacman and Richard Roberts (eds), *Cotton, Colonialism, and Social History in Sub-Saharan Africa* (London: James Currey, 1995).

[95] Allen Isaacman, *Cotton is the Mother of Poverty: Peasants, Work and Rural Struggle in Colonial Mozambique, 1938–1961* (London: James Currey, 1996), 3.

[96] The theory was seminally applied, not without criticism, by Anthony G. Hopkins, *An Economic History of West Africa* (Harlow: Longman, 1973).

output were not entirely fanciful, especially given that it was already grown in many areas. As far as cotton was concerned, it was widely assumed that successful commercial production depended on four essential criteria: fertile soil, an agreeable climate, a ready supply of labour, and the requisite infrastructure for efficient transport. Many African colonies, it was thought, possessed the first three attributes in abundance, and some seemed well on their way to acquiring the fourth as railway and road construction accelerated during the 1890s and 1900s.[97]

In reality, however, this was overoptimistic on nearly every count. First, European unfamiliarity with African soil and climate conditions invited flattering comparisons with the rich alluvial lands of the Nile valley or the cotton tracts of the American South. In fact, almost nowhere in sub-Saharan Africa were growing conditions as favourable as they were in these other areas. Second, although colonial governments initially regarded African subject populations as an ideal source of cheap manpower, labour was by no means as disposable or 'underused' as many thought; indeed, it was often extremely scarce. These first two misunderstandings begat a third: despite high hopes to the contrary, cotton exports could not be readily increased even from areas where it had long been cultivated.[98] This was largely due to a trio of related factors: the persistence of local markets that absorbed much of the cotton that was produced; the opportunities afforded by other cash crops that required less work (and often earned better returns); and, most fundamentally, the ways in which cotton fitted into existing agro-ecological systems.

Wherever cotton was grown in pre-colonial Africa it was invariably intermixed with a range of food crops such as beans, yams, rice, cassava, or maize. In northern Côte d'Ivoire and Togoland, for instance, peasants had long planted it among their maize or in yam mounds as a secondary crop.[99] Cotton was mainly grown by women, who usually sowed it along with their food crops and picked it once it matured after the peak harvest time for their chief foodstuffs, thereby avoiding a direct clash with the needs for subsistence work. The practice of growing cotton alongside other cultivars brought a number of important advantages for producers. It not only enabled them to prioritize the food supply in the event of low cotton prices or poor yields, it also minimized the effort to grow it since clearing and weeding the ground had to be done for the food crops anyway. A further benefit was that it almost certainly reduced pests by denying them large concentrations of host plants and maintaining a higher diversity of competing species.[100] All in all, these mixed cropping systems were well attuned to subsistence needs

---

[97] Schanz, 'Der koloniale Baumwollenbau', 819–26; Jonathan Robins, '"The Black Man's Crop": Cotton, Imperialism and Public–Private Development in Britain's African Colonies, 1900–1918', Commodities of Empire Working Paper no. 11 (2009), 3: <http://www.open.ac.uk/Arts/ferguson-centre/commodities-of-empire/working-papers/WP11.pdf>.

[98] As emphasized especially by Roberts, *Two Worlds*.

[99] Thomas J. Bassett, *The Peasant Cotton Revolution in West Africa: Côte d'Ivoire, 1880–1995* (Cambridge: Cambridge University Press, 2001), 57; Donna J. E. Maier, 'Persistence of Precolonial Patterns of Production: Cotton in German Togoland, 1800–1914', in Isaacman and Roberts (eds), *Cotton*, 71–95, here 77–8.

[100] As clearly recognized by some contemporaries: A. Zimmermann, *Anleitung für die Baumwollkultur in den deutschen Kolonien*, 2nd edn (Berlin: KWK, 1910), 96.

and local ecologies, and in the pre-colonial period they managed to supply substantial quantities of cotton to indigenous spinners and weavers throughout most of the continent.

The problem, as colonialists saw it, was that such methods afforded little scope for raising exports to the levels they envisaged. One solution that was repeatedly tried was to create new market incentives as a means of inducing farmers to channel a greater proportion of the cotton crop towards metropolitan markets. The difficulty, however, was that local prices were often substantially higher than European buyers were willing to pay, partly because of the cheaper costs of US cotton, and partly because of the uneven quality of the African crop.[101] Another option was therefore to 'improve' existing production methods through the adoption of new cultivation techniques, new cotton varieties, and more stringent quality controls. A third possibility was to compel farmers to grow large amounts of industrial-grade cotton via strict production quotas and forced cultivation, though this was politically risky and always controversial. As Thomas Bassett has suggested, these three opposing discourses—a belief in the 'rational peasant', a 'paternalist' approach, and a 'compulsory development' model—formed the basic architecture of cotton policies throughout colonial Africa, and were often pursued simultaneously by the various cotton-growing associations.[102] Each approach had its own environmental and social implications, but before examining them in greater detail it is worth noting that a fourth alternative also beckoned in some parts of Africa: namely, to bypass peasant production altogether by establishing centralized cotton plantations supervised by Europeans and manned by African wage labour.

Such visions of a modern, capital-intensive cotton economy were most prominent in East Africa, where early efforts to stimulate cotton production were shaped by the alienation of large areas of land for European settlement. In the 1890s and early 1900s the government in German East Africa was practically giving away land for cotton estates. British authorities likewise encouraged settlers to establish cotton plantations along the Kenyan coast, and doled out tens of thousands of hectares to European and Asian planters in Uganda.[103] Some of the largest estates were operated directly by textile firms eager to supply their own mills as a means of cushioning themselves against international price swings. The Leipzig Cotton Spinnery, for instance, leased over 300 km² of the Ruvu flood plain in Tanzania in an attempt to meet its entire raw cotton needs (around 30,000 bales per annum). By 1910 it cultivated over 2,500 hectares with the help of steam ploughs, an

---

[101] Roberts, *Two Worlds*; Isaacman and Roberts (eds), *Cotton*, 16; Louis Robert, *La Culture du coton en Afrique Occidentale Française* (Paris: Domat-Montchrestien, 1931).

[102] Bassett, *Peasant Cotton*, 55.

[103] Thaddeus Sunseri, *Vilimani: Labor Migration and Rural Change in Early Colonial Tanzania* (Oxford: Currey, 2002); Thaddeus Sunseri, 'Peasants and the Struggle for Labor in Cotton Regimes of the Rufiji Basin, Tanzania, 1885–1918', in Isaacman and Roberts (eds), *Cotton*, 180–99, esp. 189–96; Juhani Koponen, *Development for Exploitation: German Colonial Policies in Mainland Tanzania, 1884–1914* (Helsinki: Finnish Historical Society, 1995); Isaacman and Roberts (eds), *Cotton*, 24–5.

irrigation system, and a labour force of 1,500, spending no less than £75,000 in the process.[104]

For a while, at least, the expansion of such estates was lauded as a promising means of 'securing our national cotton industry', as one commentator put it.[105] But most soon ran into trouble, including even the mammoth Leipzig Cotton Spinnery plantation, which folded in 1912. As was the case with most struggling plantations, its biggest problem was labour. The challenge was twofold: while African producers were extremely reluctant to work on the estates—especially during spring planting seasons, which in many areas coincided with the harvest of the main food crops (rice, maize, millet)—the engagement of European field supervisors and engineers greatly inflated costs. The only way to acquire an adequate labour force was through blatant coercion, which provoked deep resentment among Africans as well as widespread condemnation among European critics. Many estates tried to mitigate labour bottlenecks through mechanization, but none were very successful given the scant economies of scale before the advent of mechanical cotton harvesting in the 1950s. Environmental factors also limited the scope for deploying labour-saving equipment. Local soil conditions in East Africa were often unsuitable for heavy steam ploughs, which tended to get stuck after heavy rains and which turned infertile subsoil layers to the surface by cutting too deeply below the thin top-soils.[106] Efforts to introduce ox-drawn ploughs fared little better given the presence of the trypanosome-carrying tsetse fly in many areas (see Chapter 7). Plant diseases and pests posed an additional environmental threat; in 1909 a massive outbreak of leaf-curl virus ravaged the uniform fields of the cotton estates in German East Africa.[107] Finally, political pressure also played a role. After the convulsions of the 1905 Maji-Maji rebellion—largely a response to German labour conscription and mandatory cultivation policies that forced peasants to neglect their own fields during planting and harvest time—reformers such as Colonial Minister Dernburg and Governor Albrecht von Rechenberg were convinced that smallholder production promised not only higher output but also less fuel for rebellion.[108] After experiencing similar difficulties with labour mobilization in East Africa and Uganda, British colonialists likewise concluded that 'the natives work much better on their own land than they do on European plantations'.[109]

---

[104] John Iliffe, *A Modern History of Tanganyika* (Cambridge: Cambridge University Press, 1979), 168; Moritz Schanz, 'Der koloniale Baumwollenbau', 827; Rainer Tetzlaff, *Koloniale Entwicklung und Ausbeutung: Wirtschafts- und Sozialgeschichte Deutsch-Ostafrikas, 1890–1914* (Berlin: Duncker & Humblot, 1970), 139; Sunseri, *'Baumwollfrage'*, 47.

[105] Otto Warburg, 'Die Landwirtschaft in den deutschen Kolonien', *Verhandlungen des deutschen Kolonialkongresses 1905* (Berlin: Reimer, 1906), 587–604, here 600.

[106] Zimmermann, *Anleitung*, 55–6; also H. von Nathusius, 'Der erste Stock-Motor-Pflug in Afrika', *Der Pflanzer. Zeitschrift für Land- und Forstwirtschaft in Deutsch-Ostafrika*, vol. 9 (1913), 283–7.

[107] Iliffe, *Modern History*, 145; Sunseri, 'Peasants', 194–5; Koponen, *Development*, 292.

[108] Iliffe, *Modern History*, 151–8; Koponen, *Development*, 258–71.

[109] N. M. Penzer, *Cotton in British West Africa Including Togoland and the Cameroons* (London: Murby, 1920), 10.

The commercial, ecological, and political problems of plantation culture meant that cotton was generally regarded as a 'black man's crop'.[110] But this still left the question of how to recast peasant production for the benefit of metropolitan industry. During the early years of colonial rule, the weakness of state authority on the ground meant that hopes largely rested on the ability to induce farmers to grow more (and higher-quality) cotton, and then to direct it towards European rather than local markets. Colonial governments throughout Africa implemented a range of measures to facilitate this, from railways and central ginning stations to tax incentives and price assurances. But influencing what actually happened in the fields was another matter, for it could only be practically pursued within the framework of existing African social institutions.

The key for achieving this lay in altering the cotton cultivars themselves. Around the turn of the century, French, German, and British botanists rushed to identify the most promising long-staple strains, importing seeds from the United States, Egypt, the West Indies, or India, and testing them in different climate and soil conditions. In Tanzania and Nyasaland, planters found that Egyptian strains grew remarkably well, though local disease problems kept yields far below those obtained in Egypt.[111] Breeders in Uganda quickly settled on American Upland varieties, and selected more systematically for local conditions after the establishment of a cotton experiment station at Kadunguru in 1911.[112] In French West Africa, early field trials focused on American strains in the Soudan, a mix of indigenous and American varieties in Dahomey, and Egyptian Jumel in Senegal.[113] It is worth emphasizing that these colonial breeding programmes were preceded by a much longer history of experimentation on African cotton fields. While on a scientific expedition to West Africa in 1898–9, the botanist Auguste Chevalier was struck by the wide range of cotton species in cultivation, some of them originating from far afield.[114] Generations of selection by indigenous cultivators helps explain why local varieties usually boasted higher productivity and stronger disease resistance than newly introduced species, which repeatedly produced 'much less cotton than in their places of origin'.[115] To benefit from this genetic inheritance, European botanists began to crossbreed exotic and native varieties to produce high-yielding strains for local conditions, some of which performed

---

[110] Todd, *World's Cotton*, 171; Robins, 'Black Man's Crop'.

[111] Zimmermann, *Anleitung*, 13–14, 20.

[112] J. D. Tothill (ed.), *Agriculture in Uganda* (London: Oxford University Press, 1940), 184–9; Schanz, 'Der koloniale Baumwollenbau', 827.

[113] Yves Henry, *Le Coton dans l'Afrique Occidentale Française* (Paris: Challamel, 1906), 293; Régine Levrat, *Le Coton en Afrique Occidentale et Centrale avant 1950: un exemple de la politique coloniale de la France* (Paris: L'Harmattan, 2008), 96–112.

[114] Yves Henry, *Le Coton*, 15–19, 134–5; Henry Bloud, *Le Problème cotonnier et l'Afrique Occidentale Française: une solution nationale* (Paris: Émile Larose: 1925), 170–1; Bassett, *Peasant Cotton*, 31–3.

[115] P. Coléno, 'État actuel de la culture du coton en Afrique Occidentale Française', *L'Agronomie coloniale*, vol. 18 no. 140 (Aug. 1929), 225–9, here 229. On the pest resistance of indigenous varieties: P. Vayssière and J. Mimeur, *Les Insectes nuisibles au cotonnier en Afrique Occidentale Française* (Paris: Émile Larose, 1926).

remarkably well: for example, Togo Sea-Island, Buganda Local, and Nyasaland Upland.[116]

What made these breeding efforts so important was that the provision of 'improved' seeds impinged directly on all other aspects of cotton cultivation. In order to prevent the contamination of the new strains through cross-pollination, it was necessary to suppress other local varieties. Maintaining their desired traits over the long term also meant that cultivators were unable to use seeds from the previous year's crop. Instead, colonial governments distributed specially farmed seeds free of charge, but only if cultivators agreed to follow a welter of planting, maintenance, and harvesting rules. 'It would be of little value to clear new land and to use new plants', noted one French official, 'if the methods were to remain the same and the yields inferior'.[117]

As part of their cotton improvement efforts, governments and growers' associations issued detailed instructions to micromanage field activities. The recommendations of the Kolonial-Wirtschaftliches Komitee were fairly typical, and were mirrored by French and British instructions: namely, a thorough clearance of the ground; the creation of ridges and furrows by hoe or (preferably) plough with 100–25 cm between rows; strict planting schedules according the local timing of the rains; wide planting intervals of 50–60 cm followed by reseeding after initial planting; timetables for weeding and cultivation between the rows; thinning before the roots of individual plants became intertwined; topping to encourage a bushier habit; a carefully controlled method of picking to avoid discoloration of the bolls or contamination with other plant debris, and to increase the speed of harvest; and finally, burning the stubble to deprive pests of sustenance between seasons.[118] In order to propagate such 'rational' techniques, colonial governments set up a network of demonstration farms, agricultural training schools, and extension agencies. Occasionally they even recruited cotton-growing consultants from the United States to teach locals the latest methods, most notably in Togo, where German authorities enlisted African-American experts from the Tuskegee Institute.[119]

Clearly, the improved seed varieties were much more than just a means of promoting cotton exports. They were also an important vehicle for disciplining African labour, as well as for extending state authority over the countryside and its natural resources.[120] Even so, the results were modest when measured against the goals of metropolitan cotton industrialists. Many African farmers quite readily tried the

[116] Tothill (ed.), *Agriculture*, 184–6; Zimmerman, *Alabama*, 148–9; for subsequent efforts, Matthew A. Schnurr, 'Breeding for Insect-Resistant Cotton across Imperial Networks, 1924–1950', *Journal of Historical Geography*, vol. 37 no. 2 (2011), 223–31.

[117] Quoted from Roberts, *Two Worlds*, 82.

[118] Zimmermann, *Anleitung*, 52–8, 73–6, 79–89.

[119] Tothill (ed.), *Agriculture*, 184; Torbjörn Engdahl, *The Exchange of Cotton: Ugandan Peasants, Colonial Market Regulations and the Organisation of the International Cotton Trade, 1904–1918* (Uppsala: Acta Universitatis Upsaliensis, 1999), 54; Bloud, *Problème cotonnier*, 221–32; Penzer, *Cotton*, 10; on the Tuskegee experts in Togo: Zimmerman, *Alabama*; Andrew Zimmerman, 'A German Alabama in Africa: The Tuskegee Expedition to German Togo and the Transnational Origins of West African Cotton Growers', *American Historical Review*, vol. 110 (2005), 1362–98; Beckert, *Empire*, 363–8.

[120] As emphasized by Zimmerman, *Alabama*, 148–51.

new cultivars, whose long staples were prized by local spinners and weavers. In some colonies exports rose significantly during the early 1900s.[121] But the intensive cultivation techniques promoted by colonial administrations were a different matter entirely, and the widespread resistance they encountered dimmed the prospects for further export expansion. The fundamental problem was that they disrupted well-established patterns of agricultural production—practices that had long been tailored to the rhythm of the seasons, the capabilities of the land, as well as the desire of African cultivators to maintain a measure of autonomy over their own work and subsistence.[122] It was never likely that farmers would willingly abandon these systems to focus on a risky and inedible crop, let alone to produce it in a more labour-intensive manner than before.

These basic incongruities between the ecology of commercial cotton and existing agro-ecological systems hampered cotton promotion efforts throughout colonial Africa. In southern Nigeria, the unwillingness of farmers to grow American long-staple cotton was not because it yielded poorly—in fact, it did better than native varieties when grown by itself—but rather because it did not compete well with other crops and therefore had to be grown in monoculture. Unlike the native strains that thrived amidst other crops, it diverted attention from food cultivation and was, because of the extra work required, less profitable per unit of labour than traditional cotton varieties in spite of higher yields per hectare. Tellingly, when an improved intercroppable variety was offered, local farmers gladly planted it.[123] German agronomists had a similar experience in Togo, where Ewe cultivators were reluctant to abandon the local 'Ho' variety since it thrived in association with other crops.[124] Colonial authorities in Sierra Leone likewise failed to replace local cotton varieties with Allen strains due to the poor performance of the latter when intercropped with upland rice.[125] To be sure, such opposition was not a universal response. In Buganda, where the timing of the rains and the reliable local dry season minimized the disruption to subsistence work, many peasants cultivated cotton quite willingly. In parts of Nyasaland, the ability to rotate cotton with maize and millet meant that production rested largely on peasant initiative.[126] But as a general rule, large-scale cotton cultivation was an unattractive prospect, even when sweetened with purchase assurances and price guarantees. It was not an alleged 'backwardness' or 'conservatism' that made African farmers reluctant to change their agricultural schemes, but rather a rational weighing-up of the options and advantages.

---

[121] Yves Henry, *La Question cotonnière en Afrique Occidentale Française* (Melun: Imprimerie Administrative, 1906), 101–3; Penzer, *Cotton*, 17.

[122] See also Beckert, *Empire*, 368; Zimmerman, *Alabama*, 151; Bassett, *Peasant Cotton*, 51–6; Roberts, *Two Worlds*, passim.

[123] O. T. Faulkner and J. R. Mackie, *West African Agriculture* (Cambridge: Cambridge University Press, 1933), 10–11; Penzer, *Cotton*, 17.

[124] Zimmermann, *Anleitung*, 96; Maier, 'Persistence', 84.

[125] Paul Richards, *Indigenous Agricultural Revolution: Ecology and Food Production in West Africa* (Boulder, Colo.: Westview, 1985), 23–4.

[126] Engdahl, *Exchange*, 51–60; Todd, *World's Cotton*, 174–82; Elias Mandala, '"We Toiled for the White Man in our Own Gardens": The Conflict between Cotton and Food in Colonial Malawi', in Isaacman and Roberts (eds), *Cotton*, 285–305, here 288–90; Isaacman and Roberts (eds), *Cotton*, 23.

Peasant resistance to cotton monoculture stemmed not only from the extra risks and labour it involved. It also reflected the fact that other cash crops were often more remunerative and less troublesome to grow. Groundnuts, for instance, could fetch roughly three times more per hectare in the 1910s, and moreover could be eaten if export markets turned sour.[127] This massive price differential, coupled with the relative compatibility of groundnuts with existing cultivation systems, was the main reason for the failure to develop export cotton in Sierra Leone and Gambia.[128] It also fatally undermined the BCGA's pre-war campaign to grow peasant cotton in the savannahs of northern Nigeria. The scheme was launched in 1904 in the Kano area amidst reports that it possessed such excellent cotton soil as to be capable of supplying most of Lancashire's needs. But despite years of preparation, the distribution of millions of pounds of seed, the creation of buying stations and experiment farms, even the construction of a 650-km railway from Baro (on the Niger River) to Kano in 1912, the overall result was a boom in peasant groundnut production rather than cotton cultivation. To add insult to injury, the higher local incomes generated by groundnut cultivation stimulated demand for textiles and therefore raised local cotton prices, thus diverting cotton supplies away from the export sector instead of funnelling them towards it.[129] As the BCGA project clearly illustrates, the inability of colonial states to control the decisions of rural cultivators meant that much of the land and labour in cotton-growing regions remained an 'uncaptured *corvée*'.[130]

African ecosystems were not just a physical stage for such struggles, but were a vital part of the story. Farming is, at base, a fusion of natural systems and human work, and as John Tosh emphasized long ago, the local environments in which farmers grew their crops powerfully shaped the entire 'cash-crop revolution' in tropical Africa.[131] Whether through market incentives, coercion, or a mixture of the two, the sharp rise in agricultural exports between 1890 and 1930 was ultimately based on the mobilization of surplus land and labour. Because land was by far the more abundant of the two resources, labour availability was nearly always the crucial criterion. And because environmental conditions governed the labour needs of indigenous subsistence systems—which were generally calibrated to maximize returns on labour rather than land—they profoundly influenced how and where certain cash crops could be made to work.

Environmental conditions varied enormously across the continent, but for the sake of analysis it is nonetheless helpful—following Tosh—to make a basic distinction between savannah areas and forest zones, since cash-cropping was far more

---

[127] Odet Denys, *Du rôle de l'agriculture indigène dans les colonies d'exploitation* (Paris: Jouve, 1917), 236; for later price comparisons Roberts, *Two Worlds*, 167.

[128] Penzer, *Cotton*, 25.

[129] Jan S. Hogendorn, 'The Cotton Campaign in Northern Nigeria, 1902–1914: An Early Example of a Public/Private Planning Failure in Agriculture', in Isaacman and Roberts (eds), *Cotton*, 50–70.

[130] Bassett, *Peasant Cotton*, 51–85; also Roberts, *Two Worlds*, 16–17.

[131] John Tosh, 'The Cash-Crop Revolution in Tropical Africa: An Agricultural Reappraisal', *African Affairs*, vol. 79 no. 314 (1980), 79–94.

challenging in the former than in the latter. For one thing, the agrarian systems of the forest allowed farmers to divert scarce labour into new activities much more easily than the systems of the savannah, where ecological constraints gave cultivators less flexibility. The brief rainy season in most savannah regions limited farming to only four to seven months of the year, which meant that cultivators were highly reliant on grain crops with a short growing season (e.g. sorghum and millet). These crops not only required more labour than the root and tree staples of the forest zone (e.g. yam, plantain), they also demanded intense labour inputs during peak periods at the beginning and middle of the growing season. Altogether, the organization of subsistence labour in the savannah afforded little room for error, and even the most carefully designed schemes were still frequently vulnerable to drought, especially on the fringes of the Sahel and in parts of East Africa.

Moreover, the different characteristics of the main cash crops grown in the forest and savannah zones only accentuated the agro-climatic differences. Whereas the labour demand for forest commodities such as cocoa, coffee, or palm oil tended to peak during slack periods of the subsistence crop calendar, the opposite was true for the cash crops that dominated in savannah regions (especially cotton, and to a lesser extent groundnuts). Cotton not only required large amounts of labour, it also needed it at crucial points in the tightly compressed growing season.[132] The result was yet another temporal contradiction between the designs of colonial planners and the cadence of local agricultural systems, one whose adverse consequences for food security help explain why the transition to commercial cotton was so often fraught with conflict and hardship.[133]

Because of the agro-ecological constraints of the savannahs, many of the areas targeted for cotton exports could scarcely generate the labour surpluses required to cultivate it, regardless of the availability of surplus land. And to take Tosh's argument a step further, the problems posed by environmental conditions went far beyond their relationship to subsistence work patterns. The attempt to boost African cotton exports was limited by a whole range of biophysical factors—factors that, in turn, influenced the ways in which the colonial cotton campaigns were pursued.

One issue was irregular or unpredictable rainfall patterns. Cotton grows best where there is steady moisture throughout its growing season, ideally followed by a brief dry spell just before harvest to allow the bolls to dry. Excess or badly timed rain was a common problem in the humid forest zones (especially for exotic varieties), just as droughts posed difficulties in semi-arid areas. A closely related problem was erosion and soil leaching, especially in moist regions where soils were thin and acidic and where heavy rainfall easily washed away nutrients. Less obvious, but no less important, was the question of sunlight duration. Whereas diurnal light cycles in the tropics are never far from twelve hours in length, the summer months in temperate latitudes offer much longer periods of sunshine for plant photosynthesis.

---

[132] Tosh, 'Cash-Crop', 82–5.
[133] Often the main effect was a marked deterioration in the quality of diet (due to the switch towards low-protein cassava, a less labour-intensive crop than grains) rather than a decline in subsistence production per se: Tosh, 'Cash-Crop', 92–3.

Longer days allow not only higher growth rates during the cotton plant's four- to six-month growing season, but also lower rates of carbohydrate loss at night (so called 'dark respiration'), which is further minimized by lower night-time temperatures that slow down the respiratory process. In other words, cotton plants cultivated in mid-latitudes grow significantly more during the day and lose only around half as much energy at night compared to cotton grown in the tropics.[134]

This photosynthetic differential was one of the main reasons why even the most promising cotton-growing regions of sub-Saharan Africa struggled to compete with producers in other parts of the world, above all the southern United States. It is also why cotton yields in Egypt tended to surpass those in Uganda or Tanzania by around 30 to 40 per cent regardless of the cultivation methods used.[135] Colonial agronomists were just beginning to study the effects of light duration and intensity during the inter-war years, but without any meaningful bearing on cotton policies.[136] Had the issues of sunlight, precipitation, and soil conditions figured as prominently in the calculus of colonial planners as the desire to reduce foreign dependency and market volatility, the social and ecological history of colonial cotton might have unfolded quite differently.[137]

Such environmental disadvantages had important social and political consequences, for they help to explain why the expansion of colonial cotton frequently entailed such regimented forms of work. Throughout tropical Africa, the only way to compensate for comparatively low cotton yields was to suppress wages through the strict control of labour. Of course, the link between cotton production and labour exploitation was evident in many temperate zones as well—not least the southern United States—and resulted from much more than just ecological constraints. But it was particularly severe and persistent in the colonies of sub-Saharan Africa, where the yield differential was greatest and where the focus on growing cotton for metropolitan markets was, in biophysical terms, most plainly misplaced.[138]

Across most of colonial Africa, compulsion, administrative pressure, and the threat of punishment were an integral part of colonial cotton campaigns from the very beginning. They were especially prominent wherever colonial authorities also promoted the establishment of large plantations, whose viability rested on the exploitation of cheap labour. In German East Africa, the coercive recruitment methods for the estates were mirrored in the government's approach towards indigenous cotton production. From 1902 onwards, peasants were forced to grow cotton on communal fields, which prevented them from attending to their own

---

[134] This discussion is based on Philip W. Porter, 'A Note on Cotton and Climate: A Colonial Conundrum', in Isaacman and Roberts (eds), *Cotton*, 43–9; Jen-Hu Chang, 'Potential Photosynthesis and Crop Productivity', *Annals of the Association of American Geographers*, vol. 60 no. 1 (Mar. 1970), 92–101, p. 99 for cotton yields; Jen-Hu Chang, 'The Agricultural Potential of the Humid Tropics', *Geographical Review*, vol. 58 (1968), 333–61, esp. 346–8, 352–6.

[135] Porter, 'Note', 46–7.

[136] e.g. P. Carton, 'Importance des facteurs écologiques "durée du jour" et "intensité de la lumière" en agronomie coloniale', *L'Agronomie coloniale*, vol. 22 nos 183–4 (Mar., Apr. 1933), 87–91, 120–6.

[137] A point made by Porter, 'A Note', 49.   [138] Porter, 'A Note', 47–9.

food crops at crucial points in the subsistence calendar.[139] In Côte d'Ivoire, French authorities obliged villagers in the early 1910s to cultivate a designated number of hectares on collective cotton plots under the close supervision of colonial officials or district guards, who imposed a strict method of mono-cropping and often resorted to brutal punishment as a means of enforcement.[140] These obligatory *champs du commandant*, as they were popularly known, were but one variant of the broader compulsory development model that shaped the cotton campaigns in colonial Africa. Similar devices were introduced from Haute Volta to Oubangui-Chari to the French Congo. In Kenya and Uganda too, British authorities arranged communal cotton plots on which peasants were forced to work under the supervision of allied local chiefs.[141]

Such coercive practices presaged the spread of even more repressive cultivation systems after the First World War. Following the precipitous drop in wartime imports from the United States, European governments emerged from the conflict more determined than ever to boost their supplies of colonial cotton.[142] It was all part of the broader shift towards autarky, imperial trade preferences, and state economic intervention after the war, a shift that was facilitated by the expansion of the state in colonial territories as well. The intensification of colonial rule in post-war Africa was especially evident in many inland areas where state control had hitherto been weakest. As it happened, these were often the same areas in which cotton served as the chief means of harnessing colonial resources for the recovery of metropolitan economies.

The move towards imperial autarky was particularly strong in France, where many regarded the *mise en valeur* of the colonies as the key to maintaining French economic and political power. The basic idea was to replace the ad hoc initiatives of the past with a more comprehensive, state-directed system of raw material production, and French textile industrialists were among the strongest backers of the policy.[143] In French West Africa, administrative compulsion escalated markedly after 1924. Under the supervision of a new Service des Textiles, taxes and delivery quotas were raised in an effort to boost cotton output. As the *champs du command-ant* increased in size, peasants were also instructed to intercrop cotton on their own

---

[139] Sunseri, 'Peasants', 183.　　　[140] Bassett, *Peasant Cotton*, 58–9.

[141] Levrat, *Le Coton en Afrique*, 207–51; Catherine Coquery-Vidrovitch, *Le Congo au temps des grandes compagnies concessionaires 1898–1930* (Paris: Mouton & Co., 1972), 473–9; Roberts, *Two Worlds*, 172–7; Engdahl, *Exchange*, 60–1; Isaacman and Roberts (eds), *Cotton*, 26–7.

[142] Scherer, *Cotton*, 362–3. From 1913 to 1914 the number of bales reaching Europe fell from 257,152 to 21,210. H. Heizmann, 'Amerikanische Baumwolle in den drei letzten Erntejahren sowie der Baumwollbau im Britischen Weltreich', *Der Tropenpflanzer, Beiheft*, vol. 21 no. 6 (June 1918), 97–254; Marc Michel, *Les Africains et la Grande Guerre: l'appel à l'Afrique (1914–1918)* (Paris: Éditions Karthala, 2003), 171–86; *Report of the Indian Cotton Committee* (Calcutta: Government Printing Office, 1919).

[143] Jacques Marseille, *Empire colonial et capitalisme français: histoire d'un divorce* (Paris: Éditions Albin Michel, 1984), 188–97; Levrat, *Le Coton en Afrique*, 46–67; Nicolas Stoskopf, 'La Culture impériale du patronat textile Mulhousien (1830–1962)', in Hubert Bonin, Catherine Hodeir, and Jean-François Klein (eds), *L'Esprit économique impérial, 1830–1970: groupes de pression & réseaux du patronat colonial en France et dans l'Empire* (Paris: SFHOM, 2008), 397–407; Christophe Bonneuil, *Des savants pour l'empire: la structuration des recherches scientifiques coloniales au temps de 'la mise en valeur des colonies françaises' 1917–1945* (Paris: Éditions de l'ORSTOM, 1991), 32–45.

food plots. During the late 1920s, acreage and production rose sharply in many districts of Côte d'Ivoire and Soudan.[144] Meanwhile, farmers in French Equatorial Africa were subjected to a particularly coercive system of forced cultivation organized by private concessionary companies and supervised by local clerks and indigenous chiefs. Much of the focus was on southern Chad and Oubangui-Chari, despite the fact that growing conditions in the region were, contrary to initial assessments, not especially favourable for cotton. The result was extreme hardship for cultivators, whose food production systems were severely disrupted and who saw little if any of the profits from cotton once the chiefs had taken their share.[145] Just as in West Africa, cotton acreage in Equatorial Africa rose swiftly from around 1,485 hectares in 1926 to 108,600 hectares ten years later; it eventually became the colony's chief export. Yet none of this made much difference from the standpoint of strategic provisioning. In 1930 only 2 per cent of the cotton imported into France came from its colonies.[146]

Elsewhere in Africa the inter-war cotton campaigns were even more heavy-handed. Obligatory cultivation first started in the Congo in 1917, but only truly got going after 1920 with the creation of the Compagnie Cotonnière Congolaise and the swelling influx of metropolitan capital. Throughout the 1920s, Belgian authorities doled out scores of concessions—some of them up to 800 km² in size—to the twelve main firms operating in the colony. The aim was to ensure that the Congo's vast land resources served the needs of the metropolitan economy, and with the onset of the global crisis in the 1930s, the pressure only increased. By 1936 around 700,000 households produced 96,000 tons of cotton on an area of approximately 342,000 hectares. In a bid to improve yields and quality, the Institut National pour l'Étude Agronomique au Congo experimented with American Allen hybrids in a range of different rotation systems. But since cotton was so demanding on the thin forest soils of the Congo basin, farmers were generally forced to plant it as the first crop on new clearings in order to maximize output. The ecological results were wretched, including a marked acceleration of forest clearance along with lower yields for the food crops that followed cotton on the depleted plots. Moreover, the threat this posed to local food security was further compounded by the reduction of time available for hunting, fishing, or tending other crops due to the need to clear more land.[147]

[144] Levrat, *Le Coton en Afrique*, 119–31; Bassett, *Peasant Cotton*, 66–80; Roberts, *Two Worlds*, 172–7.

[145] Levrat, *Le Coton en Afrique*, 207–51; Ulrich Stürzinger, 'The Introduction of Cotton Cultivation in Chad: The Role of the Administration, 1920–1936', *African Economic History*, no. 12 (1983), 213–25; more generally Ulrich Stürzinger, *Der Baumwollanbau im Tschad* (Zurich: Atlantis, 1980); Jean Cabot, 'La Culture du coton au Tchad', *Annales de Géographie*, vol. 66 (1957), 499–508; Coquery-Vidrovitch, *Le Congo*, 474–8.

[146] Marseille, *Empire colonial*, 197; Levrat, *Le Coton en Afrique*, 242; *VIe Congrès International d'Agriculture Tropicale et Subtropicale, Paris 15–19 Juillet 1931*, vol. 2 (Abbeville: Paillart, 1932), 99.

[147] Osumaka Likaka, *Rural Society and Cotton in Colonial Zaire* (Madison, Wis.: University of Wisconsin Press, 1997), 16–21, 37–42, 45–70, 135–6; B. Jewsiewicki, 'Modernisation ou destruction du village africain: l'économie politique de la "modernisation agricole" au Congo Belge', *Les Cahiers du CEDAF*, no. 5 (1983) 1–79, here 18–19, 49–51; G. Malengreau, *Vers un paysannat indigène: les lotissements agricoles au Congo Belge* (Brussels: Institut Royal du Congo Belge, 1949), 16–18; E. Leplae, *La Crise agricole coloniale et les phases du développement de l'agriculture dans le Congo central* (Brussels: Hayez, 1932), 20–2.

Given the grim results of the cotton drive in the Congo, the Portuguese decision to use it as a model for their own cotton policies boded ill indeed for rural cultivators in their colonies. The notorious cotton regimes in Angola and Mozambique proved to be the most oppressive and long-lived in all of colonial Africa. Whereas the other colonial powers (including Belgium) were gradually winding down forced cultivation by the late 1930s, Portuguese authorities actively expanded it in the wake of Salazar's takeover in 1938. By the mid-1940s cotton was compulsorily grown by some 800,000 households in Mozambique, many of them headed by overburdened women caught between the rapacious state demand for fibre and the unforgiving requirements of subsistence. To make matters worse, the hardship caused by forced cultivation was compounded by the technical amateurishness of Portuguese cotton policies. Apart from a few northern districts, Mozambique was far from ideal for cotton cultivation, and many peasants were forced to plant it in areas with marginal soils and adverse climatic conditions. Soil conservation was completely ignored (in stark contrast to most other colonies at the time, see Chapter 9), and the pressure on the forests was amplified by the policy of restricting cotton cultivation to newly cleared land in order to maximize yields. As Allen Isaacman puts it, deforestation and soil erosion were 'even lower priorities than food production for the state-concessionary alliance'.[148] The disregard for subjugated people was mirrored by indifference towards the lands they inhabited.

Against this background, it is scarcely surprising that the colonial cotton campaigns provoked widespread enmity among African farmers. Although outright rebellion was rare—Maji-Maji was the most spectacular instance, though cotton also figured in the Bunyoro revolt in western Uganda in 1907—more subtle forms of opposition were common, and materially shaped the outcomes of cotton policies.[149] For instance, peasants who were forced to cultivate cotton would sometimes deliberately plant it in poor soil or neglect routine maintenance work behind the backs of communal plot monitors. Another common coping strategy was to continue prohibited intercropping practices or switch to crops that were more easily combined with cotton cultivation (above all maize and cassava), though this generally entailed a decline in protein intake compared to the cereal grains they replaced.[150] As we have already seen, farmers who retained a measure of control over their labour often sold cotton to local markets rather than export agents, or grew other commercial crops such as rice, sorghum, cocoa, palm oil, or groundnuts.

Faced with such obstacles, and increasingly alert to the problems of mono-cropping and food insecurity, some officials searched for solutions more in tune with the preferences of indigenous producers. In Nigeria, British agronomists advocated

[148] Isaacman, *Cotton*, 7–12, 39–69, 148–63, 238–40, quote from p. 163; M. Anne Pitcher, 'From Coercion to Incentives: The Portuguese Colonial Cotton Regime in Angola and Mozambique, 1946–1974', in Isaacman and Roberts (eds), *Cotton*, 119–43.

[149] On Maji-Maji: Iliffe, *Modern History*, 168–202; on Bunyoro: Edward I. Steinhart, *Conflict and Collaboration: The Kingdoms of Western Uganda, 1890–1907* (Princeton: Princeton University Press, 1977), 239–54; more generally: Isaacman and Roberts (eds), *Cotton*, 36–8.

[150] Mandala, '"We Toiled"', 291–3; Sunseri, 'Peasants', 197–8.

the planting of hybrid cotton between belts of maize, partly to make it more acceptable to farmers but also because it kept the crop 'relatively free from cotton pests as compared with that grown in open fields'.[151] In Côte d'Ivoire, food shortages and pest attacks in the early 1930s prompted recommendations to plant improved varieties in intercropped fields, which demanded 'a lot less labour from the natives while furnishing them with foodstuffs and products to sell'.[152] As early as the 1900s, German agriculturists in Togo sought to integrate ploughing into local mixed cropping methods, though with little success.[153] After the First World War some agronomists began to question the wisdom of ploughs altogether given the risks of soil erosion and the loss of draught animals to trypanosomiasis. Throughout much of tropical Africa, the humble hoe was a far more appropriate cultivation tool than was initially assumed.[154]

Gradually, perhaps inevitably, the innovations imposed from outside were refracted through local social structures, land-use customs, and ecological constraints. As a number of scholars have recently argued, the story of colonial cotton was not only about displacing indigenous knowledge but also integrating it, or more precisely about the emergence of hybrid knowledge and practices on the ground—a finding that qualifies the notion of a hegemonic top-down development discourse that has shaped research agendas since the 1990s.[155]

The significance of such hybridization processes can perhaps best be glimpsed in the vast irrigated cotton projects that were launched during the inter-war period: the Gezira Scheme and the Office du Niger, two of the most ambitious environmental interventions in the entire history of colonial Africa. The Gezira Scheme was a grand attempt to create thousands of hectares of irrigated cotton fields by damming the Blue Nile near the Sudanese town of Sennar and diverting a portion of its waters across the vast, desolate plain that stretched between the Blue and White Niles south of Khartoum. The basic idea was to entice farmers on to irrigated tenancies of 30 feddans each, on the condition that they cultivate a fixed area of cotton and other crops (mainly sorghum) in specific rotations as instructed by the project managers. Building on a series of pilot irrigation schemes at Zeidab (1906) and Tayiba (1911), work accelerated rapidly after the First World War before culminating in the completion of the Sennar Dam in 1925, a massive barrage some 3 kilometres long and 39 metres high. At its formal launch in 1925

---

[151] Penzer, *Cotton*, 20.   [152] Bassett, *Peasant Cotton*, 80.

[153] Zimmermann, *Anleitung*, 96; Richard Deeken, *Die Landwirtschaft in den deutschen Kolonien* (Berlin: Süsserott, 1914), 52.

[154] See H. Fehlinger, 'Zur Lösung der Arbeiterfrage in den afrikanischen Kolonien', *Der Tropenpflanzer*, vol. 22 no. 3 (Mar. 1919), 77–80; also Tothill (ed.), *Agriculture*, 107–8.

[155] Most notably Roberts, *Two Worlds*, 14–21; Bassett, *Peasant Cotton*, 4–5, 13–14; Monica M. van Beusekom, *Negotiating Development: African Farmers and Colonial Experts at the Office du Niger, 1920–1960* (Oxford: Currey, 2002), xix–xxi. Seminal works on the development discourse are James Ferguson, *The Anti-Politics Machine: 'Development', Depoliticization, and Bureaucratic Power in Lesotho* (Cambridge: Cambridge University Press, 1990); Arturo Escobar, *Encountering Development: The Making and Unmaking of the Third World* (Princeton: Princeton University Press, 1995); also Emery Roe, '"Development Narratives": Or Making the Best of Blueprint Development', *World Development*, vol. 19 (1991), 287–300. More generally on the problems of a top-down focus on development, Hodge, 'Writing', Parts 1 and 2.

the Gezira scheme encompassed over 120,000 hectares, around a third of them under cotton. By the late 1930s it had expanded to around 420,000 hectares including nearly 90,000 hectares of cotton (an area considerably larger than all of New York City) cultivated by around 25,000 households.[156]

The twin aims of the Gezira project were to reorder both the physical and the social landscape. What had previously been a patchwork of scrub, seasonal pasture, riverine, and rain-fed plots was converted into a homogeneous gridiron of irrigated fields fed by hundreds of kilometres of ruler-straight canals. At the same time, in place of the semi-nomadic herders and subsistence-oriented farming communities in the region, it sought to create a stable society of free cotton-producing peasant households headed by male tenants.[157] From its very inception, Gezira was one of the largest irrigated settlement projects in the world, and it remains so to this day.[158] As British engineers had long known, the plain was in certain respects ideal for irrigation; its clay soils held water well, and the land gently sloped in a north-westerly direction from the Blue Nile towards the White. But if the canal system itself functioned more or less successfully, it proved much harder to make cotton production work. In the event, neither the re-engineered environment nor the people who worked it behaved as they were supposed to.

The socio-economic arrangements that developed on the ground were a far cry from what was initially envisaged. The original plan was to promote peasant wel-fare by creating an egalitarian landholding system in which individual tenants and their families were to cultivate their own allotments, thus freeing them from other debt and labour obligations. But the project ultimately had to accommodate the agendas of British managers as well as African farmers, who had their own ideas about how it should work.[159]

As elsewhere in Africa, the labour-intensity of cotton production caused serious frictions, and these frictions were scarcely alleviated by the scant revenues it gener-ated. Apart from brief spells of high cotton prices in the late 1920s and late 1940s, profits for tenants were meagre. Only the Sudan Plantations Syndicate (the private firm that managed the project on behalf of the Sudanese government and that exclusively marketed the cotton crop) got significant returns. Due to the compet-ing labour demands of subsistence production, tenants often invested as little as possible into cotton cultivation. Many hired landless workers to overcome bottlenecks at planting and harvest time. Others entered sharecropping arrange-ments with non-tenants in order to engage in more lucrative economic activities. Although officials constantly complained that tenants were acting more like lazy

---

[156] Maurits W. Ertsen, *Improvising Planned Development on the Gezira Plain, Sudan, 1900–1980* (Houndmills: Palgrave, 2016); Victoria Bernal, 'Cotton and Colonial Order in Sudan: A Social History with Emphasis on the Gezira Scheme', in Isaacman and Roberts (eds), *Cotton*, 96–118; for details and images, see *Notes on the Gezira Irrigation Project* (no publisher, January 1926); *Sennar Dam and Gezira Irrigation Works, Sudan* (undated: 1923–6).

[157] Bernal, 'Cotton', 101–2.

[158] The completion of the 1-km-long Roseires Dam in 1966 turned the plain into the largest irrigated farm in the world; it nowadays covers over 800,000 hectares.

[159] Paragraph based on Ertsen, *Improvising*, 87–108; Bernal, 'Cotton', esp. 104–15.

landlords than industrious peasants, they had little choice but to accept such practices given the high labour demands and low rewards of cotton production.

Much the same applied to the widespread prioritization of sorghum and animal husbandry over cotton, or to the diversion of household labour into various non-farming activities, all of which built on pre-colonial land use, handicraft, and trading practices.[160] According to the scheme's regulations, tenants were allowed to draw irrigation water for the cultivation of sorghum and lubia (a fodder crop), but only for their own consumption. In practice, however, this prohibition was scarcely enforceable because managers were well aware that the availability of irrigated land for grain and forage production was crucial for retaining tenants on their plots. As a result, subsistence crops, though officially regarded as nothing more than 'permissive adjuncts' to cotton cultivation, became a central element of the entire scheme.[161]

At the same time, the transformation of the physical environment also brought unexpected results. As soon as Sennar was completed in 1925, new cotton seed was imported from Egypt to boost yields. Although it responded well at first, by 1929 it was ravaged by blackarm bacteria and other pests, which together claimed up to three-quarters of the potential yield over the next several years.[162] Researchers eventually discovered that blackarm bacteria (which spreads from the fallen debris of infected plants) could not survive submersion for more than forty-eight hours, so when fields were being prepared for the 1932–3 season, managers ordered them to be heavily pre-watered just prior to sowing the crop. The decision backfired spectacularly. Although the fields were indeed cleared of blackarm, sowing was delayed well into the rainy season, and the weak growth of the seedlings on the saturated soils rendered them highly susceptible to leaf curl, a viral infection that was one of the other main threats at Gezira. As disease problems mounted, many officials suspected that the root cause was soil degradation brought on by a combination of waterlogging, salinization, and perennial weed infestation that depleted soil nitrogen even during fallow periods. According to Arthur Gaitskell, one of the chief architects of the scheme, 'within the incredibly short space of six years the virgin land which had started with such splendid crops appeared to be worthless, filthy with weed and foul with disease'.[163]

Together, these problems prompted a major overhaul of agricultural practice at Gezira. In place of the original three-year cycle (10 feddans planted with cotton, 10 left fallow, and 5 each under sorghum and lubia), managers introduced a complex eight-course rotation that ensured at least one fallow season after each cotton crop to allow for a more thorough clean-up of pests and field debris. Although this system reduced the proportion of cotton acreage on the scheme from a third to a

[160] Bernal, 'Cotton', 106, 117.

[161] Arthur Gaitskell, *Gezira: A Story of Development in the Sudan* (London: Faber & Faber, 1959), 217.

[162] H. Ferguson (Ministry of Agriculture, Sudan Government), *Notes on Cotton Growing from the Research Division* (Khartoum: Agricultural Publications Committee, 1954), 29.

[163] Gaitskell, *Gezira*, 140–4, quote p. 144; Ferguson, *Notes*, 25; see also the criticisms in Vageler, *Koloniale Bodenkunde*, 11.

quarter, it did nothing to undermine the frowned-upon practices of sharecropping and wage-employment. In fact, it further encouraged them since the most important means of controlling leaf-curl was extremely labour-intensive: namely, to pull up all of the cotton plants by the roots after harvest (each tenancy averaged around 110,000 plants).[164]

Altering the cropping system was also related to the question of water availability. Supplying the right amount of water at the correct intervals was a complex task at the best of times, and the diverse interests of state officials, Syndicate managers, and tenants made practical adjustments all the more necessary. The original design was modelled on the continuous flow systems of the Punjab and Egypt, which required cultivators to manage their water rations whenever they came, day or night. But since tenants who had 'already accepted immense changes in daylight farming, could hardly be expected to turn out at night', managers switched to a daytime-only system by turning the secondary canals into night storage reservoirs.[165]

It was a clever solution for one problem, but it soon led to others. Low night-time velocities in the canals encouraged sedimentation and the accumulation of nutrients in the channel bottom, which promoted the growth of aquatic vegetation and a further slowing of velocity rates. Breaking this positive feedback loop required expensive canal maintenance regimes, which once again added to the overall labour burden. Worse still, it created ideal conditions for the transmission of bilharzia because the clogged storage canals were an ideal habitat for snails. In turn, minimizing the bilharzia threat required new methods for protecting the canal cleaners (mainly by avoiding water contact after noontime, when the parasites generally exit the snails).[166] Such modifications to the irrigation system continued long after independence. In fact, the pressures to intensify cotton cropping after the early 1960s eventually prompted a return to continuous-flow irrigation.

The constant alterations at Gezira illustrate an essential point. Whatever the original ideas behind the project, its actual operation on the ground seemed less like an instance of 'planned development' and more like a perpetual process of adaptation and negotiation between the various human and non-human elements that together constituted the scheme.[167] Gezira was by no means unique in this respect, for the same pattern of improvisation was replicated, even magnified, by French efforts to create an irrigated cotton belt around the inland delta of the Niger River in French Soudan.

The idea of developing irrigation along the Niger reached back to the early twentieth century, though it first gained traction as part of the autarkic shift in France's post-war economic policy. The scheme originated in the early 1920s when

---

[164] Gaitskell, *Gezira*, 150–6, here 151; also Ferguson, *Notes*, 41–2; Tony Barnett, *The Gezira Scheme: An Illusion of Development* (London: Cass, 1977), 8–9.

[165] Gaitskell, *Gezira*, 123–4.

[166] William Jobin, *Dams and Disease: Ecological Design and Health Impacts of Large Dams, Canals and Irrigation Systems* (London: E & FN Spon, 1999), 321–7, 498–500; Farley, *Bilharzia*, 123–4.

[167] As convincingly argued in detail by Ertsen, *Improvising*.

Émile Bélime, an ambitious public works engineer, devised a plan to irrigate over 1 million hectares of dry savannah along the banks of the river. It soon attracted the support of the Colonial Ministry and the government-general in Dakar as an ideal vehicle for the development of West Africa's inland territories. The first barrage was completed at Sotuba, near Bamako, in the late 1920s, and was followed several years later by a much larger dam and canal system downstream at Marakala, all of which were managed after 1932 by the Office du Niger, a public body specifically charged with developing irrigated cotton and rice production in the Niger valley. Under the autocratic directorship of Bélime, the Office spearheaded the largest-ever attempt to create an intensive African cotton production system directly under French control.[168]

Like Gezira, the plan was to recruit indigenous settlers onto irrigated household plots, which tenants would cultivate according to three-crop rotations laid down by project managers. The aim was quite consciously to create a 'second Gezira' by harnessing the waters of what many regarded as West Africa's 'French Nile'.[169] But as contemporary critics pointed out, such analogies were grossly overoptimistic in view of the social and ecological conditions of the region. For one thing, the population of the mid-Niger area was scant. In addition, the long dry season, irregular rainfall, and huge seasonal river-level fluctuations (of between 5 and 8 metres) posed serious challenges for engineers.[170] Opponents argued that funds would be better spent on the development of rain-fed cotton in the Sudan or on irrigation works along the Mekong River in Cambodia. Even among those who supported Niger irrigation in principle—including Auguste Chevalier (France's most prominent tropical agronomist), Yves Henry (the leading French expert on African cotton), and most of the Association Coloniale Cotonnière—there were grave doubts about the scheme.[171]

Such misgivings were well founded, for a series of setbacks soon forced a reconsideration of the entire project. One major problem was the difficulty of attracting voluntary settlers, which meant that the vast majority of tenants had to be forced onto Office lands via compulsory labour legislation. From the beginning, recruitment tactics had to be revised in the face of widespread opposition. Occasionally, entire villages would disappear within minutes in an attempt to evade recruiters.[172] Upon their arrival at the project, many of the draftees avoided or opposed management instructions wherever they could: ignoring obligatory crop

---

[168] See generally van Beusekom, *Negotiating*; Roberts, *Two Worlds*, 118–44, 223–48; Emil Schreyger *L'Office du Niger au Mali 1932 à 1982: la problématique d'une grande entreprise agricole dans la zone du Sahel* (Wiesbaden: Steiner, 1984); Jean Filipovich, 'Destined to Fail: Forced Settlement at the *Office du Niger*, 1926–45', *Journal of African History*, vol. 42 (2001), 239–60.

[169] Bloud, *Problème cotonnier*, 134.

[170] Van Beusekom, *Negotiating*, 39; Filipovich, 'Destined', 241–3; Bloud, *Problème cotonnier*, 146–7.

[171] Roberts, *Two Worlds*, 135–43; Filipovich, 'Destined', 242–5; F. Vuillet, Yves Henry, and H. Lavergne, *Les Irrigations au Niger et la culture du cotonnier* (Paris: Émile Larose, 1922); J. Cardot, 'Le Coton en Indochine et les besoins de l'industrie cotonnière française', *L'Agronomie coloniale*, vol. 12 no. 85 (Jan. 1925), 15–19.

[172] Van Beusekom, *Negotiating*, 67–77.

rotations, cultivating land beyond their tenancies, selling a proportion of their crop to local buyers, or abandoning their plots altogether. In many parts of the scheme the planned crop rotations were abandoned almost immediately as settlers found them unsuitable for local soil and irrigation conditions. Most preferred to grow rice or millet instead of cotton anyway, and prioritized work on their own fields over project plots since the harvest from the former could be sold to whomever they chose.[173] At the same time, the Office management faced stinging internal criticism over its coercive conscription practices and the poor conditions in which the settlers and canal-building gangs lived, especially during the Popular Front era of the late 1930s. Although the Vichy government provided a more congenial atmosphere for Bélime's expansion plans, by 1944 the Office was plagued by soil degradation, canal breaches, low cotton prices, and mounting opposition from farmers within the scheme and in its main recruitment areas. In 1945 an investigation launched by the Fourth Republic's colonial ministry lambasted the project for its poor treatment of settlers, inadequate irrigation techniques, and insufficient agronomic study of the region. Finally, in 1946 the abolition of forced labour in French West Africa meant that Office managers would henceforth have to take settlers' concerns firmly into account if the project were to function at all.[174]

By the late 1940s, the dream of building an intensively cultivated, centrally managed cotton settlement on the middle Niger was giving way to a more pragmatic vision that reflected the interests of indigenous farmers and their use of the land. After 1946 the task of the new Office director, Pierre Viguier, was to determine what the agency could realistically achieve before any further expansion could be contemplated. In the absence of any detailed pedological studies to date, Viguier turned to local knowledge instead, and the benefits were immediate. Farmers' soil categorizations—based on colour, cover vegetation, and crumb structure—proved highly useful for determining crop suitability on the different soils of the project, and quickly became the basis for attempts to boost stubbornly low yields.[175] As Office agronomists subsequently turned to the problem of fertility maintenance (in particular the creation of a viable rotation system), they again adapted their plans to mesh with settler practices and soil characteristics. Green manuring was initially pushed as a solution, but the need for deeper cultivation to plough under the leguminous manure crops required mechanical traction, and the reluctance of settlers to incur the high costs of tractor services (not to mention the threat of soil compaction) eventually prompted a return to ox-drawn ploughing. Managers also experimented with chemical fertilizers to sustain yields, but these

[173] Van Beusekom, *Negotiating*, 118–46.

[174] Roberts, *Two Worlds*, 238–48; van Beusekom, *Negotiating*, xxxi, 62–3, 126–8, 152–3, 162–3; Laura Ann Twagira, '"Robot Farmers" and Cosmopolitan Workers: Technological Masculinity and Agricultural Development in the French Soudan (Mali), 1945–68', *Gender & History*, vol. 26 no. 3 (Nov. 2014), 459–77.

[175] Cotton yields varied between 110 and 233 kg/ha, approximately one-quarter to half the yields at Gezira: Filipovich, 'Destined', 257; van Beusekom, *Negotiating*, 103.

were too expensive to attract settler interest. In the end, the Office increasingly resorted to a method that had been used by locals for generations: pasturing cattle, including the herds of nomadic pastoralists in the region, directly on the fields during the dry season.

On the eve of Mali's independence in 1960, the Office had undergone a remarkable evolution. By the end of the 1950s, a combination of ecological constraints and continuous pressure from settlers for a greater voice in management decisions ensured that over six times more acreage was fertilized by grazing than by chemical inputs, and over six times more acreage was under rice than under cotton (which was eventually abandoned altogether in 1970).[176] After four decades of effort and millions of francs of investment, the challenges posed by environmental and social conditions in the middle Niger had pushed the colonial dream of irrigated cotton off the agenda.

The demand for cheap cotton, and the determination to reduce European dependence on American supplies, exacted a hefty toll on the landscapes and peoples of Europe's colonies. The strains it placed on water and soil resources were felt far beyond the land on which it was directly grown, just as the exceptionally heavy labour requirements of commercial cultivation entailed far-reaching alterations to rural life more generally. In spite of all the effort poured into colonial cotton campaigns, by and large the economic and political results fell well short of expectations, sometimes to the point of being counter-productive. In many colonies, and especially in sub-Saharan Africa, the fixation on cotton not only diverted attention from more profitable forms of land use; it also impoverished growers and nourished a sense of resentment against colonial rule.

Yet the strategic importance of cotton for European industry meant that the quest for colonial supplies was never fundamentally placed in question. The tropical colonies, so the argument went, possessed land and labour in abundance, plenty of sunshine, mild or non-existent winters, and what often appeared to be good cotton soils. All that was needed was the stimulation of European demand and the application of scientific know-how to unlock their potential. As we have seen, however, many of the areas targeted by colonial planners, even those with large indigenous textile industries, faced substantial ecological disadvantages as producers for global markets. Of all the colonial territories where cotton was grown, only Egypt was ever a match for the US Cotton Belt.

The story of colonial cotton was, above all else, a story of exploitation—of land, water, soils, and people. In many respects it epitomized the fundamental dynamics of imperialism, whose underlying purpose was to maximize the gains from the resources and labour of subjugated territories. But different commodities and crops function in different ways, and cotton was only one of many raw materials that helped to reshape global political ecology during the colonial era. As we try to

---

[176] Filipovich, 'Destined', 257–60; Roberts, *Two Worlds*, 246–81, 247; van Beusekom, *Negotiating*, 22–5, 127–9.

understand these changes it is important to recognize how the physical and biological properties of different commodities, and the diverse ways they could be produced, shaped the new social and ecological orders that they helped create. This is not to suggest that the material itself contained its own historic potential, or that it necessarily possessed a full-blown form of historical agency. But it does mean, as Chapters 2–6 show, that the stories were not all the same.

2

Bittersweet Harvest
The Colonial Cocoa Boom and
the Tropical Forest Frontier

Chocolate is by many measures Europe's favourite food.[1] The western half of the continent has long led the world in per capita chocolate consumption, and for centuries it served as the chief market for the global cocoa trade. During the years around 1900, at the high-point of Europe's colonial empire, it accounted for the vast bulk of world imports. Over a century later, Europeans consumed almost half of the 4 million tons of cocoa produced globally—nearly twice as much as North America, the second-largest import region, and despite the growing taste for chocolate in the rest of the world.[2]

At one level this sweet tooth reflects a long-standing tradition. Cocoa has been a prized luxury in Europe ever since the 1600s. From the very beginning, its costliness and exotic flavour lent it an aura of self-indulgence that it never lost over the following centuries. Nonetheless, it was mainly after the 1850s that most Europeans developed a taste for it. Over the course of the nineteenth century, chocolate was gradually transformed from a luxury item into a mass consumer good through a cluster of interrelated developments: rising incomes in Europe's industrial metropoles, the efforts of manufacturing firms to feed the growing market for non-essential foodstuffs, and the sharp upsurge of global trade and imperial expansion throughout the tropics. Towards the end of the century, the emergence of a new mass confectionery industry in Europe roused an army of cocoa growers and merchants into action, many of whom were actively encouraged by colonial governments keen to increase their export revenues. Among the various consequences of their activities was an explosion of cocoa cultivation across the humid lowlands of the tropics, from Latin America and the Caribbean to West Africa and the South Pacific.

For the past several centuries, the history of cocoa has been tightly interwoven with the global reach of European power. Starting with its 'discovery' during Europe's early modern expansion, it eventually grew into a major industry

---

[1] This chapter is largely based on material first published in Corey Ross, 'The Plantation Paradigm: Colonial Agronomy, African Farmers and the Global Cocoa Boom, 1870s–1940s', *Journal of Global History*, vol. 9 no. 1 (Mar. 2014), 49–71.

[2] Figures from UNCTAD, <http://unctad.org/meetings/en/Presentation/SUC_MEM2014_09042014_ICCO.pdf>, p. 14. In terms of per capita consumption, the top seven consuming countries are in Western Europe, led by Switzerland, with the USA in eighth place: UNCTAD, *Prospects for the World Cocoa Market Until the Year 2005* (New York: UN, 1991), 69.

during the height of imperialism, and it continued to link European consumers and tropical producers long after the demise of colonialism. At first glance, this relationship might suggest a rather smooth overarching narrative in which the growth of cocoa production and consumption forms an unbroken thread throughout the longer sweep of colonial history. But beneath the surface, the story of cocoa was anything but straightforward—economically, politically, and perhaps least of all from an environmental perspective.

Indeed, the dominant theme in the history of cocoa is not a steady flow of supply but rather a perennial cycle of boom and bust. Wherever cocoa has been produced, the basic pattern is often the same: an initial frenzy of clearing and planting is followed by either a precipitous collapse or a process of creeping decline before eventually ending in soil exhaustion, abandonment, and relocation elsewhere. Granted, cocoa is hardly unique in this respect. Sugar, coffee, and a host of other crops have also been marked by a curious mixture of volatility and endurance.[3] But of all the tropical crops that have been grown for world markets, none are more prone to cyclical extremes than cocoa.[4]

Environmental factors were not, of course, the only cause of this volatility. Economic and political changes were crucial, including shifts in trade policy, the vagaries of import markets, and, most fundamentally, the availability of cheap (often coerced) labour. All of these elements were profoundly transformed over the course of the nineteenth century with the liberalization of trade and the suppression of slavery. But ecological problems were also a constant source of trouble, from soil erosion and long-term fertility loss to pests and diseases. These factors likewise changed over the course of the nineteenth century as fresh forest land grew scarcer and as the thickening networks of global trade allowed disease pathogens to circulate further and faster than ever before.[5]

In addition, the biological characteristics of the cocoa tree (*Theobroma cacao*) itself shaped its history as a crop commodity. As an under-storey tree indigenous to the upper Amazon and Orinoco basins, its essential requirements are continual warmth and a regular supply of moisture. It grows best where rainfall is between 1,500 and 2,000 mm per year and where diurnal temperature fluctuations are between about 18 and 32 degrees Celsius. Although it dislikes prolonged or intense dry seasons, brief periods of low rainfall are advantageous for the purpose of drying harvested beans. It strongly prefers locations sheltered from strong winds and is sensitive to waterlogged soils. Some degree of shade is often beneficial, as are

---

[3] On this theme more generally: Frank Uekötter, 'Rise, Fall, and Permanence: Issues in the Environmental History of the Global Plantation', in Frank Uekötter (ed.), *Comparing Apples, Oranges, and Cotton: Environmental Histories of the Global Plantation* (Frankfurt a. Main: Campus, 2014), 7–25.

[4] The essential study is François Ruf, *Booms et crises du cacao: les vertiges de l'or brun* (Paris: Karthala, 1995).

[5] See, generally, Philip D. Curtin, *The Rise and Fall of the Plantation Complex: Essays in Atlantic History* (Cambridge: Cambridge University Press, 1990). On cocoa specifically: William Gervase Clarence-Smith, *Cocoa and Chocolate, 1765–1914* (London: Routledge, 2000); William Gervase Clarence-Smith (ed.), *Cocoa Pioneer Fronts since 1800: The Role of Smallholders, Planters and Merchants* (Houndmills: Macmillan, 1996).

deep, well-drained clay loam soils, but neither is indispensable depending on local conditions.

From an ecological standpoint, huge areas of tropical lowland forest below about 600 metres are therefore suitable for cocoa, which greatly facilitated its transfer around the globe.[6] From a commercial standpoint, however, it is a much trickier proposition, for cocoa trees require several years between planting and the first harvest. This basic attribute, which it shares with coffee and rubber, has two important effects: first, it engenders a relative inelasticity of supply; and second, it tends to encourage more long-term and individualized land tenure arrangements, whether in the form of outright land title or ownership of the crop itself. From an agricultural perspective, cocoa is easy to plant and can also be profitably grown under various forms of organization. Unlike cotton or sugar, neither the cultivation nor processing of cocoa affords any meaningful economies of scale.

As we will see in this chapter, this made it an (perhaps *the*) archetypal small-holder crop. Despite the persistence of large, centralized cocoa estates in some parts of the world, and despite the advantages bestowed on them by colonial administrations, no other tropical commodity presented so many difficulties for the modern plantation. As a result, the history of the colonial-era cocoa boom was—in stark contrast to cotton—largely driven by indigenous initiative. The story of cocoa thus illustrates how the opportunities and incentives created by imperial trade links shaped human-environment arrangements far beyond the activities of European colonizers.

But if cocoa is one of the easiest export crops to establish it is also one of the hardest to maintain over the long term. For one thing, it is quite prone to pests, disease, and wind damage. Moreover, the fact that pests and disease are generally more prevalent on second-growth lands means that replanting is almost never economically feasible so long as there is new forest land available. This need to tap the 'forest rent'—that is, the differential advantage bestowed by fresh soils and low concentrations of pests and pathogens on new clearings—has long made cocoa frontiers highly mobile.[7] And to turn the relationship around, in areas with suitable climate and available primary forest, no other cultivar has proved a more profitable vehicle for exploiting forest capital than cocoa. As a colonial-era adage put it, 'cocoa is gold, coffee is silver'.[8]

'Brown gold' is a fitting moniker in more than one sense. It points not only to the relative profitability of cocoa, but also to the 'gold-rush'-like dynamics that have often characterized its spread. Time after time, cocoa production has been marked by a sequence of boom, decline, and relocation into new areas where the entire cycle was repeated.[9] Despite efforts to boost yields on existing acreage or to replant old cocoa lands with new trees, this cyclical pattern remained largely intact. Just as the search for gold continually lured prospectors into new areas, cocoa has

[6] Allen Young, *The Chocolate Tree: A Natural History of Cacao* (Washington, DC: Smithsonian, 1994), 2–3.

[7] On the importance of 'forest rent', see Ruf, *Booms et crises*, 91–159.

[8] Paul Preuss, *Expedition nach Central- und Südamerika* (Berlin: KWK, 1901), 239.

[9] See generally Ruf, *Booms et crises*; Clarence-Smith (ed.), *Cocoa Pioneer Fronts*.

repeatedly drawn planting pioneers into the forests of the tropics. Of course, the gold-rush analogy should not be stretched too far. After all, cocoa trees have a productive life-span of anywhere from twenty to eighty years, and once the planting frontier moved on it generally left behind successor crops rather than deserted ghost-towns. But the forests that were initially cleared for cocoa have rarely returned, and the maintenance of global cocoa production has continued to rely on opening up fresh forest land as the finite fertility resources of any given region are exhausted. Ever since the colonial-era boom, there is good reason to regard the tropical forest as 'the mine of cocoa'.[10]

THE TRANSFORMATION OF THE GLOBAL COCOA INDUSTRY

Before we look at these issues in more detail, it is useful to sketch out the basic contours of the cocoa industry and how it evolved. Long before Europeans ever encountered cocoa, it was used for a variety of purposes in pre-Columbian societies. In the Orinoco and upper Amazon regions where the plant originated, the fruit was mainly collected in the wild to make a drink from the pulp coating the seeds. The deliberate domestication of the cocoa tree occurred in Mesoamerica, where chocolate substances were first made from its seeds. By the time the Spaniards arrived in Central America, cocoa seeds functioned as an important form of currency and were imbued with a rich cultural significance. As Spanish power expanded throughout the region, the consumption of chocolate increased with the abolition of cultural restrictions on its use.[11]

Cocoa was soon brought to Europe as well, though it was only with the decline of sugar prices in the seventeenth century—mainly as a result of the growth of cane plantations in Brazil and the Caribbean—that it spread very far beyond Iberia. Usually prepared as a sweetened drink, cocoa became a cherished privilege for wealthy elites across much of western and central Europe.[12] In the early nineteenth century, as prices for New World goods fell, chocolate gradually became less socially exclusive, and by the middle of the century the temperance movement gave it a further boost as an alternative to alcohol.

But the real breakthrough began around the 1880s, due partly to the expansion of global transport and rising purchasing power in Europe, and partly to a string of confectionery innovations that transformed the dominant mode of consumption from a drink to a solid.[13] As more and more people developed a taste for the 'eating chocolate' sold by firms such as Cadbury, Nestlé, and Lindt, cocoa production surged. World exports first surpassed 40,000 tons in 1885 and rose exponentially after that, reaching 95,000 tons in 1900, 280,000 in 1914, half a million tons in

---

[10] Ruf, *Booms et crises*, 20.

[11] Sophie D. Coe and Michael D. Coe, *The True History of Chocolate* (London: Thames & Hudson, 1996), 35–104.

[12] Coe and Coe, *True History*, 203–35; Clarence-Smith, *Cocoa and Chocolate*, 22–3.

[13] Coe and Coe, *True History*, 241–51.

the 1920s, and over 700,000 tons in the late 1930s. From 1900 to 1920 production increased roughly fourfold while prices sank by around two-thirds. Continental Europe was by far the largest import market, accounting for 58 per cent of the cocoa trade 1909–13, with the UK taking a further 12 per cent (26 per cent went to the USA). In the late 1930s, Europeans consumed an average of 331,000 tons of cocoa per year (over half of world production); it was not until the onset of the Second World War that US imports surpassed those in Europe, and even then only temporarily.[14]

This explosive growth of trade and consumption was inextricably linked to a shift in the geographic centre of production. When the cocoa boom began in the 1880s the crop was still overwhelmingly centred on its historic heartlands of Central/South America and parts of the Caribbean. But shortly after the turn of the century, the coastal belt of West Africa—above all the Gold Coast, but also Nigeria and to a lesser extent Côte d'Ivoire—eclipsed Latin America as the heart of the world cocoa industry. The change was as rapid as it was momentous. By the 1930s, West African farmers, many of them smallholders, accounted for around two-thirds of global cocoa production.

In turn, this shift of geographic focus was related to changes in the product itself. Cocoa is a remarkably variable species divided into three main varieties. *Criollo* types, grown mainly in Latin America, are highly prized for flavour but often suffer from low yields and disease. This combination of fussiness and superior price has made *criollo* particularly attractive to well-capitalized planters whose higher overheads could only be justified by the premium prices it could fetch. *Forastero* types, which include the *amelonado* variety that dominated in West Africa, yield a lower quality of cocoa but are more productive and more resistant to disease. Many hybrids were also developed over the years, commonly dubbed *trinitarios* after their origin on Trinidad, though most require constant maintenance and generally do not breed true. The different types of beans produced by these varieties are not regarded as the same commodity but are broadly categorized into flavour versus bulk beans, which roughly corresponds to a distinction between *criollo* and *forastero* (allowing for considerable overlap in quality and price). From the late nineteenth century onwards, the evolution of chocolate from a luxury article into a mass consumer good generally reflected a rise in the proportion of bulk beans. And since this market was increasingly dominated by African farmers, the eclipse of the noble *criollo* varieties partly reflected a decline in the proportion of cocoa grown on centralized plantations.[15]

In certain ways, then, the 'democratization' of cocoa consumption at one end of the commodity chain was mirrored in the eclipse of large-scale latifundia by small- and medium-sized farmers at the other. To be sure, the nature and magnitude of this shift varied considerably from region to region. In some areas the cocoa boom

---

[14] Vernon D. Wickizer, *Coffee, Tea and Cocoa: An Economic and Political Analysis* (London: Stanford University Press, 1951), 264, 484–5; Joseph Grunwald and Philip Musgrove, *Natural Resources in Latin American Development* (Baltimore: Johns Hopkins Press, 1970), 332, 336; Clarence-Smith, *Cocoa and Chocolate*, 238–9.

[15] Clarence-Smith, *Cocoa and Chocolate*, 176–80.

led to a proliferation of plantations characterized by centralized organization and intensive modes of cultivation.[16] This remained the case to varying degrees in the oldest producer regions in Latin America, and was particularly evident wherever the more demanding *criollo* varieties were grown. It was also common in equatorial Africa and parts of Southeast Asia. But plantations were least evident in the British colonies of West Africa, where control over land distribution was left largely in the hands of indigenous elites, and where most of the world's cocoa was eventually grown.

THE MODERN COCOA PLANTATION: PROBLEMS AND PERSISTENCE IN GLOBAL PERSPECTIVE

The evolution of the cocoa economy points to one of the more intriguing aspects of the colonial-era cocoa boom. Over time, it challenged the engrained assumption that large, centrally managed estates were the most effective vehicle for developing the 'underused' lands of the tropics and increasing the supply of sought-after crops for world markets. In the event, the modern plantation—by which I mean a large agricultural production complex employing outside capital and technology and concentrating on the intensive production of a single crop for export—proved a relatively inefficient means of bulk cocoa production. Instead, the huge increase in output came overwhelmingly from smallholder-style production—by which I mean land-extensive and mixed-cropping techniques commonly employed by smallholders but practised on farms of varying scales—primarily, though not exclusively, in the humid forest belt of West Africa. In both commercial and agricultural terms, cocoa defied the conventional script.

At the same time, however, the cocoa boom also highlights the remarkable persistence of plantation models and their associated cultivation methods long after their relative inefficiency for bulk production was plainly apparent. Despite mounting evidence to the contrary, most planters and colonial officials clung to a belief in the technical supremacy of intensive production techniques under centralized European management.[17] Even where the official policy was to promote indigenous cultivation, as in Nigeria and the Gold Coast, agricultural officials often tried to convert farmers from their supposedly archaic methods to more capital- or labour-intensive techniques.

---

[16] And frequently by coerced labour as well, as the slavery scandals of the 1900s attest: Lowell J. Satre, *Chocolate on Trial: Slavery, Politics, and the Ethics of Business* (Athens, Oh.: Ohio University Press, 2005); Kevin Grant, *A Civilized Savagery: Britain and the New Slaveries in Africa, 1884–1926* (London: Routledge, 2005), 109–34; Catherine Higgs, *Chocolate Islands: Cocoa, Slavery and Colonial Africa* (Athens, Oh.: Ohio University Press, 2012); Miguel Bandeira Jerónimo, *The 'Civilising Mission' of Portuguese Colonialism, 1870–1930* (Basingstoke: Palgrave, 2015), ch. 2.

[17] First highlighted for Ghana by R. H. Green and S. H. Hymer, 'Cocoa in the Gold Coast: A Study in the Relations between African Farmers and Agricultural Experts', *Journal of Economic History*, vol. 26 no. 3 (1966), 299–319; further elaborated by Gareth Austin, 'Mode of Production or Mode of Cultivation: Explaining the Failure of European Cocoa Planters in Competition with African Farmers in Colonial Ghana', in Clarence-Smith (ed.), *Cocoa Pioneer Fronts*, 154–75.

At one level this attachment to plantation-style cultivation no doubt reflected the disproportional power of planters in areas where they were well entrenched, where lands were considered too 'vacant' or local populations too 'idle' to build new export industries. One might also attribute it to the greater ability of state administrators to 'see', control, and generate revenue from large, concentrated estates than from scattered smallholdings.[18] Yet part of the explanation must also be sought in the realm of culture and ideas, above all in the powerful ideological devotion to plantation agriculture as an embodiment of European agronomic knowledge and a symbol of European power. By the late nineteenth and early twentieth centuries, European-run estates had many decades of experience growing a host of tropical crops. During this period they also became the focal point of the emerging field of tropical agronomy, a new body of expertise that sought to control agricultural environments and maximize yields in diverse ecological contexts. By and large the authority and universal validity of this knowledge were taken for granted; mobilizing it in the interests of productivity was the chief task of the new agricultural departments that were being established throughout the colonies. Although the conspicuous success of small-scale cocoa farmers eventually raised questions about the superiority of colonial agronomic expertise—not to mention about the viability of cocoa estates—the preferred answer was generally to improve plantation practices rather than abandon them. In other words, the increasingly trans-continental flow of agronomic knowledge and information played an important, though underappreciated, role in underpinning the status of plantations as models of organization.[19]

Of course, cocoa plantations were no more a singular entity than the numerous varieties of cocoa itself. They came in a range of different shapes and sizes, adapted a variety of methods to diverse ecological and social conditions, and employed different commercial and agricultural strategies in an attempt to maximize the profits they could coax out of the soil. Without getting bogged down in definitions, it is important to recognize that the label 'plantation' was itself used quite broadly. Reporting on his fact-finding mission to Central and South America, the German botanist Paul Preuss was struck by the broad spectrum of cocoa farms, which ranged from the 'well-tended gardens' of Suriname to the large plantations on Trinidad to the 'forests and occasionally even thickets' of cocoa in Ecuador.[20] Nor were the conditions on plantations static. Methods of planting and maintenance were influenced by new innovations—fungicides, artificial fertilizers—as well as by price trends and shifting labour laws. But despite all their differences, cocoa plantations throughout the tropics faced broadly similar problems. Over time, the increasingly global exchange of information between research stations and botanical gardens created a set of semi-standardized and expert-endorsed practices that were reflected in plantation operations in many different parts of the world.

---

[18] James C. Scott, *Seeing Like a State: How Certain Schemes to Improve the Human Condition Have Failed* (New Haven: Yale University Press, 1998).
[19] Ross, 'Plantation Paradigm'.   [20] Preuss, *Expedition*, 239–40.

The Caribbean is the best place to get a sense of these commonalities and differences. During the late nineteenth century, most would-be cocoa planters searching for the state of the art tended to look there.[21] Although the region had long been a focal point of global production, the rapid expansion of cocoa in certain territories meant that it was home to many of the world's newest plantations. In addition, the divergent climatic and soil conditions in the region meant that there was a wide range of different models on display.

Trinidad was by far the largest cocoa producer in the Caribbean, ranking third in the world at the turn of the century, behind Ecuador and Brazil. Although small amounts had been grown here since the mid-seventeenth century, nearly all of its quarter million acres (*c.*100,000 hectares) of cocoa came in a flurry of planting after the 1860s, much of it initially undertaken by smallholders but increasingly centred on larger estates.[22] Planting and maintenance methods on Trinidad generally reflected, and subsequently influenced, those in many other areas. Standard practice was as follows. First, all vegetation was cut down and burned apart from any commercially valuable wood. After drainage ditches were dug, seeds were sown at stake at wide intervals of anywhere from 12 × 12 to 16 × 16 feet (3.7 to 4.9 metres), depending on the quality of the soil (the richer the soil, the greater the distance since faster growth required more space to prevent overcrowding). Spacing at such wide intervals demanded a considerable amount of weeding, especially before the canopy thickened and shaded the ground underneath. After six or seven years the trees began to bear, and they reached full production at around ten to fifteen years.

Broadly speaking, this method of planting involved a wholesale elimination of the original forest ecosystem; little if any of the previous cover was left. But since cocoa had evolved as an under-storey tree, many of the practices on Trinidad's cocoa estates effectively mimicked the ecological 'services' otherwise provided by the original forest cover: that is, moisture retention, shade, and wind protection. Windbreaks were regarded as vital, especially wherever cocoa groves were exposed to hurricanes or tropical storms. Shade was also important for guarding against drought, avoiding high soil temperatures, and reducing erosion. For young saplings, temporary shade was often provided by cassava, chillies, or pigeon peas, which also generated an income before the trees began to yield. For mature groves the issue of shade was more controversial. Although protection from the full glare of the sun tends to extend the trees' productive life span and reduces the risk of drought, it also slows growth and limits yields.

For many decades the question of shade on cocoa estates was a source of considerable disagreement among planters and botanists, since the balance of advantages and disadvantages varied from one locality to another. At the time, most agronomists recommended some degree of permanent shade for cocoa plantings to maintain

---

[21] Including the aforementioned Paul Preuss, who was commissioned by the German Colonial Economic Committee to make recommendations for the cocoa industry in Cameroon.

[22] E. R. Moll, *Cacao in Trinidad and Tobago* (1960), 2; Kathleen Phillips Lewis, 'The Trinidad Cocoa Industry and the Struggle for Crown Land during the Nineteenth Century', in Clarence-Smith (ed.), *Cocoa Pioneer Fronts*, 45–64.

moisture and reduce soil temperatures.[23] On Trinidad it was widely deemed to be indispensable given that average rainfall was relatively low for cocoa (approximately 1,700 mm) and the risk of seasonal drought fairly high. During the late nineteenth century many Trinidadian estates planted one shade tree for every two cocoa trees, placing them at most around 12 metres apart. For outside observers this seemed excessive, and the debate eventually prompted a four-year experiment by the Trinidad Department of Agriculture, which ultimately recommended partial shade.[24] But this still left the question of which species were best suited to the task. Over the years a variety of shade trees were tried, most of them producing a catch crop—for example, bread fruit, mango, rubber, and kapok. None, however, compared with the evergreen *Erythrina* species or immortel tree, in Spanish often called 'madre del cacao'. Despite the fact that it bears no fruit and the wood is not valuable, the immortel tree is easy to propagate, forms a good canopy that retains humidity, and, best of all, often sheds some of its foliage just as the cocoa crop ripens, thereby letting the sun in at the very moment when it is most beneficial.[25] On Trinidad they were so prevalent that, as one contemporary remarked, an unsuspecting visitor might be forgiven for asking, 'Is this an Immortel plantation?'[26] At base, the strong emphasis on shade trees reflected a strategic decision to simulate certain forest conditions as the basis for the cocoa-growing environment (Fig. 2.1).

If Trinidad occupied one end of the spectrum, the other was represented by nearby Grenada, the second largest island producer in the Caribbean, whose estates were famed for their almost complete *lack* of permanent shade. One reason for the disparity was the island's high and relatively consistent rainfall (2,000–3,000 mm), which made moisture retention far less problematic than on Trinidad. Other reasons were its highly suitable clay soils and a ready supply of cheap labour. Together, these factors allowed Grenadan planters to adopt a remarkably intensive form of cultivation. Trees were planted at intervals as close as 8 × 8 feet (*c.*2.4 metres), drains were dug as necessary, and the ground was rigorously clean-weeded until the cocoa canopy closed and shaded the soil. Closure of the canopy did not take long, for compared to their slow but steady counterparts on Trinidad, which reached full production after at least ten years, Grenada's open-sun cocoa trees produced their first full harvest in only half the time and achieved roughly double the yields at maturity.

This was, of course, a major advantage, but the flip-side was that Grenada's cocoa groves tended to live fast and die young. Full sun not only wore out the trees more quickly, it also 'exploited the soil thoroughly in quick time' through a combination of high growth rates, high yields, and greater exposure of soil to the sun.[27] Whereas most of Trinidad's estates sought to minimize the loss of fertility through

[23] E.g. Auguste Chevalier, *Le Cacaoyer dans l'ouest Africain* (Paris: Challamel, 1908), 116–17; Henri Jumelle, *Le Cacaoyer: sa culture et son exploitation dans tous les pays de production* (Paris: Challamel, 1900), 77–80; Ministère des Colonies, *Manuel pratique de la culture du caféier et du cacaoyer au Congo belge* (Brussels: Van Campenhout, 1908), 76–8; Arthur W. Knapp, *Cocoa and Chocolate: Their History from Plantation to Consumer* (London: Chapman & Hall, 1920), 36–40.

[24] Knapp, *Cocoa and Chocolate*, 40.   [25] Jumelle, *Le Cacaoyer*, 79–80.

[26] Preuss, *Expedition*, 181–4; Knapp, *Cocoa and Chocolate*, 34–7.

[27] Preuss, *Expedition*, 187; C. Y. Shephard, *Report on the Economics of Peasant Agriculture in the Gold Coast* (Accra: Government Printer, 1936), 2–4.

Fig. 2.1. Cocoa grove shaded by Immortel trees, Trinidad, *c.*1920.

Source: Arthur W. Knapp, *Cocoa and Chocolate: Their History from Plantation to Consumer* (London: Chapman & Hall, 1920), p. 39.

heavy shade or the occasional planting of ground cover, on Grenada the density of plantings and the lack of cover required a more proactive regime of weeding, pruning, forking, and manuring in order to maintain fertility.[28] Although the open-sun system was notably labour-intensive, prior to the slump in cocoa prices in the early 1920s the costs were justified by higher yields and by the lower risk of fungal diseases such as witches' broom (a fungus endemic to the Amazon basin), which tended to be more problematic in shadier growing conditions.[29] By the 1910s the tendency to maximize yields per hectare on Grenada was also reinforced by a growing shortage of land.[30]

Overall, the full-sun system was well suited to the particular ecological and social conditions on Grenada, and demonstrated that there was no single answer to the fundamental question of shade. Around the turn of the century it was also being adopted elsewhere, especially on the Gulf of Guinea Islands (São Tomé, Príncipe, Fernando Pó) where planters increasingly 'mined' the soil in more marginal areas as the cocoa frontier spread beyond the most fertile districts.[31] Yet the employment of such intensive methods was due as much to a deep-seated cultural

[28] Harley P. Milstead, 'Cacao Industry of Grenada', *Economic Geography*, vol. 16 no. 2 (Apr. 1940), 195–203, here 199.
[29] Wickizer, *Coffee, Tea and Cocoa*, 297–8.   [30] Milstead, 'Cacao Industry', 202–3.
[31] Oscar Baumann, *Eine Afrikanische Tropen-Insel. Fernando Póo und die Bube* (Vienna: Hölzel, 1888), 14, 137–8; Leonard J. Schwarz, *Cocoa in the Cameroons under French Mandate and in Fernando Po* (Washington, DC: Government Printing Office, 1933), 45; Clarence-Smith, *Cocoa and Chocolate*, 185; Chevalier, *Le Cacaoyer*, 91–5, 112–13.

preference for cleanliness as to the physical conditions of the land. Undoubtedly, many Grenadan estates were highly profitable until the 1920s. But contemporaries extolled them as much for their appearance per se as for anything else. For colonialist observers, the thorough mastery of the estate environment—where 'the ground may be kept so tidy and free from weeds that they have the appearance of gardens'—embodied agricultural modernity itself.[32] Compared to the local peasant groves whose owners were allegedly 'addicted to a life of tropical indolence' and 'often do no more than chop out the weeds and harvest the crop', Grenada's meticulous estates stood as paragons of agronomic virtue and as reassuring symbols of a presumed cultural superiority.[33]

But however aesthetically pleasing they may have been, even the most orderly plantation environments were no match for adverse ecological conditions. A vivid illustration could be found in nearby Suriname, which possessed not only one of the world's most capital-intensive cocoa industries but also one of the least profitable. Located mainly in the alluvial valleys of the Suriname and Commewijne rivers, Suriname's cocoa estates boasted a reputation for tidiness and precision that surpassed even the neatest estates of Grenada.[34] After clearing the forest and digging expensive drainage works, *forastero* seeds were planted at wide intervals of 4 to 6 metres, and the soil was hoed and covered with straw to suppress weeds and retain moisture. Initial shade was provided by bananas, and mature shade by *Erythrina* varieties as on Trinidad.[35] Once established, most estates operated a particularly thorough regime of weeding and pruning that was—though it was not known at the time—almost certainly counter-productive insofar as it suppressed the breeding of pollinating midges crucial to the productivity of cocoa groves.[36] The reward for all this work was a catastrophic outbreak of witches' broom fungus, which quickly overwhelmed the humid monocultures of Suriname's cocoa plantations after 1895. Agronomists in the colony were stumped. No amount of carbolic acid, radical pruning, or dousing with Bordeaux mixture (a blend of copper sulphate and lime used since the 1880s as a fungicide for vineyards) could do more than slow the inexorable advance of the disease, which covered the colony by 1903 and had effectively killed off its cocoa industry by the 1920s.[37]

Although Suriname was an extreme example, pests and pathogens were a perennial problem in most cocoa-producing areas and were exacerbated by the (relatively) uniform character of plantation environments. A few examples must suffice by way of illustration. On Ceylon, where cocoa was introduced in the late nineteenth century in response to the devastation of coffee production by the *Hemileia vastatrix* fungus,[38] the fledgling industry was ravaged by an outbreak of cacao canker

---

[32] Knapp, *Cocoa and Chocolate*, 30.   [33] Milstead, 'Cacao Industry', 199.

[34] Preuss, *Expedition*, 168–9, 239–40; Clarence-Smith, *Cocoa and Chocolate*, 154–5.

[35] E. J. Bartelink, *Handleiding voor kakao-planters* (Amsterdam: de Bussy, 1885), 18–19, 20–3.

[36] Young, *The Chocolate Tree*, 167–71.

[37] Wickizer, *Coffee, Tea and Cocoa*, 297; Clarence-Smith, *Cocoa and Chocolate*, 155, 183–4; Bartelink, *Handleiding*, 32–3.

[38] See Stuart McCook, 'Global Rust Belt: Hemileia vastatrix and the Ecological Integration of World Coffee Production since 1850', *Journal of Global History*, vol. 1 no. 2 (2006), 177–95.

(*Phytophthora faberi*, a bark fungus) that spread like wildfire through its monocultural stands and infected 98 per cent of the trees in the colony by 1902. Although the epidemic was eventually contained by the first large-scale spraying of fungicides in the tropics, confidence in the future of cocoa never fully recovered among the planter community.[39] On São Tomé, Africa's leading producer for most of the nineteenth century, excessive forest clearance and a shift to full-sun techniques around the turn of the century contributed to a massive outbreak of thrips (a juice-sucking insect pest that is especially problematic in drier conditions) that nearly wiped out the crop during the late 1910s.[40] On the well-capitalized and carefully managed German cocoa estates around Mount Cameroon, the heavy losses to brown pod (a common fungal disease in cocoa stands) in the 1900s did not result from cross-infection from indigenous cocoa plantings, as was erroneously asserted at first, but rather from a combination of uniform stands and excessive shade in the relatively wet conditions.[41] The disease problems on Western Samoa, by far the leading cocoa producer in the South Pacific, were particularly distinctive given its fragile island ecosystem. Here, the piles of rotting shells and prunings left under the cocoa trees not only encouraged the spread of brown pod but also furnished an ideal breeding ground for the Indian rhinoceros beetle, itself a recent bio-invader without natural enemies on the island, whose exploding population threatened to wreck the island's all-important coconut industry (in the end, the beetle was bio-logically controlled with an insect fungus, *Metarhizium anisopliae*, that kills its larvae).[42] The list could continue, but it would only belabour the point that pests and pathogens continually threatened to destabilize the already unstable ecologies of the cocoa plantations.

Throughout the *fin-de-siècle* cocoa world, estates represented an attempt to mobilize the natural capital of the lowland forests through the imposition of a uniform and purportedly 'scientific' system of cultivation under a central regime of management. Like plantations growing any other tropical crop, nearly all of them reflected one of three basic scenarios: first, where European planters had a vast reservoir of landless labourers and ex-slaves at their disposal (as in much of the Caribbean); second, where they could readily import copious amounts of cheap foreign labour (most evident in Southeast Asia); and third, where they enjoyed systematic privileges in the alienation of land, which itself facilitated the mobilization of indigenous labour (as in much of sub-Saharan Africa).[43] Where none of these circumstances prevailed, as in British West Africa, cocoa plantations

[39] G. B. Masefield, *A Short History of Agriculture in the British Colonies* (Oxford: Clarendon, 1950), 117.

[40] Schwarz, *Cocoa in the Cameroons*, 10, 47; Clarence-Smith, *Cocoa and Chocolate*, 185–6; Ruf, *Booms et crises*, 120.

[41] Paul Preuss, 'Über Pflanzenschädlinge in Kamerun', *Der Tropenpflanzer*, vol. 7 no. 8 (Aug. 1903), 345–61, here 361; Friedrich Zacher, *Die wichtigsten Krankheiten und Schädlinge der tropischen Kulturpflanzen und ihre Bekämpfung* (Hamburg: Thaden, 1914), 80.

[42] K. Friederichs, 'Bericht über den staatlichen Pflanzenschutzdienst in Deutsch-Samoa 1912–1914', *Der Tropenpflanzer. Beiheft*, vol. 18 (1918), 257–94, here 257–66, 283–4; C. E. Ettling, 'Die Aussichten der Kakaokultur auf Samoa', *Der Tropenpflanzer*, vol. 7 no. 2 (Feb. 1903), 79–82; F. Reinicke, 'Gefährdung der Kakaokultur auf Samoa', *Der Tropenpflanzer*, vol. 6 no. 12 (Dec. 1902), 632–5.

[43] See I. C. Greaves, *Modern Production among Backward Peoples* (London: Allen & Unwin, 1935), 215.

stood little chance of success. To say the very least, African farmers more than made up for their absence.

THE WEST AFRICAN COCOA BOOM

The rise of the Gold Coast into the world's dominant cocoa producer is widely regarded as one of the most spectacular commodity booms in the history of tropical agriculture. Although cocoa exports only began in 1891, within two decades they reached 40,000 tons, making the colony the world's largest producer. Growth thereafter was meteoric: exports exceeded 200,000 tons in 1923 and 300,000 in the mid-1930s.[44] Although few observers at the turn of the century thought that Africans would grow a crop that took so long to pay, by the 1920s the Gold Coast cocoa industry was the envy of the other colonial powers. As a French commentator remarked in 1924, 'forget the proverb that there is nothing new under the sun—or at least cite cocoa in the Gold Coast as an exception. In the history of the world there has certainly never been such rapid development of an entire economic sector launched by the local inhabitants.'[45]

The origins of the industry reach back to around the middle of the nineteenth century when a group of Basel missionaries distributed cocoa seeds among Christian villagers. But it was mainly in the 1880s, after seeds were brought (most likely by a plantation worker) from Fernando Pó to Accra, that cocoa really caught on. The earliest planting began in the Eastern Province and quickly spread west- and northward over the following decades. The first planters were mainly merchants and commercial farmers who migrated into the sparsely populated forests of Akim Abuakwa in the extreme south-east of the colony.[46] Most were a far cry from the stereotypical 'smallholder peasant' cultivating a few acres near his village, and are better understood as agricultural entrepreneurs or even 'rural capitalists'. Many had previously grown palm oil for export; in fact, it was the collapse of palm oil prices following the rise of petroleum lubricants that initially prompted some of them to try their hand at a new crop. Using capital earned from earlier cash-crop ventures, they bought land on freehold from local chiefs, often by pooling their resources in commercial syndicates, and sometimes on the basis of kinship groups. It was these pioneers who accounted for the bulk of Gold Coast cocoa exports before the First World War, making it the biggest exporter in the world by 1911 (Fig. 2.2).[47]

As the frontier moved into other regions, above all Asante, acreage and production rose even faster. Although migrant farmers played a role here too, the substantial

---

[44] Austin, 'Mode of Production', 154.

[45] *Revue générale de botanique*, vol. 36 (1924), 190, cited in Ruf, *Booms et crises*, 177.

[46] The classic study is Polly Hill, *The Migrant Cocoa-Farmers of Southern Ghana: A Study in Rural Capitalism*, 2nd edn (Oxford: James Currey, 1997).

[47] Hill, *Migrant Cocoa-Farmers*, 15–17; see also Gareth Austin, 'Vent for Surplus or Productivity Breakthrough? The Ghanaian Cocoa Take-off, c.1890–1936', *Economic History Review*, vol. 67 no. 4 (2014), 1035–64.

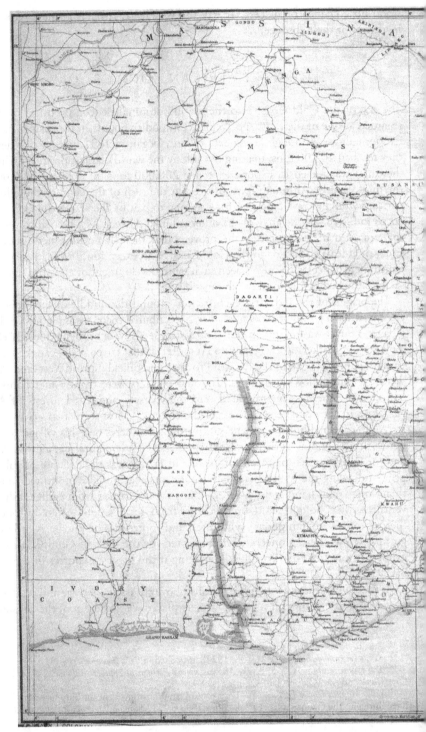

Fig. 2.2. Countries to the West of the Lower and Middle Niger, 1898. By permission
The National Archives, Image Library.
Source: CO 700/WESTAFRICA53.

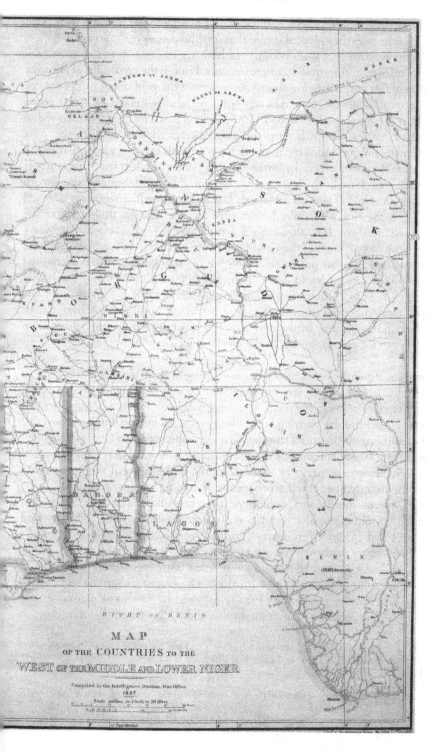

MAP
OF THE COUNTRIES TO THE
WEST OF THE MIDDLE AND LOWER NIGER

Compiled in the Intelligence Division, War Office.
1897
Scale 1640000 or 1 Inch to 10 Miles

rents charged to outsiders and the ability of Asante commoners to retain ownership rights over the trees they planted meant that smallholders were more prevalent here than in the original Akwapim boom.[48] In both regions, the spread of cocoa was crucially aided by transportation improvements. Prior to the expansion of railways, which were first constructed in the 1890s to service the gold mines in the colony, most cocoa was moved to market by means of head-porterage. Whereas cocoa growers in the Americas and on São Tomé had long relied on mules, donkeys, and horses to carry their crop to port, the prevalence of the tsetse fly on the West African mainland precluded the use of draught animals there. It was only with the spread of railways and especially lorries from the 1920s onwards that this transport bottleneck was cleared, which goes some way towards explaining why the growth of cocoa in the Gold Coast came relatively late and was so explosive once it began.[49] At the end of the First World War the estimated cocoa acreage was around 450 square miles (1,165 km², or 288,000 acres); a decade later it was reckoned that over 1 million acres (4,047 km²) of the Gold Coast were planted in cocoa.[50] By 1930 the colony dwarfed all other producers. Its output of 243,000 metric tons accounted for over 40 per cent of world production (588,000 metric tons), and was nearly three times that of its nearest rival Brazil (92,000 metric tons). By any measure, the transplantation of cocoa from its American homeland to the West African tropics was a resounding success. In the mid-1930s there were an estimated 700 million cocoa trees in the colony, mostly of the *amelonado* variety.[51]

Throughout the entire colonial era, cocoa growing in the Gold Coast was notably land-extensive: that is, increases in production came from the enlargement of the area under cultivation rather than by raising yields on existing acreage. In this respect the nature of the planting boom clearly reflected the existing ecological and social conditions on the cocoa frontier. Given the abundance of land and the relative scarcity of labour and outside capital, extensive planting strategies made sound commercial sense as a means of maximizing the exploitation of the 'forest rent'. Just as importantly, they also meshed well with existing land-use practices.

For all the commercial and social innovations that underpinned the cocoa revolution in the Gold Coast (the foundation of commercial syndicates, collective land purchases based on kinship groups, new forms of wage labour and sharecropping),[52] one of the primary reasons for its extraordinary speed was that it built upon rather than overturned long-established patterns of 'forest fallow' cultivation in the region. In this system, farmers cleared and burned a patch of forest and grew a sequence of crops—often yams, vegetables, and maize followed by cassava or plantains—for three to five years before abandoning it to secondary forest and then returning at

---

[48] On land rights in Asante: Gareth Austin, *Labour, Land and Capital in Ghana: From Slavery to Free Labour in Asante, 1807–1956* (Rochester, NY: University of Rochester Press, 2005), 258–76.

[49] Leonard J. Schwarz, *Cocoa in West Africa* (Washington, DC: Government Printing Office, 1928), 17.

[50] N. C. McLeod, *Address on Forestry in Connection with the Cocoa Industry of the Gold Coast* (Accra: Government Press, 1920), 5; Schwarz, *Cocoa in West Africa*, 1.

[51] Shephard, *Report on the Economics*, 9. The Gold Coast production figures here include output from British Togo, though this was marginal: Wickizer, *Coffee, Tea and Cocoa*, 483.

[52] Generally: Hill, *Migrant Cocoa-Farmers*.

intervals of ideally fifteen or twenty years once the land had regained its fertility. Integrating cocoa into this routine was fairly straightforward. Clearing and planting proceeded much as before, the primary difference being that cocoa was planted along with the first season's crops, usually at close intervals of as little as 6 or 7 feet. Cocoa saplings then grew alongside the food crops, which not only suppressed weeds but also provided beneficial shade. It was an ingenious innovation to traditional cultivation methods, for it essentially amounted to selecting cocoa as the main successor species once farmers left their plots to fallow. When this happened, the three- to five-year head start acquired by the cocoa saplings enabled them to out-compete other successor species, especially once the canopy closed and shaded the ground underneath. A further benefit of this system was that it provided food for most of the period before the cocoa trees came to bear, thus avoiding one of the main start-up costs.

Combined with the use of family labour, which was often supplemented by wage contracts and various sharecropping arrangements, this method of folding of cocoa into existing land-use practices enabled indigenous planters to establish a cocoa farm at a fraction of the cost of European-owned estates. Once the trees came into production, harvesting conveniently took place during the main dry season starting in November, at the nadir of annual demand for agricultural labour.[53] Even after the harvest, the beans required little processing beyond fermentation for several days, which farmers generally did by enclosing piles of beans in banana leaves followed by drying in the sun.[54] As far as labour demands and compatibility with established subsistence systems were concerned, the contrast between cocoa and cotton could hardly be more striking (Fig. 2.3).[55]

All in all this was an extraordinarily efficient system for exploiting the natural capital of the forest. Yet few British administrators believed at first that indigenous farmers would respond so quickly and effectively to market stimuli. It is sometimes misunderstood that, unlike the situation in Nigeria where European plantations were expressly forbidden, the decision to privilege African farmers in the Gold Coast was as much a consequence as a cause of the cocoa boom. Like their counterparts elsewhere in Africa, administrators in the colony initially favoured estates and only gradually changed their minds out of fear of political unrest and the recognition that African cocoa farming greatly benefited both government revenues as well as European commercial interests.[56] From the 1890s through the inter-war period, the southern Gold Coast was home to a dispersed string of plantations

---

[53] This paragraph is based on Shephard, *Report on the Economics*, 2–3; Faulkner and Mackie, *West African Agriculture*, 106–8; Austin, *Labour, Land and Capital*, 60–79.

[54] Faulkner and Mackie, *West African Agriculture*, 110–11.

[55] A point that echoes John Tosh's distinction between forest versus savannah crops: Tosh, 'The Cash-Crop Revolution'.

[56] See esp. Austin, *Labour, Land and Capital*, 253–8; Sara S. Berry, *Cocoa, Custom, and Socioeconomic Change in Rural Western Nigeria* (Oxford: Clarendon, 1975); Hubert Fréchou, 'Les Plantations européennes en Côte d'Ivoire', *Les Cahiers d'Outre-Mer*, vol. 8 no. 29 (Jan. 1955), 56–83; Jean-Pierre Chauveau and Eric Léonard, 'Côte d'Ivoire's Pioneer Fronts: Historical and Political Determinants of the Spread of Cocoa Cultivation', in Clarence-Smith (ed.), *Cocoa Pioneer Fronts*, 176–94; Coquery-Vidrovitch, *Le Congo*, 470–3; William Gervase Clarence-Smith, 'Plantation versus Smallholder Production of Cocoa: The Legacy of the German Period in Cameroon', in Peter Geschiere and Piet Konings (eds), *Itinéraires d'accumulation au Cameroun* (Paris: Karthala, 1993), 187–216.

Fig. 2.3. Farmers harvesting cocoa pods, Gold Coast, *c.*1920.
Source: Edith A. Browne, *Cocoa* (London: A & C Black, 1920), p. 9.

ranging in size from 60 to over 10,000 hectares. It quickly became apparent, however, that they could scarcely compete with the extraordinary efficiency of the indigenous planting regime. Cadbury's, one of the colony's major cocoa buyers, ran its own 'model estate', though it never produced more than a fraction of the firm's purchases and collapsed in the 1930s. A similar venture launched by the Lever Brothers met the same fate. The Agriculture Department's own model cocoa farm at Kpeve in British Togoland (initially established by the German colonial government) could only operate at a huge loss despite its technical sophistication. After a distinctly unimpressive record, the last European cocoa plantation in the Gold Coast gave up the ghost in the early 1940s.[57]

The reasons for the parlous performance of the cocoa estates were both economic and ecological. The most obvious problem was high costs, which have most commonly been attributed to the need to pay wages instead of relying on family labour.

---

[57] Roger J. Southall, *Cadbury on the Gold Coast, 1907–1938: The Dilemma of the 'Model Firm' in a Colonial Economy* (Ph.D. dissertation, University of Birmingham, 1975), 76–87; Green and Hymer, 'Cocoa in the Gold Coast', 310; Austin, 'Mode of Production', 157–9.

As Gareth Austin has shown, however, it was not so much the payment of wages per se that distinguished estates from indigenous farms (many of which also resorted to hiring outside labour for planting and maintenance), but rather the higher labour requirements demanded by their intensive cultivation techniques.[58] The conventional practice of planting in rows, heavy weeding, and pruning required a lot of work. So, too, did the regular transferral of beans between special fermentation boxes and the method of drying them on racks or in ovens, none of which appreciably improved quality over the standard practices of West African farmers.[59] In the absence of cheap labour, such techniques made little commercial sense. And in the absence of government backing for some form of coercive labour recruitment in the Gold Coast, there was little prospect of acquiring enough cheap labour. Even if intensive cultivation methods were capable of raising yields—a questionable point in itself—they would not necessarily have been more efficient in view of the extra costs incurred.

But despite their apparent shortcomings, these standard plantation practices remained a central part of the Gold Coast Agriculture Department's efforts to increase production. In essence, the department's planting recommendations boiled down to several main points: neat planting at wide intervals to maximize yields, clean-weeding, pruning, and intensive treatment of disease. For the most part, Gold Coast farmers ignored all of this.[60] Although their method of close and fairly random spacing resulted in relatively spindly trees that appeared as 'rather a shock to anyone from the American side',[61] it in fact achieved higher yields per hectare for the *amelonado* strains they were planting, especially on poorer soils. An additional advantage of close spacing was that the canopy closed quickly (usually within four years), which not only suppressed weeds but also hindered attack by capsid bugs, a sucking insect common in the coastal belt of West Africa and the main pest in the colony until the late 1930s. The indigenous method for treating capsid-infected areas also proved remarkably effective despite initial ridicule by colonial officials. Instead of adopting the more invasive measures advocated by the Agriculture Department, farmers left affected areas to fallow for three years, after which they had usually recovered and only needed to be cleared of undergrowth. As for the problem of black pod fungus, they similarly ignored Department advice to remove all infected pods and bury or burn them, which subsequent studies revealed to be useless.[62] In fact, recommendations to cut out the diseased parts of trees often made matters worse since the opening of the canopy encouraged capsid infestation.[63]

---

[58] Generally, Austin, 'Mode of Production'.

[59] Fritz Klopstock, *Kakao. Wandlungen in der Erzeugung und der Verwendung des Kakaos nach dem Weltkrieg* (Leipzig: Bibliographisches Institut, 1937), 9–10; Faulkner and Mackie, *West African Agriculture*, 110–11; Austin, 'Mode of Production', 168.

[60] Austin, 'Mode of Production', 164–8.

[61] Wickizer, *Coffee, Tea and Cocoa*, 291.

[62] Faulkner and Mackie, *West African Agriculture*, 107–8; Green and Hymer, 'Cocoa in the Gold Coast', 308–9.

[63] Masefield, *Short History*, 120–1.

It should be noted that colonial agricultural officials were not wholly dismissive of African practices. In fact, many of them regarded the 'rational peasant' as the chief agent for economic development. Nor were their prescriptions always wrong, as the struggle against 'swollen shoot' disease in the 1940s and 1950s was to prove.[64] And one should certainly not infer from the above examples that African farmers were hesitant to capitalize on outside agronomic innovations that suited them, as the adoption of cocoa itself readily attests. The point is rather that the advantages enjoyed by indigenous farmers over foreign-owned plantations were not only economic but also rested on a sound understanding of local environments and growing conditions.

Gold Coast farmers were not unique in this respect, as developments on the other cocoa frontiers of colonial West Africa clearly show. In south-west Nigeria the initial introduction of cocoa came in the 1880s as Creole merchants established farms in the Agege region. From the 1890s onwards the frontier spread throughout the Yoruba states as railway transport improved and as the end of internecine warfare facilitated the sale of forest lands for cultivation. By the 1920s there were an estimated 121,000 hectares of cocoa in Nigeria, most of it in the south-western provinces around Ibadan.[65] Although a handful of British planters tried to set up estates near Lagos, they were even less successful than their counterparts in the Gold Coast. Land distribution remained in the hands of chiefs, and the colonial government granted only occupancy rather than freehold rights to non-natives.[66] As a result, Nigeria's cocoa industry was almost entirely dominated by smallholders. The majority of farms were less than 2 hectares in size and deployed the same basic cultivation methods as in the cocoa heartlands of Akwapim and Asante. Although the growth of production was less rapid than in the Gold Coast, it nonetheless rose from 4,000 metric tons in 1911 to 95,000 by 1938, making Nigeria the world's third-largest producer behind Brazil.[67]

In Côte d'Ivoire—the world's largest cocoa producer since the 1970s—the take-off was much slower, and one of the main reasons was the different approach taken by the colonial state. In fact, the earliest stirrings of production in the 1890s were actually nipped in the bud by French authorities who were eager to tighten the south-western border with Liberia, where Kru traders had begun growing coffee and cocoa. Around 1908–10 a more enduring frontier opened in the south-eastern Indénié district, where Anyi planters turned to cocoa in response to falling rubber prices, much as the planters in south-eastern Gold Coast had responded to the collapse of the palm oil market. By 1912–13 cocoa cultivation was becoming firmly established around Asikaso, and was practised in much the same way as in the Gold Coast.[68]

---

[64] Hill, *Migrant Cocoa-Farmers*, 23–4.　　　[65] Schwarz, *Cocoa in West Africa*, 33.

[66] Berry, *Cocoa*, 54–125; Albert Viton, *Cacao: tendances actuelles de la production, des prix et de la consommation* (Rome: FAO, 1957), 14; Clarence-Smith, *Cocoa and Chocolate*, 159, 190.

[67] Figures from Wickizer, *Coffee, Tea and Cocoa*, 482; Pierre Gourou, 'Les Plantations de cacaoyers en pays Yoruba: un exemple d'expansion économique spontanée', *Annales: économies, sociétés, civilisations*, vol. 15 no. 1 (1960), 60–82.

[68] Generally, Chauveau and Léonard, 'Côte d'Ivoire's Pioneer Fronts'; Leonard J. Schwarz, *Cocoa in the Ivory Coast* (Washington, DC: Government Printing Office, 1931).

It was at this point that the French administration stepped in to encourage cocoa production on a larger scale, though the results diverged markedly from those in neighbouring British colonies. Instead of giving Anyi smallholders a free hand, they adopted a more top-down method that mirrored the concurrent cotton drive in the colony. By 1913 district officials were systematically pressuring farmers to plant cocoa, mostly on hated 'champs du commandant'. Although some villages in the region willingly complied with the planting directives, others opposed them however they could, even to the point of deliberately uprooting the cocoa saplings. Governor Angoulvant's '*methode forte*'—which meted out beatings and imprisonment to recalcitrant villagers—did little to reduce the hostility of many indigenous farmers towards prescribed crops like cocoa.

Whether this more forceful approach delayed or accelerated the expansion of cocoa in Côte d'Ivoire has been a matter of debate. Whereas some have argued that it slowed the diffusion of cocoa by up to two decades, others have suggested that it incentivized farmers who were initially wary about investing in a crop that only yielded an income several years after planting.[69] Both views seem to be correct in certain respects. Although obligatory cultivation appears to have bolstered the initial expansion of cocoa in the south-east of the colony, at a more general level the policy of forced labour probably retarded the spread of cocoa by diverting scarce labour resources towards European farms—or, indeed, towards the Gold Coast.

As a result, most of Côte d'Ivoire's cocoa stands were planted after the First World War. Centred initially on the areas around Abengourou and Agnibilekrou, cocoa cultivation soon spread westward towards Oumé and Gagnoa. Just as in Nigeria and the Gold Coast, the improvement of ground transport was crucial, as was the construction of a new loading facility at Port-Bouët, which was linked to the railhead at Abidjan by a huge floating wharf.[70] But unlike the situation in neighbouring British colonies, much of the land in Côte d'Ivoire was under state control and was available to foreigners and locals alike.[71] European planters therefore played a more prominent role here than in the rest of West Africa. Ever since the 1890s there was a handful of cocoa estates around Bingerville, but most of the European-owned plantations were established during the late 1920s between Oumé and Gagnoa. By the early 1930s they covered roughly 6,000 hectares, around half of the total cocoa surface in the colony. Unlike the estates in British West

---

[69] For the former argument: Jean-Pierre Chauveau, 'La "Mise en valeur" coloniale en pays baule: régression économique et autonomie paysanne', *Tiers-Monde*, vol. 23 no. 90 (1982), 315–20; Chauveau and Léonard, 'Côte d'Ivoire's Pioneer Fronts', 178–9; also Timothy C. Weiskel, 'Toward an Archaeology of Colonialism: Elements in the Ecological Transformation of the Ivory Coast', in Donald Worster (ed.), *The Ends of the Earth: Perspectives on Modern Environmental History* (Cambridge: Cambridge University Press, 1998), 141–71, here 167. For the opposing view: David H. Groff, 'Carrots, Sticks, and Cocoa Pods: African and Administrative Initiatives in the Spread of Cocoa Cultivation in Assikasso, Ivory Coast, 1908–1920', *International Journal of African Historical Studies*, vol. 20 no. 3 (1987), 401–16.

[70] Schwarz, *Cocoa in the Ivory Coast*, 22–31; Weiskel, 'Toward an Archaeology', 155–6.

[71] Concessions of 200–500 ha could be readily obtained from the authorities at Bingerville, with larger grants requiring approval from the AOF governor-general in Dakar: Charles Robequain, 'Problèmes de l'économie rurale en A.O.F.', *Annales de Géographie*, vol. 46 no. 260 (1937), 137–63; Schwarz, *Cocoa in the Ivory Coast*, 2–4.

Africa, they were crucially aided by privileged access to land and labour (recruited mainly from supposedly overpopulated Mossi areas to the north of the forest zone). But despite these advantages they were still no match for the African farms in the Gold Coast. Most of the planters were rank novices, having previously worked for logging or other expatriate firms before trying their hand at cocoa during the 1920s boom. They frequently planted cocoa on soils that were far too shallow or too wet, and colonial agricultural officials often derided their estates as downright shambolic.[72] A large number went under during the Depression, and many of those that struggled on over the following years gradually reverted to bush as labour shortages became more acute (and especially after obligatory labour service was abolished in May 1946).[73] In Côte d'Ivoire too, it was mainly indigenous farmers who built the cocoa industry.

SCIENCE, SMALLHOLDERS, AND THE QUESTION OF SUSTAINABILITY

To a large extent, then, the triumph of the West African cocoa boom occurred in spite of rather than because of government efforts to encourage production. In what many regarded as the most successful instance of cash-crop expansion in the colonial world, input from agricultural experts was conspicuously absent. Looking back from the vantage point of 1957, the year of Ghanaian independence, the noted botanist Duncan Hector Urquhart told the international Cocoa Conference in London: 'I would like to remind the scientists present that the world cocoa industry was very largely developed without their aid. The great cocoa industry in West Africa was developed by the skill of the farmer. That skill—you might call it the simple skill of the simple man—was great skill.'[74]

Urquhart was hardly the first to recognize this. European observers had long held a range of views about the value of indigenous agricultural knowledge, which more and more agronomists came to admire during the inter-war years.[75] The cocoa boom in West Africa was in many respects the epitome of an 'indigenous agricultural revolution',[76] a classic illustration of the value of local knowledge and the wisdom of leaving farming to farmers. Moreover, it was not an isolated development but was part of a broader trend of smallholder success within the wider

---

[72] J. Vuillet, 'Notes sur la culture du cacaoyer à la Côte d'Ivoire', *L'Agronomie coloniale*, vol. 12 no. 91 (July 1925), 1–10, here 3–5; L. Renodier, 'Le Cacaoyer en Côte d'Ivoire', *L'Agronomie coloniale*, vol. 18 no. 142 (Oct. 1929), 304–10, here 305–7. See also Schwarz, *Cocoa in the Ivory Coast*, 7, 14, Fréchou, 'Les Plantations européennes', 57–9.

[73] Fréchou, 'Les Plantations européenes', 60, 69–72.

[74] Quoted from Emma Robertson, *Chocolate, Women and Empire: A Social and Cultural History* (Manchester: Manchester University Press, 2009), 84.

[75] For heterodox views: Chevalier, *La Situation agricole*, 5; Faulkner and Mackie, *West African Agriculture*; L. D. Stamp, 'Land Utilization and Soil Erosion in Nigeria', *Geographical Review*, vol. 28 (1938), 32–45; more generally Tilley, *Africa*, 128–59.

[76] Richards, *Indigenous Agricultural Revolution*.

global cocoa economy, particularly with the fall in prices in the 1930s. During the Depression, estate managers themselves began to experiment with more extensive cultivation methods, partly under the pressure to reduce costs but also due to a growing realization that they better mimicked the natural conditions of a forest. By the mid-1930s some agriculturists even argued that 'of all plantation crops cacao is the most sensitive to environment and is least adapted to being grown under plantation conditions'.[77] Ecologically, land-extensive techniques proved remarkably effective. And both economically and politically, indigenous cultivation was less risky and more profitable for colonial administrations than a policy of privileging European estates.

But if the assumed superiority of intensive cultivation practices was no longer as unshakeable as before, it still strongly coloured the perceptions of most European observers. How did this overinflated confidence in 'modern' agriculture persist amidst the triumph of African-grown cocoa? First of all, it was necessary to explain away the success of indigenous farmers, which generally happened in two different ways. One was to give a large share of the credit to the colonial administration for what was almost entirely the result of indigenous initiative. 'In the Gold Coast the "indolent" native has created a new industry entirely native owned, and in thirty years the Gold Coast has outstripped all the areas of the world in quantity of produce,' one observer conceded in the 1920s, before perpetuating the conventional myth that 'this could not have happened without the strenuous efforts of the Department of Agriculture'.[78] Though perhaps unwittingly, French critics of the forced labour regime in neighbouring Côte d'Ivoire partially reinforced such assumptions by arguing that the future of the cocoa industry lay not in mandatory cultivation or privileging European farms but rather in 'the method of educating and persuading the native, a method which the English in the Gold Coast have deployed so brilliantly'.[79]

To be sure, not all officials were fooled by this pretence. None other than the Gold Coast governor Hugh Clifford (1912–19) opposed Agriculture Department proposals to mandate changes to African cultivation methods, noting that 'native' agricultural interests 'are capable of a rapidity of expansion and a progressive increase of output that beggar every record of the past, and are altogether unparalleled in all the long history of European agricultural enterprise in the tropics'.[80] But Clifford's views were not universally shared, particularly among technical experts who focused more narrowly on agronomic issues rather than the broader picture of commodity trade, and who were often blind to the logic of indigenous farming methods. This by no means pertained only to colonial agronomists, as the strikingly erroneous conclusions of a visitor from the US Department of Agriculture clearly attest: 'It is quite certain that the native could not have accomplished this tremendous work had he not been guided and assisted.... The native, of course, must be given credit for introducing the crop, but its rapid development must be

---

[77] Sir Arthur W. Hill, *Cacao Research*, Dec. 1935, quoted from Klopstock, *Kakao*, 5.
[78] Knapp, *Cocoa and Chocolate*, 94–6.   [79] Chevalier, *La Situation agricole*, 21.
[80] Quoted from Greaves, *Modern Production*, 209–10.

credited to those branches of the Government which planned and established the present transport system and to the agricultural department for supplying planting stock and demonstrating sound methods of cocoa culture and preparation.'[81]

The second means of rationalizing the success of African cocoa planters was more plausible and ultimately more important: namely, the idea that indigenous methods were not sustainable. During the 1930s, as the first signs of local land scarcity emerged, agricultural officials redoubled their efforts to intensify cultivation through the application of agronomic science. Without it, so the argument went, cocoa ran the risk of becoming the long-term ecological victim of its own short-term economic success. Given the proven productive capacity of African cultivation methods, the stated aim was not to suppress them entirely but rather to 'improve' them in the interests of raising yields and preventing pests and disease.

The problem, however, was a woeful lack of knowledge about these techniques and how they related to both the plant and local growing conditions. Before the founding of the West African Cocoa Research Institute at Tafo in Asante in 1937, colonial governments carried out almost no systematic research on cocoa. In the Gold Coast the assorted experiment stations were of little use since they were largely (and tellingly) geared towards supporting estate agriculture and were 'cultivated in a manner which bears little relation to native methods'.[82] An expert commission studying West African agriculture in 1938–9 found it 'difficult to see how any officer of the Department could be expected to offer correct advice on cultural or other treatment, as he had no opportunity to acquire knowledge under local conditions'.[83] The situation was similar in Côte d'Ivoire and Nigeria. Indeed, when seed selection studies were carried out in Nigeria in the 1930s they were financed not by the government but by the Ibadan Native Administration.[84] Against this backdrop it is easy to understand why local farmers ignored most department recommendations.

But the case for 'improving' indigenous methods was about more than just production. It also reflected the emergence of a more ecological way of thinking during the inter-war period, which generated a different set of concerns about the wider implications of large-scale cocoa planting.[85] One source of anxiety was the relationship between long-term yields and widespread forest clearance. Ever since the 1910s the threat of erosion was on the increase as planting moved onto more marginal, sloping land. It is worth noting that this concern was shared by African observers: the Omanhene (paramount chief) of Eastern Akim passed a by-law in 1915 prohibiting all farming and felling of trees on the hills of his territory.[86] There were also 'desiccationist' fears (see Chapters 8 and 9) about continued forest clearance creating more arid conditions that might ultimately threaten the cocoa industry itself. Conventional wisdom at the time was that a region with less than

[81] Schwarz, *Cocoa in West Africa*, 3–4.   [82] Shephard, *Report on the Economics*, 7.
[83] H. C. Sampson and E. M. Crowther, *The West African Commission 1938–1939: Technical Reports* (London: Waterlow, 1943), 40.
[84] Viton, *Cacao*, 12.   [85] More generally: Tilley, *Africa*, 115–68.
[86] McLeod, *Address on Forestry*, 4.

25 per cent forest cover was too dry for cocoa.[87] The lack of permanent shade on most African cocoa farms was therefore regarded as a major problem since plots with large shade trees maintain rainfall much better than land that has been totally cleared. In addition, the scarcity of windbreaks exacerbated the aridity problem given the seasonal threat from dry *harmattan* winds blowing southward from the Sahara. At the same time, the absence of large shade and windbreak trees was also blamed for mounting flood problems since smaller cocoa trees were unable to absorb all of the water from heavy rains.[88] In areas where the bush had been thoroughly cleared for cocoa it was reported that 'the distribution of rainfall has been altered to such an extent that in some cases farms now suffer from drought while in others the soil is water-logged'.[89] In 1920 foresters recommended that planters retain thirty of the largest trees per acre as 'standards' to maintain humidity and to reseed areas after cocoa had been abandoned.[90] The fact that such suggestions were often coloured by prejudice against 'improvident' indigenous farming methods, and were rarely adopted in practice, does not mean that they were entirely misplaced. By the 1930s there was mounting evidence of damage from arid winds on mature farms, which was plausibly attributed to the progressive clearing of surrounding forests that had initially provided adequate shelter.[91]

Another nagging concern was that the breakneck pace of expansion raised the prospect of regional land shortages. As a British forester rhetorically asked Gold Coast officials in 1920: 'Now how long do you think this country, still rich in forests could, without permanent injury, stand the drain of 450 square miles of forest cut down every twenty years to make room for cocoa, if the natives continued their happy-go-lucky style of clearing forests?'[92] Others similarly cautioned that if nothing were done 'it is obvious that the coming generation will see the destruction of the remaining forests'.[93] We now know that such catastrophist warnings were exaggerated. In fact, agricultural officials in the mid-1930s recognized that the current cocoa area (approximately 1,600 square miles, or 4,144 km^2), though vast, still represented only around 15 per cent of recent clearing in the Gold Coast as a whole.[94]

Nonetheless, in certain regions there was genuine cause for concern. By the 1930s most suitable land in the Eastern Province was already under cocoa, and

---

[87] A. Harold Unwin, *West African Forests and Forestry* (London: T. Fisher Unwin Ltd, 1920), 492; Knapp, *Cocoa and Chocolate*, 78.

[88] Klopstock, *Kakao*, 57.   [89] Schwarz, *Cocoa in West Africa*, 2.

[90] McLeod, *Address on Forestry*, 5.

[91] See the dire warnings in F. A. Stockdale, *Report by Mr. F. A. Stockdale on his Visit to Nigeria, Gold Coast and Sierra Leone, October 1935–February 1936* (London: Colonial Office, 1936), 99–100; also Shephard, *Report on the Economics*, 2, 16–20; R. S. Troup, *Colonial Forest Administration* (Oxford: Oxford University Press, 1940), 59.

[92] McLeod, *Address on Forestry*, 5, 8.

[93] H. W. Moor, 'Forestry and its Application to the Gold Coast', *Journal of the Gold Coast Agricultural and Commercial Society*, vol. 3 no. 2 (1924), 82, quoted from James Fairhead and Melissa Leach, *Reframing Deforestation: Global Analyses and Local Realities* (London: Routledge, 1998), 68.

[94] Shephard, *Report on the Economics*, 6; Fairhead and Leach, *Reframing Deforestation*, 68–9, and *passim*; see also Joseph M. Hodge, 'Colonial Foresters versus Agriculturalists: The Debate over Climate Change and Cocoa Production in the Gold Coast', *Agricultural History*, vol. 83 no. 2 (Spring 2009), 201–20.

from 1938 to 1946 the Asante Confederacy Council banned all new cocoa plant-ing in the territory for fear of a decline in staple food production.[95] Although some scholars have suggested that the link between cocoa and food shortages is a myth, citing as evidence the fact that cocoa and food cropping were usually complemen-tary for the first several years after clearing,[96] the potentially negative long-term impact on food supplies, coupled with high food prices in the towns, only added to the sense of unease about the pell-mell rush into the forests, particularly in the 'monoculture-landscape' of the main cocoa districts.[97]

All the signs pointed to the need to raise cocoa yields without further forest clear-ance. As Frank Stockdale (a leading figure in the Colonial Advisory Council for Agriculture and Animal Health) concluded from a trip to the Gold Coast in 1935–6, 'if... the total export is to be maintained there is little doubt that the time is rapidly approaching when more intensive cultivation will be necessary'.[98] Ever since the 1920s yields had begun to decline in the oldest cocoa districts as trees aged and soils became depleted. Hitherto the losses were more than compensated by further clearance elsewhere. But as Stockdale and others argued, since continual expansion into new forest was unsustainable in the long run, farmers would even-tually have to begin pruning and thinning older stands, replanting shade trees and windbreaks, applying mulches or manures, and providing better drainage. In short, they would need to abandon the land-extensive methods that had turned West Africa into the centre of world cocoa production and cultivate instead along more intensive, 'scientific' lines.

Such recommendations were, as scholars have suggested, clearly tinged by chau-vinistic assumptions about the benefits that modern agronomy could bestow upon colonial farmers. But another important reason for their persistence was that they also drew on many decades of experience with cocoa cycles in older regions of pro-duction, above all in the Caribbean colonies, which for British agronomists had long served as the key reference point for measuring how the West African industry was performing and how it might develop in the future. Trinidad and Grenada were not only long-standing producers but had also been far more thoroughly researched (especially after the Imperial College of Tropical Agriculture was estab-lished on Trinidad in 1924). By the 1930s, yields on plantations there had begun to decline sharply, partly due to the spread of witches' broom fungus (which infected over half of the cocoa acreage on Trinidad by 1932) but more importantly because of the advancing age of the cocoa trees.[99] Planting had essentially ceased on Trinidad after 1921 as prices stagnated and suitable land became less abundant. Detailed examinations of individual estates showed that yields had peaked at

---

[95] Though the ban was widely evaded: Austin, *Labour, Land and Capital*, 50, 350, 437, 445; Stockdale, *Report by Mr. F. A. Stockdale*, 7.

[96] Green and Hymer, 'Cocoa in the Gold Coast', 314–15.

[97] Quote from Klopstock, *Kakao*, 41; W. G. A. Ormsby-Gore, *Report by the Hon. W. G. A. Ormsby-Gore, M.P. (Parliamentary Under-Secretary of State for the Colonies) on his Visit to West Africa during the Year 1926* (London: HMSO, 1926), 77.

[98] Stockdale, *Report by Mr. F. A. Stockdale*, 96.　　　[99] Moll, *Cacao in Trinidad and Tobago*, 3.

around fifteen to twenty-five years of age before declining at a more or less steady rate depending mainly on soil quality.[100]

When Cecil Shephard, the agronomist who conducted these studies, was dispatched from the Imperial College of Tropical Agriculture in 1935 to make recommendations for cocoa cultivation in the Gold Coast, average yields there were estimated at around 500–600 lb per acre (560–670 kg per hectare)—similar to Grenada's intensively cultivated estates and around twice as high as on Trinidad, whose farms were mostly well past their peak. At first glance one might read this as nothing more than another instance of agricultural officials stubbornly believing in the superiority of intensive methods despite evidence to the contrary.[101] Undoubtedly such assumptions played a role, but the picture nonetheless changes once tree age is factored in. Records suggested that yields on Trinidad were slightly higher—and on Grenada appreciably higher—than in the Gold Coast at a comparable age. Although the Gold Coast as a whole was still a young producer, the first yield decreases in the oldest cocoa areas of the Eastern District were already following the familiar pattern of boom, decline, and eventual relocation that had already been seen in the Caribbean. If anything, the pattern here was even faster, since some farms were being abandoned after only twenty years.[102]

There was, to be sure, something ironic about Caribbean plantations (of all things) serving as a source of inspiration for developing a more stable and sustainable form of agricultural production in the well-established agrarian societies of West Africa. At one level it is difficult to avoid the jaundiced conclusion that this was little more than an exercise in shifting the criteria of success, a new-fangled means of asserting the agro-scientific superiority of plantation methods over the smallholder-style practices of West African farmers once the latter had clearly won the battle for commercial efficiency. But there was nonetheless good reason to assume that yields would eventually drop in West Africa in the absence of either continued forest clearance or a shift towards more intensive cultivation techniques. Since the former was not a long-term solution, officials focused their attention on the latter, looking above all to Trinidad for ideas. By the 1930s the Trinidad Department of Agriculture had undertaken extensive trials on replanting, on the development of high-yielding varieties, on pruning, draining, and fertilizer application, all of which managed to achieve considerable yield increases for ageing stands on test plots.[103]

Such promising results—all the more attractive for resonating with pre-existing suppositions about the ability of agricultural science to improve indigenous practices—quickly prompted recommendations that West African cocoa-producing regions should adopt these remedial measures since Trinidad once boasted yields like theirs.[104] But beyond the controlled conditions on the test plots, which could be managed much more carefully than was practical for commercial stands, there

---

[100] C. Y. Shephard, *The Cacao Industry of Trinidad: Some Economic Aspects. Series III–IV* (Port-of-Spain: Government Printer, 1937), 31, 70–2.

[101] As do Green and Hymer, 'Cocoa in the Gold Coast', 308–9.

[102] Shephard, *Report on the Economics*, 5.   [103] Moll, *Cacao in Trinidad and Tobago*, 4–5.

[104] Shephard, *The Cacao Industry of Trinidad*, 72.

was precious little scope for introducing them, as the Agriculture Department's own research clearly indicated. A seminal study of a single cocoa farm in the Eastern District (Koransang) in the latter 1930s showed that although replantation could be made to work through the concerted action of farmers and agriculture officials, there was little realistic prospect of success on a larger scale.[105] In fact, over the following years a similar conclusion was reached on Trinidad itself. Despite the provision of special rehabilitation subsidies, the allocation of hundreds of thousands of selected seedlings, and even the large-scale distribution of new high-yielding clones after 1945, only 10 per cent of Trinidad's cocoa was on replanted land in the late 1950s.[106]

The difficulties stemmed largely from ecological factors. Whereas planting on older forest land reduces the number of quick-growing successor species, few of whose seeds are around at first clearing, they are more numerous on previously cleared land and therefore compete more intensively with cocoa seedlings, especially on depleted soils.[107] In turn, these ecological factors translated into a significant economic problem. Given the high costs of rehabilitation and missed income while saplings matured, as well as the significant fertility and disease drawbacks of planting on previously cultivated land, it generally remained more lucrative to clear fresh forest than to replant existing farms. And where fresh forest was in short supply, it was usually more profitable to switch to other crops than to compete against farmers clearing new cocoa pioneer fronts elsewhere in the world where woodland was still abundant.

Once again, the perennial cycle of boom and decline was set to repeat itself. And once again, agricultural science was capable of raising yields, but not necessarily profits.[108] As long as forested land was available, the overall cost structure strongly favoured the land-extensive techniques that prevailed among African farmers. Refusal to abandon these methods at the behest of colonial officials did not represent an oft-alleged 'peasant conservatism' but rather an eminently rational weighing-up of the factors of production and the various alternatives at one's disposal, as well as a sound knowledge of local growing conditions.[109] The cultivation practices employed by African cocoa growers reflected the prevailing economic and ecological circumstances of the region: namely a shortage of labour and capital, a relative abundance of woodland, and eventually—as the forest rent was depleted—a transition to other crops such as maize, cassava, or pineapple that grew better on previously cleared land. In short, the exploitation of the 'forest rent' still remained the single most important factor in the economics of cocoa cultivation.

In any event, it soon became clear that the greatest problem facing the West African cocoa industry was not the prospect of land shortage or the need to intensify

---

[105] W. H. Beckett, *Koransang: A Gold Coast Cocoa Farm* (Accra: Government Printer, 1945), reprinted as Part 1 of *Koransang 1904–1970* (Legon: University of Ghana Institute of Statistical, Social and Economic Research, 1972).

[106] Moll, *Cacao in Trinidad and Tobago*, 4–6.   [107] Ruf, *Booms et crises*, 94–5.

[108] More generally: William Gervase Clarence-Smith and François Ruf, 'Cocoa Pioneer Fronts: The Historical Determinants', in Clarence-Smith (ed.), *Cocoa Pioneer Fronts*, 1–2, 14–15.

[109] As clearly recognized by some contemporaries: e.g. Faulkner and Mackie, *West African Agriculture*, 7.

production, but rather the biological vulnerability of the cocoa groves themselves. For all the attention given to replanting and fertility maintenance, it was a microscopic pathogen that ultimately posed the biggest menace. By the early 1940s 'swollen shoot' was spreading more or less unchecked throughout the cocoa groves of the region. First reported in 1936, and confirmed as a viral disease in 1939, it probably entered cocoa farms from infected native host trees in the early 1920s, remaining unnoticed until it assumed outbreak proportions. The epicentre lay in the eastern areas of the Gold Coast where it was initially discovered. By 1943 it was detected in the Ivory Coast near Abengourou, and over the next two years its presence was confirmed in Asante, the Western Provinces of the Gold Coast, as well as Nigeria.[110] Everywhere the virus spread it depressed yields by either weakening the trees or killing them outright.

Controlling the disease proved extremely difficult, and for many years the only effective treatment was to cut out infected trees. Soon after it was detected in the Ivory Coast, the colonial government mandated large-scale clearing and burning of affected areas by special 'phyto-sanitation' teams, which often incurred the wrath of indigenous farmers mistrustful of the motives behind them.[111] Authorities in the Gold Coast initially operated a voluntary system, but soon moved towards a policy of compulsory cutting-out despite widespread opposition from cocoa planters.[112] Although the Accra riots of February–March 1948—fuelled in part by popular anger at the mandatory removal of trees—forced a temporary hiatus, in 1949 compulsory cutting-out was resumed across the entire colony, tempered by more generous compensation payments for affected farmers.

Draconian though the measures were, they only gradually slowed the spread of the virus. In summer 1951 parts of the Eastern Province of the Gold Coast were written off as too damaged to warrant further sanitation efforts.[113] Outbreaks and losses continued to mount over the following years, and it was only in 1957, the year of Ghana's independence, that the disease was finally contained (rather than controlled). By this time an estimated 75 million trees had been destroyed. By 1961 around 105 million cocoa trees had been cut out in Ghana alone, and the losses were in fact far higher if one includes the trees that had died from the disease before the removal campaigns began.[114] To this day swollen shoot continues to plague the cocoa industry in West Africa. Millions of trees are still cut out each year in what is widely considered to be the largest and most expensive plant virus eradication campaign in the entire world.[115]

[110] Gold Coast, *Report on the Department of Agriculture 1944–5*, 4–5; Fréchou, 'Les Plantations européennes', 65.

[111] Fréchou, 'Les Plantations européennes', 68; Gouvernement Générale de l'A.O.F., Inspection Générale de l'Agriculture, *Organisation et action des services de l'agriculture* (Rufisque: Imprimerie du Gouvernement Général, 1952), 11, 26.

[112] Gold Coast, *Report on the Department of Agriculture 1944–5*, 4–5; *Report on the Department of Agriculture 1945–6*, 4–5.

[113] Gold Coast, *Report on the Department of Agriculture 1951–2*, 5.

[114] Viton, *Cacao*, 28–9; Hill, *Migrant Cocoa-Farmers*, 23–4.

[115] See O. Domfeh, H. Dzahini-Obiatey, G. A. Ameyaw, K. Abaka-Ewusie, and G. Opoku, 'Cocoa Swollen Shoot Virus Disease Situation in Ghana: A Review of Current Trends', *African Journal of*

As colonial agronomists clearly recognized, the swollen shoot outbreak epitomized the perils of monoculture. By the end of the 1940s the combined economic and ecological risks of over-reliance on a single crop led some to wonder whether monocultures could ever be managed safely.[116] Nonetheless, by the time swollen shoot reached epidemic proportions, cocoa was far too important for farming communities, state finances, and the regional economy as a whole to allow for a radical change of course. Quite the opposite: cocoa acreage continued to grow relentlessly, not least as a means of compensating for the losses caused by the disease. In essence the continued spread of cocoa planting was an attempt to 'escape forwards' out of the strictures of a socio-economic lock-in, and the overall result was to enlarge some of the very same problems that farmers and policy-makers were trying to avoid. As cocoa expanded across more of the West African forest belt, so did the array of pests and pathogens that plagued it. And as losses to pests escalated, so did efforts to combat them. During the 1956–7 season, the last year of colonial rule in the Gold Coast, the Agriculture Department gave farmers 11,234 subsidized sprayers and over 130,000 litres of Didimac (DDT) insecticide free of charge to fight pest attacks. At the end of the year Didimac was replaced by the more potent Gammalin 20, a highly toxic organochlorine insecticide that was excellent at killing pests but that also caused a variety of ailments for humans, livestock, and wildlife, as well as persistent damage to soils and aquatic environments, before eventually being banned in most countries.[117]

The lengths to which officials, scientists, and farmers were prepared to go in order to sustain the stricken cocoa groves illustrate some of the fundamental themes in the history of modern commercial agriculture. Large-scale monocultures, despite their appearance of strength, generally have major biological weaknesses. As a result, their seeming durability is almost always shored up by a constant series of improvisations behind the scenes. And more often than not, the solutions devised to solve one set of problems stored up new and sometimes bigger problems for the future.[118]

Producing cocoa for distant consumer markets has always been a fluid and transitory business. As François Ruf has shown, cocoa frontiers have been on the move for many centuries. In the 1600s they spread from Central America to Venezuela, Ecuador, and Jamaica. In the 1700s they reached Martinique and Guadeloupe, and in the 1800s they fanned out across Brazil, Trinidad, and the Gulf of Guinea Islands. By the late nineteenth century the first clearings were being cut out in the West African forest belt, which has dominated world production since the early twentieth

---

Agricultural Research, vol. 6 no. 22 (Oct. 2011), 5033–9; H. Dzahini-Obiatey, O. Domfeh, and F. M. Amoah, 'Over Seventy Years of a Viral Disease of Cocoa in Ghana: From Researchers' Perspective', *African Journal of Agricultural Research*, vol. 5 no. 7 (Apr. 2010), 476–85.

[116] See e.g. Masefield, *Short History*, 116–23.

[117] Ghana, *Annual Report of the Department of Agriculture for the Year 1956–7*, 7; Marvin J. Levine, *Pesticides: A Toxic Time Bomb in our Midst* (Westport, Colo.: Praeger, 2007), 229. Some of the worst effects of Gammalin 20 stemmed not from agricultural application but from its occasional use to kill fish.

[118] See Uekötter, 'Rise, Fall, and Permanence', esp. 15–20.

century. And the story did not stop there. By the close of the millennium, the main focus of growth had shifted from Ghana and Nigeria to Côte d'Ivoire, Cameroon, and to Southeast Asia as well (above all Sulawesi).[119] The one constant factor throughout this story of perpetual flux has been the supplanting of the rainforest.

But if the colonial-era cocoa boom was in some ways a continuation of a long-standing process, it also marked a new departure in several important respects. It not only led to a historic shift in the global geography of production from Latin America to West Africa, it was also primarily driven by a very different group of cocoa pioneers with their own ideas about how to grow it. Despite the continued existence of plantations, and despite the repeated attempts of colonial agricultural departments to intensify cultivation methods, the extraordinary dynamism of the West African cocoa frontier was almost entirely the product of indigenous initiative and African farming techniques. As the story of cocoa shows, Europeans were by no means the only agents of rapid environmental change in their tropical empires.

Another key difference of the colonial cocoa boom was its sheer scale, which was a harbinger of things to come. The exponential growth of output from the 1880s to 1930s made this period quite unlike earlier phases of expansion, however similar the basic pattern of frontier movement may have been. The roughly twentyfold rise in global cocoa production represented more than just an acceleration of ongoing trends; it was a fundamental step-change that reflected the unprecedented appetites that were emerging in the industrial world. Once this breakthrough occurred, the momentum continued to grow over the following decades. By the early 1960s, when most African colonies had achieved independence, world production had risen to just under 1.2 million tons, nearly twice the level of the early 1930s. From the 1960s to the early 2010s it quadrupled to 5 million tons, around three-fifths of it still produced in West Africa, with the remainder coming mainly from Southeast Asia and South America.[120]

This spectacular rise in cocoa output entailed a correspondingly gigantic ecological transformation. Although the scale of production was revolutionized, the methods of production were not. Most of the gains were achieved by extending cocoa acreage rather than boosting yields, which means that the enormous leap in chocolate consumption reflects an equivalent toll on the lowland forests of the tropics. Cocoa yields were slow to rise before the planting waves of the 1970s and 1980s. In 1961 the average yield globally was still a mere 269 kg per hectare, roughly the same as on Trinidad's ageing stands in the 1930s and barely half of what Gold Coast farmers were achieving at that time.[121] By 2012 average yields had risen to 503 kg per hectare, though some of the new hybrid varieties could achieve over 1,120 kg per hectare under optimal conditions. Consequently, the fourfold production increase from the 1960s to the 2010s was based on slightly more than a doubling of world cocoa acreage, from 4.4 million hectares in 1961 to 9.9 million in 2012.[122]

---

[119] Ruf, *Booms et crises*, 25; Clarence-Smith and Ruf, 'Cocoa Pioneer Fronts'.
[120] Figures from FAO: <http://faostat3.fao.org/>.
[121] <http://faostat3.fao.org/>; Shephard, *Report on the Economics*, 4.
[122] <http://faostat3.fao.org/>.

Ever since the late colonial period, the key challenge has been the development of more productive yet sustainable cultivation systems in the face of an ever-dwindling availability of primary forest. The doubling of average cocoa yields since the 1960s was no mean feat, but for several reasons it brought little reprieve for the forests of the main producer areas. Although technological innovations such as high-yielding hybrids, synthetic fertilizers, and pest control could, in principle, save thousands of square kilometres of primary woodland, in practice they have tended to encourage the spread of intensive full-sun farms that generate high net profits over the short to medium term.[123] Promoted by governments and leading chocolate companies as a means of boosting supply,[124] these unshaded hybrid systems rely on large inputs of fertilizer, pesticides, and (more recently) herbicides to achieve their high yields. In addition, they possess only a fraction of the biodiversity of the forest cover they replace, and are also far less varied that the mixed agro-forestry alternatives that were previously developed as a means of mimicking natural conditions and diversifying cocoa farmers' incomes. Although they do offer some scope for replanting old *amelonado* groves in parts of West Africa, these high-input techniques have not entirely offset the benefits of newly cleared forest. Cocoa trees still perform best on fresh soils, and this includes the vigorous new hybrid strains designed to respond to chemical inputs. As a result, tapping the forest rent has continued to give producers a competitive advantage wherever primary forest is available.[125]

The recent history of cocoa shows few signs that this basic pattern will change, and even less indication that consumers will lose their appetite for chocolate.[126] As long as this remains the case, the forests of the tropical lowlands will continue to be mined for the 'brown gold' they can be made to yield.

---

[123] See François Ruf, 'The Myth of Complex Agroforests: The Case of Ghana', *Human Ecology*, vol. 39 (2011), 373–88.

[124] See <http://worldcocoafoundation.org/wp-content/uploads/FINAL-CocoaAction-CDI-Press-Release-English_05202014.pdf>.

[125] Ruf, *Booms et crises*, 181–2, 262–3.

[126] Quite the opposite: surging demand for chocolate in Asia and parts of South America has led industry analysts to predict major shortfalls by 2020: see e.g. <http://www.bloomberg.com/news/2014-05-28/cocoa-shortage-looms-as-growers-opt-to-farm-rubber-commodities.html>.

3
Colonialism, Rubber, and the Rainforest

One of the chief ecological effects of global trade has been the large-scale transfer of plant species from one part of the world to another. Over the past several centuries, botanists, commercial entrepreneurs, and farmers have made enormous efforts to cultivate useful crops on different continents and to engineer host environments to accommodate these implants from afar. In tropical lands sugar cane was the trailblazer, followed by coffee, various food crops, and of course cocoa. During the late nineteenth and early twentieth centuries, the most important addition to the list of globetrotter plants was the rubber tree.

Latex substances have been used in various parts of the tropics for many centuries, whether for waterproofing, illumination, games, or other rituals. Before the 1800s rubber was little more than a curiosity in Europe, since its tendency to soften in warm temperatures and to lose elasticity in the cold severely limited its utility. Two innovations in particular were crucial for the rise of a mass market for rubber: Charles Goodyear's vulcanization process (1837), which first made rubber durable enough for an array of applications from shoe soles to electrical insulation; and above all the development of the pneumatic tyre, first conceived in 1845 and perfected by John Boyd Dunlop in 1888. From 1875 to 1900 annual world rubber production rose from around 10,000 tons to over 50,000 tons, much of it spurred by the 'bicycle craze' of the 1890s. After around 1905 the growth of the automotive industry drove a further production boom that reached nearly 120,000 tons per year by the eve of the First World War.[1]

Before the 1910s nearly all of this latex was collected in the wild from a small number of species scattered across the world's tropical lowlands. In South America the main sources were *Hevea brasiliensis* and *Manihot glaziovii*, both native to the Amazon basin. In Central America *Castilloa elastica* was most important, and among the various contenders in Southeast Asia, *Ficus elastica* led the way. In Africa the primary sources of latex were *Landolphia* vines and the towering *Kickxia* tree (*Funtumia elastica*). Of all these candidates *Hevea* yielded not only the most latex but also the highest-grade rubber, labelled Pará rubber (the standard on international commodity markets) after the coastal Brazilian state from which it was

---

[1] John Loadman, *Tears of the Tree: The Story of Rubber—A Modern Marvel* (Oxford: Oxford University Press, 2005), xxviii, 66; J. H. Drabble, *Rubber in Malaya, 1876–1922: The Genesis of the Industry* (Oxford: Oxford University Press, 1973), 222; Colin Barlow, *The Natural Rubber Industry: Its Development, Technology, and Economy in Malaysia* (Oxford: Oxford University Press, 1978), 10–16.

shipped overseas. During the era of wild rubber, Amazonia accounted for the vast bulk of world exports.[2]

As demand for rubber continued to grow, governments and investors in Europe's tropical colonies began to set up plantations as the future basis of the industry. Ever since the 1870s botanists had been experimenting with a variety of latex-bearing species, among which *Hevea brasiliensis* emerged as the planter's favourite due its high productivity, its ability to survive years of regular tapping, and its relatively straightforward cultivation requirements. *Hevea* could be grown throughout most of the world's humid tropical lowlands, especially where there was well-drained soil, little temperature variation, and consistent but not excessive rainfall (over 1,500 mm). The main prerequisites for establishing a rubber plantation were abundant supplies of forest land and adequate access to labour. Several of Europe's Southeast Asian colonies—above all parts of Malaya, Indonesia, Ceylon, and southern Indochina—had the necessary ingredients, and soon came to dominate world production.

The ensuing rubber boom marked a major ecological and social watershed across much of colonial Southeast Asia. From the 1900s to the 1930s, millions of hectares of some of the world's richest *Dipterocarp* rainforests were replaced by *Hevea* trees as waves of European planters were attracted by the promise of cheap land and big profits. Most of the heavy work on the estates was performed by thousands of migrant labourers whose arrival left an indelible imprint on the societies of the main producer areas. At the same time, the opportunities opened by rubber cultivation also brought changes for countless indigenous farming communities, expanding their engagement with the global economy and altering their systems of land use. By the 1930s, only three decades after the planting boom began, rubber had created a complex web of global linkages between the forests of Southeast Asia, the vulcanizing plants of the industrial world, and millions of consumers—especially motorists—throughout Europe and North America.

To date, the historical literature on the Southeast Asian rubber industry has focused mainly on its economic and commercial aspects.[3] Rubber was, after all, a key ingredient of industrial society and one of the most important tropical commodities traded on world markets. Although studies have long recognized the importance of the region's natural endowments and the efforts of botanists to improve latex yields, they have paid far less attention to the broader socio-ecological parameters of the rubber boom, and certainly less than has been done for the

---

[2] See, generally, Barbara Weinstein, *The Amazon Rubber Boom, 1850–1920* (Stanford, Calif.: Stanford University Press, 1983); Warren Dean, *Brazil and the Struggle for Rubber: A Study in Environmental History* (Cambridge: Cambridge University Press, 1987).

[3] The principal studies are heavily weighted towards Malaysia: Barlow, *Natural Rubber*; Drabble, *Rubber in Malaya*; John H. Drabble, *Malayan Rubber: The Interwar Years* (Houndmills: Macmillan, 1991); D. J. M. Tate, *The RGA History of the Plantation Industry in the Malay Peninsula* (Kuala Lumpur: Oxford University Press, 1996). Exceptions with an environmental focus are Michitake Aso, 'How Nature Works: Business, Ecology, and Rubber Plantations in Colonial Southeast Asia, 1919–1939', in Uekötter (ed.), *Comparing Apples*, 195–220 (on colonial Indochina); also Beinart and Hughes, *Environment and Empire*, 233–50.

Americas.[4] The purpose of this chapter is to explore how the forest ecosystems of Southeast Asia and the rise of mass rubber production shaped one another.

Like all tropical crops, *Hevea* has a number of characteristics that influence how it is grown. First of all, planters must wait several years (usually five to seven) before the trees are mature enough to yield an income. Like coffee and cocoa, and unlike cotton or sugar, the business of rubber cultivation is therefore marked by relatively long cycles. Another important feature is that rubber has been successfully cultivated on widely different scales. In contrast to cocoa, which was increasingly dominated by smallholders during the colonial era, rubber was grown on vast, carefully engineered corporate estates as well as on countless smallholdings otherwise used primarily for subsistence agriculture. At the outset, rubber cultivation was mainly centred on large plantations, but over the course of the 1920s and 1930s the proportion of smallholder rubber steadily increased, and eventually outstripped estate production in the leading export regions of Peninsular Malaya and the Dutch East Indies. In effect, estates and smallholdings constituted two separate sectors of the rubber economy, both economically and ecologically. They differed not only in their cultivation techniques and organizational forms, but also with respect to their biophysical and social effects. Despite the strong ideological attachment to what colonial authorities regarded as 'modern' plantation techniques, the success of smallholders gradually opened up a range of alternative practices designed to mitigate some of the chief environmental problems associated with plantation rubber.

The colonial rubber industry thus evolved through a complex interaction between environmental circumstances, diverse cultural predispositions, and shifting ideas about the optimal management of resources. Ultimately, the expansion of the Southeast Asian rubber frontier was rooted in the exceptional suitability of the region's lowland forests for *Hevea* cultivation—a suitability that, as we will see, surpassed even that of its Amazonian homeland. But human choices were crucial, and within the limits of ecological feasibility, a variety of different outcomes was possible.

FROM PLUNDER TO PLANTATION: THE ORIGINS OF THE NATURAL RUBBER INDUSTRY

The surging demand for rubber in the late nineteenth century unleashed a headlong rush into the forests of the Amazon basin. At Belém, the capital of Pará state, European and American purchasing agents bought tons of latex from Brazilian merchants who shipped it downriver from the various trading outlets that lined the great river system. Much of it moved through Manaus, the epicentre of the rubber boom, which at its peak in the 1890s was one of the wealthiest cities in the world. Most of the trade was controlled by a small group of rubber magnates who drew

---

[4] Dean, *Brazil*; Seth Garfield, *In Search of the Amazon: Brazil, the United States, and the Nature of a Region* (Durham, NC: Duke University Press, 2014); Mark R. Finlay, *Growing American Rubber: Strategic Plants and the Politics of National Security* (New Brunswick, NJ: Rutgers University Press, 2009).

their supplies from a network of local strong-men, or *seringalistas*, based in the Amazonian interior. As these local rubber barons carved out their fiefdoms in the jungle, they employed a swelling army of labourers—most of them immigrants from poverty-stricken areas, some of them indigenous people whose lands were seized, all of them tied to their employers by debt or the threat of violence—to tap the dispersed stands of wild *Hevea* that grew throughout the forest. The standard method for gathering the latex was to hack a gouge in the trunk and collect the sap in a bowl, which sometimes proved fatal to the tree. All things considered it was a cruel and inefficient system that relied on a constant influx of exploitable workers and a continual expansion of the extractive frontier. Nonetheless, it made Brazil the world's dominant rubber producer, accounting for nearly 90 per cent of global exports in the early 1900s.[5]

Most of the remaining latex supply came from Africa, where methods of wild rubber collection were broadly similar. In the forests of West and East Africa, rubber was mainly produced on a free trade basis whereby merchants purchased latex from tappers in the interior and hauled it to the coasts for export. Over time, traders essentially followed the tappers into the hinterlands as coastal forests became progressively depleted of latex-bearing plants. The rate of exhaustion, and thus of frontier expansion, varied according to several factors, above all the specific collection method, the degree of commercial competition, and the different target species. *Funtumia* trees were hardier than sensitive *Landolphia* vines, which often died as a result of tapping. And whereas many tappers chopped down vines or removed large rings of bark to drain latex-bearing sap as quickly as possible, others made smaller incisions from which the plants could recover. As a general rule, however, the basic pattern was one of rapid pillage that mirrored the extraction processes in the Amazon.[6]

In the humid forests of Equatorial Africa the industry worked somewhat differently than in West and East Africa, and the effects were even worse. Here rubber production was dominated by a small number of concessionary companies with little reason to worry about competitors harvesting all of their latex before they got around to it. In principle, one might expect this more regulated commercial environment to reduce the incentives for the hasty plunder of the forests. In practice, most of the concession companies were determined to cash in on their investments as quickly as possible, and committed appalling atrocities while doing so. In the Congo Free State in particular, entrepreneurs oversaw a lethal system of delivery quotas that showed little more concern for human life than for the ravaged *Landolphia* vines on which their profits depended. As collectors were forced to

---

[5] See, generally, Weinstein, *Amazon Rubber Boom*; Dean, *Brazil*.

[6] Patrick Krajewski, *Kautschuk, Quarantäne, Krieg. Dhauhandel in Ostafrika 1880–1914* (Berlin: Schwarz, 2006), 150–62; Thaddeus Sunseri, *Wielding the Ax: State Forestry and Social Conflict in Tanzania, 1820–2000* (Athens, Oh.: Ohio University Press, 2009), 19–23; J. Forbes Munro, 'Monopolists and Speculators: British Investment in West African Rubber, 1905–1914', *Journal of African History*, vol. 22 no. 2 (1981), 263–78; Raymond Dumett, 'The Rubber Trade of the Gold Coast and Asante in the Nineteenth Century: African Innovation and Market Responsiveness', *Journal of African History*, vol. 12 no. 1 (1971), 79–101; Goucher, 'The Impact', 63; John Henry Holland, *Rubber Cultivation in West Africa* (London: 1901).

travel further and further to find supplies, they often cut down the vines or stripped their bark in order to bleed out the latex. Some even killed the vines deliberately in the hope that it would make the concession companies go away. Although the end of this notorious system in 1908 is usually credited to reform activists in Britain and Belgium, it was also partly due to the exhaustion of the latex supply itself, which had already thrown the industry into disarray by around 1906.[7]

The wild rubber collection systems in Amazonia and equatorial Africa were extreme examples of frontier exploitation, and they soon faced trouble on several fronts. The political scandals they sparked off—most famously 'red rubber' in the Congo Free State, but also the M'Poko investigation in the French Congo (1906/7) and the Putamayo Affair in Peru (1909–11)—were resounding indictments of the contradictions between the rhetoric of 'free' labour and realities on the ground.[8] From an economic perspective, their long-term prospects were also dampened after the turn of the century by the stark incongruity between industrial-scale demand and primitive methods of supply. Although few feared an imminent collapse of wild rubber production—'according to the most competent authorities there is no prospect of an exhaustion of rubber in the Amazon region', noted the botanist Otto Warburg in 1900[9]—rising prices highlighted the growing inability to keep up with demand. And although large areas of Amazonia were yet to be tapped, there were already ominous warning signs in West Africa, where exports plummeted from 94,301 tons in 1898 to only 18,486 in 1902.[10] As a leading botanist put it at the time, the basic problem was that 'the European trader does not care about the source or mode of collection of the products that the native brings to his storehouse'.[11] No one expected merchants to halt the plunder since their primary concern was to generate profits. But as critics argued, any state that purported to be 'civilized' had a duty to ensure the welfare of its territory 'beyond short-term commercial success and temporarily high export revenues'.[12]

In response to the ongoing pillage, colonial governments introduced a range of measures to place rubber production on a more 'rational' footing. One was to prohibit the stripping of bark or cutting of vines and trees, though such prescriptions were scarcely enforceable on the remote extractive frontier. Throughout French

[7] Robert Harms, 'The End of Red Rubber: A Reassessment', *Journal of African History*, vol. 16 no. 1 (1975), 73–88; E. D. Morel, *Red Rubber: The Story of the Rubber Slave Trade Flourishing on the Congo in the Year of Grace 1906* (London: T. F. Unwin, 1906); Adam Hochschild, *King Leopold's Ghost: A Story of Greed, Terror, and Heroism in Colonial Africa* (London: Macmillan, 1999), 158–224; Kevin Grant, *A Civilized Savagery: Britain and the New Slaveries in Africa, 1884–1926* (London: Routledge, 2005), 39–78; Coquery-Vidrovitch, *Le Congo*, 164–86, 424–6.

[8] On the Putamayo, Michael Edward Stanfield, *Red Rubber, Bleeding Trees: Violence, Slavery, and Empire in Northwest Amazonia* (Albuquerque: University of New Mexico Press, 1998), 131–78; on M'Poko, Coquery-Vidrovitch, *Le Congo*, 177–84; on 'red rubber' in the Congo, see n. 7.

[9] Otto Warburg, *Die Kautschukpflanzen und ihre Kultur* (Berlin: KWK, 1900), 12.

[10] Auguste Chevalier, *La Situation agricole de l'Ouest Africain: enquête* (Domfront: Senen, 1906) 4–5, 7. The figures reflect the combined exports from Gambia, Sierra Leone, Gold Coast, Lagos, and Niger.

[11] Chevalier, *La Situation agricole*, 4.

[12] Louis Hoff, 'Die Kautschuk- und Guttaperchafrage in den deutschen Kolonien', *Verhandlungen des deutschen Kolonialkongresses 1905* (Berlin: Reimer, 1906), 604–17, here 616–17.

West Africa, German East Africa, and the Congo Free State, legislative bans probably did more to encourage denunciation and blackmail than to conserve latex resources. Another method was to mandate replanting in worked-out areas. In the Congo, collectors were ordered to plant fifty seedlings for every 100 kg of raw rubber they delivered, though once again enforcement was impractical despite the threat of imprisonment.[13]

For most observers, the future of the rubber industry lay in plantations rather than wild collection. Around the turn of the century, British and American entrepreneurs tried to establish concentrated *Hevea* estates in Amazonia where the tree grew naturally. But none of them were successful, partly because of commercial obstacles, but mainly due to an ecological problem: the South American leaf blight (*Microcyclus ulei*), a fungus endemic to the Amazon basin and the principal disease threat to *Hevea* trees. Over thousands of years, *Hevea* had co-evolved with the fungus in the Amazonian rainforest, surviving through a strategy of thin dispersal (generally no more than a few per hectare) among many other tree species. As a result, any attempt to cultivate a dense mono-crop of *Hevea* trees removed this natural defence and created a veritable smorgasbord for the leaf blight to attack. Despite years of effort, plant pathologists were never able to control the disease on plantations.[14] In the late 1920s, none other than Henry Ford tried to establish concentrated *Hevea* stands in Pará, but even his highly capitalized 'Fordlandia' estate proved no match for the humble fungus and eventually became a cattle ranch after its sale to the Brazilian government in 1945.[15]

Planters fared much better in Southeast Asia, where climate and soils were suitable, land and labour were readily available, and where, most importantly, there was no leaf blight. The absence of *Hevea*'s primary disease created the conditions for what biologists call 'ecological release', or the rapid expansion of a population into new ecological niches unchecked by the competitive constraints of its previous habitat. These environmental advantages played a crucial role in the emergence of Southeast Asia as the world's main rubber-producing area, and also in the choice of *Hevea* as its main cultivar.

Given the eventual dominance of Southeast Asian *Hevea* on rubber markets, it is worth emphasizing that neither of these outcomes was inevitable or obvious to contemporaries. Before the 1910s, planters experimented with a range of different latex-bearing species in many parts of the tropical world. French officials, nervously eyeing the planting boom in Malaya and the Dutch East Indies, were determined 'not to let themselves be outstripped by foreign efforts'.[16] By the early 1900s there were several small plantations growing *Hevea* in French Guinea and *Manihot* in Gabon. In Equatorial Africa, concessionary companies opted for *Manihot* over *Hevea* due to its superior ability to cope with the dry season there.[17] In Indochina,

[13] Hoff, 'Die Kautschuk', 608–13; Coquery-Vidrovitch, *Le Congo*, 424–5.
[14] Dean, *Brazil*, ch. 4, esp. 58–9.   [15] Grandin, *Fordlandia*; Dean, *Brazil*, 72–84.
[16] Henri Jumelle, *Les Plantes à caoutchouc et à gutta dans les colonies françaises* (Paris: Challamel, 1898), vi.
[17] Jumelle, *Les Plantes*, 77–123; M. du Vivier de Streel, *La Culture en Afrique Équatoriale Française* (Coulommiers: Dessaint, 1917), 32–4; Coquery-Vidrovitch, *Le Congo*, 428–31.

the only French colony ever to become a significant player in the world rubber economy, many regarded *Ficus elastica* as the most suitable cultivar for the region. It was only in 1906/7—three decades after *Hevea* was initially introduced there—that the first *Hevea* plantations of any size were established around Saigon.[18]

In the meantime, German firms in Cameroon likewise set up a string of rubber plantations, which mainly grew native *Funtumia* trees after trials with Central American *Castilloa* had to be abandoned due to beetle attacks.[19] Around the turn of the century, as German entrepreneurs turned their attention to East Africa, botanists initially recommended that they plant indigenous *Funtumia* or *Landolphia* vines rather than *Hevea*, though in the event the Amazonian *Manihot* tree became the favourite among estate directors.[20] In the late 1900s rising latex prices triggered a rash of planting in German East Africa, which resulted in around 45,000 ha of rubber by 1914. The timing could hardly have been worse. After 1910 the flood of cheap Malayan rubber onto world markets rendered the colony's *Manihot* plantations commercially unviable before they even began production. In 1914 Germany's rubber imports from its own colonies still covered only around one quarter of its needs—a strategic failure that ultimately helped launch the world's first large-scale synthetic rubber industry during the First World War.[21]

By the early 1910s the plantations of Southeast Asia had forever transformed world rubber markets. From 1910 to 1914 their combined output rose from around 11,000 to 76,000 tons, surpassing wild rubber production (which peaked in 1912) for the first time. By 1917 Southeast Asian estates outstripped wild rubber production by a ratio of nearly four to one (214,000 tons to 57,000 tons), and over the following years the quantities of wild rubber on world markets also shrank in absolute terms as falling prices made it increasingly unprofitable. By the end of the 1920s over four-fifths of world rubber exports came from Malaya and the Dutch East Indies alone.[22] It was a resounding success for the investors and planters involved, and it seemed to banish once and for all the threat of inadequate supplies for the burgeoning automotive tyre industry. But behind the

---

[18] Camille Spire and André Spire, *Le Caoutchouc en Indo-Chine: étude botanique industrielle et commerciale* (Paris: Challamel, 1906), 204–7; J. Cardot, *Note sur la production du caoutchouc en Indochine* (Paris: Agence Économique de l'Indochine, 1929), 3; Jean Vaxelaire, *Le Caoutchouc en Indochine* (Hanoi: Imprimerie d'Extrême-Orient, 1939), 7; E. Girard, *Notes sur la culture de l'hévea en Cochinchine* (Saigon: Ardin, 1918).

[19] Paul Preuß, 'Über Pflanzenschädlinge in Kamerun', *Der Tropenpflanzer*, vol. 7 no. 8 (Aug. 1903), 345–61.

[20] A. Zimmermann, 'Anzapfungsversuche mit Kickxia elastica', *Der Pflanzer*, vol. 1 (1905), 182–7; Franz Ranniger, 'Unsere Kautschuk-Plantagen und deren Zukunft', *Der Pflanzer*, vol. 3 (1907), 113–22; Dr Eduardoff, 'Über Kautschuklianen-Anpflanzungen', *Der Pflanzer*, vol. 4 (1908), 177–82; Eduard Marckwald and Fritz Frank, 'Der Kautschuk-Plantagebau in seiner Bedeutung und seinen Gefahren für die deutsche Kolonialwirtschaft', *Der Pflanzer*, vol. 7 (1911), 247–54.

[21] Richard Deeken, *Die Landwirtschaft in den deutschen Kolonien* (Berlin: Süsserott, 1914), 22–6; O. Warburg, 'Der Krieg und die koloniale Landwirtschaft', *Der Tropenpflanzer*, vol. 21 no. 1 (Jan. 1918), 7–8; *Kautschuk und die deutschen Kolonien* (Berlin: KWK, c.1917), 2–3; Eduard Marckwald, and Fritz Frank, 'Der Kautschuk-Plantagebau in seiner Bedeutung und seinen Gefahren für die deutsche Kolonialwirtschaft', *Der Pflanzer*, vol. 7 (1911), 247–54, here 250–1.

[22] Barlow, *Natural Rubber*, 53; Drabble, *Rubber in Malaya*, 220; Drabble, *Malayan Rubber*, 264.

profits and production figures lay one of the largest bouts of forest clearance ever witnessed in the tropical world.

FROM FOREST TO RUBBER FARM: THE SOUTHEAST ASIAN PLANTING BOOM

The journey of *Hevea* from Amazonia to Southeast Asia began in 1873 when Clements Markham—an India Office geographer who was also responsible for the first transplantation of cinchona (quinine) trees from Peru to India in 1860—convinced Sir Joseph Hooker of Kew Gardens to sponsor an expedition to the Amazon to collect seeds. Although only six seedlings from this cohort reached their destination in Calcutta, where they promptly died, officials in India were sufficiently interested to finance a follow-up expedition. In 1876 the British explorer Henry Wickham sent (or smuggled)[23] some 70,000 *Hevea* seeds to Kew, 2,400 of which germinated into seedlings and were subsequently sent to Ceylon to be planted at Henerathgoda Gardens in Colombo. Over two-thirds of the seedlings survived the trip, and in June 1877 twenty-two of them were transported to Singapore Botanical Gardens, nine of which were then taken to the garden of the British Resident in Perak, Sir Hugh Low. According to Henry Ridley, director of the Singapore Botanical Gardens from 1888 to 1911, this tiny handful of seedlings formed the basis for over 75 per cent of the *Hevea* that was later planted in Malaya.[24]

The first Malayan rubber plantations were established in 1896 in Malacca and Selangor. They soon attracted the attention of Chinese and European planters eager to find a substitute for coffee amidst the spread of the dreaded coffee rust fungus, and especially after the surge of Brazilian coffee production sent prices plunging.[25] At first, rubber was usually inter-planted with tapioca, gambier, or other crops as a supplemental source of income, but as the *Hevea* saplings matured most planters soon shifted to monoculture.[26] Acreage grew slowly in the beginning, expanding from 140 hectares in 1897 to 2,914 in 1902. But as prices continued to rise, they triggered a veritable explosion of planting throughout the Malayan states of Perak, Selangor, and Negri Sembalan. By 1910 rubber covered around 220,000 hectares in Malaya, and over the next four years it doubled to more than 445,000 hectares. Although much of the growth was driven by British firms (e.g. Guthries, Harrisons, and Crosfield, Barlow & Co.), by 1914 around 200,000 hectares were also in Asian hands, a third of them worked by smallholders

---

[23] Wickham's purported act of bio-piracy has long been a matter of debate and embellishment; at the time there was no Brazilian prohibition on the export of seeds: see Loadman, *Tears*, esp. 92–3; cf. the more stylized account in Joe Jackson, *The Thief at the End of the World: Rubber, Power and the Seeds of Empire* (London: Duckworth, 2008).

[24] See Loadman, *Tears*, 82–97.

[25] On the coffee rust, McCook, 'Global Rust Belt'.

[26] Barlow, *Natural Rubber*, 25.

who had entered the rubber bonanza several years after the first plantations were set up.[27]

Meanwhile, a parallel rubber frontier opened in the Netherlands Indies. Although the Dutch laid claim to the world's oldest rubber plantation (a small stand of *Ficus elastica* established in 1864 in West Java), most East Indies estates were created around a decade after large-scale planting got under way in Malaya. In 1914 rubber covered an estimated 245,000 hectares in the East Indies, rising to over 405,000 hectares in 1919.[28] At the beginning of the boom over half of this acreage was on Java, where (as in Malaya) coffee planters initially grew it as a catch-crop in the face of collapsing prices and the spread of the coffee rust epidemic.[29] By the mid-1910s, the focus of East Indies rubber planting shifted to the Outer Isles, above all to the Dutch *cultuurgebied*, or plantation belt, on the north-east coast of Sumatra (Fig. 3.1).

The rich volcanic soils in the Deli area around the town of Medan had already attracted an influx of European planters in the 1870s and 1880s, most them eager to cultivate the famous 'Deli leaf' tobacco that fetched a premium on world markets. By 1890 planters had cut down vast swathes of forest in the belief that the fancy wrapper tobacco could only be grown for one season on freshly cleared land, most of which was quickly abandoned to invasive *lalang* grass (*Imperata cylindrica*) after the harvest. As the tobacco frontier spread beyond the most suitable soils (mainly situated between the Wampu and Ular Rivers), planters experimented with a variety of tree crops as substitutes for tobacco, usually starting with coffee before eventually turning to *Hevea*.[30] In the hinterlands of Medan alone, rubber acreage rose from 22,000 hectares in 1909 to 173,000 in 1924. By 1927 Sumatra's plantation belt accounted for 49 per cent of East Indies rubber production, around half of which was shipped directly to the USA, a fifth to Britain, and a quarter to Singapore or Penang for trans-shipment to Europe or North America.[31]

In the East Indies and Malaya alike, the key prerequisite for rubber production was access to suitable forest land, which governments doled out to planters on decidedly generous terms. The first areas to be bought up were generally near the main lines of communication or existing areas of settlement. In Malaya the initial hot-spots lay along the roads that already served the tin mines in Perak and Selangor

---

[27] Drabble, *Rubber in Malaya*, 216; Barlow, *Natural Rubber*, 30–3, 308.

[28] Drabble, *Rubber in Malaya*, 219.

[29] In 1914 the vast majority of rubber in central and eastern Java was still inter-planted with *Robusta* coffee, though most Javanese rubber estates were established on the southern coast, where *Hevea* grew better due to the less persistent west-monsoon season: W. J. van de Leemkolk, *De Rubber-Cultuur en de Rubber-Handel van Nederlandsch-Indië* (Batavia: Ruygrok, 1914), 9, 17–18; *Rubber in the Netherlands East Indies* (Weltevreden: Landsdrukkerij, 1925), 2, 10.

[30] Karl Pelzer, *Planter and Peasant: Colonial Policy and the Agrarian Struggle in East Sumatra 1863–1947* (The Hague: Nijhoff, 1978), 19–23, 51–4; N. L. Swart and A. A. L. Rutgers (eds), *Handboek voor de Rubbercultuur in Nederlandsch-Indië* (Amsterdam: de Bussy, 1921), 47–53; *Rubber in the Netherlands East Indies*, 10; Pieter Honig, 'Agriculture in the Netherlands Indies', in Pieter Honig and Frans Verdoorn (eds), *Science and Scientists in the Netherlands Indies* (New York: Board for the Netherlands Indies, Surinam and Curaçao, 1945), 175–80, here 179.

[31] T. Volker, *Van Oerbosch tot Cultuurgebied: een Schets van de Beteekenis van de Tabak, de andere Cultures en de Industrie ter Oostkust van Sumatra* (Medan: Deli Planters Vereeniging, 1928), 77, 151.

Fig. 3.1. Map of colonial Southeast Asia, covering the main rubber-producing districts.

(see Chapter 4). In the late 1890s and early 1900s parcels of forest in these areas were available on long-term lease for next to nothing. Even after land rents were hiked in 1906, the price of uncleared land was still negligible in relation to profit forecasts; moreover, former estate land that had reverted to government ownership was even cheaper than forested parcels. In an attempt to streamline the process of land acquisition still further, the government of the Federated Malay States even gave the individual state Residents the authority to permit clearing before an application was formally approved.[32]

In north-eastern Sumatra, access to land was technically in the hands of the autonomous Malay sultans indirectly controlled by Batavia. In the wake of the new Agrarian Law of 1870, which terminated the state monopoly on East Indies export

[32] Barlow, *Natural Rubber*, 28–9; J. B. Carruthers, 'Rubber', in Arnold Wright and H. A. Cartwright (eds), *Twentieth-Century Impressions of British Malaya: Its History, People, Commerce, Industries, and Resources* (London: Lloyds, 1908), 345–502, here 348, 352.

crops, these local rulers sought to enrich themselves by granting large areas of vacant land to concessionary companies on highly attractive terms. But the manner in which supposedly 'unused' land was defined and distributed created deep resentment among local Batak and Simalungen cultivators, who found themselves excluded from much of the land they had long used for swidden agriculture. In response to their protests, the East Indies government introduced a 'model contract' in 1878 that set aside four bouws (2.8 hectares) of land for each household residing within concession boundaries, but this was only around a quarter of what they actually required for subsistence. Although subsequent amendments in the 1880s and 1890s went some way towards improving land access and collection rights for indigenous people, 'squatters' were continually reported on the concessions from 1900 onwards, and in the 1930s the extent of unlawful occupancy had reached such proportions as to disrupt estate operations. By 1941 virtually all the acreage that foreign corporations wanted—some 10,000 km² of the best alluvial land in the Deli region—had been granted on long-term concession.[33]

The supplanting of forests by *Hevea* estates was not a smooth or continual process, but rather advanced in fits and starts as market conditions changed and new areas opened up. The first big slow-down came in the early 1920s as the effects of wartime stockpiling and post-war economic dislocation temporarily depressed prices. In 1922 the British tried to organize a producers' cartel—the so-called 'Stevenson Scheme'—in a bid to shore up prices through planting restrictions, but the Dutch refusal to participate in the scheme undermined it from the start (indeed, the main result was to allow the East Indies to catch up with Malayan production by the end of the decade). As prices subsequently recovered in the mid-1920s, planters once again rushed into the forest. In Malaya the total rubber surface rose to just under 1.25 million hectares by 1930, roughly double that of 1920. In the East Indies, over 500,000 hectares were planted between 1925 and 1930 alone.[34]

Although this second wave of planting was in some ways a resumption of pre-war trends, it nonetheless differed from the earlier phase in several important respects. For one thing, indigenous farmers accounted for much of the increase. In the East Indies in particular, it was impossible to know exactly how much smallholder rubber had been planted, though no one doubted that the area was vast. On Sumatra, smallholder production spread rapidly across central and southern parts of the island, and on Borneo it also took off along the southern and western coasts.[35]

At the same time, a whole new planting frontier also opened in Indochina as French companies sought to gain a firmer foothold in the global rubber economy. The newfound (or belated, according to some contemporaries) French determination to boost Indochina's rubber production was not only a response to the rising prices of the late 1920s; it also reflected the increasingly autarkic direction of

[33] Pelzer, *Planter and Peasant*, 71–85; Ann Laura Stoler, *Capitalism and Confrontation in Sumatra's Plantation Belt, 1870–1979*, 2nd edn (Ann Arbor: University of Michigan Press, 1995), 2, 23–5.
[34] Drabble, *Malayan Rubber*, 308; T. A. Tengwall, 'History of Rubber Cultivation and Research in the Netherlands Indies', in Honig and Verdoorn (eds), *Science*, 344–51, here 349–50.
[35] See generally Bambang Purwanto, *From Dusun to the Market: Native Rubber Cultivation in Southern Sumatra, 1890–1940* (Ph.D. Thesis, SOAS, 1992), esp. 212–14.

French trade policy and the expanding reach of the colonial state. Before the 1920s a small number of plantations had been established on the so-called 'terres grises' (grey soils) to the east and north of Saigon, where labour was readily accessible but where production was hampered by fertility and drainage problems. Far more promising were the basaltic 'terres rouges' (red soils) situated between southern Cambodia and southern Annam.[36] Although a handful of estates had been set up on the fringes of this region before the war, large-scale planting on the more remote plateaus had to await the completion of a major post-war investment in transport infrastructure. As roads gradually penetrated the area in the mid-1920s, the colonial state granted huge concessions to planting firms, most of them comparatively large and well capitalized, and all of them French owned: Michelin, Caoutchoucs d'Indochine, Plantations de Kratié, Caoutchoucs du Mékong.

By the 1930s, over two-thirds of Indochina's rubber area was controlled by only twenty-seven companies, and much of the latex they exported came from a small number of mega-plantations over 1,000 hectares in size.[37] The underlying rationale for this policy was twofold: first, to 'do at the scale of 1,000 to 10,000 hectares what the (English and Dutch) neighbours did at the scale of 100 to 1,000'; and secondly to ensure that 'France will be able to consume French rubber, thereby removing all economic dangers in this area.'[38] Indochina's rubber industry was far more centralized and exclusive than elsewhere in the region. Unlike in Malaya or especially the East Indies, French land and labour policies ensured that indigenous farmers never accounted for more than a tiny fraction of Indochina's rubber production. Furthermore, as the plantations expanded in size (from 18,000 hectares in 1925 to around 127,000 hectares in 1937), they increasingly encroached on land used by shifting cultivators, especially once the frontier advanced into the highlands. Although special land grants were established for the 'Moï' groups that were most directly affected, the spread of rubber plantations and the influx of tens of thousands of labourers from Tonkin and Annam was nonetheless a constant source of tension.[39]

The environmental consequences of all this rubber planting were vast. From northern Sumatra to southern Indochina, the dramatic spread of *Hevea* estates came predominantly at the expense of mature forest. The basic method varied little from place to place. After a site was chosen and small pathways were cut through the undergrowth, clearing was generally done in parcels of 1 to 4 hectares depending on the thickness of the cover. The standard procedure was to cut out most of the vegetation and then pile the brush around the base of any trees too large to fell with axes, arranging the debris in such a way as to ensure a continuous burn across

---

[36] Yves Henry, *Terres rouges et terres noires basaltiques d'Indochine: leur mise en culture* (Hanoi: Gouvernement Général de l'Indochine, 1931).

[37] Four of these estates even exceeded 5,000 ha: Charles Robequain, *The Economic Development of French Indo-China*, trans. Isabel A. Ward (London: Oxford University Press, 1944), 207.

[38] Pierre Michaux, *L'Hévéaculture en Indochine: son évolution* (Paris: Exposition Internationale, 1937), 4, 14.

[39] René Mingot, and J. Canet, *L'Heveaculture en Indochine* (Paris: Exposition Internationale, 1937), 27–9; Robequain, *Economic Development*, 181–6, 213–18.

the surface. After several months—and preferably on a dry day with light wind—a fire was lit on one side of the clearing and was gradually fanned across until all the wood was consumed.[40] Although it was a seemingly simple process, a good 'burn' was crucial for releasing nutrients back into the soil and minimizing the amount of decaying material that could harbour detrimental fungi. 'The future of a rubber plantation', remarked one contemporary, 'depends in large part on a good initial clearing.'[41]

Felling these mature tropical forests was extremely arduous work. Apart from some of the largest estates in Cochin China, where clearing was often aided by machinery, it was generally carried out by hand, usually by locals working on contract.[42] Given the considerable costs and effort this involved, some of the earliest planters avoided forest plots in favour of previously cleared land, such as former tobacco estates, abandoned coffee land, or even degraded *lalang* areas.[43] There were benefits and drawbacks either way. Although cleared parcels were by and large cheaper to prepare for planting, they often yielded less well than forest plots. Moreover, getting rid of the pernicious *lalang* grass often required repeated deep-ploughing (called 'chunkling' in Malaya) and/or multiple doses of leaf poison (usually sodium arsenite, a carcinogenic toxin that is still used in herbicides today).[44] It is debatable whether the application of such chemicals or the clearing of additional woodland was ecologically worse. At the time, it was a moot point, since the sheer scale of rubber planting in the region meant that most estates were inevitably carved out of the forests.

Those who witnessed the razing of forested plots were not entirely insensitive to what was being lost in the process. In contemporary accounts, the scene after a major burn often evoked a feeling of ambivalence: 'The fire had been violent, and now only smouldering black stumps remained. The aspect of the land was desolate. The great trees had toppled down, tearing up the soil and making deep pits. All the landscape was soiled with ash and soot. Smouldering trunks lay everywhere.'[45] But despite such pangs of melancholy, most viewed the clearings as little more than pinpricks amidst the vast expanse of the region's forests. 'The plantations that seemed so large, looked, as I now saw them, like little deserts in a limitless oasis,' noted the French planter and novelist Henri Fauconnier, who worked in Malaya throughout the boom years.[46] This sense of being surrounded by an endless wilderness led many planters to regard themselves as nothing less than heroic conquerors of the unknown. In the words of one of Fauconnier's protégés, 'from the moment I set foot in Malaya I felt like a planter, with the morale of a conquistador'.[47] Few if any perceived the destruction as anything other than the justifiable cost of progress.

---

[40] Swart and Rutgers (eds), *Handboek*, 25–34, 36–8; Carruthers, 'Rubber', 348–50.
[41] Vaxelaire, *Le Caoutchouc*, 16.   [42] Robequain, *Economic Development*, 208–9.
[43] Volker, *Van Oerbosch*, 77; Pelzer, *Planter and Peasant*, 51.
[44] Swart and Rutgers (eds), *Handboek*, 42–4; Carruthers, 'Rubber', 353.
[45] Madelon Lulofs, *Rubber*, trans. G. J. Renier and Irene Clephane (Singapore: Oxford University Press, 1987), 63 (first published in Dutch as 'Rubber' in 1931).
[46] Henri Fauconnier, *The Soul of Malaya*, trans. Eric Sutton (Singapore: Oxford University Press, 1990), 36 (originally published in French as 'Malaisie' in 1930).
[47] Raoul Chollet, *Planteurs en Indochine française* (Paris: pensée universelle, 1981), 9.

The entire purpose was to carve 'a piece of civilization' from the wilderness: 'There would be a fine head-quarters with short cropped lawns and a wealth of cultivated flowers. The road would be metalled, and later, when the motor lorries arrived to fetch the latex for the factory, then he would be able to point to it all and say: "This is the piece I have reclaimed and planted. I have taken it from the forest".'[48]

As this last remark indicates, the destruction of the forest was the nucleus of a wider set of environmental impacts that rippled across the landscape, including transport infrastructure, new settlements, and a whole range of subsidiary economic activities. The plantations required huge amounts of labour, far more than local populations could generally provide. In Malaya, British authorities recruited tens of thousands of impoverished south Indian 'foreign natives' to work on the rubber estates. In East Sumatra, where autochthonous groups were generally disinclined to work on the plantations, most of the manual labour was carried out by Javanese and Chinese 'coolies' working under slave-like conditions. In all of the main rubber districts, the human population grew as rapidly as the estates themselves. In Deli, the number of inhabitants rose from around 100,000 in 1880 to 1.5 million in 1930, most of them newcomers to the area.[49] Furthermore, feeding and housing such a large labour force generated a host of secondary effects. To take one example, the Snoul estate in southern Cambodia drained a nearby marsh in order to create a 33-hectare farm that produced between 3 and 5 tons of vegetables per day for its 3,000 Tonkinese workers. It also kept 500 cattle, 800 pigs, as well as herds of sheep and goats that browsed on the surrounding forest (and that occasionally attracted unwanted predators, including tigers).[50] Besides food, estates also required significant amounts of fuel and construction timber, which was usually obtained from nearby sources to avoid the costs of buying it in.[51]

Unlike the densely populated and long-established agrarian centres of Java or Tonkin, Southeast Asia's rubber belts were essentially frontier societies peopled mainly by restless entrepreneurs and migrant labourers. Few had any ties to the land, and they treated it accordingly. Most Europeans were there to get rich before returning home, the majority of them working as estate managers and supervisors rather than as independent planters. Many of the workers who toiled under the brutal labour regime could only be kept on the estates through the threat of extreme violence for breaching their contracts (though conditions in Malaya were significantly better than in the East Indies).[52] 'Here everything and everybody was merely transient,' wrote Ladislao Székely, who began work as a planter in Deli in the late 1910s. 'It was a question of making money and getting away again. No one dreamed of settling down here; neither a Chinaman nor a European ever thought

---

[48] Lulofs, *Rubber*, 15–16.

[49] Volker, *Van Oerbosch*, 25; Pelzer, *Planter and Peasant*, 61–3; Stoler, *Capitalism and Confrontation*, 3; P. T. Bauer, *The Rubber Industry: A Study in Competition and Monopoly* (London: Longmans, 1948), 217–22.

[50] Chollet, *Planteurs*, 85–92.   [51] Swart and Rutgers (eds), *Handboek*, 25–34.

[52] Bauer, *Rubber Industry*, 221–4.

of that, nor even the Malays who came from the other islands. The country was still too young.'[53]

Domesticating this raw landscape was the basic aim of European planters and officials, and it had both an economic and a cultural logic. Establishing a rubber estate was an expensive undertaking. In Malaya it cost around $550/hectare for the initial phase of clearing, planting, and maintenance, followed by a wait of five or six years before the first income was generated.[54] Broadly speaking, European planters brought with them an 'orchard' model of cultivation that emphasized orderly rows, low tree density, weeding, and straight-edged drainage ditches wherever needed. Getting the planting right was deemed crucial. Early spacing norms of around 3 metres soon increased to 4, 5, or even 7 metres in parts of Indochina as it was discovered that yields were a function of tree girth, and that girth was inversely related to planting density.[55]

On the face of it, the methodical systems applied on the estates were designed to maximize productivity and profits. Beneath the veneer of economic rationality, however, they also served as an expression of European mastery over nature, of the 'aesthetic colonization' of the land. Székely's description of Medan in the 1910s and 1920s suggestively captures the symbolic importance of strict agronomic order amidst the untamed chaos of tropical nature: 'Forest, swamp, lianas, monkeys, jungle, thicket, stillness, dark pieces of water. Suddenly, as if marked out with a ruler, a huge clearing.... Everything one saw was carefully tended, almost exaggeratedly ordered.' Indeed, this zeal for neatness reflected not only the logic of operational efficiency but also the role of estates as metaphorical guardians of colonial order against the aboriginal forces of disarray: 'The virgin forest had disappeared. As far as the eye could see, young rubber trees stood in straight lines, like soldiers.'[56]

Such vast, serried ranks of *Hevea* rarely failed to impress onlookers, though they occasionally conjured mixed feelings. Driving the 200 kilometres from Goenoeng Malajoe to Medan, a Swiss forester in the mid-1930s was amazed by 'the endless rubber forests that appear as monochromatic walls along both sides of the road'.[57] It was highly debatable whether these were still 'forests' at all, containing as they did only a tiny fraction of the botanical diversity of the woodlands they had displaced (which, on Sumatra, was around 420 plant species per hectare in undisturbed forest).[58] Such a radical standardization of plant cover inevitably had repercussions for animal life too. A former health minister in Indochina fittingly referred to the rubber plantations as 'forests without birds'—that is, forests without the many

[53] Ladislao Székely, *Tropic Fever: The Adventures of a Planter in Sumatra*, trans. Marion Saunders (Singapore: Oxford University Press, 1979), 60–1 (first English publication in 1937).
[54] Barlow, *Natural Rubber*, 29.
[55] Carruthers, 'Rubber', 354; Drabble, *Rubber in Malaya*, 44; Chollet, *Planteurs*, 131.
[56] Székely, *Tropic Fever*, 29, 274.
[57] F. Schneider, 'Tagebuch einer Reise in Nord-Sumatra', in Honig and Verdoorn (eds), *Science*, 289–95, here 290.
[58] P. A. Sanchez, 'Science in Agroforestry', in Fergus L. Sinclair (ed.), *Agroforestry: Science, Policy and Practice* (Dordrecht: Kluwer, 1995), 5–55, here 33.

fruiting trees that sustained bird populations.[59] Numerous mammal species were also pushed out as jungle gave way to *Hevea* mono-crops, and many of those that remained were subsequently treated as pests. The progressive loss of habitat and familiar forage areas often drove large herbivores into the plantations, where they helped themselves to the tender rubber saplings and whatever else was on offer in the employees' gardens and orchards. On some estates the damage from elephants and deer ran into many thousands of trees and tens of thousands of dollars per year. Despite the concerns among conservationists about the effects of rubber cultivation on wildlife, it remained legal to shoot any animals that destroyed crops, and planters did so enthusiastically.[60]

Once the plantations were up and running, much of the work consisted of tapping, weeding, and general maintenance. Tapping, like planting, was systematized over years of experimentation. By the 1900s the basic method—devised largely by Henry Ridley at Singapore Botanical Gardens—was much as it is today, and involved the removal of a small sliver of bark with a special knife that cut just deep enough to sever the latex vessels without wounding the tree. After a specified interval (which varied according to prices, climate conditions, and different tapping regimes), another sliver was removed from the edge of the preceding cut, and the process was repeated at a controlled rate—initially in a herringbone pattern but later in spirals around the trunk—to ensure that the rate of bark usage did not exceed the rate of regrowth.[61] A skilled tapper could cut up to 350 trees per day with this method. Weeding, too, was thoroughly systematized, and was usually carried out at three-week intervals to ensure the removal of unwanted grass species before they went to seed.[62] Madelon Lulofs's portrayal of life on Deli's plantations conveys a clear sense of the mania for rationalizing such tasks: 'The days succeeded one another monotonously: tapping, weeding, tapping, weeding. The old rubber plantations needed no other attentions. But the tapping and the weeding were done to perfection. For a year, the inspectors had had nothing to do except think out new systems, and the assistants nothing to do except apply them. Everything went with the simplicity of well-oiled machinery.'[63]

The machinery analogy is fitting, for in many ways the corporate estates were more like factories than orchards, let alone forests. Like most plantations the world over,[64] in essence they were carefully designed production systems instrumentally geared towards maximizing the production of a single output. Yet for all their industrial affectation they were more than mere 'machines in the garden', technological systems intruding onto the natural landscape. The fact that they remained fundamentally based on biological processes meant there was always an element of

[59] Michitake Aso, 'Rubber Plantations, Ecology, and Colonial Rule: Industrial Agriculture and the Spread of Ecological Thinking', paper presented at the Rachel Carson Center for Environment and Society, July 2011, 4.
[60] Jeyamalar Kathirithamby-Wells, *Nature and Nation: Forests and Development in Peninsular Malaysia* (Honolulu: University of Hawaii Press, 2005), 197–8.
[61] Drabble, *Rubber in Malaya*, 8–9; Bauer, *Rubber Industry*, 254–6.
[62] Swart and Rutgers (eds), *Handboek*, 133–6.   [63] Lulofs, *Rubber*, 145.
[64] On the basic attributes of the 'global plantation', see Uekötter, 'Rise, Fall, and Permanence', 7–25.

the 'garden in the machine' as well.[65] Managing these processes was more complicated than controlling the cogs in an engine. There were many more variables at work, innumerable organisms and physical processes interconnected in an intricate web of life. Moreover, many of these organisms and processes were not very well understood. Despite the attempt to isolate and manage the various factors of production, the methodical systems employed on the rubber estates often achieved no more than the illusion of human control.

THE ECOLOGY OF RUBBER PLANTATIONS

To put the point differently, the corporate plantations created not only a new rubber economy in the region but also a new rubber ecology. Recognizing this fact, and managing the estates accordingly, were among the keys to long-term success. Few, however, saw things this way during the rubber bonanza of the early twentieth century. As planters converted huge tracts of jungle into orderly rows of *Hevea*, they unleashed a series of unanticipated ecological effects. Many of the management practices they introduced proved ill suited to the humid lowland environment, and often damaged the productivity of the land and the plantations themselves.

Among the worst offenders were the clean-weeding systems that prevailed during the early years. Removing all unwanted vegetation was standard agricultural practice in northern Europe, and was common on coffee and cocoa estates throughout the tropics. During the early rubber boom most European planters employed it almost unthinkingly, and in Malaya it continued to be 'the gospel of efficiency in estate management' until at least the mid-1920s.[66] But some observers challenged the conventional wisdom. In Malaya, the Director of Agriculture J. B. Carruthers repeatedly enjoined planters to leave some form of ground cover to hold the soil and prevent the leaching of nutrients. Although his warnings were mostly ignored at the time, they were eventually vindicated as severe erosion began to afflict many estates, especially those situated on sloping land where the formation of gullies and the exposure of roots reduced latex yields and sometimes killed entire stands.[67] Planters in the East Indies encountered similar problems, but were by and large less beholden to the doctrine of clean-weeding. On Java in particular, where intensive rice cultivation tended to push rubber onto hillsides, planters quickly abandoned the practice in the face of 'disastrous soil erosion during the

---

[65] Leo Marx, *The Machine in the Garden: Technology and the Pastoral Ideal in America* (Oxford: Oxford University Press, 1967); Edmund Russell, 'Introduction: The Garden in the Machine: Toward an Evolutionary History of Technology', in Susan R. Schrepfer and Philip Scranton (eds), *Industrializing Organisms: Introducing Evolutionary History* (New York: Routledge, 2004), 1–16.

[66] Quote from A. W. King, 'Plantation and Agriculture in Malaya, with Notes on the Trade of Singapore', *Geographical Journal*, vol. 93 no. 2 (Feb. 1939), 136–48, here 139.

[67] J. B. Carruthers, 'Report of the Director of Agriculture of F.M.S. for 1907', *Agricultural Bulletin of the Straits and Federated Malay States*, vol. 8 (Singapore: GPO, 1908), 523–48; *Report by the Right Honourable W. G. A. Ormsby Gore on his Visit to Malaya, Ceylon, and Java during the Year 1928* (London: HMSO, 1928), 30.

rainy season'.[68] On Sumatra too, clean-weeding was increasingly frowned upon by the mid-1920s, though it took many years for its after-effects to subside. Pedological studies throughout the inter-war period showed that rubber plantations were still a major source of erosion in the Deli region despite the modification of weeding practices.[69]

The impact of all this eroded soil ranged far beyond the estates themselves. Much of it inevitably ended up in the rivers draining the rubber districts, many of which became choked with silt and far more likely to burst their banks during heavy rains. As riverbed levels rose, the effects on downstream paddy farmers were occasionally severe. In the Malacca River valley, for instance, around 2,800 hectares of paddy were abandoned in the 1930s because of erosion from rubber estates.[70] On the east coast of Sumatra, silt repeatedly clogged irrigation works, caused rivers to flood low-lying fields, and in some localities raised water tables to just below the surface. In the worst affected areas, the resultant waterlogging was so severe as to create 'dying lands'.[71] As for the riverine environments themselves, Malayan reports of declining fish-catches in the 1920s were blamed in large part on clean-weeding on the rubber estates, along with the erosion caused by the mining industry (see Chapter 4). In 1939 it was estimated that erosion from rubber plantations in Peninsular Malaya amounted to 33 million tons annually, or 1.1 billion tons since 1905 (to give some sense of scale, 33 million tons is around three times as much earth as was removed by the entire Channel Tunnel project, including all three tunnels).[72] In sum, many of the costs of corporate rubber production were passed on to others downstream, generally to groups such as paddy farmers or fishermen who were less powerful than those causing the mess.

Governments introduced a variety of remedies to mitigate the damage. In the Federated Malay States, a series of enactments from 1917 onwards empowered state authorities to take action against landowners who allowed eroded material from their property to enter rivers or neighbouring land. In the East Indies, officials called for a more stringent application of 1874 laws mandating terraces on sloping terrain. In neither colony, however, was such legislation widely enforced.[73]

In the long run, a more effective solution was to promote better soil conservation, above all through the construction of silt pits, bunds, and contour drains designed to retain loose soil.[74] Despite the extra labour costs they entailed, such devices were fairly standard on new estates by the 1920s. The retention of non-invasive weed cover—or, better still, the planting of leguminous cover crops—was also broadly recommended. On Java such cover crops were all but universal on rubber estates, and on Sumatra they were also widely used despite the need for

[68] Tengwall, 'History of Rubber', 34.

[69] C. H. Edelman, *Studiën over de Bodemkunde van Nederlandsch-Indië* (Wageningen: Veenman, 1947), 285, 288–9.

[70] Sir Lewis Leigh Fermor, *Report upon the Mining Industry of Malaya*, 3rd printing (Kuala Lumpur: Government Press, 1943), 154.

[71] Edelman, *Studiën*, 289.   [72] Fermor, *Report*, 152–4.

[73] S. Robert Aiken et al., *Development and Environment in Peninsular Malaysia* (Singapore: McGraw-Hill International, 1982), 122–3; Edelman, *Studiën*, 294.

[74] Swart and Rutgers (eds), *Handboek*, 38–42.

phosphate fertilizer inputs.[75] On Indochinese estates as well, leguminous cover plants were a common feature of the 'sarclage de bande' technique, whereby workers clean-weeded only a 1-metre strip in which the trees grew while leaving the intervening spaces uncleared.[76] By contrast, planters in Malaya were slow to adopt cover plants out of fear of root competition with young trees, despite the repeated assurances of agronomists that they had little to fear.[77] The reason for this discrepancy between Malaya and neighbouring colonies is unclear, though for what it is worth, Sir Frank Stockdale surmised that Dutch planters were more likely than their British counterparts to have undergone proper agronomic training at the National Agricultural College at Wageningen before leaving Europe. Judging from a career guide for would-be Malayan rubber planters, which listed as the main prerequisites for success a 'sound physique, an aptitude for controlling native labour and a readiness to dispense with the superfluities of life', he may well have been right.[78] In any event, the lower rates of sediment loss on most East Indian and Indochinese rubber estates offered compelling evidence that erosion in Malaya was 'an evil that might have been avoided' (Fig. 3.2).[79]

Soil loss was only one of many unintended consequences. The environmental conditions on the rubber plantations also provided an ideal habitat for all manner of pathogens. Human diseases ranging from hookworm to dysentery were rife on the estates, but the biggest health problem of all was undoubtedly malaria. In Malaya, which first introduced malaria controls in 1901, mortality rates of 50/1,000 among estate workers were by no means uncommon in the 1900s and 1910s despite heavy doses of quinine. In 1911, the worst year for malarial deaths in Malaya, mortality rates reached 63/1,000, and in certain hotspots they were several times higher than that. In the state of Negri Sembilan, nearly one in five Indian estate workers died in 1911.[80] Disease problems of this magnitude were not only appalling from a humanitarian perspective, they also posed a serious obstacle to the growth of the rubber industry. As news of malarial deaths circulated in the colony, workers tried to avoid the most unhealthy estates, or at least demanded higher wages as compensation for working on them. In the words of Malcolm Watson, the physician who pioneered the anti-malaria measures in Malaya, 'the labour problem is nothing but the malaria problem, and…the solution of the malaria problem will also be the solution of the labour problem'.[81] But solving the malaria problem took time, and methods had to be modified as the rubber frontier advanced into different types of terrain.

[75] *Report by Sir Frank Stockdale on a Visit to Malaya, Java, Sumatra and Ceylon 1938* (London: Colonial Office, 1939), 17–19.

[76] In addition, leguminous cover crops performed better on the red soils of Indochina than on the more acidic soils of western Malaya: Michaux, *L'Hévéaculture*, 14–18; Vaxelaire, *Le Caoutchouc*, 18–22.

[77] Eric Macfadyen, *Rubber Planting in Malaya* (London: Malay States Information Agency, 1924), 29–32; Drabble, *Rubber in Malaya*, 120.

[78] Quote from E. Macfadyen, *Rubber Planting in Malaya* (London: Malay States Information Agency, 1924), 54; see also *Report by Sir Frank Stockdale*, 69.

[79] *Report by the Right Honourable W. G. A. Ormsby Gore*, 30.

[80] Tamils were generally thought to be more susceptible than Chinese or Malays: Barlow, *Natural Rubber*, 51–2.

[81] Sir Malcolm Watson, *The Prevention of Malaria in the Federated Malay States*, 2nd rev. edn (London: Murray, 1921), 365.

Fig. 3.2. Flat terraces on sloping terrain at a Hevea plantation in East Sumatra, 1921–6. By permission of the Nationaal Museum van Wereldculturen, coll. no. 60014052.

Watson's major innovation was to employ an 'ecological' rather than a medical approach to malaria—that is, to focus not on the bodies of infected humans but on the vectors that spread the disease. In the low-lying coastal plain where the earliest estates were located, the chief mosquito vector was *Anopheles umbrosus*, which tends to breed in stagnant pools under heavy cover. To combat this species Watson recommended a programme of swamp drainage and brush clearance, which proved sufficiently effective for planters to continue employing it as they advanced into the ravines of the foothills. As they did so, however, they found that the drainage methods designed for the lowlands were counter-productive in hilly areas, where they created ideal breeding grounds for another malaria vector, *A. maculatus*, which thrives not in heavy jungle cover but in clear water under full sunlight. These were precisely the conditions created on newly cleared estates. Drainage channels, silt pits, root holes, and the like provided *A. maculatus* larvae with a perfect habitat. The most effective remedy against this vector was the installation of subsoil drains, but this was prohibitively expensive. A cheaper and more common alternative was to leave the jungle cover intact around hilly streams to keep them shaded, though the most widely used practice of all was to douse breeding areas with kerosene or mineral oil.[82]

[82] Generally, Watson, *The Prevention*, 354–65; also Foong Kin, 'The Role of Waterborne Diseases in Malaysia', in Peter Boomgaard (ed.), *A World of Water: Rain, Rivers and Seas in Southeast Asian Histories* (Leiden: KITLV, 2007), 281–95.

As a result of such measures, mortality rates on Malayan plantations gradually declined over the course of the 1910s and 1920s, and finally dipped below 10/1,000 in 1930. In the meantime, medical officers in the East Indies and Indochina adopted many of Watson's vector-based control methods.[83] Morbidity rates in the *terres rouges* of Indochina were particularly high, sometimes reaching almost 600 per cent in the latter 1920s (i.e. an average of six bouts of malaria annually per worker); one plantation in the Thu Dau Mot province even reported a staggering 45 per cent mortality rate among its workers in 1927.[84] Given the severity of the problem, the Institut Pasteur d'Indochine pursued a dual ecological-medical approach, including the elimination of standing water within 1,200 metres of settlements, the regular treatment of all ditches and drains with larvicide, along with copious amounts of quinine. By the late 1930s infection rates dropped to around 5 per cent.[85]

Besides human diseases, the estates created breeding grounds for plant pathogens as well. Although Southeast Asia's *Hevea* trees remained unmolested by the leaf fungus that ravaged them in their native Amazonia, the huge single-species blocks nonetheless invited other problems. The most serious by far was the spread of root fungus (especially *Fomes lignosus*) from old diseased stumps or roots that had been left over from the original forest cover. Infections could spread quickly once *Hevea* stands matured and their shallow root systems intertwined, starving the trees of nutrients and eventually killing them if left untreated. By 1914 root fungus was already causing significant losses in east Sumatra, where planters tried to control it by removing all decaying vegetation from new planting areas. In Malaya too, alarm at the losses from root fungus, ants, and beetles led to an Agricultural Pests Enactment in 1913, which gave inspectors the authority to mandate sanitary measures on estates. Various forms of bark and stem kanker, mostly caused by various fungi, were also problematic.[86] In this respect the estates of Indochina enjoyed an unanticipated advantage over their counterparts in Malaya and the East Indies. The annual dry season across much of the colony, which was initially seen as a drawback for *Hevea* cultivation, eventually proved beneficial for reducing the incidence of fungal disease.[87]

To some extent such maladies were unavoidable in the perennially moist conditions of western Malaya and Deli, but they were undoubtedly exacerbated by the practice of mono-cropping. Once again, as with the practice of clean-weeding, early warnings from agronomists went unheeded. 'Though the sight of an immense area planted with rubber trees only is impressive, and calls forth an expression of appreciation for the energy and foresight displayed, yet there is something one

[83] G. Grijns and G. W. Kiewiet de Jonge, *Plantage-Hygiene* (Batavia: Javasche Boekhandel, 1914), 134–55.

[84] Michitake Aso, 'Patriotic Hygiene: Tracing New Places of Knowledge Production about Malaria in Vietnam, 1919–75', *Journal of Southeast Asian Studies*, vol. 44 (2013), 423–43, here 427.

[85] Mingot and Canet, *L'Heveaculture*, 51–4, 73–4; Chollet, *Planteurs*, 211–20.

[86] Van de Leemkolk, *De Rubber-Cultuur*, 31–2; Drabble, *Rubber in Malaya*, 119–20; Barlow, *Natural Rubber*, 154–6; generally Harold Hamel Smith, *Notes on Soil and Plant Sanitation on Cacao and Rubber Estates* (London: Bale, 1911).

[87] Cardot, *Note sur la Production*, 4; Michaux, *L'Hévéaculture*, 27–8.

does not altogether like,' remarked Herbert Wright, editor of the *India-Rubber Journal*, in 1908. 'The system is an unnatural one—that may or may not enable planters to get better results than if they strictly imitated nature—and strikes the visitor as being dangerous from the plant sanitation standpoint.'[88] Despite continued disease losses, mono-cropping remained standard practice. It was more a matter of luck than design that none of the rubber pathogens reached the epidemic proportions that witches' broom or swollen shoot assumed on many cocoa farms. In the late 1910s and early 1920s the most acute problem for the rubber estates was in fact human-made: namely 'brown bast', a bark disorder caused by excessive tapping, which reduced or stopped the flow of latex on up to 30 per cent of the trees on some estates.[89]

As disease and fertility problems mounted on the estates, the planter community instinctively put its faith in modern agronomic science to find solutions. In some ways it proved to be a successful partnership. With the help of botanists and mycologists, most planters learned from at least some of their mistakes and generally managed to keep their estates working. But keeping their estates profitable was another challenge, and in this respect the main threats were not soil wash or pathogens—important though these were in commercial terms—but rather the vagaries of international markets and the mounting competition from smallholders. Ultimately, smallholders were the more important of the two, for the threat they posed was not only economic. It was one thing that their apparently simple cultivation methods produced rubber at low cost. But the fact that they also brought other advantages posed a more fundamental challenge to the ideology of the modern scientific agro-estate.

NATURE, CULTURE, AND SMALLHOLDER RUBBER

Although the ever-rising prominence of smallholder rubber alarmed the plantation community, in many respects it was entirely unsurprising. Throughout much of the region indigenous cultivators had long engaged in commodity production for distant markets. During the nineteenth century small-scale planters in the lowlands, many of them Chinese, threw themselves into pepper, gambier, and tapioca production. Even swidden cultivators in the remote uplands busily traded resins (especially gutta-percha) and spices with outside merchants. What was new about the rubber boom was not the active participation of Southeast Asian smallholders in international commodity markets, but rather the growing scope of their involvement. After the turn of the century the voracious global demand for rubber outstripped anything the region had witnessed before. In stark contrast to colonial cotton cultivation, the main problem for peasants and small-scale planters was not that they were coerced into producing rubber for

---

[88] Herbert Wright, *My Tour in Eastern Rubber Lands* (London: McLaren, 1908), 30.
[89] Drabble, *Rubber in Malaya*, 150–3, 202; Barlow, *Natural Rubber*, 154–6; Tengwall, 'History of Rubber', 347–8.

international markets, but rather that colonial elites sought to cut them out of the profits.[90]

Smallholders near the main planting districts were generally quick to spot the opportunities presented by the rubber boom. In most localities, planting seems to have commenced around three to five years after the establishment of foreign-owned estates. Cultivation techniques were broadly similar across Malaya and the East Indies, though the distribution and ethnic profile of rubber smallholdings differed significantly between the two colonies. Whereas Malayan smallholdings were mostly concentrated in the western areas of the peninsula, in the East Indies they were more widely distributed, including not only the hinterlands of Medan but also central and southern Sumatra (Palembang, Djambi) as well as western (Pontiniak) and southern (Banjermasin) Borneo. Patterns of ownership were also noticeably different. In Malaya around half of all medium-sized and small rubber groves were owned by ethnic Chinese or, to a lesser extent, Indian immigrants, many of them absentee proprietors; furthermore, a large proportion of the nominally 'Malay' smallholders were Javanese. By contrast, immigrants played a much smaller role on Sumatra and Borneo, where the bulk of smallholdings were planted and maintained with local labour. This difference was reflected in the official definitions of 'smallholdings' versus 'estates' in the two colonies. In Malaya the key criterion was size; anything over 100 acres (40.5 hectares) was classified as an estate and anything under 100 acres as a smallholding (though medium-holdings ranging from 15 to 100 acres accounted for up to half of the acreage in this category). During the inter-war period around 40 per cent of Malayan rubber acreage was on small- or medium-holdings, and 60 per cent on large estates (three-quarters of it owned by Europeans, with most of the balance in Chinese hands). In the East Indies the categories were more closely aligned to size and ethnic ownership. Estates of over 100 acres were broadly coterminous with European or American ownership, smallholdings with 'native rubber'. Official statistics for the inter-war period attributed 46 per cent of East Indies acreage to estates and 54 per cent to smallholdings, but native rubber was almost certainly underestimated in such calculations.[91]

---

[90] Michael R. Dove, *The Banana Tree at the Gate: A History of Marginal Peoples and Global Markets in Borneo* (New Haven: Yale University Press, 2010); Jeyamalar Kathirithamby-Wells, 'Attitudes to Natural Resources and Environment among the Upland Forest and Swidden Communities of Southeast Asia during the Nineteenth and Early Twentieth Centuries', in Richard H. Grove, Vinita Damodaran, and Satpal Sangwan (eds), *Nature and the Orient: The Environmental History of South and Southeast Asia* (Delhi: Oxford University Press, 1998), 918–35; Lesley M. Potter, 'A Forest Product out of Control: Gutta Percha in Indonesia and the Wider Malay World, 1845–1915', in Peter Boomgaard, Freek Colombijn, and David Henley (eds), *Paper Landscapes: Explorations in the Environmental History of Indonesia* (Leiden: KITLV, 1997), 281–308.

[91] Indeed, the first systematic survey of smallholdings in the East Indies was only carried out 1937: Bauer, *Rubber Industry*, 3–8; Drabble, *Malayan Rubber*, 1; Jeroen Touwen, 'Entrepreneurial Strategies in Indigenous Export Agriculture in the Outer Islands of Colonial Indonesia, 1925–38', in Peter Boomgaard and Ian Brown (eds), *Weathering the Storm: The Economies of Southeast Asia in the 1930s Depression* (Leiden: KITLV, 2000), 143–70, here 149–50, 158–9; Purwanto, *From Dusun to the Market*, 184–9, 216–18; D. H. Grist, *Nationality of Ownership and Nature of Constitution of Rubber Estates in Malaya* (Kuala Lumpur: Caxton Press, 1933).

The great attraction of rubber among smallholders was based on two main factors: its profitability, and the fact that it could be neatly folded into existing patterns of swidden cultivation. The conventional hill rice or 'ladang' system that was practised across much of the region essentially consisted of forest clearance followed by one or two dry rice crops before the patch was given over to natural regrowth or 'blukar' successor species. To introduce rubber into this system, farmers planted *Hevea* seeds in relatively dense concentrations on freshly cleared *ladang* plots along with the first rice crop. After the second harvest the rubber seedlings were already over a year old and therefore had a head start over the natural *blukar* successor species, quickly forming a crown that suppressed undergrowth and that consequently minimized maintenance.[92] After another three to five years all that was needed was to slash the low-lying undergrowth for access to the mature rubber trees. In the words of P. T. Bauer, one of the most astute observers of the colonial rubber economy, 'To add rubber to this system costs nothing in effort, cash or displaced alternatives.'[93] In many ways the establishment of rubber smallholdings mirrored the dominant mode of indigenous cocoa planting in West Africa. In both cases the key was the remarkable compatibility of an exotic cash crop with existing agrarian systems, though smallholders in Southeast Asia were, if anything, even less likely to over-commit themselves to a single commodity and even more insistent on maintaining their subsistence activities.[94]

The differences between smallholdings and estates therefore went far beyond the question of size or ownership. They also reflected more fundamental distinctions over the ways in which land resources should best be used. In accordance with the Ricardian doctrine of 'comparative advantage', the large plantations specialized solely on rubber. They clear-cut forest, intercropped rarely if at all, and opted to import most of their basic needs rather than withhold any land from latex production for the purpose of growing food. By contrast, smallholdings generally grew rubber alongside rice, fruit, and other crops as a means of spreading risks. To some extent the discrepancies reflected contemporary notions of a 'dual economy' that distinguished between a dynamic, export-oriented European sector and a conservative, subsistence-based indigenous sector, each of which served quite different economic and social needs.[95] But if the theory was correct in highlighting the differences between European and indigenous approaches to land use, it failed to recognize that subsistence-oriented

[92] A. van Gelder, 'Bevolkingsrubbercultuur', in C. J. J. van Hall and C. van de Koppel (eds), *De Landbouw in de Indische Archipel*, vol. 3 (The Hague: van Hoeve, 1950), 427–75, here 446–9; V. A. Tayler, and John Stephens, *Native Rubber in the Dutch East Indies* (London: Rubber Growers' Association, 1929), 3–4; Purwanto, *From Dusun to the Market*, 114–16, 202–3.

[93] P. T. Bauer, *Report on a Visit to the Rubber Growing Smallholdings of Malaya, July–September 1946* (London: HMSO, 1948), 17.

[94] Michael R. Dove, 'Rice-Eating Rubber and People-Eating Governments: Peasant versus State Critiques of Rubber Development in Colonial Borneo', *Ethnohistory*, vol. 43 no. 1 (1996), 33–63, here 34–5.

[95] These ideas, associated above all with Julius Herman Boeke, were particularly influential during the 'ethical' period of development in the Netherlands Indies: Susanne M. Moon, 'Development and the Dual Economy: Theories of Colonial Transformation in the Netherlands East Indies, *c*.1920', in Benedikt Stuchtey (ed.), *Science across the European Empires, 1800–1950* (Oxford: Oxford University Press, 2005), 129–47.

rubber growers actually produced a large and growing proportion of colonial latex exports, and indeed did so at much lower cost. Estates needed high outputs to pay for their overheads and to recoup their investments in roads, drainage ditches, processing buildings, and the like. Smallholders needed little of this, and most of the tapping was carried out by family labour or on a sharecropping basis. In the mid-1920s it was estimated that smallholders in the Outer Isles of the East Indies invested only £5–6 per mature acre (0.4 hectare) of rubber compared to £60–80 per acre for European estates.[96]

Little wonder, then, that colonial officials and estate owners grew increasingly concerned about the threat this posed to the rubber plantations. The rivalry between these two modes of production, and the extent to which governments should intervene to control it, was a perennial source of controversy. In Malaya there were already attempts to inhibit smallholder planting before the First World War. The Malay Lands Act of 1913, which prevented sales of rice-growing land to non-Malays, was ostensibly designed to protect indigenous peasants from the effects of speculative land purchases, but it also explicitly prohibited rubber cultivation within reserve boundaries.[97] It was mainly the price slump of the early 1920s that first drew attention to the 'problem' of smallholder rubber. The 1922 Stevenson Scheme, which imposed a system of export quotas based on purportedly 'normal' production figures, strongly favoured the large estates by underestimating the amount of smallholder output. Among the various reasons why the Dutch refused to participate in the Scheme were the political risks and the practical difficulties of suppressing smallholder cultivation. They were right to do so, for over the long term the Scheme proved spectacularly counter-productive. Instead of slowing the growth of rubber acreage to keep prices stable, the maintenance of higher prices encouraged a surge of East Indies smallholder planting that merely swelled the flood of latex onto world markets after the controls were lifted in 1928.[98] Indeed, the timing could hardly have been worse for the industry, for many of the smallholder rubber groves reached maturity precisely during the trough of the Depression.

As prices plummeted after 1930, colonial administrations tried to protect the plantations in a number of ways. In Indochina, planters benefited from generous price guarantees that funnelled rubber earnings in France back to exporters in the colony.[99] In Malaya, the government issued an indefinite ban on land alienation in 1930, which scarcely affected the estates since most had ample reserves of uncleared forest land. Following the price collapse, colonial authorities in the region also agreed a temporary suspension of tapping. Although the ban was dutifully observed

---

[96] Bauer, *Rubber Industry*, 68; Touwen, 'Entrepreneurial Strategies', 158; Drabble, *Rubber in Malaya*, 100.

[97] Though the ban was widely ignored: Lim Teck Ghee, *Peasants and their Agricultural Economy in Colonial Malaya 1874–1941* (Kuala Lumpur: Oxford University Press, 1977), 50–1, 74; Drabble, *Malayan Rubber*, 104–10. Bauer, *Report on a Visit*, 39–40, 87–9.

[98] Ghee, *Peasants*, 106–16, 143–54; Barlow, *Natural Rubber*, 57–62; Touwen, 'Entrepreneurial Strategies', 159.

[99] Marianne Boucheret, 'Les Organisations de planteurs de caoutchouc indochinois et l'état du début du XXe siècle à la veille de la second guerre mondiale', in Bonin, Hodeir, and Klein (eds), *L'Esprit économique impérial*, 715–33, esp. 729–32; Robequain, *Economic Development*, 205–6.

by most estates, it was completely disregarded by smallholders in the East Indies. In 1934, in response to the ongoing slump, the governments of Britain, France, the Netherlands, India, and Siam signed an International Rubber Regulation Agreement, which once again underestimated smallholder production for the purpose of setting quotas. But despite all these discriminatory measures, smallholders continued to expand their market share.[100]

For many observers it was literally incomprehensible that indigenous farmers were able to out-compete some of most modern, well-capitalized and scientifically advanced agro-estates in the entire tropical world. Among European planters it was a worrying and downright subversive state of affairs, and it soon gave rise to a series of hopeful rationalizations.[101]

One was the idea that smallholder rubber was of poor quality and was often adulterated, but there was little evidence to support this. Indeed, the process of coagulating, mangling, and rolling the latex was simple enough to enable smallholders to produce smoked sheets comparable to those made on the estates (Fig. 3.3).[102] There was also the common accusation, echoing forestry discourses of the era, that smallholders' extensive cultivation methods made 'wasteful' use of the land by destroying more forest than necessary. Estates had a moral investment in this line of thinking since the alleged profligacy of swidden cultivation was one of the main arguments in favour of granting large concessions to foreign firms in the first place. But before the effects of new high-yielding varieties were eventually felt in the 1940s and 1950s, the thicker tree density on smallholdings meant that their per hectare yields were generally higher than those on estates—around one-quarter higher in Malaya and up to twice as high in the East Indies.[103]

Moreover, the accusation that smallholders destroyed vast swathes of virgin forest was based on a misunderstanding of how indigenous rubber was planted. Surveys in the East Indies showed that the integration of rubber into the *ladang* hill rice cycle nearly always occurred on *blukar* (secondary growth) land that had long been used for itinerant cultivation. Generally speaking, smallholders were not clearing large areas that would otherwise have remained untouched; in fact, plantations were more likely to do this.[104] Over time, the conversion of more and more *ladang* land into rubber groves inevitably pushed peasant cultivation into new areas, but this happened far more slowly than the early Cassandra calls suggested.

Once the high yields on smallholdings were grudgingly acknowledged by colonial planters, a common explanation was that they resulted from tapping too deeply and too frequently. The 'squandering of bark reserves' at an unsustainable rate would soon lead, many thought, to the degradation of trees and a marked decline in yields. But this suspicion was totally unwarranted, and smallholder yields

---

[100] Bauer, *Rubber Industry*, 370–5.   [101] See also Dove, 'Rice-Eating Rubber', 40–2.
[102] Bauer, *Rubber Industry*, 72–3, 200–2.
[103] Barlow, *Natural Rubber*, 76–7, 444–5; Drabble, *Malayan Rubber*, 253–4.
[104] Tayler and Stephens, *Native Rubber*, 3–4.

Fig. 3.3. Rolling out coagulated latex sheets on a smallholding in Palembang, Sumatra, 1920–6. By permission of the Nationaal Museum van Wereldculturen, coll. no. 10012718.

stubbornly failed to confirm such wishful thinking. An extensive investigation launched by the Malayan government in 1931–3 found no evidence of over-tapping on smallholdings, and in fact discovered that bark renewal remained well ahead of consumption. Indeed, it was soon established that bark renewal rates were actually faster on smallholdings than on estates due to their denser planting distribution and higher humidity levels.[105] None of this evidence, however, completely removed the suspicion of unsustainable tapping.[106]

Perhaps the most common accusation of all was that the unkempt native rubber gardens were incubators of disease. This was a source of great anxiety amidst the ongoing problems with fungal root infections and white ants, which many estate owners were quick to blame on nearby smallholdings. Yet once again, extensive studies in the 1920s and early 1930s found—much to the consternation of the estate lobby—that smallholdings actually suffered significantly fewer disease problems, largely due to the existence of weedy ground vegetation. For decades, the advocates

[105] H. D. Meads, *Bark Consumption and Bark Reserves on Small Rubber Holdings in Malaya* (Kuala Lumpur: Kyle, Palmer & Co., 1934), esp. 39–42; Bauer, *Rubber Industry*, 34–41; Purwanto, *From Dusun to the Market*, 247–9.
[106] e.g. Tayler and Stephens, *Native Rubber*, 6–7.

of clean-weeding thought that the removal of undergrowth would hinder the progress of root disease by denying subsurface contact points through which it could spread. As it turned out, the opposite was true. In 1932 plant pathologists at the Rubber Research Institute of Malaya found that clean-weeding promoted rather than inhibited the spread of *Fomes lignosus*. Whereas the shallow interlacing roots of *Hevea* mono-crops presented ideal conduits for the spread of underground rhizomorphs, the thick mat of small roots resulting from dense ground cover helped to block such contacts.[107] Moreover, the fact that most smallholder rubber was planted on secondary-growth land also lowered disease problems, for as Dutch observers recognized in the 1920s, *blukar* land that had previously been cleared and then left to fallow contained fewer fungal carrier roots or stumps left over from the primary cover.[108]

One of the few remaining sources of consolation for estate owners was the assumption that modern science and technical innovation would enable them to prevail over smallholders in the end. The main problem, however, was that rubber cultivation presented few economies of scale and little scope for mechanization, leaving the plants themselves as the only target for further capital investment. The development of high-yielding *Hevea* strains was therefore crucial. Attempts to select and propagate seeds from the most prolific trees reached back to the early stages of the industry, though cross-pollination made it difficult to isolate them genetically from poor yielders. The solution lay in vegetative propagation, or grafting the buds of high-yielding trees onto ordinary rootstocks, which was first successfully carried out in 1916 by Dutch botanists at Buitenzorg. During the 1920s researchers at the AVROS[109] experiment station and the Rubber Research Institute of Malaya carried out a series of long-term bud-grafting trials, and by the late 1930s they managed to produce strains capable of yielding up to 1,200 kg per hectare, or around four times more than average trees. But because of the planting restrictions imposed by the International Rubber Regulation Agreement, the proportion of high-yielding trees grew slowly. In 1936 the new strains accounted for only 6.5 per cent of acreage in Malaya and 11.1 per cent in the East Indies (but 35.4 per cent in Indochina, reflecting another latecomer advantage).[110] Significantly, all of this high-yielding acreage was on estates, which were anxious to keep the benefits of the new varieties from leaking into the smallholder sector. The failure to supply smallholders with improved planting material was symptomatic of the fact that rubber research in the colonies was geared towards the needs of plantations.[111]

While plant breeders in the research stations were busily seeking new ways to manipulate nature, others began to advocate a rather different approach. By the

---

[107] Bauer, *Rubber Industry*, 58–9, 257–8.

[108] Van Gelder, 'Bevolkingsrubbercultuur', 449; Tayler and Stephens, *Native Rubber*, 8. Readers may note the contrast to cocoa, which suffered fewer rather than more disease problems on nearly cleared land.

[109] Sumatran Rubber Growers' Association: Algemene Vereniging van Rubberplanters ter Oostkust van Sumatra.

[110] Michaux, *L'Hévéaculture*, 4; François Graveline, *Des Hévéas et des hommes: l'aventure des plantations Michelin* (Paris: Nicolas Chaudun, 2006), 70–81.

[111] Bauer, *Report on a Visit*, 42–9; Bauer, *Rubber Industry*, 275–85.

early 1930s there were growing calls within colonial agronomy and forestry circles to shift away from intrusive 'agricultural' practices—clearing ground, sowing seeds, clean-weeding—towards low-intervention 'forestry methods', which essentially managed the existing vegetation in such a way as to favour desirable species over others. What this approach entailed, more specifically, was threefold: planting *Hevea* trees at higher densities (500+/acre), leaving much of the natural ground cover intact, and removing only the most injurious species such as *lalang* grass. Although trials in the early 1930s resulted in smaller average tree size and less latex per tapping, they also raised yields per hectare and, perhaps most importantly, they dramatically reduced operating costs.[112]

To some extent this move towards low-intervention methods reflected the harsh commercial imperatives of the Depression years. As rubber prices collapsed in the early 1930s, the labour-intensive weeding and maintenance regimes that had long been criticized on agronomic grounds now became economically suspect as well. Planters who found themselves squeezed by the price slump certainly became more open to the idea of abandoning such methods, along with the Indian labourers whom they had paid to carry them out. By the end of 1932 the average costs of upkeep for a hectare of mature rubber in Malaya dropped to only one-sixth of 1929 levels.[113]

But the point was not just to make an agronomic virtue of commercial necessity. In Southeast Asia as elsewhere, the attempt to improve tropical agriculture also reflected the influence of ecological approaches and the emergence of new understandings of the natural environment.[114] As one forester put it, although *Hevea* was classified as an agricultural crop, 'a rubber plantation is none the less a forest and the ecological problems that arise in it are of general silvicultural significance'.[115]

For the advocates of forestry methods, the advantages of a less intrusive cultivation regime were not merely (or even primarily) to be found in lower costs and higher factor productivity. They also promised to improve exhausted soils and to maintain long-term fertility on plantation lands. The existence of perennial ground cover and the continual deposition of vegetable debris not only retained nitrates in the soil, it also reduced erosion. In turn, good soil husbandry would enable planters to replace ageing rubber stands at little cost, either by coppicing or by allowing *Hevea* trees to regenerate naturally from falling seeds, as foresters at the Sungei Buloh reserve in Malaya had already shown.[116] Although supporters presented this as a coherent cultivation system, certain elements were more readily accepted than others. Although most planters still harboured doubts about the benefits of natural regeneration, which deprived them of the ability to switch to high-yielding varieties, the damage caused by previous weeding regimes was

---

[112] J. N. Oliphant, 'Rubber Forestry Again', *Malayan Forester*, vol. 3 (1934), 3–6; 'Ecology and Rubber-Growing', *Malayan Forester*, vol. 4 (1935), 75–7; Drabble, *Malayan Rubber*, 54–5; King, 'Plantation and Agriculture'.
[113] Bauer, *Rubber Industry*, 367.
[114] See, more generally, Tilley, *Africa*, ch. 3; also Aso, 'Rubber Plantations'.
[115] J. G. Watson, 'Foresters and Rubber Forestry', *Malayan Forester*, vol. 4 (1935), 78–9, here 79.
[116] 'Natural Regeneration of Rubber', *Malayan Forester*, vol. 3 (1934), 206–10.

broadly acknowledged. By 1934 even the Rubber Research Institute of Malaya recommended 'controlled natural ground cover' tailored to different soil and climate conditions.[117]

In sum, the new emphasis on low intervention and adaptation to local conditions was, in the approving words of the *Malayan Forester* journal, 'just what the ecologist would expect'.[118] Interestingly enough, it was also remarkably similar to what indigenous producers had long practised. From the perspective of 'rubber forestry', the advantages of the dense planting arrangements and minimal weeding regimes on 'native' rubber holdings went far beyond the question of cost, for they also minimized erosion and leaching, aided decomposition and humus formation, stabilized soil temperature and moisture, and even reduced disease.[119] Dutch agronomists were perhaps the first to recognize the wider benefits of indigenous cultivation practices, noting as early as 1925 that 'the native intuitively took the correct path, while the European rubber planter gradually has learned to change his operations that were initially far too intensive'.[120] A small number of commercial planters—one in Malacca, another at Tjigoegoer on Java—had also been experimenting with cultivation methods that were broadly similar to those used on smallholdings.[121]

Clearly, there were some striking parallels between 'rubber forestry' and existing smallholder practices. But the promotion of low-intervention techniques had less to do with the incorporation of local knowledge than with the application of evolving principles within colonial forestry circles. Although the shift towards forestry methods encouraged more openness towards indigenous environmental knowledge, the idea that 'the native *intuitively* took the correct path' still implied that the results were more accidental than intentional. As the journal *L'Agronomie coloniale* noted (in typically social-evolutionist terms), there was something profoundly ironic about large corporate estates having 'to abandon intensive cultivation with its carefully perfected processes devised by progress, because they are too expensive, in order to go back (*revenir en arrière*) to extensive cultivation with its primitive processes as practised by the natives'.[122] Such analyses misunderstood the rationale behind the new forestry-based techniques, which represented less a backwards retreat than a sideways attempt to rethink the wisdom of the intensive, 'agricultural' model on which the rubber plantations had been based since the very beginning.

Despite the growing scientific sanction for low-intervention methods, they still met with widespread scepticism among planters, especially in Malaya. One reason was the sheer force of habit among the planter community; another was the fact

[117] W. B. Haines, *The Uses and Control of Natural Undergrowth on Rubber Estates* (Kuala Lumpur: Rubber Research Institute, 1934); Bauer, *Rubber Industry*, 258–9.
[118] 'Ecology and Rubber-Growing', *Malayan Forester*, vol. 4 (1935), 75–7, here 76.
[119] 'Kautschukkultur als Forstwirtschaft', *Der Tropenpflanzer*, vol. 35 no. 7 (July 1932), 292–4; Bauer, *Rubber Industry*, 58–9.
[120] A. A. L. Rutgers, 'De toekomst van de bevolkingsrubber in Nederlandsch-Indië', *Indische Mercuur*, vol. 48 (1925), quoted from van Gelder, 'Bevolkingsrubbercultuur', 449.
[121] 'Kautschukkultur als Forstwirtschaft', 293–4; 'Natural Regeneration of Rubber', 206–10.
[122] 'Culture forestière de l'Hévéa', *L'Agronomie coloniale*, vol. 21 no. 180 (Dec. 1932), 225–6, here 226.

that foresters tended to calculate with longer timeframes than entrepreneurs who were primarily concerned with the bottom line. But perhaps the most important factor was a deep-seated anxiety about any blurring of the racialized hierarchies associated with different forms of cultivation. Although the supporters of 'rubber forestry' presented it as a pragmatic means of ensuring the future sustainability of the plantations, both commercially and ecologically, for many observers it seemed nothing short of a capitulation to the smallholder competition. Writing in 1931, the American rubber economist H. N. Whitford noted the powerful sense of aversion towards anything that smacked of primitive and disorderly 'Asian methods'. Some planters, he reported, 'claim forestry methods are not aristocratic, implying that if the European has to go native to compete with the native, the European has no business to be in...rubber planting'.[123] In a sense this was absolutely correct, for as the British Under-Secretary of State for the Colonies had previously warned Malaya's planter community, 'the only justification for the present complicated and expensive mechanism of directors, agent firms, visiting agents, managers, and shareholders is the application of greater intelligence and skill than the native can reasonably be expected to acquire'.[124] In this context, any admission of being out-thought by 'natives' raised unsettling questions about why Europeans were there at all.

Why did a plantation sector that prided itself on deploying the latest agronomic knowledge prove so ill disposed towards this specific piece of scientific counsel? The question is revealing in itself, for what it highlights is the importance of cultural dispositions and expectations in shaping people's interaction with the environment. Ultimately, the sprawling nexus of rubber research institutes and agro-estates in Southeast Asia mirrored the wider ideological underpinnings of the imperial enterprise, which claimed to spread the benefits of European knowledge to other parts of the world by mobilizing their resources for human ends. The fact that smallholders were actually more 'efficient' (by nearly all definitions) at producing rubber did little to undermine this conviction. Indeed, the persistent faith in Europe's technical superiority long served to obscure the facts, even after certain members of its scientific priesthood had repeatedly verified them. Undoubtedly this devotion to the modern plantation was partly a reflection of European economic interests, not to mention government concerns about giving the colonies a bad name with investors. But the power of the ideology itself should not be underestimated. Given that most of the contemporary rationalizations for smallholders' success were factually wrong, and demonstrably so, suggests that they functioned not just as a ploy to discredit a commercial rival or as a pretext to justify greater state intervention in the rubber industry. They also served as a myth, a cultural response to a phenomenon that was beyond comprehension for many concerned.[125]

---

[123] Drabble, *Malayan Rubber*, 55.
[124] *Report by the Right Honourable W. G. A. Ormsby Gore*, 141.
[125] I am drawing here on Dove, 'Rice-Eating Rubber', esp. 52–3.

WAR, DECOLONIZATION, AND THE WORLD RUBBER ECONOMY

When the first *Hevea* plants were brought to Southeast Asia in the late nineteenth century, few could have imagined the changes that would eventually result. From 1900 to 1940 around 4 million hectares—an area roughly the size of the Netherlands—of rainforest were razed and converted to rubber stands. In 1939/40 Malaya and the East Indies alone accounted for over 3.25 million of these hectares (roughly the size of Belgium), and produced the bulk of the 1.1 million tons of rubber absorbed on world markets.[126] Nearly all of this output was destined for the industrial world, with around two-thirds of it going into car, bus, and truck tyres. Although few motorists were aware of the connection, the degradation of the rainforests was crucial for keeping their wheels turning. The continual flow of latex into the industrial economies represented a vital resource subsidy from the ecosystems of the tropics, one that underwrote the radical economic and social transformations of the automobile age. By the late 1930s, rubber was far and away the dominant export crop in Southeast Asia. And for the industrial powers, no other tropical commodity was of greater strategic importance as they contemplated the possibility of a war in the Pacific.

The outbreak of the Pacific war in 1941 brought enormous changes to the world rubber economy. The Japanese occupation of Malaya and the East Indies severed at a stroke the all-important trade links that had hitherto sustained the heartland of the industry. As the main consumer markets in Europe and North America faced a sudden crisis of supply, the chief production zones experienced an abrupt collapse in output. On most plantations, tapping and maintenance quickly ground to a halt. With market outlets cut off there was little revenue (or need) to pay wages to estate workers, and with no hands to tend them, rubber stands were invaded by *lalang* grass and other unwanted species. As food supplies dwindled in the plantation belts, a growing number of 'squatters', many of them former estate labourers thrown out of work, converted large swathes of rubber to rice production, including around 53,000 hectares in Malaya and a similar area in East Sumatra.[127] The Japanese occupiers had little incentive to intervene. The small dribble of latex from Malaya, Sumatra, and Borneo to the Home Islands was in any event impeded by the Allied shipping blockade, and Japan was still able to acquire sufficient rubber supplies from Vichy-ruled Indochina and the Moluccas. As a result of wartime dislocations, world production of natural rubber fell by around three-quarters to a mere 254 million tons in 1945.[128]

Such a dramatic collapse in the supply of such a key industrial resource was a major concern for planners in Europe and North America. Governments had already taken steps against the threat of a strategic rubber shortage as part of their

---

[126] Bauer, *Rubber Industry*, 380, 392.

[127] Barlow, *Natural Rubber*, 75; Stoler, *Capitalism and Confrontation*, 97.

[128] On rubber in the Second World War, William G. Clarence-Smith, 'The Battle for Rubber in the Second World War: Cooperation and Resistance', in Jonathan Curry-Machado (ed.), *Global Histories, Imperial Commodities, Local Interactions* (Hounslow: Palgrave, 2013), 204–23.

war preparations, mainly by stockpiling it up until December 1941. In addition, some states also tried to diversify their supply base by boosting production capacity in other parts of the world. In 1938 German authorities launched an ambitious programme to improve the latex yields of the *Kok-Saghyz* plant, or Russian dandelion, and after the invasion of the Soviet Union they forced farmers behind the Eastern Front to grow it, though with little success.[129] From 1941 onwards the British government tried to boost exports from Ceylon and India (the only colonies in the region that escaped Japanese occupation) as well as West Africa. French rubber firms that lost control over their Indochinese supplies encouraged latex harvesting in Côte d'Ivoire, while US authorities turned their attention to Firestone's estates in Liberia.[130]

But stockpiling and supply diversification could offset only part of the wartime rubber shortfall. In the event, most of it was covered by the synthetic rubber industry. During the First World War, Germany produced modest amounts of methyl rubber from butadiene in order to mitigate the effects of the Allied blockade. By 1926 German chemists were able to synthesize more durable types of polymerized rubber, which were soon developed into IG Farben's famous 'Buna' product in 1929. After a series of further improvements, Buna rubber became sufficiently hard-wearing for use in automobile tyres, and eventually played an important role in the German war effort (production peaked at 115,000 tons in 1943). In the meantime, several US firms were also working on synthetic rubber, most notably Du Pont, Firestone, and Standard Oil (which held a portion of the patent rights to IG Farben's Buna product). After Pearl Harbor they were the target for massive government investment, and by 1945 the production of styrene-based GR-S rubber reached 866,000 tons, enough to meet the United States' own wartime requirements as well as most of Britain's.[131]

The rise of synthetics during the Second World War forever changed the global rubber economy. After 1945, most industrialized states were eager to develop their synthetic capacity as a means of circumventing the British dominance of world rubber markets. The sharp rise in demand fuelled by post-war reconstruction, and above all the explosive growth of automobile ownership, drove an unprecedented upsurge in world rubber production after the war, from 1.67 million tons in 1946 to 10.8 million tons in 1973. The bulk of this increase—7.3 million tons—came from the expansion of synthetic rubber, which accounted for two-thirds of overall rubber output in the early 1970s.[132]

In many ways this was good news for the forests of Southeast Asia, since the growth of synthetic rubber reduced the amount of woodland that would otherwise have been converted to single-species *Hevea* stands during the post-war boom.

---

[129] Susanne Heim, *Plant Breeding and Agrarian Research in Kaiser-Wilhelm-Institutes 1933–1945*, trans. Sorcha O'Hagan (Dordrecht: Springer, 2008), 102–53.

[130] Bauer, *Rubber Industry*, 303–8; James Fenske, 'The Battle for Rubber in Benin', *Economic History Review*, vol. 67 no. 4 (2014), 1012–34; Graveline, *Des Hévéas*, 91–3; on Firestone, Tucker, *Insatiable Appetite*, 248–58, 262.

[131] Bauer, *Rubber Industry*, 287–96; Tucker, *Insatiable Appetite*, 261–5.

[132] Barlow, *Natural Rubber*, 408, 412.

But the news was not all good. For one thing, synthetic rubber was not a universal substitute for its natural competitor. Various products ranging from surgical gloves to aeroplane tyres were still primarily made from plant-derived latex due to its high tack and superior resistance to cuts and shearing; even modern radials for automobiles contained a significant proportion of natural rubber. Moreover, the huge rise in overall demand meant that natural rubber output continued to grow despite the relative dominance of synthetics. Between the mid-1940s and the early 1970s natural rubber production rose fourfold, reaching 3.5 million tons in 1973. Over two-thirds of it—a total of 2.375 million tons—still came from Peninsular Malaysia and Indonesia alone.[133] Furthermore, demand for natural rubber surged anew after the oil shocks of the 1970s, which dramatically raised the price of petroleum feed-stocks for synthetic latex. By 2014 world output of natural rubber exceeded 12 million tons, over ten times more than in 1939/40, and continued to gain ground on the 16.7 million tons of synthetics produced at the time.[134]

So despite the enormous growth of synthetics after the war, the rubber growers of Southeast Asia essentially took up where they had left off in 1941. The trees themselves were more or less unaffected by the wartime lack of maintenance and the invasion of undergrowth, which once again confirmed the futility of clean-weeding. Most of Malaya's estates recovered within a year or two; neighbouring smallholders likewise resumed tapping shortly after the war.[135] In East Sumatra the Dutch 'police action' of June 1947 returned the majority of foreign-owned estates to their proprietors, while smallholders elsewhere on the Outer Isles continued to fold *Hevea* into their cultivation cycles.[136]

But if the post-war recovery initially seemed like a return to business as usual, over the following years the Southeast Asian rubber economy was transformed in several respects. First of all, much of the production growth in the 1950s and 1960s came from the spread of high-yielding varieties that had first been developed before the war. This was especially the case on large estates, whose efforts to boost productivity mainly came to fruition in the post-colonial period. In Malaysia in particular, the development of new cloned varieties—some of which could surpass 2,000 kg of latex per hectare—enabled plantations to outstrip the average smallholder yield by around 50 per cent in the early 1970s.[137] These high-yield clones, like the growth of synthetic rubber, helped reduce the pressure to clear new land, all the more so given that they were often planted on old rubber acreage. But even so, the intensification of estate production could not entirely offset further forest clearance in the context of ever-rising demand. Malaysia's rubber area continued to expand, albeit slowly, from 1.37 million hectares in 1946 to 1.77 million in 1965 (after which it levelled off and gradually declined). By contrast, Indonesia's rubber

[133] Barlow, *Natural Rubber*, 410.

[134] Data from *Rubber Statistical Bulletin*, April–June 2015, cited in India Rubber Board, *Rubber Statistical News, Review of the Year 2014–15*, 4, available at: <http://www.rubberboard.org.in/PDF/RSNMay2015E.pdf>.

[135] Barlow, *Natural Rubber*, 76–8.   [136] Stoler, *Capitalism and Confrontation*, 112–14.

[137] Barlow, *Natural Rubber*, 76–7, 115–27, 444–5.

frontier lost none of its dynamism. After first overtaking Malaysia in the 1960s, it continued to grow to around 2.4 million hectares by 2000.[138]

This reflected another important post-war change. Unlike the early phases of rubber expansion, smallholders were now the primary drivers of growth. By 1980 they accounted for two-thirds of the acreage in Malaysia, 80 per cent in Indonesia, and no less than 95 per cent in Thailand (the chief new competitor, with 1.24 million hectares of rubber in 1980).[139] In some ways this triumph of the smallholder represented a continuation of pre-war trends, but it was also reinforced by the altered political environment.

Whereas colonial governments had generally been unsupportive or at best ambivalent towards 'native rubber' cultivation, post-colonial regimes actively encouraged it as a tool for economic development and poverty reduction. In Malaysia, the independent government incentivized rural smallholders to open up new lands through the Federal Land Development Authority (FELDA), which included Sarawak and Sabah after their merger with the Peninsular states in 1963. Although palm oil eventually surpassed rubber as the country's main export crop, *Hevea* remained one of the chief cultivars on government schemes. To promote smallholdings still further, Malaysian authorities also subdivided 146,000 hectares of foreign-owned rubber estates into smaller parcels, many of which were purchased in the 1960s and early 1970s by ethnic Chinese landlords who leased them out to tenants.[140] In Indonesia too, Sukarno's government redistributed large amounts of foreign-controlled estate land as the original leases expired, and eventually confiscated the remaining Dutch estates in 1957. Although General Suharto's 'new order' reopened the doors to foreign investment after 1965, the relentless growth of Indonesian rubber was still overwhelmingly the work of smallholders.[141] Only in southern Vietnam did plantations continue to dominate post-war rubber production, albeit with considerable difficulty. From the late 1940s onwards their operations were regularly disrupted by Viet-Minh forces, and by the mid-1960s the majority of European managers had to abandon their estates for the relative safety of Saigon.[142] Most of the plantations went into state ownership after 1975, though smallholder production gradually took root under the reformist experiments of the 1990s, and has been expanding ever since.

Since the demise of colonialism, the development of Southeast Asian rubber has in many ways been a story of trade-offs. For starters, there was a difficult balance to strike between the social and ecological benefits of different modes of production.

[138] Barlow, *Natural Rubber*, 444–5; FAOSTAT: <http://faostat.fao.org>.

[139] Figures from FAOSTAT (<http://faostat.fao.org>); Barlow, *Natural Rubber*, 444–5; Enzo R. Grilli et al., *The World Rubber Economy: Structure, Changes, and Prospects* (Baltimore: Johns Hopkins University Press, 1980), 16–20.

[140] John H. Drabble, *An Economic History of Malaysia, c. 1800–1990* (Houndmills: Macmillan, 2000), 216–24; M. C. Ricklefs, *A History of Modern Indonesia* (London: Macmillan, 1981), 215–16, 296.

[141] Generally, Adrian Vickers, *A History of Modern Indonesia*, 2nd edn (Cambridge: Cambridge University Press, 2013), 137–45, 162, 165–73.

[142] Graveline, *Des Hévéas*; also *Planteurs d'hévéas en Indochine, 1939–1954* (Amicale des Planteurs d'Hévéas, 1996), 109–44.

Although the victory of smallholders over estates has enabled a broader spectrum of the population to share in the proceeds, there can be little doubt that it resulted in higher rates of forest clearance. As plantations became more productive after the early 1950s, they were able to squeeze significantly more output from existing acreage than their smaller competitors. This yield discrepancy points to a second juggling act, namely between the interests of investors and the wider public good. Much of the research that went into the high-yield varieties was paid for by large estates and their commercial associations, which understandably sought to profit from the competitive advantages conferred by these new technologies by denying them to their rivals. In order to minimize forest clearance, the most promising strategy was to make such planting material available to smallholders (a policy most systematically pursued in Thailand), but this carried the risk of undermining future yield gains by removing the incentives for research. Herein lies yet another trade-off, for it is by no means clear that the replacement of multi-strata, low-intensity 'jungle rubber' by more input-intensive high-yield techniques is a more ecologically desirable outcome, regardless of who is doing it. As is so often the case when weighing up the advantages of different cultivation systems, growers are frequently exchanging one set of drawbacks (more forest clearance) for another (the accumulation of fertilizers and other agrochemicals).[143]

The environmental implications of synthetic rubber are similarly ambiguous, at least when viewed at a global rather than regional level. Although petroleum-based rubber production has undoubtedly spared forests in Southeast Asia, it is nonetheless a manifestly unsustainable industry that requires around ten times more energy per unit of elastomer than natural rubber.[144] Of course, the alternative—a doubling (or more) of rubber acreage—may seem far worse, especially against the backdrop of decades of rampant forest clearance for oil palm, timber, and wood pulp. But as far as tropical crops go, rubber cultivation can be done on a relatively sustainable basis. In contrast to most other agricultural systems, research has shown that mature *Hevea* stands with ample ground cover are essentially self-supporting with respect to biomass and nutrient cycling.[145] At the end of a typical thirty-year cycle, rubber parcels can usually be harvested for valuable timber. If competently managed, they are also sufficiently fertile to allow replanting with another generation of rubber or with a range of other crops. Moreover, in the mid-1990s it was estimated that the worldwide stock of *Hevea* fixed around 90 million tons of carbon dioxide per year, leading some to applaud the growth of the industry as 'a carbon dioxide fixing factory for the sustained production of timber'.[146]

---

[143] Eric Penot, 'From Shifting Cultivation to Sustainable Jungle Rubber: A History of Innovations in Indonesia', in Malcolm Cairns (ed.), *Voices from the Forest: Integrating Indigenous Knowledge into Sustainable Upland Farming* (Washington, DC: RFF, 2007), 583–605; Eric Penot and A. F. S. Budiman, 'Environmental Aspects of Smallholder Rubber Agroforestry in Indonesia: Reconcile Production and Environment', International Rubber Conference (1998): <http://www.worldagroforestrycentre.org/sea/publications/files/report/RP0056-04/RP0056-04-1.PDF>.

[144] Loadman, *Tears*, 274.

[145] Jason Clay, *World Agriculture and the Environment* (Washington, DC: Island Press, 2004), 344.

[146] Loadman, *Tears*, 275–6.

From the vantage point of the twenty-first century we might well view rubber cultivation as a relatively benign form of land use, at least in comparison to most of the alternatives. From a socio-economic perspective too, rubber has tended to bring more benefits to cultivators in the tropics than many other export crops such as sugar, bananas, or cotton. Yet any attempt to understand its historical development must also take account of the huge costs that were incurred. From the early phase of expansion through the colonial boom years, rubber destroyed enormous swathes of lowland forest across Southeast Asia. It brought hundreds of thousands of labourers into previously remote jungles, many of whom died from disease and maltreatment. In some of the main producer areas it displaced local cultivators from the best agricultural land and consigned them to a life of material and cultural poverty. As the planting frontier raced into the rainforests it eroded soils, damaged rivers, destroyed the habitat of countless species, and radically diminished local biodiversity. Although many of the rubber groves gradually stabilized as cultivation practices improved and political frameworks shifted, the woodland and soil that was lost would never come back.

Like the story of colonial cocoa, the development of Southeast Asia's rubber industry reminds us that the effects of commodity production are not culturally or ecologically predetermined. Instead, they are the result of a continuous interaction between material and social factors, which together shape the choices people make. Rubber was, and still can be, produced in different ways, on different scales, with different outcomes. The ecology of rubber has always been the historically contingent product of how it is grown, who grows it, and what it replaces. The nature of the *Hevea* tree defines the possibilities, but the trade-offs are up for grabs.

4

Subterranean Frontier
Tin Mining, Empire, and Environment
in Southeast Asia

Chapters 1–3 have focused on the role of plant commodities in reshaping the ecosystems of the tropical world.[1] Although environmental constraints clearly influenced where certain crops were grown, for the most part their story has been one of remarkable mobility. Throughout the colonial era, a host of different cultivars were transplanted via an imperial botanical diaspora as part of a concerted attempt to modify and profit from tropical ecosystems around the globe.

The relationship between mining and imperialism was somewhat different. Unlike plant-based industries, which could be deliberately built up in areas where it was politically or economically advantageous to do so, mineral wealth was more a matter of geological chance. Granted, the accessibility of coveted ore deposits was often crucially facilitated by the application of financial might and technical capability, and was not infrequently predicated on the exertion of military power. But the deposits themselves were nonetheless embedded in certain places. The fact that they had to be extracted *in situ* meant that mining tended to shape the geography of modern empire rather than the other way around. The quest for mineral resources was one of the factors that helped transform the focus of European imperialism from the control of trade to the control of territory.

The spread of industrialization in the nineteenth century created an unprecedented demand for metals on world markets. While miners burrowed holes across the topography of industrial Europe, a growing number of prospectors fanned out around the globe in search of new deposits. In many parts of the world these entrepreneurs acted as pioneers of imperial expansion, from the goldfields of Witwatersrand to the nickel pits of New Caledonia. Although few of the earliest speculators enjoyed official backing, the strategic importance of mineral ores made home governments acutely alert to questions of supply, and generally supportive of efforts to exploit the deposits that their nationals discovered. For the European powers, the ever-increasing demand for more metal—and for more types of metal— far outstripped their own resources. The lure of mineral wealth thus furnished a powerful incentive for conquest and colonization overseas.

---

[1] Sections of this chapter are largely based on material first published in Corey Ross, 'The Tin Frontier: Mining, Empire and Environment in Southeast Asia, 1870s–1930s', *Environmental History*, vol. 19 (2014), 454–79.

The mining industry, though long a favourite stomping ground of labour and economic historians, has generally been something of a stepchild of modern environmental history. In the early 2000s studies that focused on its broader ecological ramifications were still conspicuously rare.[2] Fortunately, this state of relative neglect has improved over the last decade with a handful of fine studies on the environmental history of mineral extraction, chiefly focused on the North American West.[3] But for much of the rest of the world, the role of mining in transforming regional environments remains underexposed, despite the fact that it has perennially been one of the dirtiest of all industries as well as a cornerstone of empire and global trade.[4]

There is no better example than tin, which played a central role in Europe's industrial empire in Southeast Asia. Although environmental histories of Southeast Asia have long focused on the region's vast forests, extensive plantation complexes, and dynamic rice frontiers,[5] tin mining was one of its largest industries during the colonial era. Moreover, Southeast Asia's tin fields dominated world production from the late nineteenth century through most of the twentieth.[6] Like many other metals—gold, iron, copper—tin was in high demand from the mid-1800s onwards. Few minerals, however, were so vital for the industrial economy yet so reliant on supplies from tropical territories, in particular the western foothills of the Malay Peninsula and the nearby 'tin isles' of the Dutch East Indies. The search for tin not only fuelled the extension of European power in the region, it also drove a

[2] See the comments in John R. McNeill, 'Observations on the Nature and Culture of Environmental History', *History and Theory*, Theme Issue 42 (Dec. 2003), 5–43, esp. 41. An exception he noted was Duane A. Smith, *Mining America: The Industry and the Environment, 1800–1980* (Lawrence: University of Kansas Press, 1987); another exception was Kerstin Kretschmer, *Braunkohle und Umwelt. Zur Geschichte des nordwestsächsischen Kohlenreviers (1900–1945)* (Frankfurt a. M.: Peter Lang, 1998).

[3] Kathryn Morse, *The Nature of Gold: An Environmental History of the Klondike Gold Rush* (Seattle: University of Washington Press, 2003); Andrew C. Isenberg, *Mining California: An Ecological History* (New York: Hill and Wang, 2005), 23–51; Timothy J. LeCain, *Mass Destruction: The Men and Giant Mines that Wired America and Scarred the Planet* (New Brunswick, NJ: Rutgers University Press, 2009).

[4] For Europe, see the recent collection by Peter Anreiter (ed.), *Mining in European History and its Impact on Environment and Human Societies* (Innsbruck: Innsbruck University Press, 2010). Beyond Europe and North America: Matthew Evenden, 'Aluminum, Commodity Chains, and the Environmental History of the Second World War', *Environmental History*, vol. 16 (January 2011), 69–93; Carl N. McDaniel and John M. Gowdy, *Paradise for Sale: A Parable of Nature* (Berkeley: University of California Press, 2000); B. Daley and P. Griggs, 'Mining the Reefs and Cays: Coral, Guano and Rock Phosphate Extraction in the Great Barrier Reef, Australia, 1844–1940', *Environment and History*, vol. 12 (2006), 395–434; Elizabeth Dore, 'Environment and Society: Long-Term Trends in Latin American Mining', *Environment and History*, vol. 6 (2000), 1–29.

[5] This literature is vast. For a useful overview and bibliography, see Peter Boomgaard, *Southeast Asia: An Environmental History* (Oxford: ABC-Clio, 2007).

[6] There is a sizeable literature on the economic, social, and political dimensions of the industry: see esp. Wong Lin Ken, *The Malayan Tin Industry to 1914: With Special Reference to the States of Perak, Selangor, Negri Sembilan and Pahang* (Tucson: University of Arizona Press, 1965); Yip Yat Hoong, *The Development of the Tin Mining Industry of Malaya* (Kuala Lumpur: University of Malaya Press, 1969); Francis Loh Kok Wah, *Beyond the Tin Mines: Coolies, Squatters and New Villagers in the Kinta Valley, Malaysia, c.1880–1980* (Singapore: Oxford University Press, 1988); Mary F. Somers Heidhues, *Bangka Tin and Muntok Pepper: Chinese Settlement on an Indonesian Island* (Singapore: Institute of Southeast Asian Studies, 1992); Amarjit Kaur and Frits Diehl, 'Tin Miners and Tin Mining in Indonesia, 1850–1950', *Asian Studies Review*, vol. 20 no. 2 (Nov. 1996), 95–120.

far-reaching set of social and environmental changes that profoundly transformed the physical, ethnic, and cultural landscape. Although the impact was most acute at the immediate sites of extraction, the mines also radiated complex ripple effects throughout their hinterlands. Indeed, many of the connections reached far beyond Southeast Asia itself. Like the rubber, sugar, and coffee that poured out of the region's plantations, tin was part of a global commodity network that was inextricably woven into the web of industrialization and mass consumption in Europe and North America.

For all these reasons, the tin boom in colonial Southeast Asia provides a useful lens for examining the dynamic interactions between imperial power and colonized environments. It highlights the intense ecological consequences of focusing global demand for a resource onto a limited area of supply. It demonstrates the importance of re-engineering environments to suit the needs of industry and investment. Above all, it displays many of the classic characteristics of a 'commodity frontier', an advancing boundary of trade, political control, investment, and (sometimes) settlement that together reshaped environments and the ways in which people perceived and used them.[7] Like commodity frontiers in general, the tin frontier had its pioneers and latecomers, its phases of expansion and consolidation, and it tended to reward predation over prudence. Like mining frontiers more specifically, its multi-dimensional expansion—both outward across the surface landscape and downward into lower depths and grades of ore—gave it an unusually fluid character, closing and reopening in any given area as technological advances made previously unworkable deposits both physically and economically exploitable.

Yet despite these common traits, the development of Southeast Asia's tin mines also demonstrates how social, cultural, and political peculiarities shape the ecologies of resource extraction in specific times and places. If the basic economic pressures were common throughout the global mining industry, the subterranean tin frontier was also animated by contemporary ideas about race, waste, and efficiency that fundamentally structured the colonial enterprise. As this chapter will show, the story of colonial tin mining is, at base, a story about the interactions between technology, culture, and environmental change.

BREAKING NEW GROUND: THE OPENING OF THE SOUTHEAST ASIAN TIN FRONTIER

Tin is one of the oldest metals known to humankind. Used since ancient times mainly in alloy form (bronze, pewter), by the late nineteenth century it had become a crucial component of industrial civilization. Among its numerous applications,

---

[7] On commodity frontiers generally: Alf Hornborg, J. R. McNeill, and Joan Martinez-Alier (eds), *Rethinking Environmental History: World-System History and Global Environmental Change* (Lanham, Md: AltaMira, 2007); Jason W. Moore, 'Sugar and the Expansion of the Early Modern World-Economy: Commodity Frontiers, Ecological Transformation, and Industrialization', *Review*, vol. 23 (2000), 409–33.

tin played an essential role in several key sectors of industry, from textiles (mordants, dyes) to electrical and mechanical engineering (solder, bearing metal) to military armaments (gun metal). Most tin, however, was used for tinplating, or coating sheets of steel or iron with molten tin to prevent corrosion. And among the many uses of tinplate, the most significant by far was the humble tin can. Although tin cans were first widely used by the British and French armies during the Napoleonic wars, it was mainly from around the 1860s that they became an object of everyday life. By allowing producers to conserve rural food surpluses and transport them to the industrial cities—whose burgeoning populations could only be sustained by drawing vital supplies from ever-greater distances—the tin can played a mundane but critical role in processes of urbanization and industrialization in the metropoles of the global economy. As its use expanded, demand for tin skyrocketed. World production rose from 36,000 tons in 1874 to 124,000 tons in 1914. But since European reserves (mostly in Cornwall) had been largely exhausted by this time, the bulk of supplies came from overseas, primarily from Southeast Asia, with smaller amounts imported from Bolivia and Nigeria.[8]

Nearly all tin comes from its oxide ore, cassiterite (SnO_2), which occurs in two different types of deposits: underground lodes or veins (as in Cornwall and Bolivia), and shallower alluvial deposits (the dominant type in Southeast Asia). The main Southeast Asian deposits were formed by the weathering of the tin-bearing granite ranges that run along the western side of the Malay Peninsula towards the Riouw islands, which skirt the south-east coast of Sumatra. Large parts of this region are stanniferous to varying degrees, though alluvial cassiterite, like placer gold, tends to settle quickly due to its high specific gravity and is therefore concentrated in certain spots. The biggest concentrations formed the major tin fields of the region, most notably at Larut, the Kinta valley, and Kuala Lumpur in Malaya, and the islands of Bangka, Belitung, and Singkep in the East Indies (Fig. 4.1).[9]

Tin mining was not new to these areas in the colonial period; small amounts had been extracted for many centuries. As early as 1513 Portuguese traders brought tin from the Malay Peninsula back to Europe. By the mid-seventeenth century the trade was dominated by Dutch merchants, whose hold on markets was further strengthened by the discovery of tin deposits on Bangka in 1711. Nonetheless, only small amounts of 'Banka tin' ever made it to Europe during the eighteenth century due to the proximity of Cornish supplies.[10] All of this changed in the second half of the nineteenth century. As demand soared and inter-continental transport costs sank, European mines could no longer keep up. Quality was also an important factor, since tinplating firms strongly preferred alluvial 'East tin' over Cornish lode tin for its superior colour and higher purity, which allowed them to

---

[8] Ken, *Malayan Tin Industry*, 246–7; on Nigeria: Bill Freund, *Capital and Labour in the Nigerian Tin Mines* (Harlow: Longman, 1981).

[9] H. Stauffer, 'The Geology of the Netherlands Indies', in Honig and Verdoorn (eds), *Science*, 320–35; Alex L. Ter Braake, *Mining in the Netherlands East Indies* (Bulletins of the Netherlands and Netherlands Indies Council, 1944).

[10] Ken, *Malayan Tin Industry*, 3.

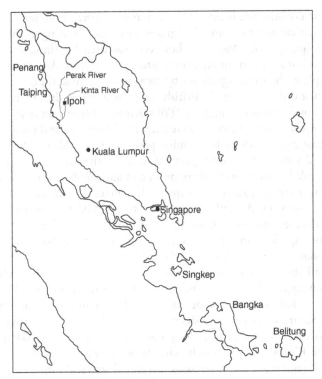

Fig. 4.1. Map covering the main tin-producing areas of colonial Southeast Asia.

achieve a thinner coating.[11] The growing scarcity of European tin deposits, along with their military significance and the lack of easy material substitutes, made Southeast Asian tin an important strategic resource. Guaranteeing a steady supply was what prompted the Dutch to rule Bangka directly from Batavia, just as the risk of disruption to the tin trade in Perak triggered the creation of the British Residency of the Federated Malay States in 1874.

Together, Bangka and Malaya marked the world's primary 'tin frontier' during the late nineteenth and early twentieth centuries. I use the term guardedly, and in full awareness of its Turnerian associations with successive waves of American pioneers creating a new civilization in the Western wilderness.[12] But leaving aside Turner's social-evolutionary logic, let alone his arguments about how it shaped the American character, the frontier concept is useful here for suggesting an interlocking set of economic, social, and cultural conditions that are either absent or less pronounced in other circumstances. As Walter Prescott Webb later formulated it, a defining characteristic of a frontier is the availability of resource 'windfalls' seemingly

---

[11] Ken, *Malayan Tin Industry*, 10.
[12] Clyde A. Milner II (ed.), *A New Significance: Re-Envisioning the History of the American West* (Oxford: Oxford University Press, 1996); William Cronon, George Miles, and Jay Gitlin (eds), *Under an Open Sky: Rethinking America's Western Past* (New York: Norton, 1992).

there for the taking.[13] These windfalls—land, wood, soil fertility, minerals—generally attract a transient population of pioneers and speculators with an instrumental attitude towards the land and with both the means and motivation to move on, thus allowing them to repeat the process of outward frontier expansion once the assets of any particular locality are exhausted. In turn, this ability to escape the consequences of one's actions, often underpinned by a weak state presence and an ideology of unending resources, imposes few social restraints against destructive behaviour, and even fewer obligations to cover the costs of depreciation—a tendency that is magnified wherever the frontier is sparsely populated or regarded as idle 'wilderness'. If one way of seeing a frontier is as a transitory boundary of settlement, trade, or technology, another is as a set of conditions that encourages short-term, extractive behaviour over other forms of land use.

Much of colonial Southeast Asia was a 'frontier' in both senses.[14] Outside the main centres of population such as Java or Bali, land was abundant and the state's power precarious. Well after the turn of the century, the bustling towns and mining camps of Malaya were still viewed as 'mere patches' in the vast expanse of forest 'that sweeps from one Sultanate to another, and is only limited by the sea'.[15] In such a seemingly endless wilderness it was relatively easy for commodity producers to move on once resources were depleted in any given area.

The early growth of the tin industry clearly exhibited these characteristics. On the Malayan Peninsula and Bangka, Malay pioneers had long mined tin via several methods. The simplest technique was panning in streams with a *dulang*, or large wooden dish. More common was the creation of a *lampan*, or ground-sluice, which essentially involved clearing the area above the would-be mine, digging a channel from a nearby stream to divert the water through a deposit, and then processing the pay dirt (*karang*) in the channel. As the light sediment washed into a tailrace, the heavy tin sand was retained by a series of small dams where it was periodically scooped out and concentrated in a sluice box (*palong*). Both methods were remarkably lucrative on unworked tin fields where the cassiterite particles were heavy enough not to be washed away. Neither, however, could tap the deeper ores just above the bedrock. To reach these deposits miners dug open pits (*lombongs*) several metres deep, usually upward into a hillside so they could wash the pay dirt in a channel below. All of these techniques were land-extensive in character; that is, miners worked the shallowest deposits and quickly moved on. They were, however, subject to fairly tight geographical constraints. Panning and ground-sluicing were only possible on slopes in close proximity to streams. Open *lombongs* could only reach deposits at a maximum depth of around 6 metres due to drainage problems, and were also dependent on streams for concentrating the pay dirt. The early Malay tin frontier was therefore largely

[13] Walter Prescott Webb, *The Great Frontier* (London: Secker & Warburg, 1953), esp. 180–202.
[14] Karl J. Pelzer, *Pioneer Settlement in the Asiatic Tropics: Studies in Land Utilization and Agricultural Colonization in Southeastern Asia* (New York: American Geographical Society, 1948); Freek Colombijn, 'The Ecological Sustainability of Frontier Societies in Eastern Sumatra', in Boomgaard, Colombijn, and Henley (eds), *Paper Landscapes*, 309–39.
[15] Sir George Maxwell, *In Malay Forests* (Edinburgh: Blackwood, 1907), 2.

limited to shallow deposits on the sides of foothills that benefited from both good drainage and good water availability.[16]

The arrival of Chinese *kongsis* (commercial syndicates fuelled by 'coolie' labour) marked a significant expansion of this frontier, both outward but more importantly downward. Appearing first on Bangka (from the late 1810s) and then in Malaya (from the late 1840s), their key innovation was to use the Chinese *chin-chia*, a traditional wooden bucket-chain mechanism driven by a water wheel, which could remove up to 3,000 gallons (13,650 litres) of water per hour and allowed miners to reach deposits 10 (and sometimes up to 25) metres deep. Apart from the lower depths it could reach, the Chinese technique was broadly similar to Malay open casting. After clearing all surface vegetation, retaining any hardwood for charcoal, and excavating the pit down to the water table, miners would divert a nearby stream to drive the water wheel and would pile the waste overburden around the mine-head to keep rainfall from running into the pit. As they burrowed into the hillside they raised the pay dirt manually, concentrated it in sluice boxes, and generally smelted the dried ore with charcoal fuel on site or at a nearby smelting house. Most of what went through the sluices ended up as waste tailings, which were simply washed downhill and deposited on the worked-out area below.[17]

In many respects the influx of Chinese miners represented a second wave of pioneers who tapped a deeper 'windfall' and moved on once it was depleted. On Bangka, their efforts made tin the third largest East Indies export by the middle of the nineteenth century. By 1900 there were around 14,000 miners on the island, the vast majority of them Chinese or *peranakan* (local-born Chinese speakers).[18] In Malaya, the number of Chinese miners in the Larut district rose from 3,000 to 40,000 between 1848 and 1872; in the Kinta valley it increased from 1,000 to 45,000 in less than a decade (1880–1889) before soaring to around 133,000 (out of a total population of *c.*185,000) by 1911, making Kinta not only the most populous and densely inhabited district in the Malay States but also the world's single largest tin field.[19]

But the Chinese tin frontier was also shaped by several key constraints. One was depth, for despite the effectiveness of Chinese open-cast methods, they grew increasingly unprofitable below 3 metres and became unsound at around 9 or 10 metres.[20] Water was another limiting factor, since the water-wheel-driven *chin-chias* depended on fairly benign rainfall conditions. The water wheels were only deployable near streams, were no use during droughts, and were not powerful enough to keep the mines dry in heavy rains. On Bangka in particular, the irregularity of

[16] Ken, *Malayan Tin Industry*, 43–7; Heidhues, *Bangka Tin*, 11–15.

[17] Heidhues, *Bangka Tin*, 37–48, 175–8; Hoong, *Development*, 19, 69–71; Ken, *Malayan Tin Industry*, 48–9.

[18] By 1920 the Bankatinwinning had over 21,000 employees, mostly Chinese; on Belitung, nearly the entire mining population was Chinese in 1920: Heidhues, *Bangka Tin*, 175–8.

[19] Wah, *Beyond the Tin Mines*, 9; Hoong, *Development*, 58–9; Salma Nasution Khoo and Abdur Razzaq-Lubis, *Kinta Valley: Pioneering Malaysia's Modern Development* (Perak Darul Ridzuan: Perak Academy, 2005).

[20] H. Zondervan, *Bangka en zijne bewoners* (Amsterdam: J. H. de Bussy, 1895), 111; see also Hendrik Merkus Lange, *Het eiland Banka en zijne aangelegenheden* (Gebr. Muller, 1850), 95f.

water supplies was considered the 'main hindrance of an increased tin production' in the late nineteenth century.[21] As one contemporary remarked, 'Bangka is rich in rivers but poor in water'; its many small, fast streams quickly emptied in the dry season.[22] The construction of reservoirs was a crucial prerequisite for working many sites on the island, but even the most extensive dam works could not guarantee adequate supplies.[23] As a result, rainfall was the main factor for determining the seasonal calendar of work. Whereas excavating was prioritized during the driest months from May to October, the rainy season from November to February was mainly reserved for washing. Water supplies also had a significant influence on overall output. Years of low production corresponded not only with low tin prices but also with years of low rainfall.[24] Although this problem was less extreme on the larger watersheds of the Malayan Peninsula, prolonged dry spells also caused mine stoppages there.[25] In short, Chinese open-cast techniques overcame only some of the constraints that had bounded the earlier mining frontier.

All of the methods on the tin frontier were highly destructive. They worked the most easily accessible surface deposits and quickly abandoned them, leaving denuded, pockmarked, and severely eroded hillsides in their wake. As the industry expanded in the late nineteenth century, some contemporaries became increasingly sensitive to the aesthetic and material costs that it entailed. 'Being full of large holes, and covered with an excavated soil of gravel and sand... such land is a great eyesore, and gives a bad impression of the country to the casual traveller,' noted a visitor to Malaya in 1904.[26] *Lampanning* was, after all, essentially a means of focusing the erosive potential of watercourses onto sloping ground that was already prone to soil wash. Moreover, the fact that it was capable of reaching only shallow ores exacerbated the damage by dotting the landscape with hundreds of derelict sites. Although the deeper open-cast mines produced more tin in relation to the surface area they destroyed, they nonetheless created gaping man-made canyons and thousands of tons of tailings with little if any regard for the after-effects of their activities (Fig. 4.2).

As production continued to rise, the forests near the mines were also severely affected. The valuable *Dipterocarp* species in the region were ideal for making charcoal, and consequently paid a heavy tribute to the smelting furnaces. 'There are certainly few mining operations that run in such cavalier fashion as the tin mines on Bangka,' remarked an East Indies medical officer in the 1870s. Neither the permanent dereliction of large areas, nor the 'ruthless devastation of the forest', nor any attempt to replant the affected woodlands was given serious

[21] Theodor Posewitz, *Die Zinninseln im Indischen Ozean II. Das Zinnerzvorkommen und die Zinngewinnung in Bangka* (Budapest: Franklin-Verein, 1886), 92.

[22] Zondervan, *Bangka*, 50–62, quote p. 50.

[23] Otto Mohnike, *Banka und Palembang nebst Mittheilungen über Sumatra im Allgemeinen* (Münster: Aschendorffs'chen Buchhandlung, 1874), 37–8; Posewitz, *Zinninseln*, 86–90.

[24] Posewitz, *Zinninseln*, 90–2.

[25] Mohnike, *Banka*, 37–8; Posewitz, *Zinninseln*, 86–92; Ooi Jin-Bee, 'Mining Landscapes of Kinta', *Malayan Journal of Tropical Geography*, vol. 4 (Jan. 1955), 1–58, here 19.

[26] John C. Willis, *A Report upon Agriculture in the Federated Malay States* (Kuala Lumpur: FMS Government Printing Press, 1904), 15.

Fig. 4.2. Yong Phin open-cast mine near Taiping, Malaya, *c.*1908.

Source: Arnold Wright, H. A. Cartwright (eds), *Twentieth-Century Impressions of British Malaya: Its History, People, Commerce, Industries, and Resources* (London: Lloyds, 1908), p. 506.

consideration.[27] As a result, by the 1890s there were already reports of wood shortages and an almost complete absence of large trees in the main mining districts. Visitors to the island noted that 'little or nothing remains of the original forest' beyond 'small islands' dispersed amidst the young secondary growth.[28] Overall, Bangka lost an estimated two-thirds of its forest between the mid-nineteenth century and the 1920s, much of it to mining operations.[29]

Similar concerns soon emerged in Malaya, first around the Larut tin mines, which had severely depleted the forests within a 20- to 30-kilometre radius by the end of the 1870s. Attempts to slow the damage—for instance, by banning inefficient smelting ovens or establishing forest reserves—were of limited effect.[30] As the frontier moved to the Kinta valley in the 1880s–1890s, the same pattern of radial deforestation repeated itself. At the turn of the century it was estimated that the Malayan mines used over half a million tons of fuel and lumber per year. Around

[27] Mohnike, *Banka*, 28–9, 45.

[28] See the overview of observations in Zondervan, *Bangka*, 69–71.

[29] Karl Helbig, 'Die Insel Bangka. Beispiel des Landschafts- und Bedeutungswandels auf Grund einer geographischen "Zufallsform"', *Deutsche Geographische Blätter*, vol. 43 nos 3/4 (1940), 137–209, here 160; Heidhues, *Bangka Tin*, 98, 108; A. M. Burn-Murdoch, 'Forests of Malaya', in Wright and Cartwright (eds), *Twentieth-Century Impressions*, 329–30. Although swidden cultivation by the indigenous Orang Gunung or Orang Darat groups had long influenced vegetation on the island, it was clear that mining accounted for most of the change: Helbig, 'Bangka', 195.

[30] Zondervan, *Bangka*, 112–13; Heidhues, *Bangka Tin*, 68; Kathirithamby-Wells, *Nature*, 62–3; Ken, *Malayan Tin Industry*, 160.

5 per cent of the 213,000 Chinese 'miners' in the Federated Malay States were, in fact, engaged solely in cutting timber.[31] Ultimately, the most important reprieve for the woodlands came not through early conservation measures but rather from the construction of coal-fired smelters on Pulau Brani island near Singapore in 1890, followed by smaller works at Butterworth and Penang.[32]

Waterways were also acutely affected as mine tailings clogged streams and eventually worked their way into the major riverine arteries. By 1885 the Larut River was so badly silted that ore could no longer be brought downriver to the coast. To bypass this problem, a new rail link was built from Port Weld (Kuala Sepetang) to Taiping, but it was not long before Port Weld also began to silt up as the tailings load carried by local rivers worked its way downstream.[33] During the Kinta valley boom of the 1890s, uncontrolled tailings emissions threatened not only the riverine environment but also the growth of the industry itself, which continued to depend on the ever-shallowing waterway for transport. The Kinta Valley Railway, completed in 1896 between Ipoh and Telok Anson on the Perak River, was explicitly built to obviate the need for navigating what was increasingly written off as a doomed river. As the 1896 Perak Annual Report unsentimentally put it, 'the competition of the Kinta River is still being felt, but should decrease as the higher part of the river becomes silted up by the operations of the miners. By special arrangement, the railway has secured the entire carriage of tin and tin-ore.'[34]

But despite all the environmental damage caused by the mines, the chief concerns for the colonial authorities were economic. Tin was a crucial source of government revenue for the Federated Malay States, Batavia, and the Palembang sultanate, and the basic problem they faced was in some ways similar to that of the wild rubber industry: namely, the growing disparity between the industrial scale of demand and primitive methods of extraction. Bangka, noted one contemporary, 'is for Holland like a hen that still lays golden eggs but which sacrifices a bit of itself with every egg, so that one can foresee a time when there is nothing left but a dead skeleton. It is therefore an imperative duty to ensure that this moment is delayed as long as possible through the most systematic, thrifty, and gentle method of exploiting the still available ores.'[35] Once it became clear that the major tin fields of the region had all been discovered (if not yet worked), the spectre of decline could only be banished by expanding the tin frontier in several directions: into deeper strata, into poorly watered areas, and above all into lower grades of ore that could not return a profit via current methods. In short, the exploration frontier had to be replaced by a frontier of technological innovation. And technology, as the 'measure of men', was to the colonial mind very much an attribute of race and culture.[36]

---

[31] Burn-Murdoch, 'Forests of Malaya', 329–30; Kathirithamby-Wells, *Nature*, 61–2.

[32] K. G. Tregonning, *Straits Tin: A Brief Account of the First Seventy-Five Years of The Straits Trading Company, Limited. 1887–1962* (Singapore: Straits Times Press, 1962), 17–25.

[33] Tregonning, *Straits Tin*, 19–20.

[34] W. H. Treacher, Resident of Perak, *Perak Annual Report* (1896), 28, quoted in Jin-Bee, 'Mining Landscapes', 22–3.

[35] Mohnike, *Banka*, 48.   [36] Adas, *Machines*.

THE INDUSTRIAL FRONTIER: MODERNIZATION, DEGRADATION, AND REMEDIATION

Calls for 'modernizing' Bangka's tin industry could already be heard in the 1850s, roughly concurrent with the start of mining operations on nearby Belitung. By the 1870s they began to mushroom amidst concerns about future production.[37] European officials were outspokenly critical of the fact that Chinese miners 'could start mines anywhere that seemed suitable to them and then quickly abandon them entirely at their own discretion'. As production rose, such practices were not only deemed 'highly disadvantageous for the ground conditions of the island' but also damaging for the industry over the long term.[38] In 1883 the first steam pumps were brought to Bangka in order to bring deeper deposits into reach, but they only became more widespread after the turn of the century.[39] In Malaya the shift towards mechanized production occurred somewhat later, above all in the wake of a new Mining Code in 1895, which was deliberately designed to encourage European investment by granting secure tenure and distributing mineral concessions in large tracts suitable only for sizeable enterprises. The aim was to make profits where older methods could not. Contemporaries estimated that *lampanning* was viable on only 2–3 per cent of a given plot. Even Chinese open-cast techniques recovered only half the available ore. Through technological innovation, so it was argued, miners could widen and deepen the tin frontier by tapping low-grade deposits and even by reopening worked-out wastelands.[40]

The problem with this line of argument was that most early attempts to modernize the tin industry were lessons in what *not* to do. Although the mines on Bangka (owned by the East Indies government) and the famous Billiton Maatschappij on Belitung (forerunner to the multinational BHP-Billiton) proved that European firms could make handsome profits, their actual operations relied almost entirely on Chinese labourers and their existing manual methods.[41] By contrast, the first wave of European miners who flocked to Malaya in the 1870s–1880s generally imported mechanized techniques from elsewhere, and nearly all were failures.[42] Rather naively, most of these entrepreneurs assumed that highly capitalized systems (with teams of surveyors, engineers, steam equipment, etc.) were inherently superior to labour-intensive methods. But as the British Resident of Perak remarked in 1893, 'after possibly a series of great hardships to the staff and disasters to the company, it is found that the tin raised is infinitesimal in value when compared with the rate of expenditure.... The company is wound up and the State gets a bad name with investors, and the only people who really enjoy

---

[37] Heidhues, *Bangka Tin*, 54, 65–6; M. F. S. Heidhues, 'Company Island: A Note on the History of Belitung', *Indonesia*, vol. 51 (Apr. 1991), 1–20.

[38] Quotes from Mohnike, *Banka*, 29.   [39] Zondervan, *Bangka*, 111.

[40] Heidhues, *Bangka Tin*, 54, 65–6; Zondervan, *Bangka*, 111; C. G. Warnford-Lock, *Mining in Malaya for Gold and Tin* (London: Crowther & Goodman, 1907), 179; Ken, *Malayan Tin Industry*, 54–8; Hoong, *Development*, 87–8.

[41] On Belitung, 92% of production was still dug by hand in 1908/9: *Gedenkboek Billiton 1852–1927* (The Hague: Nijhoff, 1927), 198.

[42] Ken, *Malayan Tin Industry*, 35–9, 46–8.

themselves are the neighbouring Chinese miners who buy the mine and plant for an old song and make several large fortunes out of working on their own ridiculous and primitive methods.'[43]

It is an intriguing remark, at once denigrating non-European techniques while conceding their commercial effectiveness. Many colonial officials found it consternating, even disconcerting, that European firms should find it so difficult to prevail over their Chinese competitors. But if this subversion of presumed civilizational hierarchies (on which more below) was one cause for concern, the main worry was that the prevailing methods of tin mining would inevitably render themselves obsolete by depleting the rich, shallow deposits within their reach. Even some Chinese operators had meanwhile reached the conclusion that 'relying upon the small workers, the yield must dwindle, for the easily treated deposits are nearing exhaustion'. Many agreed that the further expansion of the tin frontier 'depends largely upon outside capitalists and investors, to whom we look for the money to bring the deeper deposits to a producing stage with suitable mechanical processes'.[44]

But in order to attract investment it was necessary to render both the physical and commercial environment more predictable. Creating a more stable basis for investment soon became the central thrust of colonial mining policy. From the 1890s onwards the attempt to modernize the industry revolved around three main elements: new laws to facilitate concessions for large firms, the re-alienation of concessions that were left unworked, and greater control over water resources.[45] The first two measures were in effect a form of commercial discrimination against small Chinese outfits, and were followed up by ordinances against opium use, gambling, and the so-called 'truck system' (in which small operators agreed to sell ore to a creditor at a fixed price and paid their contracted labourers after the sale, often in the form of food and opium already consumed on credit).[46] The third measure sought to lure investors by precluding private monopolies of water supply and thereby making the business of resource extraction more certain.[47] But despite all of these interventions it remained difficult to attract investment, not least because it remained all but impossible to compete with Chinese *kongsis* on labour costs given their dominance of 'coolie' recruitment networks.[48] This left few options for European firms hoping to break into the industry. Ultimately, their inability to adopt capital-intensive methods due to the lack of investment, or labour-intensive methods due to the obstacles of recruitment, prompted them— much as their counterparts in the American West—to implement resource-intensive methods instead.[49]

---

[43] Frank A. Swettenham, *About Perak* (Singapore: Straits Times Press, 1893), 34.

[44] Ralph Stokes, *Malay Tin-Fields: Mining Position Broadly Reviewed* (Singapore: Straits Times Press, 1906), 36, quoting Liong Fe (owner of the large open-cast Tambun Mine).

[45] *Report and Proceedings of the Mining Conference Held at Ipoh, Perak, Federated Malay States, September 23rd to October 6th, 1901* (Taiping: Perak Government Printing Office, 1902).

[46] On the 'truck system', see Wah, *Beyond the Tin Mines*, 16–18.

[47] See Frank A. Swettenham, *British Malaya: An Account of the Origins and Progress of British Influence in Malaya* (London: Allen & Unwin, 1907), 235: 'It is impossible to over-estimate the value of this apparently simple but probably unique regulation.'

[48] Hoong, *Development*, 69–77.   [49] See Isenberg, *Mining*, 51.

The solution was hydraulic mining, a technique that targeted low-grade deposits in which the Chinese and Malay competition was uninterested. The basic method is simple. Water is collected in a reservoir at altitude and piped to the mine face where high-pressure monitors wash entire hillsides down sluices, sometimes with the aid of water- or steam-powered gravel pumps to elevate the wash-dirt onto raised chutes. Though ancient in conception, it had been perfected in the gold rushes of California and Victoria during the 1850s–1860s.[50] Despite being banned in California in 1884 due to the excessive damage it caused to local river systems, hydraulic mining was first introduced near Ipoh in 1892 and spread more widely around the turn of the century. Its crucial advantage was minimal labour input per ton of earth moved. To take one example, at the pioneering Gopeng Mine just south-east of Ipoh, water was diverted from a nearby river along a 4-km water-course and 8 km of pipe to a 2-inch (*c.*5 cm) monitor nozzle. Ten to twelve Chinese labourers broke up the mine face with the water-jet and washed the pay dirt into a nearby ditch, where some forty Malay and Tamil women panned for ore while ten more workers washed the accumulated tin sand in sluice boxes.[51] The basic technique was similar on Bangka and Belitung. Huge monitors capable of removing 50 cubic metres of earth per hour washed entire hillsides into tailraces where suction dredges (*spuitbaggers*) pumped the slurry onto raised chutes.[52] This combination of hydraulic cutting and gravel pumping made earthmoving far cheaper than ever before, costing only 13 cents per cubic yard (*c.*1.25 tons, or 0.77 cubic metres) compared to at least 61 cents by traditional open-cast techniques. Human hands could not compete. By 1916/17 hydraulicking accounted for around half of all earth moved in Belitung's mines (*c.*1.25 million cubic metres in total). In Malaya the proportion of miners in hand-dug pits fell from three-quarters in 1911–15 to only one-third by 1921–5.[53]

Hydraulicking and gravel pumping thus drove a twofold expansion of the tin frontier, first into areas located further from watercourses, and secondly into lower grades of ore. In the process, the very definition of a 'deposit' became as much a question of technological application as geological serendipity. Whereas hand-dug pits in the 1890s required a minimum of 3 lb of ore per cubic yard (*c.*1.8 kg per m^3) in order to be profitable, hydraulic mines worked deposits only one-sixth as rich, especially as prices gradually rose after 1900.[54] By 1908, it was generally agreed that 'the day when the Federated Malay States might be regarded as the happy hunting-ground for the small miner seems to have passed, and the future of the tin mining industry in the States will depend upon the economical development on a large scale of low-grade propositions'.[55]

[50] For a comparative account of these industries: David Goodman, *Gold Seeking: Victoria and California in the 1850s* (Stanford, Calif.: Stanford University Press, 1994).

[51] L. Wray, 'Some Account of the Tin Mines and the Mining Industries of Perak', *Perak Museum Notes*, vol. 2 part 2 (1898), 83–4.

[52] J. C. Mollema, *De Ontwikkeling van het Eiland Billiton en van de Billiton-Maatschappij* (The Hague: Martinus Nijhoff, 1918), 85–9.

[53] Figures from Mollema, *Ontwikkeling*, 89; Hoong, *Development*, 131, 384.

[54] Hoong, *Development*, 133.

[55] Wright and Cartwright (eds), *Twentieth-Century Impressions*, 510.

The advent of hydraulic mining thus carried considerable social costs for small operators, and its ecological costs were similarly steep. In many ways it represented what Tim LeCain has called a 'mass destruction' technique, whereby miners worked ever-lower grades of ore by shifting ever-greater burdens onto the environment.[56] As was also the case with the copper mines LeCain has studied, the key characteristic of this system was not the reduction of labour costs per se (which it also achieved), but rather a dramatic increase in throughput by means of a highly indiscriminate method of resource collection that chewed up and spat out much more than what it targeted. Contemporaries noticed the shift: 'the whole mass of the hill, rich and poor, hard and soft, is served alike; all is removed and passed through sluice boxes.'[57] As lower-grade deposits came into production, the ratio of ore to tailings shifted accordingly. For every kilogram of tin produced, five to six times more waste soil was washed away.

And where did all these tailings go? They ended up in vast 'dead zones' and ultimately in the rivers, just as in California.[58] Although local waterways had long suffered from *lampanning* and open-cast effluents, the advent of hydraulic mining greatly exacerbated the problem. As the discharge of tailings rose, especially in Perak, streams that had been 'clear as crystal' in the 1870s turned into muddy, meandering watercourses 'the colour and consistency of tomato soup'.[59] Numerous river beds were raised by several feet, some by several metres, increasing the frequency of floods and covering downstream agricultural land with sterile tailings. Among the worst affected was the Sungei Raia, a tributary of the Kinta River. Despite repeated attempts to dredge its channel and stabilize its banks, the continued deposition of sand and silt on the river plain gradually transformed a large rubber estate into a marsh of lagoons and swamp grass.[60] Large sections of the Kinta River itself (the 'River of Silt') were likewise severely affected. Whereas in 1895 it averaged between 12 and 15 feet deep (3.7–4.6 metres), by the mid-1920s the river at normal flow 'was so shallow that a matchbox could scarcely float down it', and by the 1930s the stretch near the mouths of the Sanglop and Teja Rivers presented 'as woeful a picture as any of endless swamp'.[61]

One of the most worrying upshots for colonial authorities was the increasing frequency and severity of flooding in the urban centres, especially after the 'great flood' of 1926, which inundated much of Ipoh (jokingly nicknamed the 'Malayan Venice' in the mid-1920s) and Kuala Lumpur, and which triggered major canalization and flood retention works.[62] There were even cases of mine tailings killing off

---

[56] LeCain, *Mass Destruction*, esp. 7–11.

[57] Warnford-Lock, *Mining*, 133.   [58] Isenberg, *Mining*, 30–47.

[59] Swettenham, *British Malaya*, 117; *Report by the Right Honourable W. G. A. Ormsby Gore*, 157.

[60] *Annual Report of the Drainage and Irrigation Department of the Malay States and the Straits Settlements for the Year 1937*, 86–7; Jin-Bee, 'Mining Landscapes', 35, 37.

[61] Quotes from *Annual Report of the Drainage and Irrigation Department of the Malay States and the Straits Settlements for the Year 1938*, 80; Ho Tak Ming, *Ipoh: When Tin was King* (Ipoh: Perak Academy, 2009), 461, 472.

[62] *Report of the Commission Appointed to Inquire into and Report upon Certain Matters Regarding the Rivers in the Federated Malay States* (Kuala Lumpur: Government Printing Office, 1928); Ming, *Ipoh*, 466–72.

entire settlements. Balun Bidai, a village of 2,000 paddy farmers near the mouth of the Tumboh River, gradually became a swamp in the 1900s as the river silted up. In Pahang state, the town of Bentong was threatened by mines that loaded the gorges above the Bentong River with up to 9 metres of silt and that gradually spread tailings across the entire valley below.[63] Even more dramatic was the fate of Kuala Kubu, a market town that was eventually relocated after being buried under 5 metres of tailings washed down the Selangor River from mining operations in the Peretak Hills.[64] There is also evidence that tailings damaged shad fisheries along the west coast of Malaya. Amidst declining catches around 1920, one official repeatedly 'picked up these fish by hand in a dying condition apparently choked by silt in their attempt to ascend the rivers'.[65]

Simply put, the costs of mining were passed on to others downstream. And what made the siltation problem so intractable was the difficulty of repairing the damage once it was done. Many of the worked-out sites—devoid of all topsoil and vegetation, often nothing more than exposed rock and regolith—were virtually impossible to stabilize and continued to erode at a rapid pace. On Bangka, the hundreds of washing sluices left vast flats of sterile sand where vegetation could scarcely take hold even after decades.[66] In Malaya, it was estimated in 1939 that the mines were still annually depositing 16 million tons of silt into the rivers of Perak and Selangor, much of it from abandoned sites.[67] Even after watersheds were stabilized, the silt still took decades to clear from the rivers. As a 1928 report on Malaya's rivers noted, 'today the country is faced with the problem of dealing by curative measures with a disorder, which in the nature of things is peculiarly amenable to preventive measures, and which, had adequate preventive measures been taken in the past, need never have attained very serious proportions'.[68]

By the time a new Malayan Drainage and Irrigation Department was founded in 1932 it could do little more than remedial work: dredging, channelling, and straightening watercourses into classic 'organic machines' that bore little resemblance to their previous riverine ecosystems.[69] Huge flood relief works were built for the Kinta River at Ipoh, which effectively turned a sizeable stretch of the waterway into a drainage canal. At the former site of Kuala Kubu, engineers retrained the Selangor River into a 5-km long, 30-metre wide channel that emptied into the original river bed below the abandoned old town. And while dredges on the most stricken sections of the Kinta and Larut Rivers slowly cleared the main channels,

---

[63] *Annual Report of the Drainage and Irrigation Department of the Malay States and the Straits Settlements for the Year 1937* (Kuala Lumpur: FMS, 1938), 94.

[64] Federated Malay States, *Report on the Administration of the Mines Department and on the Mining Industry*: 1914, 1920; *Annual Report of the Drainage and Irrigation Department of the Malay States and the Straits Settlements for the Year 1938*, 83; Jin-Bee, 'Mining Landscapes', 37.

[65] John G. Butcher, 'The Marine Animals of Southeast Asia: Towards a Demographic History, 1850–2000', in Peter Boomgaard, David Henley, and Manon Osseweijer (eds), *Muddied Waters: Historical and Contemporary Perspectives on Management of Forests and Fisheries in Island Southeast Asia* (Leiden: KITLV, 2005), 63–96, here 75.

[66] Helbig, 'Bangka', 195.   [67] Fermor, *Report*, 154.

[68] *Report of the Commission* (1928), 7–8.

[69] *Annual Report of the Drainage and Irrigation Department*, 1932, 1937, 1938; Richard White, *The Organic Machine: The Re-Making of the Columbia River* (New York: Hill & Wang, 1995).

a Sisyphean two-year dredging effort on the Sungei Raia only managed to lower the riverbed by less than 30 cm.[70]

These degraded mining landscapes were situated at one end of a long chain linking the kitchens and factories of the industrialized world to the forests of Southeast Asia. For many years their remote location and their indispensability for colonial coffers allowed miners to work them with scant regard for the damage they caused. On Bangka and Belitung, the quasi-official status of the industry essentially gave it a free hand. In Malaya, where early attempts to retain effluents led to 'serious friction between the Mines Department and the miners', the creation of a Tailings Commission in 1904 ultimately resulted in weak self-regulation and a lack of enforcement.[71] 'As a consequence', the Chamber of Mines later complained, 'the situation regarding the silting of rivers and water-courses which was acute in 1904 had become critical in 1914'.[72] All the same, during the First World War even these lax controls were loosened to maintain production.[73]

Yet over time, the dire effects on the region's rivers placed a new set of constraints on the industry. One limit came in the form of tighter regulation. By the 1920s and 1930s colonial governments were far more aware of such problems than they had been a generation earlier. In part this reflected the more general spread of conservationist thinking among officials, who increasingly understood their task to include both the 'development' and 'stewardship' of colonial resources. In part it also reflected hard economic interests, especially the growing power of the rubber lobby, which supported stricter mine pollution controls. In Malaya, a 1922 Control of Silt Enactment—by far the oldest such provision in the British Empire—was soon followed by a ban on hillside mining above the 250-foot contour.[74] In 1928, two years after the 'great flood' in Ipoh and Kuala Lumpur, a further enactment required explicit permission to dispose of all overburden and tailings on any given site.[75] A more fundamental constraint was the growing scarcity of exploitable deposits. By the mid-1920s engineers agreed that the hydraulic frontier had closed. There were few suitable areas left for building new reservoirs to feed the monitors, and miners had already cut down most of the workable hill sites in any event.[76] But while the soils and streams of the foothills were showing clear signs of exhaustion, world consumption of tin—and the prices it fetched—continued to

---

[70] *Annual Report of the Drainage and Irrigation Department*, 1937, 86–8.

[71] *Report on the Administration of the Mines Department and on the Mining Industry for the Year 1904*, 7.

[72] *Report of the Commission* (1928), 13–14.

[73] Imperial Mineral Resources Bureau, *The Mineral Industry of the British Empire and Foreign Countries: War Period. Tin (1913–1919)* (London: HMSO, 1922), 53; Fermor, *Report*, 165; see also 'Report of the Commission appointed to enquire into various matters affecting the tin mining industry in the FMS', in *Proceedings of the Federal Council of the FMS, 1919*, c63–c71.

[74] Sir Harold A. Tempany, *The Practice of Soil Conservation in the British Colonial Empire* (Harpenden: Commonwealth Bureau of Soil Science, 1949), 74; Jin-Bee, 'Mining Landscapes', 35–6; H. G. Harris and E. S. Willbourn, *Mining in Malaya* (London: Malayan Information Agency, 1940), 46.

[75] *Report of the Commission* (1928), 13–17.

[76] L. G. Attenborough, 'Tin Mining in Malaya', in *Empire Mining and Metallurgical Congress, Proceedings: Part II. Mining* (London: Congress, 1925), 490–514.

rise, surpassing pre-war levels by 1920 before peaking at 193,000 tons by the end of the decade.[77]

Everything pointed towards a new frontier in the lowlands, especially in swampy areas like the lower Kinta valley or Bangka's estuaries, which were known to possess tin but were unworkable via existing mining techniques. The solution, once again, was technological innovation: namely the introduction of the bucket dredge. Having already chewed up river bottoms from the Antipodes to California, the first dredges arrived in Malaya just before the First World War and systematically began eating their way across the river valleys of Perak and Bangka during the 1920s. By 1930, the hundred or so dredges operating in Malaya accounted for 30 per cent of its tin output, rising to over half by 1940.[78] They essentially combined three operations in one. A chain of buckets excavated and lifted the pay dirt, a series of jigs separated the ore from the waste, and the tailings were finally deposited at the rear, often into bunded paddocks on previously worked land.

Fuelled by copious amounts of inanimate energy, the tin dredges devoured vast swathes of low-lying alluvial land in search of the tiny (and ever-decreasing) fraction of resource that they valued. Even the early 300-horsepower dredges could lift and treat up to around 75,000 cubic metres per month, equivalent to the output of around 2,000 labourers. In the mid-1920s new models the size of apartment blocks could process up to 230,000 cubic metres per month to depths of over 30 metres. Their low operating costs—similar to the cheapest hydraulic mines—meant that ore grades as meagre as 0.4 kg per cubic metre were profitable. Like hydraulicking and gravel pumping, dredges thus extended the tin frontier in two senses. They not only opened up whole new landscapes for exploitation; they also allowed miners to work lower ore grades including even long-abandoned tailings dumps (e.g. at Larut).[79]

By utilizing a different set of land and energy resources, tin dredging opened the 'final frontier' on the wet valley floors. In addition, the different waste footprint of dredging operations took some of the pressure off erosion-prone foothills and damaged rivers. Although it would be exaggerated to claim that this was as important as economic and political considerations for inducing colonial governments to promote dredging over other methods, mitigating environmental damage did play a part, especially as the rubber industry expanded in Malaya. Dredging was, by and large, less detrimental to local hydrology. Contemporaries estimated that no more than 5 per cent of the excavated ground escaped in the form of fine slimes. Furthermore, it was centred on swampy terrain unsuited to agricultural production, and in some areas it could even ease existing drainage problems caused by mining and siltation upstream.[80]

But as is often the case, the solution for one set of problems brought new ones. Although some historians have suggested that dredging markedly reduced the

---

[77] *Minerals Yearbook 1932–3* (Washington, DC: Government Printing Office, 1933), 295.
[78] Hoong, *Development*, 126, 400.   [79] Hoong, *Development*, 133.
[80] *Report of the Commission* (1928), 139; Fermor, *Report*, 156–7; Jin-Bee, 'Mining Landscapes', 43.

ecological costs of tin mining in the region,[81] it is more accurate to say that it displaced them from the hillsides and rivers to the lowlands and coasts. For one thing, the sites themselves were demolished in the process, which mixed the ground from approximately 7 to 45 metres deep and thereby spoiled the topsoil with large amounts of infertile subsoil. Moreover, even when the finer slimes (which contained nearly all the organic matter) and coarser material were separated, the latter was often deposited on top of the former, leaving the surface effectively dead. As the dredges worked their way across valley floors, they left behind a landscape of sterile sand hummocks and miniature dunes that contemporaries regarded as 'permanently damaged'.[82] They also extended the mining footprint from terrestrial to marine environments. Bangka and Belitung soon became the world's largest offshore tin producers as dredges tore up the former alluvial river bottoms that had been inundated by rising ocean levels after the last Ice Age. Although we have no records of the damage it caused, given the indiscriminate nature of this method there can be little doubt that it devastated large areas of the sea beds around the islands, above all in the productive shallows less than 50 metres deep. Along the coasts, too, dredges slowly excavated whole new waterways that changed river and tidal flows as they chewed their way inland (Fig. 4.3).[83]

Despite repeated calls for the mandatory deposition of slimes on top of sterile sands and for stockpiling topsoil in preparation for subsequent redistribution, the failure to enact such preventive measures meant that the restoration of former mining lands, much like the repair of damaged rivers, was limited and remedial.[84] In Malaya, where rapid population growth and the expansion of rubber planting intensified the pressure for land, the Agricultural Department conducted rice growing trials on dredged sites in the 1930s, and later experimented with a variety of green dressings—especially woody shrubs of the *Mimosa* and *Crotalaria* genera—as a means of kick-starting plant succession (by contrast, former opencast or hydraulic sites were generally deemed irretrievable).[85] But despite some successes, the lack of binding regulation meant that worked-out sites were usually left infertile and derelict.[86] Once the tin frontier had encompassed a particular

[81] e.g. Headrick, *Tentacles*, 267; Ken, *Malayan Tin Industry*, 202; Donald H. McLaughlin, 'Man's Selective Attack on Ores and Minerals', in William L. Thomas (ed.), *Man's Role in Changing the Face of the Earth* (Chicago: University of Chicago Press, 1956), 851–61, here 859.

[82] Fermor, *Report*, 150; Helbig, 'Bangka', 194. Malaria was also a problem given the creation of a landscape of small artificial ponds: Mary Somers Heidhues, 'Poor Little Rich Islands: Metals in Bangka-Belitung and West Kalimantan', in Greg Bankoff and Peter Boomgaard (eds), *A History of Natural Resources in Asia: The Wealth of Nature* (Basingstoke: Palgrave, 2007), 61–79, here 71.

[83] William Robertson, *Tin: Its Production and Marketing* (London: Croom Helm, 1982), 17–18, 59, 174; Helbig, 'Bangka', 194–5.

[84] Fermor, *Report*, 157–8.

[85] F. Birkinshaw, 'Reclaiming Old Mining Land for Agriculture', *Malayan Agricultural Journal*, vol. 19 (1931), 470–6; B. A. Mitchell, 'Malayan Tin Tailings: Prospects of Rehabilitation', *Malayan Forester*, vol. 20 (1957), 181–6; see also H. N. Ridley, 'Reclaiming Abandoned Mining Lands', *Agricultural Bulletin of the Straits and Federated Malay States*, Second Series, no. 2 (1903), 63–4.

[86] *Report by Sir Frank Stockdale*, 62–3; V. M. Palaniappan, 'Ecology of Tin Tailings Areas: Plant Communities and their Succession', *Journal of Applied Ecology*, vol. 11 no. 1 (Apr. 1974), 133–50; L. H. Ang and W. M. Ho, 'Afforestation of Tin Tailings in Malaysia', Forest Research Institute Malaysia, 2002: <http://www.tucson.ars.ag.gov/isco/isco12/VolumeIII/AfforestationofTinTailings.pdf>.

Fig. 4.3. Bucket dredge on a low-lying tin-field, east of Manggar, Belitung, 1937. By permission of the Nationaal Museum van Wereldculturen, coll. no. 10007195.

site, it rarely reverted to anything resembling its former character, and in many cases the damage was too severe even to merit the label of an anthropogenic 'second nature'.[87]

Dredging was, then, another form of 'mass destruction'.[88] Like hydraulicking and gravel pumping, it expanded the tin frontier primarily at the expense of the biophysical environment. But just as with these earlier innovations, it was crucial for meeting the rising demand for tin. World production peaked in 1929 (193,000 tons) and once again between 1937 and 1941 (211,000–42,000 tons), principally thanks to output from Southeast Asia.[89] Although wartime disruption made tin one of the scarcest of the vital war materials, it remained a crucial element in numerous manufacturing processes ranging from chemicals to armaments.[90] By the Second World War dredging already accounted for around half of tin production in Southeast Asia, and after the war it became the mainstay of the industry.

---

[87] The term comes from William Cronon, *Nature's Metropolis: Chicago and the Great West* (New York: Norton, 1991).

[88] LeCain, *Mass Destruction*.

[89] *Minerals Yearbook 1932–3*, 295; *Minerals Yearbook 1941* (Washington, DC: Government Printing Office, 1943), 720. On inter-war production agreements: Hoong, *Development*, 189–263.

[90] John B. DeMille, *Strategic Minerals: A Summary of Uses, World Output, Stockpiles, Procurement* (New York: McGraw-Hill, 1947), 483.

As real energy costs fell and electrolytic techniques for thinner plating pushed tin prices downward, dredges enabled miners to process ever more minuscule percentages of ore through the ever-greater substitution of inanimate power for human energy.

RACE, WASTE, AND EFFICIENCY IN THE TIN FIELDS

The history of tin offers a particularly vivid illustration of the link between 'mass destruction' and mass consumption in the modern world. One of the basic fundaments of modern consumerism is an unprecedented ability to escape local resource limits by drawing on distant raw materials. For the industrial societies of Europe and North America, the growth of the global tin economy helped expand their ecological footprint in two ways. Directly, of course, the metal itself constituted an important material subsidy from halfway around the world, underpinning a range of vital industries and ending up in countless consumer goods. But indirectly too, it facilitated a multitude of other subsidy flows linking the industrial metropoles to their increasingly far-flung areas of supply. As one of the principal means for conserving and transporting the perishable goods that they required, the tin can quite literally fed the rise of modern consumer societies. By the late 1950s, world production of canned food reached 18 million tons. In 1962, the United States alone produced over 48 billion cans, which corresponded to around 257 per person annually.[91] Though few consumers knew it, their well-stocked cupboards were closely tied to the man-made badlands and silted rivers of Southeast Asia.

Tin was therefore a doubly important element in the globalization of consumption and imperial networks of extraction. The connections between the households of the industrial world and the subsoils of Southeast Asia typified the expanding resource frontiers and the thickening web of commodity chains during this period. This is why the tin frontier showed so many social and environmental parallels to extractive frontiers elsewhere in the world.

But if the common themes are clear enough, it is the variations that enable us to situate particular goods and industries more firmly within their historical contexts, and therefore to understand more clearly how they related to wider processes of social, cultural, and environmental change. For the specific case of tin, one such variation had to do with the nature of industrial-era mining, and in particular with the role of technological innovation as a key driver of mineral frontiers. By the early twentieth century, the mining industry at large relied progressively less on the discovery of new reserves and ever more on the ability to tap known but previously inaccessible or unprofitable deposits. In Southeast Asia as elsewhere, the progressive depletion of the richest deposits prompted miners to work declining ore grades

---

[91] Ernest S. Hedges, *Tin in Social and Economic History* (London: Arnold, 1964), 151–8; Simon Naylor, 'Spacing the Can: Empire, Modernity, and the Globalisation of Food', *Environment and Planning A*, vol. 32 (2000), 1625–39.

through greater mechanization and economies of scale.[92] Admittedly, a mineral 'reserve' is always a moving target, ever shifting in accordance with prices and methods of extraction. By this time, however, most mines had ceased to be treasure troves stumbled across by prospectors, and instead had become essentially anthropogenic sites, products of a particular constellation of closely interrelated factors: technological innovations that made mines profitable at current prices, a political system that privileged large enterprises and allowed many of the costs to be passed to the environment, and a culture broadly willing to countenance these costs in the name of 'progress'. In this sense, the mining industry epitomized frontiers of technology and investment.

Other variations were rooted mainly in socio-cultural phenomena, an understanding of which helps reduce the risk of economic tunnel vision that can sometimes plague commodity analyses.[93] The tin frontier was, like any other space, not merely a physical stage for human activity but was itself constituted by ideas and experiences, by 'mental geographies'.[94] Just as the rhetoric of 'idle lands' and profligate aborigines animated the colonization of the American West or Australian interior, perceptions of the 'waste' or 'inefficient plunder' of resources in Europe's tropical colonies both promoted and served to legitimize European dominance.[95] Viewed in this light, efforts to mechanize the tin industry reflected more than just commercial imperatives and the lure of profit (though, to be sure, there was no shortage of European-owned firms eager to work the tin sands of the region). They also mirrored the colonial ideology of the right, even duty, of Europeans to spread their mastery of nature to benighted parts of the world. Wedded to this outlook was a quasi-moral objection against permitting a resource to lie idle if it could serve human purposes. According to the sociologist Benjamin Kidd, it was imperative to avoid 'the inexpediency of allowing a great extent of territory in the richest region of the globe—that comprised within the tropics—to remain undeveloped'.[96] This same distinction between what might be called 'resource globalism' and 'resource primitivism' was equally manifest in a 1939 Malayan mining report, which asserted that anyone in control of ore deposits was 'under an onus to permit the exploitation of that mineral'.[97] As elsewhere in the tropical world, imposing industrial technology in Southeast Asia's tin fields was both a sign of European power and a means of exerting it.

Exploring these relationships between technology, culture, and power has been one of the foremost preoccupations of colonial and post-colonial historiography

---

[92] Robertson, *Tin*, 39–43.

[93] Steven Topik, 'Historicizing Commodity Chains: Five Hundred Years of the Global Coffee Commodity Chain', in Jennifer Bair (ed.), *Frontiers of Commodity Chain Research* (Palo Alto, Calif.: Stanford University Press, 2009), 37–62.

[94] Paul Carter, *The Road to Botany Bay: An Essay in Spatial History* (London: Faber, 1987).

[95] Settler complaints about the use of buffalo by Native Americans are strikingly similar to European criticisms of mining in Southeast Asia: Krech, *Ecological Indian*, 133–45.

[96] Benjamin Kidd, *Social Evolution* (London: Macmillan, 1894), 316.

[97] Fermor, *Report*, 20; on resource 'globalism' and 'primitivism', see Megan Black, 'Interior's Exterior: The State, Mining Companies, and Resource Ideologies in the Point Four Program', *Diplomatic History*, vol. 40 (2016), 81–110.

in recent years. A central leitmotif has been the concept of 'technopolitics', which has influenced work on topics ranging from colonial medicine to agricultural development. Among the many merits of this conceptual approach is its emphasis on the inextricable links—often obscured by an ideology of scientific autonomy—between control over the material and social world. As Timothy Mitchell has formulated it, technopolitics is 'a particular form of manufacturing, a certain way of organizing the amalgam of the human and nonhuman, things and ideas, so that the human, the intellectual, the realm of intentions and ideas seems to come first and to control and organize the nonhuman'.[98] Since the 1990s a vast literature has shown how the application of supposedly apolitical expertise, usually in the name of 'modernization' or 'development', carries fundamental political and social implications, even if scholars disagree on the extent of its quiet hegemonic power.[99]

Seen through this lens, the modernization of Southeast Asia's tin industry was one of many examples where the application of technical expertise, and assertions of its necessity and universal validity, served to underpin imperial power. But perhaps more than most cases, it illustrates the ways in which such expertise, far from merely parading in an 'apolitical' guise, was also overtly politicized, whether in the form of incessant complaints about superficial 'Asian' production methods or the celebration of Western miners as saviours of the industry. At one level, such evidence confirms the well-established argument that nineteenth- and early twentieth-century imperialism was animated by ideologies that measured human societies by their technical achievements.[100] But to take this argument a step further, the evolution of the tin industry also suggests that it was not just 'machines' and technical rationality per se that were regarded as the 'measure of men', but more generally the degree to which human communities were able to control the physical environment and extract wealth from it.

What was ultimately being judged in evaluations of different mining processes was not so much their level of mechanization as their level of 'efficiency'. We can get a broad sense of what this concept meant from Kidd's 1898 treatise on *The Control of the Tropics*, which declared that 'the last thing our civilisation is likely to permanently tolerate is the wasting of the resources of the richest regions of the earth through the lack of the elementary qualities of social efficiency in the races possessing them'.[101] Efficiency, in this scenario, denoted not only a superior organizational and technical aptitude but also a deeper knowledge of the natural world that permitted an appreciation of the full bounty it offered for human design— provided that design be good enough.

Such ideas were deeply engrained in the imperial project, and what made them so compelling was that they linked colonial authority not only with technological prowess but also with contemporary notions of race and environment. In the particular context of Southeast Asia's tin fields, Malays were seen to lack both of

---

[98] Mitchell, *Rule of Experts*, 42–3.

[99] Seminal works besides Mitchell include: Ferguson, *Anti-Politics Machine*; Bruno Latour, *We Have Never Been Modern*, trans. Catherine Porter (Cambridge, Mass.: Harvard University Press, 1993); Escobar, *Encountering Development*; Cooper and Packard (eds), *International Development*.

[100] Adas, *Machines*.   [101] Kidd, *Control of the Tropics*, 96–7.

the above elements of 'efficiency'. Regarded by colonial observers as 'an indolent, contented, thriftless, unambitious, polite and peaceful race', they supposedly possessed neither the urge nor the know-how to capitalize fully on the assets that lay under their feet.[102] By comparison, Chinese miners were seen to have the former trait but not the latter: though industrious and commercially astute, their technical capabilities confined them to rich, shallow deposits.[103] Only the colonizers purportedly had both the motivation and ability to maximize the extraction of available resources, and this tendency to associate race and technology was magnified by the close structural correspondence between the ethnic ownership of a mine and the techniques it deployed. By the turn of the century colonial administrations made no bones about deliberately promoting Western mining enterprise, though it was unclear whether the various mining codes, prohibitions on the 'truck system', and increasing size of concessionary plots merely amounted to or were specifically intended as a form of racial discrimination.[104]

These ideological hierarchies of efficiency and waste clearly framed contemporary perceptions of Southeast Asia's tin fields. As we have seen above, in certain ways they also helped to promote the specific policy of modernization via Western mining techniques, particularly as European entrepreneurs turned to hydraulicking and gravel pumping in order to break into the hitherto Chinese-dominated industry. When European hydraulic miners faced the prospect of tighter environmental regulations, they repeatedly cited the 'thoroughness' and 'economy' of these methods in order to counter what they saw as 'a persistent prejudice against monitor workings on the assumption that they cause immense damage'.[105] The real damage, they contended, resulted from Asian methods that did not exhaust the ground before moving elsewhere. As one hydraulic mine manager boasted in 1905, 'the most striking feature of mining affairs at present is the losing of ground by the wasteful Chinese miner, who has practically picked the eyes out of the country, and the advance of the White miner, who is making excellent profits out of ground the Chinese could not touch'.[106] The fact that Chinese miners were not slow to adopt the hydraulic monitor and gravel pump did little to undermine these racialized claims to superiority, and if anything was taken as confirmation of Europe's technological trailblazing and the benefits it brought to subject peoples. Indeed, many of the same assumptions framed the subsequent advent of dredging, which was celebrated for performing a kind of racial role reversal in the working of low-grade ores. 'It had always been the case in alluvial working, whether in California or Australia, that the patient Chinaman could come after the hasty European and obtain a living from what the European had left,' noted one engineer in the mid-1920s. The fact that 'dredging now took place in considerable part upon areas already worked and left by the Chinaman' provided 'a comfort more grateful than cocoa, and a stimulation greater than that of wine'.[107]

[102] *Notes on Perak, With a Sketch of its Vegetable, Animal and Mineral Products* (London: William Clowes, 1886), 10.

[103] Zondervan, *Bangka*, 111.   [104] Hoong, *Development*, 151.

[105] *Report and Proceedings of the Mining Conference Held at Ipoh*, 19.

[106] Stokes, *Malay Tin-Fields*, 36.   [107] *Empire Mining and Metallurgical Congress*, 523–4.

These examples illustrate an important point: despite the vast amounts of waste material they produced, hydraulicking and dredging were not considered wasteful. On the contrary, they represented the pinnacle of 'efficiency' by coaxing profits from even marginal grades of ore. What counted as profligate in the economic culture of colonialism was not the systematic destruction of entire hills, rivers, and valley floors for low-grade ore, but rather the inability to make meagre deposits pay—to allow them to run 'largely to waste under the management of races of low social efficiency'.[108] If waste therefore denoted a failure to convert a potential resource into cash, then efficiency represented a maximization of output regardless of the collateral effects. A survey of the Malayan industry summed up the matter as follows: 'efficiency of mining really means the degree of completeness attained by the miner in recovering the mineral from the ground that has been leased to him'.[109] The only thing that truly counted was profitability in relation to current world prices, including transport, fuel, and all other costs. The 'mass destruction' technologies that European firms introduced in the region worked because the costs were shifted to the environment, which did not have a column on the balance sheet.

Obvious though it may seem, it is worth emphasizing that these definitions of waste and efficiency were markedly different from—even diametrically opposed to—those that have informed more recent critiques of pioneer profligacy and 'frontier economics'. The core issue at the time was not whether natural resources were used sparingly but whether they were exploited thoroughly. This meant that, ironically, the 'waste' of untouched ore in the ground represented a greater transgression than laying waste to an entire mountain or watershed in the pursuit of low-grade ore. And what permitted the maximal extraction of the targeted resource was of course the active utilization of other natural resources—above all fossil fuels and hydrological power—that could be harnessed to this endeavour. Tapping nature's energy flows to capitalize fully on the other gifts of nature thus gave this particular brand of efficiency a double environmental dimension, though neither entered its cost calculation.

As some contemporaries noted, this narrow method of accounting was hardly unique to tin mining, or even mining at large, but increasingly characterized economic thinking in general during this period.[110] 'We have lived so long in what we have regarded as an expanding world, that we reject in our contemporary theories of economics and of population the realities which contradict such views,' remarked Carl Sauer in 1938. 'Economics unfortunately has become restricted increasingly to money economics, instead of embracing the study of *Wirtschaften*, and largely has missed this ominous fact.'[111] John Maynard Keynes likewise criticized the obsession with 'the financial results' for turning the entire conduct of life 'into a sort of parody of an accountant's nightmare.... We destroy the beauty of the countryside because

---

[108] Kidd, *Social Evolution*, 316.
[109] Fermor, *Report*, 115.   [110] LeCain, *Mass Destruction*, 212–16.
[111] Carl Sauer, 'Destructive Exploitation in Modern Colonial Expansion', in *Comptes rendus du Congrès International de Géographie Amsterdam 1938*, vol. 2, IIIc (Leiden: Brill, 1938), 494–9, here 494.

the unappropriated splendors of nature have no economic value. We are capable of shutting off the sun and the stars because they do not pay a dividend.'[112]

The expansion of the tin frontier in Southeast Asia clearly exemplified central elements of this broader economic culture. It also reflected distinctively imperialist ideas about race, technology, and efficiency that served to justify colonial power. If the main drivers of change were economic and material pressures common across much of the global mining industry—above all declining ore percentages and a corresponding need for economies of scale—the attitudes and values that framed these processes nonetheless provided an important ideological support. The colonial claim of bringing Europe's mastery of nature to the 'underused' resources of the tropical world not only abetted the entry of mechanized Western firms into the industry, it also condoned, even encouraged, the deployment of techniques more wasteful, by other criteria, than what they replaced.

The imperial tin frontier left a broad and enduring imprint on the lands it touched. During the late nineteenth and early twentieth centuries it played a central role in the construction of modern infrastructure across large parts of the region, from railways and roads to dams and waterworks. The hunger for goods, services, and energy to fuel the mining industry spurred a range of supporting activities, from logging and smelting to electrification—including Malaya's first hydroelectric plant, a 27-megawatt installation on the Perak River, which was the biggest civil engineering project in all of Southeast Asia in the late 1920s. As a leading source of export revenue for Malaysia and Indonesia, the tin mines also underwrote the rise of new secondary industries and served as an engine of economic growth long after independence. The social, economic, and ecological consequences of colonial tin production reached far beyond the mines themselves, and they lasted long after decolonization.

The most acute effects were felt in the tin fields and their nearby surroundings, especially those located downstream. From the 1860s onward the relentless quest for cassiterite denuded foothills, eroded soils, clogged rivers, and finally churned terrain across the wet lowlands. On the islands of Bangka and Belitung, it was noted by 1940 that 'not a single landscape has remained unchanged by the tin economy'. No other part of the Indonesian archipelago had witnessed such radical change, 'neither the coal finds on Sumatra, Borneo and Pulau, asphalt on Buton, ... not even petroleum on Sumatra, Java, Borneo and Tarakan have caused the same degree of equilibrium disruption through transformation of the landscape'.[113] Even in the twenty-first century the islands still serve as symbols of resource imperialism and industrial-scale devastation in the tropics.[114]

In Malaysia too, the eerie moonscapes fringing the Kinta and Klang valleys still bear witness to the destruction caused by the tin mines. Many of these sites remain

[112] John Maynard Keynes, 'National Self-Sufficiency', *The Yale Review*, vol. 22 no. 4 (June 1933), 755–69.

[113] Quotes from Helbig, 'Bangka', 192–3, 204.

[114] See e.g. the Friends of the Earth campaign to mitigate the effects of tin mining on Bangka: <http://www.foe.co.uk/sites/default/files/downloads/tin_mining.pdf> (accessed July 2016).

completely devoid of vegetation and continue to afflict nearby rivers. Studies in the 1990s still confirmed rapid erosion rates from abandoned mining lands. Sediment loads on tributaries of the Klang River increased almost fivefold as they ran through former mining sites, whose sediment yields were over eighteen times higher than disturbed forest catchments.[115] Even at the start of the twenty-first century it was estimated that only 9.7 per cent of ex-mining land had been reclaimed, and most of this area was earmarked for housing and industry rather than agriculture or forestry.[116] Although the handful of underground lode mines on the Malay Peninsula left fewer surface traces than the alluvial tin fields, they too bequeathed a troublesome inheritance. Tailings wastes from the British-run Sungei Lembing mine in Pahang—for many decades the world's largest and longest underground tin mine, comprising 322 kilometres of tunnels—still contaminate surrounding waterways with arsenic, lead, and acid drainage some forty years after operations were wound down.[117]

But the colonial tin boom left other legacies as well, for it also spurred a range of efforts—effluent regulations, forest reservation, river conservancy, agricultural reclamation—to limit or reverse the damage it caused. In part these initiatives were motivated by mounting conservationist concern about 'the cost of a scarred countryside'.[118] To some extent they also emerged within the mining industry itself, at least insofar as the danger of resource depletion and externally imposed pollution regulations threatened profits and production. Together, these partly overlapping, partly conflicting impulses gave rise to a body of environmental legislation that long outlived colonial rule, especially with regard to river protection. Over the long term the resulting legal provisions significantly reduced tailings discharge from mining operations, which once again showed that many of the worst environmental consequences of tin mining could have been avoided in the first place through tighter regulation. But as beneficial as such conservationist measures were, they were still vastly outweighed by the desire to exploit Southeast Asia's mineral resources. Profits generally came before prudence, and for the most part conservationist regulation could only make substantial headway once the costs of environmental degradation threatened the prospects for the industry itself or the interests of other powerful groups downstream, not least the plantation lobby.

Ultimately, the wealth generated by the tin industry, and the convenience it offered food shoppers in the industrial world, were an exercise in spatial and temporal displacement. Like so many industries of the nineteenth and twentieth centuries,

---

[115] G. Balamurugan, 'Tin Mining and Sediment Supply in Peninsular Malaysia with Special Reference to the Kelang River Basin', *The Environmentalist*, vol. 11 no. 4 (1991), 281–91; C. P. Lee and E. B. Yeap, 'Reclamation after Tin Mining in Malaysia', in Ming H. Wong and Anthony D. Bradshaw (eds), *The Restoration and Management of Derelict Land: Modern Approaches* (Singapore: World Scientific Publishing, 2002), 211–22.

[116] Ang and Ho, 'Afforestation of Tin Tailings in Malaysia'.

[117] Fares Yahya Alshaebi, 'Risk Assessment at Abandoned Tin Mine In Sungai Lembing, Pahang, Malaysia', *The Electronic Journal of Geotechnical Engineering*, vol. 14 (2009), bundle E:9, 2–3.

[118] 'Rationing the Ever-hungry Dredges', *Straits Times*, 15 Nov. 1937, cited in Kathirithamby-Wells, *Nature*, 154.

it not only depleted nature's capital by exploiting a subsidy from afar, it also spread the costs far into the future. A whole host of factors encouraged this process of transposition. One was the 'distancing' effect of long commodity chains, which insulates end-users from the consequences of extraction and makes the costs largely invisible. Consumers at the end of the chain had little if any inkling of where the tin in their cans originated, let alone what was sacrificed in the process. Another factor was the semi-transient character of the mining population itself, most of them Chinese or Europeans who were there to make money and then leave, and who tended to treat the land as a disposable resource. Still another reason was the importance of mining for the regional economy. In Malaysia and Indonesia alike, the problems of erosion, river pollution, and deforestation were broadly regarded as the acceptable costs of revenue generation for the state, of profits for investors, and of jobs and income creation (at least until the opening of low-cost Brazilian mines sent world tin prices tumbling in the mid-1980s).[119] From this perspective, the transformation of vast swathes of rainforest into anthropogenic badlands was not just the product of short-sighted plunder, but was rather quite systematic and deliberate. It was all part of the modern urge to make nature more legible and to regularize the flow of resources and profits that it generated.

The story of the colonial tin industry thus displayed many attributes that were common to resource frontiers in other times and places. In the beginning, the availability of a lucrative windfall attracted successive groups of entrepreneurs who serially depleted the most easily accessible resources. Before long, production could only be sustained through greater investment and new technologies of extraction: in Webb's terminology the 'secondary windfalls' of the frontier.[120] As the boom continued—driven, as so often, by an alliance of private and government interests keen to collect the resource rent of the territories they controlled—it radically transformed the landscape. Eventually the despoliation of what had previously been regarded as pristine wilderness prompted a significant conservationist response, though it nearly always lagged far behind the pace of exploitation. In all of these respects the story of Southeast Asian tin shows remarkable parallels to processes of environmental change on other resource frontiers.

Yet as this chapter has shown, the particular constellation of social, political, and technological factors that shaped the tin industry also gave it a distinctive dynamic. Compared to the growth of Southeast Asia's cash-crop industries—such as pepper, gambier, and eventually rubber—the mining frontier was peculiarly mutable and provisional. Long after the region's mineral wealth had been explored and surveyed, the frontier of production continued to advance in a series of steps as new technologies opened up ever-deeper deposits, ever-lower grades of ore, and whole new types of terrain to commercial exploitation. Of course, all resource frontiers are moulded by the technologies that enable human extraction, but the deployment of new techniques and new sources of energy loomed larger for the tin industry

---

[119] See esp. Khoo and Razzaq-Lubis, *Kinta Valley*.
[120] Webb, *Great Frontier*, 182–91.

than for the leading agricultural commodities of the region, even those, such as sugar and rubber, which were objects of extensive research.[121]

Such frontiers of technology were critical to the growth of mineral production in many parts of the world, but they possessed a special symbolic importance in colonial settings. Throughout much of the tropical world, technological innovation was more than just a means of extracting resources from colonized territory (though it certainly was this). It also served to reinforce the racial and cultural hierarchies that furnished the very scaffolding of the colonial project. In territories where large-scale European settlement was never on the agenda, the assertion of superior knowledge and technical ability was the chief justification for the European presence. And in an ideological context in which a people's level of 'civilization' and 'social evolution' was largely defined by its mastery of the biophysical environment, there was every incentive to view the methods of 'less advanced races' as wasteful and improvident, just as there was every reason to contrast them with the supposed efficiency of privileged European technologies that were, at least by some measures, even more profligate and indiscriminate in their collateral effects.

The expansion of the subterranean tin frontier thus highlights the fundamental interaction of the cultural and the material, of ideas and economics, in processes of environmental change. If the technical evolution of the colonial tin industry was driven primarily by commercial expediency, the broader ecology of the tin frontier was also shaped by an asserted cultural and racial superiority that powered and legitimized the colonial enterprise.

---

[121] For research on rubber, see Chapter 3. On sugar: Wim Van der Schoor, 'Pure Science and Colonial Agriculture: The Case of the Private Java Sugar Experimental Stations (1885–1940)', in: Chatelin and Bonneuil (eds), *Nature*, 13–20; Headrick, *Tentacles*, 237–48.

5

Peripheral Centres
Copper Mining and Colonized
Environments in Central Africa

'For the Congo, as for most of the rest of Africa, one must count above all on mining as the chief means of developing the country.'[1] Anyone aware of the enormous foreign investments that have been ploughed into Central Africa's mineral industries since the early 2000s would be forgiven for assuming that this quote derived from a recent newspaper. In fact it was written in 1932, and even then the idea that mining was the key to development in Central Africa was nothing new. Ever since the scramble for colonial territory in the late nineteenth century, dreams of tapping the potentially enormous mineral wealth of the African interior drew a growing number of explorers, prospectors, and engineers into the region. Throughout the entire colonial period, mining accounted for the vast bulk of metropolitan investment in Africa. More clearly even than in Southeast Asia, whose world-leading tin industry was eventually eclipsed by its vast rubber estates, mining profoundly transformed the social, economic, and biophysical environment in many parts of the continent. All across colonial Africa, mineral production stimulated trade, expanded the cash economy, and spurred the construction of communications infrastructure. In the process, it also integrated entire regions into the increasingly globalized flow of natural resources.

For those areas fortunate (or unfortunate) enough to possess metallic ores of sufficient quality and quantity to attract outside attention, the impact of large mining booms was often dramatic. Many parts of Africa were indelibly shaped by mineral discoveries, from the goldfields of West Africa to the diamond mines of Kimberley.[2] A particularly striking example was the copper mining region of Central Africa, which became the site of one of the most rapid and concentrated industrialization processes in the entire colonial world. Within the span of three decades, the Katanga region of southern Congo and the adjoining Copperbelt of Northern Rhodesia were transformed from sparsely populated hinterlands into what many regarded as a model of industrial progress and colonial development.

---

[1] Maurice Robert, *Le Centre africain: le domaine minier et la cuvette congolaise* (Brussels: Lamertin, 1932), 15.

[2] Raymond E. Dumett, *El Dorado in West Africa: The Gold-Mining Frontier, African Labor, and Colonial Capitalism in the Gold Coast, 1875–1900* (Athens, Oh.: Ohio University Press, 1998); Robert Vicat Turrell, *Capital and Labour on the Kimberley Diamond Fields 1871–1890* (Cambridge: Cambridge University Press, 1987).

It all began shortly after the turn of the century as Belgian and British mining interests built a fledgling mineral industry around the town of Élisabethville (now Lubumbashi), which soon spread north-west towards Kambove. During the late 1920s a second copper frontier opened along the nearby headwaters of the upper Kafue River in Northern Rhodesia, where British and American mining interests raced to build a string of competing mines. Together, the growth of these two mining clusters created a vast industrial complex in the heart of colonial Africa.

Both the scale and the pace of these changes were astonishing—so much so, in the words of one observer, as to conjure 'something of the suddenness and ruthlessness and irresistibility, on the social plane, of what, on the military plane, we have become familiar with as the German "Blitzkrieg"'.[3] By the inter-war years the region was among the world's leading producers of copper, one of the most vital natural elements of modern industry. From the 1930s through the 1950s the combined output from the Congo/Rhodesian copper fields represented around one-fifth to one-quarter of world copper production, rising from 400,000 metric tons in 1937 to just under 1 million tons in 1960. Although overall output was still exceeded by that of the United States, the world's leading copper producer, the fact that scarcely any of Central Africa's copper was used domestically meant that it was by far the biggest exporter.[4] The vast bulk of African copper was shipped to Europe, where manufacturers converted it into countless electrical gadgets and millions of kilometres of wire for delivering the electricity on which they ran. In a classic example of colonial extraction, African copper electrified metropolitan Europe (Fig. 5.1).

The production of such enormous amounts of copper brought wrenching social and environmental changes for the region, which are best captured by considering them on two different spatial scales. On one level was the remaking of the immediate mining vicinities in order to gain access to the ore deposits, to accommodate the armies of labourers that worked them, and to absorb the wastes of extraction and processing. These acute, proximal changes—from smokestacks and slagheaps to re-routed rivers—were the primary focus of the mining firms and their engineers. Just as in Southeast Asia's tin fields, such modifications reflected the ways in which the rising demand for resources in the industrial world focused much of the environmental damage on particular areas of supply. The other scale of transformation was more diffuse and far-reaching, and represented what we nowadays call the wider 'footprint' of the mining complexes. As the mines drew in resources and labour from an increasingly wide radius, they generated a markedly exploitative relationship with their own hinterlands.

In many respects the industrial centres of Katanga and the Copperbelt functioned as nodes of 'environmental sub-imperialism' within Central Africa; that is, they reproduced at the regional level a miniature version of the global asymmetry of

[3] A. Sandilands, in the preface to R. J. B. Moore, *These African Copper Miners: A Study of the Industrial Revolution in Northern Rhodesia, with Principal Reference to the Copper Mining Industry* (London: Livingstone, 1948), ix.

[4] *Minerals Yearbook 1940* (Washington, DC: Government Printing Office, 1941), 98; *Minerals Yearbook 1960* (Washington, DC: Government Printing Office, 1961), 431–2.

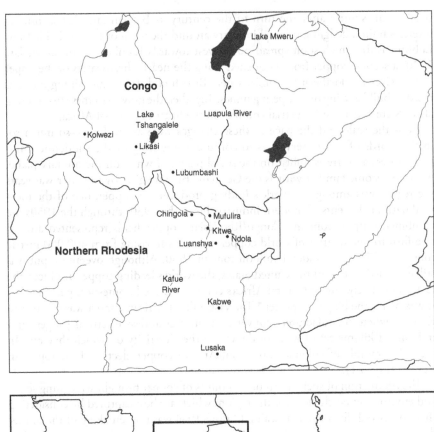

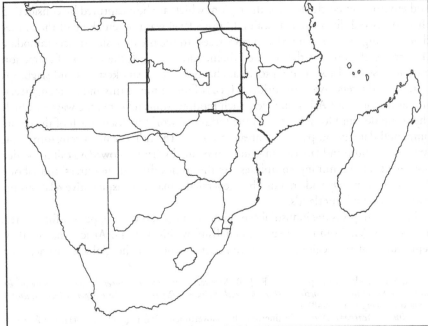

Fig. 5.1. Map of the Copperbelt and Katanga.

resource flows in which they were themselves firmly entrenched.[5] The common denominator that spanned these different spatial scales was, in world systems terminology, the principle of unequal ecological exchange.[6] The mining towns of Central Africa extracted far more from the countryside than they gave back, just as European manufacturers and consumers reaped most of the benefits of the African copper that was shipped out from the mining towns. On both the regional and global levels, nature's wealth was concentrated by funnelling resources from poorer areas to richer ones and by sending many of the environmental and social costs in the opposite direction.

These wider ripple effects, though less spectacular than the transformation of the mining sites themselves, were every bit as important for our purposes here, for they highlight the close interconnections between the technological systems created by human hand and the biophysical systems in which they were inevitably embedded. These connections have often remained under-appreciated in the scholarship on colonial mineral extraction, which has tended to view the (usually) foreign-owned mining operations as archetypal 'economic enclaves' more closely integrated with distant metropolitan markets than with nearby local economies. Although recent work has sought to bridge this dichotomy by emphasizing the many knock-on effects of large-scale mining, it nonetheless confirms the view that the 'Blitzkrieg' of industrialization in Central Africa ultimately remained limited and shallow.[7] In socio-economic terms, there is little doubt that the mining hubs of Katanga and the Copperbelt remained islands of a rather superficial process of industrial modernization. But in ecological terms, the consequences were both far-reaching and long-lasting. If there is one thing that ecology teaches us, it is that nothing is an enclave unto itself. As the story of copper in colonial Africa shows, this certainly applies to the conspicuously 'unnatural' landscapes designed and engineered by modern heavy industry.

CREATING A COLONIAL COPPER INDUSTRY

By the time the colonial powers had pushed their way into Central Africa, copper was already a key element of industrial civilization. If the age of steam had been built on

---

[5] On 'sub-imperialism': Marshall Johnson and Fred Y. L. Chiu (eds), *Subimperialism*, special issue of *Positions: East Asia Cultures Critique*, vol. 8 no. 1 (Spring 2000), esp. 1–7; Ray Mauro Marini, 'Brazilian Sub-Imperialism', *Monthly Review*, vol. 23 no. 9 (1972), 14–24; Jonathan Curry-Machado, '"Rich Flames and Hired Tears": Sugar, Sub-imperial Agents and the Cuban Phoenix of Empire', *Journal of Global History*, vol. 4 (2009), 33–56, esp. 34–6; Patrick Bond, 'Sub-imperialism as Lubricant of Neoliberalism: South African "Deputy Sheriff" Duty within BRICS', *Third World Quarterly*, vol. 34 no. 2 (2013), 251–71.

[6] See John Bellamy Foster, Brett Clark, and Richard York, *The Ecological Rift: Capitalism's War on the Earth* (New York: Monthly Review Press, 2010); J. W. Moore, 'Environmental Crises and the Metabolic Rift in World-Historical Perspective', *Organization & Environment*, vol. 13 (2000), 123–57.

[7] James Ferguson, *Expectations of Modernity: Myths and Meanings of Urban Life on the Zambian Copperbelt* (Berkeley: University of California Press, 1999), 1–14; on the continued 'enclave' status of the industry, Ray Bush, 'Conclusion: Mining, Dispossession, and Transformation in Africa', in Alastair Fraser and Miles Larmer (eds), *Zambia, Mining, and Neoliberalism: Boom and Bust on the Globalized Copperbelt* (New York: Palgrave, 2010), 237–68, esp. 252–5.

iron, many of the technologies that defined the 'second industrial revolution'—new alloys, telegraph communications, and above all electricity—had copper at their core. Up to the 1950s (when it was overtaken by aluminium), copper was the second most widely used metal behind iron. Over the first half of the nineteenth century global copper consumption grew from 9,000 to 40,000 tons. After that it rose exponentially to around 500,000 tons in 1900, 979,000 in 1913, and almost 1.4 million tons in 1918. The bulk of this copper was used in the industrial heartlands of Central and Western Europe. Germany alone consumed over one-quarter of world production on the eve of the First World War, followed closely by Britain and France. The rest was mostly used in the United States, which accounted for around one-third of copper consumption at the time.[8] But whereas the United States could rely almost entirely on its own supplies, European deposits were far too small to meet the needs of its industries. During the nineteenth century European manufacturers drew much of their copper from Chile, the world's leading producer at the time, and from 1900 to 1920 large amounts were also imported from the United States. This heavy foreign dependence for a key raw material made the acquisition of copper from colonial possessions an extremely appealing prospect.[9]

The lure of copper riches numbered among the chief attractions that drew European entrepreneurs into Central Africa in the late nineteenth century. After all, copper had been mined and smelted in Katanga for many generations, and was an important item of exchange from the shores of Angola to the Arab-dominated ports on the East African coast.[10] Tales of vast mineral deposits worked by African chiefs had long filtered out of the bush, and in the wake of the gold and diamond discoveries in South Africa, many European observers began to dream of a 'second Rand' in the heart of the continent. It took around a decade for early prospectors to determine the extent and likely profitability of these deposits. In 1892–3, the Belgian geologist Jules Cornet found extensive evidence of copper ore in Katanga but was sceptical about its commercial potential given the remoteness of the region. From 1895 to 1899 prospectors working for Cecil Rhodes's British South Africa Company confirmed the existence of a major copper field in the 'hook' of the Kafue River in Northern Rhodesia. Soon afterwards Robert Williams, the director of Tanganyika Concessions (a BSA affiliate), secured from Belgium's King Léopold the exclusive rights to prospect over 150,000 square kilometres of the upper Congo basin in exchange for a 60 per cent Belgian share in any mines that resulted.

The crucial turning point came in 1902, when an expedition led by George Grey discovered a huge string of deposits stretching from the Star of Congo site (near what was to become Élisabethville) westward through Kambove to Kolwezi. As investor confidence rose, a trio of companies was established to facilitate the industrialization of the southern Congo: the Société Internationale Forestière et

---

[8] Imperial Mineral Resources Bureau, *The Mineral Industry of the British Empire and Foreign Countries: War Period. Copper (1913–1919)* (London: HMSO, 1922), 8–10.

[9] Grunwald and Musgrove, *Natural Resources*, 155–6.

[10] Eugenia W. Herbert, *Red Gold of Africa: Copper in Precolonial History and Culture* (Madison, Wis.: University of Wisconsin Press, 1984).

Minière (Forminière), the Compagnie du Chemin de Fer du Bas-Congo au Katanga, and most importantly, the Union Minière du Haut-Katanga (UMHK), a joint venture launched by the parastatal Comité Spécial du Katanga, Tanganyika Concessions, and the Société Générale, Belgium's largest holding company. UMHK eventually became one of the biggest mining firms in the entire world, and enjoyed an overwhelming influence on the administration of Katanga throughout the colonial period. After the takeover of the colony by the Belgian government in 1908, which triggered a further wave of metropolitan investment, the final piece of the puzzle was transport. The closest railway was at Broken Hill (Kabwe) in Northern Rhodesia, where a lead and zinc mine had opened in 1906. In September 1910 the line was extended to Élisabethville, the administrative headquarters of Katanga.[11]

For the next two decades, upper Katanga was the chief target of mining investment in Central Africa. Although most of the Northern Rhodesian deposits were known by 1910, it was only in the 1920s, once Katanga's mineral wealth had been comprehensively surveyed, that large-scale mining interests began to focus on the southern side of the Congo/Rhodesian border. The slow pace of expansion into Rhodesia was due not least to the sheer size of the Katangan ore bodies, which were among the largest deposits ever discovered (an estimated 10 million tons at Star of Congo and Kambove alone). Early engineering reports spoke of 'a quantity of minerals that one can practically consider inexhaustible'.[12] Furthermore, these deposits—most of them oxides, above all malachite ($Cu_2CO_3(OH)_2$)—ranged from around 6 to 23 per cent pure copper, an extraordinarily rich grade that yielded correspondingly high profits despite the long rail journey to ports in South Africa. Best of all, they were found near the surface in low hills that rose above the surrounding plateau and were easily accessible via open-cast techniques (unlike most of the deposits on the Rhodesian Copperbelt, which demanded underground mining).

Such propitious circumstances allowed for the rapid development of the industry. Within months of the railway's arrival in Élisabethville the UMHK installed its first water-jacket furnace, replete with a 48-metre smokestack. Three more ovens were built by 1913, a further four in 1914, and by 1917 the Élisabethville smelters treated over 220,000 tons of ore yielding 26,000 tons of refined copper.[13] This early smelting plant formed the core of the region's industrial complex, and was specifically designed to process the highest-grade (>14 per cent) ores directly from the pits without any intermediate concentration. But as the richest deposits were progressively depleted—not least due to the booming demand caused by the First World War—UMHK opened a concentrator plant in 1921 on the Panda River at

[11] S. E. Katzenellenbogen, *Railways and the Copper Mines of Katanga* (Oxford: Clarendon Press, 1973), 29–35, 61–72; more generally Jean-Luc Vellut, 'Hégémonies en construction: articulations entre état et entreprises dans le bloc colonial belge (1908–1960)', *Canadian Journal of African Studies/ Revue canadienne des études africaines*, vol. 16 no. 2 (1982), 313–30.

[12] M. H. Buttgenbach, *Les Mines du Katanga* (Brussels: A. Lesigne, 1908), 12.

[13] *Union Minière du Haut-Katanga: 1906–1956* (Brussels: Cuypers, 1956), 101; *Union Minière du Haut-Katanga: évolution des techniques et des activités sociales* (Brussels: Cuypers, 1957), 123–5.

Jadotville (now Likasi) to enrich the lower-grade (6–10 per cent) ores from the surrounding western deposits in preparation for smelting at Élisabethville. Whereas the Panda plant initially recovered around half of the copper from the ore, by the late 1920s it was equipped with the newest oil flotation concentrators that recovered up to 90 per cent. In 1929 it processed over 1 million tons of ore and yielded 215,000 tons of concentrate, most of which was now sent to a new reverberatory furnace at Jadotville, which was capable of churning out 60,000 tons of copper per year.[14]

The final product from the smelters—once the solid slag was removed and various waste gases burned off—was 'blister copper' of around 99 per cent purity, so called due to its blistered appearance from forcing air through the molten matte. Although blister copper is used for various metallurgical and chemical processes, it cannot be employed for electrical applications, which requires purity levels in excess of 99.9 per cent to minimize resistance to current. Further refining was generally done via electrolysis, which is performed by passing a direct electrical current between a large anode of blister copper and a thin cathode of refined copper suspended in a dilute solution of sulphuric acid. As copper from the anode accumulates on the cathode, other impurities (gold, silver, zinc, lead) precipitate out of solution. By the early 1920s engineers had improved this century-old method through a new leaching technique that dissolved copper ores directly in sulphuric acid before subjecting them to electrolysis, thus skipping the smelting step altogether. This 'lixiviation' process was ideally suited to UMHK's needs at the time, since it was especially effective at treating low-grade ores (which were abundant in the deposits around Jadotville) unamenable to mechanical concentration. Before 1930, all Katangan blister copper had to be shipped out to Europe for further refining. In 1929, however, UMHK opened its own leaching and electrolysis plant at Jadotville-Shituru, which was capable of producing 30,000 tons of electrolytic copper per year (rising to 80,000 tons in 1942).[15]

The new refinery complex at Jadotville-Shituru was the nucleus of a much broader set of changes, for it also sparked the creation of various supporting industries designed to mobilize other resources throughout the region. Among the most important was Sogéchim (Société Générale Industrielle et Chimique du Katanga), which produced most of the chemicals that would otherwise have to be imported at prohibitive cost. The lixiviation process used around 650 tons of acid per ton of refined copper, and Sogéchim's sulphuric acid plant at Panda covered the bulk of Jadotville-Shituru's requirements by processing the sulphide ore wastes from the Prince Léopold mine at Kipushi on the Rhodesian border. Sogéchim also operated a hydrolysis plant for converting locally grown vegetable (mostly palm) oils into frothing agents for the flotation mills. Besides chemical inputs, the other major requirement of the refinery plant was cheap electricity. This was the responsibility of Sogéfor (Société Générale des Forces Hydro-Electriques du Katanga), which opened

---

[14] *UMHK: évolution*, 102–8; Robert, *Le Centre*, 104. Unlike conventional furnaces, reverberatory furnaces separate the processed ore from the fuel.

[15] *UMHK: évolution*, 161–79.

Central Africa's first hydroelectric station at Cornet Falls (now Mwandingusha) on the Lufira River in 1930. Consisting of a 500-metre dam, two feeder canals, and three groups of turbines, it supplied the bulk of electricity for the Jadotville plants located some 70 kilometres away.[16]

As the processing plants grew, so too did the pits that fed them. Mechanized excavation was critical for the Katanga mining industry, most of whose operations— apart from the Prince Léopold pit, UMHK's only subterranean copper mine—were essentially large holes in the ground. By the early 1920s the Star of Congo pit was over half a kilometre long. At Kambove, 160 kilometres north-west of Star, steam shovels operating around the clock had already converted a large hill into a crater nearly a kilometre long and up to 400 metres wide.[17] Although manual labourers did much of the work at first, perennial recruitment problems (on which more below) meant that they were soon supplemented by a fleet of steam shovels and winches, most of which were initially fuelled by wood hauled in from surrounding areas. Mechanization accelerated rapidly with the shift from high-grade to low-grade ore production after 1918. As copper prices rose during the mid-1920s, UMHK invested heavily in its massive open-cast operations, especially around Jadotville. Bucyrus shovels equipped with 2- to 3-cubic-metre buckets could do the work of 200 labourers (*c.*300 cubic metres per day) at half the cost.[18] By 1930 the company operated over two dozen steam and electric shovels, and a decade later it introduced a new generation of 400-horsepower diggers capable of excavating 3,500 cubic metres of earth in an eight-hour shift (by comparison, a manual worker could excavate at most around 2 cubic metres per shift).[19] UMHK's mechanization efforts were deliberately modelled on the latest open-cast techniques in the United States, to which it regularly dispatched engineers on fact-finding missions. Although the Katangan mines never quite reached the same scale as Utah's enormous Bingham Pit (the largest open-cast mine in the world for much of the twentieth century), they nonetheless adopted the same principle of high-throughput 'mass destruction' that Daniel Jackling had pioneered there (Fig. 5.2).[20]

Compared to the gargantuan mines in Katanga, the earliest enterprises on the Northern Rhodesian Copperbelt were downright diminutive—undercapitalized, short of expertise in low-grade ore extraction, and generally speculative. As in Katanga, the early artisanal pits focused on shallow oxide deposits; the difference was that the modest 3 to 4 per cent ore grades in the area precluded industrial-scale exploitation. What no one realized at the time was that these mediocre oxides often lay above extremely rich seams of sulphide ores. Africans had little interest in sulphides since they were unable to smelt them, so there was no prior knowledge of these deposits on which to draw. Moreover, most were only accessible via deep

---

[16] *UMHK: 1906–1956*, 150–2; Owen Letcher, *South Central Africa* (Johannesburg: African Publications, 1932), 192–4.

[17] Imperial Mineral Resources Bureau, *Copper*, 103; J. A. de Bauw, *Le Katanga: notes sur le pays, ses ressources et l'avenir de la colonisation belge* (Brussels: Larcier, 1920), 23.

[18] *UMHK: 1906–1956*, 109.   [19] *UMHK: évolution*, 77–84.

[20] See LeCain, *Mass Destruction*; see also Chapter 4.

Vue du traînage principal à la mine de Ruashi, dont la mécanisation était très développée pour l'époque (1928).

Fig. 5.2. UMHK's Ruashi mine, 1928.
Source: Union Minière du Haut-Katanga: 1906–1956 (Brussels: Cuypers, 1956), p. 149.

subterranean tunnels rather than simple open-cast techniques. So while Katanga's mines boomed, the neighbouring region of Northern Rhodesia was still regarded as a territory of questionable value. In 1924 the British South Africa Company was actually relieved to hand over the administration of Northern Rhodesia to the Colonial Office because it was costing the firm money.[21]

Things first began to change on the Copperbelt in the mid-1920s as new concessionary laws encouraged an influx of capital from Britain, South Africa, and the United States. From the very beginning, mining activities in the region were dominated by two groups: one under the umbrella of A. Chester Beatty's Rhodesian Selection Trust, and the other under Sir Ernest Oppenheimer's Rhodesian Anglo-American Ltd. The key breakthrough came in 1926 with the discovery of rich and readily workable copper sulphide ores at Roan Antelope (Luanshya). Amidst exceptionally high copper prices in the mid-1920s, this discovery prompted a frenzy of prospecting that soon uncovered highly promising sulphide deposits at several other sites in the area. By the late 1920s the 'big four' mines that would forever change the face of the Copperbelt were all under way: Roan Antelope and Mufulira by the Rhodesian Selection Trust, Nchanga (Chingola) and Nkana

---

[21] Elena L. Berger, *Labour, Race, and Colonial Rule: The Copperbelt from 1924 to Independence* (Oxford: Clarendon Press, 1974), 1–4; Kenneth Bradley, *Copper Venture: The Discovery and Development of Roan Antelope and Mufulira* (London: Parrish, 1952), 64–74.

(Kitwe) by Anglo-American.[22] Like the UMHK in Katanga, these two mining companies exerted a preponderant influence over the affairs of the Copperbelt and essentially ran it as a corporate estate until the 1950s.

The Rhodesian deposits constituted what one contemporary called 'the most spectacular discoveries that copper had ever known'.[23] Both their size and quality were extraordinary. Among the deep shales there were enormous quantities of high-grade chalcocite (Cu_2S), chalcopyrite ($CuFeS_2$), and bornite (Cu_5FeS_4), all of which could be concentrated fairly inexpensively via the new froth flotation processes recently perfected in the United States. The abundance, accessibility, and richness of the Copperbelt ores made them veritable treasure troves, and the mining companies developed them at breakneck speed. When the first discoveries were made at Roan Antelope in 1926, the site lacked even basic road connections. Five years later, when the railway extension from Ndola to Roan was completed, most of the complex was already in place: concentrators, boilers, pulverizers, a flotation mill, and an entire township to house the workforce. Roan produced its first concentrates in June 1931 and shipped out its first consignment of blister copper that same November. The three other mines on the Copperbelt were not far behind. Although the 1931 price slump temporarily halted operations at Mufulira, Nkana, and Nchanga, production expanded with a vengeance once markets bounced back.[24] From 1933 to 1938 the combined output of the Copperbelt doubled from 104,000 long tons (roughly equivalent to metric tons) to 213,000 tons, easily surpassing UMHK's gross copper production of around 150,000 tons. Output grew even faster after the Second World War, exceeding 300,000 tons in 1951, 400,000 tons in 1957, and over 600,000 tons by 1964.[25]

Production figures like this made Central Africa's copper mines a major strategic asset. From the perspective of Whitehall and Brussels they represented a prime opportunity to break the decades-long dominance of the United States over the international copper industry. This was no minor consideration for European governments at the time. The First World War made the pitfalls of foreign copper dependence all too clear. Germany in particular struggled to secure adequate supplies, and copper was its most important mineral import (for which it relied heavily on the United States).[26] The experience of the Second World War reinforced the lesson by demonstrating not only the risks of dependence but also the strategic and financial advantages of colonial copper resources. Whereas Britain

---

[22] L. J. Butler, *Copper Empire: Mining and the Colonial State in Northern Rhodesia, c.1930–1964* (Houndmills: Palgrave, 2007), 15; Bradley, *Copper Venture*, 79–86; Berger, *Labour*, 5; John Phillips, 'Alfred Chester Beatty: Mining Engineer, Financier, and Entrepreneur, 1898–1950', in Raymond E. Dumett (ed.), *Mining Tycoons in the Age of Empire, 1870–1945: Entrepreneurship, High Finance, Politics and Territorial Expansion* (Farnham: Ashgate, 2009), 215–38.

[23] Ira B. Joralemon, *Copper: The Encompassing Story of Mankind's First Metal* (Berkeley: Howell-North, 1973), 279 (first published in 1934 under the title *Romantic Copper*).

[24] Joralemon, *Copper*, 289; Berger, *Labour*, 20.

[25] Figures from Charles Perrings, *Black Mineworkers in Central Africa: Industrial Strategies and the Evolution of an African Proletariat in the Copperbelt, 1911–1941* (New York: Africana Pub. Co., 1979), 245; Berger, *Labour*, 238–9.

[26] See Kolonial-Wirtschaftliches Komitee, *Kupfer und die deutschen Kolonien* (Berlin: KWK, 1917), 1–2.

initially acquired over half of its wartime copper from North America, by 1945 over two-thirds came from Northern Rhodesia. Moreover, Copperbelt exports remained critical after the war. Amidst the severe post-war dollar shortage they helped shore up Britain's precarious balance-of-payments position, indeed on two fronts: first by obviating the need for copper purchases from the United States, and secondly by generating significant dollar earnings once the US government began stockpiling strategic minerals in the late 1940s.[27] Much the same could be said of Katanga's mines. During the German occupation of Belgium, the UMHK reserved its entire production for the British government, delivering some 800,000 tons of copper to the Allies from 1940 to 1944 (as well as uranium for the Manhattan Project from its Shinkolobwe mine). After 1945 it provided the bulk of the copper needed for economic reconstruction in France, Italy, and Belgium, once again sparing precious dollar reserves.[28] Over the following years Katanga's vast mineral wealth lost none of its geopolitical importance for the major industrial powers. In 1960, when Katangan secessionists launched an ill-fated attempt to detach the province from the newly independent Republic of the Congo, the ensuing 'Congo Crisis' became one of the bloodiest proxy conflicts of the entire Cold War.

Apart from their strategic significance, Central Africa's copper mines also possessed a remarkable symbolic importance. More than perhaps any other development scheme in colonial Africa, they were regarded by economists, officials, and engineers alike as a vivid illustration of what Western science and enterprise could accomplish even in the most challenging of environments. Like India's celebrated railways or the construction of the Panama Canal, the rise of Central Africa's mining complexes was feted as one of the most glorious victories over tropical nature in human history. What so impressed onlookers was not only their size and technical sophistication (which rivalled the greatest mining sites in Europe or North America) but also their juxtaposition against the vast untamed landscapes of what had been, only a few decades earlier, one of the most remote and unknown places in the Western geographic imagination. 'The spectacle presented by the smelter, especially in the evening, is truly grandiose,' remarked a Belgian visitor to Élisabethville in 1920. The 'flames and sparks escaping from the furnaces', the 'glow of a thousand electric lamps illuminating the mine face', and the 'din of the locomotives carrying their loads of coke and ore' stood in uncanny contrast with 'the calm of the tropical night'. Most astounding of all was the fact that all of this activity was situated 'in the centre of Africa and that perhaps, at this very instant, not far from here, a lion is shaking the forest with his ominous roar'.[29]

The towering smokestacks were a particular source of virile pride for the mining companies. The 48-metre chimney at Élisabethville was touted as a key 'symbol in

---

[27] DeMille, *Strategic Minerals*, 139, 151–5; Berger, *Labour*, 54; Bradley, *Copper Venture*, 26.

[28] *L'Exploitation des richesses minières du Congo belge et du Ruanda-Urundi* (Brussels: Centre d'information et de documentation du Congo belge et du Ruanda-Urundi, 1955), 56; *UMHK: 1906–1956*, 195; M. Legraye, 'La Production minière du Congo Belge et son rôle dans le relèvement économique de la Belgique', *Annales de la Société Géologique de Belgique*, vol. 68 (1945), 157–74.

[29] De Bauw, *Le Katanga*, 24.

the bosom of the Katanga bush'.[30] In Northern Rhodesia such accolades generally went to the gigantic 91-metre stack at Nkana, one of the largest in the world in the 1930s. Other modern marvels included the 58-metre steel head-frame at Roan Antelope, which surpassed any structure on the Witwatersrand gold fields. Flanked by huge concentrator plants and rows upon rows of workshop buildings, such structures served, in the words of one contemporary, as 'a monument to organisation and technical ability amidst the background and setting of the Northern Rhodesian forest belts'.[31] For European observers, the quintessence of the mining areas was the contrast between the primeval bush and the 'industrial giants that pound and thunder in their silence'.[32]

As self-congratulatory as such rhetoric was, this sense of incongruity reflected more than just a romantic cultural conceit. After all, one of the greatest difficulties faced by the mining firms was to secure an adequate supply of raw materials, especially labour, in such a sparsely populated region. Ever since the turn of the century the colonial authorities in Katanga were eager to integrate the local population into the cash economy via hut taxes (*impôt indigène*) and various market controls, and directly assisted labour recruitment for the mines through the imposition of *corvée* laws mandating sixty days of work per year. But despite such measures, UMHK still had to seek workers from a wide radius, sometimes as far afield as Angola and Mozambique.

Recruitment practices were often coercive and occasionally violent. At a general level they were organized by parastatal agencies such as the Bourse du Travail du Katanga or the Force Publique, though much of the actual conscription on the ground was done by independent contractors.[33] In the early years, labour arrangements at the Katangan mines followed a short-term migratory pattern in which most workers would sign up for three- to six-month stints and then temporarily return to their villages before entering another contract. The rationale for this system, which mirrored standard practice in South Africa, was twofold: to avoid the creation of an uprooted African proletariat, and to uphold colour-bar policies that reserved semi-skilled jobs for whites. During the first half of the 1920s the annual turnover of UMHK's workforce (which totalled between 10,000 and 15,000 employees) was approximately 96 per cent. By contrast, after 1926 the Katangan administration promoted the creation of a more settled urban labour force as a means of improving worker productivity and reducing the disruptive impact of labour migration on rural society. Minimum three-year contracts soon became the norm, and by the early 1930s turnover at UMHK dropped to a mere 7 per cent.

[30] *UMHK: 1906–1956*, 101.
[31] Letcher, *South Central Africa*, 211, 218.   [32] Bradley, *Copper Venture*, 20.
[33] Perrings, *Black Mineworkers*, 27–71; John Higginson, *A Working Class in the Making: Belgian Colonial Labor Policy, Private Enterprise, and the African Mineworker, 1907–1951* (Madison, Wis.: University of Wisconsin Press, 1989), 8–9, 51–2. UMHK even launched an abortive attempt to recruit Chinese 'coolies' in 1910–11: Aldwin Roes, 'Centre or Periphery? The Colonial Administration and the Valorization of Congolese Natural Resources, 1885–1914', paper presented at the London School of Economics, 28 Apr. 2010, 18–20; also Ian Phimister, 'Foreign Devils, Finance and Informal Empire: Britain and China c.1900–1912', *Modern Asian Studies*, vol. 40 no. 3 (2006), 737–59.

This policy of workforce stabilization transformed the Katanga mining centres in a number of respects. From 1925 to 1940 the proportion of women and children in the settlements rose from eighteen and six (respectively) per hundred men to fifty-eight and fifty-nine per hundred men.[34] In turn, the presence of miners' families also led to better housing, education, and medical services, all of which tended to keep workers in the towns.

The Northern Rhodesian mines eventually followed a similar process of workforce stabilization, though the transition away from migratory labour came around two decades later than in Katanga. One reason for the delay was a deep concern about the possible effects of 'detribalization' and the threat that it posed to the structures of chiefly authority on which the British system of indirect rule was based. Another factor was the reluctance to create an urban labour force that was wholly dependent on the mines for their livelihood. The risks of such a policy had already been illustrated by the mass lay-offs during the Depression, which reduced the Copperbelt workforce from 31,941 in September 1930 to only 6,677 at the end of 1932.[35] Although employment figures recovered by the mid-1930s, the unwillingness to create a more settled African 'proletariat' on the Copperbelt was reinforced by periodic strikes in 1935 and 1940, followed by major disturbances in Katanga in 1941. But if the social and political dangers of a settled urban workforce were plain to see, they nonetheless had to be balanced against the hazards of turning the townships into vast migrant slums. Eventually the unfavourable comparisons with the superior housing and education facilities in Katanga prompted the Northern Rhodesian authorities to adopt a similar policy of labour stabilization. Although the initial expectation was that most workers should return to their villages after two years, this repatriation clause was difficult to enforce, and by the early 1950s it was clear that most of the Copperbelt's mineworkers were there to stay.[36]

Like it or not, from the 1910s to the 1950s the colonial copper industry created a string of new mining centres inhabited by an increasingly settled industrial workforce. The task of sustaining and managing these new urban environments brought its own set of changes.

ENVIRONMENTAL TRANSFORMATION
IN THE COPPER TOWNS

Due to the high labour demand of the mines, the settlements that grew alongside them—Lubumbashi/Élisabethville and Likasi/Jadotville in Congo; Kitwe, Luanshya, Mufulira, and Chingola in Northern Rhodesia—grew as quickly as the pits themselves. Lubumbashi, which began as no more than a 'corner of the bush pompously named Élisabethville', soon became the largest town in the region and the second

---

[34] *UMHK: évolution*, 221–2.   [35] Berger, *Labour*, 20.
[36] J. Clyde Mitchell, 'A Note on the Urbanization of Africans on the Copperbelt', *Rhodes-Livingstone Journal*, no. 12 (1951), 20–7, here 22; J. L. Parpart, *Labor and Capital on the African Copperbelt* (Philadelphia: Temple University Press, 1983), 32; Berger, *Labour*, 12–19.

most populous city in the entire Congo (numbering around 200,000 inhabitants in the late 1950s).[37] The population of the Copperbelt, which was estimated at no more than 1,000 people before the advent of the mines, numbered over 400,000 by the early 1960s, mostly concentrated in the cities or sprawling peri-urban shanty towns.[38]

All of these settlements were essentially colonial creations, outposts of foreign power that owed their very existence to the metropolitan demand for copper.[39] The so-called 'native townships', which were initially no more than lodging camps for the mines, developed with scant regard for the needs of locals, let alone for the precepts of urban planning. As one contemporary put it, 'like Topsy they "just growed"'.[40] It took years to establish even the basics of municipal administration, utilities, and transport infrastructure, partly because of the investment priorities of the mining firms and partly because of the legal ambiguities between company rights and state authority.[41] As a result, the newly minted copper towns were plagued by a host of political and social problems. Some of their most fundamental challenges, however, were ecological.

Foremost among them was disease. Sickness and epidemics were especially problematic on the Copperbelt, most of which was covered by bush, streams, and *dambos* (swampy sites of poor drainage) that harboured malaria, blackwater fever, and all manner of waterborne pathogens. By comparison, the drier heights of Katanga presented a less malign disease ecology, though Belgian claims about its healthy climate, which were intended to attract European settlers, were greatly exaggerated (indeed, the Lubumbashi River running through Élisabethville was a breeding ground for the malaria-carrying *Anopheles funestus*).[42]

In both regions, the concentration of mineworkers into dense settlements was a recipe for elevated morbidity. During the early years in particular, the high inherent disease risks of the lodging camps were greatly exacerbated by harsh living conditions and poor hygiene. During the 1910s, workers at Kambove obtained their drinking water from the same pipe that supplied five steam shovels, two locomotives, and a variety of other machines. To avoid long queues in the mornings, many drew water from muddy streams or stagnant pools near the camp, which

[37] Quote from de Bauw, *Le Katanga*, 22; see also Bruce Fetter, *The Creation of Elisabethville, 1910–1940* (Stanford, Calif.: Hoover Institution Press, 1976), 173.

[38] Mitchell, 'Note', 20; Berger, *Labour*, 16.

[39] A core theme of Bruce Fetter's study of Élisabethville, though equally applicable to the Copperbelt towns: Fetter, *Creation*, 177–80.

[40] J. Merle Davis (ed.), *Modern Industry and the African: An Enquiry into the Effect of the Copper Mines of Central Africa upon Native Society and the Work of Christian Missions made under the auspices of the Department of Social and Industrial Research of the International Missionary Council* (London: Macmillan, 1933), 78.

[41] F. Grévisse, *Le Centre extra-coutumier d'Élisabethville: quelques aspects de la politique indigène du Haut-Katanga industriel* (Brussels: Institut Royal Colonial Belge, 1951); John Gardiner, 'Some Aspects of the Establishment of Towns in Zambia during the Nineteen Twenties and Thirties', *Zambian Urban Studies*, no. 3 (1970), 25–8.

[42] Buttgenbach, *Les Mines*, 9; Pierre Forthomme, *La Véritable Signification du Katanga pour la Belgique: des moyens de l'accentuer* (Brussels: Hayez, 1911), 21; Sir Malcolm Watson, *African Highway: The Battle for Health in Central Africa* (London: Murray, 1953), 204.

repeatedly led to acute outbreaks of dysentery and enteritis. Pneumonia was also a recurrent problem in the mining camps, and infected no less than one-third of Élisabethville's 2,000-man workforce in 1916. Other diseases and epidemics of varying degrees of severity were common. The worst by far was the influenza pandemic of 1918, which temporarily raised the mortality rate among Élisabethville's African inhabitants to a staggering 30 per cent, and triggered a mass efflux of panicked workers out of the mining camps.[43]

None of these disease problems were helped by what the Congolese governor called the 'repulsive filthiness' of Élisabethville's African district (*cité indigène*), where the first sanitary measures came only in the 1920s.[44] Sanitation was little better in the fledgling townships of the Copperbelt, where communal cesspits were described as 'so horrific that, in spite of the risk of arrest, the surrounding land is fouled with night soil'.[45] Although the Rhodesian authorities continually increased the number of sewage buckets and septic tanks in an attempt to improve sanitary standards, the pace of urban expansion continually outstripped their capacity. The perpetual migration of workers between the mines and the countryside only added to the cocktail of microbes swirling around the towns. A high proportion of the epidemics during the early years coincided with the influx of large cohorts of new recruits, many of whom came from areas with different disease pools and arrived in the mining camps with suppressed immunity due to the physical rigours of the trip. This connection between disease and labour migration worked both ways, for as workers returned to their villages at the end of their contracts they often exported urban crowd diseases to rural areas. In the 1920s, yaws and smallpox emanating from the mining towns covered much of southern Katanga and had also spread into Northern Rhodesia.[46]

Taken together, the continuing series of disease outbreaks amounted to a creeping mortality crisis for the mining centres. Even apart from the mounting medical costs, the thousands of sick days and associated work delays were a constant source of concern for company bosses. What alarmed them most of all was not the immediate impact on work plans, but rather the potential for the mortality crisis to turn into a labour crisis as well. Fears of illness not only undermined efforts to recruit new workers to the mining settlements—a morbid joke told to European travellers from Cape Town was that they should not bother buying a return ticket[47]—it also led to high rates of 'desertion' among African workers already on site.[48] For the mining industry to function efficiently, it was imperative to lower disease rates. One means of accomplishing this was the construction of water mains and sewers,

---

[43] *UMHK: évolution*, 340; Higginson, *Working Class*, 33–4; Fetter, *Creation*, 37. By comparison, the mortality rate among European workers during the 1918 pandemic was only 5 per cent.

[44] Grévisse, *Le Centre extra-coutumier*, 5.

[45] Quote from Davis (ed.), *Modern Industry*, 80; see also Ministry of Local Government and Social Welfare, *Report on the Preliminary Investigation into the Complaints as to the Conduct and Management of the Affairs of the Municipal Council of Luanshya* (Lusaka, 20 Nov. 1959), 5.

[46] See Higginson, *Working Class*, 44; Perrings, *Black Mineworkers*, 168–72.

[47] L. H. Gann, *A History of Northern Rhodesia: Early Days to 1953* (London: Chatto & Windus, 1964), 209.

[48] Perrings, *Black Mineworkers*, 173–82.

which first came to Élisabethville in 1926–7 and were soon installed in the Copperbelt towns as well.[49] Another was the establishment of clinics and general medical services, where the UMHK clearly led the way.[50] But a third approach was to focus not on unhealthy bodies but rather on unhealthy environments, the 'curing' of which required a fundamental alteration of the area's waterways.

The most far-reaching campaign to 'sanitize' the local surroundings focused on the many swamps and streams of the Rhodesian Copperbelt. In 1929 the Rhodesian Selection Trust enlisted the Ross Institute for Tropical Hygiene to investigate the soaring disease rate at Roan Antelope, the largest of the Rhodesian mines at the time. The head of the institute's malarial department was none other than Malcolm Watson, the physician who had earlier pioneered the Malayan government's anti-malarial efforts on the colony's rubber plantations. Following the same vector-based approach that Watson had applied in Malaya, the Ross Institute team sought to deprive *Anopheles* mosquitoes of their breeding grounds. When the institute's chief hydrologist C. R. Harrison (who had also previously worked in Malaya as a drainage expert and former rubber planter) arrived on the Copperbelt in 1929, he found *A. gambiae* to be pervasive. He quickly realized, however, that the high concentration of mosquitoes resulted as much from the changes wrought by the mining firms as from the inherent characteristics of the natural surroundings. The construction of mine-works, processing facilities, and housing created countless ditches, puddles, and tyre-tracks, all of which furnished an ideal habitat for *A. gambiae*, which thrives in small pools. Harrison therefore immediately set to work filling holes and building drains throughout the mining complex, and by April 1930 *A. gambiae* had largely been eradicated from the controlled area.[51]

It was a remarkably effective solution, but it was only the first step of a much broader anti-malaria campaign. The most prevalent adult vector in the area was not *A. gambiae* but rather *A. funestus*, which lives in swamps rather than pools and breeds in the partial shade afforded by marsh vegetation. The local *dambos* provided ideal habitat for *A. funestus*, and there were so many *dambos* along the course of the Luanshya River that nearly all of the residential buildings at Roan were within half a mile of one. This posed a serious challenge since the flight radius of anopheline mosquitoes was thought at the time to be around half a mile (it is actually considerably greater, as soon became apparent). But once again, mining activities significantly aggravated the problem by impeding the smooth flow of the Luanshya and by creating more swampy breeding grounds through the construction of dams, road crossings (or 'drifts'), and other obstructions.[52] From the perspective of the mine's managers there was little alternative but to drain the Luanshya River and

---

[49] Grévisse, *Le Centre extra-coutumier*, 6–7.

[50] Mortality rates for UMHK declined from 46/1,000 in the latter 1920s to under 10/1,000 in the mid-1940s. Medical services in the Copperbelt towns were generally passable though slower to develop: *UMHK: évolution*, 314, 322–5; Perrings, *Black Mineworkers*, 199.

[51] Watson, *African Highway*, 23–6; Lyn Schumaker, 'Slimes and Death-Dealing Dambos: Water, Industry and the Garden City on Zambia's Copperbelt', *Journal of Southern African Studies*, vol. 34 no. 4 (Dec. 2008), 823–40, here 826–7.

[52] Watson, *African Highway*, esp. 24–5.

dry up the local *dambos*. Towards this end, engineers employed a range of tried and tested measures: cleaning out the river channel, cutting drainage channels through the swamps, and clearing the riverbanks of overhanging vegetation that shaded the water and gave shelter to larvae. Weekly spraying with paraffin or kerosene was also used to eliminate vegetation and larvae, and by 1931 workers were dousing the Roan surroundings with nearly 7,000 litres of oil each month.[53]

In many respects the anti-malarial campaign at Luanshya mirrored prior experience with vector-based sanitation methods in Malaysia. The involvement of the Ross Institute, and the many personnel links it entailed, all but guaranteed a significant degree of similarity. Yet the measures on the Copperbelt involved more than just a straightforward transfer of practices from one place to another. For all the parallels between the two cases—above all the close linkage between malaria epidemics and the human transformation of the landscape—the vast mining works presented opportunities to alter the local disease environment that were quite different from those available on Southeast Asia's rubber plantations.

By the beginning of the 1930s the Roan Antelope mine was already producing millions of tons of waste material every year, mainly soil overburden, smelter slag, as well as fine tailings that were spewed out of the processing plants. Whereas most of these dry solids were simply piled up in immense waste-heaps, the liquid-suspended tailings required the construction of large dams and settling ponds to prevent the discharge of particulate matter into local rivers. While thousands of tons of waste were accumulating behind the main tailings dam (which happened to be located along a stretch of the Luanshya River between two *dambos*), engineers were simultaneously tasked with drying out the malarial swamps below. It did not take long for them to connect the dots. From 1930 onwards mine engineers pumped huge quantities of mine tailings into these low-lying sections of the Luanshya, and the effects on local hydrology were revolutionary. By 1950 the river was unrecognizable—its upper *dambos* completely dry, covered with sterile tailings, and devoid of nearly all of their previous plant and animal species, including *A. funestus* (Fig. 5.3).[54]

By transferring huge amounts of mine tailings into the local swamps, the engineers at Roan Antelope effectively turned a useless waste product into a beneficial sanitation tool. The effects were clearly visible in declining malaria rates. Monthly infections fell from 61/1,000 in the 1929–30 rainy season to 31.6/1,000 the following year, and were nearly halved again to 17.5/1,000 by 1931–2.[55] In view of these results, the destruction of the local wetlands was broadly welcomed by Luanshya's residents, both European and African alike. Echoing a widely held view, one local administrator celebrated the barren swathe of flotation plant tailings covering the valley below the town as a splendid silvery plain of progress: 'you may get some satisfaction from reflecting that no slag-heap could shine so beautifully

[53] Watson, *African Highway*, 40–5, 51.
[54] Watson, *African Highway*, 49–50, 54, 74; also Schumaker, 'Slimes', 831.
[55] Schumaker, 'Slimes', 827. Mortality among African employees also fell sharply at Roan from 34.6/1,000 in 1930 to 6.6/1,000 in 1938: Watson, *African Highway*, 70.

Fig. 5.3. Swampy area drained and filled with tailings below the tailings dam at Luanshya.
Source: Sir Malcolm Watson, *African Highway: The Battle for Health in Central Africa* (London: Murray, 1953), Plate 29.

or, if it comes to that, could so mould itself to the landscape.'[56] But such triumphant rhetoric obscured the fact that malaria was by no means the only ailment among mine workers. Poor nutrition and various waterborne pathogens continued to plague the African workforce long after malaria rates had subsided. Indeed, pneumonia claimed more lives than any other disease during the initial crisis of the early 1930s. As Lyn Schumaker has noted, the main reason why malaria attracted the bulk of medical attention was not because it posed the greatest health threat (serious though this was), nor because of the complexity of its disease aetiology (which was significant), nor even because it affected Europeans as well as Africans, but rather because it was a problem that was particularly amenable to a technical solution that did not call into question the broader social and political inequalities that underlay patterns of public health. Unlike the other diseases in the mining camps, malaria did not require sanitation officers to draw unwanted attention to the far lower standards of housing and nutrition for African workers in comparison with European residents.[57]

The technical success of the anti-malarial innovations at Roan soon prompted replication elsewhere on the Copperbelt. At Mufulira, a large natural depression just north of the mine was entirely filled with tailings, while a 20-hectare *dambo* near the African compound was dammed by a huge barrage over 20 metres tall and 400 metres long. The Mufulira River itself was drained and channelled in the 1930s to prevent the formation of stagnant pools, and from 1940 to 1950 the

---

[56] Bradley, *Copper Venture*, 22.   [57] Schumaker, 'Slimes', 835–6.

large, swampy loop of the river that skirted the edge of the township was covered with a stratum of tailings 6 metres deep and over 3 kilometres long.[58] The Nkana mine near Kitwe was situated among several tributaries of the Kafue River, each of which hosted dangerous breeding grounds. To rid the area of mosquitoes, the Kitwe stream just north of town was extensively drained, while the Uchi swamp to the south was filled in with a layer of tailings 9 metres deep. At the Nchanga complex near Chingola, the last of the 'big four' Copperbelt mines to open (in 1936), officials immediately drained eight large swamps in the vicinity and eventually turned one of the tailings-filled *dambos* into the municipal golf course. Across the border in Katanga, where malaria controls were initially focused on prophylactic doses of quinine, the Lubumbashi River was gradually sanitized by accelerating its flow, clearing its banks, and spraying its surroundings with DDT. So confident were the Élisabethville authorities in the healthiness of the city's waterways that they eventually channelled a stream from the river through a municipal garden to feed an artificial lake next to the concrete swimming pool—though their confidence was soon dented by an infestation of bilharzia-carrying snails that infected swimmers and eventually forced the closure of the lido.[59]

The sanitation campaign was not the only factor behind the transformation of the local hydrosphere. The engineering requirements of the mines brought a whole other set of parallel changes. Keeping the underground tunnels dry was an ongoing challenge. At Kipushi, UMHK's largest subterranean mine, the influx of water could be as great as 2,000 m^3 per hour, which meant that around 20 tons of water had to be pumped out for every ton of ore extracted.[60] In the Northern Rhodesian Copperbelt, around 340 million litres were pumped out of the mines every day—a flow of water to the surface so large as effectively to create a second major regional waterway alongside the Kafue River itself (340 million litres per day was roughly equivalent to the Kafue at low flow).[61] Most of this 'produced water' went straight to the flotation works and other processing facilities adjacent to the mines, which together consumed around 230 million litres per day. And while this river-sized current was being pumped to the surface, many of the area's natural waterways—especially those lying above ore bodies earmarked for exploitation, such as the Luanshya River, the Mufulira River, and the Mindolo stream at Rhokana—were dammed, straightened, and diverted to prevent them from running into the mines in the first place. As a 1959 survey put it, such rivers should no longer be regarded as natural features but should instead be 'classed as "industrial" or "mining" streams'.[62] Lacking large numbers of downstream users, and rendered all but unusable for non-mining purposes anyway, they scarcely even qualified for the hybrid label of 'organic machine'.[63]

[58] Watson, *African Highway*, 112–13, also plates 40, 41.
[59] Watson, *African Highway*, 139, 148–50, 153, 158–9, 192–5, 204, also plate 42.
[60] *UMHK: évolution*, 90.
[61] *First Report on a Regional Survey of the Copperbelt 1959* (Lusaka: Government Printer, 1960), 23–5.
[62] *First Report on a Regional Survey of the Copperbelt 1959*, 112.
[63] White, *Organic Machine*.

If watercourses were a particular focus of intervention around the mines, both for medical and industrial reasons, the urge to discipline and 'improve' the local environment was perhaps most clearly manifested in the design of the new copper towns themselves. During the inter-war period the expansion of the mining settlements was shaped by the 'garden city' movement that was currently transforming the landscape around the industrial centres of Europe. Élisabethville and Luanshya were the trailblazers in this respect, and their development shaped the growth of the other towns in the region. Both were deliberately conceived as miniature 'neo-Europes'. Luanshya, one administrator declared, 'is not Central Africa at all, but Pittsburgh or Wigan or Johannesburg'.[64] Furnished with gardens, parks, and sporting facilities, they were celebrated as islands of health, prosperity, and 'civilization' in the wild and untamed heart of Africa.

But despite the many parallels with Europe's garden cities, the new copper towns were also spatial expressions of colonial hierarchy and racial segregation. The strict separation of white and African quarters meant that some residents experienced the pleasures of suburban living much more than others. Whereas Europeans enjoyed golf courses, cricket pitches, pools, and leisure clubs, recreation facilities for Africans remained rudimentary at best until the end of the 1940s, especially on the Rhodesian Copperbelt.[65] Likewise, whereas Europeans generally lived in spacious bungalows situated on garden plots, the standard of African housing ranged from modest to poor. African accommodation was relatively good at Élisabethville and Luanshya, where residential areas were interspersed with shade trees and where workers were encouraged to tend kitchen gardens to supplement their mine rations. The worst forms of housing were the hated barrack-type huts at Nkana, a perennial source of grievance that helped fuel the strikes of 1935 and 1940.[66] By almost any standard these were peculiar urban landscapes. An anthropologist studying Luanshya in the early 1950s was struck by their bizarre look: neat rows of small, whitewashed bungalows standing in the shadow of huge processing plants situated amidst a forest of red anthills 1 or 2 metres high.[67]

Like many garden cities the world over, the wholesome and orderly appearance of the mining towns was deceptive. It not only masked grotesque social inequalities, it also concealed some ugly pollution problems. Although there is frustratingly

[64] Bradley, *Copper Venture*, 21.
[65] This was the context in which the Mbeni and Kalela dance groups emerged as an important element of local popular culture, and eventually of anti-colonial sentiment: J. Clyde Mitchell, *The Kalela Dance: Aspects of Social Relationships among Urban Africans in Northern Rhodesia*, Rhodes-Livingstone Papers no. 27 (Manchester: Manchester University Press, 1956); Albert B. K. Matongo, 'Popular Culture in a Colonial Society: Another Look at Mbeni and Kalela Dances on the Copperbelt', in Samuel N. Chipungu (ed.), *Guardians in their Time: Experiences of Zambians under Colonial Rule 1890–1964* (London: Macmillan, 1992), 180–217, esp. 183–7.
[66] *Report of the Commission Appointed to Enquire into the Disturbances in the Copperbelt of Northern Rhodesia* (London: HMSO, 1935), 60; *Report of the Commission Appointed to Enquire into the Disturbances in the Copperbelt of Northern Rhodesia* (Lusaka: Government Printer, 1940), 32.
[67] Hortense Powdermaker, *Copper Town: Changing Africa. The Human Situation on the Rhodesian Copperbelt* (New York: Harper & Row, 1962), 5; see, generally, the pioneering work of A. L. Epstein, *Scenes from African Urban Life: Collected Copperbelt Papers* (Edinburgh: Edinburgh University Press, 1992).

little material on the effects of mining pollution during the colonial period, there are enough indices to confirm that it was extensive. Air contamination was clearly acute, especially near the smelters. At Élisabethville, most of the smelting and processing plant was located east of the city, which meant that the prevailing east–west winds carried large amounts of sulphur dioxide and trace metals into town, stunting plant growth and raising the risk of pulmonary disease.[68] Around Jadotville, acid precipitation had become so severe by the early 1930s that it forced garden 'squatters' near the town to abandon their plots and move upstream.[69] On the Copperbelt, which mainly extracted sulphide rather than oxide ores, the potential for soil and water acidification was even higher than in Katanga. Smelting such ores generally produces around two tons of sulphur dioxide gas for every ton of copper, and although the Rhodesian ores contained fewer toxic metals than most comparable deposits elsewhere in the world (e.g. the western United States), only a tiny portion of the waste fumes was captured for the production of sulphuric acid. The vast bulk of sulphur-containing gas—indeed, all of it at Mufulira, which had no sulphur-capture facilities at all—was discharged into the atmosphere, which damaged plant life for miles around the stacks.[70] This is not to say that the mines had an entirely free hand in discarding their waste. Northern Rhodesian legislation explicitly obliged operators to use 'all reasonably practicable methods and processes . . . to minimise the escape of gases, fumes or smoke'. But this obligation was rendered virtually meaningless by the parallel provision of 'smoke areas' stretching 7 to 10 miles (c.11 to 16 kilometres) around the smokestacks, within which it was impossible to take legal action against any damage caused by 'gases or fumes or smoke or any other exhalations from any smelter or other mining or metallurgical plant'.[71] In practice, smelter emissions on both sides of the border remained all but uncontrolled throughout the colonial period.[72]

Water pollution likewise took a heavy toll. Organic run-off from sewage or topsoil erosion degraded rivers below all of the mining towns, most severely on the Lubumbashi River downstream from Élisabethville. Chemical effluent from ore

---

[68] Contemporary evidence of such problems is very scarce, though useful pointers can be found in Marie Mazalto, 'Environmental Liability in the Mining Sector: Prospects for Sustainable Development in the Democratic Republic of the Congo', in Jeremy Richards (ed.), *Mining, Society, and a Sustainable World* (Berlin: Springer, 2009), 289–317; Réseau Ressources Naturelles, *L'Impact de l'exploitation minière sur l'environnement du Katanga: table ronde* (Lubumbashi: Réseau Ressources Naturelles, 2007), esp. 19–20: <http://www.congoforum.be/upldocs/table%20ronde%20du%2010%20 fevrier2007%20Impact%20mines%20sur%20env%20Kat.pdf>.

[69] Higginson, *Working Class*, 142–3.

[70] World Bank, *Copperbelt Environment Project: Project Appraisal Report* (Report No: 25347-ZA), 14 Feb. 2003, 5, available at <http://www-wds.worldbank.org/external/default/WDSContentServer/ WDSP/IB/2003/03/29/000094946_03030604005362/Rendered/PDF/multi0page.pdf>; Sir Ronald Prain, *Copper: Anatomy of an Industry* (London: Mining Journal Books, 1975), 201–2; *First Report on a Regional Survey of the Copperbelt 1959*, 90.

[71] *Northern Rhodesia Government Gazette, Ordinances, 1959* (Lusaka: Government Printer, 1960), 144–5.

[72] N. P. Perera, 'Mining and Spoiled Land in Zambia: An Example of Conflicting Land Use in the Third World', *Geojournal*, Supplement 2 (1981), 95–103, esp. 98–9; Jean-Pierre van de Weghe et al., *Profil Environnemental—République Démocratique du Congo—Rapport provisoire* (European Commission, EURATA, Jan. 2006), 23.

processing was another problem, and was particularly acute below the leaching plant at Nchanga on the Copperbelt.[73] But the most serious threat to the rivers came from physical run-off, above all from the thousands of hectares of tailings dumps that covered the regional watershed in a patchwork of sterile dead zones. The slimes pumped to these sites were composed mainly of fine mud particles that drained poorly and were extremely prone to erosion. Efforts to stabilize such areas were scanty and ineffectual, partly because the lack of soil nutrients impeded plant growth, but also because of the reluctance to replant dump sites containing trace amounts of copper that might be profitably reprocessed in the future. As this fine inert material was washed down the rivers, it clogged channels, choked vegetation, and occasionally damaged soils on the fertile floodplains, especially when it came in large amounts during the rainy season or, worst of all, in the event of a dam failure. When the tailings dam at Mufulira catastrophically failed in 1952, it smothered the banks of the Kafue River with a thick coat of sterile slimes that killed fish and aquatic plants for over 30 kilometres downstream.[74]

As the effects of sediment pollution mounted, mining engineers gradually became more sensitive to the problem of tailings silt, especially in the wake of the 1952 Mufulira disaster.[75] By the 1950s managers sought to preserve as much natural vegetation as possible around the dumps in order to hold back run-off and minimize the formation of erosion channels. There were also efforts to protect vegetation along stream-banks and to encourage the growth of reeds that tolerated the slimes.[76] As subsequent studies have shown, the most important protection for downstream waterways was actually provided by the remaining *dambos*, which filtered out sediment and chemical effluents at the cost of becoming pollutant traps themselves.[77] All of these pollution problems eventually raised the broader question of how far some watercourses should be sacrificed for the benefit of others. For officials on the Copperbelt, the primary concern was to protect the Kafue River (the main waterway in the region), but there was a range of views over the degree to which its tributaries should soak up the pollution pressure given that at least ten of them (including the Luanshya and Mufulira) were already badly affected by effluents. While some administrators protested against the further degradation of

---

[73] Michel LeBlanc and François Malaisse, *Lubumbashi, un écosystème urbain tropical* (Lubumbashi: Université Nationale du Zaire, 1978), 106; *First Report on a Regional Survey of the Copperbelt 1959*, 91.

[74] *First Report on a Regional Survey of the Copperbelt 1959*, 91; more generally, see H. Matschke, 'River Pollution by Mine Effluence in the Kitwe Region', in Ian D. Elgie (ed.), *Kitwe and its Hinterland* (Lusaka: Zambian Geographical Association, 1974), 125–32.

[75] Northern Rhodesia, Mines Department, *Annual Report for the Year 1952* (Lusaka: Government Printer, 1953), 8; *Report of a Soil and Land-Use Survey of the Copperbelt, Northern Rhodesia* (Lusaka: Government Printer, 1956), 118.

[76] Perera, 'Mining and Spoiled Land in Zambia', vols 99–100; *First Report on a Regional Survey of the Copperbelt 1959*, 91.

[77] C. J. von der Heyden, and M. G. New, 'Groundwater Pollution on the Zambian Copperbelt: Deciphering the Source and the Risk', *Science of the Total Environment*, vol. 327 (2004), 17–30; C. J. von der Heyden, and M. G. New, 'Sediment Chemistry: A History of Mine Contaminant Remediation and an Assessment of Processes and Pollution Potential', *Journal of Geochemical Exploration*, vol. 82 (2004), 35–57.

These regional-level processes of land conversion were mirrored on a smaller scale in the immediate vicinity of the mining towns. Generally speaking, the mining firms tolerated or promoted local food production, whether by market-gardeners or by the mineworkers themselves. Roan Antelope explicitly encouraged its employees to sow their own plots, and moreover allowed them to sell any surplus produce at market rates.[85] Few residents needed much prompting to do so. Even for those receiving mine rations, high local food prices furnished a powerful incentive to grow one's own food, and for those without rations the motivations were even stronger. During the early 1930s the number of peri-urban gardening plots sky-rocketed as thousands of laid-off workers joined the semi-rural communities that had sprung up around the mining towns. In order to reduce the tensions of mass unemployment, the UMHK tried to persuade such 'squatters' to grow produce for the remaining workforce. At Jadotville, managers even went so far as to provide them with maize seed, artificial fertilizers, and goats for this purpose.

The whole issue of local land availability soon became a source of considerable tension. Around Élisabethville, where the authorities distributed garden allotments to the wives of workers in the early 1930s, the failure to provide fertilizers or to allocate new plots after the Depression years gradually led to soil exhaustion, and became one of the many grievances that fed into the strikes of 1941.[86] On the Rhodesian Copperbelt too, one of the main recommendations after the 1940 labour disturbances was the distribution of small farming allotments for workers, especially those 'who have lost touch with tribal life' and were unlikely to return to their ancestral villages (the 'detribalization' concept at work).[87] Although Luanshya was the only Copperbelt town that formally followed this recommendation, authorities in the other centres turned a blind eye to the expansion of small-scale cropping, which mostly focused on maize, cassava, groundnuts, pumpkins, and potatoes.[88] By the late 1950s it was estimated that anywhere from 400 to 1,200 hectares were cultivated around the main Copperbelt cities, which significantly aggravated what were already severe local erosion problems.[89]

But the effects of the mines on regional agriculture went far beyond the question of feeding their workforces. As some contemporaries were well aware, the under-lying tension between the demand for more labourers and the demand for more food put a huge strain on agricultural communities in the areas that served as labour reservoirs for the mines—above all the Bemba and Bisa regions to the north-east and Barotseland to the south-west. In her landmark 1939 study of *Land, Labour and Diet in Northern Rhodesia*, the anthropologist Audrey Richards emphasized how the creeping exodus of young male workers from the villages undermined the

---

[85] In 1932 some 18,000–23,000 kg of produce was sold on this basis: Davis (ed.), *Modern Industry*, 74–5.

[86] Fetter, *Creation*, 147; Higginson, *Working Class*, 142–3.

[87] *Memorandum by the Anti-Slavery and Aborigines Protection Society on the Report of the Commission Appointed to Enquire into the 1940 Disturbances in the Copperbelt of Northern Rhodesia* (London: ASAPS, 1941), 8.

[88] W. V. Brelsford, *Copperbelt Markets: A Social and Economic Study* (Lusaka: Government Printer, 1947), 9.

[89] *First Report on a Regional Survey of the Copperbelt 1959*, 90.

customary 'citemene' system of shifting agriculture that had long been practised in the region. At the core of this system was the annual cutting and burning of trees or branches (performed by men), which left behind a layer of ash-enriched soil on which cultivators (generally women) first planted millet and then a succession of other crops—groundnuts, maize, vegetables—until yields fell and the plot was left to fallow. Although colonial officials disdained the practice as wasteful and inefficient, in fact it was remarkably well suited to the nutrient-poor soils and the lengthy dry season that characterized most of the area.[90]

By the 1930s, the outflow of male tree-cutting labour to the mining centres was recognized as a central cause of the escalating food shortages throughout the region. Most alarming was the situation in Bemba areas, where male absenteeism was especially high due to the dearth of alternative cash-earning opportunities and the attraction of sizeable wage bonuses for dangerous underground work, for which Bemba men, who took pride in their image as fierce warriors, were highly regarded. Richards calculated that around 40 to 60 per cent of Bemba men left their villages each year to find work elsewhere, mostly in the copper mines of Katanga and Northern Rhodesia.[91] In an insightful reappraisal of Richards's study, Henrietta Moore and Megan Vaughan have shown that the connections between male absenteeism and food shortage were more complex than was thought at the time, due partly to the decline of circulatory migration between the villages and urban centres by the 1940s, and partly to the ways in which women creatively combined cash-cropping and kinship-based subsistence strategies.[92]

Yet despite these complexities it was clear that the mines had a major effect on rural society, which even contemporary observers thought was 'in many ways worse off than before'.[93] What made their impact so damaging was the vicious circle of scarcity and migration that they initiated. The more labour they drew from the villages, the poorer the villages became; and the poorer the villages became, the greater the motivation for young men to leave for the industrial centres. In the absence of a solution for the push-factor of poverty, one possible remedy was to reduce the urban pull-factor via the 'dual wage' system, which kept African mine wages far below those of Europeans. But this blatantly discriminatory practice could only achieve so much, and in any event was becoming less effective as urban work-forces began to stabilize. Although it would seem logical to assume that the policy of labour stabilization should have mitigated the problem of rural out-migration,

[90] It was especially productive when supplemented by other practices such as mound cultivation of tuber crops: see Audrey I. Richards, *Land, Labour and Diet in Northern Rhodesia: An Economic Study of the Bemba Tribe* (London: Oxford University Press, 1939); on early attempts to ban *citemene* cultivation, see Mwelwa C. Musambachime, 'Colonialism and the Environment in Zambia, 1890–1964', in Chipungu (ed.), *Guardians in their Time*, 8–29, here 9–12.

[91] Richards, *Land, Labour and Diet*, 22–3; Henrietta L. Moore and Megan Vaughan, *Cutting Down Trees: Gender, Nutrition and Agricultural Change in the Northern Province of Zambia, 1890–1990* (London: James Currey, 1994), 48–9.

[92] Such strategies often involved the substitution of protein-rich millet by protein-poor cassava as the key staple crop in response to the absence of male tree-cutting labour: Moore and Vaughan, *Cutting*, esp. 47–9, 79–89, 140–4.

[93] Godfrey Wilson, *An Essay on the Economics of Detribalization in Northern Rhodesia*, Part 1 (Livingstone: Rhodes-Livingstone Institute, 1941), 38.

in the event its implications were ambiguous. While on the one hand it helped alleviate the gender imbalance in the villages by enabling wives and children to accompany male workers to the mining towns, on the other hand it also brought improvements to urban welfare facilities that made the towns more attractive to young people living in the countryside. It was a dilemma that post-colonial governments struggled to resolve as well.

Labour and food were by no means the only regional resources that were exploited by the mines. Wildlife was also acutely affected by the appetites of the industrial towns, both for meat and for sport. Game was in fact one of the more plentiful resources in the area; in the late 1920s most of the European personnel on the Copperbelt reportedly flocked into the bush 'hunting anything they could see'.[94] As the mines grew, the quantity and diversity of local fauna correspondingly declined. By the 1950s game populations were 'virtually non-existent' across much of the Copperbelt, partly because of habitat loss, but mostly due to what officials saw as 'indiscriminate, if not actually illegal' overhunting by urban residents, both European and African.[95] Paradoxically, the tightening of hunting regulations in Northern Rhodesia in 1948 probably worsened the situation on the Copperbelt by making it more attractive for European residents to seek nearby hunting opportunities rather than travel further afield. In Katanga too, workers occasionally went absent for weeks at a time in search of game and fish, whether for their own consumption or for commercial sale. Eventually their forays into the surrounding countryside led to clashes between the UMHK and local chiefs, particularly when workers damaged important spawning grounds by dynamiting for fish.[96]

During the early years of expansion, the local game resource furnished an important food subsidy for the mining centres. But it could hardly meet all of their protein requirements over the longer term, which meant that the task of obtaining a more regular source of meat was crucial for sustaining the growth and the productivity of the mines. By far the largest provider was the Compagnie d'Élevage et d'Alimentation du Katanga (ELEKAT), a commercial ranching concern that supplied around 90 per cent of the UMHK's meat purchases by the early 1930s. Established in 1925, it incorporated sixteen butcheries, seven dairies, as well as numerous grazing concessions, the largest of them a 100,000-hectare ranch on the high plateau of Biano. It also purchased and processed meat from a plethora of subsidiary suppliers, some as far away as Southern Rhodesia, Ruanda-Urundi, and Lake Kivu.[97]

Building a mass-production livestock industry in Central Africa required significant biological adaptations, both to the organisms being reared and to the environments in which they were kept. First of all, ranchers needed highly productive cattle that were able to cope with the region's climate and vegetation. Towards

[94] Watson, *African Highway*, 174.

[95] *Report of a Soil and Land-Use Survey of the Copperbelt*, 132.

[96] Higginson, *Working Class*, 139.

[97] The largest of which was the massive 300,000-hectare concession run by the Compagnie des Grands Élevages Congolais: Letcher, *South Central Africa*, 199–201; Michael Hubbard, *Agricultural Exports and Economic Growth: A Study of the Botswana Beef Industry* (London: KPI, 1986), 235.

this end, they cross-bred local cattle with different exotic varieties; the Laiterie Coopérative du Katanga, for instance, bred African cows with Devon, Hereford, and Friesland bulls, the latter obtained from farms in South Africa.[98] Second, they needed to control the local disease ecology to minimize livestock loss. The most serious threat was trypanosomiasis, which was a central factor in decisions about the location of ranching operations. While parts of Katanga were relatively safe, the Copperbelt was swarming with tsetse flies when work commenced there in the 1920s. At Luanshya only two of the 500 cattle imported in 1928 were still alive in 1930, and nearly all the imported dogs perished as well. Although bush clearance and hunting reduced the tsetse area to small pockets by the 1940s, commercial ranching never took off on the Copperbelt, not least because of well-founded fears that the overgrazing of what was mostly marginal browsing land would cause acute sheet erosion on the Kafue watershed.[99] As a result, the Northern Rhodesian mines drew meat from as far away as Botswana, where they sparked a wave of borehole drilling and herd expansion after 1945.[100]

Perhaps the biggest impact of the mines' protein requirements was felt not on the terrestrial environment but on the aquatic ecosystems of the region. This was especially true of the UMHK, which relied more heavily on fish supplies than the Rhodesian companies did. In 1911, the Belgian administration encouraged the rapid development of local fisheries in order to wean the mines off expensive beef imports from the south. The main supply areas were Lake Mweru and the Luapula River, which lay on the Congolese/Rhodesian border just over 200 kilometres east of Élisabethville. At the behest of the Belgian authorities, a group of expatriate (mostly Greek) traders migrated into the area in the 1910s to act as middlemen between local fishermen and the UMHK. The volume of fish purchases rose markedly after the completion of the first all-weather road between Élisabethville and Kasenga (situated on the Luapula River) in 1918, and was boosted yet again in the 1930s by the construction of an ice plant there. Once this infrastructure was in place, the colonial government encouraged the Greek merchants to move directly into fishing on the assumption that they could provide a cheaper and more reliable source of proteins than their African suppliers could. Using large boats and long gill nets, they in fact netted far more than the local fishermen could catch in their canoes. From 1919 to 1949 the overall catch from Mweru-Luapula rose from 160 tons to over 6,000 tons, around half of it the prized *mpumbu*, or Luapula salmon, an important fish for the local economy and the target species for delivery to the mines.[101]

---

[98] A. Gavage, 'L'Essor de la colonisation agricole européenne dans le Haut-Katanga', *VIIe Congrès International d'Agriculture Tropicale et Subtropicale: comptes-rendus et rapports* (Paris, 1937), 47–52.

[99] *First Report on a Regional Survey of the Copperbelt 1959*, 89; *Report of a Soil and Land-Use Survey of the Copperbelt*, 134; Watson, *African Highway*, 174.

[100] Hubbard, *Agricultural Exports*, 70, 123–7.

[101] David M. Gordon, *Nachituti's Gift: Economy, Society and Environment in Central Africa* (Madison, Wis.: University of Wisconsin Press, 2006), 70, 90; Mwelwa C. Musambachime, 'Rural Political Protest: The 1953 Disturbances in Mweru-Luapula', *International Journal of African Historical Studies*, vol. 20 no. 3 (1987), 437–53, here 440–1.

As pressure on fish stocks rose, the effects quickly snowballed. The spawning period of the Luapula salmon had long been a highlight of the local fishing calendar. The peak came just after the first heavy rains in February/March as huge shoals from Lake Mweru ascended the rapids of the Luapula River and its tributaries, where they occasionally made the water in the spawning grounds so cloudy with sperm milt as to render it temporarily undrinkable. Throughout the first half of the year, local fisherman could haul in hefty catches without jeopardizing long-term population numbers. But the advent of the mines altered the equation. The first clear indications of overfishing came in the late 1930s, and grew increasingly plain during the Second World War as Belgian authorities encouraged bigger catches to feed the inflated wartime workforce. After the war—and despite conspicuous warning signs—the Greek fishermen introduced bottom-set gill nets on Lake Mweru in order to boost the catch during what had previously been the low season from July to December. It was a fateful blow to an already stressed fishery. In 1949 the salmon population abruptly collapsed, threatening severe consequences for the rural communities that relied on it. In response to this entirely unnatural disaster, authorities on both sides of the Congolese/Rhodesian border agreed a stricter set of regulations including a total fishing ban during the spawning season, minimum mesh sizes, and mandatory apertures in fish traps to allow small fry to escape. But the blanket enforcement of these conservation measures infuriated locals, who understandably felt that they were being unfairly punished for a problem caused by Europeans. Many Northern Rhodesian officials privately agreed, though their sympathy did not stop the controversy from becoming a magnet for anti-colonial sentiment in the 1950s.[102]

Besides food, the mining centres also consumed vast amounts of wood. When work first started in Katanga, firewood provided most of the fuel for the boilers as well as the locomotives. During the first decade of UMHK's operations the demand for fuel-wood was enormous, and so were the consequences for nearby woodlands. In the early 1920s managers were already alarmed at the extent of local deforestation and the imminent prospect of wood shortages. A botanist who was studying the region suggested that 'the whites, only just installed in the area, are changing... the face of the countryside to such an extent that the indigenous vegetation of Katanga will soon be completely modified'.[103] After the First World War, rising coal imports (which increased from 100 million tons in 1920 to 400 million in 1930, mostly from the Wankie colliery in South Rhodesia) took some of the pressure off local woodlands, as did the discovery of coal deposits at Luena around 130 kilometres north of Kolwezi.[104] The Rhodesian mines were less reliant than UMHK on fuel-wood, since coal from the Wankie colliery played a central role

---

[102] Gordon, *Nachituti's Gift*, 115–20, 129–38; Musambachime, 'Rural Political Protest', 441–2.

[103] Émile de Wildeman, *Contribution à l'étude de la flore du Katanga* (Brussels: D. Reynaert, 1921), xcii, liii.

[104] Robert, *Le Centre*, 140–1; R. E. Birchard, 'Copper in the Katanga Region of the Belgian Congo', *Economic Geography*, vol. 16 (1940), 429–36, here 432; on Wankie colliery, Ian Phimister, *Wangi Kolia: Coal, Capital and Labour in Colonial Zimbabwe, 1894–1954* (Johannesburg: Witwatersrand University Press, 1994).

from the outset. But even so, their need for construction lumber put a major strain on local forests. In the 1940s the 'big four' mines on the Copperbelt required around 1.8 million cubic feet of sawn timber and poles annually.[105] When wartime shipping disruptions temporarily cut off Canadian and Australian supplies, which provided most of the large beams used for underground tunnels, local forests were the only thing that kept the mines running. After the war these woodlands remained an important source of lumber, while also furnishing a much-needed fuel supplement to offset the growing coal shortages from Wankie colliery, which was unable to keep up with demand during the post-war boom.[106]

Furthermore, the demand for wood was not limited to the mines themselves. Household consumption took a heavy toll on the forests near the industrial townships. Urban residents initially collected fuel-wood wherever they could find it. On the Copperbelt there were already fears of an 'exhaustion of free forest lands' by the late 1930s, which soon prompted the Northern Rhodesian government to set aside special reserves near the cities. Few people, however, were willing to pay the associated charge of 2s. 6d. per cord for reserve wood, and some took the risk of gathering it without payment. As residents had to trek further and further to collect free wood, the despised surcharge on nearby forest reserves became one of the many grievances that sparked the strikes of 1940.[107]

But despite the complaints among city dwellers, forest conservation on the Copperbelt became increasingly stringent as urban populations continued to rise. In the early 1950s the Copperbelt cities consumed around 8,000 hectares of local woodland each year, and the trend was clearly upward. In an attempt to ensure adequate wood supplies for the future, the government set up a gigantic 6,000-square-kilometre forest estate in the Western Province of Northern Rhodesia. On the Copperbelt itself, it also created twenty-seven forest reserves and four protected areas, which together covered over 200,000 hectares. But the price of enclosing these woodlands was high, both socially (by denying access to unauthorized users) and ecologically (by replacing vast swathes of native *miombo* bush with fast-growing Oregon pine plantations).[108] Overall it is estimated that around 150,000 hectares of Copperbelt woodland were cleared between 1937 and 1962, either by urban residents or by colonial forestry officials. Although much of this area was eventually converted to exotic species such as Oregon pine, around a third failed to regenerate over the following decades due to poor management.[109]

---

[105] Moore, *These African Copper Miners*, 120.

[106] In 1954 this amounted to 1.25 million tons of fuel-wood: *Report of a Soil and Land-Use Survey of the Copperbelt*, 186.

[107] *Report of the Commission* (1940), 34; also Godfrey Wilson, *An Essay on the Economics of Detribalization in Northern Rhodesia*, Part 2 (Livingstone: Rhodes-Livingstone Institute, 1942), 30.

[108] *Report of a Soil and Land-Use Survey of the Copperbelt*, 186–8; *First Report on a Regional Survey of the Copperbelt 1959*, 10–12, 54–8; H. M. N. Less, *Organisation for the Production of a Working Plan for the Forests Supplying the Copperbelt of Northern Rhodesia* (Lusaka: Government Printer, 1962), 1; Kate B. Showers, 'Electrifying Africa: An Environmental History with Policy Implications', *Geografiska Annaler: Series B, Human Geography*, vol. 93 no. 3 (2011), 193–221, here 209–10.

[109] E. N. Chidumayo, 'Land Use, Deforestation and Reforestation in the Zambian Copperbelt', *Land Degradation & Development*, vol. 1 no. 3 (1989), 209–16.

The damage to the forests, significant though it was, would have been far worse without the development of hydroelectricity in the region. As mentioned above, the UMHK invested heavily in hydroelectric generation once the commercial viability of electrolytic refining had been established. When the first plant was completed on the Lufira River in 1930 (Francqui station at Mwandingusha) it not only provided power for the new electrolytic refinery at Panda/Jadotville; it also served notice to the many wood- and coal-powered steam turbines that had hitherto generated the electricity for the mining and processing facilities. As the western mines of Kolwezi, Musonoi, and Ruwe came on stream, additional turbines were added at the station to cover their energy needs. By the end of the 1930s Francqui's output had doubled to nearly 250 million kWh, and a decade later it doubled again to just under half a million kWh. In conjunction with the new colliery at Luena, the expansion of hydroelectric generation brought a dramatic reduction in the UMHK's reliance on foreign coal imports, which fell from 400 million tons in 1930 to only 77 million tons in 1937. At the same time, it also significantly reduced the pressure on regional woodlands.[110] But the provision of cheap hydro-electricity nonetheless brought its own environmental costs. The construction of the Francqui station and the creation of its artificial lake (now Lake Tshangalele) destroyed around 40 kilometres of riverine habitat and no less than 400 km² of forest.

The advent of hydroelectricity did not, therefore, reduce the energy footprint of the mines so much as rearrange it. In essence it gave the mines a new means of exploiting the energy flows of their hinterlands, and the Francqui hydropower station was only the beginning. As post-war copper prices boomed, another 250 million kWh turbine centre was opened in 1950 10 kilometres downstream from Francqui. Two years later came the 560 million kWh Delcommune installation on the nearby Lualaba River, whose 160-metre dam created an artificial lake (now Lake Nzilo) around 200 km² in size. In 1956 the completion of the nearby Le Marinel complex signalled a whole new scale of operations: with a production capacity just short of 1.5 billion kWh, it rivalled the largest hydroelectric plant in Western Europe at the time (Génissiat on the Rhône).[111] Le Marinel not only ended the lingering energy bottlenecks in Katanga, it also ushered in a new era for the distant mines (and forests) of Northern Rhodesia. Woodland clearance on the Copperbelt peaked in 1956 and fell rapidly over the following years as the demand for fuel-wood declined. During the late 1950s the Copperbelt mines annually imported around 750,000 kWh (half of their total electricity needs) from Le Marinel.[112] Thanks to the construction of long-distance 220,000-volt transmission lines, the Rhodesian mines could now harness the power of a river system some 350 kilometres away.

Yet even Le Marinel was dwarfed by what came next. The Kariba Dam—by far the largest infrastructural project ever launched in sub-Saharan Africa—formed

[110] Birchard, 'Copper', 432; Robert, *Le Centre*, 140–1, 168.

[111] *UMHK: 1906–1956*, 147, 177–9, 214–15.

[112] Northern Rhodesia Chamber of Mines, *Yearbook* (1959), 11; Showers, 'Electrifying', 210–11; Gerhard Everwyn, 'Which Way in Katanga?', *African Affairs*, vol. 61 no. 243 (Apr. 1962), 149–57, here 156.

the definitive linkage between the mines and waterways of Central Africa. Spanning a remote stretch of the Zambezi River, it ranked (and still ranks) as one of the chief engineering wonders of the world. The dam itself is gargantuan: 128 metres high and 620 metres long. During the five years after its initial closure in 1958, it slowly but surely created the largest artificial lake in the world, Lake Kariba. Although it was designed to serve several purposes—including the provision of irrigation water and the creation of a major inland fishery—the chief aim was to provide electricity for the newly created Federation of Rhodesia and Nyasaland. From the outset, the main recipient of this power was not the regional population but rather the copper mines located some 550 kilometres to the north. By the early 1960s, the Kariba power station annually sent over one billion kWh to the Copperbelt via special 330 kV long-distance lines that transported more power over a longer distance than anything hitherto attempted on the continent.[113] As Kate Showers has argued, the Kariba project epitomized how science and technology were deployed to connect 'widely separated islands of Neo-European technological modernity over the heads of excluded African majorities'.[114]

Kariba fulfilled its engineering aims magnificently, but it did much else besides. For one thing, it involved the traumatic resettlement of around 57,000 Tonga people, who were forced to vacate their riverine lands for higher ground that was less fertile and supported far fewer livestock.[115] Although advocates of the resettlement plan argued that the plentiful fish harvests from the new lake would compensate for the loss of rich floodplain pastures, as it turned out the Tonga found it difficult to secure access rights to the lakeshore. Moreover, even those who were able to fish the lake found their catches declining steeply over the course of the 1960s, as the initially high nutrient and mineral levels (caused by decaying vegetation on the new lakebed) fell to normal levels.[116] To add insult to injury, most of the resettlement villages never even received electricity; indeed, the majority still lacked it over sixty years later.[117]

---

[113] Crucially, Kariba supplied around two-thirds of the Copperbelt's electricity needs during the early 1960s as fighting disrupted supplies from the Congo: Northern Rhodesia Chamber of Mines: *Yearbook* (1962), 11; Northern Rhodesia, *Annual Report of the Mines Department for the Year 1963* (Lusaka: Government Printer, 1964), 9; Showers, 'Electrifying', 199.

[114] Showers, 'Electrifying', 207; see also Julia Tischler, *Light and Power for a Multiracial Nation: The Kariba Dam Scheme in the Central African Federation* (Houndmills: Palgrave, 2013).

[115] Elizabeth Colson, *Social Organisation of the Gwembe Tonga* (Manchester: Manchester University Press, 1960); Elizabeth Colson, *The Social Consequences of Resettlement: The Impact of the Kariba Resettlement upon the Gwembe Tonga* (Manchester: Manchester University Press, 1971); Thayer Scudder, *The Ecology of the Gwembe Tonga* (Manchester: Manchester University Press, 1962); JoAnn McGregor, *Crossing the Zambezi: The Politics of Landscape on a Central African Frontier* (Oxford: James Currey, 2009), esp. chs 6–9; JoAnn McGregor, 'Living with the River: Landscape and Memory in the Zambezi Valley, Northwest Zimbabwe', in William Beinart and JoAnn McGregor (eds), *Social History and African Environments* (Oxford: James Currey, 2003), 87–105.

[116] Eugene K. Balon and André G. Coche (eds), *Lake Kariba: A Man-Made Tropical Ecosystem in Central Africa* (The Hague: Junk, 1974).

[117] Julia Tischler, 'Cementing Uneven Development: The Central African Federation and the Kariba Dam Scheme', *Journal of Southern African Studies*, vol. 40 no. 5 (2014), 1047–64; Baboki Kayawe, 'Electricity for All but Those the Kariba Dam Displaced', *Inter Press Service*, 26 Mar. 2013: <http://www.ipsnews.net/2013/03/electricity-for-all-but-those-the-kariba-dam-displaced/>.

More generally, the flooding of 5,580 km² of the Zambezi plain—home to large herds of elephant, hippopotami, antelope, and zebra, as well as top predators such as lions and leopards—represented perhaps the single largest act of habitat destruction in colonial history. It is therefore no coincidence that Kariba was also the site of the single greatest wildlife rescue operation to date: the aptly named Operation Noah, which captured over 6,000 animals (ranging from birds to rhinos) for relocation to higher ground, mainly to the new Matusadona National Park on the southern bank of the new lake.[118] From 1958 to 1964 the rescue campaign above the Kariba Dam was one of the primary rallying points for nature preservation groups around the globe.

Lake Kariba remains one of the largest anthropogenic objects on the planet, and in view of the conservationist furore that surrounded its creation, it seems more than a little ironic that its shimmering waters and dramatic shoreline were eventually celebrated as wonders of 'nature' themselves. Among many Euro-Zimbabweans, at least, the lake fulfilled a deep cultural yearning for water in the semi-arid region, and it soon became an object of conservation in its own right.[119] The sense of irony is by no means diminished by the intimate connection between the beauty of the lake and the scarred and polluted mining landscapes of the Copperbelt.

It is generally agreed that industrialization marked a profound turning point in the relationship between human society and the biophysical environment. As the deployment of new energy-intensive technologies helped bring about an unprecedented acceleration of economic activity, industrial cities pulled in resources and emitted wastes on a correspondingly unparalleled scale. Although the point is usually made with reference to nineteenth-century Europe, in many respects it is applicable wherever and whenever processes of industrialization have taken hold. From the 1910s to the 1960s, the mining hubs of Katanga and Northern Rhodesia were, despite all the obvious differences with industrial cradles such as the Midlands or the Ruhr, epicentres of an industrial upheaval that echoed throughout the surrounding region. 'We in Northern Rhodesia to-day are living in a revolution, the intensity of which, as far as we can judge, has not been equalled in thousands of years,' wrote the anthropologist J. Clyde Mitchell in 1951.[120] Even though Mitchell, like most contemporary observers, was mainly interested in the social impact of Western industrialism on what he called the 'traditional way of life', the environmental consequences of this upheaval were no less revolutionary.

For most contemporaries, however, none of these consequences seemed very important when balanced against the profits, revenues, and tens of thousands of jobs generated by the mines. Nearly everyone in the region—the company managers and state officials, the workers in the pits and their union representatives—was heavily invested in the copper industry and the wealth it created. For all the

[118] Charles Lagus, *Operation Noah* (London: William Kimber, 1959); Eric Robins and Ronald Legge, *Animal Dunkirk: The Story of Lake Kariba and 'Operation Noah', the Greatest Animal Rescue since the Ark* (London: Herbert Jenkins, 1959).

[119] David McDermott Hughes, 'Whites and Water: How Euro-Africans Made Nature at Kariba Dam', *Journal of Southern African Studies*, vol. 32 no. 4 (Dec. 2006), 823–38.

[120] Mitchell, 'Note', 20.

bitter disputes over how this wealth should be distributed, virtually all parties were agreed on the aim of extracting as much of it from the ground as they could. The result was a kind of socio-environmental lock-in that was difficult to escape, and that was equally familiar to mining centres in many other parts of the world. Within this context, the pollution of air or water was generally regarded as an unavoidable side-effect of an otherwise vital activity. Moreover, such logic generated a powerful socio-political momentum that was hard to deflect off its current course. This was true even in open democratic societies, as the long history of civic campaigns against industrial pollution in Europe and North America clearly shows. Such inertia was all the more difficult to resist in colonial contexts where there was far less political scope for dissent and remediation. The role of the mining firms as the prime export earners in the Congo and Northern Rhodesia gave them far-reaching discretion to run their own affairs, and generated little incentive among officials to constrain their effects on the physical environment. The basic pattern was hardly unique to the copper industry, but was broadly replicated across the entire mining sector of colonial Africa.[121]

This situation changed little after the demise of colonial rule. The nationalization of UMHK into La Générale des Carrières et des Mines (Gécamines) in 1966, and the subsequent nationalization and conglomeration of the Rhodes Selection Trust and Anglo-American into Zambia Consolidated Copper Mines (ZCCM) from 1970 to 1982, made almost no difference with respect to environmental regulation. If anything, it made managers and politicians even more determined to maximize profits and even less responsive to environmental concerns given the overwhelming importance of the mines for the revenues of post-colonial states (and, in the case of Gécamines in particular, for lining the pockets of Zairean officials). What's more, after the oil crisis of the 1970s sent copper prices tumbling, pollution problems were the last thing on anyone's mind. The collapse of global demand for primary commodities spelled trouble for most post-colonial economies, but the overwhelming dependence of Zambia and Zaire on copper revenues meant that it dealt them a particularly devastating blow. As debts continued to swell in the 1980s, environmental protection was scarcely a government priority amidst the incessant demands for 'structural readjustment' by the IMF and World Bank, which, for their part, strongly encouraged poor debtor countries with mineral resources to privatize their mines and boost production as a means of literally digging themselves out of a hole. It was only in the 1990s, and especially since 2000, that the main international lending bodies incorporated environmental impact studies and regulatory mechanisms into the standard package of 'neo-liberal' reforms.[122]

[121] See generally Greg Lanning and Marti Mueller, *Africa Undermined: Mining Companies and the Underdevelopment of Africa* (Harmondsworth: Penguin, 1979).

[122] Michael Goldman, *Imperial Nature: The World Bank and Struggles for Social Justice in the Age of Globalization* (New Haven: Yale University Press, 2005), esp. 97, 119; on the Copperbelt specifically, Dan Haglund, 'From Boom to Bust: Diversity and Regulation in Zambia's Privatized Copper Sector', in Fraser and Larmer (eds), *Zambia, Mining, and Neoliberalism*, 91–126, esp. 95–7; also John Craig, 'Putting Privatisation into Practice: The Case of Zambia Consolidated Copper Mines Limited', *Journal of Modern African Studies*, vol. 39 (2001), 389–410.

Around the turn of the millennium, as Gécamines and ZCCM were in the throes of re-privatization, the World Bank commissioned two major studies into the environmental legacies of nine decades of copper mining in Central Africa. What they found was sobering, though not surprising. In both Katanga and the Copperbelt, heavy emissions of sulphur dioxide—especially at Nkana, Mufulira, and Lubumbashi—had severely contaminated the soil and rendered vegetation virtually 'non-existent' downwind from the smelters (revealingly, the temporary closure of the Lubumbashi smelter from 1993 to 1999 allowed a gradual return of vegetation). Nitrous oxides, heavy metal dust particles, toxic reagents from the concentrators, and PCB-based oil from electricity transformers had entered food-chains and caused serious damage to aquatic ecosystems. Perennial run-off and leakages from the thousands of hectares of waste dumps and tailings compounds were still exerting 'widespread negative impacts' in the rivers of the Kafue basin. More acute problems followed the occasional failure of tailing dams, such as the collapse of TD 33C at Nkana in 1997, which released around 1 million tons of tailings into the Chibuluma River and wrecked farmland many kilometres down-stream. Arguably the worst single pollution incident was the enormous accidental discharge of heavy metal effluents from the control dam at Nchanga in November 2006, which turned the Muschishima stream (as well as stretches of the Kafue River) a garish turquoise colour, deprived some 2 million district inhabitants of drinking water for two days, and eventually triggered a wave of lawsuits from poisoned residents. But despite such spectacular events, it was the creeping, cumulative build-up of toxicity that was perhaps the most ominous threat over the long term. In parts of the Kafubu valley below the tailings dump of the Kipushi mine, Congolese activists discovered soil concentrations of copper and cobalt over sixty times higher than international thresholds.[123] It is generally agreed that these problems are only the tip of the iceberg. Over a century after the birth of Central Africa's copper industry, the full costs have yet to be counted.

[123] World Bank, *Copperbelt Environment Project*, Rep. No. 25347-ZA (2003), 5, 18, 27, 73–9, 105–16; SNC-Lavalin International, *Étude sur la restauration des mines de cuivre et de cobalt*, République Démocratique du Congo, Apr. 2003, esp. 43–50; Réseau Ressources Naturelles, *L'Impact de l'exploitation minière sur l'environnement du Katanga*, 16–20. On the 2006 Nchanga incident, Jean-Christophe Servant, 'Mined out in Zambia', *Le Monde diplomatique* (May 2009): <http://mondediplo.com/2009/05/09zambia>; 'Konkola Copper Mines Negligence Blamed for Kafue River Pollution', *Times of Zambia* (15 Nov. 2006).

6

Oil, Empire, and Environment

In the preceding chapters we have investigated how Europe's empire was shaped by natural resources, and how the exploitation of these resources helped maintain and augment its global dominance. From Malaya's rubber to Katanga's copper deposits, control over tropical nature was both a reflection and a source of Europe's imperial power. As we turn our attention to oil it is worth pausing, very briefly, to consider the nature of this imperial 'power' and what we mean by the concept.

The fundamental bases of power and the ways in which it is constructed and exerted are, of course, questions that scholars have grappled with for a very long time. From Marx to Weber to Foucault and beyond, generations of theorists have pondered these issues, and have profoundly shaped historical debates in the process. For all the differences of opinion, the common aim has been to understand power as a social phenomenon, one rooted in the creation or maintenance of a particular constellation of people, institutions, and values that (re)produces differentials of wealth and influence. By and large, historians have been far less concerned, if at all, with power in the physical sense of the term, defined most elementally as energy converted into action. At first glance this might seem a naively banal observation, one that merely reflects the multiple meanings of a word whose different uses mirror the disciplinary divisions between the social and natural sciences. But as a number of scholars have recently pointed out, the relationship between these two meanings merits closer attention, for in certain ways the distinction is misleading.[1] When looked at more closely, physical and social power can be seen as more than just separate phenomena accidentally sharing the same label. On the contrary, they have various traits in common and are in some respects closely linked.

The basic connection is energy, because harnessing energy is fundamental to both physical and social power. Just as all material systems are propelled by flows of energy, so too do all societies rely on the capture of energy and its conversion into particular types of work. Over the centuries humans have devised many different schemes for this purpose. Before the nuclear age they revolved almost exclusively around harnessing solar energy in some form or another, most of it captured directly or indirectly via photosynthesis—grain and other crops for

---

[1] Edmund Russell et al., 'The Nature of Power: Synthesizing the History of Technology and Environmental History', *Technology and Culture*, vol. 52 no. 2 (Apr. 2011), 246–59; Mitchell, *Carbon Democracy*; Timothy Mitchell, 'Carbon Democracy', *Economy and Society*, vol. 38 no. 3 (Aug. 2009), 399–432.

food, grass for animal fodder, wood or fossilized biomass for fuel. Some systems tapped other energy flows, though even the wind and river currents used for transport, milling, or turbines ultimately derive from weather systems driven by solar energy. As Alfred Crosby has reminded us, in the final analysis we are all 'children of the sun'.[2]

But regardless of its source, one of the key physical traits of energy is that it can be concentrated and stored in various forms, whether in wheat silos, forest reserves, coal sheds, or reservoirs. This characteristic has important social implications, for the greater one's access to energy—whether through control over its dispersal or the possession of larger stocks—the greater is one's ability to convert it into action. As a consequence, tracing energy flows and analysing how they are concentrated, governed, distributed, and deployed is a remarkably useful tool for mapping the basic structures of social and political power.[3]

Viewing Europe's imperial power through this lens helps to highlight just how much it derived from the application of unprecedented amounts of fossilized energy to a multitude of new industrial, military, and commercial activities. The mass conversion to coal in the nineteenth century first allowed Britain, then parts of continental Europe and North America, to undertake a wholesale reorganization of their energy systems, with momentous consequences for world history.[4] The windfall provided by millions of years of concentrated solar energy helped sustain otherwise unattainable levels of economic expansion, which in turn formed the basis of Europe's global pre-eminence. By the middle of the century, this energy shift was already reflected in the power differential that had opened up between the industrial and non-industrial world.[5] By the 1870s, it also helped propel the wave of imperial conquest that swept the tropics. Coal powered the ships and railways that enabled Europe's military forces to control territories that had hitherto resisted their advances. Over the following years it also fuelled the enormous expansion of inter-continental trade and the ecological transformations that flowed from it. By the turn of the century, the increasing diffusion of coal-based energy systems had boosted the metabolism of the entire global economy.[6] Few aspects of the modern world, and Europe's role within it, can be understood without reference to this energy shift.

The subsequent rise of oil around 1900 was in some ways a continuation of this story, though in certain respects it opened a whole new chapter. Compared to coal, petroleum is an even more concentrated source of energy with even greater potential to be converted into social, economic, and political power. Its chief physical characteristics—fluidity and a higher energy-to-weight ratio than coal—had

[2] Alfred Crosby, *Children of the Sun: A History of Humanity's Unappeasable Appetite for Energy* (New York: Norton, 2006); Vaclav Smil, *Energy in World History* (Boulder, Colo.: Westview, 1994). Strictly speaking, of course, solar energy is itself a form of nuclear energy.

[3] Russell et al., 'Nature of Power', esp. 249–55; Mitchell, *Carbon Democracy*.

[4] See generally Sieferle, *Subterranean Forest*.

[5] Pomeranz, *Great Divergence*; E. A. Wrigley, *Continuity, Chance, and Change: The Character of the Industrial Revolution in England* (Cambridge: Cambridge University Press, 1988), 68–97.

[6] Bruce Podobnik, *Global Energy Shifts: Fostering Sustainability in a Turbulent Age* (Philadelphia: Temple University Press, 2006), 23–33.

important social and political implications. For one thing, they made oil easier and more cost-effective to transport over large distances, which meant that its production and distribution tended to operate on a more global scale than other sources of energy. In turn, this global scale helps explain why the petroleum industry has historically been dominated by large multinational corporations—a consciously pursued organizational form, to be sure, but one that was also encouraged by the need, unlike coal, for extensive refining and processing before most products reached end consumers. Moreover, the easy portability of liquid hydrocarbon, which replaced furnace stokers with pumps and heavy coal bunkers with small tanks, meant that oil had more potential applications than coal. Its remarkable versatility, especially when wedded to the internal combustion engine, spawned a multitude of new ways to apply fossil energy to human designs, and soon led to the emergence of a whole new energy regime that revolutionized economies, transformed consumer expectations, and reshaped global politics.[7]

Oil thus became a source of immense power over the course of the twentieth century, and as such it influenced the geography of Europe's empire in numerous ways. The contest for control over oil flows was a key element in the closing stages of European expansion, especially in the waning Ottoman Empire. By the 1910s it was increasingly regarded as a strategic resource of the utmost importance, and it played a vital role in both world wars (the Second far more than the First). As the search for petroleum opened new frontiers of trade and investment, it brought profound changes for local societies and economies, from the influx of foreign goods and labourers to the formation of new lifestyles and social hierarchies. Its ecological consequences were also momentous, and broadly fell into two main categories: the modification of environments for oil exploitation, and the problems arising from the limits of human control over the material forces that people sought to master.

These biophysical aspects of petroleum extraction are the focus of this chapter, which surveys the connections between oil, environmental change, and empire from the late nineteenth century to the Second World War. Though less familiar than the political and economic aspects of the story, it is nonetheless an enormous topic that can only be outlined here. We will focus on key parts of Europe's petroleum empire in Southeast Asia, the Middle East, and the Caribbean, which included territories both formally and informally under European domination. The chapter will begin by sketching the rise of colonial oil extraction in the context of the growing strategic importance of petroleum, before examining some of the main environmental consequences of oil production and the technological innovations that shaped it. Given the central role of non-European powers (above all the United States) in the global oil industry, it is necessary to frame the story as part of a broader international system that crossed political boundaries and bound together

---

[7] For overviews, see Daniel Yergin, *The Prize: The Epic Quest for Oil, Money and Power* (New York: Free Press, 2009); Podobnik, *Global Energy*, 49–57, 68–91. The term 'energy regime' comes from McNeill, *Something New*, 297. On the political implications of oil's physical properties, Mitchell, 'Carbon Democracy', esp. 406–9.

distant places through flows of energy, capital, and technology. These spatial linkages are important, but they are not the only ones that concern us here. Equally
crucial are those that united the human and the non-human, the social and the
physical. As we will see, the imperial network of oil connected a multitude of
entities together: the geologist and the forest, the driller and the desert, the motorist
and the subsoil.

THE EARLY PETROLEUM INDUSTRY AND
THE COLONIAL OIL FRONTIER

Mineral oil was put to a variety of human uses long before its deployment as fuel
in the twentieth century. In ancient Mesopotamia, asphalt and bitumen obtained
from ground seepages were employed as medicine, sealant, building mortar,
and weapons. Oil was produced in China as early as 200 BCE, and by the tenth and
eleventh centuries Arab peoples had already begun to distil it for illumination.
For most of the millennium that followed, petroleum products were chiefly used
for lighting and, to a lesser extent, heating. With the onset of industrialization,
demand for lighting oil, lubricants, and (eventually) fuel skyrocketed, above all
in Europe and North America.[8]

Before the middle of the nineteenth century, Europe drew most of its lubricant
and lighting oil from whaling fleets, but as industrial demand outstripped what
marine ecosystems could provide, businesses soon looked to other sources.[9]
Petroleum had long been produced in Romania and Galicia (which became significant producers in the early twentieth century), but the traditional hand-dug shafts
in use at the time could yield only limited amounts. The key breakthrough came
with the introduction of hard-rock drilling near Oil Creek in western Pennsylvania,
based on salt extraction techniques first devised centuries earlier in China. Two
years after Edwin Drake drilled the first 'commercial' well in 1859, a series of
gusher strikes in the area sparked the world's first oil rush, and soon led to the creation of Rockefeller's Standard Oil company.[10] A decade later, huge strikes around
Baku touched off an even bigger oil rush along the shores of the Caspian Sea.
Before long, a cluster of Russian-based firms, above all the Nobel Brothers
Petroleum Company, competed with Standard in the all-important European market for lighting kerosene, the chief petroleum product until the 1900s. Subsequent
strikes from California to the Caucasus sparked yet more booms and boosted
world production still further.

So rapid was the increase in petroleum output that the main producer con-
glomerates were, by the beginning of the twentieth century, just as interested in
restricting oil supplies as in augmenting them. As Timothy Mitchell has emphasized,

---

[8] R. J. Forbes, *Studies in Early Petroleum History* (Leiden: Brill, 1958).
[9] For an overview of early modern whaling: Richard Ellis, *Men and Whales* (New York: Knopf,
1991); Richards, *Unending Frontier*, 574–616.
[10] Brian Black, *Petrolia: The Landscape of America's First Oil Boom* (Baltimore: Johns Hopkins
University Press, 2000).

the history of oil exploration and concession-bargaining during this period should be viewed not merely as a search for new supplies to support an increasingly energy-intensive way of life, but also as a series of efforts to limit and channel these flows of energy in order to keep prices high and enhance the power of the oil firms and their government backers.[11] In the late nineteenth century, the US and Russia dominated world production; Europe, like most of the rest of the world, imported the bulk of its petroleum products from there. But with the growth of Asian kerosene markets, a surge of exploration swept across Europe's eastern empire.

The first colony to attract such attention was Upper Burma, and the manner in which its petroleum industry developed highlights the vital role played by imperial states and military power in enabling oil companies to control these flows of energy. In the area around Yenangyaung, a dry and scrubby strip of land along the Irrawaddy River about 480 kilometres north of Rangoon, locals had extracted oil from hand-dug pits for at least two centuries, reportedly producing up to 25,000 barrels annually by the 1790s. Interest in this so-called 'Rangoon oil' grew sharply after the first Anglo-Burmese war of 1824–6, and by the 1850s Burmese paraffin was being sold to Britain for candle-making. In the wake of the second Anglo-Burmese War of 1852, after which most of Lower Burma was annexed to India, the industry in Yenangyaung had grown to around 130 wells producing up to 46,000 barrels per year. Most of this oil went to the distillation works at Dunnedaw, located at the confluence of the Rangoon and Pegu Rivers just south of Rangoon city, where it was turned into paraffin wax and kerosene for sale on the Indian and British markets. During the 1850s and 1860s the Dunnedaw works were upgraded to handle the expanding flow of Burmese crude, and with the founding of the Irrawaddy Flotilla Company in 1865, which provided a faster and more reliable means of transport than the rafts that had previously hauled petroleum downstream from Yenangyaung, the industry seemed poised to expand. A Burmese oil frontier beckoned (Fig. 6.1).[12]

For European merchants eyeing the situation, there were two main obstacles in the way. First, traditional extraction methods offered limited scope for boosting output, and certainly nothing on the scale envisaged by would-be investors. The hand-dug wells, some of which reached depths of over 60 metres, were as dangerous as they were primitive. Lowered down on ropes, diggers literally waded in the oil that seeped into the well-bottoms and hurriedly baled it into buckets before being hoisted back to the surface to avoid succumbing to the noxious fumes.[13] The introduction of mechanical drills and pumps was clearly necessary for expanding production. But the peculiar way in which oil extraction was organized in Yenangyaung—the second obstacle—presented scant opportunity for such innovations.

---

[11] Mitchell, *Carbon Democracy*, 45–7.
[12] T. A. B. Corley, *A History of the Burmah Oil Company 1886–1924*, vol. 1 (London: Heinemann, 1983), 6–11; E. H. Pascoe, *The Oil-Fields of Burma* (Calcutta: Geological Survey of India, 1912), 6–10; Marilyn V. Longmuir, *Oil in Burma: The Extraction of 'Earth-Oil' to 1914* (Bangkok: White Lotus, 2003).
[13] Longmuir, *Oil*, 43–4; Corley, *Burmah*, vol. 1, 6.

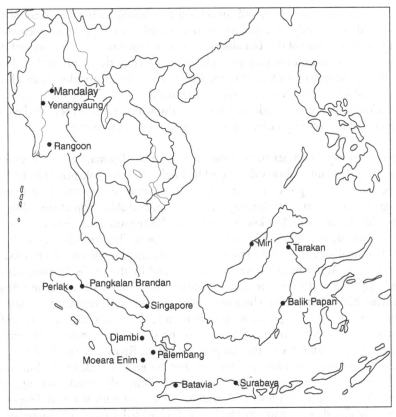

Fig. 6.1. Map indicating the main oilfields of colonial Southeast Asia.

Before the 1880s Upper Burma and its oilfields were still governed as an independent kingdom from Mandalay, and after the second Anglo-Burmese War, King Mindon Min (1853–78) established a royal monopoly that explicitly excluded Europeans from both the production and distribution of crude. Oil extraction had long been controlled by a syndicate of local *twinzayo*, headmen of the two dozen families that held a hereditary royal concession at Yenangyaung. Together, they governed the operations of the individual *twinza*, or well owners, working the oilfield.[14] In exchange for the royal concession, the *twinzayo* sold the entirety of their output to the Crown, which then sold it on for a hefty mark-up through a network of agents who often insisted on taking their own cut from purchasers. This royal monopoly on the energy flow from Yenangyaung made access difficult for the European refiners based in Rangoon. Furthermore, it meant that the richest known oilfield in the region could not be developed on an industrial scale. In response,

---

[14] See, generally, Longmuir, *Oil*.

several European companies tried to circumvent these obstacles by searching for oil in British-controlled Lower Burma, though with little success.[15] The historic oilfields of Upper Burma remained a promising prospect, but only if new production techniques could be deployed. In essence, getting more crude out of the Burmese subsoil required a major investment in Yenangyaung, which ultimately hinged on transforming how it was governed.

As so often the case in the history of resource frontiers, the crucial breakthrough came through military conquest. The third Anglo-Burmese War of November 1885, which resulted in the ousting of King Thibaw and the British annexation of Upper Burma, created a whole new political and legal framework for industrial-scale extraction in Burma. To be clear, the region's petroleum deposits were not among the primary incentives for the British invasion. Tensions had been mounting ever since Thibaw's bloody ascension to the throne in 1878, and the immediate trigger for the war was a dispute over teak extraction payments rather than oil royalties.[16] Yet the petroleum business was certainly one of the chief beneficiaries of the conflict, for it was the annexation of Upper Burma in 1886 that finally opened Yenangyaung to European investment.

No sooner had the war ended than David Cargill, the owner of a small Dunnedaw refinery, secured a small Yenangyaung concession and founded the Burmah Oil Company to work it. Backed by a group of merchants connected to the Scottish shale oil industry, the firm quickly set about prospecting for sites, purchasing additional concessions for exploration, and hiring experienced North American drillers to operate the rigs and supervise the gangs of labourers that serviced them. The company's wells soon reached strata several times deeper than anything dug by hand, and by the early 1890s the drillers were averaging a new well every month. Whereas Burmese output in 1886 had totalled around 50,000 barrels, all of it produced by *twinzas*, by 1891 output had risen to 144,000 barrels, over half of it coming from the Burmah Oil Company alone.[17] As more firms piled into Yenangyaung, and as geologists discovered the rich Singu field around 50 kilometres further north, the industry began to boom. By 1898 Burmese production had swelled to over 500,000 barrels and continued to grow rapidly, surpassing 1 million barrels in 1901, 2 million in 1903, and 3.5 million in 1905.[18]

Building a petroleum industry on this scale inevitably brought significant changes to the region's economy and ecology. At Yenangyaung the local oil-diggers were quickly overrun by the influx of labourers from India and other parts of Burma. Although the *twinzayo* continued to enjoy their hereditary extraction rights under British authority, the industrialization of production in the 1890s and

---

[15] Corley, *Burmah*, vol. 1, 23–4.

[16] For background, Thant Myint-U, *The Making of Modern Burma* (Cambridge: Cambridge University Press, 2001), 186–92. For an eccentric ecological interpretation of the conflict, C. L. Keeton, *King Thebaw and the Ecological Rape of Burma: The Political and Commercial Struggle between British India and French Indo-china in Burma 1878–1886* (Delhi: Manohar, 1974).

[17] Corley, *Burmah*, vol. 1, 30–9. On the drillers, see Christina Burr, 'Some Adventures of the Boys: Enniskillen Township's "Foreign Drillers", Imperialism, and Colonial Discourse, 1873–1923', *Labour/Le Travail*, vol. 51 (Spring 2003), 47–80.

[18] Corley, *Burmah*, vol. 1, 320.

1900s increasingly consigned them to the margins. At the same time, the scrubby bush that had long covered the soils of Yenangyaung was also gradually displaced by a thicket of derricks, pipelines, pump-houses, and collection tanks. Regulations on the oilfield were lax, and operations often messy. In some areas drillers sank wells no more than 60 feet (18 metres) apart in a race to maximize their share of the underground loot, turning the entire surface into a greasy morass and inviting frequent fires that scorched the earth and blackened the sky.[19] Travellers venturing up the Irrawaddy were sometimes jarred by the change of scenery. 'Though in general so fertile', noted one observer in 1908, the section of river running through the 'great oil-field of the country' was one where the hills were barren and the land-scape 'hot and uninviting by comparison', its vegetation replaced by 'the chimneys of pumping stations which stretch for miles along the hills and river-bank'.[20]

Further downstream, the need to convert the swelling flow of crude into saleable products also transformed the landscape around Rangoon. Nearby Dunnedaw was already home to numerous oil-works, sawmills, and other installations before the turn of the century. The oil-works were dirty operations; Burmah's early refinery distilled around half of its feedstock into kerosene, another quarter or so into par-affin, and turned the remaining sludge into furnace fuel by mixing it with rice husks and straw. Although the plant was overhauled in the 1890s to cope with rising crude supplies, its close proximity to Rangoon posed a perennial pollution nuisance and a major fire hazard. Such considerations were, in fact, among the chief reasons behind the construction of a large new facility across the Rangoon River at Syriam, which soon became the main refining centre of the colony.[21]

In order to feed this growing refinery complex, engineers also had to bypass the natural obstacles that lay between it and the oilfields upstream. Burmah Oil was the Irrawaddy Flotilla Company's largest customer by the turn of the century, and although the steamship service between Yenangyaung and Rangoon was generally reliable, its ability to link up the production and processing ends of Burma's great hydrocarbon chain was still beholden to the seasonal vagaries of the Irrawaddy. Like all great flood rivers, the Irrawaddy continually changed course, scraping off parts of the bank in one place and depositing them as irksome sandbars or shallows in another. In a bid to escape the natural vicissitudes of the river, and thereby make the flow of petroleum more predictable, the company built a 480-kilometre steel pipeline connecting its collection tanks at Yenangyaung with the refineries outside Rangoon. Completed in 1908, the pipeline immediately proved its worth: 1908 was the worst year on record for Irrawaddy navigation, and was followed by a season of exceptionally severe monsoon floods in Upper Burma.[22]

Contrary to the picture that is often painted in company histories, this re-engineering of the landscape was much more than just the handiwork of heroic oil pioneers determined to capture the bounty of nature. Rather, it reflected a

---

[19] Longmuir, *Oil*, 228–32; M. V. Longmuir, 'Twinzayo and Twinza: Burmese "Oil Barons" and the British Administration', *Asian Studies Review*, vol. 22 no. 3 (Sept. 1998), 339–56; Corley, *Burmah*, vol. 1, 122–3.

[20] R. Talbot Kelly, *Burma* (London: Black, 1908), 32.

[21] Corley, *Burmah*, vol. 1, 37–40.   [22] Corley, *Burmah*, vol. 1, 60–2, 125–6.

whole bundle of factors including strong state support, long-term financial sponsorship, market privileges, and, of course, the oil itself. Burmah Oil's rise into a major supplier was largely a result of favourable tariff arrangements, which gave it a virtual monopoly within Burma and a dominant position in India's growing kerosene market. It was also thanks to British concessionary policy that Burmah was able to swallow up many of its smaller competitors while simultaneously keeping Standard Oil at bay during the early 1900s. Scientists from the Geological Survey of India played a key role in developing the oilfields at Yenangyaung and Singu, and in 1905 a provisional agreement to provide fuel oil to the Admiralty opened an important potential outlet for Burmese production, which rose to nearly 7 million barrels (around 2 per cent of world output) in 1913.[23] But what ultimately fuelled this network of political and commercial interests was the vast store of energy buried underground, and its supply was limited. By 1912, crews at Yenangyaung had to drill over 600 metres (twice the average depth of 1905) to keep the crude flowing. As wells were successively tapped out, water increasingly seeped in.[24] Although geologists scoured the area in search of additional reserves, they found no other commercially attractive sites beyond those already under development at Singu. On the eve of the First World War Burma's oil frontier was already closing.

By this time, attention had long since shifted to other parts of Southeast Asia, above all the Dutch East Indies. Local knowledge of oil and gas vents in the East Indies was ancient, and explorers' accounts in the sixteenth century already reported the use of petroleum as balm for stiff limbs. By the mid-1860s the East Indies Department of Mines had identified over fifty oil seepages across the archipelago.[25] The first attempt at commercial exploitation came in 1872 when a general-store owner named Jan Reerink began to drill around a well-known seep in the Madjalengka area of West Java. As it turned out, his 'Madja Petroleum' was an unusually light crude ideal for producing kerosene, but it only briefly competed with imported US lamp oil on the Javanese market before the wells tapped out and operations ceased.[26] After this sobering experience it took around a decade before investors once again tried their luck in the East Indies. But when they did, they unwittingly laid the foundations for one of the great corporate oil giants of the twentieth century.

It all started in 1880 when the manager of a Deli tobacco firm, Aeilko Jans Zilkjer, was shown an oil seep near one of the company's coastal plantations in north-east Sumatra. Zilkjer immediately recognized the commercial potential, and after sample tests confirmed a high proportion of kerosene, he quickly acquired

[23] Raja Segaran Arumugam, *State and Oil in Burma: An Introductory Survey* (Singapore: Institute of Southeast Asian Studies, 1977), 4–5; Corley, *Burmah*, 46, 67, 321; R. W. Ferrier, *The History of the British Petroleum Company*, vol. 1: *The Developing Years 1901–1932* (Cambridge: Cambridge University Press, 1982), 3.

[24] Corley, *Burmah*, vol. 1, 174.

[25] J. P. Poley, *Eroïca: The Quest for Oil in Indonesia (1850–1898)* (Dordrecht: Kluwer Academic Publishers, 2000), 5–6, 37–41; F. C. Gerretson, *History of the Royal Dutch*, vol. 1 (Leiden: Brill, 1958), 20–2.

[26] Poley, *Eroïca*, 65–72; Gerretson, *Royal Dutch*, vol. 1, 43–6.

a concession from the local Sultan of Langkat. The concession, known as Telaga Said, was a remote 1,000-hectare strip of dense, marshy jungle near a bend in the Lepan River some 10 kilometres above the Balaban River, which empties into the Strait of Malacca.

Once again, political and military backing was crucial, and sheer luck played a role as well. The fledgling enterprise could count on solid support from the colonial government in Batavia, which was keen to reduce the colony's reliance on US kerosene imports, and was also eager to strengthen the Dutch presence in an area still scarcely under its control. It was only with the help of the East Indies Mines Department that drilling commenced in July 1884. After nearly a year of drilling dry holes, oil and gas finally erupted from a shallow test well in June 1885. Encouraged by this find, investors financed the arduous transportation of deep-drilling equipment to the site. But as so often in the early days of oil exploration, it proved to be a false dawn. Over the following years new strikes were elusive, and to make matters worse, operations were regularly hampered by disease, accidents, and attacks by Achinese warriors resisting Dutch encroachment in the region. By the end of the decade the entire enterprise was in peril, but in 1890 the company's fortunes suddenly turned. While visiting the Netherlands, Zilkjer managed to convince a group of Amsterdam's leading business figures to back the venture, and the confidence this generated disposed King William III to take the unusual step of allowing the enterprise to call itself the 'Royal' Dutch Petroleum Company.[27] Obtaining royal approval was a major coup for the firm, but for Zilkjer himself it was a short-lived triumph: on his return journey to Sumatra he suddenly took ill and died in Singapore.

When the new manager, Jean Baptiste August Kessler, arrived at Langkat in October 1891, the company could finally ramp up production in what he despairingly called 'this god-forsaken, out-of-the-way place'.[28] Biophysical and climatic conditions at the site were indeed challenging. One of the biggest initial problems was the severity of the rainy season. No sooner had workers completed the 10-kilometre railway from the river to the wells than torrential rains washed whole sections of the track away. When new rails were relaid on tree trunks, they too were swept from low-lying areas as the Lepan River flooded. Similar problems hampered the construction of a short pipeline from the wells to the new refinery site at Pangkalan Brandan, a deep spot of the Babalan Bay where ships could be loaded. As labourers worked for days in waist-deep water, food and other supplies ran perilously low due to the unnavigable state of the local rivers. At one point a detail of eighty Chinese workmen was dispatched to a village 20 kilometres away to carry back a few sacks of rice.[29]

If heavy seasonal rains posed periodic difficulties, the remoteness and sparse population of the area presented more enduring challenges. Most of the labourers had to be recruited from Java, Singapore, or Penang, and the harsh working conditions meant that few were very eager to stay. Discipline was correspondingly

[27] Gerretson, *Royal Dutch*, vol. 1, 67–70, 81–3, 93–102.
[28] Quote from Gerretson, *Royal Dutch*, vol. 1, 129.   [29] Gerretson, *Royal Dutch*, 132–3.

severe; many of the workers laboured under forms of indenture similar to those used on the coastal plantations of Deli. Locals were mostly uninterested in joining the work crews, and were hard to enlist even as contractors for wood-cutting and other supplementary tasks. The ironic result was that, despite being surrounded by dense forest, it was difficult to procure adequate wood supplies for manufacturing the cases in which the tins of kerosene were shipped out (the company eventually resorted to using a pair elephants to fell and transport timber to Pangkalan Brandan). Disease regularly compounded the ongoing labour problems. The European staff was repeatedly racked with fever, and work crews were frequently decimated by dysentery and other illnesses. Moreover, for those who remained healthy there was also the continual risk of attacks by Achinese fighters. In May 1893 some 300 Achinese mounted a full-scale assault on Pangkalan Brandan, killing several workmen and burning much of the settlement before withdrawing (for good, as it turned out) from the area.[30]

This whole incident underscores the dependence of colonial oil firms on military security, for it was only with the arrival of Dutch-led troops that the company could focus its full attention on boosting output. After 1893 operations advanced quickly as new wells came into production and pumping capacity grew. Once the wells were mechanized and adequate security arrangements put in place, the final unresolved problem was the woeful inefficiency of the refining operation at Pangkalan Brandan. The early processing plant was a fairly primitive setup. Crude oil arriving from the wells was first piped to a gigantic tree that had been left standing when the site was cleared. Here it ran through a series of 15-metre pipes supported by the tree—a curious amalgam of the organic and the industrial—which allowed the volatile gases in the crude to escape into the air. From there it went to a large storage tank before arriving at a bank of stills where the liquid was heated to drive off the lighter hydrocarbon fractions. The vapours from the stills were collected in a condenser cooled by water piped from the river, though the apparatus was so ineffective and the fumes around it so thick that they regularly knocked passing workers unconscious.[31]

All in all it was a remarkably wasteful operation that generated more pollution than product. Over half of the crude was classed as unwanted benzene (which included most of the fractions later used for gasoline), and the total yield of refined lighting oil was initially a mere 35 per cent.[32] Although yields and refining capacity soon improved, Pangkalan Brandan continued to spew large amounts of hydrocarbon waste into the air and watercourses of the surrounding area. In the summer of 1895 it received 9 million litres of crude per month and produced 4 million litres of refined oil, with nearly all of the remainder (apart from a small amount used as fuel for the boilers) either driven off as fumes, dumped as residue in the sea, or burned in a gravel pit a short distance behind the site. As the quantities of crude

---

[30] Joost Jonker and Jan Luiten van Zanden, *A History of Royal Dutch Shell*, vol. 1: *From Challenger to Joint Industry Leader, 1890–1939* (Oxford: Oxford University Press, 2007), 22–31; Poley, *Eroïca*, 95–7; Gerretson, *Royal Dutch*, vol. 1, 127–32, 165–8, 170–1.

[31] Gerretson, *Royal Dutch*, vol. 1, 139–40.   [32] Gerretson, *Royal Dutch*, vol. 1, 169.

from Telaga Said steadily rose (reaching around 18,000 barrels per day by 1898), this stream of refinery refuse swelled proportionately. So much unwanted by-product was incinerated in the waste pit that the resulting inferno could be seen for miles around, and for many years served as a beacon for ships passing through the Strait of Malacca.[33]

By the late 1890s the rising profits of Royal Dutch, along with recent strikes by the Dordtsche Petroleum Maatschappij in eastern Java,[34] triggered a flurry of oil exploration in the East Indies. With commercial viability now proven it was much easier to obtain capital from the Netherlands, whose financial markets were gripped, in the words of Dordtsche's director, by 'a real petroleum fever'.[35] Given the sizeable kerosene market on Java and Madura, many of the new start-ups focused their exploration efforts there. By 1904 there were no fewer than thirty-six concessions on the two islands. But for those willing and able to sell to distant markets, it was the 'outer isles' that still promised the biggest rewards.

On Sumatra, prospectors soon moved south from the Deli region into the Palembang and Djambi provinces, where a number of seeps had been known even before the arrival of the Dutch. In the hills of south-west Palembang, the Moeara Enim Petroleum Maatschappij commenced work on a highly promising oilfield in 1897—so promising, in fact, as to draw the attention of Standard Oil, whose attempt to take over the company was blocked by the colonial government. Some 100 kilometres to the north, another set of seepages along the upper Musi River was developed by the Moeara Enim and Moesi Ilir Companies, which joined forces to construct a large refining complex downriver at Pladju, a settlement just below Palembang town. Further north still, Royal Dutch hit gushers in the coastal zone near the Djambi frontier and hastily built a refinery at Bajung Lentjir on the nearby Lalang River.[36]

The bulk of these finds, like most early wells, resulted more from trial-and-error guesswork than from the application of specialized knowledge. Reconnaissance efforts bore little resemblance to the surveys that guided drillers in later years, and many of the biggest strikes were found by 'wildcat' teams that essentially tried their luck near surface seepages. The problem was that such a scatter-gun approach, based on scant knowledge of subterranean structures, provided a shaky basis for investment. Royal Dutch managers were all too aware of this. By the end of 1897 the company's wells at Telaga Said were beginning to produce brine rather than oil, which triggered an increasingly desperate search for new sources elsewhere. Wildcatters working for the company sank no fewer than 110 wells, but came up empty-handed. In this context, the aforementioned finds along the Palembang/ Djambi border were a major stroke of luck, for they effectively kept Royal Dutch afloat while it tried to acquire a concession in Perlak (in the far north of Sumatra), an area that the government was keen to see developed after recently acquiring it in a brutal war with the Sultan of Aceh. Once the Perlak concession was agreed,

[33] Jonker and van Zanden, *Royal Dutch*, 27; Gerretson, *Royal Dutch*, vol. 1, 140, 242–6; vol. 2, 40.
[34] See Poley, *Eroïca*, 105–14.   [35] Gerretson, *Royal Dutch*, vol. 2, 42.
[36] Gerretson, *Royal Dutch*, vol. 2, 55–7, 76–86.

Royal Dutch managers were anxious to find a more reliable survey method in order to minimize the exploration risks that had nearly wrecked the company. Here they put their faith in geologists rather than wildcatters, and in December 1899, only a week after securing the approval of the local Rajah, they hit their first gusher. Within a year the Perlak field was producing 5,000 barrels per day, and by 1901 it was linked by pipeline all the way to Pangkalan Brandan.[37] The whole episode was symptomatic of a broader trend within the industry towards the accumulation of specialist knowledge and the deployment of geological 'experts' as a new means of controlling the flow of oil energy.

In the meantime, oil exploration was also underway on the east coast of Borneo, where Dutch coal prospectors had noted petroleum seeps ever since the 1840s. In 1888, Jacobus Hubertus Menten (a former mining surveyor who, coincidentally, had spent several years on Bangka's tin-fields before founding his own coal mining firm in east Borneo) caught wind of the Dordtsche's strikes on Java and managed to obtain a vast 2,500-km² concession just south of the Mahakam River. After several years of fruitless prospecting, he desperately needed a financial backer. In 1895 he managed to convince Marcus Samuel, the owner of a flourishing shipping syndicate (soon to be rechristened the Shell Transport and Trading Company) to put up the exploration capital. Armed with Samuel's funding, Menten hired a crew of Canadian drillers and Chinese workers, cleared a patch of jungle near the Sanga-Sanga River, hacked a 6-kilometre path along the Sungei Minjak Tanah ('Earth-oil River'), and began drilling in 1896 at a place locally known as the 'Black Spot', a wide asphalt basin that oozed thick petroleum.[38] Operations progressed slowly due to the remoteness of the area—most of the supplies had to be shipped over 1,600 kilometres from Singapore—and the inability to persuade the local Dayak population to join the labour crews. Disease was also rampant, and the workers who stayed fit struggled to keep the evergreen rainforest from reclaiming everything they built. After finally striking commercial quantities of oil in February 1897, managers chose a refinery site 65 kilometres south on the deep-water bay of Balik Papan, where the construction of the refinery reprised the same litany of problems—labour shortages, missing equipment, poorly functioning stills—as at Pangkalan Brandan. Pollution and waste were similarly pervasive. When drillers hit a powerful gusher at Tandjung Tokong, a clearing just above Balik Papan, it flowed uncontrolled for several months and covered the sea with a pearlescent film as far as 16 kilometres offshore.[39]

But the biggest challenge for the new enterprise was the chemical composition of the Bornean crude itself, which points to a much broader issue. Oil was not just oil; there were many different types and grades, and these material differences clearly mattered. Throughout the entire history of the oil industry, the precise

[37] Jonker and van Zanden, *Royal Dutch*, 52–4; Gerretson, *Royal Dutch*, vol. 2, 39–51; 89–97, 135–44; Poley, *Eroïca*, 134–7; Stephen Howarth, *A Century in Oil: The 'Shell' Transport and Trading Company 1897–1997* (London: Weidenfeld & Nicolson, 1997), 55.

[38] Howarth, *Shell*, 44–5; Hubert Jezler, *Das Ölfeld Sanga Sanga in Koetei* (Berlin: Scholem, 1916), 4; Gerretson, *Royal Dutch*, vol. 2, 152–67; Poley, *Eroïca*, 121–6.

[39] Gerretson, *Royal Dutch*, vol. 2, 165–9; Yergin, *Prize*, 99–100; Poley, *Eroïca*, 127–9.

material properties of different crudes were sufficiently important, in both a technical and economic sense, to qualify as a form of non-human agency. To take the example of Bornean crude, the problem was that it was unusually heavy and therefore yielded little marketable kerosene. Its only saving grace was that it served well as fuel oil, even without refining. The Shell Company, making a virtue of necessity, soon burned Bornean oil in its ships, but managers also recognized the huge market that could open up if others could be persuaded to do the same. After all, Russian ships on the Caspian had been burning refinery residues for years, and there were already voices within the Royal Navy—by far the world's largest fleet—advocating a shift from coal to petroleum. Vice Admiral Sir John Fisher was a vociferous champion of the virtues of oil-powered ships, which would be easier to fuel, produce less visible exhaust, have greater range and speed, and be capable of carrying more powerful guns. He and Samuel soon teamed up to lobby a sceptical Admiralty, and despite initial rebuffs they eventually secured agreement for a public trial of fuel oil in June 1902 at Portsmouth Harbour.[40]

The trial itself was a shambles. After steaming out under coal and switching its burners to oil, the *HMS Hannibal* was quickly enveloped in a cloud of dark smoke. The display was so unconvincing that it effectively delayed the Royal Navy's switch to petroleum for nearly a decade. But despite the bitter disappointment for Fisher and Samuel, the incident nonetheless pointed to the future in two key respects. First, those who saw fuel rather than illumination as the future for the oil industry were soon proven right. With the spread of the electric light-bulb from the 1880s onward, lighting oil was a commodity whose days were numbered, especially in the markets of the industrial world. As traditional markets shrank, it was critical for the oil companies to find, or create, new outlets for their product. At the turn of the century the horseless carriage was still the preserve of a tiny elite, but by the 1910s the steady expansion of the automobile—along with the introduction of diesel-powered ships and a fledgling aviation industry—became the cornerstones of a new petroleum-based energy system. And as this system began to materialize, it confirmed a second important foreshadowing that could be glimpsed through the smoke wafting over Portsmouth Harbour: namely, the enormous military implications of oil conversion and the strategic significance of controlling flows of petroleum energy.[41]

OIL-FLOWS AND IMPERIAL RIVALRY

The expansion of oil and electricity in the early twentieth challenged not only the hegemony of coal but also the global power structures that had been built upon it. As Britain's economic and political dominance declined, the fortunes of other industrial powers—above all the USA and Germany, which were at the forefront

---

[40] Howarth, *Shell*, 58, 63–4; Yergin, *Prize*, 100.
[41] Podobnik, *Global Energy*, 51–2; Mitchell, *Carbon Democracy*, 45, 59–61; Yergin, *Prize*, 62–3, Howarth, *Shell*, 85.

of the petroleum and electrical industries—correspondingly rose. The early 1900s were thus marked by an intensification of geopolitical competition, and this rivalry made it all the more important for the leading industrial powers to harness the power of oil, not least to augment the fighting capacity of their armed forces. Well before the First World War, military planners began to experiment with petroleum-based systems for combat. Europe's overseas colonies played an important role in the process, both as testing-grounds for new equipment—the first combat use of aircraft was by Italian forces in Libya in 1911, followed by the French deployment of aeroplanes against Algerian insurgents in 1913—and, more importantly, as sources of supply.[42]

It was above all the mounting naval competition of the 1900s that put petroleum on the geopolitical agenda, and for the admirals the question of supply was paramount. The US Navy, the first to move decisively towards all-oil firing, was the only major fleet that could run on domestic petroleum sources. By contrast, the Royal Navy was reluctant to trade the security of Britain's domestic coal supplies for the uncertainty of foreign oil reliance. But as dual-fuel ships became more common, and as Germany's naval construction programme accelerated, the benefits of oil-fired propulsion increasingly outweighed the risks. By 1912 it was decided that all future British battleships should burn oil, prompting other navies to follow suit. The key, as Winston Churchill (then First Lord of the Admiralty) emphasized, was to ensure ownership or at least control over sufficient overseas reserves.[43] In 1905 the British government arranged for the Burmah Oil Co. to supply the Royal Navy in exchange for an effective monopoly on sales in India. Leaders in Russia and the Netherlands also enjoyed a degree of oil sovereignty thanks to the reserves under their control. But the French and German governments, bereft of colonial supplies, were forced to look elsewhere, above all towards Ottoman-ruled territories, Eastern Europe, and the Caspian.

During the lead-up to the First World War, oil security became an important factor in the strategic calculus of all the major European powers. But what 'security' meant was more than just a matter of finding adequate supplies. Production capacity in the Americas, Russia, and colonial Asia was more than sufficient to cover demand, even for the potentially huge fuel requirements of the Royal Navy. The main concern, once again, was not a lack of oil but a lack of control over its flow. And this question of control was not just about territory but also about the commercial dimensions of the industry. All governments wanted to avoid the risk of rendering their military capacity susceptible to the monopolizing power of Standard Oil and Royal Dutch/Shell, regardless of whether they were foreign-owned.[44]

[42] Michael Paris, 'The First Air Wars—North Africa and the Balkans, 1911–13', *Journal of Contemporary History*, vol. 26 no. 1 (Jan. 1991), 97–109; Michael Paris, 'Air Power and Imperial Defence, 1880–1919', *Journal of Contemporary History*, vol. 24 no. 2 (Apr. 1989), 209–25; Podobnik, *Global Energy*, 64–6.
[43] Podobnik, *Global Energy*, 66–7; Yergin, *Prize*, 137–40.
[44] See Mitchell, *Carbon Democracy*, 60.

It is against this background that we must examine the opening of oil production in the Middle East, and the nature of government involvement there. For the leading oil firms, the scramble for concessions and exploration rights in the region did not reflect an immediate need for additional supplies, but rather a bid to delay production and thereby curb competition by controlling the main sites of extraction and distribution. This underlying motive helps explain why the first large oilfield to be developed in the region was not along the banks of the Tigris in northern Mesopotamia—whose vast oil reserves were well known by the turn of the century, and were assiduously kept off the market by the main concessionaires—but instead among the more isolated hills of western Persia.[45]

The reserves in western Persia were first developed by William Knox D'Arcy, a British engineer who in May 1901 managed to obtain exclusive oil and pipeline rights to around three-quarters of the entire country. After finding no more than small pockets of oil near the north-west border with Mesopotamia (a concession that conveniently blocked a possible pipeline route that could have brought Baku oil to the Gulf and from there to the Asian market), Knox's syndicate was rescued in 1905 by none other than the Burmah Oil Company. Burmah's investment in Persia was partly conceived as a hedge against its Burmese wells drying up, but mostly as a means of protecting its Indian markets from Middle Eastern competition. Armed with new funding, D'Arcy's drilling operation moved into the mountainous terrain of Khuzestan in south-west Persia, where in May 1908 it hit a large gusher at Masjid-i-Suleiman, the site of an ancient fire temple. Subsequent wells soon confirmed the existence of an enormous limestone reservoir some 25 kilometres square, all of it notionally under British control. None of its contents were initially brought into production out of a concern for the possible effects on oil prices. Tellingly, Burmah's directors in Scotland took nearly a year to establish the Anglo-Persian Oil Company (APOC, which later evolved into BP) to exploit the find (Fig. 6.2).[46]

Despite APOC's ownership of an enormous underground lake of oil, the survival of the fledgling company required strong political backing on at least two fronts. One was the need to keep Mesopotamian oil in the ground, which was eventually achieved through the negotiated establishment of the multinational Turkish Petroleum Company. The other was to find an outlet for the Persian oil that it produced, whose high sulphur content made it unsuitable for lamp kerosene. Just as in Borneo, the physical properties of the crude played a crucial role in subsequent developments. And once again, the only practical option was to sell it as fuel oil. Accordingly, APOC's directors, like Shell's, appealed to the Admiralty to conclude a long-term supply contract. Despite initial rejection, the Royal Navy soon warmed to the suggestion amidst rising concerns about the power of the oil monopolies, as well as the demands of coal miners and railway workers during the 'Great Unrest' of 1910–14. In 1912 the Admiralty acquired a 51 per cent stake in APOC, which not only enabled it to circumvent the domestic political constraints

[45] Mitchell, *Carbon Democracy*, 47–9.
[46] Stephen Helmsley Longrigg, *Oil in the Middle East: Its Discovery and Development* (Oxford: Oxford University Press, 1954), 16–22; Mitchell, *Carbon Democracy*, 54; Yergin, *Prize*, 130.

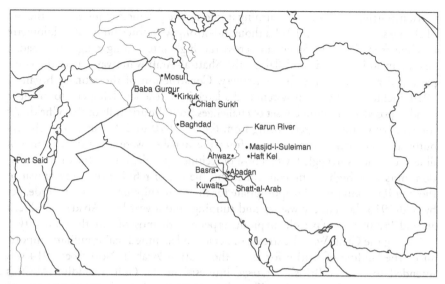

Fig. 6.2. Map indicating the main oilfields of the Middle East in the early twentieth century.

on its energy supplies, but also provided a secure market for the Persian oil that its own company was producing. Though ostensibly private-owned, APOC was for all intents and purposes a state-run concern. It was majority-owned by the British Treasury, the Royal Navy was its main customer, and the government of India provided a detachment of troops to guard operations from local pastoralists who resented its incursions into their rangelands.[47]

APOC's oil wells soon numbered among the most productive in the world, and the business of channelling all of this energy quickly transformed the surrounding region. The oilfield itself—the Maidan-i-Naftan, or 'plain of oil'—lay amidst the dry, broken foothills giving on to the Bakhtiari Mountains, the natural barrier between the central Persian plateau and the desert plains to the south. It was a harsh landscape, used mainly for winter grazing by Bakhtiari herders who were largely independent of Tehran's authority. Conditions for the oil workers were punishing at first. Available food was 'rather trying for any digestion', and drinking water was 'best described as water with dung in suspension'.[48] Nearly everything had to be brought from afar. Equipment and provisions were initially hauled in by river and pack-animal before the completion of a 56-kilometre road between the oilfield and Dar-i-Khazineh, the highest navigable point on the Karun River. Much of the workforce was Indian or European, and water had to be pumped over 60 kilometres from the Karun River.[49]

---

[47] Mitchell, *Carbon Democracy*, 54–61; Yergin, *Prize*, 118–48; generally, Ferrier, *British Petroleum*, 15–201.

[48] Ferrier, *British Petroleum*, 79.

[49] J. W. Williamson, *In a Persian Oil-Field: A Study in Scientific and Industrial Development* (London: Ernest Benn, 1927), 91.

Transporting the crude and turning it into usable products required a further set of changes. From 1909 to 1911 a thousand-strong workforce built a 222-kilometre pipeline from Masjid-i-Suleiman across the high intervening ranges to Abadan Island, an uninhabited mud-flat on the Shatt-al-ʿArab waterway where the company had acquired a site for its refinery. Construction of the refinery began in 1910, including a light rail system and a large jetty. The low-lying environment at Abadan posed a very different set of challenges from the arid hills of the oilfields. As the refinery workforce grew (rising from 632 in 1910 to 2,825 in 1913), cholera outbreaks and malarial mosquitoes from the marshes were a constant source of illness. Engineers struggled with a host of technical problems too. The early distillation units were highly temperamental, and the use of refining practices similar to those in Rangoon proved inappropriate for the more sulphurous Persian crude. Yet by mid-1913 the refinery was up and running, and a year later Abadan produced around 25,000 tons of petroleum products per month, most of it for the Admiralty.[50]

During the Great War, the stream of Persian oil acquired major military importance. The landing of British forces on the Shatt-al-ʿArab in November 1914 was intended to protect British 'strategic interests' in the Gulf, including APOC's petroleum assets, from attack by Turkish troops. Apart from three months in early 1915, when the pipeline between the oilfields and Abadan was cut by local clans incited by German and Turkish agents, the current of hydrocarbon energy continued to swell.[51] Wartime drilling on the Maidan-i-Naftan multiplied APOC's crude production from 274,000 tons in 1914 to 1.1 million in 1919, and necessitated a doubling of pipeline capacity to handle the output. As more oil flowed out, the inward stream of food, equipment, and other supplies was facilitated by new roads and bridges that reduced the journey time between the oilfields and Abadan from five days to only eight hours. Refinery capacity at Abadan correspondingly grew to over a million tons by the end of the war, around two-thirds of it fuel oil for the Royal Navy.[52]

The swelling current of Persian petroleum was all part of a broader assemblage of energy flows that sustained Britain's worldwide military power. In Egypt, a nationalized Shell subsidiary struck oil on the shores of the Red Sea in 1913 and built a lucrative refinery at Suez. In Sarawak, strikes near the mouth of the Miri River in 1911 produced over 1,200 barrels per day by summer 1914.[53] On the other side of the world, the nascent oil industry on Trinidad was also spurred by naval demand. Commercial production on the island had begun in the 1900s, nestled mainly among the former cocoa and coconut groves of Guapo on the south-west cape, before spreading north to the Tabaquite field. By 1914 there were around eighty companies on Trinidad collectively producing 1 million barrels per year, and by the end of the war output had doubled to over 2 million barrels,

[50] Ferrier, *British Petroleum*, 122–53, 271–2; Longrigg, *Oil*, 19–20, 34; Williamson, *Persian Oil-Field*, 133–3.
[51] Ferrier, *British Petroleum*, 279–80.
[52] Ferrier, *British Petroleum*, 271, 275; Longrigg, *Oil*, 35.
[53] Howarth, *Shell*, 88–91; Jonker and van Zanden, *Royal Dutch*, 98; Mitchell, *Carbon Democracy*, 49.

two-thirds of it refined on the island, mainly at Point-à-Pierre and Point Fortin. Most went directly to the Admiralty, and as Trinidad's oil production grew, the great West Indian coaling stations were soon wound up.[54]

During the First World War, the extensive reserves of the East Indies were likewise harnessed to the Allied cause. Output from the colony had grown rapidly following the amalgamation of Royal Dutch and Shell in 1907. The new conglomerate enjoyed an effective monopoly on local production, and it also invested heavily in refining capacity, turning Balik Papan into the most important processing site in the entire archipelago. By 1912 the Royal Dutch/Shell 'Group' had become a genuine rival to Standard, and was even selling its gasoline in California. Though majority-owned by Royal Dutch and officially based in the neutral Netherlands, during the war it clearly identified its interests with the UK and its allies.[55] Shell's tanker fleet—then the largest private fleet in the world—became the main supplier of gasoline and aviation spirit to the Allied land and air services, delivering around 3,700 barrels of petrol per day from the East Indies and the Americas to the depots of the various fronts.

Engine fuel was not the only military use to which this oil energy was put. Well before the war, Bornean crude was known to contain significant amounts of toluol, an essential ingredient for the manufacture of high explosive. At the time most toluol was produced from coal, though Shell's Rotterdam refinery had begun to extract it from Bornean crude in 1908. By the end of 1914 it was clear that coal-based production was wholly inadequate for meeting wartime needs. While British and French stocks of high explosive ran perilously low, German companies were able to use Rotterdam's toluol output for the manufacture of TNT (trinitrotoluene). On the night on 30 January 1915—with prior approval from the Group's executives and tacit support from the Netherlands government—the entire Rotterdam toluol refinery was quietly dismantled and shipped to London. Two months later the plant reappeared at Portishead in Somerset, and for the remainder of the war Bornean toluol met the bulk of British and French requirements.[56] In this way, Shell's network of oil forged a direct link between the subsoils of eastern Borneo and the cratered landscape of the Western Front.

The wartime activities of Royal Dutch/Shell and APOC highlight an important point. The opening of colonial petroleum resources and the disproportionate control over oil flows by British, US, and sympathetic Dutch firms gave their home governments a significant strategic advantage. The preferential petroleum access enjoyed by Allied governments played a role in the outcome of the First

[54] George E. Higgins, *A History of Trinidad Oil* (Port of Spain: Trinidad Express, 1996), esp. 102–3; A. Beeby-Thompson, *Oil Pioneer: Selected Experiences and Incidents Associated with Sixty Years of World-Wide Petroleum Exploration and Oilfield Development* (London: Sidgwick & Jackson, 1961), 105–44.

[55] *The Royal Dutch Petroleum Company, Diamond Jubilee Book* (The Hague: Royal Dutch, 1950), 15; Jonker and van Zanden, *Royal Dutch*, 104–5.

[56] Howarth, *Shell*, 103–5; Yergin, *Prize*, 158–9; Ernst Homburg, 'Operating on Several Fronts: The Trans-National Activities of Royal Dutch/Shell, 1914–1918', in Roy M. MacLeod and Jeffrey Allan Johnson (eds), *Frontline and Factory: Comparative Perspectives on the Chemical Industry at War, 1914–1924* (Dordrecht: Springer, 2006), 123–44, here 131–2.

World War, however modest compared to that of Second. This was increasingly true as the war dragged on, for although the initial clashes of 1914—the so-called 'last battles of the nineteenth century'—were still based largely on organic energy, on the muscle-power of men and especially horses, by the end of the conflict the battlefield from ground to sky was more and more characterized by the deployment of oil-powered machinery, especially once the static fronts in the West began to move.

The history of oil in the First World War also confirmed yet again that the power of petroleum was as much about limiting supplies as accessing them. Perhaps its most important contribution to the Allied war effort lay in the advantages it gave the Royal Navy in its maintenance of the continental blockade. The blockade exacerbated what was already an adverse oil situation for the Central Powers, which had plenty of coal but little access to petroleum. Before the war Germany imported all of its oil from abroad (mostly from North America or Russia), and once the war began it depended overwhelmingly on Romanian supplies. Not even the occupation of Romania in 1916 could do much for German oil security since the Allies destroyed most of the installations before German troops reached them. The paradoxical result was that Germany, the land of Daimler, Benz, and Diesel, was at a distinct disadvantage when it came to mechanized warfare. The only competitive benefit it derived from the internal combustion engine came from the diesel-electric power-plants of its submarine fleet, which were used to disrupt supplies of oil and other necessities to Britain and France throughout 1916–17. Yet in the final analysis, even this success was ultimately self-defeating since the unrestricted submarine campaign was what eventually drew the oil-rich USA into the war.[57]

The cessation of hostilities in 1918 did not stop the imperial contest over oil resources, but instead marked the beginning of what some called a 'secret war for petroleum'.[58] Just days after the armistice, Senator Henry Béranger, wartime director of France's Comité Général du Pétrole, proclaimed that 'as oil has been the blood of war, so it would be the blood of the peace. At this hour, at the beginning of the peace, our civilian populations, our industries, our commerce, our farmers are all calling for more oil, always more oil, for more gasoline, always more gasoline.'[59] During the war years global oil consumption rose by 50 per cent, and against the background of political destabilization in Russia, European governments emerged from the conflict more determined than ever to secure control of overseas reserves.[60]

By the mid-1920s French crews were hunting for oil in New Caledonia, Madagascar, Algeria, Morocco, Tunisia, Gabon, and Indochina, and German teams were even

---

[57] This discussion is based on Dietrich Eichholtz, *Deutsche Ölpolitik im Zeitalter der Weltkriege* (Leipzig: Leipziger Universitätsverlag, 2010), 96–187; W. G. Jensen, 'The Importance of Energy in the First and Second World Wars', *Historical Journal*, vol. 11 (1968), 538–54, here 538–45.

[58] Antoine Zischka, *La Guerre secrète pour le pétrole* (Paris: Payot, 1933).

[59] Quotes from Yergin, *Prize*, 167; see also Podobnik, *Global Energy*, 69–70.

[60] Figure from Brian Black, *Crude Reality: Petroleum in World History* (Lanham, Md: Rowman & Littlefield, 2012), 80.

surveying parts of their ex-colony Cameroon.[61] But the main focal points of exploration were the spoils of the former Ottoman Empire, and above all the vast oil resources of Mesopotamia.[62] As part of the San Remo Agreement of 1920, it was decided that Mesopotamia would become part of a British mandate in exchange for the French takeover of the confiscated 22.5 per cent Deutsche Bank stake in the Turkish Petroleum Company (soon renamed the Iraq Petroleum Company), which had been founded before the war in conjunction with Anglo-Persian and Royal Dutch/Shell for the purpose of developing Mesopotamia's reserves.[63] The deal was essentially a Franco-British stitch-up, and sparked a prolonged diplomatic offensive by the US government to secure access for American companies.[64]

Over the following years, the geopolitical tensions between Western governments were exacerbated by rising commercial strains between the major oil companies. Despite initial post-war fears of a looming shortage, by the late 1920s the problem for the industry was not too little oil but rather too much. From 1919 to 1929 world crude production soared from 77 million tons to 204 million tons, and not even the swelling fleet of automobiles—up from 157,000 to 1.1 million in France, 187,000 to 1.1 million in Britain, and 8.1 to 23 million in the USA between 1920 and 1930—could absorb supplies.[65] The ensuing glut on world markets threatened a collapse of prices and a ruinous bout of price wars between the leading firms. What the oil companies wanted was an easing of political tensions and a stabilization of oil markets to avoid the dangers of unbridled competition. Delaying the development of Middle Eastern production was a crucial part of this strategy. In July 1928, Royal Dutch/Shell, the Compagnie Française des Pétroles (which held the French shares in the Iraq Petroleum Company), APOC, and a Standard-led consortium concluded the so-called 'Red Line' agreement, which committed the signatories to the joint development of the oilfields of Iraq, Turkey, the Levant, and most of the Arabian Peninsula. The following month a parallel marketing pact effectively fixed international oil prices, reduced competition in key markets, and cemented the dominance of the existing oil majors by making it harder for new participants to gain a foothold.[66]

---

[61] Honoré Paulin, *Le Pétrole: recherches et indices de gisements de pétrole dans les colonies françaises et pays de protectorat* (Paris: Librarie d'Enseignement Technique, 1924), 3–11; Armand Rabichon, *Le Pétrole en Algérie* (Paris: Lafayette, 1921); L. Joleaud, *Le Pétrole dans l'Afrique du Nord* (Paris: Revue Pétrolifère, 1926).

[62] Marian Kent, *Oil and Empire: British Policy and Mesopotamian Oil, 1900–1920* (Houndmills: Macmillian, 1976); Eichholtz, *Ölpolitik*, 10–95.

[63] Or rather delaying development. Drilling in northern Iraq finally commenced in 1927 after two decades of delays, and even then the firms that controlled the Iraq Petroleum Company sought to hold back production to avoid exacerbating the existing glut on oil markets: Mitchell, *Carbon Democracy*, 102.

[64] Yergin, *Prize*, 168–87; for the wider diplomatic context, Fiona Venn, *Oil Diplomacy in the Twentieth Century* (Houndmills: Macmillan, 1986), 54–82; Fiona Venn, 'Oleaginous Diplomacy: Oil, Anglo-American Relations and the Lausanne Conference, 1922–23', *Diplomacy & Statecraft*, vol. 20 no. 3 (2009), 414–33.

[65] Venn, *Oil Diplomacy*, 5.   [66] Yergin, *Prize*, 187–211, 243–8.

Taken together, these twin agreements represented a kind of oil armistice between the leading imperial powers. By dividing up the spoils and retaining their control over the main sites of production and distribution, they created a more stable framework in which the oil companies could invest with confidence and in which their home governments could secure ready access. In essence, the agreements ensured that the precious flow of liquid energy would continue to enhance their wealth and power. But keeping the oil flowing required more than just the maintenance of a favourable political environment. First and foremost, it involved a far-reaching transformation of the physical environment.

PETROLEUM LANDSCAPES: TECHNOLOGICAL AND ENVIRONMENTAL CHANGE IN EUROPE'S OIL COLONIES

Even in the early days, the business of extracting, transporting, refining, and distributing petroleum entailed major ecological changes. At the immediate sites of production the ground surface had to be thoroughly cleared to make way for oil camps, storage tanks, processing plants, and pipelines. In the surrounding areas water sources were tapped, channelled, and piped to lubricate the drilling rigs, cool the condensers, and sustain the workers who operated them. At the same time, the need for building material and boiler fuel placed heavy demands on local woodlands. Further afield, waterways were dredged and harbours bulk-headed to facilitate the shipment of oil to distant markets, while road networks and railways criss-crossed the land to bring in supplies and equipment. Throughout the late nineteenth and early twentieth centuries, the quest for oil razed forests, drained swamps, and scarred deserts in Europe's colonies. And as the search intensified after the war, so too did its footprint.

From 1919 to 1939 global oil production nearly quadrupled from around 77 million tons to 285 million tons.[67] For the most part this reflected the development of new oilfields in the Americas. But production also rose rapidly in the Middle East and Asia (from around 5.1 million to 25.2 million tons combined), and above all in south-west Persia, which still accounted for over two-thirds of Middle Eastern output in 1939.[68]

Ramping up production on this scale not only involved a host of changes at the drilling and refining sites, it also obliged oil companies to strengthen their grip on the surrounding landscape. From 1919 to 1924 the workforce at APOC's Masjid-i-Suleiman oilfield trebled in size, which effectively led to the construction of a whole new town in the desert. In order to supply it, the company built 2,500 kilometres of roads, as well as a light railway to the loading wharves at

[67] Figure from the Shift Project dataset: <http://www.tsp-data-portal.org/Energy-Production-Statistics#tspQvChart>.
[68] Longrigg, *Oil*, 276–7; Shift Project dataset: <http://www.tsp-data-portal.org/Energy-Production-Statistics#tspQvChart>.

Dar-i-Khazineh on the Karun River. Further upriver at Godar Landar, APOC built a new moveable pump-house (specially designed to cope with the Karun's extreme seasonal fluctuations, which varied by as much as 14 metres) to meet its rising water needs, while electrical power was transmitted from a new generating station beside the Tembi River.[69] Meanwhile, some 55 kilometres south-east of Masjid-i-Suleiman, the discovery of another vast petroleum reservoir at Haft Kel in 1928 opened a whole new oilfield and set off a similar cascade of changes.[70]

By the inter-war years, most major discoveries like Haft Kel drew on an increasingly detailed understanding of the lithosphere. The use of seismic survey techniques spread quickly to Europe's oil colonies after their successful deployment in Texas and Mexico in the mid-1920s, and they greatly enhanced the oil companies' ability to 'read' the ground under their feet. Aerial surveying also became increasingly common, and was particularly advantageous in the 'outer isles' of the East Indies where heavy forest cover and a scarcity of roads made prospecting especially arduous.[71] During the 1920s and 1930s these new exploration techniques helped engineers open several oilfields in the Djambi and Palembang provinces of Sumatra, including the Talang Akar field, which soon became the most prolific in the entire archipelago. They were also used in east Borneo, where eight new production sites were added to the existing oilfields at Sanga-Sanga and on Tarakan Island. By the end of the 1930s East Indies production had risen to just under 8 million tons (up from 2.4 million in 1920), around two-thirds of it from Sumatra, a quarter from Borneo, and the remainder from Java, Madura, and Ceram.[72] During the Depression petroleum was about the only sector of the East Indies economy that grew rather than shrank.[73]

Processing and transporting the swelling flow of crude generated a range of impacts on nearby ecosystems. Such changes were clearly visible at Abadan, which became the world's single largest refinery by the end of the 1920s. Between 1919 and 1925 its workforce grew from 3,379 to 14,670 employees, and by the late 1920s the entire complex of tank farms, distillation equipment, jetties, bungalows, and barracks covered around 1,200 hectares. Maintaining public health in these low, humid mud-flats brought its own set of environmental interventions, from fumigation and rat-trapping campaigns to the construction of a modern water-borne sanitation system (though housing in Abadan remained notoriously inadequate). Nor were the effects confined to terrestrial ecosystems. From 1925

---

[69] Williamson, *Persian Oil-Field*, 93–4, 170–1; Ferrier, *British Petroleum*, 414, 423; Longrigg, *Oil*, 52–3.

[70] Ferrier, *British Petroleum*, 447; Longrigg, *Oil*, 53–4.

[71] Aerial surveys were first trialled in the 1920s in Sarawak and Brunei before commencing in earnest over Sumatra and Dutch New Guinea after 1930: *The Royal Dutch*, 39–40; Jonker and van Zanden, *Royal Dutch*, 329–33.

[72] Stauffer, 'Geology of the Netherlands Indies', 335; Venn, *Oil Diplomacy*, 174–5; Jonker and van Zanden, *Royal Dutch*, 264–9.

[73] J. Thomas Lindblad, 'Structural Origins of the Economic Depression in Indonesia during the 1930s', in Boomgaard and Brown (eds), *Weathering*, 123–42, here 138–9; J. Thomas Lindblad, 'The Petroleum Industry in Indonesia before the Second World War', *Bulletin of Indonesian Economic Studies*, vol. 25 (1989), 53–78.

onwards dredgers repeatedly deepened and widened the Shatt-al-'Arab channel to accommodate the ever-larger tankers mooring at Abadan. In the process they altered tidal currents and almost certainly disturbed feeding and spawning grounds of important commercial fish and shrimp species.[74] In the East Indies too, the refineries at Balik Papan, Pladju, and Pangkalan Brandan grew rapidly. As a traveller to north-east Sumatra noted in 1936, 'in Pangkalan Brandan one can see from a distance the smokestacks of the great petroleum refineries... There are numerous well sites along the coast in the mangrove swamps and in the heart of the jungle near the mountains . . . Gas eruptions, too, are not uncommon, and are visible from far around as high, blazing perennial fires in the forest.'[75] By the 1930s the previously formidable jungles of the area had become a hybrid land-scape, its forests interspersed with oil derricks and its marshes lined with oil-storage ponds.

Meanwhile, around 18,000 kilometres to the west, even bigger changes were in store for the small islands of the Dutch West Indies, which became home to two of the largest refinery complexes in the entire world. In December 1922 a massive blowout at one of Shell's wells on the shores of Venezuela's Lake Maracaibo—estimated to have flowed uncontrolled at 100,000 barrels per day—sparked a frenzy of drilling in the region. By the end of the decade, Venezuela had become the world's second largest oil producer (19.9 million tons per year), overtaking the East Indies as the main source for Royal Dutch/Shell in 1929, and surpassing Persia as the single largest supplier for Britain in 1932.[76] Much of its crude passed through refineries on Curaçao and Aruba, which provided the oil companies with a welcome safe-haven against the threat of political turmoil and possible nationalization on the mainland. The Isla refinery on Curaçao, which was initially built in 1918 to process the modest amount of heavy Venezuelan crude that was then flowing from Shell's wells, quickly grew to cover most of the northern shore of the Schottegat, the deep natural harbour that opens behind the protected inlet at the capital city of Willemstad. On Aruba, two refineries were opened in the late 1920s, one just west of Oranjestad (operated by Shell), and a much larger one built by the Lago Company (a Standard subsidiary) on the eastern Sint-Nicolaasbaai, whose protective reef and bottom were extensively dredged to facilitate shipping access. Isla and Lago were colossal installations by contemporary standards. In the late 1930s Isla's annual throughput of over 12 million tons was six times the combined capacity of all the refineries in the Dutch East Indies, making it by far the largest refinery in the Royal Dutch/Shell Group. Lago's capacity was greater still, and by the end of the 1930s

[74] Williamson, *Persian Oil-Field*, 133–8; Ferrier, *British Petroleum*, 431, 436–7, 444–5, 449–52, 669; on conditions at Abadan: Stephanie Cronin, 'Popular Politics, the New State and the Birth of the Iranian Working Class: The 1929 Abadan Oil Refinery Strike', *Middle Eastern Studies*, vol. 46 no. 5 (2010), 699–732; on the Shatt-al-'Arab: Abdulaziz H. Abuzinada et al. (eds), *Protecting the Gulf's Marine Ecosystems from Pollution* (Basel: Birkhäuser Verlag, 2008), 214–17.

[75] Schneider, 'Tagebuch', 290. See also *The Royal Dutch*, 141–3; Jonker and van Zanden, *Royal Dutch*, 333–4: Balik Papan alone had 45 kilometres of narrow-gauge railway by 1940.

[76] *The Royal Dutch*, 62; Yergin, *Prize*, 216–20; Jonker and van Zanden, *Royal Dutch*, 245–55; Howarth, *Shell*, 131–2; B. S. McBeth and Alan Knight, *Juan Vicente Gomez and the Oil Companies in Venezuela, 1908–1935* (Cambridge: Cambridge University Press, 2002).

the two complexes ranked second and third in the world behind Abadan.[77] For the islanders living next to them, the refineries brought both benefits and drawbacks. Although they generated considerable wealth—by the end of the 1920s no less than a quarter of Curaçao's 44,000 residents worked directly for the industry—they also caused chronic air pollution, choked nearby reefs, and blackened the waters and shorelines. Around Sint-Nicolaasbaai some villages were even abandoned as a result of intense pollution.[78]

For most observers at the time, and certainly for the oilmen themselves, the transformation of desert, marsh, and jungle into bustling oilfields and refineries was nothing short of a heroic achievement. As a visitor to APOC's installations remarked in 1927, 'to reflect that but a few short years ago there was nothing at Fields but a hilly wilderness and at Abadan only a bare desert, is to realise what a great thing has been done for Persia, for Britain and for civilisation in this area of the Middle East'. Most inspiring of all, he added, was that it all stemmed from 'British enterprise, industrial organisation and, not least of all, from the steady, persistent application, continuously directed from the head, of scientific knowledge and methods to the whole business of getting and refining a black liquid from the bowels of the earth'.[79] From this viewpoint, the towering drill-rigs, orderly rows of storage tanks, and miles of arterial pipelines were the very epitome of progress, a testament to human ingenuity and to the vigorous masculine dominion over nature.

But despite all of the engineering swagger on display, the oil companies' control over nature was always far from complete. If the petroleum landscapes they created bore all the hallmarks of industrial modernity, they also testified to the limits of their technical mastery of nature. Extracting large amounts of highly flammable material from deep underground was (and remains) an intrinsically hazardous business, especially when dealing with reservoirs under high pressure. Yet in the haste to cash in on their concessions, which some companies had to do simply in order to stay afloat, the oilmen were frequently overwhelmed by the power of the material forces they released.

Fires were perhaps the most common problem, especially in the early days. The origin of many, if not most, oilfield fires was the prevailing idea that wells should be drilled until they spouted. This was, for instance, the root cause of the first major fire on Royal Dutch's Telaga Said field in spring 1893. After initially hitting a slow flow at just over 90 metres, workers at well No. 7 continued to drill until a plume of gas and oil burst into the air. Such gusher-strikes were usually a cause for celebration, but in this case the result was panic as the uncontrolled stream of oil

---

[77] Jonker and van Zanden, *Royal Dutch*, 251, 363–5, 447–8; Henrietta M. Larson, Evelyn H. Knowlton, and Charles S. Popple, *History of Standard Oil Company (New Jersey): New Horizons, 1927–1950* (New York: Harper & Row, 1971), 201; <http://www.lago-colony.com/STORIES_REFINERY/LAGO_HISTORY_DJ.htm>.

[78] Jeroen J. H. Dekker, *Curaçao zonder/met Shell: een bijdrage tot bestudering van demografische, economische en sociale processen in de periode 1900–1929* (Zubphen: Walburg, 1982); <http://www.historiadiaruba.aw/index.php?option=com_content&task=view&id=28&Itemid=42>.

[79] Williamson, *Persian Oil-Field*, 188.

was ignited by the flame of a nearby field boiler and quickly spread the fire to the neighbouring well No. 6. In the end it took two full days to extinguish the blaze.[80] The burning gusher at Telaga Said also points to a second factor that commonly increased the risk of fire, namely the close proximity of drilling rigs to one another. The closeness of drill-rigs was especially problematic on Burma's Yenangyaung oilfield, where fires were exceptionally common among the smaller wildcat outfits. The densely packed, oil-spattered wooden derricks (some standing as little as 18 metres apart) caught fire easily, and many of the storage tanks and oil-burning pump stations were also dangerously close to one another. By 1908 the problem had reached such proportions that the colonial government directly intervened with a clutch of stricter fire regulations.[81]

Conflagrations were hardly confined to the oilfields, but rather flared up all along the hydrocarbon production chain, from drill-sites to refineries to the tankers that carried products away. The authorities in Rangoon were well versed in the associated risks. In 1900, one of the Burmah Company's first two tankers, the *Kokine*, burned at Rangoon before embarking on its maiden voyage. In 1909, only a year after the government clampdown at Yenangyaung, a major tank blaze at the Syriam refinery complex blackened the skies south of the city.[82] And while fires were sometimes caused by human error—an injudicious cigarette or, in the case of the *Kokine*, lowering the flash point of its fuel oil by mixing in too much unsaleable naphtha—others had natural causes. Lightning strikes were a common problem in many tropical oilfields. In 1924–5 they caused two major blazes in less than two years at the Brighton Refinery on Trinidad. The first inferno at Tanks 7 and 8 was fanned by strong easterly winds that rained crude over the nearby settlement of Coon's Town, most of which was burned down before a channel was dug to divert the flaming oil out across the sea. The fire was so intense that it was visible from Port of Spain some 50 kilometres away, and over the following two days huge explosions darkened the skies for miles around. The after-effects were still visible the following year when the same thing happened to Tank 14.[83]

But not all blazes were accidental, for fire was also systematically deployed as a cheap means of disposal. On the oilfields it was common practice to burn off excess crude after collecting it away from gushers, leaking pipelines, or newly completed wells, creating huge clouds of putrid smoke and shrivelling nearby vegetation in the process. In addition, most of the output from exploration wells was simply torched since there was usually no means to transport it to market before a commercially viable level of supply was assured. Around the Iraqi towns of Kirkuk and Mosul, the frenzy of exploration in the 1920s generated 'immense palls of smoke [that] rose heavenwards from the oilfields at frequent intervals'.[84] In 1938, the incineration of the oil from the first free-flowing development well on Kuwait's Burgan field created a fire so intense that it turned the sandy walls of the

[80] Gerretson, *Royal Dutch*, vol. 1, 164.
[81] Longmuir, *Oil*, 228–32; Corley, *Burmah*, vol. 1, 122–3.
[82] Corley, *Burmah*, vol. 1, 49.   [83] Higgins, *Trinidad Oil*, 96–7.
[84] Beeby-Thompson, *Oil Pioneer*, 430.

collection reservoir into glass.[85] Moreover, the practice of burning surplus crude did not stop once an oilfield was established. When output pressures at one of the Masjid-i-Suleiman wells suddenly spiked in early 1912, thus overwhelming the capacity of the pipeline that served it, APOC managers simply burned off the excess— some 400 tons per day, or 146,000 tons per year—in a smoke-belching blaze that continued for a full five years until the completion of a larger pipeline.[86]

Fire was the standard method for dealing not only with excess crude but also with the various by-products of petroleum production. As we have seen, early refineries incinerated huge quantities of the light fractions for which there was no market, especially during the early years when even the fractions that went into gasoline were regarded as nothing more than waste. But long after the automobile revolution had created a mass market for gasoline, refineries continued to flare off large volumes of unsaleable gases. At the oilfields too, huge quantities of excess hydrocarbon went up in smoke. On newly opened sites in particular, companies often faced an urgent financial need to get the crude processed and on the market as quickly as possible. The gas that bubbled up with it was dealt with summarily at the outset. Because it was both highly flammable and often poisonous (especially when it contained significant amounts of hydrogen sulphide), it was generally piped a safe distance away from the wellheads and burned off continuously, night and day. On the hilltops around Masjid-i-Suleiman, where vapours from the sulphurous crude had previously made the whole area smell 'like a cataract of rotten eggs', APOC burned off some 2.1 million cubic metres of gas per day in the mid-1920s—enough, it was reckoned, to light the whole of London. The resulting flares rose over 30 metres into the air, creating a landscape of controlled infernos that one night-time observer described as one of 'the most wonderful and weird spectacles ever, surely, associated with industrial development'.[87]

As the prevalence of fire shows, intense local pollution was not so much a side-effect as an integral part of petroleum production during this period. Fouling the nearby surroundings was generally regarded as the inevitable price of oil extraction, and indeed as a price that neither producers nor consumers were actually obliged to pay. Nothing illustrated this fundamental connection between pollution and production more clearly than the iconic gusher, the ultimate goal of the drillers and the most spectacular cause of environmental contamination on the oilfields. Before the 1930s the initial opening of new wells ordinarily involved some degree of excess oil flow, which was usually diverted into earthen storage reservoirs where it seeped into the soil and was either pumped out or burned. In most cases the flow could be stopped quickly by packing off the drill hole and installing valve collars at the surface. Occasionally, however, the pressure of escaping oil and gas was too great to control, creating a 'runaway' well that endangered workers and caused extensive damage to nearby fields, forests, and waterways (Fig. 6.3).

[85] Yergin, *Prize*, 283.   [86] Ferrier, *British Petroleum*, 270.
[87] Quotes from Williamson, *Persian Oil-Field*, 64; Ferrier, *British Petroleum*, 420, 456.

Fig. 6.3. An oil-gusher on Sumatra, 1895–1915. By permission of the Nationaal Museum van Wereldculturen, coll. no. 60037693.

Runaway wells could occur on most oilfields, but some were more prone to them than others. Piercing through the reservoir crust always carried significant risks in Persia and Iraq due to the unusually high temperatures and pressures of their oil-bearing structures. High pressure was one of the many advantages of these oilfields, which they shared with the subsequent finds in Arabia. What made them so profitable was not only the sheer size of their subterranean reservoirs but also the extraordinary output of individual wells. In the 1920s APOC's

wells were by far the most prolific in the world. Whereas the average well productivity in the USA was around 4,000 tons per year, APOC's B17 well could
produce an astonishing 880,200 tons per year (and its F7 well a further 586,000 tons)
with no need for pumping.[88] It was not always possible to control such colossal
forces from deep underground, as the very first commercial strike in Iraq clearly
illustrated. On 15 October 1927 drillers at Baba Gurgur, just north-west of
Kirkuk, hit a gusher so powerful that it could be seen almost 20 kilometres
away. It was a prospector's dream but an environmentalist's nightmare. The
gusher flowed uncontrolled for over a week, dousing the surrounding area with
some 95,000 barrels per day and creating a river of crude large enough to threaten
Kirkuk, whose inhabitants reportedly 'witnessed with awe a spectacle of unusual
grandeur and novelty'.[89]

Drilling into oil formations was especially hazardous on Trinidad, where the
problem of high pressure was amplified by the loose, sandy substrata sitting atop
the main reservoirs. In the 1910s the island's Guapo oilfield was perennially slath-
ered with gushers and choked with the smell of gas. On one occasion a single well
at Guapo spouted no fewer than six times in a fortnight while its output was
gathered in a makeshift earthen pond before the arrival of steel storage tanks from
Britain. In 1913, when drillers at the Morne L'Enfer No. 4 well hit the high-pressure
oil-sands, the resulting eruption blew drilling cable, tools, sand, and oil 30 metres
into the air before sending an estimated 200,000 barrels streaming downhill
over the next three days. Worse was to come at the Forest Reserve field in 1920,
where drillers at the No. 3 well hit a rich oil-sand at 330 metres that blew out at
the surface and rained crude in a wide radius around the rig. Although most of the
inhabitants of the neighbouring village of Fyzabad were drafted in to help dam
the flow, their makeshift barrage soon broke, releasing a flood of oil and water into
the nearby John River. Soon afterwards a spark from a boiler that was running one
of the pumps ignited the entire basin of crude behind the failing dam. Derricks
reportedly lit up 'like torches' as the fire spread down the valley and into the nearby
cocoa plantations, destroying around 25 hectares and leaving residual coke in the
ditches between tree rows. The next morning, as the sun rose clearly in the east, the
entire western half of the sky was shrouded by an enormous black cloud stretching
slowly seaward. A team of test-diggers then worked their way along the stricken
John River and channelled the remaining unburnt oil into the Orupuche mangrove
swamp—probably the worst possible expedient from an ecological perspective, since
mangroves are not only among the most productive and diverse ecosystems on Earth,
but also exceptionally sensitive to oil spills.[90] Overall, around 100,000 barrels

---

[88] Ferrier, *British Petroleum*, 398.

[89] Quote from Beeby-Thompson, *Oil Pioneer*, 414–15; J. H. Bamberg, *The History of the British
Petroleum Company*, vol. 2: *The Anglo-Iranian Years 1928–1954* (Cambridge: Cambridge University
Press, 1994), 157–60; Howarth, *Shell*, 147–8; Yergin, *Prize*, 188.

[90] This is because the smothering of their aerial roots impairs gas exchange, while the absorption
of oil into the subsoil also damages the salt-exclusion capacity of their underground roots:
International Maritime Organization, *Field Guide for Oil Spill Response in Tropical Waters*
(London: International Maritime Organization, 1997), 20–33.

of oil were incinerated in this single incident. According to an eyewitness the 'fried alligators and fishes attracted the vultures from as far away as Port of Spain', and the soot from the blaze harmed flowering trees over 10 kilometres away.[91]

For many years such damage was simply accepted by company managers as an unavoidable part of the oil business. Indeed, in the case of another Trinidad gusher in 1912, which smeared the banks of the Vance River and covered nearby beaches with oily sludge, the company owner—clearly oblivious to the shortcomings of his logic—actually refused any outside help to bring the well under control 'on the grounds that [he] did not intend to interfere with nature'.[92] Yet within the industry there was also a mounting sense of disapproval about the colossal amounts of waste involved, not to mention the dangers posed to workers and the threat of compensation payments to landowners whose fields and forests were ruined. As demand rose after the First World War, companies increasingly sought to gain more control over the oil they tapped, and also to maximize the capture of the energy that it contained.

'Rationalization' was a key buzzword of the inter-war period, and technological developments within the petroleum industry clearly reflected this preoccupation. For the oil majors, the application of efficiency-enhancing and waste-reducing technologies was more than just a formula for boosting profits; it was also their preferred means of contending with the problems of pollution.[93] Although many of the key innovations originated in the United States, they were quickly applied in Europe's main oil colonies as well. In the 1920s, the development of blowout preventers (essentially a stack of valves attached to the steel well casing) and special drilling muds significantly reduced the risk of oil loss that was previously associated with opening new high-pressure wells.[94] Basically, this involved routing the drill-string through a blowout preventer to the boring bit below, and feeding heavy, viscous muds (often containing finely ground barium sulphate or haematite) into the well casing. The column of mud served several purposes: it lubricated the bit, enabled the cuttings to be lifted out, and, most importantly, provided hydrostatic pressure to prevent fluids and gas from entering the borehole. Simple versions of valve containers were used in Persia by the mid-1920s, and allowed drillers to bring wells of up to 3,000 tons per day into production with no loss of oil at the surface.[95] On Trinidad, drilling muds and blowout preventers were critical for controlling the high pressures and loose sands that otherwise entered the wells and damaged valve equipment. First introduced in the late 1920s, they became widespread in the 1930s with the availability of barites from Germany (which were, incidentally, traded for cocoa). Soon they enabled Trinidad's drillers to bring deposits into production that had hitherto defied all attempts to control their flow.

---

[91] This paragraph is based on Higgins, *Trinidad Oil*, 89, 95, 295–7.

[92] Higgins, *Trinidad Oil*, 307.

[93] At least until the 1950s–1960s, as pressures for outside pollution regulation grew: see Hugh S. Gorman, *Redefining Efficiency: Pollution Concerns, Regulatory Mechanisms, and Technological Change in the U.S. Petroleum Industry* (Akron, Oh.: University of Akron Press, 2001).

[94] Howarth, *Shell*, 129–30; *The Royal Dutch*, 51–2.

[95] Williamson, *Persian Oil-Field*, 48–9.

But as ever, the new techniques were not fail-safe. In 1928, a blowout preventer failure at the Dome oilfield not far from Fyzabad caused a massive explosion that killed sixteen people, the worst oil-related accident in Trinidad's history.[96]

Reduction of spillage at the wellhead was mirrored by a decline in the proportion of crude and gas discarded as waste. During the 1920s the most volatile high-pressure gases were increasingly siphoned off in separator units, while new absorption plants allowed for the recovery of low-pressure gases that could be used for making gasoline. By the late 1920s APOC was extracting 1.7 million cubic metres of gas per day, some of which was used to fuel its boilers, heaters, and generators, and the remainder of which was converted into an additional 450,000 litres of gasoline—a far better solution, one observer noted, than sending it 'in flame and smoke to the Persian skies'.[97] In the 1930s the burgeoning petrochemical industry also turned excess gas into a multitude of new products, from benzole and carbon black to insecticides, fertilizers, and detergents.[98]

Yet one of the biggest challenges for oil producers was the skyrocketing demand for gasoline, which made it difficult to bring refining output into balance with the market. The rapid spread of automobiles in the inter-war years left APOC with a large surplus of heavy fuel oil. Likewise, the Royal Dutch/Shell Group, with its abundance of heavy crude supplies, was perennially short on gasoline but long on bitumen. One solution was to recycle excess products back underground. In the early 1930s gas re-injection became a common method for maintaining reservoir pressures and reducing waste. APOC re-injected excess fuel oil at a rate of nearly 1 million tons per year into the Masjid-i-Suleiman reservoir in an effort to maintain both well pressures and fuel prices.[99] But the key was to increase the yield of gasoline per barrel of crude, which was accomplished by 'cracking' the long hydrocarbon chains of heavy oils and distillates into shorter molecules through treatment under high temperatures and pressures.

By the end of the 1910s there were several industrial cracking systems on the market, some cleaner and more efficient than others. On Trinidad, the 'Greenstreet' cracking unit built in 1921 at Point-à-Pierre belched out so many noxious fumes that 'trees in the vicinity of the plant exhibited glorious autumn tints as a preliminary to dying, birds passed away in the atmosphere of hydrocarbon vapours and hydrogen sulphide and the whole neighbourhood was rendered uninhabitable'.[100] Here as elsewhere, the main turning point came with the spread of so-called Trumble units and Dubbs crackers from the mid-1920s. APOC began cracking in 1925 and acquired its first Dubbs converter in 1927; from 1920 to 1932 the company's gasoline sales increased more than sevenfold, nearly twice the rate of fuel oil and diesel growth.[101] By 1926 Royal Dutch/Shell obtained 40 per cent of its gasoline from cracking plants in Balik Papan, Trinidad, Suez, and Curaçao, the

[96] Higgins, *Trinidad Oil*, 104–7, 394–410.
[97] Williamson, *Persian Oil-Field*, 65–6, quote 68; Ferrier, *British Petroleum*, 420–1, 456–7.
[98] Jonker and van Zanden, *Royal Dutch*, 345–66; Howarth, *Shell*, 147.
[99] Ferrier, *British Petroleum*, 421–2; Higgins, *Trinidad Oil*, 116; Jonker and van Zanden, *Royal Dutch*, 335–6.
[100] Higgins, *Trinidad Oil*, 206.   [101] Ferrier, *British Petroleum*, 455, 466.

latter boasting no fewer than thirteen Trumble units and twenty Dubbs crackers by the mid-1930s.[102]

These technological improvements in refining and extraction meant that the development of Europe's oil empire was not only a story of wanton environmental destruction, but also included attempts to reduce waste and pollution, at least insofar as this had a clear engineering and commercial rationale. But even so, it was hardly a win-win game, since the underlying political ecology of the colonial oil industry continued to create a fairly clear set of winners and losers. As one might expect, the main winners were the oil companies, their shareholders, and consumers in the industrial world. Among the local winners one might add the elites and landholders who were able to profit from the industry, and, to a lesser extent, anyone who managed to earn better wages by working for it. By contrast, the main losers were the people and the multitude of other plant and animal species that had to make way for oil exploitation or had to live with its dirty consequences.

In this sense, oil production followed the classic pattern of ecological imperialism in which an existing power differential allows one group of people to control and extract natural resources from areas inhabited by less powerful groups, all of which augmented the power differential still further. As for the damage and pollution this caused, it is difficult to say whether the effects in the colonies were any worse than they would have been in metropolitan settings given the absence of a European oil industry at the time. Certainly the fact that so many colonial oilfields were located in sparsely populated 'wildernesses' hardly heightened concerns about environmental degradation. Nor, for that matter, did the industry's heavy reliance on a transient labour force recruited from afar. It is worth noting, however, that the oilfields of the United States and Canada were also treated in a highly instrumental manner during this period, just as many of the coal-producing landscapes of Europe were written off for what was regarded as the common good. Few waterways anywhere in the colonies were as polluted as the infamous Cuyahoga River (the 'river that caught fire', indeed on multiple occasions) or the sludge-laden Emscher in the Ruhr valley (dubbed 'the river of hell'[103]), just as few coastlines were more thoroughly trashed than the North Sea shores that were used as waste dumps for the collieries of county Durham. Throughout this period it seems that most fossil fuel-producing localities were treated like 'subject' landscapes, areas that were sacrificed for the sake of the energy they harboured.

Either way, the peculiar structure of the petroleum empire also meant that there were relative winners and losers even among the industrial societies that principally benefited from the resources that it mobilized. For those who actually controlled rather than merely consumed the resulting flow of fossilized solar energy, it significantly augmented their power. For those excluded from direct involvement in the global oil system, it was a major cause of international tension.

---

[102] Jonker and van Zanden, *Royal Dutch*, 334–5, 447.

[103] Thomas M. Lekan, *Imagining the Nation in Nature: Landscape Preservation and German Identity, 1885–1945* (Cambridge, Mass.: Harvard University Press, 2004), 33.

WAR AND THE RESHAPING OF EUROPE'S OIL EMPIRE

If the First World War demonstrated the strategic link between oil energy and power, the Second World War, and the build-up to it, emphatically underscored the point. At the end of 1918, the British, French, and US governments were keenly aware of the petroleum advantage they had enjoyed over their erstwhile opponents, and were not inclined to relinquish it during the years that followed. The series of political agreements reached during the 1920s effectively kept the other industrial powers—Germany, Japan, and Italy—from gaining direct access to the prolific reserves of the Middle East and Southeast Asia. The commercial arrangements between the existing oil majors had much the same effect, and moreover enabled them to dominate the domestic oil markets of importing countries by shutting out new competitors. By the 1930s, Germany, Japan, and Italy relied almost entirely on foreign-owned companies for their supplies of a key energy resource. Against the backdrop of mounting geopolitical tensions, leaders in all three countries were determined to acquire independent sources of petroleum, not least in order to fuel the expansion of their armed forces. Enhancing their control over oil energy was vital for boosting their political and military power. Ultimately they attempted to create their own petroleum empires.

Throughout the 1930s the Axis powers sought to reduce their oil vulnerability in three principal ways: by manufacturing synthetic fuel, by purchasing from friendly countries, and by acquiring reserves of their own. Germany and Italy—deprived of their pre-war shares in Middle Eastern oil, and locked out by the Red Line Agreement—tried in vain to gain access to the huge finds in Saudi Arabia during the 1930s. In response, they bought large amounts of oil from Central and South American suppliers, especially from the newly nationalized industries of Mexico and Bolivia. Nazi Germany and Fascist Italy were Mexico's two largest customers after the expropriation of the industry by the Cárdenas government in 1938, which triggered a British-led embargo on Mexican exports.[104] But it was not long before US pressure curtailed oil sales to the Axis powers, and as these deliveries sank, the development of synthetic fuel became all the more important.

Germany, as part of its self-sufficiency drive, invested heavily in the construction of hydrogenation plants for manufacturing gasoline from its abundant coal supplies. By 1939 it had become the world's largest producer of synthetic fuel and was able to cover around half of its peacetime consumption.[105] But on the eve of the war Germany still imported over two-thirds of its oil, and once the fighting broke out, the additional requirements of its military operations, coupled with the need to supply Fascist Italy, created serious bottlenecks. After the fall of France, which brought still more net-oil-importing territory under German authority, Romania was the only secure foreign supplier for the Nazis' growing continental empire. The

---

[104] Myrna I. Santiago, *The Ecology of Oil: Environment, Labor, and the Mexican Revolution, 1900–1938* (Cambridge: Cambridge University Press, 2006), 205–341.
[105] Eichholtz, *Ölpolitik*, 96–278; Venn, *Oil Diplomacy*, 84–5; Yergin, *Prize*, 257–8; Podobnik, *Global Energy*, 86.

only other oilfields within reach lay in Russia, which sold considerable amounts to Germany under the Molotov–Ribbentrop Pact. Securing direct control over these energy sources was one of the main motivations behind the invasion of the Soviet Union in June 1941, and in particular the drive towards the Caucasus in 1942. The subsequent failure to capture Russia's petroleum wealth thus dealt a critical strategic blow to the German military machine, denying it much-needed liquid fuel while embroiling it in a drawn-out, gas-guzzling land war across the entire eastern front. By 1943 gasoline shortages increasingly hampered German military operations, and by late 1944 the opening of a second front in the west rapidly depleted Germany's remaining fuel stocks.[106]

Japanese policy was shaped by similar needs and constraints. Although oil accounted for only 7 per cent of Japan's energy consumption in the 1930s, it was nonetheless crucial for the army and navy. Moreover, Japan's modest synthetic fuel industry meant that the acquisition of foreign oilfields was even more important than it was for Germany. The aspiration for self-sufficiency in strategic raw materials was the foundation for the imperial concept of an Asian 'new order' and 'co-prosperity sphere', which would be free from the influence of the Western powers. Enhancing Japan's oil security was one of the motives behind the invasion of Manchuria in 1931, and it also prompted the formation of an overambitious synthetic fuel plan after 1937. But despite these initiatives, Japan (and the territories it controlled) still produced only 7 per cent of the oil it used at the end of the 1930s. The vast bulk of its supplies were still imported from the USA (80 per cent), with a further 10 per cent coming from the Dutch East Indies. This left Japan highly vulnerable to the threat of petroleum sanctions, especially in the context of rapidly deteriorating relations with its principal supplier. The occupation of Indochina in July 1941 finally brought matters to a head, triggering what was effectively an oil embargo by the USA, Britain, and Dutch East Indies. With no more than eighteen to twenty-four months' reserves at its disposal, the government now deemed it imperative to secure control over its own petroleum supplies. Japanese naval commanders had long set their sights on the East Indies, which could, if ruled directly, meet most of the country's oil needs. In essence, the attack on Pearl Harbor was a pre-emptive strike designed to provide a window of opportunity for conquering the resource-rich colonies of Southeast Asia, and above all for invading the oil-rich East Indies in January 1942. By the end of February 1942 the archipelago was firmly under Japanese control, followed a month later by Malaya and Burma.

The conquest of Southeast Asia's oilfields temporarily gave Japan its own longed-for petroleum empire. Despite the demolition of rigs and refineries by retreating Allied personnel, by 1943 Japanese engineers had managed to restore East Indies production to three-quarters of its pre-war level. In a remarkable stroke of luck, Japanese drillers also hit the largest oilfield ever discovered in Southeast Asia—at

---

[106] Eichholtz, *Ölpolitik*, 366–561; Adam Tooze, *The Wages of Destruction: The Making and Breaking of the Nazi Economy* (London: Allen Lane, 2006), 381–2, 411–12, 493–4.

Minas in central Sumatra—with their single wildcat well of the entire war.[107] But if the oil wells of the so-called 'southern zone' were flowing freely, relentless US submarine attacks ensured that the Japanese Home Islands received only a small portion of what they produced. By early 1944 tanker sinkings had already cut imports by half, and by the end of the year the flow was reduced to a trickle. Japan's synthetic fuel programme was completely unable to make up the shortfall, covering at most 5 per cent of its requirements. From 1944 onwards the resulting shortages severely constrained Japanese military operations, while in the Home Islands oil grew so scarce that essential vehicles were retrofitted with special condensers to run on charcoal- or wood-gas.[108]

In short, the Allies' privileged access to oil resources, and their ability to move it across the seas, was a decisive factor in the outcome of the war. The USA still produced over two-thirds of the world's petroleum, and after 1941 its vast reserves were firmly harnessed to the Allied war effort. Although German U-Boats posed a serious threat to Britain's oil lifeline up until spring 1943, even in 1942 Britain managed to import over 10 million tons.[109] Moreover, the USA was by no means the only source of oil for the Allies. Venezuela, Trinidad, Aruba, and Curaçao made significant contributions, while Persia nearly doubled its output to around 17 million tons after the loss of Burma and the East Indies to Japan. The strategic significance of these colonial oil resources was obvious, and British authorities did everything they could to protect them. In July 1940 French shares in the Iraqi Petroleum Company were seized to keep them out of Vichy hands, and in April 1941 British troops forcibly deposed a group of pro-Axis army officers that had temporarily taken over the government in Iraq. Shortly after the invasion of the Soviet Union, British forces landed in southern Persia to protect APOC's oil installations, and as German columns advanced towards Baku a year later, Royal Engineers plugged oil wells throughout Iraq.[110]

It was not only the sheer quantity of oil from the colonies that was important, but also the range of different products they provided. Allied ships could draw on abundant fuel oil supplies from Persia and the Caribbean, in stark contrast to the shortages faced by the German Navy. Gasoline production also rose sharply through the installation of additional cracking and hydrogenation units. Most notable, perhaps, was the role of colonial oilfields in the provision of high-octane aviation fuel. In the late 1930s the development of catalytic hydrogenation, polymerization, and alkylation enabled refineries to engineer new molecules out of various hydrocarbon compounds rather than merely 'cracking' heavy fractions into lighter ones. British authorities were quick to hitch these technologies to their war preparations, and by 1940 new alkylation and polymerization units were operating at Abadan, Aruba, Curaçao, and Trinidad (Point-à-Pierre) to supply the Royal Air Force with 100-octane spirit. The shipments from the Caribbean proved crucial

---

[107] Yergin, *Prize*, 338–9; Albert Rolff, *Erdöl in Südostasien und seine volkswirtschaftliche Bedeutung für Westeuropa* (Berlin: Duncker & Humblot, 1978), 22. The rig and equipment had recently been brought in by the US firm Caltex, which had previously identified the field.

[108] Yergin, *Prize*, 340.　　[109] Tooze, *Wages*, 412.　　[110] Longrigg, *Oil*, 120–6.

during the Battle of Britain, for they gave the RAF's Spitfires and Hurricanes a significant advantage over the Luftwaffe, which relied entirely on synthetic fuel that could not be converted into 100-octane spirit. Meanwhile, Abadan became a vital supplier of aviation fuel for other theatres of operation, including the Soviet Union, and by the end of the war it was producing over a million tons of 100-octane spirit per year.[111]

As the scale of production grew, so did the environmental consequences at the main processing centres. The almost unlimited need for gasoline and aviation fuel significantly altered the market mix and created a large surplus of heavy products such as fuel oil and asphalt. In Persia, most of this excess was pumped back into the reservoirs at Masjid-i-Suleiman and Haft Kel. But recycling was not an option for the refinery complexes on Aruba and Curaçao, which obtained their crude from wells on the Venezuelan mainland. Curaçao's Isla refinery, which had already produced large quantities of asphalt from the heavy crude it processed, simply dumped the excess—around 2 million tons by the end of the war—into pits along the shores of the Buscabaai, not far from Willemstad. It was a short-term expedient with a long-term legacy, for it created a vast asphalt lake that continued (and, as of this writing, continues) to emanate toxic fumes and ensnare unsuspecting birds and other animals well into the twenty-first century.[112]

Furthermore, the environmental impacts of elevated wartime demand reverberated far beyond the oil hubs themselves. Perhaps the most tragic example stemmed not from the actual production of oil but rather from the inability of Japanese authorities to acquire enough of it. While US torpedoes severed the supply line from the East Indies, which regularly covered the South China Sea in flaming oil slicks, the Japanese government made an increasingly frantic attempt to squeeze petroleum substitutes out of the ecosystems of the Home Islands. In spring 1945 the Imperial Navy, now desperate for fuel, resorted to a quixotic campaign to mobilize ordinary civilians, even schoolchildren, to dig up pine roots all across the country under the slogan 'two hundred pine roots will keep a plane in the air for an hour'. By June the monthly production of pine root oil had risen to around 70,000 barrels. Due to refining difficulties, however, it only ever yielded 3,000 barrels of gasoline, and even this paltry amount was found to be unusable by post-war tests on US jeeps, whose engines soon seized when burning the fuel. The campaign was worse than futile, adding nothing to Japanese fuel stocks while needlessly stripping entire mountainsides of the tree cover that had long held their erosion-prone soils intact.[113]

---

[111] Larson et al., *Standard Oil*, 164–5, 198, 396; Jonker and van Zanden, *Royal Dutch*, 447; Stephen Howarth, and Joost Jonker, *A History of Royal Dutch Shell*, vol. 2: *Powering the Hydrocarbon Revolution, 1939–1973* (Oxford: Oxford University Press, 2007), 14; Higgins, *Trinidad Oil*, 120–2; Bamberg, *British Petroleum*, 217–19, 242–6.

[112] On Persia: Bamberg, *British Petroleum*, 239; Longrigg, *Oil*, 129. On Curaçao: Howarth and Jonker, *Royal Dutch*, 36; Colin Woodard, 'Curaçao's Crude Legacy', *Christian Science Monitor*, 28 Nov. 2008: <http://www.csmonitor.com/Environment/2008/1128/curacaos-crude-legacy>; FOE Netherlands, <http://royaldutchshellplc.com/2011/11/08/shells-toxic-legacy-in-curacao/>.

[113] William M. Tsutsui, 'Landscapes in the Dark Valley: Toward an Environmental History of Wartime Japan', in Richard P. Tucker and Edmund Russell (eds), *Natural Enemy, Natural Ally: Toward*

Probably the most spectacular effects occurred at the oil hubs that got caught up in the actual fighting. In early 1942, plans to prevent the petroleum assets of Southeast Asia from falling into Japanese hands were put into effect as soon as individual installations came under threat. The oilfields in Sarawak—the most vulnerable to Japanese attack—were demolished almost immediately after Pearl Harbor. Off the north-eastern coast of Borneo, the Tarakan oilfields were set alight on 10–11 January, and at Balik Papan the oilfields, refinery, and even wharves were destroyed two weeks later as Dutch forces opened the tank valves and ignited their contents. Once Singapore came under attack in February, the oilfields of Sumatra were also systematically destroyed. The fire at the flagship Pladju refinery was so intense that it lit up the night sky in nearby Palembang. Throughout the next day, the smoke obscured the entire town under a 'ghostly twilight, like that caused by the ash raining down after a volcanic eruption'.[114] In early March, when it was clear that Rangoon, too, would fall, the whole process was repeated. As the wells on Upper Burma's oilfields were set ablaze, demolition squads in Rangoon torched the vast refinery complexes south of the city, sending a huge black smoke cloud over 6 kilometres into the air. The updraft of the conflagration was so powerful that it sucked large quantities of the heavier oil fractions into the atmosphere, which subsequently condensed and fell in a sticky, black rain across the area. It took another two months before the fires finally went out.[115]

It was, as one eyewitness remarked, an 'outrage to the bounty of Nature' that 'the earth with its flowing riches should be torn and rent and destroyed in an ideological struggle between peoples'. Yet it was the very contest over these 'flowing riches' that helped trigger the struggle in the first place. Nor was this the last time that the soils, air, and jungles of Southeast Asia would be doused with burning hydrocarbons and enveloped in smoke. After salvaging as much as they could from the wreckage, Japanese forces eventually carried out their own programme of asset-denial as they retreated back to their oil-deprived Home Islands. At the end of the war, the twice-demolished Balik Papan site reportedly 'presented a gloomy, doomed picture, its mud-pools brown with rust on which the oil floated in a kaleidoscope of gold, green and purple; the beach too, with its burned, collapsed jetties, its charred palm stumps, its ghostly shadows several fathoms under water, the motor-boats riddled with leaks, and cars and lorries driven into the sea, and already embedded into the sandy bottom'.[116]

The mess left behind on the shores of eastern Borneo broadly typified the state of Europe's oil colonies in Southeast Asia at the end of the war: wrecked, charred,

an Environmental History of Warfare (Corvallis, Ore.: Oregon State University Press, 2004), 195–216, here 203; Yergin, *Prize*, 345–6, 348.

[114] Johan Fabricius, *East Indies Episode: An Account of the Demolitions Carried out and of Some Experiences of the Staff in the East Indies Oil Areas of the Royal Dutch-Shell Group during 1941 and 1942* (London: Shell, 1949), 12–13, 46–53, 86–117, quote 116.

[115] T. A. B. Corley, *A History of the Burmah Oil Company*, vol. 2: *1924–66* (London: Heinemann, 1988), 70–2, 82–99; Pagan U Khin Maung Gyi, *Memoirs of the Oil Industry in Burma* (Rangoon, 1989), 23.

[116] Quotes from Fabricius, *East Indies*, 137, 139.

polluted, and degraded. In some ways it also reflected the condition of colonialism itself in the region, for just like the oil in the demolished storage tanks and refinery units, the basis of Europe's imperial power in Asia had largely gone up in the smoke of the conflict. Unlike much of Africa and the Caribbean, where colonialism remained entrenched for nearly two more decades, European rule never fully recovered from the carnage of the war in this part of the world, despite rearguard efforts to maintain it. But even so, this hardly spelled the end of Europe's petroleum empire, in Southeast Asia or anywhere else. Although it had to be reshaped in the post-war world, a world in which Europe's imperial power was not only weaker but also seemed increasingly anachronistic, the oil empire that had been built up since the first colonial strikes of the 1870s–1880s continued to channel ever-growing amounts of energy from petroleum landscapes overseas.

PART II

CONSERVATION, IMPROVEMENT, AND ENVIRONMENTAL MANAGEMENT IN THE COLONIES

7

Tropical Nature in Trust
The Politics of Colonial Nature Conservation

In 1857, while travelling through the Aru Islands in what is now eastern Indonesia, the explorer-scientist Alfred Russel Wallace was initially overjoyed by his first successful capture of a King Bird of Paradise (*Paradisea regia*), one of the most beautiful and enigmatic animals to be found anywhere in the world. As he later recounted in his bio-geographical treatise *The Malay Archipelago*, finding this species was one of the primary aims behind his trip to the East, and the emotions stirred by finally gazing upon this 'perfect little organism' required 'the poetic faculty fully to express them'.

But no sooner had Wallace bagged his prized specimen than he was gripped by feelings of ambivalence, even melancholy. 'It seems sad that on the one hand such exquisite creatures should live out their lives and exhibit their charms only in these wild inhospitable regions, doomed for ages yet to come to hopeless barbarism; while on the other hand, should civilised man ever reach these distant lands, and bring moral, intellectual, and physical light into the recesses of these virgin forests, we may be sure that he will so disturb the nicely-balanced relations of organic and inorganic nature to cause the disappearance, and finally the extinction, of these very beings whose wonderful structure and beauty he alone is fitted to appreciate and enjoy.'[1]

Wallace was, of course, an unusual observer. He was one of the most celebrated naturalists of the Victorian era, perhaps best known for the so-called 'Wallace Line' that separates the faunal zones of Asia and Australia. Were it not for Darwin, he would almost certainly be remembered as the founder of evolutionary theory.[2] But if Wallace himself was atypical, many of the sentiments he expressed were not. His portrayal of the tropical lands that Europeans were penetrating, as well as the implications of this looming encounter, encapsulated some of the most fundamental ideas, impulses, and anxieties of the imperial era. Like most of his contemporaries, he revelled in the notion of tropical landscapes as pristine wilderness, as 'virgin' territory unsullied by human alteration. He was fascinated by the plethora of life they contained, and especially by the exotic creatures (like the Bird of Paradise) that served as iconic symbols of tropical nature. His perceptions were strongly

---

[1] Alfred Russel Wallace, *The Malay Archipelago: The Land of the Orang-utan, and the Bird of Paradise. A Narrative of Travel, with Studies of Man and Nature* (New York: Harper, 1869), 448–9.

[2] Michael Shermer, *In Darwin's Shadow: The Life and Science of Alfred Russel Wallace* (Oxford: Oxford University Press, 2002).

moulded by current conceptions of 'civilization' and 'barbarism' that ranked different societies according to their capacity to understand and control the natural world. Part of the excitement he felt about capturing his new specimen stemmed from being so far removed from civilization amidst 'the wild luxuriant tropical forest' and the 'rude uncultured savages who gathered round me'.[3]

Europe's imperial powers took immense pride in their capacity to bend nature to their will—a capacity that not only furnished the practical tools for conquest, but also engendered a sense of licence for it. But just as the 'march of progress' in Europe provoked regrets about the loss of tradition, so too was the enthusiasm for tropical wilderness tinged by fears of its vulnerability in the face of modern technology and trade. In a sense, Wallace's reflections about the simultaneous discovery and endangerment of nature's beauty recalls the so-called 'observer effect', or the changes that the act of observation makes on the phenomenon being observed. If the expansion of European power promised a better understanding of tropical nature, it also threatened to transform it on an unprecedented scale. By the late nineteenth century some of the most cherished flora and fauna in tropical Asia and Africa in fact began to disappear, and as losses mounted, observers placed even greater value on what was under threat. By the turn of the century such concerns gave rise to a new framework of laws, agreements, and institutions designed to curb the destruction of wildlife and natural habitats in Europe's colonies.

The motives behind these efforts were complex, and grew increasingly so as the twentieth century progressed. In part they reflected a growing sense within Europe about the need to safeguard treasured landscapes and endangered species from the threats posed by rapid industrialization. To a large extent they also arose from specific circumstances in the colonies, above all the impact of commercial hunting and the desire to control the trade in animal parts. As it happened, these two dimensions were tightly entangled, for the evolution of conservation involved a multifaceted exchange of ideas, norms, and practices between metropoles and colonies, as well as between rival empires.[4]

As recent scholarship has shown, Europe's tropical colonies played a central role in the rise of modern nature conservation more generally. Although this initially had much more to do with concerns about resource availability than with a budding 'environmentalist' consciousness, many of the world's earliest and most far-reaching protection measures were developed there.[5] The prominence of tropical colonies in the history of conservation was based on a wide range of factors: the

---

[3] Wallace, *Malay Archipelago*, 448.

[4] Generally, MacLeod (ed.), *Nature and Empire*; David Anderson and Richard H. Grove (eds), *Conservation in Africa: People, Policies and Practice* (Cambridge: Cambridge University Press, 1987); Tilley, *Africa*; Donal P. McCracken, 'Fraternity in the Age of Jingoism: The British Imperial Botanic and Forestry Network', in Benedikt Stuchtey (ed.), *Science across the European Empires, 1800–1950* (Oxford: Oxford University Press, 2005), 49–62; MacKenzie (ed.), *Imperialism*. On parks specifically: Bernhard Gißibl, Sabine Höhler, and Patrick Kupper (eds), *Civilizing Nature: National Parks in Global Historical Perspective* (New York: Berghahn, 2012).

[5] Cf. Grove, *Green Imperialism*; Grove, *Ecology*. See, more generally, Beinart and Hughes *Environment*; David Arnold and Ramachandra Guha (eds), *Nature, Culture, Imperialism: Essays on the Environmental History of South Asia* (Delhi: Oxford University Press, 1995).

European fascination with unspoiled tropical paradises, the rapid changes unleashed by imperial conquest and trade, and a cluster of anxieties about the potentially destructive effects of European economic and technological forces on distant shores. But perhaps most important of all was the structure of colonial domination itself, which enabled Europeans to impose their own visions of tropical nature onto these environments with scant regard for the interests of rural communities living there. Throughout Europe's colonies, efforts at nature conservation rarely involved the assent, let alone participation, of the peoples they affected. Indeed, they often excluded locals from certain areas altogether. If the history of colonial conservation is partly about the attempt to limit the destructive consequences of imperial expansion, it is also very much about the spread of European domination and state power.

Accordingly, both the design and the effects of colonial conservation measures were shaped by much more than just the ecological changes they sought to redress. Social and political dynamics were crucial, including the economic designs for individual territories, their different forms of government, the relative capacity of colonial states to enforce their writ, and the actions of indigenous peoples who variously opposed, undermined, or made the best of the conservation measures imposed upon them. Here we will examine how these criss-crossing strands were woven into a new fabric of nature conservation in Europe's colonies—a fabric whose loose ends trailed far beyond the colonial era.[6]

PRIMEVAL NATURE AND THE CIVILIZING MISSION

Self-evident though it may seem today, the idea of protecting 'nature' from the threat of degradation is a relatively recent phenomenon. At one level it is a universal notion: the protection of revered sites and other expressions of 'sacred ecology' are common to most rural cultures the world over, and have functioned since time immemorial to set limits on the human transformation of nature.[7] Yet throughout human history, nature has just as often been an article of fear as veneration. For agrarian societies, 'wilderness' traditionally connoted barrenness, infertility, and danger. The wild places beyond the cultivated fields and coppices were at best an object of conquest, at worst a realm of savagery and peril. The emergence of what we would nowadays recognize as conservationist sensibilities was a quintessentially modern phenomenon, one rooted in new understandings of nature and moulded by processes of territorial state-building, industrialization, and colonial expansion. It was driven by many different ideas and impulses, from a pragmatic interest in resource conservation to Romantic notions of the spiritual need for unspoiled

---

[6] Sections of this chapter are based on material first published in Corey Ross, 'Tropical Nature as Global *Patrimoine*: Imperialism and International Nature Protection in the Early Twentieth Century', in Paul Betts and Corey Ross (eds), *Heritage in the Modern World: Historical Preservation in Global Perspective* (supplement of the journal *Past & Present*, 2015), 214–39.

[7] Fikret Berkes, *Sacred Ecology*, 2nd edn (London: Routledge, 2008).

nature. What bound them all together was a shared aspiration to safeguard flora, fauna, and landscapes against the depredations of modernity.[8]

By the second half of the nineteenth century, the rise of preservationist concern in Europe became increasingly bound up with nationalistic programmes of cultural renewal. The idea of a close connection between the development of a people and its indigenous nature was commonly evoked to generate a sense of rootedness in the national soil, an organic bond to the biophysical homeland. Nature, in this view, was both a cornerstone of national identity and a source of moral strength, a salutary antidote to the ills of industrial civilization. For societies increasingly living in dirty, unwholesome cities and subjected to the dehumanizing rhythms of industrial work, an idealized countryside—whether the pastoral landscapes of Merrie England or the primeval German *Urwald*—represented a fount of physical and spiritual renewal. As the notion of 'wilderness' evolved from an object of fear into one of reverence, untamed nature became a repository of untrammelled authenticity, a place in which the individual could escape the pressures of social conformity and where an elemental virility could still assert itself against the effeminizing constraints of industrial society. As a complementary mirror of civilization, wilderness represented a sublime heritage that anchored the nation in time and space.[9]

As Europeans went to other continents they took these multifaceted ideologies with them. In the neo-Europes of the Americas and Australasia, wilderness played a vital role in the construction of national identities. The vast and seemingly empty (or rather, emptied) expanses of these 'new worlds' were generally regarded as *terra nullius*, unoccupied territory ripe for settlement by industrious pioneers.[10] In national mythology, the frontier between wilderness and civilization became a site of heroic self-definition, an essential means of distinguishing these societies from their Old World progenitors by celebrating the values of self-sufficiency that enabled them to carve a new home out of forest, bush, and desert. But as their frontiers began to close in the late nineteenth century, observers grew increasingly concerned about the disappearance of wild areas and what this implied for the national character. In the United States in particular, early conservationists responded by redefining 'wilderness' not as a threat to civilization but as a source of purification and renewal.[11]

---

[8] For a recent overview, see Charles-François Mathis, 'Mobiliser pour l'environnement en Europe et aux États-Unis: un état des lieux à l'aube du 20ᵉ siècle', *Vingtième Siècle: revue d'histoire*, no. 113 (Jan.–Mar. 2012), 15–27. For national studies: David Evans, *A History of Nature Conservation in Britain*, 2nd edn (London: Routledge, 1997); Friedemann Schmoll, *Erinnerung an die Natur. Die Geschichte des Naturschutzes im deutschen Kaiserreich* (Frankfurt a. Main: Campus, 2004); A. Cadoret (ed.), *Protection de la nature: histoire et idéologie* (Paris: Harmattan, 1985).

[9] Max Oelschlaeger, *The Idea of Wilderness: From Prehistory to the Age of Ecology* (New Haven: Yale University Press, 1991); on nature and nation, see Lekan, *Imagining*.

[10] James Belich, *Replenishing the Earth: The Settler Revolution and the Rise of the Anglo-World, 1783–1939* (Oxford: Oxford University Press, 2009).

[11] Roderick Nash, *Wilderness and the American Mind* (New Haven: Yale University Press, 2001, orig. 1967); Thomas R. Dunlap, *Nature and the English Diaspora: Environment and History in the United States, Canada, Australia, and New Zealand* (Cambridge: Cambridge University Press, 1999).

By the turn of the twentieth century, these shifting sensibilities had helped spawn a profusion of nature protection societies throughout Europe, North America, and Australasia. Although their scope and emphasis varied, their common purpose was to protect the wonders of nature from despoliation by humankind. The question of what should be preserved, and how, sparked extensive debates between those who advocated the 'rational use' of resources and those who were primarily concerned with preserving elements of unspoiled nature for the sake of posterity.[12] Within Europe, the work of Hugo Conwentz, a senior forester in Berlin, was particularly influential. As commissioner of the Prussian Staatliche Stelle für Naturdenkmalpflege—founded in 1906 as the world's first state-supported office for nature protection—he travelled widely to promote his concept of the *Naturdenkmal*, or natural monument. The underlying idea was simple, namely that a 'monument' as a vehicle of commemoration could apply to nature just as readily as to anthropogenic artefacts, and that natural monuments should therefore 'be given the same care and attention as has long been successfully expended upon the memorials of earlier art'.[13]

As European nature protection groups sought to determine their priorities and practices, most followed the broad guidelines set out by Conwentz, who defined a natural monument as 'an original—that is, entirely or almost entirely untouched by cultural influences—and characteristic feature of the landscape or an original and characteristic natural living condition of extraordinary, general, patriotic, scientific, or aesthetic interest'.[14] It was a fuzzy concept open to all manner of interpretation. But two aspects of this 'conwentzional nature protection' (as critics called it)[15] are worth highlighting. First, the terminology of a monument focussed attention on individual areas or objects of natural history rather than on larger biophysical systems or communities. This was symptomatic of the concern of early nature protection—quite unlike environmentalism in the late twentieth century—with symbols of nature rather than matters such as pollution or health. Second, and more fundamentally, nature was primarily associated with the 'untouched' and 'pristine'. It resided only where people did not.

[12] The classic study is Samuel P. Hays, *Conservation and the Gospel of Efficiency: The Progressive Conservation Movement, 1890–1920* (Cambridge, Mass.: Harvard University Press, 1959); see also Stephen R. Fox, *The American Conservation Movement: John Muir and his Legacy* (Madison, Wis.: University of Wisconsin Press, 1985).

[13] Hugo Conwentz, *Die Gefährdung der Naturdenkmäler und Vorschläge zu ihrer Erhaltung* (Berlin: Borntraeger, 1904), 206.

[14] Conwentz, *Gefährdung*, 186. Conwentz was particularly influential in Britain, where his 1907 lecture to the British Association for the Advancement of Science formed the basis of his widely cited book *The Care of Natural Monuments with Special Reference to Great Britain and Germany* (Cambridge: Cambridge University Press, 1909). Among the principal nature organizations of the period were the Société pour la Protection des Paysages de France (1901), Bund Heimatschutz (1904, of which Conwentz was a founder member), Vereeniging tot Behoud van Natuurmonumenten (1904), Ligue Suisse pour la Protection de la Nature (1909), and British Society for the Promotion of Nature Reserves (1912).

[15] Friedemann Schmoll, 'Schönheit, Vielfalt, Eigenart. Die Formierung des Naturschutzes um 1900, seine Leitbilder und ihre Geschichte', in Hans-Werner Frohn and Friedemann Schmoll (eds), *Natur und Staat. Staatlicher Naturschutz in Deutschland 1906–2006* (Bonn: Bundesamt für Naturschutz, 2006), 13–84, here 59–60.

This created a problem for conservationists inasmuch as there was little 'untouched nature' left to salvage in Europe. As Conwentz himself explained, his broad definition of a natural monument derived from the recognition that 'completely untouched landscapes, here as in other civilized countries (*Kulturstaaten*), hardly survive any longer'.[16] For most nature advocates, as for other heritage enthusiasts, the prime culprits of this despoliation were obvious: modern industry, economy, and finance, the same forces that were responsible for all the other unwanted side-effects of modernity (alienation, artificiality, the trampling of tradition, etc.). But if the basic problem was the 'advance of civilization' itself, then the aim for the future was to ensure that the same mistakes were not repeated as 'civilization' spread. One could still take solace in the thought of vast stretches of wilderness in other parts of the world, especially in the recently colonized tropics. These exotic lands represented an opportunity to experience a pristine nature long since vanished from the domesticated and defaced landscapes of Europe. But first of all they required protection. The spread of European sovereignty into the tropics provided nature conservation with an enormous field of action.

The idealized image of tropical Edens that underpinned these concerns was by no means new at the turn of the century. Anxieties about the destruction of island paradises stretched back centuries, and travelogues of explorers had long conjured primeval wildernesses brimming with exotic creatures and sparsely populated by primitive tribes.[17] Nonetheless, a number of developments around the turn of the century intensified these perceptions. For one thing, the 'new imperialism' coincided very closely with the rapid expansion of communications and commercial entertainments (mass-circulation papers, cinema, urban leisure industries) that helped to assemble and popularize such stereotypes. Moreover, this was also the heyday of 'social evolutionism', during which it was taken for granted that the technical mastery of nature was what separated the civilized from the primitive and what legitimized European rule over those more subservient to nature.[18] In this respect, the 'untamed wilds' of the tropics represented both a foil to a domesticated Europe as well as a reflection of its own past. The use of terms such as 'Eden', 'original', or 'authentic' reflected the current evolutionist tendency to temporalize spatial differences.[19] The vocabulary is revealing: the 'primeval' forests in Sumatra or the 'aboriginal' herds in East Africa were perceived not merely as different geographic environments, but as throwbacks to an earlier stage of history before the advent of civilization. In this sense, tropical savannahs and jungles became landscapes frozen in time, relics of human heritage.

At the same time, the closing of the 'global frontier' under the impact of steam and telegraph made nature seem less vast and more vulnerable than ever before. Whereas human history since the dawn of time had been dominated by the struggle against nature, it was, as one contemporary put it, 'first since the close of the

---

[16] Conwentz, *Gefährdung*, 5–6.
[17] See generally Grove, *Green Imperialism*; Oelschlaeger, *Idea*. [18] Adas, *Machines*.
[19] See Johannes Fabian, *Time and the Other: How Anthropology Makes its Object* (New York: Columbia University Press, 1983).

nineteenth century that civilized peoples are becoming fully aware not only that humanity requires protection against the forces of nature, but also, conversely, that nature requires protection from human activity'.[20] The recent spate of well-publicized extinctions or near-extinctions—from the South African quagga to the American bison—was already encouraging a more global perceptual framework of environmental decline.[21] With the massive overseas extension of European authority, the threat to tropical Edens posed by capitalist trade and technical progress generated a powerful urge to 'salvage what could still be salvaged' of the primeval purity that had already been extirpated in the industrial world.[22]

In addition, the formal extension of European sovereignty itself made a difference, for the direct stake in governing overseas territories furnished a clearer opportunity to pursue conservation through appeals to national pride or imperial obligation. As the self-proclaimed guardians of their tropical dependencies, governments could be called upon to protect wildernesses as a matter of imperial stewardship. In the realm of nature as in the realm of culture, imperialism and heritage preservation became mutually reinforcing enterprises.[23] While protecting a threatened inheritance against human exploitation served to legitimize imperial intervention, ensuring that nature was adequately preserved became a badge of imperial credibility, a measure of a nation's fitness to rule abroad.[24] Paradoxically, the threat posed by the 'advance of civilization' meant that nature protection became an integral part of the civilizing mission.

FROM PLUNDER TO PROTECTION: THE RISE OF COLONIAL WILDLIFE CONSERVATION

There was, after all, ample cause for concern. By the late nineteenth century it was impossible to overlook the effects of European expansion on the flora and fauna of the Americas, Asia, Africa, and Australasia. Even if the overall impact did not

---

[20] Max Haushofer, *Der Schutz der Natur* (Munich, 1906), 3.

[21] The strident warnings of William T. Hornaday were influential not just in the United States but also in Europe: *The Extermination of the American Bison* (Washington, DC: Smithsonian Institution Press, 2002) (originally 1889); more generally, William T. Hornaday, *Our Vanishing Wildlife: Its Extermination and Preservation* (New York: New York Zoological Society, 1913); Mark V. Barrow Jr, *Nature's Ghosts: Confronting Extinction from the Age of Jefferson to the Age of Ecology* (Chicago: University of Chicago Press, 2009); on the decline of the bison, Andrew C. Isenberg, *The Destruction of the Bison: An Environmental History, 1750–1920* (Cambridge: Cambridge University Press, 2000); on South Africa, William Beinart, *The Rise of Conservation in South Africa: Settlers, Livestock, and the Environment 1770–1950* (Oxford: Oxford University Press, 2003), here 196.

[22] Quote from F. B. v. Schellendorf, *Internationaler Wildschutz in Afrika* (Munich, 1900), 7.

[23] Astrid Swenson, 'The Heritage of Empire', in Astrid Swenson and Peter Mandler (eds), *From Plunder to Preservation: Britain and the Heritage of Empire, c.1800–1940* (Oxford: Oxford University Press, 2013), 3–28, esp. 8–14; also William H. Rollins, 'Imperial Shades of Green: Conservation and Environmental Chauvinism in the German Colonial Project', *German Studies Review*, vol. 22 (1999), 187–213.

[24] On heritage preservation as cultural 'yardstick', Astrid Swenson, *The Rise of Heritage: Preserving the Past in France, Germany and England, 1789–1914* (Cambridge: Cambridge University Press, 2013), 273–328; Betts and Ross (eds), *Heritage*.

amount to the apocalypse that some observers conjured, in certain areas it was nonetheless quite devastating.[25] From the depredations of the North American fur trade to the expansion of sheep farming in New Zealand, endemic species were often carelessly and sometimes ruthlessly extirpated in a bid to exploit the resources of conquered territories. Although the temperate zones of mass European settlement witnessed some of the most far-reaching changes, there were also dramatic effects in the trading hubs of the tropics. The rapid despoliation of 'tropical island Edens' had already stimulated new ways of thinking about the environmental impact of colonial conquest, and by the middle of the nineteenth century these ideas were evolving into more systematic models of resource conservation in the mainland colonies of South Asia and North Africa.[26] If the 'new imperialism' was animated by a brash ideology of political and economic conquest, it was also shot through with environmental anxieties.[27]

The decades straddling the turn of the century witnessed a flurry of conservation initiatives throughout Europe's tropical colonies. Such efforts were part of a global surge of conservationist activity at the time, spearheaded mainly by scientists and hunter-naturalists alarmed at the decline of threatened plant and animal species. During the 1870s–1880s the world's first national parks were created in the United States and British Dominions (Yellowstone in 1872, Australia's Royal National Park in 1879, Banff in 1885, and New Zealand's Tongariro in 1887). Over the following years activists in Europe and North America established the first large-scale organizations for the protection of particular landscapes (e.g. Sierra Club, 1892; Société pour la Protection des Paysages, 1901) or animals (Society for the Protection of Birds, 1889; Audobon Society 1905, Ligue pour la Protection des Oiseaux, 1912).[28] All of these initiatives were echoed in Europe's tropical colonies, though by and large it was the threat to prized game species that prompted the most far-reaching interventions.

Some of the earliest game protection regulations came in India, where the landmark Forest Act of 1878 (see Chapter 8) enabled the government to restrict hunting and to close off demarcated sanctuaries whenever game numbers appeared to decline. It was quickly followed by legislation limiting the capture and hunting of wild elephants to instances of self-defence or the prevention of damage to property. Other species soon came into the frame as well. In the Nilgiri Hills of Madras, the favourite summer retreat for the regional British authorities, the local Game Association successfully lobbied in 1879 for a closed season and licence requirement for anyone wishing to hunt or fish in the area. Eight years later the provisions of the Nilgiri Game and Fish Preservation Act were extended throughout the whole of British India, though their enforcement remained extremely patchy. In 1912 the Wild Birds and Animals Protection Act was passed in an attempt to standardize regional legislation, though its brevity and faunal imprecision rendered

[25] Mackenzie, 'Empire and the Ecological Apocalypse'.
[26] Grove, *Green Imperialism*; Grove, *Ecology*; Grove, 'Historical Review'.
[27] See James Beattie, *Empire and Environmental Anxiety: Health, Science, Art and Conservation in South Asia and Australasia, 1800–1920* (Basingstoke: Palgrave, 2011).
[28] On parks: Gißibl, Höhler, and Kupper (eds), *Civilizing*. On organizations: Mathis, 'Mobiliser'.

it largely ineffective. As a result, many declining species remained not only unprotected but actively targeted for eradication. Wild buffaloes, wild pigs, and especially tigers were reviled by the colonial state, which took a decidedly unsentimental approach to wildlife conservation. Tigers were a particular focus of the 'protective hunts' that so vividly symbolized the imperial paternalism of intrepid white men defending helpless Indian villagers.[29]

In Southeast Asia too, there was an upsurge of conservationist alarm around the turn of the century, largely focused on bird pelts sought for the millenary trade in Europe. The plumes of Wallace's beloved Birds of Paradise were an especially valuable commodity. Their beautifully iridescent feathers had been traded in Southeast Asia for centuries, reportedly reaching Europe after Magellan's first circumnavigation in the early sixteenth century.[30] By the late nineteenth century a 'plumage craze' in the fashion industry created a brisk trade to Europe and North America, where the feathers served as a prime symbol of exotic tropicality and an article of conspicuous consumption (and where anxieties about the over-hunting of indigenous avian populations had already sparked a significant conservationist response).[31]

By the 1880s, restrictions on the hunting of bright-plumaged birds were already in place in the Straits Settlements, Perak, and Johor.[32] But the main source of millenary feathers was New Guinea, especially the Dutch-administered half of the island, where the introduction of guns from the 1870s and the establishment of a regular steamship connection in the 1890s boosted exports to London, Amsterdam, and Paris.[33] In the mid-1890s Dutch naturalists urged the government in Batavia to prevent the further slaughter of such striking animals. Bird protection played a key role in the rise of nature preservation more broadly in the Dutch East Indies, where the Nederlandsch-Indische Vereeniging tot Natuurbescherming, founded in 1912, adopted the Bird of Paradise as its logo. Yet progress was slow, and even after the passing of a Protection of Wildlife Ordinance in 1909, the legislation contained

---

[29] Mahesh Rangarajan, *India's Wildlife History* (Delhi: Permanent Black, 2001), 22–6, 46–58; Mahesh Rangarajan, 'The Raj and the Natural World: The War against "Dangerous Beasts" in Colonial India', in John Knight (ed.), *Wildlife in Asia: Cultural Perspectives* (London: Routledge, 2004), 207–32; Vijaya Ramadas Mandala, 'The Raj and the Paradoxes of Wildlife Conservation: British Attitudes and Expediencies', *Historical Journal*, vol. 58 no. 1 (Mar. 2015), 75–110, strongly emphasizes the pragmatism of wildlife conservation in India; John M. MacKenzie, *Empire of Nature: Hunting, Conservation and British Imperialism* (Manchester: Manchester University Press, 1988), 283–6; M. S. S. Pandian, 'Hunting and Colonialism in the Nineteenth-Century Nilgiri Hills of South India', in Grove, Damodaran, and Sangwan (eds), *Nature*, 273–97.

[30] Pamela Swadling, *Plumes from Paradise: Trade Cycles in outer Southeast Asia and their Impact on New Guinea and Nearby Islands until 1920* (Boroko: Papua New Guinea National Museum, 1996).

[31] Robin W. Doughty, *Feather Fashions and Bird Preservation* (Berkeley: University of California Press, 1975); Bernhard Gißibl, 'Paradiesvögel. Kolonialer Naturschutz und die Mode der deutschen Frau am Anfang des 20. Jahrhunderts', in Johannes Paulmann, Daniel Leese, and Philippa Söldenwagner (eds), *Ritual-Macht-Natur. Europäisch-ozeanische Beziehungswelten in der Neuzeit* (Bremen: Überseemuseum, 2005), 131–54.

[32] Kathirithamby-Wells, *Nature*, 195–200.

[33] Estimates of exported pelts range from 30,000 to 80,000 per year for the early twentieth century, the majority apparently from the Dutch half of the island: Reichskolonialamt, *Jagd und Wildschutz in den deutschen Kolonien* (Jena: Fischer, 1913), 146; Stuart Kirsch, 'History and the Birds of Paradise: Surprising Connections from New Guinea', *Expedition*, vol. 48 no. 1 (2008), 15–21, here 16.

too many loopholes to make much difference on the ground. A more effective measure was the blanket ban passed by the German authorities on their half of New Guinea in 1913 (tellingly, the same year the United States outlawed the import of feathers). Eventually the Dutch introduced a similar prohibition on their half of the island in 1922, one year after Britain passed its own import ban.[34] As the timing of these injunctions suggests, it was the conservationist pressure placed on metropolitan governments—along with a gradual change in fashion— rather than colonial regulation that made the biggest difference to the fate of these animals. Other threatened species were not so fortunate. Even such charismatic creatures as the Javan rhinoceros, orang-utan, and Sumatran elephant had no effective legal protection until long after the First World War.[35] And in the meantime, 'vermin' such as tigers and crocodiles remained a scourge to be extirpated, often with the help of cash incentives paid out for collected crocodile eggs or proof of any tiger killed.[36]

Yet it was in colonial Africa that the most extensive and influential wildlife protection measures were developed. By the early twentieth century the set of laws and regulations that governed hunting in South, East, and Central Africa far surpassed anything on the statute books in the Asian colonies. There were several reasons for the difference, not least the sheer abundance of spectacular fauna in these regions, as well as the large commercial (and touristic) hunting industry that arose to exploit it. But it was also partly due to the 'environmental memory' of earlier wildlife losses on the southern tip of the continent, which strongly shaped conservationist impulses elsewhere in Africa.[37] As imperial control expanded into the game-rich savannahs of Central and East Africa in the 1880s and 1890s, previous transgressions on the Cape furnished a stark warning about what could go wrong in the process.

Southern Africa was home to an exceptional wealth of game species. For millennia, indigenous peoples hunted a variety of animals without causing lasting damage to overall population numbers. With the arrival of white settlers and the penetration of commercial markets, the fate of the region's fauna radically changed.[38] Whereas European settlers in the seventeenth century encountered grasslands teeming with wildlife, by the beginning of the nineteenth century the once prolific herds of elephant, rhinos, wildebeest, and antelope were severely depleted. When the British assumed power on the Cape in 1806, some species

[34] Robert Cribb, 'Birds of Paradise and Environmental Politics in Colonial Indonesia, 1890–1931', in Boomgaard, Colombijn, and Henley (eds), *Paper Landscapes*, 379–408; Peter Boomgaard, 'Oriental Nature, its Friends and its Enemies: Conservation of Nature in Late-Colonial Indonesia, 1889–1949', *Environment and History*, vol. 5 (1999), 257–92, here 264–6, 279–80.

[35] Boomgaard, 'Oriental Nature', 264–5; J. H. Westermann, 'Wild Life Conservation in the Netherlands Empire: Its National and International Aspects', in Honig and Verdoorn (eds), *Science*, 417–24.

[36] Peter Boomgaard, *Frontiers of Fear: Tigers and People in the Malay World, 1600–1950* (New Haven: Yale University Press, 2001), 87–106; Mohnike, *Banka*, 162–7.

[37] On environmental memory generally, see Frank Uekötter (ed.), *Ökologische Erinnerungsorte* (Göttingen: Vandenhoeck & Ruprecht, 2014).

[38] On indigenous hunting, Mackenzie, *Empire*, 55–84.

were already either extinct (the blaubok) or on the verge of extinction (the quagga). Others survived but had long since disappeared from areas of white settlement. Different species were, of course, hunted for different reasons: some for meat, others for tusks or hides. Both of these aspects of the game resource—digestible protein and tradable goods—furnished a crucial subsidy for the process of colonial expansion in southern Africa. As animal populations retreated in the face of agricultural settlement, the commercial hunting frontier moved further and further northward. And with each additional step that hunters made into the interior, game populations receded still further. As the frontier advanced, generally with the search for ivory leading the way, indigenous hunters became increasingly drawn into the trade as well, greatly to the detriment of game populations.[39]

Close behind the hunting frontier came the northward spread of European farms and ranches, which in many ways paralleled the westward expansion of settlers across North America.[40] This, too, had a major impact on the region's fauna, especially those species that competed with domestic animals for grass and water or that posed a threat to livestock. As Boer settlers moved further inland, they shot predators, reserved water-holes for domestic herds, and disrupted the seasonal migrations of wild herbivores in an attempt to convert millions of hectares of bush into fields and pasture. The process accelerated markedly during the Great Trek of the 1830s, when tens of thousands of Afrikaner *voortrekkers* set out from the Cape to colonize new territory in what became the Transvaal and Orange Free State. Once again, the huge herds of game they found provided a crucial source of food and animal products that could be traded for cash or other goods. All throughout this period hunting was an integral element of the settlement frontier, both economically and culturally. It not only furnished an important material subsidy, but was also seen as a basic right for the pioneer and an expression of one's masculinity and dominance over nature.[41]

Over time, these two principal modes of hunting—for profit and for subsistence—were increasingly accompanied by a third: the pursuit of game for pleasure. During the second half of the nineteenth century, a growing influx of European hunter-adventurers, many of them British officers on their way to service in India, sought their own share of southern Africa's wildlife treasures. Venturing far up country, they shot animals in prodigious numbers, mostly to indulge their taste for 'sport' but also out of a naturalist passion for collecting. Once again the game resource provided these tourist hunters with an important subsidy. Many financed their trips through the sale of ivory, and most fed their hunting parties with meat from the kills. Upon return to the coast they sent thousands of skins and specimens back to Europe, where they ordinarily wound up in the private collections of grand

[39] Generally, MacKenzie, *Empire*, 86–119; Beinart and Hughes, *Environment*, 58–75.

[40] William Beinart and Peter Coates, *Environment and History: The Taming of Nature in the USA and South Africa* (London: Routledge, 1995), chs 2, 4.

[41] Beinart and Hughes, *Environment*, 63–4; John M. MacKenzie, 'The Imperial Pioneer and Hunter and the British Masculine Stereotype in Late Victorian and Edwardian Times', in J. A. Mangan and James Walvin (eds), *Manliness and Morality: Middle-Class Masculinity in Britain and America, 1800–1940* (Manchester: Manchester University Press, 1987), 176–98.

The late lamented Pilipili helped us to shoot him

Fig. 7.1. African safari porters seated atop a trophy, early 1930s.
Source: Count Zsigmond Széchenyi, *Land of Elephants: Big-Game Hunting in Kenya, Tanganyika and Uganda* (London: Putnam, 1935), p. 83.

houses or in the display cases of new public museums. A few of the hunter-adventurers also sent back vivid accounts of their exploits, which found an eager audience among the expanding readerships of the imperial metropoles, and especially among the hunting-obsessed elites of Britain and Germany. Books by William Harris, R. G. Cumming, and William Charles Baldwin were bestsellers of the Victorian era. Their tales of hunting prowess—which generally glossed over their heavy dependence on local knowledge and African guides—gained them notoriety as intrepid men of action, and helped assemble the somewhat misleading cultural stereotype of the dominant white male hunter.[42] Baldwin alone undertook no fewer than seven major expeditions, each of them chasing the retreating ivory frontier with the help of African trackers. Although his hunting parties could sometimes go many days without making a kill, Baldwin once shot eight elephants in half an hour (Fig. 7.1).[43]

By the 1860s the effects of all this blood-sport were increasingly obvious both to the hunters themselves and to the African rulers who allowed them to shoot. The spread of single-shot muzzle loaders had already caused widespread carnage across southern Africa, and the introduction of the breech-loading rifle in the 1870s made hunting easier still. Elephants attracted most of the attention, and were killed in their thousands to meet the ballooning demand for ivory ornaments,

[42] See Angela Thompsell, *Hunting Africa: British Sport, African Knowledge and the Nature of Empire* (Basingstoke: Palgrave Macmillan, 2015), esp. chs 2, 4.
[43] MacKenzie, *Empire*, 108.

billiard balls, and piano keys. By the 1870s the search for ivory compelled hunters to venture further north into Zimbabwe and eastern Zambia. One of them was Frederic Selous, the most famous of all Victorian hunter-adventurers, who later became a leading figure in the wildlife conservation movement. Another was the German explorer Karl Mauch, who 'discovered' the ruins of Great Zimbabwe in 1871 while attached to a hunting party.[44] As the influx of hunters grew, it was not long before the elephant herds in these areas were depleted as well. A rough-and-ready measure of the killing can be gleaned from the Cape's ivory exports, which rose from 26,480 kg in 1861 to a peak of 73,200 kg in 1876, followed by a steep decline to only 4,659 by 1882.[45] After this point ivory exports were mainly channelled through ports in East Africa.

By the 1880s–1890s, the nagging fears about the destruction of southern Africa's wildlife became increasingly acute. Many of the underlying concerns had been around for a long time. The first attempts to limit hunting reached back to the seventeenth century. In the 1820s closed seasons and licensing were introduced on the Cape, followed in the 1850s by similar regulations in the Orange Free State and South African Republic. But none of these laws were widely enforced. A watershed of sorts came in 1886 with the Act for the Better Preservation of Game, which not only sharpened existing legislation in the Cape Colony but also included the first special protections for threatened species such as the elephant, zebra, and quagga (which was already extinct in the wild). Although the Act itself was too little too late (it explicitly enshrined the right of private landowners to shoot game on their own property, and much of the big game on the Cape had already been hunted out anyway), it nonetheless catalysed the introduction of protective legislation elsewhere in the region. Over the following two decades its measures were refined and updated by a series of new acts, and from the 1890s onward the basic precepts of Cape legislation—closed seasons, licensing, prohibition of most African hunting techniques, game schedules—were extended and adapted throughout Britain's other African colonies.[46]

The grisly record of game extermination in southern Africa thus served both as a warning for what could happen elsewhere and as a model of what could be done about it. During the late nineteenth century, these 'lessons of the Cape' served as a lens through which developments in East and Central Africa were viewed. But like all lenses, they sharpened the perception of certain objects while distorting the vision of others. While on the one hand they helped officials spot the early warning signs of unregulated hunting, on the other hand they made it easy to overestimate the threat. During the 1880s–1890s the escalation of the ivory trade and the concomitant decline of elephant herds along the Kenyan and Tanzanian coasts led many to conclude that the South African tragedy was repeating itself, and that similarly rigorous conservation measures were necessary in order to avoid it.

---

[44] MacKenzie, *Empire*, 148; Eva Maria Verst, *Karl Mauch als Forschungsreisender. Wissenschaft und Karriere zwischen Deutschland und Südafrika* (St Ingbert: Röhrig, 2012).
[45] Beinart and Hughes, *Environment*, 67.
[46] MacKenzie, *Empire*, 202–5.

Such fears were stoked by eyewitness reports from the region, especially those of Joseph Thomson, who led a Royal Geographical Society expedition to East and Central Africa in 1878–80. During fourteen months of travel around the Great Lakes he encountered not a single elephant, and what made this so worrying was that David Livingstone had reported large numbers of pachyderms in many of the same areas merely a decade earlier. The apparent cause was the penetration of the area by hunters and traders, which also explained why only the remotest parts of Central Africa were still reportedly producing any ivory. The overall prognosis for the elephant was grim: 'an iron band of ruthless destroyers is drawing round it; and it may be safely predicted that in twenty years, the noble African elephant will be a rare animal.'[47]

In fact, Thomson's dire forecast was belied by abundant herds of elephant still roaming across parts of Uganda, Congo, and southern Sudan. These rich pickings continued to attract professional hunters for the next several decades, especially in remote areas or border regions where game laws were lax or unenforceable.[48] But against the backdrop of what had happened on the Cape, Thomson's ominous warnings struck a chord, and were subsequently echoed by a host of other European observers in the region. Although few went so far as the explorer Gustav Fischer, who declared the elephant 'completely extinct' in German East Africa as early as 1885, fears about its imminent demise rose sharply over the following years as ivory exports from Zanzibar began to slump.[49]

Furthermore, the anxieties roused by the 'elephant scare' were soon compounded by a catastrophic Rinderpest epizootic, which tore through the region's wildlife herds during the 1890s. The Rinderpest virus, which had long been present in Egypt, reached Khartoum by the mid-1880s with the expansion of Anglo-Egyptian influence in the area. By 1890 it was spreading like wildfire across the plains of East Africa, most likely triggered by the introduction of Indian cattle into Somaliland in 1889. As the virus moved southward it killed huge numbers of ruminant herbivores, including domestic cattle, buffalo, eland, giraffe, and various other ungulate species. German and British observers gave vivid accounts of collapsing herds. While travelling in Kenya in 1890, Frederick Lugard saw entire plains covered in buffalo carcasses, and estimated that in some areas at least 90 per cent of the cattle had perished. Further south in Maasai country, Oskar Baumann reported the near-total annihilation of cattle in 1891. Over the following years, Rinderpest destroyed the livelihoods of numerous African pastoralist groups, who were already suffering from smallpox, plague, and a cluster of other diseases associated with colonial penetration. It was especially devastating for those who depended on cattle for food; Baumann

[47] MacKenzie, *Empire*, 149–51, quote p. 150; on Thomson more generally, see Robert Irwin Rotberg, *Joseph Thomson and the Exploration of Africa* (London: Chatto & Windus, 1971).
[48] MacKenzie, *Empire*, 152–6.
[49] Bernhard Gißibl, *The Nature of Colonialism: Hunting, Conservation and the Politics of Wildlife in the German Colonial Empire* (Ph.D. Dissertation, Universität Mannheim, 2009), 72–4, quote p. 72.

estimated that up to two-thirds of the Maasai died in the famine that followed the Rinderpest outbreak.[50]

For all these reasons the 1890s are generally regarded as a calamitous decade for East Africa, one marked by hunger, disease, and widespread violence.[51] It was, undoubtedly, a period of enormous social hardship and political turmoil throughout the region. It was also a time of profound ecological upheaval, whose effects shaped the landscape for many years to come. As human and livestock populations shrank, the area used for cultivation and grazing correspondingly contracted. And with the parallel decline in the numbers of wild herbivores, large stretches of open grassland became covered with bushier vegetation. One of the consequences of these changes was a significant expansion of the tsetse fly, which, as we will see, posed a whole series of problems for European officials and settlers over the following decades. But if the effects of the Rinderpest epizootic caused difficulties for colonial governments, on balance they probably aided the establishment of imperial power in the region. Although the destruction of game temporarily reduced food supplies and trade revenue, Lugard noted that 'in some respects it has favoured our enterprise. Powerful and warlike as the pastoral tribes are, their pride has been humbled and our progress facilitated by this awful visitation. The advent of the white man had else not been so peaceful.'[52]

As it turned out, the long-term effects of the Rinderpest outbreak on animal populations proved less apocalyptic than many feared at the time. For one thing, its impact varied greatly from one species to another. Whereas cattle, buffalo, giraffe, and many types of large antelope were all but wiped out in the worst affected areas, rhinoceros, elephant, hippopotamus, and wildebeest were left unscathed. Moreover, even the most susceptible species rebounded quickly over the following years, as numerous contemporary accounts attest.[53]

At the time, however, the precipitous die-offs of the 1890s generated a profound sense of ecological crisis. Many onlookers drew parallels to earlier bouts of wildlife destruction in the American West and especially South Africa, and therefore concluded that the only way to ward off the threat was through the introduction of strict game laws. As scholars have long noted, the first to sound the alarm were generally the big-game hunters themselves, 'penitent butchers' determined to ensure a continuing supply of game in the future.[54] Among them were not only acclaimed adventure authors such as Frederick Selous, but also high-ranking colonial officials like Hermann von Wissmann, governor of German East Africa, or Harry H. Johnston, the first commissioner of British Central Africa. From the

---

[50] Kjekshus, *Ecology*, 127–30; MacKenzie, *Empire*, 157–8; Oskar Baumann, *Durch Massailand zur Nilquelle. Reisen und Forschungen der Massai-Expedition des deutschen Antisklaverei-Komité in den Jahren 1891–1893* (Berlin: Reimer, 1894); Clive Spinage, *Rinderpest: A History* (New York: Kluwer Academic, 2003).

[51] Kjekshus, *Ecology*, 126–43; Iliffe, *Modern History*, 124–5.

[52] Lord (F. D.) Lugard, *The Rise of our East African Empire* (1893), vol. 1, 527, cited in MacKenzie, *Empire*, 158.

[53] MacKenzie, *Empire*, 158–60.

[54] Quote from Richard Fitter, *The Penitent Butchers: The Fauna Preservation Society, 1903–1978* (London: FPS, 1978).

early 1890s onwards these hunter-conservationists played an instrumental role in persuading colonial governments to safeguard wildlife, whether through the implementation of closed seasons and licensing, or through the establishment of game reserves.

Despite decades of British game protection in southern Africa, the most influential legislation of the 1890s was actually introduced in German East Africa. The Game Ordinance of 1896, written by Governor von Wissmann himself, not only spurred the neighbouring British authorities into action, it also served as a foil for conservation initiatives as far away as India.[55] Many aspects of the law mirrored practices on the Cape: a schedule of protected species (elephant, rhino, etc.), a licensing system for hunters, and a blanket ban on the killing of females and juveniles. But what distinguished it from previous legislation was the demarcation of large areas as game sanctuaries. Within the boundaries of these wildlife reserves, hunting was forbidden to all but a handful of privileged sportsmen, and during breeding seasons it was prohibited for them as well. The first two reserves in German East Africa were gazetted on sites that von Wissmann expressly chose for the purpose, one along the Rufiji River and the other just west of Kilimanjaro. Although he occasionally referred to such areas as 'national parks', they were actually more akin to European hunting domains than to the Yellowstone model of a 'natural monument'. The idea proved popular among the German elite, and it found a strong resonance among British officialdom as well. By the time the British Foreign Office received a translation of von Wissmann's law, Lord Salisbury—then acting as both Prime Minister and Foreign Secretary—had already recommended territorial sanctuaries in Africa as a means of halting the 'indiscriminate slaughter' of animals.[56] By 1899 all of the British colonies bordering on German East Africa added game reserves to their existing palette of conservation measures.

Of course, the specific forms that colonial conservation took were determined by more than just the desire to shore up animal populations. They were also moulded by the socio-economic framework of empire and by the cultural assumptions that Europeans brought with them. One of the most important factors shaping game protection measures was the deep-rooted cult of hunting among British and German elites, which strongly favoured the 'chase' over the killing of animals for subsistence. Both countries boasted a long tradition of privileged game access on designated hunting estates, and in both countries hunting for pleasure rather than for the cooking-pot was an important marker of social status. As John MacKenzie has argued, the expansion of imperial power during the late nineteenth and early twentieth centuries brought a transition from a broadly functional hunting ethos towards a more recreational approach in which 'sporting' values and social exclusivity came to symbolize white dominance in the colonies, much as the traditional rituals of The Hunt had long signified the prestige of social elites in

---

[55] Gißibl, *Nature*, 404; Mark Cioc, *The Game of Conservation: International Treaties to Protect the World's Migratory Animals* (Athens, Oh.: Ohio University Press, 2009), 32–3; MacKenzie, *Empire*, 205.

[56] Gißibl, *Nature*, 404–5; MacKenzie, *Empire*, 204–6.

Europe.[57] Although this argument perhaps implies too sharp a distinction between hunting for economic gain and hunting for pleasure—the two could and often did go hand in hand[58]—there can be little doubt that the valorization of the self-restrained sportsman over the self-interested stalker mirrored the racialized moral hierarchies that structured colonial discourse more generally.[59]

The conservationist disdain for 'unsportsmanlike' hunting had important consequences on the ground, for its translation into colonial legislation effectively excluded most Africans from hunting. Whereas the use of guns and bag limits was considered 'humane' and sustainable, the majority of African hunting techniques—pits, snares, poison, nets, fire—were expressly forbidden as cruel and profligate. This is not to say that there was universal agreement over the threat posed by indigenous hunting. Many European observers thought that white hunters and settlers were even worse, at least those who lacked 'true sportsmanship' (what the Germans called *Weidgerechtigkeit*) and therefore killed excessively. Von Wissmann complained bitterly about 'how every European who possesses a gun on board a Congo steamer fires in the most reckless fashion...without having any regard as to whether or not he can possess himself of the animal when killed'.[60] Other leading figures such as the British conservationist Edward North Buxton and the German hunter Carl Schillings emphasized that African hunting methods had been used for centuries without destroying game herds.[61] It was generally accepted that Africans had a right to defend their crops and livestock from marauding animals. German authorities in East Africa even granted formal exemptions for certain 'hunter' tribes such as the Wabahi, Watindiga, and Wandorobo.[62] But even among those who blamed the slaughter on trigger-happy whites, it was widely agreed that the changes wrought by colonialism—above all the influx of guns and the expansion of commercial hunting—demanded tight restrictions on indigenous hunting. Colonial governments enacted strict gun laws to keep firearms out of African hands, and although some states allowed Africans to acquire hunting licences, few non-Europeans could actually afford the fees.[63] Not that any of this put a stop to African hunting, which the threadbare net of state surveillance was scarcely able to curtail in practice.

By the early 1900s, then, colonial wildlife conservation was firmly set on the course of social exclusion and indigenous hunting suppression that was to characterize it throughout most of the twentieth century. Through the establishment of game reserves, closed seasons, and licensing, colonial states placed the interests of a foreign elite and the wildlife they prized above the ability of locals to access animal

[57] John M. MacKenzie, 'Chivalry, Social Darwinsim and Ritualised Killing: The Hunting Ethos in Central Africa up to 1914', in Anderson and Grove (eds), *Conservation*, 41–62; also Gißibl, *Nature*, 240–1.

[58] As pointed out in Beinart and Hughes, *Environment*, 68.

[59] See Thompsell, *Hunting Africa*.   [60] Quote from Cioc, *Game*, 32; Gißibl, *Nature*, 95–6.

[61] E. N. Buxton, *Two African Trips* (London: Stanford, 1902), 139, cited in William M. Adams, *Against Extinction: The Story of Conservation* (London: Earthscan, 2004), 109; also Gißibl, *Nature*, 119.

[62] Kjekshus, *Ecology*, 79.

[63] H. Jürgen Wächter, *Naturschutz in den deutschen Kolonien in Afrika (1884–1918)* (Münster: LIT, 2008), 22; MacKenzie, *Empire*, 209.

resources. But given that neither ivory smugglers nor migrating animals showed much concern for colonial boundaries, it soon became apparent that some degree of trans-border coordination was necessary. The trade in animal parts had long been a matter of competition between the colonial powers, all of which were eager to profit from the flow of tusks and hides to the coast. As the traffic from the interior dwindled around the turn of the century, what had once been a source of rivalry became an important field of inter-imperial cooperation, especially between British and German authorities. In 1897 Governor von Wissmann proposed an international agreement on game preservation, which was immediately welcomed by the British Foreign Office. After three more years of preparation, the result was the 1900 London Convention for the Preservation of Wild Animals, Birds and Fish in Africa.[64]

Widely recognized as the 'first ever "international" environmental conference', the 1900 Convention was a prime example of 'imperial internationalism', an attempt to realize colonial aims via closer trans-imperial cooperation.[65] Encompassing all of Africa's major colonial powers, its basic aim was to establish a uniform set of game regulations between the twentieth parallels north and south of the equator, including gradated lists of protected species, licensing, closed seasons, as well as common tariffs and controls on traded animal carcasses or parts. There is no need here to reiterate the story of the convention in detail, which has ably been done elsewhere.[66] For our purposes, two main points deserve emphasis. First, the agreement was essentially a hunting treaty based on a utilitarian desire for the sustainable management of game, especially the ivory trade, rather than on any transference of metropolitan notions of 'nature protection' to the colonies.[67] Second, apprehensions about the loss of ivory revenue, especially on the part of the French and Belgian governments, ultimately prevented the treaty's formal ratification by the signatories.

The 1900 Convention thus highlighted both the appeal and the limits of trans-imperial cooperation. But despite the difficulties surrounding its endorsement, it nonetheless marked an important milestone in the history of colonial nature preservation in several respects. For starters, it served as a key reference point for wildlife conservation until at least the early 1930s, since nearly every colonial government in Africa came to observe the agreement over the following years. In addition, it created a set of internationally recognized norms and methods—closed seasons, licences, endangered species lists, and the concept of reserves—whose implementation increasingly required 'expert' input. Most fundamentally, it established wildlife protection as an arena of truly international concern. Despite the failure to ratify the convention, the principles it espoused were vital: namely that threatened species should be preserved from destruction, and that preventive

---

[64] The text of the resulting treaty is reprinted in Cioc, *Game*, 154–61.

[65] Quote from Ramachandra Guha, *Environmentalism: A Global History* (New York: Longman, 2000), 45; on the convention as 'imperial internationalism', Gißibl, *Nature*, 416–27.

[66] Cioc, *Game*, 34–40; MacKenzie, *Empire*, 207–12; Gißibl, *Nature*, 416–27.

[67] The utilitarian motivation is emphasized in particular by Cioc, *Game*, 34–40.

action formed part of an international standard for civilized behaviour.[68] By the turn of the twentieth century, conservation had become an indispensable marker of enlightened rule, and as such it also became an integral part of the colonial enterprise.

TROUBLE IN PARADISE: CHALLENGES TO CONSERVATION

As a general rule, laws and treaties need to be approved in order to achieve anything. Although campaigns for particular statutes can occasionally influence lawmakers without ending in formal authorization, it is unusual for a political agreement to carry much force without official endorsement. The 1900 London Convention was one such exception. Indeed, it was doubly exceptional, for it was in many ways the very failure to achieve ratification that gave the greatest impulse to the cause of colonial nature preservation.

Disappointed by the lack of an international agreement, and increasingly impatient with the inadequacy of colonial protection measures, conservationists in Europe did two things: they used the convention as a tool for prodding officials into action, and they became more organized. In France, the Société Nationale d'Acclimatation became a vocal advocate of colonial conservation after the turn of the century, and was joined in 1905 by the Société des Amis de l'Éléphant. In Germany, conservationists within the Colonial Society established Wildschutzkommissionen in 1907 and 1911 to persuade the government to tighten protective legislation in East Africa.[69] The most important new organization was the Society for the Protection of the Wild Fauna of the Empire (SPFE), founded in 1903 to encourage 'the protection of the wild fauna in all British possessions'. Its membership included not only leading colonial officials, aristocrats, and top political figures, but also most of the prominent African hunters of the era. From its very inception, the SPFE organized public meetings, published its own journal (renamed *Oryx* in 1950), and sent high-powered deputations to the Colonial Office, where delegates were warmly received by successive Secretaries of State. It was also the driving force behind a series of Parliamentary Papers on game preservation published between 1906 and 1913. Although nominally a private pressure group, the SPFE's small elite membership and extraordinary access to government gave it a level of influence unmatched by any of its counterparts in continental Europe, including the German Wildschutzkommissionen, which modelled its approach on the SPFE's discrete lobbying within upper-class hunting circles.[70]

During the 1900s–1910s these organizations proved highly adept at promoting the conservationist cause within the halls of power. But their voice was hardly the

---

[68] A general theme of Gißibl, *Nature*; Cioc, *Game*.

[69] See *Les 'Amis de l'éléphant', société fondée à Paris, le 6 décembre 1905* (Paris, 1907); Deutsche Kolonial-Gesellschaft, *Bericht über die Arbeiten der Wildschutz-Kommission der Deutschen Kolonial-Gesellschaft* (Berlin: Süsserott, 1912).

[70] Fitter, *Penitent Butchers*; Gißibl, *Nature*, 428–31; Mackenzie, *Empire*, 211–16.

only one seeking the ear of government. The white settler lobby exerted a powerful influence of its own, especially in British and German East Africa and in Southern Rhodesia, and for the most part it was ill disposed towards wildlife protection, especially game reserves.[71] At best, white settlers regarded the great herds of wild herbivores as unwanted competitors with domestic livestock, at worst as nothing more than pests. From their perspective, game reserves not only provided sanctuaries for undesirable predators and grazers, but were also suspected of functioning as disease reservoirs. Many colonial officials shared their scepticism about the 'excessive' protection of wild animals or the sequestration of land that could potentially be put to more profitable use. The German Colonial Secretary Bernhard Dernburg, for instance, deemed it inevitable that 'the entire appearance of a land undergoing colonisation changes fundamentally', which included 'unfortunately the entire fauna. First the wild and dangerous animals disappear, and in most cases the European sets a bounty on their elimination. The untameable but useful animals (*Nutztiere*) also disappear, hunted for their ivory, their skins and the like.'[72] In order to avoid any hindrance to valuable economic activity, most reserves were located far from railways and major rivers and were deliberately situated on land deemed unsuitable for other uses. But even so, the continued expansion of agriculture generated a constant stream of demands for the revision of reserve boundaries.

Conservationists were in little doubt that the protection of wildlife would always come second to the sacred prerogative of economic development, whether in the form of white settlement, the growth of concessionary companies, or even the spread of indigenous farming. Although it can scarcely be said that colonial governments consistently prioritized the interests of African cultivators over those of the game lobby, many officials were far more interested in the needs of agriculture than in what they saw as the extravagant passions of hunter-naturalists. This was most plainly the case in West Africa, where the discretionary power of indigenous elites and the existence of major export crop industries meant that hunting was widely permitted for meat, body parts, and crop protection despite the gradual introduction of tighter regulations.[73] It was also evident in parts of Central Africa, where the damage to farming communities from wildlife prompted some officials to call for a reversal of game protection measures. In Uganda in particular, elephants, hippos, and buffalo caused widespread crop damage as well as significant loss of life. In 1908, just over a decade after the Rinderpest epizootic, Governor Hesketh Bell complained that 'the native population is suffering severely, both in life and property, from the attacks of the wild animals that are protected by our game laws'.[74] In 1925 the Ugandan government even established an Elephant Control Department to deal with the problem.[75] Yet the attempts of colonial states to promote indigenous farming (to which we turn in Chapter 9) had ambivalent

---

[71] See, generally, Adams, *Against Extinction*, 70–2, 159–62; MacKenzie, *Empire*, 214–16.
[72] Bernhard Dernburg, *Zielpunkte des deutschen Kolonialwesens* (Berlin: Mittler, 1907), 5–6.
[73] Reichskolonialamt, *Jagd*, 72–8, 126–35.
[74] Quoted from Adams, *Against Extinction*, 74.   [75] MacKenzie, *Empire*, 249–50.

implications for the cause of wildlife protection. Although agriculture departments opposed the protection of animals they regarded as pests, their aspiration to sedentarize shifting cultivators tended to encourage the spatial separation of humans and wild animals, which in some ways complemented the efforts of conservationists to establish discrete game reserves.

In the early twentieth century, the thorniest problem facing the cause of African wildlife protection was the threat of disease, above all trypanosomiasis, more commonly known as sleeping sickness. Sleeping sickness (whose animal equivalent is often called *nagana* after a Zulu word) is a parasitic ailment caused by protozoa of the genus *Trypanosoma*, which are endemic throughout much of sub-Saharan Africa. The trypanosomes spend part of their life cycle in the bloodstream of host animals, mainly in certain wild ungulates (buffalo, warthogs, and antelope) that are immune or resistant to their effects. When the tsetse fly (*Glossina sp.*) feeds on a host, the ingested trypanosomes multiply in its gut and are then transmitted to another host through a subsequent bite. The disease ecology of sleeping sickness is therefore composed of several interlocking elements: the trypanosomes themselves, wild host species, the tsetse fly vector, a suitable habitat for the fly (generally warm conditions with sufficient humidity and bushy vegetation cover), and finally humans or livestock as end-hosts.[76] As far as wildlife protection was concerned, the main issue for contemporaries was whether game reserves promoted the spread of the disease by furnishing a haven for hosts and for the blood-sucking tsetse flies that transmit the parasites to humans and livestock.

Known for centuries as a lethal disease, trypanosomiasis was most prevalent in the lightly settled parts of the 'tsetse belt', which stretched from the moist savannahs and woodlands of West Africa to the south-east of the continent. Although Africans and Europeans alike had long associated outbreaks of sleeping sickness with the presence of game and tsetse, its precise aetiology was not well understood in the early twentieth century. In view of the grave threat it posed to human and animal health, it soon became the focus of a trans-imperial medical effort that engaged some of the leading scientists of the time. In 1894 the Scottish microbiologist David Bruce conclusively demonstrated that the trypanosome which caused *nagana* (the eponymous *T. brucei*) was carried in the blood of certain game animals, which served as a reservoir for transmission to livestock via tsetse flies. In 1903 the human disease was also linked to tsetse, and from 1910 to 1912 researchers identified the species that were most dangerous to humans: *T. gambiense*, associated mainly with the riverine tsetse fly (*G. palpalis*), and *T. rhodesiense* carried by the savannah tsetse (*G. morsitans*). These breakthroughs provided scientists with many pieces of the puzzle, but the precise relationship between flies, victims, and game nonetheless remained a matter of profound disagreement for years to come.[77]

[76] The seminal study of the disease is John Ford, *The Role of the Trypanosomiases in African Ecology: A Study of the Tsetse Fly Problem* (Oxford: Clarendon, 1971).

[77] On the trypanosomes, Ford, *Role*, 2–3; on scientific debates, John M. MacKenzie, 'Experts and Amateurs: Tsetse, Nagana and Sleeping Sickness in East and Central Africa', in MacKenzie (ed.), *Imperialism*, 187–212.

Colonial attempts to curtail trypanosomiasis have been the focus of extensive historical research, and studies of the subject have played a crucial role in integrating natural history and human history in Africa.[78] The immediate problem at the time was the rapid advance of tsetse and the recurrent outbreaks of human sleeping sickness that resulted. As John Ford argued in his landmark 1971 study of the disease, both of these developments were directly linked to the colonial incursions of the late nineteenth century.[79] The Rinderpest epizootic initially wiped out so many cattle and wild animals that the tsetse fly was temporarily on the retreat. Over the following years, however, tsetse-bearing bush began to expand into previous farming and grazing lands as game numbers recovered and areas of dense human settlement shrank due to the combined effects of famine, disease, and colonial 'pacification' campaigns. In German East Africa, for instance, the fly was thought to infest no less than one-third of the entire territory by 1913.[80] The huge scale of this expansion has led some historians—above all Kjekshus—to contrast a pre-colonial era of relative human 'control' over tsetse from a subsequent post-incursion period in which the tables were turned. Although more recent studies have convincingly rejected such a neat distinction, it is nonetheless clear that the ecological tumult caused by colonial intrusion greatly facilitated the expansion of fly belts throughout Central and East Africa.[81] One of the chief results was the spread of extensive no-go zones for livestock herds, many of which had to be rebuilt after the Rinderpest outbreak from cattle stocks that had not previously been exposed to trypanosomes. Worse still was the terrible series of sleeping sickness epidemics that ravaged the region during the 1900s, especially in Uganda and the Congo, where it is likely that over half a million people died from the disease over the course of the decade.[82]

In their search for a remedy, colonial authorities throughout sub-Saharan Africa solicited the latest scientific advice to guide their policies. But opinions were mixed on the epidemiology of sleeping sickness, and therefore on the best means of combating it. The prevailing explanation at the time was the recent upsurge in human migration. The basic hypothesis was that, prior to colonial conquest, the combined effects of tribal warfare and slave raiding kept population movements to a minimum and encouraged people to live in more concentrated settlements, which allowed them to develop a degree of resistance to local pathogens. By contrast, the *pax colonial* brought an increase in trade, security, and mobility, which together encouraged a dispersal of human populations and therefore exposed people to

---

[78] Ford's work strongly influenced subsequent historiography: for an overview, see Beinart and Hughes, *Environment*, 184–99.

[79] Ford, *Role*.   [80] Iliffe, *Modern History*, 164.

[81] Kjekshus, *Ecology*; for critical views, see Koponen, *Development*, 645; Iliffe, *Modern History*, 163–6; Isaria N. Kimambo, 'Environmental Control and Hunger: In the Mountains and Plains of Nineteenth-Century Northeastern Tanzania', in Gregory Maddox, James Giblin, and Isaria N. Kimambo (eds), *Custodians of the Land: Ecology and Culture in the History of Tanzania* (Oxford: James Currey, 1996), 71–95.

[82] Maryinez Lyons, *The Colonial Disease: A Social History of Sleeping Sickness in Northern Zaire, 1900–1940* (Cambridge: Cambridge University Press, 1992), 102–36; Kirk Hoppe, *Lords of the Fly: Sleeping Sickness Control in British East Africa, 1900–1960* (Westport, Conn.: Praeger, 2003), 27–79.

more diseases. From this perspective, the epidemics of the early colonial period were the flip-side of greater peace and stability. Consequently, early countermeasures often focused on curtailing population movement. In French Equatorial Africa, where acute outbreaks of sleeping sickness killed perhaps half of the population of the Niari plain between 1898 and the early 1910s, the colonial authorities sequestered thousands of people into quarantine camps. In the Congo, Belgian authorities created *cordons sanitaires* around outbreak areas and forcibly transferred infected people into special lazarets that were soon likened to 'death camps'. In Uganda, entire villages were evacuated from the shores of Lake Victoria to be resettled in fly-free zones.[83] Although German authorities in East Africa were more sceptical about the need for such radical population movements, they too advocated evacuation from hard-hit areas where population densities were low.[84] Despite continuing disagreements over the efficacy of resettlement measures, they nonetheless remained an integral part of anti-trypanosomiasis efforts until well into the 1950s.[85]

In the event, these policies proved not only ineffective but often counterproductive, for they were based on the misconception that humans were the prime reservoir of the disease. Since the main hosts were in fact various game species, the decline of livestock grazing and agricultural cultivation in evacuated zones merely encouraged the further expansion of tsetse-bearing bush. There were, however, other approaches to follow. One was to focus on immunization and trypanocidal drugs, which was most common among French and Belgian health authorities. The other was to concentrate on the link between wildlife and tsetse, as British and German scientists increasingly did. We do not need to go into the details of these scientific debates, which rumbled on for decades and have been analysed elsewhere.[86] The point is that the latter 'ecological' approach largely amounted to an attack on the tsetse fly and on the animals that harboured trypanosomes, which placed the entire policy of wildlife protection and game sanctuaries in question. It should be noted that, even for those who advocated the 'ecological' control of sleeping sickness, the practical implications were not entirely straightforward. While game reserves were viewed as incubators of infection, they also presented a practical means of keeping wildlife away from humans and livestock. By the 1930s some conservationists even suggested that the presence of the fly was a blessing in disguise, since it kept people out of certain areas and therefore acted as a 'trustee of the land for future generations'.[87] But by and large, the tsetse problem put the conservationist cause on the defensive.

[83] Coquery-Vidrovitch, *Le Congo*, 494–5; Lyons, *Colonial Disease*, 103–25; Hoppe, *Lords*, 55–73.

[84] Dr Meixner, 'Die Bekämpfung der Schlafkrankheit', *Verhandlungen des deutschen Kolonialkongresses 1910* (Berlin: Reimer, 1910), 257–78, here 268.

[85] Hoppe, *Lords*, 105–42.

[86] See, generally, Lyons, *Colonial Disease*, 103–25; Hoppe, *Lords*; James Giblin, 'Trypanosomiasis Control in African History: An Evaded Issue?', *Journal of African History*, vol. 31 (1990), 59–80.

[87] G. V. Jacks and R. O. Whyte, *The Rape of the Earth: A World Survey of Soil Erosion* (London: Faber & Faber, 1939), 69–70; see also T. W. Kirkpatrick, 'East Africa and the Tse-Tse Fly', *East African Agricultural Journal* (1936), 411–15, cited in Kjekshus, *Ecology*, 175.

The problem faced by conservationists was that the suspension of shooting restrictions and the deliberate extermination of game in infected zones was a relatively effective, albeit contentious, means of controlling tsetse. Mass wildlife culling was most common in colonies with a vocal white settler lobby, such as Southern Rhodesia (where it began in 1901), but it was also widely employed elsewhere (e.g. Nyasaland and Natal). The policy had powerful scientific backers. Among them was David Bruce, who pointedly argued in 1915 that 'it would be as reasonable to allow mad dogs to live and be protected by law in our English towns and villages. Not only should all game laws restricting their destruction on fly country be removed, but active measures should, if feasible, be taken for their early and complete blotting out.'[88] The renowned German bacteriologist Robert Koch, who had initially pinned his hopes on inoculation, also gradually came around to this view. By 1908 he openly called for the extermination of large ungulates and wild pigs 'wherever tsetse prevails'.[89]

As the tsetse debate intensified, so too did lobbying efforts against the dilution of hunting regulations and especially against the policy of game extermination. The SPFE maintained that there was no irrefutable connection between game and the fly since the former were spread over large areas where the latter was absent. As Edward North Buxton complained to the British Colonial Office in 1905, 'science has not yet arrived at the point that you can justly condemn all species; and we deprecate its being used as an excuse for the destruction of game generally'.[90] The issue similarly galvanized the German Wildschutzkommissionen, especially after Koch publicly advocated a policy of local extermination. Their protests in Berlin were so vehement as to persuade the administration in German East Africa to abandon the policy of culling in favour of destroying fly habitat through the use of brush fires.[91]

Opposition to prophylactic game clearance arose on three main levels. First of all, conservationists continually highlighted the uncertainties of the scientific evidence. Indeed, they actively tried to increase the sense of uncertainty by using their connections to secure positions on key policy bodies, most notably the British Interdepartmental Committee on Sleeping Sickness, which was established in 1914.[92] Second, they rejected the idea that wildlife preservation was necessarily a brake on economic development. Big game animals, they argued, constituted a lucrative economic asset, both as a magnet for tourism and as a sustainably managed source of food and trade goods. Third, and perhaps most importantly, they challenged the policy on ethical as much as on practical grounds. From their

---

[88] MacKenzie, *Empire*, 237–42, quote from p. 240; see also MacKenzie, 'Experts', 201.
[89] Koch also mistakenly singled out crocodiles for eradication. Gißibl, *Nature*, 172–4, quote p. 174; Meixner, 'Bekämpfung', 266–7.
[90] Cioc, *Game*, 46.
[91] Wolfgang U. Eckart, *Medizin und Kolonialimperialismus. Deutschland 1884–1945* (Paderborn: Schöningh, 1997), 340–9; Gißibl, *Nature*, 174–81; MacKenzie, *Empire*, 237–9; Koponen, *Development*, 481.
[92] MacKenzie, 'Experts', 199–204.

perspective, wildlife preservation was not merely sound policy; it was a moral imperative of imperial stewardship for any people that claimed to be civilized.

No single episode encapsulated this moral dimension better than the so-called 'Rechenberg slaughter' of summer 1910, when the German East African Governor Albrecht Freiherr von Rechenberg, a reformer with little sympathy for the big-game hunting lobby, took the radical step of ordering the clearance of all game within a 50-kilometre strip along the borders with Kenya and Uganda in order to retard the spread of disease to domestic livestock herds. Although the specific threat in this instance was a reported Rinderpest outbreak, officials understandably viewed the matter through the lens of the ongoing tsetse controversy, not least through Koch's recent proclamations about the inability of livestock and wildlife to coexist in Africa.[93] And although the story only broke around a year after the actual event, once it went public it elicited howls of protest from the conservation lobby in Germany and abroad. The article that sparked the controversy, penned by the prominent hunter-conservationist Hans Paasche and luridly titled 'mass murder in East Africa', in many ways set the tone.[94] Reprinted in numerous newspapers, it portrayed a functional quarantine measure—one widely supported by the settler lobby, agricultural officials, and pathologists alike—as a fundamental moral failing, a barbaric and indiscriminate slaughter of innocent life both contrary to the civilizing mission and grimly symbolic of the threat to nature worldwide.

We can only guess how many animals perished in this operation; undoubtedly the number is somewhere between official reports of under 5,000 and conservationists' estimates of up to 30,000. But regardless of the actual death toll, its main significance lies in the backlash it generated. The resulting scandal not only cost Governor von Rechenberg his job, it also accelerated the expansion of wildlife reserves in East Africa and dampened the enthusiasm of German officials for the policy of game eradication.[95] More generally, it illustrated the rising public profile of colonial conservation after the turn of the century. By 1910 the practice of discrete petitioning was gradually giving way to a programme of public campaigning. Although the SPFE in particular continued its elite lobbying efforts, colonial conservation was acquiring a broader public constituency beyond the confines of hunter-naturalist circles. As a result, the protection of tropical wildlife was increasingly couched in the language of imperial obligation and the stewardship of nature. And what lent the cause a broader popular appeal was its emphasis on the teeming savannahs and jungles of the colonies as 'wonders of nature', and especially on the charismatic fauna (giraffes, elephants, rhinos) that symbolized the exotic allure of faraway paradises—the very same attributes that made them prized hunting trophies in the first place.

---

[93] Gißibl, *Nature*, 204–10.

[94] Hans Paasche, 'Der Massenmord in Ostafrika', *Deutsch-Ostafrikanische Zeitung*, vol. 13 (13 May 1911).

[95] Wächter, *Naturschutz*, 79–80; Gißibl, *Nature*, 211–18, 224.

IMPERIALISM, INTERNATIONALISM, AND THE SCIENCE OF NATURE PROTECTION

Well before the First World War, then, the protection of tropical 'wilderness' was becoming a matter of morality as much as utility. For conservationists the world over, the destruction of threatened species not only defied the logic of sound resource management; it also breached the standards of civilized behaviour, on aesthetic as much as on scientific grounds. Yet while some advocates deployed this rhetoric in order to influence colonial governments, others became convinced that a truly effective framework of nature preservation had to extend beyond the formal institutions of empire altogether. At a purely practical level, this idea arose from the fact that many of the species under threat—migratory animals or species strongly exposed to international trade—could not be adequately protected within the boundaries of single states or even empires. It also reflected a growing conviction that the duty to preserve the treasures of nature transcended the competence of individual states. As the tsetse controversies made abundantly clear, the task of protecting wild creatures regardless of their economic utility could not reliably be left to governmental discretion. If they were truly a legacy for 'all humankind' they required an international body to monitor their safekeeping.

This was, in a nutshell, the programme of the 'world nature protection' movement that emerged just before the First World War. Both the term and the agenda it denoted were closely associated with the explorer and naturalist Paul Sarasin, a leading figure in the Swiss League for Nature Protection whose 1914 book 'on the responsibilities of world nature protection' served as a manifesto for international conservationists in the early twentieth century.[96] Sarasin's vision was in many ways a direct challenge to colonial conservation as hitherto practised. His experiences on Ceylon and Celebes in the late 1880s–1890s had made him highly critical of colonialism, and convinced him that human relationships with nature should be arranged on an ethical and non-utilitarian basis. Above all, they convinced him of the need to establish a truly global framework of nature protection beyond the remit of any single power. Instead of entrusting the matter to state authorities—in thrall as they were to the interests of business, politicians, and administrators—he advocated the creation of an international commission of scientific experts whose task was to establish and supervise 'total reservations' that would be legally sacrosanct vis-à-vis their territorial governments.

Sarasin envisaged such reserves eventually stretching 'from pole to pole', but it was the areas in between that exercised him most, especially the preservation of the 'African megafauna, and furthermore those of the entire tropical belt of the world'. The aim was not merely to ensure protection from further harm, but also to promote the restoration of damaged landscapes into what was regarded

---

[96] Paul Sarasin, *Ueber die Aufgaben des Weltnaturschutzes* (Basel: Helbig & Lichtenhahn, 1914); also Paul Sarasin, *Weltnaturschutz: Global Protection of Nature* (Basel, 1911). Sarasin's 1914 book is often described as one of the two seminal texts of the period alongside Hornaday, *Our Vanishing Wildlife*.

as a more original state: to recreate 'biocenoses such as adorned Africa before the arrival of the white man, this terrible destroyer'. Unusually for the time, his reserves also envisioned humans as part of the picture. The 'protection of the so-called *Naturvölker* from extermination' was, for Sarasin, the 'most important and simultaneously most honourable' task of all. For like the landscapes they inhabited, these peoples offered Europeans 'a glimpse of our own past', a pristine remnant of an earlier 'transitional stage (*Durchgangszustand*) of our own culture'.[97]

Given the radical nature of Sarasin's plans, he and his backers chalked up a remarkable series of achievements before 1914. In 1910 he persuaded the International Zoological Congress to establish a commission for the global protection of nature, and in 1913 he convened the Conférence Internationale pour la Protection Mondiale de la Nature in Bern to obtain formal recognition from governments across Europe, along with the United States, Japan, and Argentina.[98] But it was not long before this new world order of environmental governance ran into difficulties. For one thing, it had powerful adversaries even among leading conservationists. Hugo Conwentz, for instance, had no intention of allowing outside regulation of his own activities in Prussia. His keynote address to the 1913 conference made clear his opposition to any external interference in the conservationist measures taken by 'civilized' countries, and his misgivings were strongly echoed by the British delegation.[99] The sponsorship of the conference by the Swiss government was also sceptically viewed as yet another instance of states without overseas colonies supporting 'internationalism' as a means of gaining influence beyond their borders.[100] In this sense, Sarasin's agenda was part of a broader contest between 'competing visions of world order', and one whose anti-imperial implications were plain to see.[101] Like so many optimistic visions of the Belle Époque, it was quickly consumed in the fires of the First World War. Ratification of the international commission stood no chance of success after the outbreak of hostilities in 1914, and in the post-war period Sarasin's attempts to revive it under

---

[97] Sarasin, *Ueber die Aufgaben*, quotes from 29, 38–9, 53, 55. For an overview of his 'anthropological nature protection', Anna-Katharina Wöbse, 'Paul Sarasins "anthropologischer Naturschutz": Zur "Größe" Mensch im frühen internationalen Naturschutz. Ein Werkstattbericht', in Gert Gröning and Joachim Wolschke-Bulmann (eds), *Naturschutz und Demokratie?!* (Munich: Martin Meidenbauer, 2006), 207–13; also Andrew Zimmermann, *Anthropology and Antihumanism in Imperial Germany* (Chicago: University of Chicago Press, 2001).

[98] There is surprisingly little on Sarasin in English. The best overview is Anna-Katharina Wöbse, *Weltnaturschutz. Umweltdiplomatie in Völkerbund und Vereinten Nationen 1920–1950* (Frankfurt a. M.: Campus, 2012), 36–53. For a brief biography, see also Stefan Bachmann, *Zwischen Patriotismus und Wissenschaft. Die schweizerischen Naturschutzpioniere (1900–1938)* (Zurich: Chronos, 1999), 271–9.

[99] *Recueil des Procès-Verbaux de la Conférence Internationale pour la Protection de la Nature. Berne, 17–19 Novembre 1913* (Bern: Wyss, 1914), 83–98, 119–24.

[100] Madeleine Herren, *Hintertüren zur Macht. Internationalismus und modernisierungsorientierte Außenpolitik in Belgien, der Schweiz und den USA 1865–1914* (Munich: Oldenbourg, 2000), 352–62; see also Bachmann, *Zwischen Patriotismus und Wissenschaft*, 271–9.

[101] Sebastian Conrad and Dominic Sachsenmaier (eds), *Competing Visions of World Order: Global Moments and Movements, 1880s–1930s* (Houndmills: Palgrave, 2007).

the aegis of the League of Nations once again foundered on the sovereignty claims of the victorious powers.[102]

But despite these setbacks, international cooperation and exchange grew increasingly important during the inter-war years, especially for conservationists working in the French, Dutch, and Belgian colonies. In 1923 the Congrès International pour la Protection de la Nature (explicitly conceived as a successor to the 1913 Bern conference) gave a visible push to protective legislation throughout the French Empire. Backed by scientific luminaries like the botanist Auguste Chevalier, a spate of new measures was introduced over the following two years, including the first hunting regulations in Cochin China, tightened prohibitions in French West Africa, a ban on the use of explosives for fishing around New Caledonia, and the formation of five national parks in Algeria.[103] In the Netherlands Indies, new legislation in 1924 introduced general licensing for all hunting activities, and greatly expanded the list of protected bird and mammal species.[104] Most conspicuous of all was the 1925 establishment of the King Albert (now Virunga) National Park in the Belgian Congo, the first such park in Africa, followed a year later by the Kruger National Park in the Transvaal.

This flurry of colonial legislation during the mid-1920s was mirrored by a wave of organizational activity within Europe. The Netherlands Commission for the International Protection of Nature, the French Permanent Committee for the Protection of Colonial Fauna and Flora, and the Belgian Committee for the International Protection of Nature were all founded in 1925–6. In 1928 the International Union of Biological Sciences formed an Office International de Documentation et de Corrélation pour la Protection de la Nature in Brussels, which was modelled on the International Agricultural Institute in Rome, the forerunner of the FAO. Spearheaded by the influential Dutch conservationist Peter G. van Tienhoven and his Belgian protégé Jean-Marie Derscheid (a zoologist by training), the Office International formed the inter-war genealogical link between Sarasin's ill-fated 1913 commission and the International Union for the Protection of Nature, which was founded in 1948.[105]

The most decisive advances in cross-border conservation came in the early 1930s. In July 1931, delegates at the second international congress for the protection of

---

[102] Paul Sarasin, 'La Protection mondiale de la faune sauvage', in *Congrès International pour la Protection de la Nature* (Paris, 1925), 34–44, here 43–4; more generally Wöbse, *Weltnaturschutz*, 54–64; Wöbse, 'Der Schutz der Natur im Völkerbund—Anfänge einer Weltumweltpolitik', *Archiv für Sozialgeschichte*, vol. 43 (2003), 177–90.

[103] *Congrès International pour la Protection de la Nature* (Paris, 1925). These were part of a more ambitious set of plans submitted to the Colonial Ministry, focusing above all on total hunting bans for particular species and the creation of over two dozen parks in AOF, AEF, Madagascar, and Indochina.

[104] Boomgaard, 'Oriental Nature', 268–9.

[105] *La Protection de la nature et l'Union Internationale des Sciences Biologiques: communications présentées aux assemblées générales de 1925, 1926, 1927 et 1928* (Brussels, 1929), 11–18; G. A. Brouwer, *De Organisatie van de Natuurbescherming in de verschillende Landen* (Amsterdam: De Spieghel, 1931), 37–8; Johann Büttikofer, *Report on the Conference for the International Protection of Nature* (Basel: Swiss League for the Protection of Nature, 1946), 63; 'Conference for the Establishment of the International Union for the Protection of Nature: General Information', UNESCO report, Paris, 20 July 1948, pp. 1–2, available at: <http://unesdoc.unesco.org/images/0015/001547/154739eb.pdf>.

nature (held in Paris within the framework of the 1931 Colonial Exhibition) resolved to update the existing conservation measures previously agreed at the 1900 London Convention.[106] The resulting London Conference, held in the House of Lords in October–November 1933, was another major milestone for international nature protection, surpassing even its 1900 predecessor in several respects. For one thing, it deliberately pursued a more global agenda by including representatives from several countries that did not possess African colonies (the USA, Netherlands, and India). Furthermore, unlike the 1900 agreement, its provisions were not limited to the twentieth parallels north and south, but extended to the entire African continent; indeed, they eventually influenced conservation measures throughout much of colonial Asia as well. Most importantly, the range of issues it addressed went far beyond the turn-of-century focus on shooting, trading, and licensing. Although the 1933 London Convention did update these older protocols, its central thrust was, in the words of its preamble, to promote 'the constitution of national parks, strict natural reserves, and other reserves within which the hunting, killing or capturing of fauna, and the collection or destruction of flora shall be limited or prohibited'.[107]

Support for such a territorial approach to conservation grew rapidly after the First World War. By the beginning of the 1920s there were dozens of official wildlife sanctuaries dotted around the globe, including most European countries, several colonial territories, parts of Central and South America, and of course the US and British dominions. Within colonial Africa, the Belgian authorities were perhaps the most enthusiastic proponents of the park model. The creation of the Albert National Park gave Belgian scientists like Jean-Marie Derscheid and the palaeontologist Victor van Straelen (director of the Musée Royal d'Histoire Naturelle de Belgique, and later president of the Congolese national parks institute) considerable clout within international conservation circles. Throughout the late 1920s and 1930s they urged British authorities to establish analogous reserves in neighbouring colonies (especially Uganda), and were broadly supported by their associates in the SPFE. In 1930 the SPFE commissioned a report from R. W. G. Hingston, a noted medical officer and naturalist, which concluded that there were four main challenges confronting wildlife conservation in Africa: the inexorable spread of cultivation, commercial hunting for body parts, the effects of indigenous hunting, and the tsetse menace. The solution to all of them, Hingston suggested, lay in the establishment of inviolable game sanctuaries. For the British authorities, this report provided much of the initial impetus behind the 1933 London conference.[108]

---

[106] *Deuxième Congrès International pour la Protection de la Nature* (Paris, 1932). The connection of the conference to the Exhibition precluded any official delegation from Germany given the French takeover of previously German colonies, though German delegates attended in an unofficial capacity: Anna-Katharina Wöbse, 'Naturschutz global—oder: Hilfe von außen. Internationale Beziehungen des amtlichen Naturschutzes im 20. Jahrhundert', in Frohn and Schmoll (eds), *Natur und Staat*, 625–727, here 647.

[107] The treaty is reprinted in Cioc, *Game*, 161–76, here 162.

[108] Adams, *Against Extinction*, 89–91.

The new London agreement formally came into force in 1936 and committed signatories to fulfil their pledges about the creation of parks within two years of ratification. For various reasons, however, most of the great national parks of East Africa only came into being after the Second World War (see Chapter 10). In the 1930s British officials still thought that the establishment of national parks was premature in their Central and East African colonies, which lacked the sizeable urban population and easy tourist accessibility that was deemed necessary to fund the employment of park rangers and guards (and that underpinned the success of Kruger National Park in South Africa).[109]

As a result, some of the most immediate effects of the 1933 convention were felt beyond Africa. In India it significantly strengthened the SPFE's case for new legislation, which culminated in the establishment of the Hailey (now Corbett) National Park in 1936.[110] In Malaya, the King George V National Park was created in 1939 after years of lobbying by the conservationist pioneer Theodore Hubback.[111] Although the Netherlands were not party to the convention, the colonial government in Batavia had already brought its legislation into line with the preparatory committee's recommendations through a new Game Protection Ordinance of 1931, which extended its 1924 legislation to the entire archipelago, as well as a new Natural Monument and Wildlife Reserve Ordinance of 1932, which formed the basis for the creation of twenty wildlife reserves by the end of 1941.[112] Among French naturalists there was a chorus of calls for the creation of parks and wildlife refuges in Indochina, West Africa, and Equatorial Africa.[113] Conservationists prepared for a third London convention scheduled to take place in 1939, but in the end it was abandoned due to the outbreak of the Second World War.[114]

In short, the coordination of conservation efforts across national and imperial boundaries was increasingly marked by a shift towards permanent parks and sanctuaries as the most appropriate vehicles for nature protection. These two trends, though partly distinct from one another, were closely interlinked, for the growing emphasis on the need to separate human and animal populations reflected wider international debates about the purpose of nature conservation and the most

---

[109] On Kruger, Jane Carruthers, *The Kruger National Park: A Social and Political History* (Pietermaritzburg: Natal University Press, 1995); MacKenzie, *Empire*, 271–7.

[110] MacKenzie, *Empire*, 287–9.   [111] Kathiritamby-Wells, *Nature*, 208–17.

[112] Charles Kies, *Nature Protection in the Netherlands Indies* (Cambridge, Mass.: American Committee for International Wild Life Protection, 1936); Cornelis van Steenis, *Album van Natuurmonumenten in Nederlandsch-Indië* (Batavia: Nederl.-Indische Vereenig. tot Natuurbescherming, 1937); Boomgaard, 'Oriental Nature', 269–71. For a full list of parks and reserves, see Paul Jepson and Robert J. Whittaker, 'Histories of Protected Areas: Internationalisation of Conservationist Values and their Adoption in the Netherlands Indies (Indonesia)', *Environment and History*, vol. 8 (2002), 129–72, here 158–61.

[113] André Aubréville et al., *Contribution à l'étude des réserves naturelles et des parcs nationaux* (Paris: Lechevalier, 1937); P. A. de Keyser and A. Villiers, 'Recherche scientifique et protection de la nature', *Institut Français d'Afrique Noire*, no. 2. (undated, c.1950), 1–3; *Congrès International pour la Protection de la Nature* (Paris, 1925), esp. 352–9.

[114] H. Humbert, *La Protection de la nature dans les territoires d'outre-mer pendant la guerre* (Paris: Société d'Éditions Géographiques, Maritimes et Coloniales, 1940), 6–7.

effective means of pursuing it. As before, practical concerns about sustainable resource management continued to coexist alongside more ethically oriented approaches; if anything, the two were becoming more and more difficult to disentangle.[115] But within conservationist circles there was a general move away from the focus on hunting regulations towards a more holistic approach that sought to protect integral habitat for diverse flora and fauna.

Broadly speaking, there were two dominant models to follow. One was the notionally American national park, the apotheosis of the 'natural monument', whose purpose was to preserve spectacular landscapes and make them accessible for recreation. Combining scientific and tourist aims, it inspired the creation of Kruger National Park in the Transvaal (1926) as well as plans for the great East African national parks that were established after 1945.[116] The other model followed a stricter scientific rationale for the protection of entire ecosystems (usually referred to as 'biocenoses' before the term 'ecosystem' was coined in 1935), and was exemplified by the Parc National Suisse, founded in 1913 in a remote alpine region.[117] This latter prototype furnished the mould for the Albert National Park, which was conceived as a 'réserve intégrale' for 'exclusively scientific aims'.[118] It also underpinned various French conservation efforts, most notably on Madagascar, where ten 'réserves naturelles' were established in 1927 exclusively for scientific research.[119]

The increasingly apartheid approach to conservation during the inter-war years was, then, neither unique to Europe's colonies nor entirely new. To understand why it took such a powerful hold during this period we must consider a broader set of developments that together inscribed the exclusion of people firmly into the agenda of colonial nature preservation.

One factor was the growing capacity of colonial states. However weak these 'shoestring regimes' remained, colonial bureaucracies were generally more capable of enforcing game (and other) laws after the First World War than before. As it happened, the relationship between the state and nature preservation was mutually beneficial insofar as hunting regulations, reserves, and game departments bolstered colonial security, perhaps especially in settler colonies. As one observer remarked on Algeria, 'from the perspective of fauna conservation—as well as for the security of French *colons*—we can only deplore the excessive

---

[115] At least in the British empire: Peder Anker, *Imperial Ecology: Environmental Order in the British Empire, 1895–1945* (Cambridge, Mass.: Harvard University Press, 2001), chs 4, 6. Caroline Ford argues that they remained more distinct in the French context: 'Nature, Culture and Conservation in France and her Colonies 1840–1940', *Past & Present*, no. 183 (May 2004), 173–98.

[116] Carruthers, *Kruger*; on Serengeti, Jonathan S. Adams and Thomas O. McShane, *The Myth of Wild Africa: Conservation without Illusion* (Berkeley: University of California Press, 1996), 37–48; see also MacKenzie, *Empire*, 269–71.

[117] Patrick Kupper, 'Translating Yellowstone: Early European National Parks, *Weltnaturschutz* and the Swiss Model', in Gissibl, Höhler, and Kupper (eds), *Civilizing*, 123–39; Bachmann, *Zwischen Patriotismus und Wissenschaft*, 117–80.

[118] Sarasin, 'La Protection mondiale', 42; *Les Parcs nationaux et la protection de la nature* (Brussels: Institut des Parcs Nationaux du Congo Belge, 1937), 6.

[119] Georges Petit, 'Les "Réserves naturelles" de Madagascar', in Aubréville et al., *Contribution*, 229–40.

opportunities given to the natives to arm themselves to European standards'.[120] Moreover, colonial administrations were often in a stronger position than metropolitan governments when it came to the establishment of permanent reserves. After all, the nature of colonial rule made it much easier to sequester territory and curtail local access without having to engage in extensive consultation or compensation efforts.

A less tangible—though no less important—factor was the cultural fallout of the First World War, which intensified existing anxieties about the self-destructive character of industrial society. Although we can only speculate about the connection, this post-war sense of pessimism seems to have bolstered apprehensions about the squandering of resources and the destruction of natural landscapes.[121] Writing in 1922, the acclaimed naturalist William Hornaday declared that 'there was nothing more terrible to contemplate at the time than the grinding and devastating power of modern civilization as it is exerted, not only on animal life generally, but on vegetable life and on all the products of nature; that the human race ... is also increasing in its power and ingenuity to destroy'. Most lamentable of all was the transference of particular technologies—above all firearms—to 'savage tribes' still incapable of appreciating the power of these modern marvels and therefore even more complacent about their destructive consequences than the societies that invented them. Hornaday estimated the ratio of nature protectors to destroyers at around 1:500 for New York, 1:1,000 in the American West, and 1:100,000 in Africa.[122] Steeped in notions of civilizational hierarchy and racialized expertise, one can hardly find a clearer rationale than this for the exclusionist brand of conservation that took hold in the inter-war years.

Most important of all, however, was the shifting scientific basis of conservation efforts, and in particular the importance of ecology as a source of knowledge. In many ways the inter-war years marked the coming of age for ecology, as earlier organicist paradigms (that viewed nature as a community of beings collectively displaying attributes of a single organism) were increasingly challenged by more mechanistic models designed to facilitate the rational management of nature's economy. In the tropical world, ecology exhibited a certain 'subversive' potential as field researchers grew more sympathetic to subaltern knowledge and more critical

---

[120] 'Creation de parcs nationaux en Algerie', in *Congrès International pour la Protection de la Nature* (Paris, 1925), 351.

[121] There is, of course, a vast literature on the cultural effects of the war. For its resonance in the imperial context, see Adas, *Machines*, 380–401. Especially influential among contemporary naturalists was Henry Fairfield Osborn and H. E. Anthony, 'Close of the Age of Mammals', *Journal of Mammalogy*, vol. 3 no. 4 (Nov. 1922), 219–31; also R. L. Sherlock, *Man as a Geological Agent: An Account of his Action on Inanimate Nature* (London: Witherby, 1922); Carl Ortwin Sauer, 'Theme of Plant and Animal Destruction in Economic History' (1938), repr. in John Leighley (ed.), *Land and Life: A Selection from the Writings of Carl Ortwin Sauer* (Berkeley: University of California Press, 1963), 145–54; Sauer, 'Destructive Exploitation'.

[122] See Hornaday's comments on Osborn and Anthony, 'Close of the Age of Mammals', 231–2.

of colonial interventions.[123] But despite this shift of perspective, and despite the growing attention paid to disturbed habitats, there was still a powerful disciplinary fascination with pristine ecosystems devoid of human interference. This fascination continued to inform the conservation discourse of the inter-war period, which for the most part remained rooted in the language of natural equilibrium and homeostasis. Frederic Clements' famous model of plant succession—whereby disturbed floral communities pass through a series of stages before returning to a stable 'climax'— retained much of its influence, and if anything gained ground in francophone circles.[124] Within this framework, humans largely appeared as disruptions.

When translated into concrete conservation measures, the rising influence of ecological perspectives tended to encourage a policy of separation and exclusion. According to Georges Petit, a scientist at the Muséum National d'Histoire Naturelle and the founder of the reserves on Madagascar, the absence of human presence was the fundamental principle of a 'réserve naturelle intégrale'. Unlike the 'American' national-park-as-spectacle, his concept of a 'purely biological' reserve was a place in which people represented an external interference.[125] The same idea informed the management of Albert National Park. In the words of Victor van Straelen (then president of the Congolese national parks institute), within its boundaries 'nature must submit only to her own laws. The biological equilibrium, essentially labile, can freely oscillate there without any of its constituent parts being influenced by anthropogenic intervention of any sort.' In a telling choice of metaphor, he likened the park to 'a vast enterprise of experimental ecology'.[126] The analogy neatly expressed the perception of intact tropical ecosystems as quasi-laboratories for scientific study and for new forms of environmental management. As Jean-Marie Derscheid put it, 'for those preoccupied by the protection of species, natural communities, and sites of interest, the Belgian colonial empire offers an incomparable field of action, not merely by virtue of its immense expanse (more than eighty times the size of the mother country) but also of the great variety of bio-geographic regions that are represented there'.[127]

In view of all this scientific pretence, it is worth emphasizing that colonial efforts to preserve supposedly pristine remnants of 'nature' in Europe's tropical empire

[123] On ecology's subversive potential, see Tilley, *Africa*, ch. 3. On the rise of the 'new ecology' associated with Charles Elton and Arthur Tansley, see Donald Worster, *Nature's Economy: A History of Ecological Ideas*, 2nd edn (Cambridge: Cambridge University Press, 1994), 291–315. On the imperial dimension more broadly, Anker, *Imperial Ecology*, chs 3, 4; Libby Robin, 'Ecology: A Science of Empire?', in Griffiths and Robin (eds), *Ecology*, 63–75.

[124] Pascal Acot and Jean-Marc Drouin, 'L'Introduction en France des idées de l'écologie scientifique américaine dans l'entre-deux-guerres', *Revue d'histoire des sciences*, vol. 50 no. 4 (1997), 461–80.

[125] Georges Petit, 'Protection de la nature et questions de "définitions"', in Aubréville et al., *Contribution*, 5–14.

[126] Victor van Straelen, 'La Protection de la nature: sa nécessité et ses avantages', in *Les Parcs nationaux et la protection de la nature* (Brussels: Institut des Parcs Nationaux du Congo Belge, 1937), 41–87, here 42, 82.

[127] J.-M. Derscheid, 'La Protection de la nature au Congo Belge', in *La Protection de la nature et l'Union Internationale*, 39–46, here 39.

came largely at the expense of a more accurate understanding of these landscapes and how they developed. The rhetoric of unspoiled Edens framed tropical environments as timeless, intact wildernesses rather than as changing landscapes in which people actually lived. As also happened in the American West, the attempt to preserve wilderness generally involved the disruption and erasure of human influence.[128] Few recognized that most of the landscapes they sought to protect in a state of pristine equilibrium had long been shaped by human use. Even the noted evolutionary biologist and conservationist Julian Huxley, when visiting Africa for the first time in 1929, regarded it as 'a continent which had hardly changed in the last five hundred years'.[129] That such views were mistaken became clear as these landscapes unexpectedly changed due to the suppression of human activities such as hunting, herding, farming, and fire-setting. In Albert National Park, the 1929 decision to suppress fire, which ended a long-established indigenous practice of burning scrub to encourage grass growth, led not only to a greater diversity of plants and small animals (as anticipated), but also to the displacement of grasses by spiny or woody plants and a consequent migration of large herbivores to other areas (not anticipated). To ensure sufficient fodder for herds, park authorities soon reinvented the traditional African practice of burning.[130] In later years a similar process unfolded in Serengeti, where park officials likewise burned bush to encourage a reversion to open grassland.[131]

Just as the rhetoric of eternalized nature sought to remove these environments from history, it also detached them from politics. The protection of 'tropical wilderness', when defined as a moral obligation for all civilized peoples, constituted an unassailable objective that transcended the structures of colonial power. Nature preservation—especially though not exclusively in colonial contexts—thus presented a fertile field for the application of 'apolitical expertise' impervious to questions about its social implications.[132] Although this technocratic tendency is often associated with the advent of development 'experts' after the Second World War, in the realm of nature conservation its roots reached back at least to the beginning of the twentieth century. As Hugo Conwentz remarked in 1909, a committee of international experts 'might, without impropriety, make suggestions or

---

[128] See Mark David Spence, *Dispossessing the Wilderness: Indian Removal, National Parks, and the Preservationist Ideal* (Oxford: Oxford University Press, 1999); Karl Jacoby, *Crimes against Nature: Squatters, Poachers, Thieves and the Hidden History of American Conservation* (Berkeley: University of California Press, 2001); Christopher Conte, 'Creating Wild Places from Domesticated Landscapes: The Internationalization of the American Wilderness Concept', in Michael Lewis (ed.), *American Wilderness: A New History* (Oxford: Oxford University Press, 2007), 223–42.

[129] Julian Huxley, *Memories* (London: Allen & Unwin, 1970), cited in Adams, *Against Extinction*, 105.

[130] Victor van Straelen, 'Les Parcs nationaux du Congo belge', in Aubréville et al., *Contribution*, 181–210, here 204–5.

[131] Holly T. Dublin, 'Dynamics of the Serengeti-Mara Woodlands: An Historical Perspective', *Forest and Conservation History*, vol. 35 no. 4 (Oct. 1991), 169–78; more generally, Roderick P. Neumann, *Imposing Wilderness: Struggles over Livelihood and Nature Preservation in Africa* (Berkeley: University of California Press, 1998).

[132] See Ferguson, *Anti-Politics Machine*; Mitchell, *Rule of Experts*; Cooper and Packard (eds), *International Development*; also Joseph Morgan Hodge, *Triumph of the Expert: Agrarian Doctrines of Development and the Legacies of British Colonialism* (Athens, Oh.: Ohio University Press, 2007).

recommendations to the States concerned, on such an uncontroversial matter as the preservation of natural monuments'.[133]

But if the expansion of hunting laws, nature reserves, and national parks was posited as a universal good beyond partisan interests, it nonetheless represented a radical assertion of power over land use. Ultimately it helped determine which areas were worth preserving and which were open to economic exploitation. At base, these measures were part of the rational allocation of land to different purposes, a quintessentially modern means of circumscribing a space outside of which the 'advance of civilization' could proceed apace. To this extent they functioned as nothing less than a means of delimiting sustainability itself.

This is why, for all the undeniably noble motives that underpinned them, such conservation efforts cannot be detached from the broader framework of colonial domination, whose hierarchical assumptions and exclusionist land-use practices they so clearly embodied.[134] It is also why they remained objects of resentment, avoidance, and sometimes resistance among the rural communities that were directly affected. In essence, the attempt to safeguard what Europeans defined as wilderness paradises or natural monuments represented an imperialist expropriation of tropical landscapes for metropolitan purposes. Indeed, the story of colonial conservation involved a twofold conquest of 'tropical nature'—both as a biophysical entity, and as an idea.

---

[133] Hugo Conwentz, *Care*, 185.

[134] Cf. Jepson and Whittaker, 'Histories', which argues against an 'orientalist', imperialist, and self-serving reading of the motivations behind nature protection in Indonesia.

8

Forests, Ecology, and Power in
the Tropical Colonies

The imperial surge of the late nineteenth and early twentieth centuries was a major historical watershed for the forests of the tropical world. The bulk of territory that came under European control during this period was forested. In colonial Asia even the most densely populated heartlands still had large hinterlands of jungle, and in sub-Saharan Africa the extent of high rainforest and sparsely populated bush seemed well-nigh limitless. These tropical woodlands were a hugely valuable resource on many different levels and for many different groups. For merchants and traders, the myriad species of durable hardwoods they contained—used for everything from fine furniture to shipbuilding—were a rich commercial prize. For colonial officials, railway builders, and naval commanders, they were an important strategic asset. For planters, the availability of 'vacant' forest land was the essential basis for the creation of commercial estates. For indigenous communities, the forests were a potential reservoir of arable land as well as a vital supply of building material, fuel, fodder, trade goods, and sometimes food.

Of course, human societies have been clearing, thinning, and altering forests since time immemorial. Tapping the wealth of forest ecosystems was a central part of social and economic life in the tropics long before the advent of European rule. But during the colonial era, the collective effects of commercial growth, transport innovations, and the expansion of agricultural settlement unleashed an unprecedented onslaught on the woodlands. Although the details are scant for some areas, the overall pattern is clear. Between 1850 and 1920 an estimated 152 million hectares of the world's tropical forests were converted to crops or grasslands, 94 million of them in sub-Saharan Africa, South Asia, and Southeast Asia, the main centres of colonial expansion.[1] Taken as a whole, the rate of forest loss during this period was roughly four to five times faster than over the previous century and a half. In the eyes of most colonialists, and for many indigenous cultivators too, the economic benefits of all this forest clearance were well worth the costs. But by the middle of the nineteenth century there was also a growing sense of apprehension about the consequences of large-scale deforestation for the long-term economic, social, and ecological welfare of Europe's tropical colonies. Over time, these concerns gave rise to a wide-ranging set of conservation practices that

---

[1] Michael Williams, *Deforesting the Earth: From Prehistory to Global Crisis* (Chicago: University of Chicago Press, 2003), 335.

exerted a profound influence on environmental management throughout much of the world.

Forests were a key focal point of colonial attempts to control conquered territories and profit from their natural resources. The establishment of centralized forestry systems formed a cornerstone of colonial state-building efforts, providing revenue and raw materials for economic growth while simultaneously extending the reach of state power. Foresters in Europe's tropical colonies created some of the most extensive apparatuses of resource management to be found anywhere in the world. In the process, the woodlands they administered became sites of a multidimensional set of transformations: ecological, social, and political. The interrelated acts of mapping and delineating forests, codifying them as state territory, and imposing new systems of forest management had profound consequences for their biotic makeup and for the communities that depended on them. Even the seemingly simple step of demarcating forest from agricultural land was fraught with difficulties. The boundaries were fuzzy, and any attempt to clarify them raised a host of thorny questions about customary ownership and access. Nor did such difficulties cease once a tract was reserved. Attempts to regulate forest usage were a constant source of tension, since they often deprived people of resources whose availability was regarded as a traditional right.

All of these changes were closely interlinked, and in order to understand them it is necessary to approach the forests not only as geographic or biological entities but also as social and political formations. Defined taxonomically according to vegetation, and classified legally as unused land sequestered by the state, the 'political forest'[2] became a space in which a complex set of interrelated agendas was simultaneously pursued. Economically, it enabled forest officials to construct a system of extraction and production designed to maximize revenues for colonial development. Politically, it comprised a realm in which governments could monitor and discipline subject populations that had long escaped close state control. Culturally, it furnished a sphere in which 'scientific' forestry—above all the achievement of a 'maximum sustained yield' of valuable timber—could assert its superiority over the supposedly irrational and wasteful practices of indigenous users. And ecologically, it enabled conservation-minded officials to protect areas of woodland that were deemed to be under threat or essential for local food and water supplies.

As a result, historians have often viewed colonial forestry regimes as instruments of imperial authority and resource exploitation. Undoubtedly they were a powerful tool for extracting value from conquered lands. But even as we recognize this, it is important not to overstate the case or to conjure up images of a pre-colonial golden age of sustainable forest use.[3] As we will see, many of the principles that guided

---

[2] Nancy Lee Peluso and Peter Vandergeest, 'Genealogies of the Political Forest and Customary Rights in Indonesia, Malaysia, and Thailand', *Journal of Asian Studies*, vol. 60 no. 3 (Aug. 2001), 761–812.

[3] These debates have been most intense with respect to India, where colonial forestry has commonly been portrayed as fundamentally repressive, extractive, and ecologically disruptive; most seminally in Gadgil and Guha, *Fissured Land*. More recent studies have offered a convincing corrective: e.g. S. Ravi

colonial forest policies were hardly new, but rather drew on European precedents and occasionally on pre-colonial arrangements. By and large their aim was not to consume the forest resource but rather to ensure its perpetual exploitability by conserving it over the long term. Nor were forestry institutions unchanging or homogeneous in their attitudes towards indigenous peoples, whose rights to forest resources were the subject of considerable debate. In purely practical terms, the limits of state surveillance and the local antagonisms that it could arouse meant that the actual ability of foresters to enforce regulations varied greatly from place to place. Colonial forestry systems thus had diverse origins and effects, and this diversity resists blanket categorization as a callous instrument of extraction.

All the same, by the early decades of the twentieth century colonial forest departments governed vast expanses of territory throughout the tropical world, and had a major impact on the landscape, the people who lived there, and the evolution of resource conservation more generally. Given the complexity of this story and the rich historical literature it has produced, this chapter can only outline some of the main issues and developments. It does so in three steps: first, by examining the rise of state forestry regimes in South and Southeast Asia, where many of the key precedents were set; second, by investigating the chief social and ecological consequences they generated; and third, by tracing the spread of these forestry regimes to other parts of the colonial world, above all in Africa.

FORESTRY, CONSERVATION, AND THE STATE IN COLONIAL ASIA

In the latter half of the nineteenth century the colonies of South and Southeast Asia still boasted huge expanses of woodland that included some of the richest and most biodiverse forests in the entire world. In 1880, the Indian subcontinent as a whole (India, Bangladesh, and Sri Lanka) contained just under 110 million hectares of forest, forested wetlands, and interrupted woods, an area roughly equivalent to the entire area under cultivation. In the more sparsely populated colonies of mainland Southeast Asia the ratio of forest to cropland was much higher (150.3 million to 8 million hectares), and in insular Southeast Asia it was higher still (215.4 million to 8.1 million hectares).[4] Naturally, these broad geographical categories mask some stark local differences. Whereas the Gangetic plain, Java, and Bali had already lost most of their forests to agriculture by the 1880s, there were still enormous tracts

---

Rajan, *Modernizing Nature: Forestry and Imperial Eco-development 1800–1950* (Oxford: Clarendon, 2006); Mahesh Rangarajan, *Fencing the Forest: Conservation and Ecological Change in India's Central Provinces, 1860–1914* (New Delhi: Oxford University Press, 1996); K. Sivaramakrishnan, *Modern Forests: Statemaking and Environmental Change in Colonial Eastern India* (Stanford, Calif.: Stanford University Press, 1999); K. Sivaramakrishnan, 'Histories of Colonialism and Forestry in India', in Paolo Squatriti (ed.), *Nature's Past: The Environment and Human History* (Ann Arbor: University of Michigan Press, 2007), 103–44.

    [4] John F. Richards and Elizabeth P. Flint, 'A Century of Land-Use Change in South and Southeast Asia', in Virginia H. Dale (ed.), *Effects of Land-Use Change on Atmospheric CO_2 Concentrations: South and Southeast Asia as a Case Study* (New York: Springer, 1994), 15–63, esp. 20, 34, 36.

of woodland in India's upland provinces. In the 'outer isles' of the East Indies (Sumatra, Kalimantan, Sulawesi) there were many areas that scarcely felt the impact of colonial forest policies until well after the First World War. Writing about Peninsular Malaya in 1907, George Maxwell (later Chief Secretary of the Federated Malay States) remarked that 'the inhabited area, every yard of which has been won from, and hacked out of, the forest, is infinitesimal in comparison with the extent of the forest that remains untouched'.[5]

Yet far from being genuinely 'untouched', most of the forests of colonial Asia had, to varying degrees, been shaped by human hand long before Europeans arrived. The greatest impacts arose from the expansion of indigenous agriculture, and especially the widespread practice of burning to clear land for temporary rice cultivation or grazing. Itinerant farmers regularly moved from place to place as the soils of their clearings were depleted, usually every one to three years depending on the quality of the land. All but the very largest trees were felled and burned in the process. Once abandoned, the plots quickly reverted to young regrowth, and ideally were left to recover for at least fifteen years before being cleared and cultivated once again. Adequate intervals were not always observed, and wherever fallow periods were too short, the land gradually degraded and was frequently overtaken by pernicious *lalang* grass. Even where clearing cycles were long enough to enable the secondary forest to regenerate, the resulting woodlands were different from—and generally less biodiverse than—'primary' forest. The spread of sedentary farming of course entailed more radical changes to vegetation cover. By the late nineteenth century it had already resulted in the enduring loss of forest cover across large areas of the well-watered lowlands. Although sedentary farming required far less land per person than shifting cultivation, the overall cultivated surface area continued to grow, claiming around 25 million hectares of forest from 1880 to 1920, plus another 30 million hectares 1920–50.[6]

Aside from subsistence farming, commercial agriculture and the trade in forest products also ate away at the woodlands for many centuries. The production of pepper and other spices for Chinese and Indian markets claimed large areas of forest in Southeast Asia, and often left behind a degraded landscape of *lalang* grass, for instance in the Aceh province of northern Sumatra.[7] Even in the most remote areas of the Indonesian archipelago, the extraction of aromatic woods was an important economic activity long before colonial conquest. Contrary to popular clichés of ecological innocence, the supposedly isolated peoples of the Bornean interior had in fact engaged in long-distance trade for centuries, extracting spices, rattans, gums, and resins while simultaneously meeting their subsistence needs through relatively sustainable itinerant cultivation systems.[8] Nor was pre-colonial

---

[5] Maxwell, *Malay Forests*, 2–3.   [6] Richards and Flint, 'Century', 17.

[7] Anthony Reid, 'Humans and Forests in Pre-colonial Southeast Asia', *Environment and History*, vol. 1 no. 1 (Feb. 1995), 93–110.

[8] Bernard Sellato, 'Forests for Food, Forests for Trade—Between Sustainability and Economic Extractivism; The Economic Pragmatism of Traditional Peoples and the Trade History of Northern Kalimantan', in Reed Wadley (ed.), *Histories of the Borneo Environment* (Leiden: KITLV, 1995), 61–86; Cristina Eghenter, 'Histories of Conservation or Exploitation? Case Studies from the Interior of Indonesian Borneo', in Wadley (ed.), *Histories*, 87–107; Dove, *Banana Tree*.

forest use as equitable as is sometimes assumed. In India, access to forest land for hunting or farming was often jealously guarded by local rulers or village headmen, and farmers' rights to certain forest resources (fuel, construction wood, green fodder) generally did not extend to the 'tribal' groups that practised shifting cultivation in the uplands.[9]

In many respects, then, the advent of European rule did not mark the neat ecological caesura that some accounts have suggested. As recent scholarship has shown, it is simply inappropriate to demarcate a long pre-colonial era of harmony between human needs and forests from a subsequent period of rapid depletion and social exclusion.[10] But this does not mean that colonial conquest, and above all the intensification of resource use that accompanied it, did not bring major changes for the forests of South and Southeast Asia, especially for woodlands near the key centres of population and commercial activity or those that contained exceptionally rich and accessible stands of hardwood. Throughout the nineteenth century a growing number of loggers and cultivators literally made inroads into forests that had previously been either too remote or too expensive to reach. In this context, the principal aim of colonial governments was not so much to encourage the exploitation of the woodlands as to regulate and control it.

The earliest attempts to do so were triggered by fears about the depletion of teak, whose exceptional suitability for shipbuilding (owing to its oiliness and resistance to rot and warping) made it a valuable strategic resource for the navies of the imperial powers. As early as 1805 the diminution of teak supplies along the Malabar Coast prompted the East India Company to reserve all teak stands for its own exclusive use.[11] After the first Anglo-Burmese war of 1824–6 there was a sudden rush of clear-cutting in coastal Tenasserim (the southernmost region of Burma), which observers feared would 'lead in a short time to the extermination of all the available teak forests'.[12] By 1841 the colonial government was sufficiently concerned to appoint a superintendent for the district's forests, but the failure to overturn the hitherto laissez-faire approach to the wood trade undermined protective measures.[13] After the Second Anglo-Burmese War of 1852, when the British annexed the even richer teak forests of Pegu, local officials were determined to protect them from the same fate. The establishment of the Burma Forest Department in 1856, and the appointment of the German botanist Dietrich Brandis as its superintendent, effectively marked the inauguration of 'scientific forestry' in the British Empire.[14]

---

[9] Mahesh Rangarajan, 'Imperial Agendas and India's Forests: The Early History of Indian Forests, 1800–1878', *Indian Economic and Social History Review*, vol. 21 (1994), 147–67.

[10] A point emphasized by Williams, *Deforesting*, 335–6, 340–2; also Rangarajan, 'Environmental Histories', 232–7; cf. Gadjil and Guha, *Fissured Land*.

[11] Grove, *Green Imperialism*, 391–2.

[12] J. W. Helfer to Government of Bengal: E. P. Stebbing, *The Forests of India*, vol. 1 (London: Bodley Head, 1922), 151.

[13] Raymond L. Bryant, *The Political Ecology of Forestry in Burma 1824–1994* (London: Hurst & Co., 1997), 32–4.

[14] Bryant, *Political Ecology*, 36–42; Michael Adas, 'Colonization, Commercial Agriculture, and the Destruction of the Deltaic Rainforests of British Burma in the Late Nineteenth Century', in Richard P. Tucker and J. F. Richards (eds), *Global Deforestation and the Nineteenth-Century World Economy* (Durham, NC: Duke University Press, 1983), 95–110, here 96–7.

Ten years later, Brandis became the first inspector-general of India's forests, and the system that he helped create on the subcontinent was admired and eventually replicated in many other parts of the world, including the United States.[15] In the meantime, Dutch authorities in the East Indies were moving in a similar direction. In the 1860s, as the demand for teak gradually exhausted Java's coastal forests, the upland teak stands of central and eastern Java became the hub of a forest administration system remarkably similar to the one in India.[16] Just as in Burma, what originally began as a set of controls on the Javanese teak trade gradually evolved into a territorial system of forest reserves that governed millions of hectares of woodland across the East Indies.

The expansion of forest administration in the 1850s and 1860s was closely related to the advent of railway building in the region. From mid-century onward the growing appetite for cross-ties, construction timber, and locomotive fuel placed a huge strain on local wood supplies, and especially on certain tree species. In India, each mile (1.61 km) of track required between 1,760 and 2,000 cross-ties, which had to be replaced every thirteen to fourteen years in the case of hardwoods (e.g. teak, sal, or deodar) and roughly every five years for softer woods. By the 1870s the most desirable species were already in short supply, and as railway construction peaked around the turn of the century it was estimated that nearly 50,000 hectares of forest were destroyed each year for railway ties alone. Added to this was the demand for wood-fuel for the locomotives, whose effects, though clearly substantial, are more difficult to calculate. For what it is worth, estimates suggested that by 1910 the needs of India's railways required as much as 427,000 hectares of reserved forest (assuming a seventeen-year production cycle) to cover demand on a sustainable basis.[17]

If the direct effects of railway construction on the forests were thus considerable, the indirect effects were even greater. The huge expansion of transportation capacity and the associated decline in carrying costs gave a powerful boost to commercial agriculture, and thus to the large-scale clearance of scrub or woodland. In long-established farming regions, the availability of cheap and efficient rail transport often pushed cultivation onto more marginal lands as farmers devoted more area to export crops such as cotton, indigo, or sugar. In more remote localities, it often caused the rapid disappearance of high forest cover, for instance in the tea-growing centres of Assam, Kerala, or upland Sri Lanka.[18] Better transport connections also

[15] On the global impact of the Indian model, see Gregory Barton, *Empire Forestry and the Origins of Environmentalism* (Cambridge: Cambridge University Press, 2002).

[16] Nancy Lee Peluso, *Rich Forests, Poor People: Resource Control and Resistance in Java* (Berkeley: University of California Press, 1992), 48–55; Peter Boomgaard, 'Forest Management and Exploitation in Colonial Java, 1677–1879', *Forest and Conservation History*, vol. 36 (1992), 4–14.

[17] Williams, *Deforesting*, 358–60.

[18] Michelle B. McAlpin, 'Railroads, Prices, and Peasant Rationality: India, 1860–1900', *Journal of Economic History*, vol. 34 (1974), 662–84; Richards and McAlpin, 'Cotton Cultivating'; Richard P. Tucker, 'The Depletion of Indian Forests under British Imperialism: Planters, Foresters, and Peasants in Assam and Kerala', in Worster (ed.), *Ends*, 118–41; Jayeeta Sharma, 'Making Garden, Erasing Jungle: The Tea Enterprise in Colonial Assam', in Kumar, Damodaran, and D'Souza (eds), *Environmental Encounters*, 119–41; Nihal Karunaratna, *Forest Conservation in Sri Lanka from British Colonial Times, 1818–1912* (Colombo: Trumpet, 1987).

encouraged loggers to move into previously inaccessible areas such as the sub-montane forests of the western Himalayas or the highlands of eastern Java, where the Dutch forest service built around 1,000 kilometres of track by the First World War.[19] In the meantime, the railways also extended the resource-reach of towns and cities. Because urban areas still relied heavily on wood for fuel and construction needs, forests and scrublands were rapidly denuded all along the track lines. All in all, the railways generated a kind of self-reinforcing dynamic of forest depletion. The greater the demand for commercial crops or timber, the stronger the incentive to construct railways into hitherto remote regions; and the larger the railway network became, the easier it was to transport commercial crops, timber, and fuel to market, all of which came at the expense of forest cover.

Important though they were, the railways were more a catalyst than a root cause of colonial forest conservation. Long before the 1850s–1860s there were already urgent calls to counter the rising pace of woodland clearance in the colonies, especially in India. To understand the nature of these concerns and why they arose when they did, we must look beyond the question of export revenues and commercially valuable species to consider how these economic impulses interacted with a broader set of anxieties about the effects of forest loss on climate, rainfall, run-off, and food security, which ultimately touched on the very political and social stability of colonial rule.

By the middle of the eighteenth century, a small number of scientists working in the British, Dutch, and French maritime empires (especially on Mauritius, St Helena, and in the eastern Caribbean) became convinced that the destruction of tropical island forests by logging and farm clearance was directly linked to a decline in precipitation, which posed a serious threat to agricultural production and public health. As European states extended their power in the nineteenth century, this 'desiccation-ist' discourse shaped responses to deforestation in the continental empires of Asia and Africa.[20] In India in particular, such ideas became bound up with concerns about food and water shortages, especially after a series of drought-related famines in the late 1830s. By the 1840s desiccation theory formed the scientific basis for an increasingly influential campaign to conserve India's forests. Championed by a network of medical officers in the East India Company—Hugh Cleghorn, Alexander Gibson, John McClelland—it underpinned the establishment of the first forest departments in the Bombay (1847) and Madras (1855) Presidencies.[21] By the 1860s the concept of anthropogenic desiccation was fairly widespread within colonial officialdom, and from the 1870s onwards it was powerfully reinforced by a series of extreme El Niño droughts and devastating famines in southern Asia.[22]

---

[19] Peluso, *Rich Forests*, 49–50.

[20] Generally, Grove, *Green Imperialism*; Richard H. Grove, 'Conserving Eden: The (European) East India Companies and their Environmental Policies on St. Helena, Mauritius and in Western India, 1660 to 1854', *Comparative Studies in Society and History*, vol. 36 no. 3 (1993), 318–51.

[21] Grove, *Green Imperialism*, 380–473; Rangarajan, 'Imperial Agendas'; Pallavi Das, 'Hugh Cleghorn and Forest Conservancy in India', *Environment and History*, vol. 11 no. 1 (Feb. 2005), 55–82.

[22] Grove, 'Historical Review', 160–6.

Together, this jumble of ecological, agricultural, and climatic concerns raised unsettling questions about the long-term viability of colonial economies in the face of resource exhaustion and environmental degradation. The rapid loss of forest cover threatened not only to diminish the productivity of the land, but also to increase the scope for social unrest. Fears about the political and security implications of food or water shortages were especially acute after the 1857 uprising in India, which made the extension of the state's presence into remote forest areas all the more attractive to the colonial government.[23] The desire to control the activities of potentially 'unruly' subject populations was one of the main reasons why colonial officials were so eager to regulate the movements of itinerant groups living on the forested fringes of agrarian society. Not only was it difficult to police such groups or harness their labour for the colonial economy, most officials also regarded their land-use practices as wasteful and destructive.[24] The desire to protect the forests from overexploitation was only one of many motives behind the introduction of reserves and conservation measures. State forest management was not only about regulating resource use; it was also a powerful means of social control that penetrated previously obscure realms of colonial society and sought to curtail behaviours that were deemed profligate or unproductive.

Consequently, the extent to which colonial forestry arose from a nascent environmentalist consciousness, as opposed to more statist concerns about revenue and security, has been interpreted quite differently. Whereas some historians have argued for the primacy of *raison d'état* and commercial profitability, others have emphasized the attempt to introduce management systems that were, or at least aimed to be, sustainable over the long term and that were animated by a sense of moral duty to protect rainfall, soils, food, and water supplies.[25] Over the past two decades scholars have shown how such broadly conceived conservationist impulses played an important role in debates about deforestation in the tropical colonies, and eventually influenced the emergence of 'environmentalist' sensibilities more generally.[26] What's more, such impulses were by no means confined to India, but were evident throughout the region. In the East Indies, climate stability and the prevention of erosion and excess run-off were important stimuli for forest conservation, especially on mountain slopes.[27] In Indochina too, some of the earliest

---

[23] Grove, 'Historical Review', 165; Rangarajan, 'Environmental Histories', 236.

[24] Jacques Pouchepadass, 'British Attitudes towards Shifting Cultivation in Colonial South India: A Case Study of South Canara District 1800–1920', in Arnold and Guha (eds), *Nature, Culture, Imperialism*, 123–51, here 134–7, 149; Raymond Bryant, 'Shifting the Cultivator: The Politics of Teak Regeneration in Colonial Burma', *Modern Asian Studies*, vol. 27 (1994), 225–50; Mathieu Guérin, *Paysans de la forêt à l'époque coloniale: la pacification des aborigènes des hautes terres du Cambodge, 1863–1940* (Caen: Association d'histoire des sociétés rurales, 2008); Ajay Pratap, *The Hoe and the Axe: An Ethnohistory of Shifting Cultivation in Eastern India* (Delhi: Oxford University Press, 2000).

[25] For the former view, Gadjil and Guha, *Fissured Land*, esp. 119–59; for the latter, Grove, *Green Imperialism*, 399–462.

[26] Apart from Grove, *Green Imperialism*, see esp. Barton, *Empire Forestry*, who, in contrast to Grove, emphasizes the importance of deforestation in North America and Europe, and in particular the work of George Perkins Marsh, in the rise of environmental thought.

[27] Edelman, *Studiën*, 283–4; Peluso, *Rich Forests*, 44–55; Boomgaard, 'Forest Management'.

advocates of a centralized forest service highlighted the climatic and hydrological benefits of forest cover.[28]

Whatever the precise admixture of ideas and motives, the central point is that colonial forest management reflected a closely interlocking set of ecological, economic, and political arguments.[29] As pressure on the woodlands grew, governments were convinced that they could better protect and more efficiently utilize the forests by corralling subject populations into circumscribed areas and setting aside state-owned reserves for the sustainable production of timber under 'scientific' management.

In many respects, this marked a new departure for the forests of the tropics. Although state woodland management per se was not uncommon in pre-colonial societies, the colonial-era systems were nonetheless distinctive with regard to their rationale, their practices, and their sheer scale. Royal monopolies on particular tree species, or the reservation of forested tracts for elite hunting, had deep roots in South and Southeast Asia, but by and large such interventions were limited in scope. The extraction of timber, fuel, and other products was hitherto governed by local custom rather than a desire to maximize yields. Pre-colonial regulations rarely involved complete, perpetual control over entire tracts of territory—the essence of the modern forest reserve—but instead focused on supervising the trade in forest products. Such territorial controls as were in place (e.g. princely hunting grounds or protected areas for elephants) were in any event dwarfed by the forest reserves that followed.[30]

But if colonial administration brought significant changes for tropical forests, it also reflected important continuities in European woodland management.[31] Ever since the eighteenth century, 'scientific' forestry had been an integral part of state-building efforts across much of Europe, stimulated not least by cameralist doctrines of government-centred social and economic modernization. As European power spread, it is perhaps unsurprising that some of the key precepts of this emerging forestry regime—centralized control, maximum sustained yields, suppression of unauthorized use—were exported to overseas colonies.

The German concept of the *Hochwald*, or high forest, was crucial. It was in the German-speaking states of central Europe, bereft of overseas colonies and largely reliant on their own wood resources, that foresters first developed systems of long-term rotation designed to maximize yields of timber and firewood, usually through

---

[28] J. Prades, *Déboisement—incendies—rays: préservation et reconstitution de la forêt* (Hanoi: Imprimerie Tonkinoise, 1921), 1–2; Marlène Buchy, 'Histoire forestière de l'Indochine (1850–1954)—perspectives de recherche', *Revue française d'histoire d'outre-mer*, no. 299 (1993), 219–50, here 223; Mark Cleary, 'Managing the Forest in Colonial Indochina c.1900–1940', *Modern Asian Studies*, vol. 39 no. 2 (May 2005), 257–83, here 270–1.

[29] As convincingly argued by Rajan, *Modernizing Nature*, 61–74.

[30] Chetan Singh, 'Forests, Pastoralists and Agrarian Society in Mughal India', in Arnold and Guha (eds), *Nature, Culture, Imperialism*, 21–48; Richards, *Unending Frontier*, 25–38; Peluso and Vandergeest, 'Genealogies', 787.

[31] As argued especially by Rajan, *Modernizing Nature*, 79–96.

the creation of fast-growing softwood monocultures.[32] Unlike the traditional practices of communal forests, which were often managed by locals on short coppicing patterns intended to meet their own fuel needs, the 'high' production forest demanded systematic supervision over several decades, including elaborate felling cycles, detailed surveying, and strict planting schedules (the so-called 'working plan'). By the end of the eighteenth century the core tenets of scientific silviculture had begun to spread from central Europe to other areas, above all France, whose École Nationale des Eaux et Forêts, established at Nancy in 1824, was directed by a series of German-trained foresters.

This distinctive brand of forest management had important consequences for European woodlands, on both sides of the Rhine. The long rotation cycles that were required to grow tall timber stands strongly encouraged a system of permanent tenure, which usually meant state control and the spatial consolidation of forested tracts. It also generally entailed a much clearer demarcation of forests from agricultural or pastoral land, which in turn brought far-reaching ecological changes through the replacement of mixed tree cover (a hallmark of multi-use woodlands) by monocultures of the most commercially valuable species. All of these alterations also had a major impact on rural communities. In many areas the gazetting and transformation of forests in Europe bred acute social resentment by excluding farmers from local woodlands, depriving them of age-old foraging or gathering rights, and even blaming them for forest degradation in the first place.[33] As these management practices moved to the colonies, such antagonisms were a harbinger of things to come.

Broadly speaking, it is fair to say that the forestry systems of the colonial world, as well as the social conflicts they caused, echoed earlier patterns of land enclosure and resource conservation in Europe.[34] Many of the basic concepts, practices, and effects of imperial forest management were, in other words, not uniquely 'colonial'. But despite all the continuities with European traditions of state forestry, nor were they simply a rerun of previous developments there. Given the peculiar character of colonial governance and the very different modes of land use in many tropical colonies—especially the pervasiveness of itinerant agriculture and communal rights of access—the introduction of state-based forest management faced a rather different set of opportunities and challenges than in Europe.

---

[32] Joachim Radkau, 'Das hölzerne Zeitalter und der deutsche Sonderweg in der Forsttechnik', in Ulrich Troitzsch (ed.), *Nützliche Künste. Kultur- und Sozialgeschichte der Technik im 18. Jahrhundert* (Münster: Waxmann, 1999), 97–118; Joachim Radkau, 'Holzverknappung und Krisenbewusstsein im 18. Jahrhundert', *Geschichte und Gesellschaft*, vol. 9 (1983), 513–43; more generally Franz Heske, *German Forestry* (New Haven: Yale University Press, 1938).

[33] On France, see Tamara L. Whited, *Forests and Peasant Politics in Modern France* (New Haven: Yale University Press, 2000), esp. chs 2, 3 on peasant revolts; Louis Badré, *Histoire de la forêt française* (Paris: Arthaud, 1983); Andrée Corvol, *L'Homme aux bois: histoire des relations de l'homme et de la forêt (XVIIe–XXe siècle)* (Paris: Fayard, 1987); Andrée Corvol, *Forêt et montagne* (Paris: Harmattan, 2015); Peter Sahlins, *Forest Rites: The War of the Demoiselles in Nineteenth-Century France* (Cambridge, Mass.: Harvard University Press, 1994).

[34] Rajan, *Modernizing Nature*, 102–7; also noted in Ramachandra Guha, *The Unquiet Woods: Ecological Change and Peasant Resistance in the Himalaya* (Delhi: Oxford University Press, 1989), 187–90.

All across South and Southeast Asia, the first issue to address was which forests belonged to the state. One of the implicit assumptions of colonial sovereignty was that the government maintained jurisdiction over any unused or unalienated land. But colonial administrations were by no means agreed on how to define these categories, and nor was there a consensus on the extent to which they should be justified on the basis of customary laws or rights of tenure.[35] In India, the Forest Act of 1865—the first attempt to codify state control over the forests of the subcontinent—sparked a protracted debate among state officials. One group, led by the senior civil servant B. H. Baden-Powell, argued for total state control over all unalienated forest land. This 'annexationist' position was based on a wilfully selective reading of Indian precedents, in particular the idea that all forest rights had traditionally been the formal prerogative of the territorial sovereign, and that local communities therefore had no rights that were not officially and explicitly granted. To reinforce this argument, annexationists also continually suggested that 'native' land-use practices posed the principal threat to the forests. Directly opposed to this view was a 'populist' position championed above all by officials in the Madras Presidency, who rejected Powell's fixation on written sanction and who regarded customary grazing, collecting, and hunting practices as tantamount to formal property rights. They contended that the denial of such rights was both unjust and unwise since it would exacerbate rural poverty and therefore increase the potential for social unrest. Between these two poles, pragmatists such as Dietrich Brandis argued for strict state control over forests of vital strategic or climatic importance, while at the same time leaving other woodlands under customary communal rights.[36]

Once the dust finally settled, it was the annexationist view that prevailed. The Indian Forests Act of 1878, which subsequently served as a legislative reference point throughout the British Empire, established three basic categories of woodland: reserved forests, which were placed under close state control and were managed for long-term exploitation; protected forests, which allowed limited rights for grazing and collecting various forest products; and village forests where customary access rights were generally maintained (but which were relatively rare compared to the other two categories). By 1900 over one-fifth of India's entire land surface was governed as state forest, including no less than 211,000 square kilometres of reserves.[37]

These vast forest reservations not only furnished an ideal arena for 'scientific' management, they also effectively dispossessed rural populations across large parts of India. In addition, they set a portentous precedent for other British colonies. The 1881 Burma Forest Act was even more restrictive than the 1878 Indian law on

[35] See generally Peluso and Vandergeest, 'Genealogies', 771–9.

[36] Ramachandra Guha, 'An Early Environmental Debate: The Making of the 1878 Forest Act', *Indian Economic and Social History Review*, vol. 27 (1990), 65–84; Rangarajan, 'Imperial Agendas'; Gadgil and Guha, *Fissured Land*, 124–32.

[37] Figures from Rangarajan, 'Environmental Histories', 237; Ramachandra Guha and Madhav Gadgil, 'State Forestry and Social Conflict in British India', *Past & Present*, no. 123 (May 1989), 141–77, here 147.

which it was modelled. It created only one class of reserved forests and made no explicit provision for popular access outside their boundaries, which, among other things, facilitated the subsequent expansion of the reserves.[38] In Malaya, where the advocates of village rights quickly lost out to the annexationists, the coalescence of federal forest legislation in 1907 largely followed the stringent Burmese example.[39] The most striking exception was Madras, a populous agrarian region with well-established communal forest rights, whose relatively permissive 1882 legislation was not emulated elsewhere.[40]

In all of these regions the delineation of 'forests' was not so much about defining a botanical entity—indeed, many forested areas were explicitly slated for agricultural expansion—as about regulating land use within specific boundaries. This 'territorialization' of forest control was by no means confined to British-ruled parts of Asia. On Java, a succession of German-inspired laws starting in 1865 placed entire regions under direct state management. Most of the reserved forests encompassed areas suitable for teak production, though certain 'wild woods' were also managed for the protection of vulnerable watersheds. Within reserve boundaries, customary rights of access were abrogated or severely curtailed to make way for elaborate production systems that effectively turned the island's upland forests into teak plantations. The whole process continued over the following decades, and by the 1920s a carefully policed network of state forests covered roughly one-quarter of Java's surface.[41] By the late nineteenth century similar changes were under way in Indochina, where French authorities largely followed the Dutch and British examples. Although state forest services were not formally centralized until 1901–3, by 1939 reserves covered some 2.25 million hectares in Indochina.[42] Even Siam, which maintained formal independence from colonial rule, operated a comparable system that was managed by British foresters.[43]

In short, the scientific management of state-owned forest reserves became a cornerstone of land-use policy throughout colonial Asia. In British, Dutch, and French territories alike, these forestry regimes were the most visible manifestation of an increasingly influential ideology of state-based conservation and efficient resource use. Yet despite the shared aims of such systems, we should not overlook the many variations on the ground. For all the commonalities that linked the trans-imperial forestry network together, in practice the management of tropical woodlands was shaped by a whole raft of local particularities: the relative concentration and accessibility of commercially valuable timber, the productivity of

---

[38] Bryant, *Political Ecology*, 56–61.   [39] Kathirithamby-Wells, *Nature*, 74–6.
[40] Berthold Ribbentrop, *Forestry in British India* (Calcutta: GPO, 1900), 112–13; Dietrich Brandis, *Suggestions Regarding Forest Administration in the Madras Presidency* (Madras: Government Press, 1883), 20–2.
[41] Peluso, *Rich Forests*, 50–5, 76–7; Peluso and Vandergeest, 'Genealogies', 789–90.
[42] Frédéric Thomas, *Histoire du régime et des services forestiers français en Indochine de 1862 à 1945* (Hanoi: Thé Giói, 1999), 41–146; Buchy, 'Histoire forestière', 223–5; Pierre Gourou, *L'Utilisation du sol en Indochine Française* (Paris: Hartmann, 1940), 381–96.
[43] David Feeny, 'Agricultural Expansion and Forest Depletion in Thailand, 1900–1975', in John F. Richards and Richard P. Tucker (eds), *World Deforestation in the Twentieth Century* (Durham, NC: Duke University Press, 1988), 112–43.

different soils and climates, the needs and scope of domestic industry and trade, as well as the strength of local people's claims to timber, fuel, and other forest products. Moreover, the actual capacity of forestry departments to enforce regulations and control extraction varied enormously from one place to another.[44]

Surveying the literature on colonial forestry, dominated as it is by studies on India and to a lesser extent Java, it is easy to forget how feeble colonial power was throughout much of the region. The differences were clearly reflected in the size of the various forestry departments. India's Forest Service was gargantuan: in 1916 it numbered well over 14,000 staff, including 468 senior officers, 1,600 rangers, 2,000 foresters, and 10,500 forest guards (and these figures mirrored a significant wartime loss of staff to other duties).[45] The only comparable department was on Java, whose 5,969 employees (in 1929) dwarfed all the other forestry services of Southeast Asia combined. Its closest rival, the Federated Malay States, had 580 staff.[46] Indochina had only 117 European officers in 1934, and the shortage of trained personnel was a perennial source of complaint.[47] Elsewhere the forest departments were no more than skeletal. Sarawak had a total of eighty-one staff in 1929, and Dutch Borneo only eighteen. These enormous differences in management capacity are even starker when surface area is factored in. Whereas Java's forest service had one member of staff for every 4 km² of reserved forest, the ratio in Malaya was 1:34 km² and for Borneo 1:200 km².[48] Amidst the vast jungles of Kalimantan the task of simply surveying the forests, let alone managing them, was a huge challenge. In Sarawak the Brooke administration had little choice but to content itself with regulating the trade in certain tree species and non-timber forest products rather than trying to police the forest itself, and pragmatically allowed the bulk of land to be administered by community-based systems. On Borneo, the inability of Dutch colonial authorities to control land use was reflected in the far greater importance attached to *adat*, or customary law, than on Java.[49]

In these peripheries of Europe's Asian empire, the actual impact of colonial forest legislation on the ground diverged little from pre-colonial norms, and created far less scope for social grievance than in the epicentres of colonial power and trade. By contrast, across large parts of India and Java the advent of forest reserves and strict production schedules greatly reduced the accessibility and biodiversity of the woodlands, largely to the detriment of local users. For millions of rural people, the regulations laid down by the forest departments were—alongside the exactions of the tax collector—the primary manifestation of the colonial state at large. By the closing decades of the nineteenth century, state forest management was a spearhead

---

[44] For this counter-perspective, see esp. Peter Vandergeest and Nancy Lee Peluso, 'Empires of Forestry: Professional Forestry and State Power in Southeast Asia', Parts 1 and 2, *Environment and History*, vol. 12 (2006), 31–64, 359–93.

[45] R. S. Troup, *The Work of the Forest Department in India* (Calcutta: Superintendent Government Printing, 1917), 9–10.

[46] Figures for Java and Malaysia from Peluso and Vandergeest, 'Genealogies', 772; Vandergeest and Peluso, 'Empires', Part 1, 36.

[47] Buchy, 'Histoire forestière', 226.   [48] Peluso and Vandergeest, 'Genealogies', 772.

[49] Amarjit Kaur, 'A History of Forestry in Sarawak', *Modern Asian Studies*, vol. 32 no. 1 (1998), 117–47, here 126–30; Peluso and Vandergeest, 'Genealogies', 774–7.

of centralized authority that penetrated rural life and land use more deeply than ever before.

COLONIAL FORESTS: CONFLICTS
AND CONSEQUENCES

One of the fundamental features of most colonial forestry regimes was the strict demarcation of forests from agricultural land. At one level such spatial distinction was little more than an administrative device, a bureaucratic means of establishing different taxation levels and user rights much like any other form of land zoning. But at another level it also represented a deliberate attempt to separate forested land from indigenous people and their livestock. After all, the spread of cultivation was the single greatest cause of deforestation in most colonies. Between 1880 and 1920 it accounted for around two-thirds of all woodland loss in South and Southeast Asia as a whole, driven mainly by the rapid growth in human (+87 million) and livestock (+50 million) numbers.[50] By the late nineteenth century even the most vociferous advocates of agricultural development agreed on the need for strict controls on forest usage, especially wherever the human population was expanding. John Augustus Voelcker, author of an influential 1893 report on Indian agriculture, was convinced that 'the people, left to themselves, have never been able to manage forests properly', and that colonial forestry had rescued the woodlands 'which, if left to the people, would have been ruthlessly destroyed'.[51]

But the problem with any clear legal distinction between agricultural and forest land was that it often clashed with realities on the ground. Because rural communities commonly relied on woodlands for many of their basic needs, any neat separation between these categories was bound to contravene long-established land-use practices.

The kinds of tensions that resulted were plainly apparent in India, where the 1878 Forest Act disrupted rural life in multiple ways. Perhaps the biggest source of resentment was the reduction of access to wooded forage land, which was an important part of the Indian livestock economy. Many farmers had long grazed their animals in nearby woodlands. As soon as an area was gazetted, however, the priority of state foresters was tree regeneration rather than forage, which meant preventing livestock from devouring seedlings or indeed anything else. Popular access to timber and fuel supplies was also squeezed. The inaccessibility of firewood was doubly problematic for farming communities since it deprived them not only of fuel but also of much-needed manure for their fields. By the 1880s the burning of cow dung was becoming more and more common wherever fuel-wood was in short supply. As state officials clearly recognized, 'the supply of wood to serve as fuel forms one of the most important factors in maintaining the fertility of the soil, or, in other words, the prosperity of agriculture'.[52] Access to a whole range of other woodland resources

---

[50] Richards and Flint, 'Century', 20, 34, 36.　　　[51] Voelcker, *Report*, 135.
[52] Voelcker, *Report*, 137.

was likewise curtailed by the new forest regulations, and posed a particular hardship for poor tenants and sharecroppers who had previously supplemented their incomes through the sale of fuel, fodder, and forest products. Throughout India, rural people increasingly had to pay for forest products that had once been freely available. In this sense, the process of forest reservation was part of the broader commercialization of natural resources that pushed people into the cash economy and exposed them more directly to the vagaries of markets (see Chapter 1).[53]

The adverse social consequences of India's forest laws were broadly paralleled in other colonies. Javanese peasants also found their access rights truncated as the government restricted them to land earmarked solely for agricultural use. Collecting wood or other items within the reserves required a permit from the forest police, which most farmers could scarcely afford.[54] In Burma, cultivators faced a raft of irksome restrictions on what they could and could not gather from the reserved forests, and moreover were banned from collecting some species—such as *sha*, the source of cutch, used in tanning and dyeing—outside the reserves as well. Grazing was generally prohibited within reserve boundaries, and the use of fire to encourage the growth of fodder crops was vigorously suppressed.[55] In Indochina too, there were strict regulations on the collection of fuel and resins and on the felling of trees below a certain size.[56] Virtually everywhere in colonial Asia, forest policies that were designed to prevent a shortage of wood actually made it far less available for indigenous people.

To a large extent, the social and ecological effects of colonial forest management were driven by its commercial orientation. Forest departments, like colonial administrations in general, were normally expected to pay for themselves, and ideally to generate earnings through the collection of export duties and the sale of cutting licences. Officials made no bones about this priority. In the 1860s the Indian government openly declared that 'it is necessary that the administration of the public forests should be so conducted as to yield the largest possible amount of revenue, compatible with a due regard for the maintenance and improvement of these important public domains'.[57] Towards this end the Raj was remarkably successful: annual forest revenue rose from 5.5 million rupees in the 1880s to 21 million rupees by 1920.[58] But as critics pointed out, this fiscal surplus brought costs elsewhere. Agricultural departments questioned the economic logic of prohibiting cultivation in forested areas that could be profitably farmed. As J. A. Voelcker's 1893 report on Indian agriculture pointedly remarked, the aims of the forest department 'were in no sense agricultural, and its success was gauged mainly by fiscal considerations…Indeed, we may go so far as to say that its interests were opposed to agriculture, and its intent was rather to exclude agriculture from than to admit it to participation in its benefits.'[59]

[53] Gadgil and Guha, *Fissured Land*, 140–1, 159; Guha and Gadgil, 'State Forestry', 158–9.
[54] Peluso, *Rich Forests*, 67–9.   [55] Bryant, *Political Ecology*, 74–6, 92–3.
[56] Cleary, 'Managing', 274.
[57] Quoted from E. P. Stebbing, *The Forests of India*, vol. 2 (London: Bodley Head, 1923), 38.
[58] Sivaramakrishnan, 'Histories of Colonialism', 113.
[59] Voelcker, *Report*, 135–6; similar arguments were made on Java: Peluso, *Rich Forests*, 74.

Over time, the pressure to generate profits radically altered the very biological makeup of the reserved forests. One of the central aims of forest departments was to increase the proportion of commercially valuable species, usually through the use of fire, girdling, or ringing. In India, the most lucrative species (depending on the ecological zone in question) were teak, sal, and various fast-growing pine and cedar varieties, all of which were prized for construction or fuel-wood purposes but were of little use for agriculture or grazing. By contrast, trees such as oak and various members of the *Terminalia* genus (sometimes called 'tropical almond') grew too slowly for commercial exploitation and were gradually replaced, despite the fact that they were an important source of nuts and fodder for farmers.[60] In this sense, the deliberate creation of teak and conifer plantations effectively involved the replacement of what one might call subsistence trees with commercial species. Furthermore, the expansion of such plantations also meant that what began as a *de jure* distinction between agricultural and forest land—a paper exercise designed for zoning and tax purposes—gradually acquired a *de facto* form as the forest reserves lost their agricultural value. Colonial forest management not only sequestered woodland resources, it also deliberately modified them.[61]

It was all but inevitable that such measures would provoke resentment among rural communities. Violations of the forest codes were rife, ranging from wood theft and illegal burning to refusals to pay fines. On Java, the groundswell of agrarian unrest around the turn of the century was fuelled not least by restrictions on access to wood; in 1905 alone there were some 45,000 arrests for forest 'crimes'. Although much of the opposition to forest codes was passive and sporadic, it occasionally assumed a more organized form. A notable example was the Samin movement on Java, which called for a mass retreat into the forests as a means of resisting Dutch administrative interference in village life, and which attracted around 3,000 families at its peak in the late 1900s. Though principally non-violent, the movement nonetheless alarmed officials by posing an open challenge to their authority in the very heart of the island's teak forests.[62]

Not all expressions of discontent were so peaceful. Although forest-related grievances could often be settled by petitioning local officials, when such legal appeals failed to achieve the desired results the response occasionally turned violent. In India the abrogation of forest rights sparked periodic outbreaks of open confrontation, some of which managed to wring significant concessions out of state authorities.[63] In the Himalayan foothills of Uttarakhand (later home to the famous Chipko movement), an organized campaign to burn the blocs of chir pine that had been planted in the early 1920s made it impossible for the administration to apply its working plan across large areas of woodland.[64] On the Chotanagpur plateau (centred on the modern-day state of Jharkhand in eastern India), the so-called Munda Rebellion of 1899–1900 prompted a major review of forestry regulations,

---

[60] Oak and *Terminalia* stands were, however, protected in some areas and were occasionally cultivated for farm use and timber: Stebbing, *Forests of India*, vol. 2, 112, 126, 148, 412.
[61] Sivaramakrishnan, 'Histories of Colonialism', 118; Gadgil and Guha, *Fissured Land*, 142, 147.
[62] Peluso, *Rich Forests*, 69–76.   [63] Guha and Gadgil, 'State Forestry', esp. 158–63.
[64] Guha, *Unquiet Woods*, 110–20; Guha and Gadgil, 'State Forestry', 162–3.

eventually culminating in 1908 in the Chotanagpur Tenancy Act, which formally recognized customary land tenure and placed many 'tribal' areas under a separate system of administration.[65] As numerous studies have shown, it was often impossible for officials to enforce deeply unpopular regulations even in the heavily policed forests of the Indian subcontinent. The overall result was a patchwork of pragmatic compromises that reflected both the fissures within the colonial state as well as the multiplicity of local interests among landlords, tenants, men, women, and diverse ethnic groups.[66]

As a general rule, the process of forest reservation was especially hard on itinerant groups. The suppression of shifting cultivation was one of the key aims of state foresters during the entire colonial period. Swidden agriculture was prevalent throughout most of the tropical world at the time, and probably expanded with the onset of European rule as the *pax colonia* encouraged more dispersed patterns of settlement.[67] In South and Southeast Asia it was most common in hilly areas that fringed the main centres of agricultural settlement. Known locally by a variety of names—*kumri, jhum, taungya, rây*—there were innumerable variants based on different ecological conditions and social conventions. As Harold Conklin elaborated in his famous study of the Hanunóo, whereas some groups practised swidden as a sideline or 'partial' activity designed to supplement other sources of income, for more self-contained groups it formed an 'integral' part of their entire cultural system and way of life.[68] But despite the many variations, all of these systems shared a core set of practices: cutting and burning the forest to provide fertilizing ash for the soil; cultivating staple grains and vegetables for several (usually one to four) years before abandoning the plot to fallow; and returning to the same plot to repeat the process after an interval of anywhere from ten to twenty-five years. Compared to sedentary cultivation, these systems required far more land but significantly less labour per unit of output. Many were remarkably productive in terms of their effort-to-reward ratio, and moreover were broadly sustainable so long as there was enough land available to allow for sufficient fallow periods.

For most colonial officials, however, shifting cultivation was the epitome of backwardness. Itinerant groups were seen to occupy a kind of halfway house on the social-evolutionary ladder from hunter-gather societies to agricultural civilization. By the middle of the nineteenth century this engrained cultural condescension was magnified by concerns about environmental degradation and the profligate use of resources, in which shifting cultivation was generally regarded as a primary cause of deforestation and soil erosion. The forestry literature of the colonial era is peppered

---

[65] Paul Basu and Vinita Damodaran, 'Colonial Histories of Heritage: Legislative Migrations and the Politics of Preservation', in Betts and Ross (eds), *Heritage*, 240–71, here 266–8; S. P. Sinha, *Conflict and Tension in Tribal Society* (New Delhi: Concept, 1993), 30–90.

[66] See generally Sivaramakrishnan, *Modern Forests*; Sivaramakrishnan, 'Histories of Colonialism', 122–6.

[67] Peter Boomgaard, 'Introducing Environmental Histories of Indonesia', in Boomgaard, Colombijn, and Henley (eds), *Paper Landscapes*, 1–26, here 11–13.

[68] Harold C. Conklin, *Hanunóo Agriculture: A Report on an Integral System of Shifting Cultivation in the Philippines* (Rome: FAO, 1957), 2–3.

with adjectives such as 'primitive', 'wasteful', even 'barbaric'. Fairly typical were the comments of an official in the Canara District of southern India, who opined in 1847 that 'the practice of *kumri* cultivation is one of so wasteful and improvident a nature that it appears to me it ought not to be tolerated except in a very wild and unpeopled country'.[69]

In fact, many observers thought that shifting cultivation should not be tolerated anywhere. While travelling through southern Sumatra in 1880, the naturalist Henry Forbes noted that 'the original forest is rapidly disappearing; each year sees immense tracts felled for rice fields, more than is actually necessary, and also much wanton destruction by wilful fires. Trees of the rarest and finest timber are hewed, half burned, and then left to rot; amid their prostrate trunks a couple of harvests are reaped, then the ground is deserted, and soon fills up with the fast-growing and worthless woods, or falls a prey to the ineradicable *alang-alang* grass.'[70] French foresters in Indochina were resolutely hostile towards *rây* cultivation, which one official condemned as a 'nefarious practice' carried out by 'ravaging natives' who needed to be rescued from themselves.[71] Even on New Guinea, European travellers were startled by the 'huge stretches of land' used for shifting cultivation, which made a decidedly negative impression compared to the 'magnificent' old-growth forests.[72] Although the spread of commercial agriculture undoubtedly accelerated the pace of forest loss in Southeast Asia, there is clear evidence that indigenous cultivation and the use of fire for hunting had already degraded large expanses of woodland long before the colonial era, even in scantily populated regions such as Pahang, the Batak areas of northern Sumatra, or central Sulawesi.[73]

Colonial efforts to ban or curtail shifting cultivation arose from a jumble of different concerns. Apart from ecological considerations, the fact that it was often practised by groups on the fringes of state power provided a further incentive to suppress it, as did the (partly erroneous) idea that it was incompatible with the regular payment of revenue or with the notion of private landownership.[74] Such motives were scarcely new in the nineteenth century; pre-colonial rulers in many areas had long sought to control and settle nomadic groups as part of their state-building efforts.[75] The main difference between colonial governments and their predecessors was their capacity to act on these motives. This was especially evident

---

[69] T. L. Blane, reprinted in Hugh Cleghorn, *The Forests and Gardens of South India* (London: W. H. Allen, 1861), 127.

[70] Henry Forbes, *A Naturalist's Wanderings in the Eastern Archipelago: A Narrative of Travel and Exploration from 1878 to 1883* (London: Low, Marston, Searle & Rivington, 1883), 132.

[71] Prades, *Déboisement*, 2.

[72] W. Kolbe, 'Die Kulturpflanzen der Eingeborenen von Neuguinea', *Der Tropenpflanzer*, vol. 7 no. 5 (May 1903), 211–24, here 222–3.

[73] Boomgaard, 'Introducing', 11–13; Peter Boomgaard, 'Hunting and Trapping in the Indonesian Archipelago, 1500–1950', in Boomgaard, Colombijn, and Henley (eds), *Paper Landscapes*, 185–213, esp. 203–4; Kathirithamby-Wells, *Nature*, 176–7.

[74] Pouchepadass, 'British Attitudes', 134–7, 149.

[75] James C. Scott, *The Art of Not Being Governed: An Anarchist History of Upland Southeast Asia* (New Haven: Yale University Press, 2009), esp. 98–126; C. A. Bayly, *Indian Society and the Making of the British Empire* (Cambridge: Cambridge University Press, 1988), 30–2; Richards, *Unending Frontier*, 125, 255; also Radkau, *Nature and Power*, 41–6.

wherever land was being alienated for European use—as in north-east Sumatra or western Malaya—where complaints about the wastefulness of shifting cultivation helped to justify the confiscation of large expanses of forest.[76] Similar objections facilitated the establishment of new reserves in more remote areas too, for instance in the upland forests of Indochina.[77]

Yet opinions among colonial officials were not entirely unanimous with respect to shifting cultivation, and even if they had been, forest departments were not always able to enforce their writ. Hugh Cleghorn, the influential conservator of forests in Madras (who later became inspector-general of Indian forests), took a more measured view than most. Although he agreed that *kumri* was a 'wasteful system', his sharpest criticism was reserved for 'unscrupulous contractors and traders' rather than shifting cultivators. In his view it was neither possible nor desirable to suppress swidden systems altogether given their importance for local subsistence. Instead, *kumri* was allowed to continue in Madras under a state-controlled system of permits and charges, albeit '*greatly limited...* and *not permitted* on the banks of navigable rivers, on the sea-shore, close to trunk roads, or in any locality where superior timber exists'.[78] Most colonial administrations were less obliging than in Madras, though officials on the ground had to make concessions to reality. In Burma, foresters held little hope for blanket bans on shifting cultivation since local Karen communities would inevitably circumvent the restrictions anyway. Likewise, the Malayan administration grudgingly tolerated shifting cultivation in upland areas where it was impossible to put forestry codes into effect.[79] Curtailing swidden practices was completely impractical on Borneo, where they were widely treated as customary rights. In Sarawak they even found explicit legal sanction within certain designated areas.[80]

By the inter-war period attitudes towards shifting cultivation were softening in any event. To some extent this reflected the greater emphasis on 'native welfare' after the First World War, but an equally important factor was the gradual reassessment of shifting cultivation itself. As scientists acquired a better understanding of how different swidden systems worked, some concluded that they were not as destructive as had often been assumed. The renowned French geographer Pierre Gourou, for example, argued that *rây* cultivation in Indochina was 'a less maladroit technique than it may first appear. It allows for several harvests, albeit meagre ones, without unleashing excessive soil erosion... and without ruining the soil by laterisation, which would be a major worry if the same ground were continually

[76] Pelzer, *Planter*, 71–3; Stoler, *Capitalism*, 23–5; Kathirithamby-Wells, *Nature*, 176.

[77] Cleary, 'Managing', 271–2.

[78] Cleghorn, *Gardens of South India*, pp. v, 126–7; more generally, Pouchepadass, 'British Attitudes', 133–5, 145–7; Marlène Buchy, 'The British Colonial Forest Policy in South India: A Maladapted Policy?', in Chatelin and Bonneuil (eds), *Nature*, 33–58.

[79] Bryant, *Political Ecology*, 68–71; Timothy N. Harper, 'The Politics of the Forest in Colonial Malaya', *Modern Asian Studies*, vol. 31 (1997), 1–29, here p. 9; Timothy N. Harper, 'The Orang Asli and the Politics of the Forest in Colonial Malaya', in Grove, Damodaran, and Sangwan (eds), *Nature and the Orient*, 936–66.

[80] Peluso and Vandergeest, 'Genealogies', 793–5; Kaur, 'Forestry'.

cultivated.'[81] Besides these pedological advantages, shifting cultivation also brought benefits for natural fauna. From the viewpoint of nature conservationists, the bigger threat to tropical wildlife was not the land-extensive practices of shifting cultivators, which actually promoted the diversity of animal species by encouraging the growth of grasses and wild fruits, but rather the intensive production methods of the forest services, which were governed by a 'tyranny of budgetary receipts' that allowed little scope for sensitivity towards the interconnectedness of forest ecosystems.[82]

Even among professional foresters there was a variety of different views on shifting cultivation.[83] By 1940 many agreed with the pragmatic conclusion of Robert Troup (director of the Imperial Forestry Institute at Oxford) that 'whatever may be said for or against shifting cultivation, forests must remain the basis of native agriculture over extensive areas until science has devised better methods to take its place'.[84] In practice, it was usually more productive to try to integrate rather than suppress swidden techniques as a part of forest management schemes. There was strong precedent for doing so; in fact, none other than Dietrich Brandis sponsored just such an approach in South Asia. Shortly after his arrival in Burma in 1856, Brandis persuaded Karen groups in the Pegu region to inter-plant teak seedlings with their cereal crops on newly cleared *taungya* plots. The basic idea was to propagate teak as the chief successor species once the clearings were abandoned and left to fallow—in essence, the same technique by which 'native rubber' plots were established throughout much of Southeast Asia around half a century later. It was a simple and ingenious method for harnessing the labour of shifting agriculturalists to the cause of forest management. As Berthold Ribbentrop (India's Inspector-General of Forests) approvingly remarked in 1900, the '*taungya* method' of afforestation had 'transformed these tribes... from an antagonistic nuisance to forestry conservancy into the most loyal servants of the Department'. By 1898 some 21,000 hectares of Burmese teak had been planted on this basis, and by 1924 the figure had nearly doubled to 40,000 hectares.[85]

Given the pervasiveness of shifting cultivation in the tropics, the so-called *taungya* method was eventually replicated in many other regions as well. In India it allowed swidden practices to continue or even resume in certain areas where it would otherwise have been banned.[86] On Java it was widely deployed under the local name '*tumpang sari*', and by 1928 it accounted for over 94 per cent of reforestation in Java's state reserves.[87] In the early 1900s it also crossed the ocean to East Africa, where German and British foresters deployed mixed techniques of teak

[81] Gourou, *L'Utilisation*, 179–81, see also 351–7; also Robequain, *Economic Development*, 185–6.
[82] Quote from F. Évrard, 'Biogéographie indochinoise et réserves naturelles', in Aubréville et al., *Contribution*, 257–67, here 260; more generally, Jeya Kathirithamby-Wells, 'Human Impact on Large Mammal Populations in Peninsular Malaysia from the Nineteenth to the Mid-Twentieth Century', in Boomgaard, Colombijn, and Henley (eds), *Paper Landscapes*, 215–41.
[83] Rajan, *Modernizing Nature*, 171–9.
[84] R. S. Troup, *Colonial Forest Administration* (Oxford: Oxford University Press, 1940), 244.
[85] Ribbentrop, *Forestry*, 191–4, quote p. 193. See, more generally, Bryant, 'Shifting the Cultivator'; Bryant, *Political Ecology*, 110–13.
[86] Gadgil and Guha, *Fissured Land*, 158.   [87] Peluso, *Rich Forests*, 63–4.

and crop cultivation under the label of 'forest *shamba*'.[88] By the 1920s it also spread into West Africa with the influx of forestry personnel and know-how from the Asian colonies. Early *taungya* trials in southern Nigeria were quickly copied in Sierra Leone, Gold Coast, and Côte d'Ivoire, where sequestered land was temporarily granted to cultivators rent-free on the condition that they plant tree seedlings as stipulated by forestry officers.[89] All the same, such hybrid or cooperative afforestation methods did not convince everyone, and nor did they redeem shifting cultivation per se in the eyes of colonial foresters. Although the *taungya* method was, if properly administered, one of the cheapest and most effective means of regenerating the woodlands, many officials regarded it as a temporary compromise rather than a system of truly sound forest management.[90]

The spread of the *taungya* method may have been a small chapter in the history of colonial forestry, but it nonetheless illustrates a number of central themes. First, it shows that the overall aim was control. Although grazing, wood-gathering, and shifting cultivation were widely suppressed, these censured practices were not universally or inevitably regarded as incompatible with effective forest management, provided they were carefully regulated. Secondly, it also highlights the limits of state control. In practice, the doctrines of scientific forestry often had to be adapted or relaxed to mesh with local needs and land-use customs, especially in areas where the state's presence was weak. Perhaps most importantly, it reflects the emergence of a globalized and trans-imperial framework of knowledge, which provided an increasingly standardized set of practices and normative models for resource management. As European foresters grappled with the enormous diversity of the tropical woodlands in the colonies, they understandably sought solutions from seemingly analogous situations elsewhere. Like the transferral of desiccationist theories from tropical islands to mainland colonies, or the transplantation of German *Forstwirtschaft* to Europe's colonies overseas, the spread of the *taungya* method was one of many instances in which the history of state forestry seemed to repeat itself. It was, however, a rather unusual example, for the more common pattern of recurrence was one of exclusion rather than integration, one of conflict with rural communities rather than cooperation.

COLONIAL EXPANSION AND AFRICAN FORESTS

Well before the scramble for Africa in the 1880s, colonial states in southern Asia were surveying, cataloguing, and gazetting large stretches of forest for protection or

---

[88] Büsgen, 'Forstwirtschaft in den Kolonien', *Verhandlungen des deutschen Kolonialkongresses 1910* (Berlin: Reimer, 1910), 801–17, here 813; Alfonso Peter Castro, 'Southern Mount Kenya and Colonial Forest Conflicts', in Richards and Tucker (eds), *World Deforestation*, 33–55, here 41.

[89] André Aubréville, *La Forêt coloniale: les forêts de l'Afrique Occidentale Française* (Paris: Société d'Éditions Géographique, Maritimes et Coloniales, 1938), 172–4, which noted that this implied a feminization of forest work by associating it with growing food crops; see also E. P. Stebbing, *The Forests of West Africa and the Sahara* (London: Chambers, 1937), 48–51, 164–93.

[90] Rajan, *Modernizing Nature*, 175–6; Troup, *Colonial Forest Administration*, 243–4.

controlled exploitation. Parallel conservation processes were also under way in parts of the Maghreb and the Cape, where fears of deforestation and soil erosion first emerged in the 1830s–1840s and were in full force by mid-century.[91] But in the vast expanse of land between the northern and southern fringes of Africa, European knowledge of the continent's woodlands was patchy at best, and it remained so long after the ink had dried on the treaties of colonial partition. Even in the 1920s many of Africa's tropical forests were still 'completely unknown' to Europeans.[92] Against this backdrop, it is scarcely surprising that forest management in sub-Saharan Africa drew heavily on the knowledge, organizational forms, and practices in colonial Asia, the Maghreb, and the Cape. By the late nineteenth century, foresters in these older established colonies had acquired extensive experience with a range of forest ecosystems that appeared broadly comparable to those in the more recently conquered territories of tropical Africa. As a result, Africa's tropical forests were generally viewed through the same lens of anthropogenic deforestation and desiccation that already informed management regimes elsewhere. Consequently, foresters in colonial Africa reprised many of the well-worn indictments of native profligacy and woodland destruction discussed above, along with the segregationist conservation policies designed to combat them. As Michael Williams has put it, 'it was the Indian story all over again but with a vengeance, always working to the detriment of the shifting agriculturalist and indigenous farming practice, and denying the peoples' livelihood and history'.[93]

The Indian and South African stories were a very direct prelude to forest management in British East and Central Africa, where they provided not only the legislative framework but also many of the key personnel. In Kenya, the first steps towards a centralized forest administration were taken around the turn of the century amidst an influx of European settlers and timber companies. In order to control their activities, as well as to curb potential woodland damage by indigenous groups, the East African Forestry Regulations of 1902 established a system of reserves, royalties, permits, and penalties modelled directly on the India Forest Act and Cape Forest Ordinance.[94] The bulk of actual survey work was carried out by foresters trained in India or South Africa, most notably David E. Hutchins, who had worked in both. His 1907 and 1909 reports on the forests of British East Africa furnished the basic blueprint. Following Indian precedent, they called for state regulation rather than private control, and they displayed the same amalgam of economic, ecological, and political aims that governed forest administration in the subcontinent: watershed protection and climatic stability, revenue generation, preventing commercial overexploitation, and curtailing 'irrational' use by locals.

---

[91] Diana K. Davis, *Resurrecting the Granary of Rome: Environmental History and French Colonial Expansion in North Africa* (Athens, Oh.: Ohio University Press, 2007); Beinart, *Rise of Conservation*, 77–88; Grove, 'Early Themes in African Conservation: The Cape in the Nineteenth Century', in Anderson and Grove (eds), *Conservation*, 21–39.

[92] A. Bertin, 'Les Bois coloniaux', *L'Agronomie coloniale*, vol. 6 nos 43–5 (July–Sept. 1921), 4–22, 52–62, 84–9, here 13.

[93] Williams, *Deforesting*, 402.

[94] The regulations were subsequently updated by a series of amendments 1911–16: R. S. Troup, *Report on Forestry in Kenya Colony* (London: Waterlow, 1922), esp. 9–13, 24–5.

Over the following years the fledgling forestry regimes in Uganda and the Rhodesias were similarly based on the workings of the Indian Forest Service.[95]

As one might expect, this common genealogy ensured that there were numerous parallels between the forestry systems of East and Central Africa, all of which excluded indigenous users from the forests through the gazetting of woodlands or the granting of large concessions to outside timber firms. But even so, the existence of large numbers of white settlers in Kenya and Southern Rhodesia gave developments in these colonies their own dynamic. In both territories, the large-scale alienation of land for European farms sharpened the conflicts between foresters and indigenous groups, many of whom were denied access to woodlands for grazing, pasturage, gathering timber, even collecting honey. In Kenya in particular, the resulting antagonism was compounded by the policy of situating white-owned farms as buffers between 'native lands' and reserved forests, partly in order to prevent the woodlands from being overexploited by allegedly 'reckless' peoples (such as the Kikuyu and Tugen), and partly to keep them from being used as a refuge in the event of civil disturbances. This two-pronged alienation of land was, as some field officers recognized, a serious blow for peasants and pastoralists who had long relied on the forests as an integral part of their subsistence strategies, especially during drought periods. To make matters worse, the resulting disputes between indigenous groups and state authorities were further aggravated by the exceptionally stringent set of conservation measures demanded by the settler lobby, which served as a means of rationalizing the discriminatory land policies that underpinned their livelihoods in the first place. This peculiar political constellation left little scope for a more conciliatory approach to forest management. Any alleviation of tensions over the following decades derived less from a deliberate relaxation of forest policy than from the sheer difficulty of enforcing deeply unpopular measures amidst a perennial shortage of forestry personnel.[96]

The political landscape was somewhat different in neighbouring Tanganyika, though here too the expansion of white settlement and the transposition of forestry practices from Asia and central Europe led to a host of problems. When German foresters first arrived in the colony in the 1890s the principal focus was on the production of mangrove poles in the Rufiji delta, which Arab loggers were already supplying for the Indian Ocean trade.[97] As they devised a working plan for the delta, it seemed only natural to borrow from existing mangrove management techniques in India, where the German forester Wilhelm Schlich had led the effort to 'rationalize' timber production in the Sundarbans. But the schemes that were developed for India soon proved inappropriate in the very different social and

[95] D. E. Hutchins, *East Africa Protectorate: Report on the Forests of Kenia* (London: HMSO, 1907); D. E. Hutchins, *Report on the Forests of British East Africa* (London: HMSO, 1909); Troup, *Colonial Forest Administration*, 298–9.

[96] Castro, 'Southern Mount Kenya', 37–42; David Anderson, 'Managing the Forest: The Conservation History of Lembus, Kenya, 1904–63', in Anderson and Grove (eds), *Conservation*, 249–68, here 253, 258–62; A. Fiona D. Mackenzie, *Land, Ecology and Resistance in Kenya, 1880–1952* (Edinburgh: Edinburgh University Press, 1998), 65–75.

[97] Büsgen, 'Forstwirtschaft', 812; Sunseri, *Wielding the Ax*, 26–37.

environmental circumstances of the Rufiji Delta, above all due to the inaccessibility of much of the Delta as well as the acute shortage of labour in the area. Efforts to boost teak exports suffered from similar problems. Paul Eckert, the colony's chief forester, found that his prior experience on Java was of little use amidst the transport and labour difficulties in the region.[98] Such obstacles made it difficult to generate surpluses, and the lack of revenue flow consequently hampered the expansion of forest administration in German East Africa. In 1909/10 the entire colony had only four trained foresters, thirteen forest protection officers, and a handful of indigenous forest guards. By 1914 reserves covered a mere 1 per cent of the colony's land surface, and given the dearth of personnel, the forest department was not even able to manage this area effectively.[99]

But if forest administration in German East Africa was limited in scope, it nonetheless provided abundant fuel for conflict. The Crown Land Ordinance of 1895 established the basic legal framework by declaring all supposedly unused land to be state domain. In 1904 it was followed by a Forest Protection Ordinance that empowered the colonial government to expel inhabitants from newly created reserves, which was one of the many grievances that eventually sparked the Maji-Maji rebellion the following year.[100] This pair of regulations, like so many conservation decrees in the tropical colonies, reflected a deep-seated scepticism towards indigenous land stewardship. In the humid forests near the coast, local and Arab loggers were accused of wasting timber and causing widespread erosion. In the drier woodlands further inland, the powerful hold of desiccation theory led German foresters to overestimate the extent of previous woodland cover and therefore to exaggerate the scale of forest loss due to indigenous cultivation.[101] In the highlands of the north, these ideas were readily seized upon by white farming interests to justify further land alienation, much as in Kenya. But foresters in German East Africa were by no means mere tools of the settler lobby, and nor did they shy away from imposing restrictions on European landowners as well. Like most of their counterparts in other colonies, they may have lacked a detailed understanding of tropical forest ecosystems, and therefore overestimated the damage caused by indigenous land use, but by and large they did so according to their own disciplinary logic.[102] If the expansion of forest departments bolstered state authority on the ground, their assertion of scientific autonomy could also thwart other colonial interests.

This tendency to misread the landscape was a pervasive feature of forestry, agriculture, and pastoral management throughout the tropical colonies. Given the limited

[98] Koponen, *Development*, 533.

[99] Figures from Büsgen, 'Forstwirtschaft', 811; Sunseri, *Wielding the Ax*, 69; see also Hans G. Schabel, 'Tanganyika Forestry under German Colonial Administration, 1891–1919', *Forest and Conservation History*, vol. 34 no. 3 (July 1990), 130–43.

[100] Sunseri, *Wielding the Ax*, 50–1.

[101] Koponen, *Development*, 529–36; Friedrich Jentsch, 'Die Entwicklung des Forstwesens in den deutschen Kolonien', *Mitteilungen des deutschen Forstvereins*, vol. 25 (1914), 71–81.

[102] This point is made more broadly by Rajan, *Modernizing Nature*, ch. 5; see also Sunseri, *Wielding the Ax*, 53, 65; Tobias J. Lanz, 'The Origins, Development and Legacy of Scientific Forestry in Cameroon', *Environment and History*, vol. 6 (2000), 99–120.

understanding of how tropical ecosystems and land-use practices worked, it cropped up nearly everywhere—and everywhere it appeared, it worked to the detriment of local cultivators and pastoralists.

Nowhere were such misinterpretations more evident than in the forests and wooded savannahs of West Africa. When Europeans expanded their authority across the region in the 1880s–1890s, they had only a vague idea of the botanical makeup and geographic extent of its forests despite centuries of trade contact along the coast. It was only around the turn of the century that French and British botanists began a systematic survey of West Africa's woodlands, and they were immediately enthralled by what they found. As Auguste Chevalier remarked in 1909, not even the current gold rush in the region could compare with the vast arboreal wealth it contained: 'the real gold mine of the Côte d'Ivoire is its immense virgin forest.'[103] From the very beginning, however, the sense of excitement was tinged by apprehensions about the degradation of these botanical treasure-troves. Unregulated logging was a major worry. Among the worst-affected species was African mahogany (often called 'acajou' in French), which was subjected to 'a veritable pillage' in littoral areas and along the main communication routes. Chevalier despaired at the waste of valuable timber caused by careless logging practices, and estimated that no less than half of all the mahogany felled in Côte d'Ivoire was left to rot for lack of transport.[104] H. N. Thompson likewise lambasted the 'haphazard methods of exploiting the mahogany forests' in the Gold Coast, while in Sierra Leone the timber trade was widely—though exaggeratedly—blamed for destroying huge areas along the coast and rivers.[105] During the 1890s and 1900s one of the principal aims of foresters in West Africa was simply to ensure that commercial loggers could extract all the trees they cut down.[106] But over the longer term, their chief focus inexorably shifted towards the effects of indigenous farming and pastoral practices on the woodlands.

By the late nineteenth century the well-worn trope of 'native profligacy' dominated colonial forestry discourse not only in British-ruled India and South Africa but also in the French colonies north of the Sahara. Ever since the middle of the century, officials in the Maghreb had been steeped in a narrative of environmental degradation that blamed centuries of despoliation by Arab herders for ruining lands that had once served as the ancient 'granary of Rome'. On a political level, this narrative functioned as a classic morality parable of the victors, a cautionary tale of civilizational decline that affirmed the French right to govern the area while conveniently legitimizing the process of land expropriation and French settlement. But as an account of bio-geographical change, it also significantly influenced

---

[103] Auguste Chevalier, *Première Étude sur les bois de la Côte d'Ivoire* (Paris: Challamel, 1909), 7.

[104] Chevalier, *Première Étude*, 49–53, quote p. 48.

[105] H. N. Thompson, *Gold Coast: Report on Forests* (London: HMSO, 1910), 5, quoted from James Fairhead and Melissa Leach, *Reframing Deforestation: Global Analysis and Local Realities: Studies in West Africa* (London: Routledge, 1998), 76, also 139–45; Michael S. Asante, *Deforestation in Ghana: Explaining the Chronic Failure of Forest Preservation Policies in a Developing Country* (Lanham, Md: University Press of America, 2005), 62–5.

[106] A. Jolyet, *Le Transport des bois dans les forêts coloniales* (Paris: Challamel, 1912).

scientific discourse in the region, above all by encouraging speculation about the difference between its 'actual' vegetation and the 'potential' flora that it could carry under alternative forms of land use.[107] Given what was known about ancient plant cover in the Maghreb, and given current understandings of the relationship between forests and climate, there was no reason—so the logic went—why the area could not once again become a breadbasket if its vegetation were managed in such a way as to increase regional humidity levels.

When French and British botanists began to map the flora of their West African colonies, these socially constructed notions of 'potential vegetation' in the Maghreb shaped perceptions south of the Sahara as well. During the early twentieth century, one of the central issues that preoccupied foresters in West Africa was the relationship between current vegetation patterns and local climate conditions—or, in contemporary terminology, whether the observed plant cover represented the 'climax' vegetation that could be supported by local geo-climatic conditions, or rather a community of vegetation that had been degraded by human intervention, in particular by shifting agriculture and repeated burning.

In certain respects the climatic and floral geography of West Africa encouraged this kind of analysis.[108] Broadly speaking, the woodlands of the region can be divided into three different zones running parallel to the coast and defined by declining rainfall isohyets the further northward one moves towards the desert. Moist high evergreen and semi-deciduous forest is largely confined to a coastal strip extending around 300 kilometres inland in Liberia and the Ivory Coast, before gradually tapering down through Ghana and eventually ending at the Dahomey Gap, a corridor of savannah-woodland that interrupts the coastal rainforest belt from south-east Ghana through Togo and Benin. East of the Dahomey Gap the rainforest then resumes, with a slightly different species composition, into southern Nigeria, Cameroon, and beyond. To the north of this moist forest strip is a 200–400 km forest-savannah transition zone that becomes progressively drier and less wooded as one moves inland. Beyond the transition zone lies another 300–400 km belt of grassland with only isolated forest patches along watercourses, which is in turn followed by the Sahel.

During the early 1900s this series of bio-geographic belts came to be understood as distinctive 'botanical zones'.[109] Subdivided according to climatic and soil conditions, these zones provided a normative basis for conceptualizing the 'standard' or 'natural' vegetation of the region, and consequently furnished a yardstick for measuring the extent of any perceived deviations. The existence of such a typological baseline influenced forestry thinking in a number of ways. First of all, it heightened suspicions of human-induced degradation wherever the vegetation was scrubbier or sparser than what local soil or rainfall conditions seemed 'naturally'

---

[107] Davis, *Resurrecting the Granary*, esp. 89–130.

[108] Fairhead and Leach, *Reframing*, 164–6.

[109] Auguste Chevalier, 'Les Zones et les provinces botanique de l'Afrique–Occidentale française', *Comptes rendus des séances de l'Académie des Sciences*, vol. 130 no. 18 (1900), 1202–8; A. Harold Unwin, *West African Forests and Forestry* (London: T. Fisher Unwin Ltd, 1920), 17–19.

capable of supporting.[110] It also encouraged observers to view extreme weather events as warnings about the potential effects of deforestation. What contemporary foresters feared most of all was a self-reinforcing cycle of progressive desiccation whereby anthropogenic tree clearance would cause a decline in local humidity that would then hinder subsequent forest regeneration, thus allowing the 'advancing desert' to push the various vegetation zones ever further southwards. Such anxieties were clearly heightened by the severe droughts in the Sahel between 1900 and 1903, and were further amplified by the calamitous drought and famine—possibly the worst of the entire twentieth century—1910–15 (peaking in 1913).[111] These disasters formed the grim backdrop against which the initial forest surveys by Chevalier, H. N. Thompson, and Harold Unwin were carried out, and helped stoke fears of a bio-climatic domino effect in which desert encroached on savannah and savannah invaded the forest (Fig. 8.1).

From the very beginning, colonial forestry in West Africa was therefore preoccupied with the threat of a sequential degradation from 'virgin' to secondary forest, and from secondary forest to semi-arid grassland. In the humid forest, where the most valuable timber reserves were found, it was widely thought that colonial 'pacification' had accelerated the pace of woodland clearance by encouraging the expansion of bush fallow farming and a corresponding transition to secondary vegetation. As noted above, the idea that colonial conquest encouraged agricultural expansion was not altogether wrong; commercial cropping spread rapidly during the late nineteenth and early twentieth centuries. The problem was the declensionist narrative that accompanied this idea, for the relationship between past and present conditions was almost always viewed as one of inexorable decline. In the absence of detailed historical data, the task of determining precisely what constituted the 'natural' cover of the various botanical zones had to rely on inferences about previous vegetation based on current scientific theories, which held that 'climax' vegetation prevailed wherever the natural equilibrium remained intact. The corollary of this line of thought was that, in Chevalier's words, 'as soon as man makes breaches in the forest, the equilibrium is destroyed'.[112] Conclusions about natural cover were inevitably based on educated guesswork, but in making their guesses foresters were quick to blame indigenous cultivation as the prime culprit for any signs of degradation. To cite an extreme example, the forester C. E. Lane-Poole exclaimed in 1911 that no less than 99 per cent of the rain forests in Sierra Leone 'have been destroyed by the natives in their wasteful method of farming'.[113]

---

[110] Fairhead and Leach, *Reframing*, 10–15, 165–7.

[111] Michael Mortimore, *Adapting to Drought: Farmers, Famines and Desertification in West Africa* (Cambridge: Cambridge University Press, 1989), 12–15; Michael Watts, *Silent Violence: Food, Famine and Peasantry in Northern Nigeria* (Berkeley: University of California Press, 1983), 285–93; Beusekom, *Negotiating*, 8.

[112] Chevalier, *Première Étude*, 46.

[113] C. E. Lane-Poole, *Report on the Forests of Sierra Leone* (Freetown, 1911), 4, quoted from Fairhead and Leach, *Reframing*, 138.

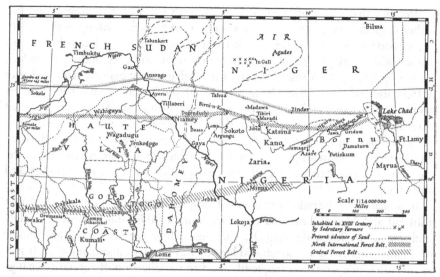

Fig. 8.1. Colonial-era map of vegetation belts in West Africa.
Source: E. P. Stebbing, *The Forests of West Africa and the Sahara* (London, Edinburgh: W. & R. Chambers, 1937), p. 21.

The evidence for such a process of bio-geographic decline seemed clearest to the north of the humid belt, where the open woodlands of the forest-savannah transitional zone were easily interpreted as an intermediary stage in the regression of primary forest to scrub. The first botanical surveys of the early 1900s already expressed concerns about the progressive loss of forest to savannah through burning and cultivation. By the inter-war period such fears were an integral part of conservationist orthodoxy, and eventually culminated in André Aubréville's concept of 'desertification', the final stage of a transformative process that began with the 'savanisation' of humid forest.[114] One of key factors that encouraged this reading of the forest-savannah belt was the existence of substantial yet isolated patches of verdant deciduous woodland that included species found mainly in the moist coastal forest. To most European observers such woodlands appeared to be remnants of the 'original' vegetation that must once have covered the surrounding savannah. In turn, this inference gave rise to the notion of 'derived savannah', a grassland landscape produced not by environmental conditions that precluded forest growth, but by recurrent disturbances of the natural process of vegetative succession through shifting cultivation and repeated burning.[115]

---

[114] André Aubréville, *Climats, forêts et désertification de l'Afrique tropicale* (Paris: Société d'Éditions Géographique, Maritimes et Coloniales, 1949), 309–44. The term was actually used before Aubréville's work, though he did more than anyone else to flesh out and propagate the concept: Tor A. Benjaminsen and Gunnvor Berge, 'Myths of Timbuktu: From African El Dorado to Desertification', *International Journal of Political Economy*, vol. 34 no. 1 (Spring 2004), 31–59, esp. 41–9.

[115] Aubréville, *Forêt coloniale*, 80–6.

The idea that much of West Africa's savannah was not natural grassland but rather 'degraded forest' soon became a mainstay of forestry thinking in the region. What made it so plausible was that it resonated not only with local observations but also with seemingly equivalent scenarios in the semi-arid woodlands of South Asia. As E. P. Stebbing, the former director of the Indian Forest Service, remarked after a 1934 tour of West Africa, large portions of the 'so-called savannah forest or savane' were actually 'only a varied form of what in India the forest officer termed degraded mixed deciduous forest, of which I had been acquainted with extensive areas'. Employing this 'more correct term', he argued, was crucial for devising an effective management plan for such areas, which should ultimately lead to the creation of a 'reconstituted high forest through the two agencies of closure and strict fire protection'.[116]

In actual fact, 'degraded forest' was hardly the correct term at all. As James Fairhead and Melissa Leach have shown, much of this land is more accurately understood as 'afforested savannah'. Their research on the forest-savannah mosaic of colonial Guinea has demonstrated how French foresters, and many of their successors after independence, frequently misread the direction of vegetative change by assuming that sparse tree cover was a sign of woodland degradation rather than (re)generation. Among the factors that encouraged such confusion was the parallel misunderstanding of the effects of human population growth, for the process of savannah afforestation in Guinea did not result from an absence of human influence, as the notion of 'wasteful natives' would have it, but rather from the expansion of agricultural settlement, cultivation, and livestock rearing. Far from destroying the tree cover, agriculturists actually encouraged tree growth around savannah villages for reasons of security, grazing, subsistence reserves, and protection from fire.[117] Subsequent analyses in other parts of the region have found a similar pattern of anthropogenic afforestation across large portions of the forest-savannah belt, stretching even to farmed parkland in the Sahel. Although there were enormous variations between different agro-ecological zones, and although many local areas have yet to be studied, recent research has effectively turned conventional accounts of deforestation and population growth on their head.[118]

The basic upshot of these studies is that the extent of the humid forest in the distant past, and therefore the scale of deforestation in more recent times, has often been grossly overestimated. This certainly does not mean that deforestation has not taken place; indeed, there is little doubt that it accelerated markedly over the past century or so. It does show, however, that the history of West Africa's forests was far more complex than a simple narrative of anthropogenic decline can allow, and that the changes wrought by human hand have not been universally negative or unidirectional.

[116] Stebbing, *Forests of West Africa*, 7, 231.

[117] James Fairhead and Melissa Leach, *Misreading the African Landscape: Society and Ecology in a Forest-Savanna Mosaic* (Cambridge: Cambridge University Press, 1996).

[118] Generally: Fairhead and Leach, *Reframing*; on the importance and complexity of local arrangements, see Reginald Cline-Cole and Clare Madge (eds), *Contesting Forestry in West Africa* (Aldershot: Ashgate, 2000).

Against this backdrop, it is worth emphasizing that colonial foresters were neither blind to such complexities nor entirely agreed on a linear thesis of woodland
loss in the region. As Fairhead and Leach themselves point out, some foresters
recognized the reverse process of woodland encroachment into the savannah, and
accordingly rejected the gloomy assessments offered by the likes of E. P. Stebbing.[119]
Even Aubréville himself—the chief author of the 'desertification' thesis—dismissed
the assumption that pockets of high forest species in the savannahs were necessarily
a vestige of a once-larger forest from a distant past. Characteristically, however, he
attributed these forest patches to 'natural' regeneration (that is, to seed dissemination from neighbouring stands) rather than to the effects of human land use.[120]
Like nearly all of his contemporaries, Aubréville could scarcely conceive that
agricultural settlement might actually increase forest cover. For most colonial
observers, the hegemonic idea of natural equilibrium led them not only to overlook but to downright invert the role of human activity in promoting these patches
of woodland. As the forest inspector of Côte d'Ivoire explained, the spread of
woodland into the savannah only took place wherever people did not burn or
farm, thus confirming that natural vegetation could successfully re-colonize
favourable geo-climatic zones in the absence of such disturbance. As ever, the
'grave problem' was human disruption, which caused the woodlands to be 'nibbled
away' by grasslands, with desert following in turn.[121]

Perversely, this predetermined conclusion meant that the spread of forest into
the savannah invited the very same policy response as the encroachment of the
savannah into the forest: namely, the reservation of woodlands and the suppression
of indigenous land use. Throughout West Africa this package of measures became
the standard formula for colonial forest management, much as it had throughout
colonial Asia. Yet once again, the actual ability to impose such policies varied significantly from place to place. Wherever land use was still controlled by local elites,
as in Nigeria and the Gold Coast, the mechanisms of indirect rule made it difficult
to introduce centralized conservation measures until well after the First World
War. This was a sore point among British foresters, many of whom were alarmed
at the rate of forest clearance by cocoa farmers and timber firms.[122] Harold Unwin,
one of the leading British foresters in the region, expressed his frustrations in
revealingly paternalistic terms: 'a child is not allowed to play with fire, although it
may very much like to see the flames; in the same way the British people, as locally
represented by the Gold Coast Government, cannot allow the inhabitants of the
district to play fast and loose with their priceless treasures, the African forests, well

---

[119] e.g. L. Dudley Stamp, 'The Southern Margin of the Sahara: Comments on Some Recent
Studies on the Question of Desiccation in West Africa', *Geographical Review*, vol. 30 no. 2 (Apr.
1940), 297–300; Fairhead and Leach, *Reframing*, 80–1.

[120] Aubréville, *Forêt coloniale*, 86.

[121] M. Martineau, 'Protection de la forêt en Côte d'Ivoire', in *Deuxième Congrès*, 247–52, here 248.

[122] Richard H. Grove, 'Chiefs, Boundaries and Sacred Woodlands: Early Nationalism and the
Defeat of Colonial Conservationism in the Gold Coast and Nigeria, 1870–1916', in Grove, *Ecology*,
147–78; Edmund Onyemeke Egboh, *British Forest Policy in Nigeria: A Study in Colonial Exploitation
of Forest Produce (1897–1940)* (Ph.D. Dissertation, University of Birmingham, 1975).

knowing that the country will be permanently injured thereby'.[123] In theory, land tenure arrangements in the French colonies of West Africa were more favourable to state-based woodland management. From the 1890s onwards all nominally unoccupied land (much of which was in fact forest fallow land periodically used for shifting cultivation) was classified as state domain, which allowed the French forest services to adopt a more interventionist approach than their British counter-parts—or, as Stebbing put it, to have a more 'Indian' outlook.[124] But in practice, the perennial shortage of personnel and resources meant that French colonial for-esters were also scarcely capable of imposing effective conservation measures until well after the First World War.[125]

Once the forest services got going, their management methods built directly on the established discourse of anthropogenic deforestation. Some of the most decisive interventions occurred on the northern edges of the savannah, where the encroachment of the Sahara had been a matter of grave concern since the begin-ning of the century.[126] Although scientists disagreed on whether recent changes reflected a southward progression of desert conditions or rather a series of periodic climate oscillations,[127] fears of the advancing desert were remarkably persistent and grew increasingly acute during the 1930s in view of the unfolding disaster of the US Dust Bowl and concurrent droughts in East Africa (see Chapter 9). 'In reality, the indigenous populations, by destroying immense areas of tropical forest, have created desert in their wake,' remarked a French agronomist in 1935. 'In the future, the primary role of the colonizer . . . is therefore to monitor the destructive actions of the natives, to prevent them, to stave off bush burning, to prohibit deforestation at all costs.'[128]

Many British observers agreed, and none more so than Stebbing, who exclaimed that 'the people are living on the edge, not of a volcano, but of a desert whose power is incalculable and whose silent and almost invisible approach must be dif-ficult to estimate. But the end is obvious: total annihilation of vegetation and the disappearances of man and beast from the overwhelmed locality.'[129] From Lake Chad in the east to the Ségou region (in current-day Mali) in the west, the Sahara was estimated to be advancing by as much as 1 kilometre per year. The only way to halt this 'invasion of the sands' was to create shelter belts or curtain reserves against dry *harmattan* winds, ideally composed of mixed deciduous or acacia forests that would be completely protected from grazing and fire (much like the 'great green

[123] Unwin, *West African Forests*, 91–2.   [124] Stebbing, *Forests of West Africa*, 233.

[125] Claude Garrier, *L'Exploitation coloniale des forêts de Côte d'Ivoire: une spoliation institutionnalisée* (Paris: l'Harmattan, 2006), 86, 139–42, 165–6.

[126] Mortimore, *Adapting*, 12–13; Henry Hubert, 'Le Desséchement progressif en Afrique Occidentale', *Bulletin du Comité d'Études Historiques et scientifiques d'AOF* (1920), 401–67; M. J. Lahache, 'Le Desséchement de l'Afrique française est-il demontré', *Bulletin de la Société de Géographie et d'Études Coloniales de Marseilles*, vol. 31 (1907), 149–85.

[127] Aubréville, *Forêt coloniale*, 25–35.

[128] Frédéric Martin, *Principes d'agriculture et d'économie rurale appliqués aux pays tropicaux* (Paris, 1935), 96.

[129] Stebbing, *Forests of West Africa*, 16.

wall' projects in Algeria in the 1970s and currently planned across the entire African Sahel).[130]

In order to provide a firm scientific basis for such efforts, a joint Anglo-French Forestry Commission was established in 1936–7 for the express purpose of ascertaining the extent of desert encroachment across West Africa and the degree to which it was being accelerated by human action. After a series of surveys stretching from the Niger River to Lake Chad, the Commission reached the resounding conclusion that the Sahara was not advancing and that fears of desert encroachment were groundless. It discovered no instances of large-scale sand movement; on the contrary, it found that the dunes had been largely stable since the desiccation of the Sahara in Late Quaternary times. Although there were clear signs of localized sand encroachment due to the cultivation of marginal soils, this was offset by evidence of countermovement in other areas. Ground water levels did not suggest any general climatic desiccation in recent times, and nor was there much evidence of receding woodlands: 'there is no lack of natural regeneration and in places it is even abundant.'[131] While afforestation efforts were recommendable in certain localities, the idea of creating an enormous green barrier along the desert fringe was unnecessary since there was already a natural belt of savannah forest up to 160 kilometres wide that was too dry to cultivate and that effectively separated farming areas from the desert.

In sum, the Anglo-French Forestry Commission concluded that 'under present climatic conditions there appears to be no imminent and general danger of desiccation'.[132] But if the spectre of climatic desertification was dismissed, the Commission nonetheless maintained that 'there is unquestionably an impoverishment of the sylvan conditions of the country'. Indeed, the fact that signs of forest degeneration could not be attributed to a changing climate meant that the blame fell even more squarely on human activity, in particular on the 'uncontrolled expansion of shifting cultivation as a result of the security afforded by European administration'.[133] After highlighting once again the well-known litany of problems—overgrazing, cultivation of marginal soils, consequent erosion—the Commission concluded that the real threat to West Africa's woodlands was not a desert invasion from without but rather a human attack from within. Shortly after the report appeared, Aubréville (one of the leading voices on the Commission) summed up the general consensus as follows: 'when one ascertains the diminution, disappearance, or physiological impoverishment of forest vegetation, one must, apart from rare exceptions, blame Man. Deforestation is the outcome of systematic and age-old destruction by the native.'[134]

---

[130] Jean Meniaud, 'La Déforestation des territoires tropicaux et ses conséquences pour l'agriculture', *L'Agronomie coloniale*, vol. 24 no. 206 (Feb. 1935), 33–40, esp. 39; E. P. Stebbing, 'The Encroaching Sahara: The Threat to the West African Colonies', *Geographical Journal*, vol. 85 (1935), 506–19, esp. 518; Stebbing, *Forests of West Africa*, 29; Fairhead and Leach, *Reframing*, 169–70; for the longer view, see the wide-ranging study by Diana K. Davis, *The Arid Lands: History, Power, Knowledge* (Cambridge, Mass.: MIT Press, 2016).

[131] *Report of the Anglo-French Forestry Commission 1936–37* (Lagos: Government Printer, 1937), 7.

[132] *Report of the Anglo-French Forestry Commission*, 8.

[133] *Report of the Anglo-French Forestry Commission*, 9.

[134] Aubréville, *Forêt coloniale*, 42; cf. Stamp, 'Southern Margin'.

The proposed solution was as obvious as it was familiar—familiar, at least, to anyone acquainted with colonial conservation efforts elsewhere in the tropics. Over the long term, an effective forestry regime could only work in tandem with sustainable forms of sedentary agriculture. As long as shifting cultivation continued, and as long as the agricultural frontier continued to expand, foresters harboured little hope of halting, let alone reversing, the inexorable process of degradation. In its final recommendations, the Anglo-French Commission thus reiterated a long-standing aim of colonial states throughout the tropics, namely to replace extensive forms of shifting cultivation with 'permanent farmlands, properly demarcated, regularly manured, adequately timbered with trees of local economic importance and with an assured supply of water'.[135] The specific model it had in mind was based on the mixed agriculture practices that had long been used by farmers in the 'close settled' zones of northern Nigeria, and that were promoted from the 1920s onwards by a handful of colonial agronomists with experience of comparable systems in India.[136]

But the obstacles that stood in the way of this reformist vision were equally familiar to anyone acquainted with agricultural improvement in the tropics. According to a seasoned French official, persuading indigenous farmers to abandon cherished land-use customs was only part of the challenge. Even more difficult was the need to devise and implement 'more rational methods of cultivation and husbandry that the environment, the soils and the available means do not always—far from it—make easy to impose'.[137] As we will see in Chapter 9, this task of negotiating the nexus of colonial expertise, indigenous know-how, and environmental variability was no easier in the fields and farmyards than in the forests of the tropical world.

[135] *Report of the Anglo-French Forestry Commission*, 9.

[136] Reginald Cline-Cole, 'Redefining Forestry Space and Threatening Livelihoods in Colonial Northern Nigeria', in Cline-Cole and Madge (eds.), *Contesting*, 36–63.

[137] J. Meniaud, 'Les Forêts des colonies françaises, leur importance et leur role: les raisons qu'a la métropole de s'en préoccuper', in *VIIe Congrès International d'Agriculture Tropicale et Subtropicale: comptes-rendus et rapports* (Paris, 1937), 339–42, here 342.

9

Cultivating the Colonies
Agriculture, Development, and Environment

One of the central leitmotifs of colonial rule was the 'development' of Europe's tropical dependencies. As the British Colonial Secretary Joseph Chamberlain proclaimed to Parliament in 1895, 'I regard many of our colonies as being in the condition of undeveloped estates,' raw assets that must be 'developed for the benefit of their population and for the benefit of the greater population which is outside'.[1] Through the application of Western capital, scientific knowledge, and expertise, European colonizers had not only the ability but also the duty to assist the 'less advanced races' in exploiting the prodigious natural wealth of the lands they inhabited.

This programme of colonial development was composed of many different elements, including all the hallmarks of progress (railways, roads, sanitation, education) that the European powers claimed to bestow upon subject peoples. As we have seen in Chapters 1–8, it also involved the rapid expansion of commodity production, along with whole new systems of resource governance. But what ultimately underpinned all of these activities was agriculture. Throughout the colonial period, the cultivation of food and fibre crops remained the fundamental basis of domestic economies across the tropical world. Agriculture was the sole or primary occupation of the vast bulk of the population, and it provided the calories and protein needed to sustain the growing workforces of the railways, mines, and plantations geared towards export markets. For 'development' to happen at all, stimulating agricultural production was essential. Few could disagree with Albert Milhe-Poutingon (a prominent member of the Union Coloniale Française) that agriculture constituted 'the prime factor in the economic development of the colonies'.[2]

Yet what 'agricultural development' actually meant was a matter of interpretation. In the late nineteenth and twentieth centuries, 'modern' agriculture was increasingly conceived as a means of accumulating capital rather than merely growing food. Before the First World War, colonial agricultural departments, botanical gardens, and experiment stations focused overwhelmingly on the needs of commercial plantations and the requirements of particular export crops. By contrast, subsistence cultivars received little attention at all. Not even the renowned Dutch botanical gardens at Buitenzorg—the 'Mecca of the tropical agriculturalist'—gave much consideration to staple food crops until well into the

[1] Quoted from Hodge, *Triumph*, 8.
[2] Speech at the 1897 International Colonial Congress in Brussels, quoted from Drayton, *Nature's Government*, 256.

twentieth century, and they were even more peripheral to research agendas at the gardens of Peradeniya, Singapore, Victoria, or Saigon.[3] Apart from the promotion of exports, the 'development' of indigenous agriculture initially meant little more than the extension of croplands into previously uncultivated wastes.

Over time, an assemblage of factors brought food crops and subsistence systems more sharply into focus. During the late nineteenth century, the devastating series of famines in South and Southeast Asia forced colonial governments to pay much closer attention to the question of food security. Likewise, the grim succession of colonial scandals—from Max Havelaar's attack on the Dutch Cultivation System to the 'red rubber' campaigns of the 1900s—made indigenous welfare in the colonies a focus of public scrutiny. After the First World War and the establishment of the League of Nations, the renewed need to justify colonial rule led to a greater emphasis on the duty of imperial powers to develop the economies of subject territories (perhaps most famously articulated in Frederick Lugard's concept of the 'dual mandate'). Agriculture was the main economic activity in the colonies, so any attempt to improve livelihoods would have to start there.

But the question of how 'native agriculture' should be developed, and by whom, was a complicated one. Answers were shaped by a range of different interests and issues: departmental rivalries, agricultural modernization in the metropoles, prevailing perceptions of tropical environments, and current understandings of indigenous farming systems. Persistent stereotypes of 'lazy natives' and tropical cornucopias led many officials to conclude that the chief obstacle to higher food production was the innate conservatism of the stagnant, tradition-bound societies they were governing. If peasants failed to adopt more advanced techniques or respond to new economic stimuli, then the solution was to impose innovations from outside. By contrast, some agronomists maintained that the problem was not an alleged cultural conservatism—farmers embraced some exotic cultivars with alacrity—but rather the inherent shortcomings of indigenous farming practices, which could be remedied through the deployment of superior methods.

Common to both perspectives was a belief in the need for technical innovation, and an assumption that European agriculture showed the way. After all, by the turn of the century farmers in Europe and North America were achieving unprecedented yield increases through the use of artificial fertilizers, improved crop varieties, and new cultivation methods.[4] Even in the early 1900s, long before the package of high-input mechanized agriculture had fully taken hold in Europe, Western observers tended to think that their intensive cropping systems were not only superior to those of the tropics (an argument that would have been much harder to sustain a century earlier) but also, with suitable adaptation, broadly replicable there. As European farming practices underwent radical change, so too did prescriptions for agriculture in the colonies. From the industrializing perspective

---

[3] *Report by the Right Honourable W. G. A. Ormsby Gore*, 120; see generally Harro Maat, *Science Cultivating Practice: A History of Agricultural Science in the Netherlands and its Colonies 1863–1986* (Dordrecht: Kluwer, 2001), 66–70; Headrick, *Tentacles*, 215–31.

[4] J. L. van Zanden, 'The First Green Revolution: The Growth of Production and Productivity in European Agriculture, 1870–1914', *Economic History Review*, vol. 44 (1991), 215–39.

of metropolitan agronomy, colonial food shortages were not the result of socio-economic inequalities or unpredictable weather events, but rather stemmed from deficiencies in agricultural technology.

Such an analysis was, of course, highly characteristic of modern states, and especially of their penchant for technical 'fixes'. Over the past two decades this tendency to privilege technological solutions in response to social, political, and environmental problems has been explored, dissected, and criticized by a multitude of historians and social scientists.[5] Time and again, 'high modernist' visions of scientific planning—whether for the model city, the rationally managed forest, or the factory farm—bracketed out forms of vernacular knowledge that did not suit their own internal logic of simplified standardization, and that consequently sowed the seeds of their own demise by grossly underestimating the complexity of the social or ecological systems they sought to master. Without a doubt, the history of colonial agriculture provides its fair share of examples. For all the remarkable achievements in the fields of plant transfer, disease control, and crop breeding, efforts to 'improve' tropical agriculture were repeatedly marred by ill-conceived interventions into poorly understood agro-ecosystems.

Yet not all aspects of the story fit this high modernist picture so neatly. For some of the leading agronomists of the day, the more they learned about tropical environments and farming systems, the more they realized they did not know. Over a period of several decades the gradual accretion of knowledge from the field led to a greater appreciation of the fragility of tropical soils and the diverse adaptations of indigenous agricultural techniques to local environmental conditions. Although the focus of colonial governments was chiefly fixed on export commodities and the 'modernization' of cultivation techniques, by the inter-war period the growing influence of ecological approaches gave rise to more holistic understandings of agricultural improvement, which powerfully shaped development policies over the following decades.

This chapter will explore the principal aims, methods, and effects of colonial agricultural development and how they evolved over the late nineteenth and early twentieth centuries. It does so in four steps, focusing first on the expansion of croplands and the intensification of farming techniques in tropical Asia, before turning to sub-Saharan Africa and the increasingly determined efforts to conserve agricultural resources from the threat of overexploitation.

AGRICULTURAL EXPANSION AND FRONTIER SETTLEMENT IN COLONIAL ASIA

Of all the environmental changes that took place in colonial Asia, the largest in purely spatial terms was undoubtedly the extension of the area under permanent or long-term cultivation. In many ways there was nothing uniquely 'colonial' about these changes, which represented the continuation of a centuries-old trajectory of

[5] Led most notably by Scott, *Seeing*; and Mitchell, *Rule of Experts*.

agricultural expansion driven by land-hungry peasants and revenue-hungry states. But even so, this ongoing process escalated markedly during the colonial era. Both the scale and pace of land conversion varied greatly from region to region, as did the factors that propelled it: commercial cropping in some areas, the spread of plantations or demographic expansion in others. Throughout most of colonial Asia the pre-eminent driver was the inexorable if uneven rise in the human population and the growing demand for food.

Across the whole of South Asia (India, Bangladesh, and Sri Lanka, but excluding modern Pakistan), large parts of which had been densely settled for many centuries, the best estimates of the cultivated area indicate a net rise of 25 million hectares—slightly larger than the surface of the United Kingdom—between 1880 (110.7 million ha) and 1950 (135.6 million ha). The fact that land conversion lagged noticeably behind the rate of population growth over the same seventy-year period (increasing from 253.1 million to 412.2 million) reflected a rise in the proportion of cultivated land that was cropped more than once per year. In mainland and island Southeast Asia (Myanmar, Cambodia, Laos, Vietnam, Thailand, Malaysia, Brunei, Singapore, Indonesia, Philippines), much of which was sparsely populated in comparison to the subcontinent, the changes were more drastic. Here the cultivated area roughly trebled between 1880 (16.1 million ha) and 1950 (45.7 million ha)—a net increase slightly smaller than the size of modern Italy—and was accompanied by a commensurate rise in population from 57.4 million to 177.1 million.[6]

We can get a clearer sense of the dynamics underlying these figures by considering the role of different crop categories. Taking South and Southeast Asia together, the fastest rate of expansion (from 9.4 million to 17.9 million ha, or a rise of 90 per cent) was registered for perennial crops, most of which were bound for overseas markets: for example, rubber, coffee, oil palm, tea, and coconut. In other words, the high growth rate for perennials was chiefly driven by the boom in long-distance trade and commodity exports during the colonial era. In terms of absolute surface area, however, it was the expansion of annual crops—above all rice, with wheat and maize playing secondary roles—that accounted for the bulk of land conversion (117.4 to 163.4 million ha, or a net gain of 46 million ha), even if the rate of growth (39 per cent) was less than half that for perennials. This reflected the simple fact that temporary crops covered approximately ten times more land area than perennial crops, a ratio that scarcely changed throughout the entire colonial period. Since annuals roughly corresponded to what we might call subsistence crops, and perennials to commercial crops, the numbers indicate that food production was the single most important factor driving land conversion. Of course, the equations were complex and differed substantially from place to place. Not all annual crops were grown for subsistence; cotton, sugar, and tobacco (all annuals) were among the oldest export crops in the region. In some areas (lower Burma, Cochin China) a large portion of the temporary food crop was destined for export, while in other localities (western Malaya, north-east Sumatra) clearance for export crops far

---

[6] Figures from Richards and Flint, 'Century', 20, 34, 36.

outstripped subsistence cultivation. But in general the production of food for local consumption accounted for most of the additional acreage.[7]

What these statistics illustrate is not only the central role of agricultural expansion for land conversion, but also, to turn things around, the crucial importance of land availability for agricultural growth. At base, they highlight the land-extensive character of much of what we might call 'agricultural development' in the Asian colonies. Despite the spread of double-cropping and other methods for squeezing more output from existing acreage, the rising demand for food and other crops—regardless of whether it was driven by demographic growth, higher consumption, new kinds of commodities, or trade links—was still met primarily by clearing and planting previously uncultivated land.

There was a clear economic logic behind this extensive pattern of growth, since land was far more abundant than either labour or capital throughout most of colonial Asia. But this was not universally true, and as a general rule surplus land was least available precisely where the pressure was greatest, namely in the densely populated lowlands where agricultural resources were already under considerable strain. In India's North-West Provinces, there were already 'large tracts where trees, much less forests, are almost unknown' in the 1890s.[8] By the 1920s forests covered only around 20 per cent of the entire surface of Java (most of it in the uplands), while in the heavily populated deltas of Tonkin and North Annam there was reportedly 'not a patch of earth uncultivated'.[9] As rural populations continued to swell, there was ever-increasing pressure to bring new land under the plough, most of which would have to be carved out of the forests. But as we saw in Chapter 8, this directly clashed with the efforts of colonial forest departments to conserve woodlands around settled areas, where fuel-wood and timber were in short supply.

Partly as a result of these demographic push factors, and partly due to the pull of new economic and trade opportunities, the search for fresh farmland brought more and more people into areas too marginal or remote to have attracted large farming populations in the past. During the late nineteenth and early twentieth centuries, such backwaters and 'wastelands' in fact witnessed some of the most dramatic environmental transformations in the entire tropical world. From the swampy river valleys of mainland Southeast Asia to the arid steppes of north-western India, a massive inward migration of peasants opened a string of new agricultural frontiers that fundamentally reshaped landscapes and economies across the region.

Although these pioneer movements in colonial Asia have attracted less scholarly attention than the agricultural colonization of the Americas or Australasia, the changes they unleashed were both profound and far-reaching. Like the 'neo-European' settlement of the temperate zones, they were driven by a bundle of interrelated factors: a growing shortage of arable land in population centres, swelling market demand, the introduction of land tenure systems that encouraged settlement, and a thickening network of communications that allowed merchants to connect farmers to distant markets. Many of the effects on regional societies and economies recalled

---

[7] Richards and Flint, 'Century', 27–9.   [8] Voelcker, *Report*, 151.
[9] Robequain, *Economic Development*, 53; Peluso and Vandergeest, 'Genealogies', 772.

those of the main European settlement frontiers. They provided an outlet for demographic pressures, they marginalized or displaced indigenous groups, and they created some of the largest food-exporting areas in the world. There were also numerous ecological parallels, given that all of these frontiers involved an enormous influx of people, plants, and domesticated animals into areas which, though hardly 'pristine' or untouched, were nonetheless relatively undisturbed by agrarian activities, or had at least been exploited in less intrusive ways. If the conversion of forest and steppe in colonial Asia was perhaps less epoch-making than the agricultural bio-invasion of the 'neo-Europes', it nonetheless entailed a thorough displacement of existing ecosystems.[10]

Some of the most far-reaching changes occurred in the great river deltas of mainland Southeast Asia.[11] Formed over millennia by silt deposition from their mountainous interiors, and protected from the sea by extensive mangrove swamps fringing the coast, the fertile alluvial soils of the Irrawaddy Delta in Burma and the Mekong in southern Indochina (as well as the Chao Phraya in central Thailand, which escaped formal colonial rule) were still covered in thick monsoon forests or grasslands when the colonial powers first took over. During the late nineteenth and early twentieth centuries these sprawling deltaic plains were cleared, dyked, drained, and sown in one of the most feverish bouts of pioneer agricultural settlement anywhere in the world. In no more than half a century, their complex riverine ecosystems were transformed into the world's leading rice-exporting area.

The first of these frontiers opened in the lower reaches of the Irrawaddy Delta. When Lower Burma was annexed by the British in 1852, only around 3,200 of its 40,000 km² of marshy grasslands and rich *kanazo* (*Heritiera fomes*) forest had been cleared for cultivation. With the establishment of British control, the pace of land clearance accelerated sharply, though less as the result of specific colonial policies than of the indirect effects further upstream. One of the most important consequences of colonial rule in Lower Burma was the disruption of established trade patterns with the more densely populated region of Upper Burma, which was still independent from European control but which relied on surpluses from the Delta to supplement its drought-prone dry-rice food economy. As population pressures mounted in the inland Dry Zone, peasants were quietly allowed to migrate southwards where they were welcomed by British authorities eager to develop the lowland economy. In the early 1880s a series of poor rice harvests brought matters to a head; in 1884 alone around a quarter of a million people left the southern Mandalay provinces for the Delta.[12]

---

[10] On the frontier characteristics of agricultural expansion in colonial Asia, see Michael Adas, 'Continuity and Transformation: Colonial Rice Frontiers and their Environmental Impact on the Great River Deltas of Mainland Southeast Asia', in Burke and Pomeranz (eds), *Environment*, 191–207; David Biggs, *Quagmire: Nation-Building and Nature in the Mekong Delta* (Seattle: University of Washington Press, 2010); Imran Ali, *The Punjab under Imperialism, 1885–1947* (Princeton: Princeton University Press, 1988), 3–7.

[11] Adas, 'Continuity'.

[12] Keeton, *King Thebaw*, 143; more generally Michael Adas, *The Burma Delta: Economic Development and Social Change on an Asian Rice Frontier, 1852–1941* (Madison, Wis.: University of Wisconsin Press, 1974).

Colonization of the Irrawaddy Delta was, then, well under way by the time the British conquered Upper Burma in 1885/6, though the process sped up markedly in the wake of formal annexation. In a bid to boost land and export revenues, British authorities encouraged yet more Upper Burmese settlers to brave the Delta's malarial swamps and clear its mangrove forests for rice cultivation. Railway construction, which first began in the 1870s, was stepped up to connect the main rice-growing provinces with coastal ports. Roads and river transport were also improved. The Irrawaddy Flotilla Company, founded in 1868 as a quasi-state enterprise, operated over 600 vessels by 1932. Hundreds of kilometres of canals were dug in order to extend the reach of the river's floodwaters and to link up the vast network of paddy fields that was taking shape, especially in the eastern sections of the Delta.

Farmers came to the area in droves, mostly from the Dry Zone of Upper Burma but also from the east coast of India, swelling the Delta's population from around 1.5 million in 1852 to over 4 million by the turn of the century. For the ecosystems of the region, the overall result was the rapid disappearance of mangrove, swamp, and jungle. Paddy acreage rose by 76 per cent during the 1890s alone, and in some areas the rate of clearance was so fast as to cause local land shortages by 1897. Although the pace of land conversion slowed somewhat after 1900—by which time the most accessible sections of the Delta had already been cleared—overall acreage continued to rise through the inter-war years. From 1852 to the early 1930s the area under rice grew from approximately 284,000 hectares to more than 3.4 million hectares. Over the same period rice exports correspondingly shot up from 162,000 to almost 3 million tons, making Lower Burma a key supplier for the world food market and especially for the expanding mine and plantation workforces dotted around Southeast Asia.[13]

Meanwhile, a similar process of frontier expansion was under way in the Mekong Delta.[14] Long before the piecemeal conquest of the Delta by the French, Khmer and Vietnamese emperors had constructed a series of canal systems to encourage the settlement of Vietnamese peasants and to consolidate their influence in the region.[15] The French, for their part, began to extend these pre-colonial waterworks in the 1860s, though most of their canal-building came after the turn of the century with the deployment of mechanized dredges. From 1900 to 1930 French dredgers removed some 165 million cubic metres of mud and soil. To give a sense of scale, this made the canalization of the Mekong Delta the third largest earth-moving exercise in history (ranking only behind the construction of the Suez and Panama canals).[16] By the 1930s around 2,600 kilometres of primary and secondary

---

[13] Adas, *Burma*, 35, 128–9; Adas, 'Continuity', 195.

[14] Pierre Brocheux, *The Mekong Delta: Ecology, Economy and Evolution, 1860–1960* (Madison, Wis.: University of Wisconsin Press, 1995); Biggs, *Quagmire*; Martin J. Murray, *The Development of Capitalism in Colonial Indochina (1870–1940)* (Berkeley: University of California Press, 1980).

[15] On pre-colonial settlement, Biggs, *Quagmire*, 59–70.

[16] David Biggs, 'Managing a Rebel Landscape: Conservation, Pioneers, and the Revolutionary Past in the U Minh Forest, Vietnam', *Environmental History*, vol. 10 no. 3 (July 2005), 448–76, here 456.

canals linked the western provinces of Cochin China to the rice mills at Cholon and the main port at Saigon.[17]

The main function of these hydraulic works was to facilitate transport and to allow an expansion of seasonal flood-based rice cultivation, much like the parallel infrastructure in Lower Burma. But given that the entire Mekong Delta rises scarcely more than 2 metres above sea level (which is roughly equivalent to the highest China Sea tides), its waterworks were also designed to drain salt water away from low-lying sections and to protect croplands from periodic storm surges. Irrigation in the form of water storage and uninterrupted availability was not the central purpose (though the network of channels did enable some planters to regulate water levels on their fields rather than rely entirely on the region's irregular precipitation). The key task was to control and harness the volatile seasonal flows of the Mekong, a challenge that would have been far more difficult were it not for a remarkable natural buffer mechanism: the Tonlé Sap (or Grand Lac) in Cambodia, a huge natural reservoir that absorbs the river's floodwaters during the monsoon period and releases them during the dry season. In essence, the system of canals and dykes was designed to absorb and channel this run-off into an ever-expanding grid of paddy fields. From 1880 to the 1930s the combined paddy area of Cochin China rose from 522,000 to 2.2 million hectares, with rice exports growing even faster from 284,000 to over 1.5 million tons.[18]

Of course, colonial officials liked to claim the credit for 'improving' these previously 'unproductive' lands. But in fact, the transformation owed as much to peasant initiative as to colonial development policies. As is usually the case with processes of pioneer agricultural settlement, there was a close convergence of interests between rulers eager to extend their revenue base and farmers keen to improve their own lot. Most of the hard work of clearing and sowing the Delta was done by settlers from the densely populated lowlands of central and northern Vietnam, long the key centres of peasant migration into the Mekong floodplain.[19] The French authorities, like their British counterparts, tried to attract migrants into the Delta through low taxes and promises of land, though in contrast to British land policies in Burma they also granted large concessions to French *colons* and wealthy Vietnamese or Chinese investors, especially in the southern and western sections of the Delta (which produced a disproportionate share of exports). Over time, the expansion of these estates, in conjunction with mounting smallholder indebtedness and associated land foreclosure, led to a steady rise in the number of tenant farmers working more or less at subsistence levels for large rice-producing *latifundia*. The resulting social disparities were grotesque. In 1930, 48 per cent of the Delta's paddy land was owned by only 4 per cent of the population, while nearly three-quarters of rural households had no land at all.[20] Although such glaring

[17] Robequain, *Economic Development*, 110–11; on canal-building and dredging, Biggs, *Quagmire*, 30–48.

[18] Gourou, *L'Utilisation*, 284–95; Robequain, *Economic Development*, 220.

[19] Biggs, *Quagmire*, 70–1.

[20] J. F. Le Coq, G. Trébuil, and M. Dufumier, 'History of Rice Production in the Mekong Delta', in Peter Boomgaard and David Henley (eds), *Smallholders and Stockbreeders: History of Foodcrop and*

levels of inequity did not spark uprisings on the same scale as in other parts of colonial Vietnam, they were certainly no recipe for political or social stability.[21]

The ecological changes on these rice frontiers were similarly severe. Although details about fauna populations are sketchy, it can safely be assumed that the replacement of some of the world's most biodiverse forests by millions of hectares of rice monocultures destroyed the habitat of countless species, from birds and reptiles to elephants and tigers. Moreover, the fallout was by no means confined to the land. In the Mekong Delta in particular, which was home to nearly 2 million hectares of mangrove forest, land clearance and the construction of hydraulic works eliminated huge areas of protective habitat for fish and crustaceans.[22]

Nor were the effects temporally limited to the initial act of agricultural colonization, for the alteration of the terrestrial and riverine environments eventually led to problems for the new agro-ecosystems themselves. The thousands of kilometres of canals and dykes gave farmers greater control over seasonal water supplies, but they also reduced the delivery of nutrient subsidies from upstream. Without monsoon floods there was far less silt deposition, and without the annual supply of silt, the intensively cropped soils of the deltas gradually lost fertility.[23] By reducing the periodic ebb and flow of the rivers, the new canals also prevented farmers from draining away standing water that, if left too long on their paddies, became increasingly acidic and stunted plant growth by encouraging the build-up of alum salts.[24] In addition, the relatively homogeneous crop cover invited its own problems. The rice monocultures of the river deltas comprised only a small number of different strains, and this lack of crop diversity was further magnified by the tendency, especially among large landholders, to maximize rice exports by buying in other foodstuffs rather than growing them locally. In the lower Mekong Delta, stem borers alone destroyed around 10 to 15 per cent of the crop each year, and there were further losses to beetles, rats, crabs, and leaf hoppers. Overall, between 15 and 30 per cent of the annual rice crop was lost to pests and disease.[25]

By any standard, these were huge environmental transformations. Yet when viewed in global perspective, the colonization of Southeast Asia's river deltas appears less destructive overall than the concurrent frontier movements in the Americas.[26] Despite extensive deforestation on the deltaic plains, the creation of paddy fields did not always supplant high rainforest or mangrove. In some areas it meant little more than the substitution of a particular type of marsh grass—rice—for other species of marsh grass. The fact that the canal systems generally allowed for a partial (albeit reduced) continuation of seasonal flooding meant that they did not entirely halt the delivery of nutrient-rich silt that had created the fertile deltas in the first place. Furthermore, the traditional wet rice cultivation techniques that prevailed before the 1960s and 1970s were relatively sustainable, and indeed

Livestock Farming in Southeast Asia (Leiden: KITLV, 2004), 163–85, here 169, 172; Gourou, *L'Utilisation*, 269–83.

[21] Biggs, *Quagmire*, 91–195; Adas, 'Continuity', 197.
[22] Generally: Brocheux, *Mekong*; Biggs, *Quagmire*, 75; Adas, 'Continuity', 199.
[23] Murray, *Development*, 444; Adas, *Burma*, 131.   [24] Biggs, *Quagmire*, 95–6.
[25] Murray, *Development*, 446.   [26] This is based on Adas, 'Continuity', 201–2.

functioned with little exogenous input from commercial firms or state-sponsored scientific experts. As a result, the overall scope of ecological transformation in Southeast Asia's river deltas was less extreme than the annihilation of forests by Brazilian coffee planters or the plough-up of prairies by settlers in North America.

The same can scarcely be said for the enormous expansion of cropland in the arid steppes and deserts of north-western India. During the late nineteenth and early twentieth centuries, the attempt to turn these barren landscapes into the granary of the subcontinent represented a radical alteration of the biophysical environment spearheaded by an enthusiastically interventionist colonial state.

Once again, the key to the transformation was the control of water. Water was a major constraint on agricultural production across large parts of South Asia, but it was especially acute in those areas that did not benefit from monsoonal rainfall, above all in Sind and the western reaches of the Punjab. The floodplains of this region were, despite their arid climate, among the oldest agricultural centres in all of India. The annual floodwaters of the Indus River, which originate from the snow-covered peaks of the Himalayas, have been harnessed by farmers for over 4,000 years. The river is fed by a group of tributaries that descend south and west through the Punjab (the 'land of five rivers') before converging just above the Sind province.

Controlling these waters was crucial for cultivating the region as well as for governing it. Long before the British arrived, a series of rulers—including the Mughal emperors and their successors—constructed seasonal inundation canals in an attempt to expand their agricultural base and consolidate their power. After the British conquest in the 1830s–1840s, the initial focus was on the restoration and extension of existing waterworks, which mainly channelled the seasonal floods into fields immediately adjoining the rivers.[27] Before long, however, a new cohort of hydraulic engineers devised more ambitious plans to irrigate the extensive *doabs*, or slightly elevated areas that stretched between the tributary rivers of the Punjab, in a bid to strengthen British authority in what was still effectively a frontier zone. In the 1880s the British began building a vast system of permanent weirs and perennial canals designed to convey a reliable year-round supply of water to millions of hectares of the western Punjab and Sind. By the early twentieth century it had grown into one of the largest irrigation systems in the world, covering roughly 5 million hectares by 1918 and around 7.5 million hectares (an area slightly larger than Ireland) by the mid-1940s.[28]

This gigantic irrigation network opened colonial India's single greatest agrarian frontier. From the 1880s onwards it permitted the permanent settlement and cultivation of vast tracts of previously desolate scrub and desert. The nuclei of the transformation were the so-called 'canal colonies', planned farming settlements built to attract an influx of peasant migrants from the more crowded districts of

[27] David Gilmartin, 'Scientific Empire and Imperial Science: Colonialism and Irrigation Technology in the Indus Basin', *Journal of Asian Studies*, vol. 53 no. 4 (1994), 1127–49, figures p. 1143; Ali, *Punjab*, 5.

[28] Gilmartin, 'Scientific Empire', 1143n.; David Gilmartin, *Blood and Water: The Indus River Basin in Modern History* (Berkeley: University of California Press, 2015), esp. 144–81.

eastern and central Punjab. The settlement colonies were the focal points of a two-sided process of socio-ecological change, one that supplanted the sparse desert vegetation with lush fields of grain and fodder crops while simultaneously displacing (or sedentarizing) the scattered pastoralist groups that had previously roamed the area. The results were remarkable. By the 1910s the once barren *doabs* of western Punjab were the breadbasket of the Raj. For the remainder of the colonial period the Punjab yielded prodigious wheat crops for commercial export, provided herds of horses and camels for the army, and generated more tax revenue than any other province of India. Its peasantry was among the most prosperous in the entire empire, and despite rising tensions over water rights and caste privileges, it dutifully repaid the Crown by providing around half of the manpower for the Indian Army. The largest agricultural expansion project in colonial India thus strengthened the Raj on two different levels. It not only reinforced British control over the territories bordering the sensitive north-west frontier, it also helped secure Britain's military position throughout the rest of the subcontinent.[29]

For all these reasons the colonization of the Indus desert was long celebrated as a model of state-led agricultural development and a showpiece of enlightened colonial rule. The irrigation systems themselves were of global engineering significance, and served as a key source of expert knowledge for canal-building projects in many other parts of the world. But all of these changes came at considerable cost, and the costs only mounted as time progressed.

Perhaps the biggest problem was malaria, which soon became the scourge of India's canal-irrigated tracts. Infection rates rose more or less in line with the expansion of the irrigation network, and were punctuated by periodic outbreaks, including a major epidemic that swept the Punjab in 1908. By the early 1920s, endemic malaria in the canal colonies had become so serious as to raise fundamental questions about the wisdom of canal-building schemes.[30] Waterlogging and soil salinization also caused severe problems. By the 1900s the struggle against rising water tables was one of the primary tasks of the Punjab Irrigation Institute in Lahore, and in 1918 the incidence of waterlogging had become so alarming that the Punjab government established a special Drainage Board (superseded in 1925 by a Waterlogging Enquiry Committee) to devise solutions for the stricken canal commands.[31] But despite such reclamation efforts, the problem continued to spread. By the 1940s waterlogging and salinity reduced yields by as much as 75 per cent across large parts of the Punjab, and each year took some 20,000 hectares out of cultivation altogether.[32]

---

[29] Generally: Ali, *Punjab*; M. Mufakharul Islam, *Irrigation, Agriculture and the Raj: Punjab, 1887–1947* (New Delhi: Manohar, 1997); Gilmartin, *Blood*, 27–68.

[30] Elizabeth Whitcombe, 'The Environmental Costs of Irrigation in British India: Waterlogging, Salinity and Malaria', in Arnold and Guha (eds), *Nature, Culture, Imperialism*, 237–59, here 254–7; I. Agnihotri, 'Ecology, Land Use and Colonisation: The Canal Colonies of Punjab', *Indian Economic and Social History Review*, vol. 33 no. 1 (1996), 37–58.

[31] Nirmal Tej Singh, *Irrigation and Soil Salinity in the Indian Subcontinent: Past and Present* (Bethlehem, Pa: Lehigh University Press, 2005), 159–63.

[32] Whitcombe, 'Environmental Costs', 255; Gilmartin, *Blood*, 235–40.

In certain respects the agricultural colonization of India's north-western steppes followed the classic frontier pattern of boom and decline. The newly opened farmland initially paid a handsome dividend, but returns steadily fell as the negative effects of disease and soil degradation took hold. The parallels with other instances of frontier agricultural settlement were not lost on contemporaries. As one agronomist pointedly remarked, 'When the engineers, by means of perennial canals, enabled the surplus population of the congested areas of the Eastern Punjab to conquer the desert, a system of exploitation of the virgin soil took place not unlike that in North America when the great Western movement occurred.'[33]

All told, the expansion of agricultural land in colonial Asia claimed around 62 million hectares of grassland, desert, forest, and swamp between 1880 and 1950.[34] As long as new cropland was readily available, this overall pattern of land-extensive growth remained the default response to the needs of a growing population and rising market demand. Long after the settlement of the western Punjab and the deltas of the Mekong and Irrawaddy, there were still large areas of forest, grassland, and swamp that could be (and subsequently were) converted to cropland, especially in Southeast Asia and the mountainous districts of India. But if the outward agrarian frontier was nowhere near 'closing' during the colonial era, local land shortages nonetheless placed tight restrictions on agricultural growth in the main heartlands of settlement. By the early twentieth century it was clear that any attempt to raise agricultural production above population growth would require not only more hectares of cropland but also more crops per hectare. The ensuing campaign to make tropical agriculture more productive opened a whole new horizon for colonial agricultural intervention. Instead of merely converting undomesticated ecosystems into farmland, the focus now lay on optimizing agro-ecosystems themselves.

INTENSIFICATION AND IMPROVEMENT

When Europeans built their colonial administrations in Asia they found themselves presiding over a wide range of sophisticated agricultural systems. Throughout the region, long-settled peasant societies cultivated a broad assortment of food and fibre crops, often supplementing them with home gardens and fruit trees. Wheats and millets predominated in the alluvial plains of northern and western India, along with smaller amounts of maize and barley. Pulses (e.g. gram, pigeon peas) were found nearly everywhere on the South Asian peninsula, and were generally grown in rotation with cereals as a means of restoring soil nitrogen. Rice dominated throughout Southeast Asia, and was the primary staple of India's monsoon-watered lowlands encircling the Bay of Bengal. In addition to the 'wet rice' cultivation methods that prevailed among settled farmers (that is, bunded fields

---

[33] Howard, *Crop Production*, 36–7.
[34] Figure based on Richards and Flint, 'Century', 17; Gilmartin, 'Scientific Empire', 1143n.

that were inundated during most or all of the growing season), dry or rain-fed rice was the main subsistence crop for most shifting cultivators.[35]

Many of these systems had been developed over centuries of experimentation and evolved into a bewildering variety of permutations suited to local ecological circumstances. Wheat and rice had been grown in parts of India for around 8,000 years; wet rice or 'sawah' techniques dated back at least 2,000 years on Java. Some of these methods were remarkably productive. Wet rice cultivation in particular could achieve yields far in excess of most European cropping regimes, and sustained far higher population densities until well into the nineteenth century. What's more, it also stood the test of time. For European agronomists who lacked much familiarity with aquatic cultivars, it was puzzling to find that rice paddies could, under favourable conditions, be cultivated almost indefinitely without significant yield declines or loss of fertility. In some cases fertility even increased over time as soil nutrients were replenished by irrigation water, nitrogen-fixing blue-green algae, the ploughing under of rice stalks, and the manure of oxen that were pastured on the paddies after harvest. These rice-growing systems were among the most productive and stable forms of agriculture anywhere in the world.[36]

Improving them was no small challenge, and the attempt to do so centred on the same issues that engrossed agricultural modernizers the world over: better irrigation, more intensive cultivation techniques, and better crop varieties. All three elements were closely interrelated. The benefits of extra water and fertility could only be fully realized by cultivars that were specially bred to respond to them, just as the selected crop varieties required controlled growing conditions if they were to outperform existing strains. On all of these fronts, colonial advances broadly paralleled developments in the industrial world. In tropical and temperate zones alike, the basic aim was to harness agro-ecosystems more tightly to human designs through the application of scientific knowledge and modern cultivation practices, which were to be administered on the ground by newly created bureaucracies and agricultural extension services. But despite the many parallels with metropolitan agronomy, agricultural development in the colonies was also shaped by the particularities of tropical ecosystems, as well as by debates about whose strategies and interests should be prioritized.

Irrigation was the paramount tool of colonial agricultural modernization. The technological manipulation of water played a key role not only in opening new agrarian frontiers but also in better exploiting the labour and soils of long-established agricultural regions. For all the resources that were poured into India's

---

[35] A smaller amount of dry rice was also grown on permanent fields: Howard, *Crop Production*, 100, 111, 162–3; Boomgaard, *Southeast Asia*, 223–7; see also John F. Richards, Edward S. Haynes, and James R. Hagen, 'Changes in the Land and Human Productivity in Northern India, 1870–1970', *Agricultural History*, vol. 59 no. 4 (Oct. 1985), 523–48.

[36] Generally: Francesca Bray, *The Rice Economies: Technology and Development in Asian Societies* (Berkeley: University of California Press, 1986), 8–19. As regards sustainability, the methane production associated with wet rice cultivation is nowadays recognized as a significant contributor of greenhouse gases, and perhaps one of the oldest sources of anthropogenic climate-change: W. F. Ruddiman, *Plows, Plagues, and Petroleum: How Humans Took Control of Climate* (Princeton: Princeton University Press, 2005); Adas, 'Continuity', 204–5.

canal colonies or Southeast Asia's new paddy networks, most colonial irrigation schemes were built to enhance productivity in existing centres of cultivation. There were two main aspects to this task, one spatial and the other temporal. Spatially, the aim was to extend irrigation to previously un-watered croplands, especially in areas that were prone to periodic drought. Temporally, it was to make water available throughout the entire year, thus allowing farmers to crop their fields more frequently. Both involved a substantial reordering of pre-colonial environments, and both were animated by a desire to increase yields and prevent famine. Yet there were various ways to achieve these aims, and the fact that they were mainly pursued through the construction of large, centrally managed systems demonstrates that irrigation was always about more than just boosting agricultural output.

As historians have long recognized, canal projects were shaped by a range of different influences and served a multitude of purposes: raising revenue, improving transport, and enhancing military security. Just as important, they also reflected a subtle but important shift in the understanding of rivers (along with much of the rest of the natural world) during the nineteenth and twentieth centuries. Colonial irrigation schemes were part of an increasingly globalized discourse of water engineering that sought to transform the hydrosphere into a knowable set of mathematical flows and units of capacity that could be calculated, harnessed, distributed, bought, and sold to maximum economic advantage, especially that of the state.[37] Like the 'scientific' management of the forests, this was a distinct form of water knowledge that helped secure colonial domination over subject environments through a claim to greater efficiency and rationality. And as such, it also tended to devalue traditional irrigation systems, especially those controlled by ordinary farmers.

Many of colonial Asia's agricultural heartlands boasted irrigation works that dated back centuries if not millennia. The fertile alluvial plains of northern India were criss-crossed by a network of ancient tanks, canals, and barrages that harnessed the seasonal melt-water flowing from the Himalayas. In the coastal deltas of Madras, Tonkin, and Annam, dense farming populations had long channelled and stored monsoonal run-off to inundate their rice fields and carry them through the dry season. The rice terraces of Java, Madura, and Bali were extraordinary feats of local engineering, fed by elaborate channels that turned entire hillsides into staircases of carefully contoured *sawah* plots. Most systems were initially designed and controlled by elites to augment their political power, but routine maintenance and supervision was commonly organized on a local or communal basis. Many pre-colonial societies were therefore 'hydraulic', though not necessarily 'despotic', long before Europeans governed them.[38]

---

[37] David Gilmartin, 'Models of the Hydraulic Environment: Colonial Irrigation, State Power and Community in the Indus Basin', in Arnold and Guha (eds), *Nature, Culture, Imperialism*, 210–36, here 212–14.
[38] The terminology of course comes from Karl Wittfogel, *Oriental Despotism: A Comparative Study of Total Power* (New Haven: Yale University Press, 1957). See generally Elizabeth Whitcombe, 'Irrigation', in Dharma Kumar and Meghnad Desai (eds), *The Cambridge Economic History of India*, vol. 2 (Cambridge: Cambridge University Press, 1983), 677–736; Anne Booth, *Agricultural Development in*

The extent to which such traditional water harvesting systems were displaced by a new 'colonial hydrology' has long been a matter of debate.[39] Clearly the effects of colonial interventions were not uniform. While some pre-existing waterworks (e.g. in marginal areas of southern India) showed signs of decline long before the onset of colonial rule, others (e.g. in western Rajasthan) successfully coexisted with modern canal technologies well into the twentieth century.[40] Yet on balance, colonial hydro-engineering projects not only tended to marginalize older irrigation methods, they were often quite consciously designed to do so.

During the great canal-building boom in nineteenth-century India, much of the existing hydrological infrastructure was ignored or overlaid in the rush to build massive irrigation systems that could deliver water to larger areas and thus generate higher revenues. As money was poured into the Ganges and Jumna Canals, and subsequently into the gargantuan works of the Punjab, many older systems—the inundation canals of Bengal, the tank and channel systems of South Bihar, the small dams of Tamil Nadu—fell into disrepair. The last of colonial India's great canal projects, the Sarda Canal in Oudh (commissioned in 1928) was expressly designed to replace the existing patchwork of small-scale irrigation works in the name of productivity and efficiency.[41]

The situation was broadly similar in the East Indies, where the initial focus on improving ancient waterworks gave way to a more ambitious approach by the late nineteenth century. In 1890 the government in Batavia launched a 'General Irrigation Plan' that sought to irrigate some 577,000 bouws (just over 400,000 hectares) spread across nineteen different projects. Much of the effort centred on the construction of modern flood controls and feeder canals in central and eastern Java, which were designed to replace the small reservoirs and channels that had previously tided peasants over during the dry season.[42]

But colonial canal-builders did not have it all their own way. In some agricultural centres the local topography afforded little scope to override existing irrigation systems, forcing engineers to work within them instead. In the densely populated Tonkin Delta, for instance, local farmers had long confined the meandering streams of the Red River between high dykes, which had to be periodically elevated as sedimentation raised stream beds. Because these dykes determined the

---

Indonesia (London: Allen & Unwin, 1988), 73–81; David Hardiman, 'Small-Dam Systems of the Sahyadris', in Arnold and Guha (eds), *Nature, Culture, Imperialism*, 185–209.

[39] For a brief historiographic overview, Rohan D'Souza, 'Water in British India: The Making of a "Colonial Hydrology"', *History Compass*, vol. 4 no. 4 (2006), 621–8; see also Peter L. Schmitthenner, 'Colonial Hydraulic Projects in South India: Environmental and Cultural Legacy', in Kumar, Damodaran, and D'Souza (eds), *British Empire*, 181–201; Rohan D'Souza, *Drowned and Dammed: Colonial Capitalism and Flood Control in Eastern India* (New Delhi: Oxford University Press, 2006); Elizabeth Whitcombe, *Agrarian Conditions in Northern India: The United Provinces under British Rule, 1860–1900* (Berkeley: University of California Press, 1972); Ian Stone, *Canal Irrigation in British India: Perspectives on Technological Change in a Peasant Economy* (Cambridge: Cambridge University Press, 1985).

[40] David Mosse, *The Rule of Water: Statecraft, Ecology, and Collective Action in South India* (New Delhi: Oxford University Press, 2003); D'Souza, 'Water', 624.

[41] Whitcombe, 'Environmental Costs'; Whitcombe, 'Irrigation', 726.

[42] Wim Ravesteijn, *De zegenrijke heeren der wateren: irrigatie en staat op Java, 1832–1942* (Delft: Delft University Press, 1997), 111–206, *passim*.

location of villages and cultivated fields—some of which, especially around Hanoi, lay several metres below the river level—it was 'not possible to start brand new projects in this region as it would be in open country or new territory; all that can be done is to restore, correct and develop'.[43] In contrast to the hydraulic works in the Mekong Delta, French engineers in Tonkin focused mainly on improving the existing lacework of canals and the dykes that contained them, especially in the wake of a catastrophic burst in 1915 that flooded a quarter of the entire delta and destroyed crops and villages over an area of around 1,000 square kilometres.[44]

One of the chief attractions of large-scale irrigation projects was that they appealed to so many disparate interests: agronomists, landowners, private investors, and advocates of 'native welfare' alike. But this did not render them immune to criticism, especially as the costs and side-effects began to mount up. In India, revenues from the major canal works persistently fell short of overheads. Despite the overriding focus of canal designers on profitability and revenues, and despite high charges for users, India's canal network operated in the red until well after the First World War.[45] Moreover, much of the water it supplied was wasted anyway. In the early 1920s it was estimated that the wheat fields of Upper India were overwatered by between 30 and 50 per cent. Much also ended up where it was not wanted, or in excessive amounts that diminished rather than increased crop productivity.[46]

The consequences of these defects were visible not only in the account books of canal companies, but also, as we have seen, in extensive waterlogging and salinization of soils. In some of the worst affected areas, for instance around Amritsar, waterlogging was so severe that special tube-wells had to be built for subsoil drainage. Along the Nira Left Bank Canal in Deccan, approximately one-third of the scheme's 33,000-hectare command area was damaged by alkali build-up.[47] Worse still were the lethal malarial outbreaks that followed the opening of new canals along all the major systems. It is telling that such soil and disease problems were more acute in the Ganges and Indus basins of northern India, which were fed by snow melt and dominated by large perennial irrigation canals, than in southern parts of India where water supplies relied on the monsoon and where colonial irrigation works were more likely to incorporate older systems that periodically allowed soils to dry out and become aerated.[48] Characteristically, however, attempts to remedy these problems centred on yet more technical fixes—surface drains, canal lining, oiling of ponds, quinine distribution—rather than any fundamental questioning of large-scale irrigation works per se.

[43] Robequain, *Economic Development*, 53.

[44] Gourou, *L'Utilisation*, 217–27; Robequain, *Economic Development*, 223–6; Rémi Dumont, *La Culture du riz dans le delta du Tonkin: étude et propositions d'amélioration des techniques traditionnelles de riziculture tropicale* (Paris: Société d'Éditions Géographiques, Maritimes et Coloniales, 1935).

[45] Whitcombe, 'Irrigation'; Whitcombe, 'Environmental Costs', 238.

[46] Howard, *Crop Production*, 29.　　　　[47] Howard, *Crop Production*, 29.

[48] Whitcombe, 'Irrigation'; Schmitthenner, 'Colonial Hydraulic Projects'; Hardiman, 'Small-Dam Systems'.

In essence, perennial irrigation sought to 'correct' for the local shortcomings of nature. Wherever insufficient or unpredictable water supplies were the chief brake on agricultural output, they could be remedied in the interests of economic growth. Yet more often than not, the attempt to level out such natural variations ended up creating new discrepancies. As a general rule, perennial irrigation enhanced productivity wherever soil conditions and surface topography permitted sufficient drainage. But wherever circumstances were unfavourable, the presence of excess water actually reduced output. Irrigation thus had highly divergent effects in different localities. While in some areas it resulted in 'oases of good soils, well watered and attended by the benefits of the optimum in natural resources', in others it led to 'saline deserts and bald patches of alkalinity, the swamps and waterlogged tracts, the erosion of riverine areas'.[49]

Perennial irrigation systems also affected the agricultural potential of the land in other ways. Above all, they tended to deplete soil fertility on two fronts. While dams and barrages eliminated or reduced the deposition of beneficial silt onto cultivated fields, they simultaneously raised demands on soil fertility due to the upsurge of multiple-cropping that was made possible in the first place by the continual availability of irrigation water. Both of these changes had significant long-term implications for agricultural production, and contemporaries were by no means unaware of this. When the renowned hydrological engineer William Willcocks was asked in the 1920s to advise on the problem of slumping yields in the deltas of central and western Bengal, he was scathing about the suppression of seasonal inundation systems by modern irrigation works. Whereas the new channels were stagnant and clogged with sediment, the ancient overflow canals had carried a yearly supply of nutrient-rich silt that long maintained fertility on the cultivated delta plain. Just as important, they brought a beneficial influx of fish that fed on harmful mosquito larvae while also providing farmers with a valuable source of dietary protein.[50]

The advent of modern irrigation works thus altered much more than just water supplies. It modified entire agro-ecosystems, and many of the changes were detrimental to the land and the people working it. Both Willcocks and the malariologist Charles Bentley, Director of Public Health in Bengal, argued that the recent irrigation schemes should be restructured or even abandoned in favour of older inundation technology: 'If there is one thing one has learnt in Bengal it is that health and wealth have accompanied the "overflow irrigation" of the ancients, and malaria and poverty have followed its abandonment.'[51] But such high-profile critics remained the exception among British officialdom. Despite widespread recognition of the negative consequences of perennial irrigation, the scale of hydraulic works continued to grow in the late Raj.

---

[49] Whitcombe, *Agrarian Conditions*, 275; Whitcombe, 'Environmental Costs', 239–40, 258–9.
[50] Sir William Willcocks, *The Restoration of the Ancient Irrigation of Bengal* (Lecture to the British India Association, 6 Mar. 1928) (Calcutta: Calcutta General Printing Co., 1928), 3–8.
[51] Willcocks, *Restoration*, 17; Charles A. Bentley, *Malaria and Agriculture in Bengal: How to Reduce Malaria in Bengal by Irrigation* (Calcutta: Bengal Secretariat Book Depot, 1925); see also Iftekhar Iqbal, *The Bengal Delta: Ecology, State and Social Change, 1840–1943* (Basingstoke: Palgrave, 2010).

Against this backdrop it is interesting to note the rather different trajectory of irrigation development in the East Indies. Although Dutch officials were every bit as keen to modify the physical environment to economic advantage, the specific political context in the East Indies, and the overarching imperative to provide water for both sugar and rice production, prompted a more thorough reconsideration of large irrigation systems as vehicles of agricultural improvement. Debates revolved around several key issues. One was the recognition that early colonial irrigation systems (e.g. the Sampean River works in eastern Java, one of the first integrated systems completed on the island) often benefited the Dutch-controlled sugar industry more than rice cultivation.[52] Another was the risk of large barrages curtailing the deposition of the exceptionally rich and abundant volcanic silt from Java's uplands.[53] Soil salinization and malaria outbreaks, though far less widespread than in India, posed another set of problems, especially on the Tjihea plain in the west of the island, where a combination of inadequate drainage and heavy soils triggered a major public health scare in the 1910s.[54] Most important of all, perhaps, was the vexed question of the socio-economic cost–benefit ratio of large waterworks.

An important change in the prevailing wind came with the failure of the gargantuan Solo valley scheme in central Java. This was by far the largest irrigation project ever planned in the East Indies, encompassing an area of some 225,000 bouws (*c.*160,000 hectares). Designed to control flooding on Java's longest river and to provide perennial irrigation for one of the island's poorest regions, it formed the centrepiece of the 'General Irrigation Plan', consuming nearly half of its entire budget of 35.5 million gulden. Launched with great fanfare in 1893, the Solo scheme soon ran into trouble. Huge cost overruns prompted Colonial Minister J. T. Cremer to call a temporary halt in 1898. Five years later, as doubts about its socio-economic benefits crystallized, Cremer's successor A. W. F. Idenburg finally pulled the plug.[55]

The termination of the Solo project was a big decision, and it was based on more than just financial considerations. The contemporary political context in the East Indies was crucial, namely the emphasis on indigenous well-being as the principal moral duty of the colonial government. It was no coincidence that Colonial Minister Idenburg was a key champion of 'ethical policy'. Like the other leading advocates of the ethical programme, he was not convinced that large-scale irrigation was the most useful way to promote Javanese agriculture. After all, water control was only one of many factors influencing rice yields. Whereas some colonial projects clearly benefited indigenous farmers—such as the Pemali River works, which trebled local rice yields 1904–12 and became the model for many subse-

[52] Ravesteijn, *De zegenrijke heeren*, 53–107.

[53] Wim Ravesteijn, 'Controlling Water, Controlling People: Irrigation Engineering and State Formation in the Dutch East Indies', *Itinerario*, vol. 31 (2007), 89–118, here 101–2. It was estimated that the Solo River carried more than twice the amount of suspended solids (6 kg per m³) as the 'muddy Mississippi' at New Orleans: *Report by the Right Honourable W. G. A. Ormsby Gore*, 128; Edelman, *Studiën*, 290.

[54] Suzanne Moon, *Technology and Ethical Idealism: A History of Development in the Netherlands East Indies* (Leiden: CNWS, 2007), 27.

[55] Ravesteijn, *De zegenrijke heeren*, 173–206.

quent schemes[56]—in other cases the effects were less favourable, and sometimes plainly negative. From the perspective of the agricultural department, the gargantuan scale and cost of the Solo valley works represented not only an inefficient use of finite resources; it was also an example of what many officials, including the Director of Public Works, regarded as 'irrigation fanaticism'.[57] In the wake of the project's closure even A. G. Lamminga, the founding father of modern irrigation on Java, acknowledged that the supporters of large-scale works often exaggerated the advantages in relation to costs.[58] Over the long-term, the demise of the Solo valley scheme did not fundamentally alter the overall approach to irrigation in the East Indies, which continued to revolve around the provision of water for rice and sugar within the same command areas, and which largely remained the preserve of engineers rather than agronomists. It did, however, foster a move to 'hou het klein' (keep it small) after the turn of the century.[59] In the 1920s and 1930s, as the pace of construction once again accelerated, new irrigation projects were based on a more rigorous cost–benefit analysis and occasionally sought to improve rather than override existing irrigation works.[60]

In short, large-scale, centralized irrigation systems were no longer perceived as the panacea they once were, at least within agricultural circles. By the turn of the century there was good reason to question their effectiveness for promoting farmers' prosperity, or, for that matter, even averting food shortages. The evidence was as plain as it was tragic. Thousands of kilometres of canals did not prevent the devastating series of famines that swept across much of South and Southeast Asia from 1896 to 1904. As some contemporaries recognized, these crises derived more from the problems of food availability than food production.[61]

Yet boosting agricultural output remained a central goal, and in this respect irrigation advocates still proclaimed three interrelated benefits: reliable water supplies, more crop harvests per year, and the opportunity to raise yields per crop by permitting the optimal use of fertilizer and seed. By and large colonial irrigation schemes achieved the first two objectives. Water supplies became more predictable, and the

[56] Maurits Ertsen, *Locales of Happiness: Colonial Irrigation in the Netherlands East Indies and its Remains, 1830–1980* (Delft: VSSD, 2010), 95–106; Ravesteijn, *De zegenrijke heeren*, 111–44.

[57] Ravesteijn, *De zegenrijke heeren*, 192, 207–42.

[58] A. G. Lamminga, *Beschouwingen over den tegenwoordigen stand van het irrigatiewezen in Nederlandsch-Indië* (The Hague: van Langenhuysen, 1910), 24.

[59] Ravesteijn, *De zegenrijke heeren*, 193–5; Ravesteijn, 'Controlling Water', 104–5; Moon, *Technology*, 26–8. Ertsen lays more emphasis on the engineering continuities of the Dutch irrigation regime: Ertsen, *Locales*, 187.

[60] Ravesteijn, *De zegenrijke heeren*, 245–93.

[61] George Lambert, *India, the Horror-Stricken Empire: Containing a Full Account of the Famine, Plague, and Earthquake of 1896–7, including a Complete Narration of the Relief Work through the Home and Foreign Relief Commission* (Elkhart, Ind.: Mennonite Publishing Company, 1898), 1–29; John Dacosta, *Facts and Fallacies Regarding Irrigation as a Prevention of Famine in India* (London: W. H. Allen & Co., 1878), 1–19; Davis, *Late Victorian Holocausts*; Michelle McAlpin, *Subject to Famine: Food Crises and Economic Change in Western India, 1860–1920* (Princeton: Princeton University Press, 1983); David Arnold, *Famine: Social Crisis and Historical Change* (Oxford: Blackwell, 1988); M. R. Fernando, 'Famine in a Land of Plenty: Plight of a Rice-Growing Community in Java, 1883–84', *Journal of Southeast Asian Studies*, vol. 41 no. 2 (2010), 291–320.

rapid expansion of double- and even triple-cropping appreciably raised yields per hectare in many areas. But the third anticipated benefit—higher yields per crop— largely failed to materialize. Even on the sophisticated *sawah* plots of Java and Bali the heavy expenditure on irrigation made no appreciable impact on average crop yields.[62] The end result was a significant gain in land productivity but not labour productivity; or, to put it differently, a rise in output per hectare rather than output per capita, which would have allowed for an improvement in farmers' living stand- ards. On Java in particular, which faced the twin pressures of high population growth and high export demands (mainly related to sugar), the overall outcome was the intensification rather than alteration of existing cultivation techniques— what Clifford Geertz famously dubbed 'agricultural involution'.[63]

Beginning in the early 1900s, the focus of agricultural intervention gradually moved beyond the question of water availability to include several other aspects of tropical agro-ecosystems. Boosting soil fertility was a central consideration, and there were several ways in which agricultural departments tried to achieve it. One was to improve traditional techniques of fertility maintenance such as the cultiva- tion of leguminous crops (whether in rotation or as green manures), though obser- vers soon recognized that they had little to teach Asian farmers in this respect.[64] A more promising approach was to develop new composting practices along the lines of those used in China and Japan. Applying the right blend of organic residues in the right stage of decomposition was critical, and was the subject of extensive investigations in the East Indies and at the Institute of Plant Industry at Indore in central India, where Albert Howard—one of the founding figures of modern organic agriculture—developed his famous 'Indore Process' of humus manufacture in the late 1920s, one of the core tenets of the organic farming gospel.[65]

Other agronomists argued that artificial fertilizers such as those used in Europe (ammonium sulphate, superphosphates) were necessary to stimulate crop produc- tion. By the inter-war period scientists in India and the East Indies were experi- menting with a range of nitrogenous and phosphate fertilizers on a variety of different soils and crops, though the effects were largely confined to the test farms. The main problems were not technical but rather economic. The high price of such fertilizers meant that only the wealthiest farmers were able to purchase them, whereas the vast majority of small farmers were much more interested in the green manures (such as the leguminous *Crotalaria* species) that colonial agricultural departments were trying to promote.[66] Artificial fertilizers were rare in the river deltas of Southeast Asia, despite the strongly commercial orientation of many

---

[62] Booth, *Agricultural Development*, 38, 130.

[63] Clifford Geertz, *Agricultural Involution: The Process of Ecological Change in Indonesia* (Berkeley: University of California Press, 1963).

[64] Edelman, *Studiën*, 19–20; Howard, *Crop Production*, 36–9, 113–14, 117–18.

[65] Albert Howard, *An Agricultural Testament* (orig. 1940) (Oxford: Oxford City Press, 2010), 47–128. It was later discovered that Japanese field-manuring practices frequently depressed yields compared to established local techniques: Madhumita Saha, 'The State, Scientists, and Staple Crops: Agricultural "Modernization" in Pre-Green Revolution India', *Agricultural History*, vol. 87 no. 2 (Spring 2013), 201–23, here 214.

[66] Edelman, *Studiën*, 19–20, 129–41; Moon, *Technology*, 110–11; Howard, *Crop Production*, 38–40.

farms in the region, and despite rising concerns about soil depletion due to silt reduction from upstream. In the Mekong Delta, French efforts to promote artificial fertilizers in the late 1920s and early 1930s backfired due to haphazard application and correspondingly poor results. In Lower Burma the high costs meant that there was little uptake even among the large landowners of the Irrawaddy Delta.[67]

Efforts to upgrade agricultural equipment had a similarly mixed record. The most successful interventions generally revolved around small improvements to indigenous implements rather than the wholesale introduction of more glamorous mechanical devices. In Burma there were around sixty tractors in the lower Delta by the late 1920s, but given the surplus of cheap labour and the high cost of fuel and spare parts, they were sparingly used, and were no good on the wettest soils in any event. The attempt to promote soil-inverting ploughs over the traditional 'hte' plough fared somewhat better, but they, too, were only used occasionally.[68] In southern Indochina the arrival of subsidized tractors and threshers in the 1920s met with great interest among Vietnamese farmers, but once again the tractors were expensive and of no use on marshy ground. Moreover, the need for yet more animal traction to pull heavy ploughs or to power mechanical threshers promised to exacerbate an already acute shortage of draught animals. To remedy the problem, French authorities imported water buffaloes from Cambodia, which they hoped would outperform oxen on the wet, heavy delta soils. Upon arrival, however, the buffalo were ravaged by epizootics.[69] Equally fruitless was the attempt to create a large, fully mechanized rice plantation just north of Palembang on Sumatra. The Selatdjaran project, brainchild of the new agriculture director J. Sibinga Mulder (an ex-sugar planter), was launched in 1919 in an effort to replicate the success of California's rice industry. Within four years it was abandoned due to cost overruns, technical problems, and principled criticism from 'ethically minded' Dutch officials who pointed out that such high-tech schemes, by decoupling food production from peasant farmers, did nothing for the cause of 'native development'.[70]

Against this backdrop, many agronomists thought that the most promising means of raising yields was to improve the plants themselves. By the early twentieth century the potential of high-yielding varieties was already becoming visible in the crop-fields of Europe, North America, and Japan.[71] The basic procedure was to select a small number of crop strains with the desired characteristics (higher yield, shorter growing season, early ripening) and then isolate them through controlled reproduction to attain a homogeneous seed population that would breed true and behave predictably in the field. All in all it was an expensive and time-consuming process, and when scaled up into a full-blown crop-breeding programme, it stretched the means of most colonial agriculture departments. The creation of an improved variety took many generations of selection on protected seed farms in

---

[67] Brocheux, *Mekong*, 61; Robequain, *Economic Development*, 228; Adas, *Burma*, 130–1.
[68] Adas, *Burma*, 132.
[69] Brocheux, *Mekong*, 62–5. As early as 1900 an attempt to deploy tractors on a large French-owned estate was similarly unsuccessful: Robequain, *Economic Development*, 193.
[70] Maat, *Science*, 187–9; Moon, *Technology*, 83–90.   [71] Bray, *Rice Economies*.

order to avoid cross-fertilization from surrounding strains. Even after this initial development phase, a careful system of distribution, extension work, and continued experimentation was needed in order to integrate the new varieties into farming practices and to maintain the selected strains.

Some of the earliest advances in tropical crop selection were made in India, where state authorities already established a plant breeding agency before 1900.[72] Although the initial emphasis was on cotton (see Chapter 1) and sugar, the principal food crops also gradually came into focus. In the case of wheat, a 1905 botanical survey of Indian strains led to the selection of a handful of high-performing varieties that covered over 10 million hectares by 1915.[73] Most of the breeding work centred on the improvement of native wheat strains, though hybridization with exotics was also used to improve particular crop characteristics, especially at the Pusa Agricultural Research Institute in Bihar and in the canal colonies of the Punjab. In the case of rice, several of India's provincial agricultural departments— Bengal, Burma, Madras—developed high-performing strains selected from the wide range of cultivars in use. Yet compared to wheat, the breeding and distribution of improved rice varieties proceeded more slowly due to the lack of a systematic botanical survey and the limited supply of selected seed. Even in export-oriented Burma, high-yielding rice varieties still accounted for only 2 per cent of the cultivated area in 1929–30,[74] and the results were broadly similar in the deltas of colonial Indochina. Although the Office Indochinois du Riz (founded in 1930) operated several experiment farms and distributed tons of selected seed to planters, its ability to maintain the improved strains amidst the 2,000 or so varieties in cultivation was severely undermined by the habit of Chinese middlemen to mix all their seed rice together after purchase.[75]

The situation was rather different in the Netherlands Indies, which boasted by far the most extensive rice improvement programme in the colonial world. Dutch attempts to boost rice production stretched back to the 1860s, and the selection of high-yielding varieties was a central concern of the Department of Agriculture from its very inception in 1905. Its first director, Melchior Treub (also the director of Buitenzorg Botanical Gardens), wasted little time in collecting rice samples from across Java and Madura as the basis for trials. The department also set up an Experiment Station for Rice and Secondary Crops for the purpose of classifying and indexing the different strains, along with an extensive network of demonstration fields designed to encourage the adoption of improved varieties and to educate farmers about their cultivation requirements (Fig. 9.1).[76]

In many ways these measures laid the basis for what might have been a colonial-era 'green revolution'—that is, a far-reaching agricultural transformation in

[72] John H. Perkins, *Geopolitics and the Green Revolution: Wheat, Genes and the Cold War* (New York: Oxford University Press, 1997), 76–85.

[73] Howard, *Agricultural Testament*, 200; Howard, *Crop Production*, 100–10.

[74] Howard, *Crop Production*, 118–20; Adas, *Burma*, 131.

[75] R. Caty, 'L'Amélioration des plantes de culture indigène aux colonies', *L'Agronomie coloniale*, vol. 25 nos 217–18 (Jan., Feb. 1936), 34–42, 78–89; Edmond Carle, *Le Riz en Cochinchine: étude agricole, commerciale, industrielle, avec diverses notes concernant cette culture dans le monde* (Cantho: Imprimerie de l'Ouest, 1933); Brocheux, *Mekong*, 61–2; Robequain, *Economic Development*, 228–9.

[76] Maat, *Science*, 68–70, 179–87; Moon, *Technology*, 51–4, 60–1.

Fig. 9.1. Lessons at the Agricultural School at Buitenzorg, *c.*1908. By permission of the Nationaal Museum van Wereldculturen, coll. no. 60041673.

which the plethora of local varieties cultivated across the East Indies would be replaced by a standardized set of high-yielding strains selected for their responsiveness to tightly controlled growing conditions. Treub himself, who modelled his new Agriculture Department on the USDA, and who greatly admired the large-scale rice production systems in Italy, seemed to envision the crop selection programme as the platform for just such a policy. With hindsight, Treub's strategy can be interpreted as a kind of productivist prelude to the cultivation practices that eventually emerged in Indonesia with the 'Green Revolution' proper in the 1960s and 1970s.

Given the initial impulses behind it, what is perhaps most remarkable about the crop-breeding programme in the East Indies is that it ended up doing something quite different. Instead of pursuing a narrow set of standard solutions for general application, the Agriculture Department soon opted for a more localized, small-scale approach. The parallels with irrigation policy are striking, and once again the contemporary political context in the East Indies was just as important as technical considerations. The shift of rationale had much to do with Treub's succession in 1909 by the more 'ethically' minded Herman Lovink, who redirected the departmental focus towards methods that would cause as little disruption as possible to existing techniques, and therefore minimize the resistance to adoption among indigenous farmers.

The policy signalled not only a new relationship between agronomists and farmers, but also a different approach towards local growing environments. Under Lovink's guidance the emphasis of agricultural research was on the operation of field trials under diverse ecological conditions. In methodological terms it was quite unlike Treub's carefully maintained experiment fields at Buitenzorg, which sought to isolate and control for the many variables that, to the laboratory mind, 'interfered' with research, but which, to the field scientist's or cultivator's mind, constituted the very essence of farming. Rather than insisting on a standardization of growing conditions for a small number of high-yielding strains, researchers tried to develop a wide range of productive rice varieties that were well suited to the diverse soil and climate conditions across the colony. Towards this end the department conducted multi-year trials in a range of different localities. At the same time, its extension service consciously employed indigenous rather than European field agents in order to facilitate the adoption of improved strains and to communicate information about local techniques and cultivars back to researchers.[77]

The decision to bring the experimental fields to the farmers rather than the other way around was important in two ways. It not only promised greater receptiveness on the ground, it also enabled agronomists to tap the rich store of indigenous knowledge about the very crops and cultivation systems they were trying to improve. In the process, researchers discovered that traditional rice varieties often equalled or outperformed the newly selected strains, whose yields fluctuated markedly in different locations. Louis Koch, one of the lead researchers at the Experiment Station for Rice and Secondary Crops, conclusively demonstrated that pure strains performed relatively poorly as soon as soil and moisture conditions varied beyond optimal levels, and accordingly advised growers to sow a mixture of seeds to spread risk.[78]

Over time, such findings led to a greater appreciation of the skill of indigenous farmers. After a visit to Java in 1938, a leading British agronomist remarked that the disappointing yield increases obtained by pure-line selection were 'undoubtedly due to the care which this crop has received from the cultivators over many generations. There has been going on for years, if not for centuries, a natural selection by the growers themselves.'[79] Furthermore, paying attention to farmers' concerns also led to the recognition that higher yields were not the only measure of 'improvement'. When a hardy, high-yielding, and disease-resistant new rice strain (*Skrivimankotti*) was brought to Java from Suriname, it was broadly rejected by local farmers—not because it yielded poorly (in fact it yielded well) but because it was more difficult to harvest and its flavour did not suit local tastes. Experiences like this had two important consequences. First, they encouraged a more fine-grained understanding of diverse ecological and socio-cultural conditions and their relationship to agricultural techniques. And second, they nourished a growing sense that the best means of improving cultivation was by taking careful account of local practices.[80]

---

[77] Drawn from Moon, *Technology*, 41–2, 51–68; Maat, *Science*, 73–80, 179–80; Edelman, *Studiën*, 129–41.

[78] Maat, *Science*, 186–7.　　[79] *Report by Sir Frank Stockdale*, 75.

[80] Moon, *Technology*, 66–9. This particularist approach was also evident in research on maintaining *sawah* fertility: Edelman, *Studiën*, 129–41.

Such positive reassessments of indigenous cultivation methods were by no means confined to the East Indies. As early as 1893, the British agriculturist John Augustus Voelcker remarked that 'I do not share the opinions which have been expressed as to Indian Agriculture being, as a whole, primitive and backward, but I believe that in many parts there is little or nothing that can be improved.' Even where there was room for improvement, he argued that the best way to achieve it was 'by the transference of a better indigenous method from one part, where it is practiced, to another where it is not'.[81] When Albert Howard began studying plant diseases at the Pusa Agricultural Research Institute in 1905, he found that the crops grown by local cultivators were remarkably free from pests of any kind. He quickly concluded that he could do no better than to acquire their traditional knowledge of cultivars and growing techniques, and for the next five years he regarded the local peasants (and local crop pests) as his 'professors of agriculture'. By 1910 Howard was able to grow crops virtually disease-free, without the aid of artificial chemicals or fertilizers or 'all the other expensive paraphernalia of the modern Experiment Station'. Over the following two decades he used this knowledge as the basis for broader investigations into the underlying relationships between plants, pests, and soil conditions.[82]

Nor were such reconsiderations of local or 'traditional' techniques necessarily limited to small-scale interventions, as events at the Krian project, by far the largest irrigation scheme in colonial Malaya, serve to demonstrate. Completed in 1906, Krian was the epitome of a large, centralized irrigation scheme, boasting a 25-km² reservoir and 258 kilometres of canals covering 20,000 hectares of paddy. The original plan was based on the wholesale transfer of selected rice strains and cultivation methods from India, but it was soon found that the results fell far short of local Malay techniques. Managers initially responded by importing selected seeds from Thailand, only to discover that the long stalks of the Thai varieties often lodged (fell over) and spoiled the crop. After years of experimentation with fast-maturing exotic varieties, mechanized cultivation, and different types of fertilizer—none of which worked well on local paddy fields—botanists at Krian found that the best results were achieved by indigenous rice varieties and local cultivation techniques. By the 1920s plant breeders were working with some 1,300 local strains, and by the early 1930s the focus of rice research in all three of Malaya's main agricultural stations (Pulau Gadong, Teluk Chengai, Titi Serong) was on native varieties.[83] Once again, the demonstration fields and extension services that were designed to transmit technical improvements to peasants ended up functioning as sites of dialogue between farmers and scientific 'experts'.

The emergence of such a dialogue does not, of course, mean that power was equally distributed or that indigenous know-how was equally valued. In Malaya, the more holistic socio-environmental approach of botanists like H. W. Jack or D. H. Grist had little wider impact on a colonial administration that was less

---

[81] Voelcker, *Report*, vi.   [82] Howard, *Agricultural Testament*, 173–6.
[83] John Overton, *Colonial Green Revolution? Food, Irrigation and the State in Colonial Malaya* (Wallingford: CAB International, 1994), esp. 116–19.

politically committed than its Dutch counterpart to 'close contact' with farmers.[84] Even in the East Indies, the repeated attempts to mechanize rice production show that top-down conceptions of agricultural development remained a powerful force. 'Ethically' minded officials were primarily concerned with boosting indigenous confidence in European expertise rather than valorizing local techniques for their own sake.[85] Many of those who praised the immaculately maintained terraces and 'the high standard of native agricultural practice' on Java still erroneously attributed it to the locals' 'wonderful knowledge of modern scientific methods'.[86] And to turn the perspective around, farmers often resented the seemingly capricious advice they were given. When asked by an off-duty Dutch official what he thought of the local administrators, a Javanese farmer sarcastically remarked that 'one week they come and tell us to hoe with our backsides towards the sun and the next week they tell us we should be hoeing with our backsides away from the sun'.[87]

But despite the limits of this knowledge exchange, the rising interest in indigenous agricultural techniques reflected a new sensitivity to ecological variability and a growing recognition of the skill with which cultivators adapted to it. In time, these insights raised broader questions about what 'agricultural development' actually meant. The more locally oriented approach that emerged after 1900—especially, but not exclusively, in the East Indies—was in some ways a hybridization programme itself, one that blended European expertise and indigenous knowledge and that opened spaces, however limited, in which farmers could be the subjects as well as the objects of agricultural improvement. Although it never became the dominant paradigm of colonial agronomy, it nonetheless pointed to an evolving understanding of tropical environments that influenced thinking in other parts of the world.

COLONIAL AGRONOMY AND AFRICAN FARMERS

In many respects the evolution of colonial agronomy in Africa followed the same basic pattern as in Europe's Asian colonies. During the early years of colonial rule the focus was almost entirely on the expansion of cash crops. Beginning in the 1890s, colonial governments built a new institutional framework of research and extension services primarily to support commercial planting ventures. It was mainly after the First World War that African agricultural systems and food crops came into focus. Broadly speaking, this outline mirrored developments in the older Asian colonies, with a time-lag of a decade or so.

Yet in other respects colonial efforts to improve agricultural practice differed significantly between the two regions. At the time, most Europeans regarded African societies as distinctly backward compared to the complex agrarian civilizations of Asia.

---

[84] Overton, *Colonial Green Revolution*, 96–7.
[85] Moon, *Technology*, 42; see also Marieke Bloembergen and Remco Raben (eds), *Het koloniale beschavingsoffensief: wegen naar het nieuwe Indië, 1890–1950* (Leiden: KITLV, 2009), which emphasizes the parallels between 'ethical policy' and other imperial 'civilizing missions'.
[86] *Report by the Right Honourable W. G. A. Ormsby Gore*, 125.
[87] Quoted from Pelzer, *Pioneer Settlement*, 233.

When European agronomists first began to 'improve' African cultivation methods, they distinguished between what could be expected from Indian or Javanese farmers as opposed to 'primitive Negroes'.[88] As late as the 1950s one could still hear complaints that the fundamental agricultural problems in Africa were due to the fact that 'the agriculturalist was an unskilful peasant who could provide little assistance himself to their solution'.[89] As a result, Africa's vast natural abundance seemed to lie dormant. Even more than the natural riches of tropical Asia, African agricultural resources were ripe for development. The question was how best to exploit them.

The main aim of colonial administrations throughout sub-Saharan Africa was to create profitable export industries by mobilizing African labour and natural resources. This much was common across the continent, though the specific methods varied from one place to another. In Equatorial Africa, French and Belgian authorities presided over a mixture of foreign-owned plantations, compulsory cultivation systems, and strict collection quotas, most infamously in the Congo Free State under Léopold's regime. In West Africa (especially in British-controlled territories) there was a greater focus on the development of 'native' export industries, though coercive planting and labour practices were hardly unknown there either. Colonial administrators in East Africa initially looked to European settlers as the principal agents of economic development, but the commercial tribulations of foreign-owned estates and the antipathy caused by large-scale land alienation soon led to the view that 'the focal point of colonial agriculture over the long-term lies in indigenous small-scale cultivation'.[90]

More than anything else, it was the desire to determine which commodities could successfully be grown where that drove agricultural research in colonial Africa. In the 1890s British authorities set up a string of botanical gardens in Lagos, Gold Coast (Aburi), Sierra Leone, Gambia, and Uganda (Entebbe), which were soon mirrored by German facilities in Cameroon (Victoria), Dar es Salaam, and later at Amani in Tanzania.[91] French research capacity developed more slowly in its overseas territories; apart from the small botanical garden at Libreville, most activities were based in Paris at the Jardin des Plantes and Jardin d'Essai Colonial.[92] As colonial states in Africa expanded in the early 1900s, most established agricultural departments alongside forestry and veterinary services.[93] By and large their

---

[88] W. Busse, 'Ueber Aufgaben des Pflanzenschutzes in den Kolonien', *Verhandlungen des deutschen Kolonialkongresses 1905* (Berlin: Reimer, 1906), 30–44, esp. 40.

[89] Masefield, *Short History*, 66.

[90] Warburg, 'Die Landwirtschaft', 590; Deeken, *Die Landwirtschaft*, 52.

[91] G. B. Masefield, *A History of the Colonial Agricultural Service* (Oxford: Clarendon, 1972), 26; G. Volkens, 'Die Entwickelung des auf wissenschaftlicher Grundlage ruhenden landwirtschaftlichen Versuchswesens in den Kolonien', *Verhandlungen des deutschen Kolonialkongresses 1910* (Berlin: Reimer, 1910), 60–76.

[92] Christophe Bonneuil and Mina Kleiche, *Du jardin d'essais colonial à la station expérimentale, 1880–1930: éléments pour une histoire du CIRAD* (Paris: CIRAD, 1993); Headrick, *Tentacles*, 222–7.

[93] Tilley, *Africa*, 124–5; Charles Jeffries, *The Colonial Empire and its Civil Service* (Cambridge: Cambridge University Press, 1938; repr. 2014), 162–75; 'Organisation des Services d'agriculture et de l'apprentissage agricole à la Côte d'Ivoire, en Guinée, dans le Haut- Organisation des Services Sénégal-Niger et au Dahomey', *L'Agronomie coloniale*, vol. 2 (Jan.–June 1914), 25–8; Leplae, *La Crise agricole*, 3–4.

focus remained on export crops rather than staple foodstuffs; in 1909, Uganda's new Agriculture Department comprised only two officials while its Cotton Department had a staff of nine.[94] They were also based on the idea that, in the words of Georges Wéry (director of France's Institut National Agronomique), 'it is not the native to whom one must turn for maximizing the productivity of the country, but rather to science'.[95] Even among those who championed peasant production over foreign-owned estates, there was an assumption that European plantations served as demonstration grounds for raising indigenous cultivation standards.[96]

Yet as the list of failed plantations grew longer, and as field surveys began to catalogue Africa's agricultural resources, researchers became more interested in 'native agriculture'. Shortly after the turn of the century, a series of territorial studies commissioned by the British Colonial Office expressed great admiration for indigenous cultivation systems in certain areas. 'There is little we can teach the Kano farmer,' noted the reformer Edmund Morel after a tour of northern Nigeria. 'There is much we can learn from him.'[97] In 1905, following a survey of French West Africa, Auguste Chevalier similarly concluded that 'the indigenous cultivator is not the contemptible lay-about... that is so often represented'. On the contrary, a greater familiarity with African farming techniques could, he argued, have helped avoid the huge waste of time and money squandered on ill-conceived European planting enterprises.[98] German researchers were likewise alert to the benefits of drawing on indigenous knowledge: 'there is no cause for disdain... for as regards the agricultural value or otherwise of the different soil types in relation to the overall locality, especially the potential of irrigation, the native farmer has very sound ideas that make mistakes in this direction very rare—rarer than among his white colleagues'.[99]

Although the study of African farming systems lagged behind developments in Asia, there were nonetheless some significant early advances, most notably at the Kaiserliches Biologisch-Landwirtschaftliches Institut at Amani in German East Africa.[100] Founded in 1902 in the Usambara Mountains, and initially established to support the new coffee plantations in the area, the Amani Institute was the first colonial facility in sub-Saharan Africa to focus explicitly on the study and improvement of indigenous cultivation methods. During the 1900s–1910s it represented

---

[94] Masefield, *Colonial Agricultural Service*, 34.

[95] G. Wéry, *L'Organisation scientifique de l'agriculture aux colonies* (Paris: Baillière, 1919), 9, quoted from Bonneuil, *Savants*, 39.

[96] Warburg, 'Die Landwirtschaft'; F. Stuhlmann, 'Entwickelung und Aussichten der europäischen Pflanzungen in unseren tropischen Kolonien', *Verhandlungen des deutschen Kolonialkongresses 1910* (Berlin: Reimer, 1910), 788–801; Deeken, *Die Landwirtschaft*, 14; Leplae, *La Crise agricole*, 30.

[97] Tilley, *Africa*, 127.

[98] Chevalier, *La Situation agricole*, 5; Auguste Chevalier, *Exploration botanique de l'Afrique Occidentale Française* (Paris: Lechevallier, 1920), vii–xiii.

[99] Paul Vageler, 'Landwirtschaftliche Eindrücke aus Deutsch-Ostafrika', *Deutsche Kolonialzeitung*, vol. 27 (1910), 228f., quoted from Detlef Bald and Gerhild Bald, *Das Forschungsinstitut Amani. Wirtschaft und Wissenschaft in der deutschen Kolonialpolitik Ostafrika 1900–1918* (Munich: IFO, 1972), 97.

[100] The following is drawn from Bald and Bald, *Forschungsinstitut*; Christopher A. Conte, 'Imperial Science, Tropical Ecology, and Indigenous History: Tropical Research Stations in Northeastern German East Africa, 1896 to the Present', in Gregory Blue, Martin Bunton, and Ralph Croizier (eds), *Colonialism and the Modern World* (London: M. E. Sharpe, 2002), 246–61.

the nearest African equivalent to the likes of Buitenzorg or Pusa, albeit on a much smaller scale. The parallels were no coincidence: Amani was directly modelled on Buitenzorg, and several of its key staff—including the directors Albrecht Zimmermann and Franz Stuhlmann, both outspoken advocates of 'native agriculture'—had previously worked there. Before the First World War, Amani served as a kind of inter-continental conduit for transferring colonial agronomic know-how from Asia to sub-Saharan Africa.[101] In turn, it disseminated this knowledge to other research facilities through its journal *Der Pflanzer. Ratgeber für tropische Landwirtschaft.* There was nothing else quite like it in Africa at the time.

The first studies of indigenous agriculture at the Amani Institute focused on staple crops and their diseases, mainly rice, cassava, and sorghum.[102] After 1907—as part of Colonial Minister Dernburg's 'scientific colonization' programme[103]—it began a more systematic evaluation of native cultivars and fertility maintenance, including the use of fire and penned livestock.[104] Significantly, the research programme at Amani was supported by some of the earliest detailed examinations of African soils, most notably by the agricultural chemist Paul Vageler. Vageler was among the first to study the fragility of tropical soils, whose fertility is overwhelmingly dependent on surface plant growth and decomposition rather than deeper layers, and which is therefore quickly leached away once the ground is cleared. He was also an outspoken critic of some of the madcap development schemes sponsored by colonial lobbyists in Germany, who fancifully sought to create a 100,000-hectare irrigated settlement in the steppe between Arusha and Lake Victoria (the plan was shelved after a damning soil and meteorological survey by Vageler).[105] Unusually for the time, the institute's recommendations for different temperature, precipitation, and elevation gradients were consciously based on African cultivation techniques. Moreover, the exchange of knowledge moved in both directions: some of the novelties introduced by colonial agronomists—such as potatoes and new poultry breeds—were readily adopted by local farmers.[106] Even if these early studies failed to generate specific 'improvement' measures, they clearly broke new ground. The Amani Institute was eyed with envy by the other

[101] F. Stuhlmann, 'Studienreise nach Niederländisch- und Britisch-Indien', *Der Tropenpflanzer. Beiheft*, vol. 4 (1903), 1–58; Otto Warburg, 'Über wissenschaftliche Institute für Kolonialwirtschaft', in *Verhandlungen des deutschen Kolonial kongresses 1902* (Berlin, 1903).

[102] A. Zimmermann, 'Die Kräuselkrankheit des Maniok', *Der Pflanzer*, vol. 2 (1906), 182–3; A. Zimmermann, 'Einige Bemerkungen über Maniok, Kassave', *Der Pflanzer*, vol. 2 (1906), 257–71; A. Zimmermann, 'Die Deutsch-Ostafrikanischen Maniok-Varietäten', vol. 3 (1907), 258–69; Walter Busse, 'Über die Krankheiten der Sorghumhirse in Deutsch-Ostafrika', *Der Tropenflanzer*, vol. 7 no. 11 (Nov. 1903), 517–26.

[103] Ruppenthal, *Kolonialismus als 'Wissenschaft und Technik'.*

[104] 'Notizen über einige Eingeborenen-Kulture', *Der Pflanzer*, vol. 3 (1907), 138–42; K. Braun, 'Bestimmungstabellen für die Eingeborenenkulturen von Deutsch-Ostafrika. Die Hülsenfrüchte', *Der Pflanzer*, vol. 7 (1911); 'Beiträge zur Kenntnis einiger Eingeborenen-Nahrungsmittel', *Der Tropenpflanzer*, vol. 21 no. 7 (July 1918), 191–201; Dr Sommerfeld, 'Verwendung von Düngemitteln durch ackerbautreibende Eingeborenenstämme in Deutsch-Ostafrika', *Der Pflanzer*, vol. 8 (1912), 91–3.

[105] Paul Vageler, *Über die Düngungsfrage in den deutschen Kolonien* (Berlin: Süsserott, 1911), 4–16; Paul Vageler, 'Moderne Bodenuntersuchung und landwirtschaftliche Praxis', *Der Pflanzer. Zeitschrift für Land- und Forstwirtschaft in Deutsch-Ostafrika*, vol. 9 (1913), 3–16; Bald and Bald, *Forschungsinstitut*, 95.

[106] Conte, 'Imperial Science', 252–6.

powers in Africa, and after the British took it over in the 1920s, the rechristened East African Agricultural Research Station continued to function as a leading centre for the study of African agriculture.[107]

During the 1920s and 1930s research on African soils, crops, and farming methods became much more extensive and systematic.[108] This largely reflected contemporary changes within agronomic science itself, in particular the increasingly 'ecological' focus on the manifold interconnections between soils, crops, disease, and climate. Girolamo Azzi was a key figure for bringing the two fields together; his 1928 book *Agricultural Ecology* was a kind of manifesto for the new discipline, even if some scientists were already conducting agro-ecological research *avant la lettre*.[109] The potential benefits of such an approach were considerable, all the more so in tropical territories whose ecosystems were poorly understood. 'If ecology, which studies the relations between living organisms and the surrounding environment, is capable of rendering major but as yet under-recognised services to agriculture in metropolitan France', wrote one agronomist, 'it is of even greater interest for agriculture in our overseas possessions.'[110]

One of the earliest and most extensive surveys of African agriculture was carried out in 1919–20 by the ecologist Homer Shantz, an official with the USDA and a former student of Frederick Clements. His 1923 report on the vegetation and soils of Africa furnished the first detailed map of the agricultural potential of different parts of the continent. Although it did not include an explicit discussion of indigenous cultivation techniques, Shantz nonetheless studied them closely while conducting his fieldwork in Africa, and found much to admire.[111] In subsequent publications he highlighted the remarkable ingenuity of African farmers in adapting to diverse and often hostile growing environments. Their skill in matching crops to different soil and moisture conditions led Shantz to conclude that, contrary to widespread assumptions, 'the Native is an excellent agriculturalist'. He accordingly cautioned against the temptation to interfere with their practices on the basis of the 'dogmatic teaching' of modern agriculture, much to the approval of reform-minded colonial officers who were already thinking along similar lines.[112]

Just over a decade later, a ground-breaking 'ecological survey' in Northern Rhodesia emphatically confirmed Shantz's portrayal of African agricultural skill. It found that African farmers possessed a detailed knowledge of the connections

[107] Bald and Bald, *Forschungsinstitut*, 99–101; William Nowell, *The Agricultural Research Station at Amani* (Dar es Salaam, 1933).
[108] Generally, Tilley, *Africa*.
[109] Girolamo Azzi, *Ecologia agraria* (Turin, 1925), published in English in 1956; see also P. Carton, 'L'Écologie: importance de son enseignement dans les écoles supérieures d'agriculture', *L'Agronomie coloniale*, vol. 25 no. 227 (Dec. 1936), 165–75. Pierre Carton, chief of the meteorological bureau in Indochina, was also a member of the newly founded Commission Internationale de Climatologie et d'Écologie Agricole.
[110] Jean Adam, *De l'écologie agricole à l'écologie coloniale* (Paris: Imprimerie Nationale, 1937), 2.
[111] H. L. Shantz and C. F. Marbut, *The Vegetation and Soils of Africa* (New York: NRC and AGS, 1923).
[112] On Shantz's views and influence, see Tilley, *Africa*, 134–7, quotes 136–7.

between vegetation cover and soil fertility, and that the cultivation techniques they deployed were, for the most part, highly appropriate. Spearheaded by Colin Trapnell, a protégé of the Oxford ecologists Charles Elton and Arthur Tansley, the Northern Rhodesian Ecological Survey probably did more than anything else to dispel notions of the 'primitive' African farmer, at least among British officials and agronomists. Through painstaking fieldwork covering tens of thousands of square kilometres, it showed that 'native agricultural systems are normally admirably adapted to their environment [and] any criticism of them must for this reason be made with the greatest caution'.[113] Along with Audrey Richards's 1939 study of *Land, Labour and Diet in Northern Rhodesia*, the Ecological Survey also underlined the need to examine the environmental and sociological dimensions of agricultural systems together in order to understand them 'in the round'. It was widely seen as a model for 'the ecological interpretation of the country and its mode of life', and it helped pave the way for E. B. Worthington's landmark review of *Science in Africa* published in 1938.[114]

The success of the Northern Rhodesian Ecological Survey soon prompted calls for similar investigations elsewhere. Although no such surveys were carried out until after the Second World War, a number of agronomists in West Africa were already conducting detailed studies of indigenous cultivation methods. At the forefront was the Nigerian Agricultural Department under the direction of Odin Faulkner, who had worked for many years in India and made the study of local farming techniques a key priority upon his arrival in Nigeria in 1921. In a widely read 1933 treatise on *West African Agriculture*, Faulkner and his deputy James Mackie tackled a range of misconceptions about agricultural development in the region, starting with the conventional emphasis on exotic export crops at the expense of native cultivars. Their basic point was that any genuine 'improvement' had to be based on a sound understanding of farmers' current techniques and how they related to social, ecological, and economic circumstances, above all the crucial importance of labour inputs (the key constraint in most African agricultural systems) in the calculation of overall incomes. This meant, among other things, abandoning tired stereotypes of the 'conservative native farmer', who, in their experience, was often 'much less conservative than most English farmers'. Indeed, given the rather poor track record of colonial agricultural policy in the past, it was 'not surprising that the African farmer is suspicious of advice given by Europeans'.[115]

The problem, according to critics like Faulkner, was that Europeans were too quick to assume that African methods were inefficient. Such assumptions soon led to an overconfident belief that they could devise something better, when in fact there was no shortage of instances where this was clearly not the case. 'Such failures

---

[113] C. G. Trapnell and J. N. Clothier, *The Soils, Vegetation and Agricultural Systems of North Western Rhodesia: Report of the Ecological Survey* (Lusaka: Government Printer, 1937), quoted from Tilley, *Africa*, 149.

[114] Quote from Sampson, Crowther, *West African Commission*, 53; E. B. Worthington, *Science in Africa: A Review of Scientific Research Relating to Tropical and Southern Africa* (London: Oxford University Press, 1938); more generally, Tilley, *Africa*, 146–53, 159–68; Helen Tilley, 'African Environments and Environmental Sciences', in Beinart and McGregor (eds), *Social History*, 109–30.

[115] Faulkner and Mackie, *West African Agriculture*, 4–7.

not only discredit the European in the eyes of the native farmer, but arouse in him a justifiable suspicion of all new ideas, which suspicion, once acquired, is not readily forgotten.'[116] Just how deep this suspicion could run is illustrated by an encounter between the young Oswald Voelcker (later director of the West African Cocoa Research Institute in the Gold Coast) and a north Cameroon chief in 1929. In order to gain the chief's cooperation, Voelcker tried to convince him of the benevolent intentions of agriculture officers, regardless of what he thought about other colonial officials: 'Administrative Officers always wanted labourers to work on roads; Education Officers wanted to remove their children to school; Forestry Officers to take their land for reserves but Agricultural Officers only wanted to put money in their pockets by growing the things needed.' As Voelcker recalled: 'the Chief looked at me with bleary eyes and said, through an interpreter, "When I see a snake I kill it. I find out afterwards if it is poisonous".'[117]

What all of this added up to was, as one observer put it, the 'rehabilitation of the African farmer'.[118] The more familiar European researchers became with African agro-ecosystems and cultivation practices, the more they found themselves revising conventional wisdom.

A key example was the widespread practice of intercropping. Although colonial officials often disparaged the seeming disorder of African farming plots, agronomists soon recognized the benefits of growing various cultivars together. As early as 1919, German research in Togo suggested that 'there is no reason to alter existing practices' in this respect, since mixed cropping helped to reduce pests, maintain fertility (through nitrogen-fixing legumes), and retain moisture (through the cultivation of creepers such as peanuts, beans, and yams).[119] By the 1930s such views were more common. G. Howard Jones, a mycologist who worked in Nigeria during the late 1920s, was adamant about the advantages of intercropping:

'If one looks at it more closely there seems a reason for everything. The plants are not growing at random, but have been planted at proper distances on hillocks of soil arranged in such a way that when rain falls it does not waterlog the plants, nor does it pour off the surface and wash away the fine soil: the stumps of bushes and trees are left for the yams to climb upon and the oil palms are left standing because they yield valuable fruit: and although several kinds of plants are growing together, they were not sown at the same time nor will they be reaped together: they are rather successive crops planted in such a way that the soil is always occupied and is neither dried up by the sun nor leached out by the rain, as it would be if it were left bare at any time.'[120]

---

[116] Faulkner and Mackie, *West African Agriculture*, 7.

[117] Recorded in Bernard Silk, *Post-War Food and Cash Crop Production in Former Colonial Territories* (Oxford Development Records Project, 1985), 8.

[118] Quote from Jean-Paul Harroy, *Afrique: terre qui meurt. La Dégradation des sols africaines sous l'influence de la colonisation* (Brussels: Académie Royale de Belgique, 1944), 183; H. Scaëtta, *Les Famines périodiques dans le Ruanda* (Brussels: Hayes, 1932); Auguste Chevalier, *L'Agriculture coloniale: origines et évolution* (Paris: Presses Universitaires de France, 1942).

[119] H. L. Hammerstein, 'Die Landwirtschaft der Eingeborenen Afrikas', *Der Tropenpflanzer. Beiheft*, vol. 22 no. 7 (July 1919), 45–123, here 53.

[120] G. Howard Jones, *The Earth Goddess: A Study of Native Farming on the West African Coast* (London: Longmans, 1936), 35.

In French West Africa too, researchers began to understand the pattern of crops that previously seemed to 'pop up at random': 'Is it negligence? *Laisser-aller?* It does not seem so. On closer inspection one recognizes it as a technique of mixed cultivation.'[121]

Another subject for reconsideration was soil tillage. For most Europeans the plough was a fundamental symbol of civilization, and during the early years of colonial rule it was a central feature of 'improvement' efforts in Africa.[122] Agriculture departments advocated ploughing for several reasons. Technically, it allowed for a deeper cultivation of the soil while also enabling farmers to work larger areas, which theoretically permitted them to grow cash crops while still producing sufficient food. Socially, it was hoped that ploughs would encourage a transition towards sedentary farming and private property by allowing a more intensive cultivation of the land. And culturally, it was thought that they would promote the European norm of patriarchal nuclear families by significantly reducing the amount of labour required on subsistence plots (which were mainly worked by women) and therefore weakening the rationale for polygamous households. The plough thus promised to transform not only African agricultural techniques but also patterns of sexuality and family life.[123] In many respects it was a tool for 'masculinizing' African agriculture along European lines.

But despite all of these presumed benefits, ploughs often did more harm than good. In Uganda, the massive expansion of ploughing in the Teso district (from 282 ploughs in 1923 to 15,388 in 1937) led to a surge of erosion and a gradual degradation of forest fallow plots due to the removal of tree stumps and shrubs from which the original vegetation had previously regenerated under hoe cultivation.[124] In French Soudan, ploughing was linked to a shortening of fallows and a corresponding decline in fertility.[125] By the end of the 1910s some German agronomists were openly questioning the utility of the plough as a basis for agricultural development in Africa: 'Let us for now leave the Negro with his tried-and-tested hoe cultivation before we try to replace it with a different technique that has hitherto not yet proved itself in the very different circumstances there.'[126] In the 1930s British agronomists in West Africa concluded that ploughing was 'more dangerous to the ultimate welfare of the inhabitants than the existing system' of

---

[121] Jules Blache, 'La Campagne en pays noir: essai sur les caractères du paysages rural en Afrique occidentale', *Revue de géographie alpine*, vol. 28 no. 3 (1940), 346–88, here 378.

[122] 'Grâce à l'emploi de la charrue l'agriculture se développe en Guinée Française', *L'Agronomie coloniale*, vol. 12 no. 95 (Nov. 1925), 236; Otto Warburg, 'Einführung der Pflugkultur in den deutschen Kolonien', *Verhandlungen des Kolonial-Wirtschaftlichen Komitees* (1906), 4–9; Tothill, *Agriculture*, 54–5; van Beusekom, *Negotiating*, 40–1.

[123] Zimmermann, *Alabama*, 143; van Beusekom, *Negotiating*, 40–2.

[124] Tothill, *Agriculture*, 82; Pierre Gourou, *The Tropical World: Its Social and Economic Conditions and its Future Status*, 4th edn (London: Longmans, 1966), 187.

[125] Van Beusekom, *Negotiating*, 48.

[126] Hammerstein, 'Die Landwirtschaft', 52; also H. Fehlinger, 'Zur Lösung der Arbeiterfrage in den afrikanischen Kolonien', *Der Tropenpflanzer*, vol. 22 no. 3 (Mar. 1919), 77–80.

tillage, and it was even suggested that the plough had previously been used in the region but was deliberately abandoned due to the erosion problems it caused.[127]

By 1930 even the oft-reviled practice of shifting cultivation came in for reassessment. At the same time as colonial foresters were trying to integrate itinerant farmers into their management plans, there was a parallel effort among agronomists to improve swidden techniques rather than eliminate them entirely. In Northern Rhodesia, extensive studies of the *citemene* system found not only that it yielded nearly three times more millet than conventional European practices, but also that the fertility effects of burning plant cover (a practice that attracted widespread criticism) were markedly superior to those of animal manure or synthetic fertilizers on the area's acidic and leach-prone soils.[128] In Nigeria, Faulkner's research on shifting cultivation led him to suggest that the practice 'would be more accurately described as a system of rotational "bush fallows"', and indeed one that, with adequate periods of rest, 'involves no deliberate waste and gives fair returns'.[129] Just as in Northern Rhodesia, field experiments in West Africa demonstrated the agronomic value of fire as a means of bush clearance. Even when deploying green manure crops, the Nigerian Agriculture Department found that burning them rather than ploughing them under increased the supply of base elements in the soil.[130] In French West Africa there was a similar recognition of the soil-rejuvenating effects of bush-burning, at least in areas where regrowth was deemed certain: 'the forest in this sense becomes a type of agricultural fallow'.[131] When soil fertility began to plummet on the Ugandan Agriculture Department's own experiment farms, officials who had long criticized shifting cultivation found that the best means of reversing the trend was to replace their green manure systems with a period of rest under grass cover, which effectively meant reverting to a form of swidden.[132]

All of this indicated a revision of the earlier insistence on sedentary, intensive cultivation, which severely damaged soils in many parts of Africa despite various efforts to make it work. By the end of the 1940s it was no exaggeration to say that 'the wheel has, indeed, come full circle, for the agricultural scientist of today would be more likely to describe continuous cultivation in the scathing words [previously used for swidden], and would point out that under shifting cultivation a sparse peasant population had been in ecological balance with its environment'.[133] The problem, as many colonial officials saw it, was that rapid demographic expansion was disturbing this balance. Wherever the demand for uncultivated land outstripped supply, the reduction of fallow periods threatened

---

[127] Quote from F. A. Stockdale, *Report by Mr. F. A. Stockdale*, 16; Sampson and Crowther, *West African Commission*, 54.

[128] Moore, Vaughan, *Cutting*, 26–30; Tilley, *Africa*, 141–3.

[129] Faulkner and Mackie, *West African Agriculture*, 44.

[130] Sampson and Crowther, *West African Commission*, 37.

[131] Georges Aubert, *Les Sols des régions tropicales de la France d'outre-mer: leur nature, leur conservation, leur prospection, leur étude* (Paris, 1944), 8–9.

[132] Tothill, *Agriculture*, 107–8; Masefield, *Short History*, 78–9.

[133] Masefield, *Short History*, 76–7; *Congrès du Perfectionnement de l'Agriculture Indigène* (Quinzaine Nationale de la Production Agricole d'Outre-mer, 1931), 3–4.

long-term soil fertility, and wherever fertility declined, so too did the capacity to boost agricultural output.

For all the newfound appreciation of African farming techniques, the task of colonial agronomists was still to improve them. Yet the fact that such efforts were increasingly based on existing practices marked a significant change of tack. As a prominent French observer put it, agricultural research had become 'tropicalized'.[134] Although such hybrid approaches never commanded a consensus, and although they exerted more influence on agronomic science than on actual colonial policy, by the 1930s the rise of ecologically minded research had substantially altered understandings of African farming methods and the biophysical environments they cultivated.[135]

SOIL CONSERVATION AND THE QUEST FOR SUSTAINABILITY

If ecological science offered a new lens for looking at tropical agriculture, it also allowed viewers to draw many different conclusions. On the one hand, more holistic understandings of the relationships between soil, vegetation, disease, and climate furnished scientists with powerful new tools for extracting wealth from tropical ecosystems, not least at the various commodity research stations. On the other hand, it made them more sensitive to the long-term sustainability of production systems and the need to safeguard resources. As a result, many colonial agronomists—much like their colleagues in the forestry departments—became vocal advocates of conservation measures. And what concerned them more than anything else was the state of tropical soils in the face of ever-increasing exploitation.

By the early twentieth century the evidence of soil degradation was all too obvious in many areas. Over the preceding few decades, huge expanses of forest had been brought into cultivation, and it was clear that a better understanding of tropical soil structure and chemistry was necessary if the colonies were to realize their agricultural potential. Pedological research had been under way in the Asian colonies since the late nineteenth century, and in East Africa the pre-war studies at Amani were extended through the work of Geoffrey Milne, whose 'Provisional Soil Map of East Africa' explicitly incorporated Paul Vageler's earlier work on regional soils and their relationship to local vegetation and climate.[136]

The inter-war years were a period of rapid progress in the field of pedology, and Europe's colonies played an important role in the process. In fact, some of the major breakthroughs of the era were made at research stations in the East Indies

---

[134] Gourou, *Tropical World*, 191.   [135] Generally: Tilley, *Africa*, 115–68.
[136] On Asia, see Edelman, *Studiën*, 19–20; Howard, *Crop Production*, 10–50. On Amani: Geoffrey Milne, *A Provisional Soil Map of East Africa* (Southampton: Ordnance Survey, 1936), 8, 20, 33. Vageler, in turn, praised Milne's innovative 'soil catena' system of classification: Vageler, *Koloniale Bodenkunde*, 14–15. On Milne more generally, see Hodge, *Triumph*, 154–6.

and Sudan.[137] As studies of tropical soils proliferated, their findings quickly circulated between different territories and across imperial boundaries. Research agendas were strongly influenced by contemporary trends in agronomy and ecology, and broadly echoed the more critical view of colonial agricultural policies that was emerging at the time. By the 1930s the myth of the 'richness of tropical soils' was well and truly buried among scientists and technical officers, even if some policy-makers still failed to recognize it. Vageler reckoned that over three-quarters of all plantation failures were 'due to the choice of unsuitable land': 'if ever appearances are deceptive they are so in the tropics and subtropics'.[138] Numerous studies confirmed that African farmers' knowledge of the soil and what it could support was often far superior to that of European planters, many of whom overworked the land in a manner that 'is not worthy to be designated farming, but can only be termed soil exploitation'.[139]

As field researchers soon discovered, African cultivators not only understood the soil but often conserved it just as well. After travelling to Nigeria, the geographer Dudley Stamp concluded that local farming techniques 'afford almost complete protection against soil erosion and loss of fertility' and could scarcely be improved upon.[140] A British survey of West Africa in 1938–9 found that gully erosion was a relatively recent problem arising from cash-cropping and new cultivation practices (especially ploughs), and that there was little sign of it where traditional methods prevailed.[141] In the Congo, Belgian agronomists readily conceded the fertility advantages of traditional fallow systems, which they were busily trying (without much success) to improve.[142] In the most densely populated districts of Uganda, where even the steepest slopes were cultivated, officials discovered that 'the native has developed his own anti-erosion measures: he grows his crops in strips across the slopes, with intervening strips of uncleared land, and this system leads to the formation of natural terraces'.[143] Given the effectiveness of such practices, local officers wisely focused on refining them rather than introducing unfamiliar conservation measures.[144]

From a pedological perspective such findings were clearly encouraging. Yet in the event, they did little to assuage the rampant fears of catastrophic soil degradation during the inter-war years. As historians have often suggested, the spectacle of the Dust Bowl in the United States certainly intensified the sense of alarm

---

[137] Yvon Chatelin, 'Genèse, mutation et éclatement des paradigmes: le case de la science des sols tropicaux', in Chatelin and Bonneuil (eds), *Nature*, 141–54; Vageler, 'Moderne Bodenuntersuchung', 269.

[138] Paul Vageler, *An Introduction to Tropical Soils*, trans. H. Greene (London: Macmillan, 1933), 9–10; Vageler, 'Moderne Bodenuntersuchung'; M. Etesse, 'Les Engrais aux colonies: importance de l'amélioration des sols coloniaux', *L'Agronomie coloniale*, no. 189 (Sept. 1933), 65–71, here 65–6; Henry, *Terres rouges*, 7–11.

[139] Worthington, *Science*, 405.   [140] Stamp, 'Land Utilization'.

[141] Sampson and Crowther, *West African Commission*, 14.

[142] G. de Groof, 'Conservation des sols congolais et politique agricole', *Bulletin agricole du Congo belge*, vol. 35 (1944), 118–36.

[143] Tothill, *Agriculture*, 87.

[144] Grace Carswell, *Cultivating Success in Uganda: Kigezi Farmers and Colonial Policies* (Oxford: James Currey, 2007).

among colonial officers in the 1930s. But the roots of these worries went much deeper, and drew directly on desiccationist narratives that had long framed perceptions of semi-arid environments.[145] By the turn of the century, anxieties about 'soil mining' and overgrazing were already common among officials in South Africa and the Maghreb.[146] After the First World War these concepts increasingly coloured perceptions of land use in other parts of the continent, especially in the dry parts of Central and East Africa.[147] In the late 1920s the British Colonial Office established the Imperial Bureau of Soil Science as a kind of information centre for the battle against erosion and soil depletion throughout the empire. Over the next several years, droughts in East Africa triggered a wave of new conservation initiatives in Kenya and Tanganyika, which were partially replicated in Uganda as well.[148] In the mid-1930s such regional efforts were coordinated under the Colonial Advisory Council on Agriculture and Animal Health (established in 1929), and in particular under the guidance of Frank Stockdale, an agriculture adviser to the Colonial Office who had introduced a range of anti-erosion measures on Ceylon while serving as the colony's agricultural director.[149]

Most colonial agronomists, including the admirers of indigenous farming, understood their primary tasks to be the improvement of cultivation practices and the protection of soil resources from swelling numbers of people and livestock. Without firm intervention, Stockdale noted in 1937, 'a bankrupt domain of ruined lands is likely to be the inevitable result'.[150] What made soil degradation so alarming was that it lay at the nexus of several interrelated concerns: mounting population growth, the reduction of fallows, rapid deforestation, and creeping 'desertification'. Together, these issues generated a potent conceptual link between soil husbandry and the wider menace of environmental decline.

The extraordinary magnitude of such fears was reflected in the apocalyptic depictions of soil erosion at the time. The most striking example was the seminal 1939 survey *The Rape of the Earth*, whose very title captures the prevailing tone. Authored by G. V. Jacks and R. O. Whyte, both based at the Imperial Bureau of Soil Science, it argued that human-induced soil erosion represented 'the gravest danger threatening the security of the white man and the well-being of the coloured man in the tropical and subtropical lands of Africa and India'.[151] The root of the problem, they contended, lay in the spread of European civilization to other parts of the world, which included the transfer or adaptation of intensive

[145]   See, generally, Davis, *Arid Lands*.

[146]   Beinart, *Rise of Conservation*; Davis, *Resurrecting the Granary*.

[147]   David M. Anderson, *Eroding the Commons: The Politics of Ecology in Baringo, Kenya 1890s–1963* (Oxford: James Currey, 2002), 70–189; David M. Anderson, 'Depression, Dust Bowl, Demography, and Drought: The Colonial State and Soil Conservation in East Africa during the 1930s', *African Affairs*, vol. 83 no. 332 (July 1984), 321–43.

[148]   Including a pasture rehabilitation scheme and erosion convention in 1929, a Standing Soil Erosion Committee in 1931, and a conference of East Africa soil chemists at Amani in 1932.

[149]   Hodge, *Triumph*, 158–9, 163–5; Anderson, *Eroding the Commons*, 21; Carswell, *Cultivating Success*, 55.

[150]   F. A. Stockdale, *Report by Sir Frank Stockdale on his Visit to East Africa, January–March 1937* (Colonial Office: 1937), 5.

[151]   Jacks and Whyte, *Rape*, 20.

agricultural techniques from temperate zones to tropical or subtropical environments where they resulted 'almost invariably, in a catastrophic decrease in fertility'.[152] Just as important, European expansion also led to a fateful rise of population levels spurred by Western sanitation and enhanced economic opportunities. In India, the main driver of soil degradation was the rapid demographic increase under British rule, which shortened fallow periods and drove cultivation onto more marginal land. In parts of Africa too, rising human numbers led shifting cultivators to return to the same plot more frequently than before. In both areas 'European influence has been responsible for the rapid, and in places now uncontrollable, biological deterioration of the land'.[153]

Over the following years, Jacks's and Whyte's pessimistic indictment of colonial degradation was echoed by a string of other works. Most prominent in francophone circles was Jean-Paul Harroy's *Afrique: terre qui meurt*.[154] Drawing on a similar blend of Clementsian ecology and social evolutionism, its basic argument was that imperialism had severely disrupted the equilibrium between animals, vegetation, soils, and humans that had formerly prevailed in Africa for thousands of years: 'It is incontestably the intervention of the European colonizer that carries the bulk of responsibility for the fall of African fertility.'[155] African land-use practices had been 'established over centuries of experience and adapted, often perfectly, to the previous economic and ethnographic conditions'. Contrary to widespread assumptions, it contended that the root cause of the problem was 'the brutal transformation of these conditions' rather than the supposed profligacy of indigenous land-use methods. Covering many of the same themes as Jacks and Whyte, and expressing a similar sense of urgency, Harroy argued that the fight against 'the biological degradation ... of Africa as well as several other continents' was among the 'most pressing duties' of colonial sovereignty.[156]

In many respects these books can be read as prime examples of a budding 'green anti-imperialism' during the inter-war period. By shifting the blame for environmental decline from 'improvident natives' to the changes wrought by colonization itself, they encapsulated and amplified the more subtle currents of auto-critique that were emerging among field researchers and technical officers. But if their diagnosis of soil degradation pinned the blame on imperial intrusion, their proposed solutions amounted to a further extension of colonial control. Although both painted a picture of ecological harmony between the 'age-old customs' of indigenous farmers and 'the former balanced scheme of Nature', there was little doubt that such customary practices had become 'destructive under civilized conditions' of rapid population growth, higher levels of trade, and more intensive exploitation of resources.[157]

One hypothetical solution was to allow colonized peoples to revert to an earlier state of existence. 'War and disease, nomadism and shifting cultivation would soon

[152] Jacks and Whyte, *Rape*, 26.   [153] Jacks and Whyte, *Rape*, 62, 86, 247.

[154] Harroy was secretary of the Institut des Parcs Nationaux du Congo Belge at the time, and later became secretary-general of the IUPN.

[155] Harroy, *Afrique*, 4.   [156] Harroy, *Afrique*, 183, 548.

[157] Jacks and Whyte, *Rape*, 248.

give Nature the short respite she requires in which to recuperate.' The problem with this approach, according to Jacks and Whyte, was that the intense contact between the 'native' and the 'white man' was like a forbidden fruit. Once sampled, there was no going back. 'For better or worse, the seeds of civilization have been sown, and Africa can never revert to its former condition, where the forest, savannah and veld maintained the stern and efficient laws of the jungle.'[158] Moreover, allowing such a regression would be an abdication of imperial responsibility, in at least two ways. At a moral level, the idea that soil degradation was caused mainly by imperial expansion meant that Europeans were obliged to repair the damage. And at a technical level, only the colonial powers had the ability to do so in any event. 'The white man's burden in the future will be to come to terms with the soil and plant world, and for many reasons it promises to be a heavier burden than coming to terms with the natives.'[159]

Regardless of the motivations (charitable or otherwise) behind such arguments, it was obvious that the main burden would, as ever, fall on the 'natives'. Since whites were purportedly not cut out for hard labour in the tropics, and since blacks allegedly lacked the necessary know-how, only a more openly 'feudal' arrangement promised to avert the impending environmental disaster. 'We suggest that some system which will leave the responsibility for organizing, and the power to enforce, soil conservation in the hands of the few while the many do the work either voluntarily or by indenture is indicated as the probable future basis of land tenure in tropical Africa under European influence. In every way the European is fitted to be the overlord and the native to be the villein.'[160]

The metaphor is revealing, for it eloquently expresses the authoritarian undercurrents that characterized much of the 'conservation imperialism'[161] of the late colonial period. Given the scale of the perceived challenge, many officials thought that the threat of soil degradation could only be countered through radical intervention. It was, to be sure, a risky approach, which was likely to arouse indigenous opposition. But in view of what was at stake, it was a risk that had to be taken. Scientific necessity must prevail over political expediency. As Jacks and Whyte suggested in 1939, 'nowhere yet has the conflict between what the ruling race demands from the land and what the land demands from its cultivators led to an open conflict between the conquerors and conquered, but that such may occur in the future is more than a possibility'.[162]

As it turned out, this ominous prediction was not so wide of the mark. As we will see in Chapter 10, the scale-up of conservation measures during the final years of colonial rule led to widespread popular opposition. It was all part of a renewed post-war drive to 'modernize' African agriculture, a campaign that in many ways

---

[158] Jacks and Whyte, *Rape*, 263.   [159] Jacks and Whyte, *Rape*, 249.
[160] Jacks and Whyte, *Rape*, 260–1.
[161] Ramachandra Guha, 'The Authoritarian Biologist and the Arrogance of Anti-Humanism: Wildlife Conservation in the Third World', in Vasant K. Saberwal and Mahesh Rangarajan (eds), *Battles over Nature: Science and the Politics of Conservation* (Delhi: Permanent Black, 2003), 139–57, here 154.
[162] Jacks and Whyte, *Rape*, 254.

marked the culmination of the developmentalist agenda that spanned the entire history of colonial agronomy.

From the late nineteenth century to the middle of the twentieth, efforts to improve tropical farming systems were animated by a faith in Western agronomy and an aspiration to remake tropical agriculture in its image. The key tools for enhancing agricultural productivity—modern irrigation, synthetic fertilizers, crop breeding, mechanization—reflected technological and scientific development in the metropoles, where a highly intensive farming system was currently taking shape. As this model grew more dominant it shaped the agenda of agronomic research, and as the thinking that underpinned it circulated throughout the colonies, it progressively marginalized other modes of agriculture and other forms of knowledge. In the process, tropical agronomy, like other fields of science in the colonial world, reinforced discourses of difference between the 'traditional' and the 'modern', the 'backward' and the 'rational', and thus helped reproduce the asymmetrical relations of power between rulers and ruled.

Throughout the colonial period, the central aim of agricultural development was to coax more wealth from tropical soils through more effective and sustainable land-use practices. Beyond this common denominator, what is perhaps most striking is not the uniformity of policy prescriptions but rather the proliferation of different ideas and approaches. Agricultural research in the colonies was certainly influenced by developments in Europe, but it was much more than just an offshoot of metropolitan trends. Indeed, much of it was focused on alternatives to the increasingly mechanized, high-input farming practices that were becoming standardized across the industrial world. As field researchers became more familiar with the agro-ecosystems they sought to manage, many concluded that the best outcomes came through a detailed understanding of local agro-ecosystems and cultural expectations rather than large-scale, centralized solutions. Agricultural development in the colonies was not always 'high modernist' and rigidly top-down. In the crop fields of Europe's tropical empire, small was often seen as beautiful long before Ernst Friedrich Schumacher pointed it out in the 1970s.[163]

The more multifaceted tropical agronomy became, the more it resists being pigeonholed as an authoritarian 'colonial science' in the service of imperial states or metropolitan commercial ventures.[164] Undoubtedly, the campaign for 'agricultural improvement', like 'scientific forestry', had adverse effects on farming communities, and state policy was still based on the assumption that colonial economies should prioritize the export of cash crops. Even the most dissident agronomist voices were not seeking to undermine the colonial enterprise, but rather to reform and improve it through the development of sustainable agricultural systems and the creation of prosperous and stable rural communities. Yet figures such as Howard, Faulkner, Chevalier, Vageler, or Lovink show that colonial agronomy did not always conform

[163] See Moon, *Technology*, esp. 150; E. F. Schumacher, *Small is Beautiful: A Study of Economics as if People Mattered* (London: Abacus, 1974).

[164] For an insightful discussion and critique: Beinart, Brown, and Gilfoyle, 'Experts', 424–5; also Mark Harrison, 'Science and the British Empire', *Isis*, vol. 96 no. 1 (2005), 56–63.

to imperial agendas or uphold presumed hierarchies. It also followed its own disciplinary reasoning, and it occasionally opened up new understandings of tropical environments by drawing on local knowledge. Helen Tilley's portrayal of inter-war British Africa as an 'environmental laboratory'—one in which re-evaluations of subaltern knowledge were bound up with new approaches to agricultural development—has its parallels in other parts of colonial Africa and Asia.[165]

From the 1890s to the 1940s, tropical agronomy in Europe's colonies evolved from a productivist, export-oriented enterprise into a syncretic, conservationist body of knowledge that was increasingly focused on the long term and that sought solutions to complex problems (soil protection, food security) that transcended the boundaries of the social and natural sciences. Its evolution reflected the broader transformation of 'colonial development' from an agenda of resource extraction into a multifaceted programme combining economic growth and social progress with responsible stewardship over natural resources. But these various goals were no easier to harmonize then than they are now. Looking ahead, the key question was how far they could be reconciled amidst the unprecedented population growth, commercial expansion, and rising social expectations of the post-war world.

[165] Tilley, *Africa*, 115–68.

PART III

ACCELERATION, DECLINE, AND AFTERMATH

10

Progress and Hubris
The Political Ecology of Late
Colonial Development

The decade following the Second World War was full of contradictions for Europe's imperial enterprise. On the one hand, the immense strains of wartime mobilization, the interruption of colonial authority in much of Asia, and the growing challenge of independence movements left it in a state of crisis. For most states in Western Europe, the enormous task of economic reconstruction at home, coupled with the strategic reliance on a US government that had rather different ideas about the post-war international order, made a far-flung empire seem like a luxury that they could ill afford to maintain. On the other hand, the urgent demand for raw materials and the pressing need to earn US dollars highlighted the potential of colonial territories as a source of national strength. Amidst the bottlenecks and acute financial pressures of post-war recovery, overseas colonies seemed like necessities that Europe could ill afford to relinquish.[1]

The upshot was a mixture of imperial retreat and imperial reinforcement, in which the specific intentions and outcomes varied greatly from place to place. The Netherlands, whose domestic economy was heavily dependent on its links with the East Indies, waged two brutal campaigns to retain as much of its political and economic authority as possible in the archipelago; as the old Dutch saying went, 'Indië verloren, rampspoed geboren' (losing the Indies will lead to ruin).[2] By contrast, Britain's exit from India, though anything but peaceful on the ground, was essentially a pragmatic withdrawal in the face of a powerful independence movement that could no longer be contained. But wherever the European powers remained entrenched—which by the end of the 1940s was mostly in Africa and parts of the Caribbean—they approached their empires with renewed vigour.

---

[1] Nicholas J. White, 'Reconstructing Europe through Rejuvenating Empire: The British, French, and Dutch Experiences Compared', in Mark Mazower, Jessica Reinisch, and David Feldman (eds), *Post-War Reconstruction in Europe: International Perspectives, 1945–1949*, *Past & Present* Supplement 6 (Oxford: Oxford University Press, 2011), 211–36.

[2] H. L. Wesseling, *Indië verloren, rampspoed geboren: en andere opstellen over de geschiedenis van de Europese expansie* (Amsterdam: Bakker, 1988). At the end of the 1920s, 12 per cent of the Netherlands' national income and as much as one-fifth of the Dutch population were directly linked to the East Indies via trade or investment: Stoler, *Capitalism*, 20–1. As the CIA recognized, the Netherlands' 'police action' in the East Indies was clearly about maintaining Indonesia as a major contributor to its trade balance and source of dollar credits: 'Consequences of the Dutch "Police Action" in Indonesia', 27 Jan. 1949, p. 3, <https://www.cia.gov/library/readingroom/docs/DOC_0000258552.pdf>.

Confronted by massive debts and daunting economic problems, many political leaders looked to their empires for salvation. In the post-war spirit of dirigiste intervention, Europe's colonies were increasingly governed as part of a carefully planned, technocratic programme of developmental imperialism. The fundamental rationale was twofold: to modernize colonial economies, and to support metropolitan reconstruction efforts. The key for achieving both aims was rapid economic growth through an upsurge of production in the tropics.[3]

This was a remarkably ambitious agenda, for it ultimately entailed a major overhaul of colonial governance. Colonial states that had long operated on a shoe-string budget would have to be far more proactive than ever before—intervening in markets, investing in infrastructure, and marshalling resources for maximum productivity. In the late 1940s, British, French, and Belgian authorities devised detailed colonial development plans that in many ways sought to realize, at long last, the unfulfilled aspirations of imperial reformers such as Joseph Chamberlain and Albert Sarraut. The chief ingredients of the post-war development recipe were in themselves hardly new: namely, promoting commodity exports, improving transportation, raising agricultural production, and cataloguing valuable resources. The crucial difference lay in the scale and scope of post-war initiatives, which far outstripped anything that had come before. This required money, which was allocated in record amounts via the French Fonds pour l'Investissement en Développement Économique et Social (FIDES, 1946), the British Colonial Development Corporation (CDC, 1947) and Overseas Food Corporation (OFC, 1947), along with various five- and ten-year plans.[4] It also required a closer relationship between policy-making and scientific knowledge, for the vast increase in investment could, it was believed, only repay itself through the rigorous application of technical expertise. Science was a critical part of the late-colonial development programme, both for defining its aims and for providing the means to achieve them.[5]

What all of this added up to was an unprecedented escalation of state intervention into the lives of rural people, their use of the land, and the environments they inhabited. Buoyed by metropolitan grants and rising commodity revenues, the so-called 'second colonial occupation' was the heyday of the scientific expert, the comprehensive plan, and the monumental mega-project.[6] But if the underlying aim was to shore up the authority of colonial states by converting a greater share of their natural riches into economic growth, the effects of the post-war development

---

[3] Bonneuil, Savants, 83–95, Michael Havinden and David Meredith, Colonialism and Development: Britain and its Tropical Colonies, 1850–1960 (London: Routledge, 1993), 206–34.

[4] To give a sense of scale, whereas the French government spent the equivalent (1951 value) of 21 billion francs on colonial development 1938–47, from 1947 to 1955 the figure leapt to 195 billion: Le Plan quadriennal d'equipement et de modernisation de l'A.O.F. (1953–1957), 3. The Belgian government raised its investments in the Congo on a similar scale within the framework of its 'Plan décennal': Bulletin agricole du Congo belge et du Ruanda-Urundi: volume jubilaire (Brussels: Place Royale, 1960), 109–10.

[5] Hodge, Triumph, 207–53; Bonneuil, Savants, 90–5.

[6] The term originates from D. Low and J. Lonsdale, 'Introduction', in D. Low and A. Smith (eds), The Oxford History of East Africa (Oxford: Oxford University Press, 1976), 1–64.

programme were often very different. As we will see, the accelerating pace of socio-ecological change bred also new tensions that ultimately helped undermine the colonial order.

There was, in other words, an important environmental dimension to both the regeneration and degeneration of late colonialism, one that was inextricably entwined with the political, social, and economic sides of the story. During the twilight years of empire, colonial development largely revolved around the attempt to enhance the productivity of tropical territories through the more intensive management of their biological and mineral resources. As one French contemporary put it in suggestively Clementsian terms, the task of colonial governments was to engineer a new anthropogenic conclusion to the process of ecological succession: 'By means of research, capital, time and technical expertise, humankind might well succeed in progressing from the various *natural climaxes* of tropical Africa to genuine *climaxes of domestication*.... It is necessary because the advancement of the black world is at stake. That is the essential goal.'[7] This chapter will explore several key aspects of the late colonial intervention into tropical ecosystems, starting with the shift towards more intensive forms of agriculture before turning towards the redoubled efforts of colonial states to conserve and govern valuable resources.

A COLONIAL AGRICULTURAL REVOLUTION?

At its core, the post-war development drive was a response to a powerful set of countervailing forces. On one side there was a strong economic pressure from metropolitan governments to produce more export commodities (tin, rubber, cocoa, vegetable oils) for sale on world markets. At the same time, there were equally strong political demands for better social services, faster economic growth, and higher living standards for colonized peoples. It was clear from the beginning that these two imperatives would have to be pursued in tandem, since the sale of export goods would provide many of the resources for welfare improvements. Equally clear was that neither could be achieved without increasing food output, since higher agricultural productivity was vital for boosting peasant prosperity and for channelling land and labour into export production in the first place. In the words of a leading French agronomist, 'underdevelopment in agriculture seriously affects the entire economy. It is inseparable from the lack of industry and underdevelopment in general.'[8] Put somewhat differently, development meant raising the 'carrying capacity' of the land and the productivity of its agro-ecosystems.

---

[7] Jean Richard-Molard, 'Les Terroirs tropicaux d'Afrique', *Annales de géographie*, vol. 60 (1951), 349–69, here 349, italics in the original; see also R. Portères, 'Climax de domestication et systèmes de culture', *L'Agronomie tropicale*, vol. 4 (1949), 165–9.

[8] René Dumont, *False Start in Africa*, trans. Phyllis Nauts Ott (London: Andre Deutsch, 1966), 31. For the long view of the importance of agriculture for international development debates in the twentieth century, see Corinna R. Unger, 'Agrarwissenschaftliche Expertise und ländliche Modernisierungsstrategien in der internationalen Entwicklungspolitik, 1920er bis 1980er Jahre', *Geschichte und Gesellschaft*, vol. 41 (2015), 552–79.

Although it was hardly a new goal in itself, the challenge for colonial agriculture departments was to scale up productivity to a level commensurate with the heightened socio-economic ambitions of post-war administrators and populations alike. The key question was how best to go about it. As we saw in Chapter 9, many colonial agronomists were by now firmly convinced that the basis of any genuine improvement was a better understanding of existing agro-ecological systems and how they related to the social and economic needs of local people. During the 1930s, the shift towards a more 'holistic' approach had proven not only more ecologically appropriate than previous methods, but also more economically prudent. Subsistence-oriented farmers generally weathered the price shocks of the Depression far better than those who gambled on a narrow range of crops or relied on external capital inputs. Maintaining the fertility of fragile tropical soils was the top priority, and throughout the 1940s and 1950s researchers in Africa continued to highlight the suitability of indigenous techniques such as mound cultivation, intercropping, and controlled burning.[9] Among British agronomists there were many who preached the organic gospel of 'humus', and even more who emphasized the importance of adjusting to local circumstances.[10] In the French colonies, agricultural officers likewise sought to build upon the existing 'adaptation of the black peasant to his surroundings': 'He artfully uses innumerable varieties of every cultivated plant according to local conditions. He adapts his methods of cultivation with a care that is all the greater insofar as his peasant traditions have been conserved.'[11]

But not everyone was convinced by this approach. In the eyes of many officials, especially metropolitan policy-makers, such a policy of incremental change was simply not up to the challenge of delivering a marked improvement of yields and living standards. Even among veteran agronomists in the colonies there had always been advocates of a more productivist approach, and after the war this perspective was broadly shared by a younger generation of agricultural officers who were eager to apply the technocratic solutions that had been deployed to such effect on the wartime home front.[12] As the Economics Director in the British Colonial Office remarked in 1947, 'there is today general agreement that African Agriculture cannot secure the improvements in productivity which are necessary by continued dependence on the efforts of the individual family working with primitive tools and that radical changes in the system of agriculture are required in order to permit

---

[9] On British colonies: Hodge, *Triumph*, 230–5. On French territories: Aubert, *Les Sols des régions*, 8–9; Georges Aubert, *Les Sols et l'aménagement agricole de l'Afrique Occidentale Française* (Paris, 1951).

[10] Hodge, *Triumph*, 233–4.

[11] Jean Dresch, 'La Riziculture en Afrique occidentale', *Annales de géographie*, vol. 58 (1949), 295–312, here 295.

[12] This was true for all of the colonial powers: on French agronomy, see Christophe Bonneuil, Gilles Denis, and Jean-Luc Mayaud (eds), *Sciences, chercheurs et agriculture: pour une histoire de la recherche agronomique* (Paris: L'Harmattan, 2008); Jean Boulaine, *Histoire de l'agronomie en France* (Paris: Tec & Doc-Lavoisier, 1996); for Britain, Hodge, *Triumph*, 234, notes the importance of generational change; see also Andrew Bowman, 'Ecology to Technocracy: Scientists, Surveys and Power in the Agricultural Development of Late-Colonial Zambia', *Journal of Southern African Studies*, vol. 37 no. 1 (2011), 135–53; for the East Indies, J. H. Boeke, *Ontwikkelingsgang en toekomst van bevolkings- en ondernemingslandbouw in Nederlandsch-Indië* (Leiden: Brill, 1948), 102–3.

operations on a larger scale, with increased use of mechanical assistance and with the basic object of increased productivity'.[13]

The pursuit of such 'radical changes' represented an important shift of emphasis from the 1930s. It mirrored the broader evolution of the colonial state in which the district official who 'knew his natives' was increasingly replaced by a technically trained corps of experts less attuned to conditions on the ground. 'Development' was fundamentally about achieving social and economic progress, and for most observers the end point on this road to modernity was embodied in metropolitan society itself.[14] From this perspective, advancement along the continuum of civilization meant travelling at least some distance towards the model that prevailed in Europe, which was rapidly moving towards a new system of industrialized, high-input agriculture. Of course, some doubted that such a transition could ever be achieved among the supposedly primitive societies inhabiting much of Africa. But while presumptions of persistent backwardness provoked widespread scepticism, they also invited the notion that African societies were readily malleable and thus ripe for social engineering.[15] The perception of Africa as a kind of technological *tabula rasa* bolstered the already powerful desire to introduce European agrarian practices as the basis for a revolutionary breakthrough in colonial agriculture. It also enhanced the attraction of top-down, technology-driven schemes that would enable agricultural experts to circumvent (rather than engage with) what was seen as a stubbornly conservative and immutable peasantry. Transmitting European knowledge and translating it into technological improvements were the twin prongs of post-war agricultural modernization in the colonies. Between them they left little room to consider the complexities of local environmental conditions or the ways in which indigenous farmers adapted to them.

The post-war combination of unprecedented funding levels and the desire for quick results meant that the appeal of large-scale prestige projects was never greater. The most (in)famous example by far was the East African Groundnut Scheme, the flagship development project in British Africa at the time. Although the stated aim of the scheme was to remedy the acute shortage of fats on world markets (and thereby generate revenue for the Tanganyikan government), an equally important goal was to demonstrate what the colonial state could achieve by deploying the full panoply of Western planning and agronomic expertise. Originally proposed by the United Africa Company (a subsidiary of Unilever), and strongly backed by the former Director of Agriculture in Tanganyika, the plan certainly did not lack for ambition. Over a five-year period, 1.3 million hectares of land were to be developed in units of 30,000 acres (12.140 hectares) each, at a total estimated cost of some £24 million. By the fifth year, planned output of groundnuts was to reach around 600,000 tons, thus alleviating Britain's fats shortage and generating a tidy profit for the sterling area on world markets. After obtaining formal approval in

---

[13] Sydney Caine, quoted from Frederick Cooper, *Decolonization and African Society* (Cambridge: Cambridge University Press, 1996), 210.

[14] See Nick Cullather, 'Development? It's History', *Diplomatic History*, vol. 24 (2000), 641–53; also Hodge, 'Writing', Parts 1 and 2.

[15] Cooper, *Decolonization*, 176–7.

late 1946, the plan was to clear and plant just over 60,000 hectares at Kongwa by the end of 1947 so that the first harvest could take place in early 1948. The scheme was always about more than just groundnuts. It was also conceived as the vanguard of industrial agriculture in colonial Africa, a model of technological development that African farmers would wish to emulate and that would present a compelling alternative to the Soviet collective farm concept.[16]

Despite high hopes, however, the Groundnut Scheme was one of the biggest failures in the history of overseas development. It soon ran into trouble on a variety of levels: logistical, economic, administrative, and not least ecological. It was ultimately the unsuitability of soil and climate conditions—or more precisely, the failure to study them adequately—that undermined the project from the beginning. The local brush and baobab trees proved much harder to remove than originally anticipated. Clearing them wrecked most of the tractors (some of them converted Sherman tanks) that had been brought in for the job. Managers eventually resorted to stretching a ship-anchor chain between two bulldozers in order to clear the brush, but this method still failed to remove the tangled root systems, which subsequently damaged the seed-drilling equipment at planting time. In the first season of the project, heavy rains delayed planting, destroyed several buildings, washed away a rail embankment, and sent a plague of scorpions over the Kongwa settlement.[17] During the subsequent dry season, the sun baked the now unshaded and compacted clay into a hardpan that was well-nigh impenetrable. By 1949, insect pests and weeds had become a serious problem, and the effects were further exacerbated by periodic drought. When the British government finally pulled the plug in early 1951, fewer than 20,000 hectares had been converted to groundnuts—a sizeable area, to be sure, but a tiny fraction of the original plan.[18] After spending around twice the original budget of £24 million, managers had little more to show than thousands of hectares of ruined land (Fig. 10.1).

The East African Groundnut Scheme was one of the largest and most high-profile colonial development projects ever undertaken, and its humiliating demise sparked a flurry of recriminations and debates. Against this backdrop, what is perhaps most striking is how the same mistakes were repeated elsewhere in spite of ubiquitous calls to draw the appropriate lessons.

Just as the debacle unfolded in Tanzania, French authorities embarked on a remarkably similar (albeit less grandiose) project in the central Casamance area of southern Senegal.[19] Directly inspired by the British scheme at Kongwa, the basic plan of the Compagnie Générale des Oléagineux Tropicaux (CGOT) was to convert around 100,000 hectares of marginal land—in this case wooded savannah

---

[16] The essential study remains Alan Wood, *The Groundnut Affair* (London: Bodley Head, 1950), figures pp. 252–6.

[17] Underground arthropods commonly surface after heavy rains to escape rising groundwater levels.

[18] Wood, *Groundnut*, 85–101, 205–10, acreage figure p. 155; also Matteo Rizzo, 'What Was Left of the Groundnut Scheme? Development Disaster and Labour Market in Southern Tanganyika, 1946–1952', *Journal of Agrarian Change*, vol. 6 no. 2 (Apr. 2006), 205–38.

[19] Marina Diallo Cô-Trung, *La Compagnie générale des oléagineux tropicaux en Casamance: autopsie d'une opération de mise en valeur coloniale (1948–1962)* (Paris: Karthala, 1998), 92–109, 182–3.

Fig. 10.1. The Groundnut Scheme at Kongwa, Tanzania, *c.*1950.
Source: Alan Wood, *The Groundnut Affair* (London: Bodley Head, 1950), p. 80.

recently emptied by an outbreak of sleeping sickness—into groundnut fields that would be worked by African wage labourers using the latest mechanized cultivation methods from the United States. The most notable feature of the project was that CGOT officials knowingly proceeded with it in 1948 despite awareness of the problems emerging in Tanganyika, and despite vocal criticism by prominent French agronomists.[20]

The methods used in Casamance were strikingly similar to those in Tanganyika. Tractors and anchor chains were once again deployed for clearing, followed by deep ploughing to prepare the massive plots, some of which measured a full kilometre in length. The results broadly replicated those in Tanganyika as well. Clearing was painfully slow, and the tangle of roots that was left in the ground damaged planting equipment. Once cleared, the bare and unshaded soil became too wet during the rains and too hard in the dry season. Weeds soon smothered the crops, and by 1950 there were also signs of severe soil erosion on all but the flattest terrain (in one spot, a ravine 1.7 km long had washed out in less than four years). But despite these warning signs, and despite the fact that even government scientists deemed only one-third of the earmarked land to be suitable for mechanized cultivation 'without grave danger of erosion', more and more parcels were prepared by tractor and plough.[21] After four years the project had little to show for all the effort and investment it had absorbed. In 1952 motorized cultivation was abruptly

[20] e.g. Auguste Chevalier, 'Amélioration et extension de la culture des arachides au Sénégal', *Revue de botanique appliquée* (May 1947), 173–92; Dumont, *False Start*, 56–8.
[21] Roger Fauck, *Érosion et mécanisation agricole* (Bureau des Sols en A.O.F., Sept. 1956), 10–19, quote p. 19.

curtailed, and with closure of the entire scheme looming, the CGOT quickly re-fashioned itself into a research station for the gradual mechanization and improvement of indigenous cultivation techniques (in which form it survived decolonization as the Société pour le Développement Agricole et Industriel de la Casamance).[22]

The Groundnut Scheme spin-offs did not stop there. The Mokwa agricultural project in western Nigeria, launched in 1949 and terminated five years later, also repeated many of the same mistakes, though on a smaller scale. Once again there was insufficient prior study of soils and suitable crops, which was not helped by the complete lack of input by local farmers. As a result, what was supposed to be a mechanized demonstration farm quickly turned into an experiment farm, since 'with such inadequate knowledge', one of its officers recounted, 'there was virtually nothing to demonstrate', least of all to indigenous cultivators whose two traditional sorghum strains yielded better than any of the ninety-three cross-varieties and exotics that were grown at the project.[23] In defence of the Mokwa scheme, it should be noted that the full scope of the failures in Tanganyika was not yet apparent when clearing commenced. The same could not be said for the Gonja groundnuts project in the northern Gold Coast, which commenced in 1950. Here, as at Mokwa, the plan was to create a mechanized agricultural colony by attracting settlers from crowded districts to a sparsely populated tract of savannah around 12,000 hectares in size. But Gonja made almost no headway at all, collapsing in 1957 with fewer than 600 hectares planted.[24]

The Groundnut Scheme was by no means the only mega-model for subsequent projects to follow. The Office du Niger (see Chapter 1) likewise spawned imitators. The Richard Toll rice project in Senegal, for instance, was essentially a miniature version of the Office minus the cotton. First conceived during the Second World War (in response to rice shortages caused by the disruption of shipping from Indochina), the project began operation in 1949 along the lower Senegal River as an intended archetype of irrigated, mechanized cultivation. Before long, it ran into the usual problems: high machinery costs, declining fertility, soil deterioration, weakening of selected cultivar strains. It also faced an additional threat from an unexpected (though again, with proper study, not unpredictable) quarter, namely vast flocks of *Quelea* (the world's most abundant avian species), small sparrow-like birds with a big appetite for rice and other seeds. After receiving around 4 billion francs of investment, the Richard Toll project cultivated merely a third of the planned surface.[25]

[22] Cô-Trung, *Compagnie*, 13, 237–8, 246–50.

[23] Kenneth D. S. Baldwin, *The Niger Agricultural Project: An Experiment in African Development* (Oxford: Blackwell, 1957), 168. Of the 13,000 hectares originally planned, only 3,885 were ever cleared, and at no point was the scheme economically viable.

[24] Jeff D. Grischow, 'Late Colonial Development in British West Africa: The Gonja Development Project in the Northern Territories of the Gold Coast, 1948–57', *Canadian Journal of African Studies*, vol. 35 (2001), 282–312.

[25] *Le Plan quadriennal*, 14; Dumont, *False Start*, 304–5.

According to the tropical geographer Pierre Gourou, French colonial development failures generally received less publicity than their British equivalents, 'perhaps because they were less grandiose, but partly because in France there has been rather less criticism and rather more discretion'.[26] Be that as it may, the list of setbacks grew longer over the course of the 1950s. Gambia was home to an abortive attempt to convert 4,000 hectares into a mega-battery-farm for poultry. In the Belgian Congo, a project to increase local protein supplies through the creation of over 122,000 fish ponds—many of them poorly sited, as it turned out—produced only a fraction of the expected yields despite massive inputs of nutrients and feed. In Dahomey, FIDES spent around 900 million CFA francs on the planting of 7 million high-yielding oil palm trees, only to see many of the new plantations damaged by fires, invaded by *Imperata* grass (which cannot be uprooted without damaging the shallow oil palm roots), and abandoned to bush by 1961.[27]

Such sobering experiences never fundamentally undermined the post-war faith in scientific expertise as the key to managing the natural world. They did, however, take some of the lustre off glitzy prestige projects. For starters, they sensitized officials to what one contemporary called the 'twin dangers in all development projects of grandiosity and arrogance'.[28] We can see this, for instance, in the shift towards smaller-scale hydraulic schemes in French West Africa after the disappointments of the Office du Niger, or in the return to more traditional flush irrigation methods in the Scarcies Delta of Sierra Leone after new rice polders caused an unexpected rise in soil acidity and salinity.[29] More importantly, such experiences helped validate the idea that agricultural development should focus on the refinement of existing cultivation methods rather than the imposition of radical changes from above. After all, small farmers still accounted for the vast bulk of agricultural production in the colonies, and field researchers continued to highlight the remarkable effectiveness of many of their techniques (in particular the studies of William Allan in Northern Rhodesia and Alfred Grove in Nigeria).[30] As Auguste Chevalier remarked, indigenous agriculture may have appeared backward, 'but it is perfectible'.[31]

A good example of such 'perfection' efforts were the *lotissements agricoles* in the Belgian Congo, the cornerstone of the colony's *paysannat* scheme, one of the largest agricultural settlement programmes in all of colonial Africa. Before the 1940s, agronomists generally denounced the shifting cultivation systems that prevailed in

---

[26] Gourou, *Tropical World*, 191.

[27] Havinden and Meredith, *Colonialism*, 292; *Bulletin agricole du Congo belge*, 154; Dumont, *False Start*, 60–3.

[28] S. Herbert Frankel, in Baldwin, *Niger*, xi.

[29] Dumont, *False Start*, 54; Richards, *Indigenous Agricultural Revolution*, 31.

[30] William Allan, *Studies in African Land Usage in Northern Rhodesia*, Rhodes–Livingstone papers no. 15 (Cape Town: Oxford University Press, 1949); A. T. Grove, *Land Use and Soil Conservation in Parts of Onitsha and Owerri Province* (Kaduna: Nigerian Government, 1951); A. T. Grove, *Land Use and Soil Conservation on the Jos Plateau* (Kaduna: Nigerian Government, 1952); more generally, Richards, *Indigenous Agricultural Revolution*, 32–3.

[31] Auguste Chevalier, *Révolution en Agriculture* (Paris: Presses Universitaires de France, 1946), 277–8.

the Congo basin as wasteful and damaging to the forests. Over time, however, their inability to devise an alternative means of maintaining fertility on the region's thin soils led them to recognize the efficacy of long forest fallows, and thus to focus on the improvement rather than elimination of indigenous swidden methods.[32] At the *paysannat* settlements, land was divided into alternating 20-metre bands of field and forest, which were initially cultivated on a nineteen-year cycle comprising three years of cultivation followed by sixteen years of fallow. Although agronomists debated the ideal length of fallow periods—some arguing for sixteen years, some longer, some for as few as twelve years on plots where no cotton was grown—the standard nineteen-year formula was remarkably similar to the traditional cycles in the region, which were usually around twenty years. When managers at the Paysannat Turumbu tried to reduce the fallow period to twelve years in order to boost productivity, they soon found that it harmed soil fertility and were forced to revert to the customary Turumbu system.[33]

In effect, researchers in the Congo, like many of their counterparts in other colonies, were forced to acknowledge the suitability of indigenous cultivation methods, and often tailored their improvement efforts accordingly. The *lotissements agricoles* were a prime example of this amalgamation of African and 'expert' knowledge after the war, and offer yet another illustration of the complexities and compromises that characterized the late colonial development discourse on the ground.[34] But even so, this should not obscure the fact that such hybrid practices were themselves a means of penetrating rural communities and exerting colonial power. Ultimately, schemes such as the Congolese *paysannats* were about control—about imposing geometric order on the landscape, gathering statistics, and domesticating indigenous cultivation methods through experiment and observation. As one contemporary revealingly noted, 'the Bantu agricultural system has remained intact in its principles and in the techniques it deploys, *but it has been disciplined'*.[35]

A focus on indigenous farming methods rather than centralized mega-projects did not, therefore, necessarily indicate a less 'top-down' perspective. Nor did it automatically signal a 'hybrid' approach to agricultural development, let alone an adherence to the organic, ecological perspectives that had shaped tropical agronomy during the inter-war period. There was a broad range of ideas about how best to improve indigenous agriculture, and by the late 1940s many officials were convinced that

---

[32] Malengreau, *Paysannat*, esp. 13; G. Tondeur and B. Bergeroo-Campagne, *L'Agriculture nomade*, vol. 1: *Congo belge, Côte d'Ivoire* (Rome: FAO, 1956), 48–69; Jewsiewicki, 'Modernisation', 51–4.

[33] Tondeur and Bergeroo-Campagne, *L'Agriculture*, 74–86, 91–7; Malengreau, *Paysannat*, 60–1.

[34] Hodge, 'Writing', Part 2; Joseph Hodge, 'The Hybridity of Colonial Knowledge: British Tropical Agricultural Science and African Farming Practices at the End of Empire', in Bennett and Hodge (eds), *Science and Empire*, 209–31; Roberts, *Two Worlds*, 14–21; Bassett, *Peasant Cotton*, 4–5; van Beusekom, *Negotiating*.

[35] Tondeur and Bergeroo-Campagne, *L'Agriculture*, 88, italics in the original; see also Christophe Bonneuil, 'Development as Experiment: Science and State Building in Late Colonial and Postcolonial Africa, 1930–1970', *Osiris*, vol. 15 (2000), 258–81, here 272–4; *Bulletin agricole du Congo belge*, 125; Malengreau, *Paysannat*, 90–1.

sufficient productivity gains could only be achieved through the large-scale deployment of modern machinery and artificial fertilizers. Such assumptions were clearly manifested in the colonial economic plans of the period, and by the end of the decade they were enshrined in agricultural policy as well.[36] As the British Select Committee on Colonial Development noted in 1948, 'a large-scale advance in agriculture means reaching into every village, forming farmers' groups and agricultural societies, demonstrating new techniques on farmers' holdings, promoting cooperatives and providing fertilisers, improved tools and cattle'.[37] All across Africa, colonial governments pinned their hopes on the kinds of technical innovations that were currently driving the transition towards industrialized agriculture in Europe.

It was a characteristically high modernist response to a multifaceted challenge. The great attraction of technologies such as artificial fertilizers and agricultural machinery was (and largely still is) that they promised to simplify inherently complex biological and social processes. For a while, at least, heavy doses of fertilizer boosted output almost irrespective of the other factors of plant growth. The mechanization of farm tasks likewise promised to alleviate the labour bottlenecks caused by the drain of agricultural workers into mining and export-cropping.[38] On the face of it, these technologies offered a panacea for all ills, and a remarkably effective one at that. Their mass deployment in post-war Europe and North America was already producing dramatic yield increases, and it would take another quarter-century or so before the disastrous environmental side-effects of overuse came more fully into view.[39] But as veteran agronomists knew, there were limits to what fertilizers and mechanization could realistically achieve in the context of tropical farming systems. In the event, an all-too familiar set of problems awaited this would-be colonial agricultural revolution.

Economic obstacles were a perennial source of difficulty. Although the production of fertilizer skyrocketed in the wake of the Second World War, it was still too expensive for most farmers in the colonies, and only came into widespread use—for good and ill—with the massive fertilizer subsidy programmes after independence.[40] Mechanization efforts made somewhat more headway, but were commonly inhibited by the mismatch between the high price of equipment and the small size of most peasant farms, which made it difficult to realize the economies of scale necessary to make the acquisition of machinery worthwhile. One solution was to establish collective equipment stations, but tractor cooperatives could rarely break even once the costs of depreciation were factored in. Technical snags only compounded the economic hurdles. In many parts of Africa the huge variation in soil firmness from wet to dry seasons called for vastly different power and traction requirements, which made the tropical equivalent of the multi-use

---

[36] Richards, *Indigenous Agricultural Revolution*, 34; *Le Plan quadriennal*, 7; Bowman, 'Ecology'.
[37] Havinden and Meredith, *Colonialism*, 306.   [38] Cooper, *Decolonization*, 194–5.
[39] On the social function and resilience of panaceas in modern agriculture, see Frank Uekötter, 'Why Panaceas Work: Recasting Science, Knowledge and Fertilizer Interests in German Agriculture', *Agricultural History*, vol. 88 no. 1 (2014), 68–86.
[40] Vaclav Smil, *Enriching the Earth: Fritz Haber, Carl Bosch, and the Transformation of World Food Production* (Cambridge, Mass.: MIT Press, 2001), 114–16.

'Farmall' tractor frustratingly elusive. Furthermore, the interlocking lateral root systems of bush savannah were notoriously hard on discs and ploughs.[41] In the end, only lavish state subsidies allowed the 'tractorization' wheels to start rolling. In the late 1950s, the mechanical cultivation scheme in Sierra Leone consumed a full 80 per cent of the Agriculture Department's budget, despite the fact that only 4 per cent of the total rice crop was grown with the aid of machinery.[42]

Besides economic and technical considerations, there was a host of agronomic misgivings about large-scale mechanization as well. The dangers of ploughing up tropical soils, especially sandy or light, silty soils, were by now fairly axiomatic among colonial agriculture officers. Cutting deeper and exposing more earth to blazing sun and pounding rain reduced humus content and accelerated the processes of nutrient leaching, laterization (the concentration of insoluble iron and aluminium oxides), and erosion. Moreover, the practice of laying out fields lengthwise in order to allow long runs for tractors was an affront to the conservationist principle of slope-contouring as a means of minimizing soil loss. The severe erosion of groundnut fields at the CGOT in Senegal was only one example of what could happen. At the Mokwa project in Nigeria, it took only two years for plough furrows running downhill to create a gully nearly 2 kilometres long.[43] Little wonder that colonial agronomists were extremely wary of the enthusiasm for agricultural machinery among project engineers.[44] As Gourou put it, '"tractoritis" is a disease fatal to progress'.[45]

Perhaps most importantly, the large-scale use of machinery and fertilizers also raised some thorny social and political issues, for as successive study missions concluded, they almost inevitably would involve significant changes in landownership. The underlying logic was that agricultural intensification demanded a greater investment of time, effort, and other resources, and that farmers' readiness to make this investment would require greater security of individual land tenure, inheritance rights, and rights of disposal over the product of their labour.[46] On a political level, the key problem was that individualized ownership often entailed a fundamental transformation of land tenure arrangements, especially in those colonies where land rights and obligations were rooted in kinship-based systems supervised by indigenous elites. In British-governed territories, such 'customary' structures of authority were an important element in the framework of colonial rule, which meant that any diminution of elite control over access to land posed serious political risks. On a social level too, the implications were deeply unsettling.

[41] Generally, J. W. Y. Higgs et al., *Report of a Survey of Problems in the Mechanization of Native Agriculture in Tropical African Colonies* (London: HMSO, 1950), 35–6, 68–70, 84; Baldwin, *Niger*, 110–25.

[42] Richards, *Indigenous Agricultural Revolution*, 35.   [43] Baldwin, *Niger*, 178–81.

[44] G. Labrousse, 'La Conférence d'Entebbé, sur la mécanisation de l'agriculture tropicale', *L'Agronomie tropicale*, vol. 11 (1956), 106–11, here 108; M. Gaudy, *La Conservation des sols en A.O.F.* (Gouvernement Générale de l'AOF, 1953), 63.

[45] Gourou, *Tropical World*, 191.

[46] This was essentially a 'Boserupian' analysis *avant la lettre*, linking demographic growth to agricultural innovation and the emergence of new land rights: Ester Boserup, *The Conditions of Agricultural Growth: The Economics of Agrarian Change under Population Pressure* (London: Allen & Unwin, 1965).

The long experience of colonial land reform in the Caribbean gave good reason to fear the potential consequences of extensive private landholding in Africa, worst of all a vicious circle of wealth concentration, peasant indebtedness, and eventual landlessness. In short, the logic of full-scale agricultural modernization conjured the spectre of dangerous social upheaval and political destabilization, which was precisely the opposite of what the policy was trying to achieve.[47]

The late colonial development campaign therefore threw officials onto the horns of a dilemma. Should the main aim be an increase in agricultural productivity, or rather the preservation and stabilization of rural communities through the incremental improvement of sustainable cultivation practices? Both of these aspirations had broad support, and the question of which should be prioritized—and how, if at all, they could be wedded together—was extensively debated, at least among those (unlike African farmers themselves) with much say in the matter.

Yet for all the differences of opinion, there was one point of general agreement. Neither goal could be achieved without combating the threat of soil degradation, erosion, and deforestation. If the development of agrarian economies demanded a more intensive utilization of the land, it also called for rigorous safeguards to protect agricultural resources from reckless overexploitation. Both of these issues were central to the new 'climax of domestication' in the tropics. Both were based on mounting fears about population growth and the carrying capacity of the land. And both were highly intrusive into rural environments and the communities that lived in them.

RESOURCE CONSERVATION AND LATE-COLONIAL DEVELOPMENT

During the post-war years, the drive to capitalize more fully on the resources of the colonies was mirrored by a major scale-up of conservation efforts. Here we will focus on three distinct but overlapping sets of concerns: forest depletion, wildlife decline, and soil deterioration.

Just as in previous decades, late-colonial conservation initiatives served a variety of different purposes. Aside from the protection of natural assets, they also dovetailed with the desire to boost raw material exports and to bolster state authority over resources and populations. In many European colonies the forests were a particular focus of attention. In part this reflected the large revenues that could be generated by the export of forest products, but during the immediate post-war years in particular, it was also amplified by the security risks they posed. During the late 1940s and early 1950s, such concerns were particularly acute in the forests of Southeast Asia, where one of the principal aims after the war was simply to re-establish a measure of state control after years of Japanese occupation.

---

[47] For a detailed analysis of these debates, see Hodge, *Triumph*, 238–51.

The Second World War had taken a heavy toll on the woodlands of Southeast Asia.[48] Even apart from the effects of actual combat, large areas of forest were depleted by the many indirect effects of the war. These included not only the transport and fuel needs of military installations, but also the influx of tens of thousands of woodcutters and 'squatters' trying to escape food shortages or labour conscription, as well as the more general disintegration of colonial-era management systems that had previously governed access and extraction. The Japanese military authorities did little to fill the managerial void they had created, and in the few places where they did establish formal forestry services (above all Java) the results bore little resemblance to the sophisticated management systems that operated on the Home Islands.[49] Instead of maintaining current rotation schemes, Japanese authorities ransacked the island's teak stands; instead of restricting access to production forests, they allowed them to become riddled with farming settlements. After the war, the inhabitants of these settlements, most of them previously landless peasants, vigorously (and sometimes violently) resisted Dutch attempts to re-impose previous forest ordinances.[50] Re-establishing state authority was even more difficult in the forests of the 'outer isles' and mainland Indochina, where colonial-era controls never really recovered during the closing years of empire. In many areas it was well after independence before comparable restrictions were back in place.

Malaya was in some respects an exception due to the relatively successful post-war restoration of colonial rule, which formally lasted until 1957. But even so, the challenges confronting foresters there broadly illustrated the problems across Southeast Asia. During the war, large numbers of Chinese and Malay settlers decamped to the forests in response to severe rice shortages and the collapse of the tin and rubber industries. Although the precise figures are uncertain, the scale of inward migration was clearly large. So, too, were its environmental effects, which included acute erosion on sloping plots, the spread of stubborn *Imperata* grass, and an increase in silt loads and flood problems.[51]

Immediately after the war, British attempts to refill the power vacuum in the forests were severely hampered by the sheer lack of security. Forest guards were frequently attacked when they tried to stop unauthorized activities. Most of them refused to enter certain areas at all, and the colonial government eventually had to dispatch armed troops to halt illegal clearing in trouble spots. Few of the 'squatters' who had moved into the forests were willing to relinquish the lives they had built for themselves during the war years, whether as subsistence farmers, tapioca cultivators, or unregulated loggers. None wanted a return of colonial forest laws, and some had even waged a long guerrilla campaign against the Japanese with the

---

[48] For an overview, Richard P. Tucker, 'The World Wars and the Globalization of Timber Cutting', in Tucker and Russell (eds), *Natural Enemy*, 110–41.

[49] Kathirithamby-Wells, *Nature*, 229–38; Peluso, *Rich Forests*, 93–7; Yoshiya Iwai, *Forestry and the Forest Industry in Japan* (Vancouver: UBC Press, 2002), 3–158.

[50] Peluso, *Rich Forests*, 97–102.

[51] Timothy N. Harper, *The End of Empire and the Making of Malaya* (Cambridge: Cambridge University Press, 1999), 96–7; Kathirithamby-Wells, *Nature*, 238–46.

explicit support of the British colonial government.[52] As a result, the attempt to re-establish state control grew into a protracted contest over the forests of the Malaysian peninsula.[53]

With the declaration of the 'Malayan Emergency' in 1948, land-use and forest policy became tightly enmeshed with the military effort to quash the Communist-led insurgency. Depriving the Malayan National Liberation Army of new recruits and safe operating zones were key aims, and both were facilitated by the resettlement of hundreds of thousands of people into a series of 'New Villages' reclaimed from the forest. These planned settlements not only gave farmers more land, they were also strategically located to prevent the use of certain areas for guerrilla activity. From 1951 onwards, this vast state-sponsored migration programme cleared forests, diverted rivers, and transformed local disease ecologies across the peninsula. By 1954, well over half a million people had been resettled in 480 'New Villages', and by the end of the Emergency in 1960 over one-seventh of the entire Malaysian population had been moved. After independence, a series of new settlement schemes administered by the Federal Land Development Authority (FELDA) and Federal Land Consolidation and Rehabilitation Authority (FELCRA) claimed a further 2 million hectares of forest by the late 1980s.[54]

Among the various effects of the settlement programme was an unprecedented squeeze on Malaya's woodlands, which had serious consequences for the upland forests and for the 100,000 or so *Orang Asli* ('first peoples') living there. As sedentary farming expanded, many of the areas that were now gazetted for timber exploitation lay within their hereditary lands in the central highlands of the peninsula. Whereas foresters and government officials had previously tolerated shifting cultivation in these remote areas, the booming timber market of the 1950s— driven above all by soaring demand in Japan—led to a hardening of attitudes. And whereas many of these forests had previously been too inaccessible for profitable logging anyway, the introduction of the chainsaw and caterpillar tractor fundamentally changed the commercial equation. Together, the combination of high prices and new logging technologies meant that the continuation of swidden practices now represented a significant loss of income for the state and for the growing number of timber outfits operating on the peninsula.[55] Such pressures were felt across much of Southeast Asia, even in regions where aboriginal farming rights had long been formally protected. In Sarawak, the replacement of the Brooke dynasty by Crown rule in 1946 was soon followed by a series of forest reservations, cultivation restrictions, and attempts to sedentarize nomadic groups, all of which soured relations between the government and 'upriver' peoples like the Penan, and indeed

---

[52] See Christopher A. Bayly and Timothy N. Harper, *Forgotten Armies: Britain's Asian Empire and the War with Japan* (London: Penguin, 2005).

[53] Kathirithamby-Wells, *Nature*, 239–42; Harper, *End of Empire*, 103–4.

[54] Harper, *End of Empire*, 149–77; see also *Resettlement and the Development of New Villages in the Federation of Malaya, 1952* (Kuala Lumpur: Government Press, 1952); Barbara Watson Andaya and Leonard Y. Andaya, *A History of Malaysia*, 2nd edn (Houndmills: Palgrave, 2001), 295–6, 304–6.

[55] Kathirithamby-Wells, *Nature*, 242–53; Harper, *End of Empire*, 271–2; Harper, 'Politics of the Forest'.

continued to do so long after Sarawak joined the independent Federation of Malaysia in 1963.[56]

Efforts to tighten forest management after the war were by no means confined to the remnants of Europe's Asian empire. Across the Caribbean too, rising population pressures prompted stricter controls on tree-cutting. Even in the Middle East, British forestry initiatives, based partly on inter-war precursors, became part of the broader attempt to shore up London's informal authority in the region.[57] But apart from Southeast Asia, the most extensive changes came in Africa, and especially in the transitional forest-savannah zones where fears of a creeping 'desertification' had long exercised colonial officials (see Chapter 8).

The Second World War had ambivalent consequences for forest conservation in Africa. While the pressures of wartime mobilization brought a temporary halt to the expansion of reserves, the search for additional manpower and resources extended the reach of colonial bureaucracies and rendered them significantly more capable of pushing through unpopular conservation policies after the war. Post-war forestry measures were still characterized by a tendency to overestimate the extent of woodland loss in the region, and few scientists doubted that the pace of deforestation would accelerate amidst rising population numbers and buoyant demand for agricultural exports.[58] By the end of the 1940s, restrictive forest controls had returned with a vengeance, partly due to the enhanced capacity of the state, but perhaps most importantly as a result of the enhanced power of science as a foundation for state policy.

After the war, scientific forestry not only received far more funding than ever before, it also achieved greater political traction.[59] Ever since the early twentieth century, leading foresters such as Chevalier, Thompson, Unwin, and Aubréville had created a sizeable body of knowledge on African forests, along with a new corps of experts to transmit, apply, and further augment that knowledge. Since many of these younger disciples now manned the bureaucracies of the post-war colonial state, calls for tighter forest legislation stood a better chance of competing with the interests of agriculture, mining, and other activities. At the same time, forest conservation also became more internationally coordinated under the aegis of the Franco-British Commission for Technical Cooperation in sub-Saharan Africa, which organized the first inter-African forestry conference in 1951.[60]

---

[56] Peluso and Vandergeest, 'Genealogies', 784, 796; Kaur, 'Forestry', 136.

[57] Gregory A. Barton, 'Environmentalism, Development and British Policy in the Middle East 1945–65', *Journal of Imperial and Commonwealth History*, vol. 38 (2010), 619–39; Robert S. Anderson, Richard H. Grove, and Karis Hiebert (eds), *Islands, Forests and Gardens in the Caribbean: Conservation and Conflict in Environmental History* (Oxford: Macmillan Caribbean, 2006), 12–15.

[58] Generally Fairhead and Leach, *Reframing Deforestation*; Williams, *Deforesting*, 405.

[59] My discussion here follows James Fairhead and Melissa Leach, 'Desiccation and Domination: Science and Struggles over Environment and Development in Colonial Guinea', *Journal of African History*, vol. 41 (2000), 35–54, esp. 44–5, whose points on Guinea are more widely applicable; also Bonneuil, *Savants*, 91; Masefield, *Colonial Agricultural Service*, 45–7.

[60] Commission de Coopération Technique en Afrique au Sud du Sahara, *1ère Conférence forestière interafricaine: Abidjan, 4–12 décembre 1951* (Paris: de Jouve, 1952). On the Commission more generally: John Kent, *The Internationalization of Colonialism: Britain, France and Black Africa, 1939–1956* (Oxford: Clarendon Press, 1992), 263–85.

Such international cooperation was important for at least two reasons: it not only permitted a more rapid dissemination of ideas and techniques; it also enhanced the scientific credibility of forestry proposals, which made it harder for colonial governments to ignore them.

But if science-based conservation enjoyed widespread support within official-dom, things looked very different from the perspective of the rural communities that were affected by it. Once again, events in Africa largely echoed previous developments in India and the Maghreb, where growing environmental bureaucracies based their policies on a perceived antagonism between the activities of local farmers and the long-term stability of woodland cover and regional climate. And once again, forest reserves and access restrictions became a prime target for anti-colonial resentment. In French West Africa, some reserves were so detested that they were de-gazetted in the late 1950s as a matter of political expediency. This is not to say that African responses to colonial forest policies were uniformly hostile. The fault lines were complex, and some groups even appropriated the desiccationist discourse as a means of advancing their own interests within local land disputes. But the political costs were remarkably high, and they tended to rise in proportion to the level of disregard that was shown for local farming concerns.[61]

Against this backdrop, the great irony is that the 1950s were in fact an unusually wet decade for West Africa. All across the Soudan and Sahel regions, annual rainfall levels were above (and some years well above) long-term means, right through the early 1960s. The effects on regional vegetation were unmistakable, and eventually led even Aubréville (the leading champion of the 'desertification' concept) to revise his previous analysis of the links between deforestation and climate. During the final decade of colonial rule, higher rainfall and overall vegetation patterns were conspicuously out of sync with rising levels of conservationist activity. The incongruity is revealing, for it shows that the post-war wave of forest protection in colonial Africa had less to do with actual changes in the biophysical environment than with the shifting goals and enhanced political status of conservation science.[62] Deforestation may well have been on the rise, but what was expanding fastest of all was the 'environmental-management state' itself.[63]

Much the same applies to the post-war campaign to protect African wildlife. Despite clear signs that large mammal populations were either stable or increasing in many regions, the fifteen years after the end of the war witnessed a boom of animal conservation throughout colonial Africa, above all through the establishment of dozens of national parks. As ever, this surge of activity was driven by a range of different influences, including a marked rise in tourism and the growing

---

[61] This draws on Fairhead and Leach, 'Desiccation', 46–51.
[62] For a recent overview of climate trends in the region: Sharon E. Nicholson, 'The West African Sahel: A Review of Recent Studies on the Rainfall Regime and its Interannual Variability', *ISRN Meteorology*, vol. 2013 (2013), Article ID 453521, 32 pages, doi:10.1155/2013/453521, esp. 8–10; Gufu Oba, *Climate Change Adaptation in Africa: An Historical Ecology* (London: Routledge, 2014), 225–8; see also Fairhead and Leach, *Reframing Deforestation*, 176; Fairhead and Leach, 'Desiccation'.
[63] Rome, 'What Really Matters'.

importance of international conservation organizations as global agenda-setters. But the chief factor, just as with forestry, was the drive to develop colonial economies on the basis of scientific expertise. During the final years of colonialism, wildlife preservation was part of the wider management of the biophysical environment in the interests of modernization.

The most sweeping changes came in East and Central Africa, where British authorities established a series of national parks and wildlife sanctuaries in the 1940s and 1950s (Tsavo, Amboseli, Serengeti, Murchison Falls, to name just a few).[64] After a hiatus of conservation initiatives during the war years, calls for tighter regulation soon returned after a string of alarmist reports on the slaughter of African wildlife. In May 1947, the Conference on the Fauna of British Eastern and Central Africa was held in Nairobi to coordinate protective legislation on the basis of the latest scientific data. One of its central resolutions was the strict curtailment of African hunting, which was once again singled out as the chief threat to the region's fauna and the primary cause of a purportedly sharp decline in wildlife numbers.

The idea that wildlife populations were shrinking was by no means universally shared among colonial administrators. From the perspective of local officials, the biggest problem in many areas was controlling wildlife numbers rather than maintaining them. But despite such differences of opinion, a clutch of new ordinances and national park laws were soon applied across Kenya, Tanganyika, Southern Rhodesia, and Uganda. To administer the new legislation, game departments were expanded through the appointment of wildlife biologists whose job was to survey animal populations and to ensure that protective controls were focused where they were most needed. Over the course of the 1950s, this increasingly scientific approach towards wildlife conservation led to an ever more uncompromising panoply of land-use restrictions, grazing bans, forced livestock reductions, and even mass evictions. Among the most contentious measures were the mass expulsions from the Matopos Hills of Southern Rhodesia, which were completely cleared of human settlement between 1950 and the early 1960s. Similar steps were taken in the Serengeti, where repeated clashes between Maasai pastoralists and park authorities led to a revision of park boundaries and the complete exclusion of human habitation by the end of the 1950s.[65]

Meanwhile, French authorities also sought to expand their conservation regimes and place them on a more scientific footing. No sooner had the war ended than a new cadre of *inspecteurs des chasses et de la protection de la nature* was appointed to review hunting regulations in French West Africa and oversee its protected spaces. By 1950 they were joined by a team of zoologists responsible for studying threatened animal populations and devising appropriate means of protecting them.[66] As critics pointed out, however, the main shortcoming in French West Africa was

---

[64] This discussion is based on Roderick P. Neumann, 'The Postwar Conservation Boom in British Colonial Africa', *Environmental History*, vol. 7 (2002), 22–47, esp. 30–4.

[65] Terence O. Ranger, *Voices from the Rocks: Nature, Culture and History in the Matopos Hills of Zimbabwe* (Oxford: James Currey, 1999), 149–94; Neumann, *Imposing Wilderness*, 135–8.

[66] P. A. de Keyser and A. Villiers, 'Recherche scientifique', 3; P. A. de Keyser and A. Villiers, 'Protection des animaux', *Institut Français d'Afrique Noire*, no. 4. (Jan. 1951).

the lack of regulatory control on the ground. Most of the regional parks that had been founded after the 1933 London Convention continued to 'exist only on paper'; indeed, the majority were 'neither delimited, nor guarded, nor studied' due to a lack of funds. Even the cherished *réserves intégrales* that were set aside exclusively for scientific study were continually plagued by poaching.[67] What was required was not only a stricter enforcement of existing legislation, but also the extension of protective measures to more areas and more animal species. The plan of the AOF government was to accomplish both goals at once through the creation of the federation's first 'national parks': Niokolo-Koba in south-eastern Senegal, the 'Boucle du Baoulé' in south-eastern French Sudan, and the 'Parc du W' (named after a W-shaped meander of the Niger River) straddling Dahomey, Haute-Volta, and Niger. All three were established in August 1954 on the basis of existing reserves, and all three modelled their management practices on the Congo's Albert National Park, the oldest park in Africa.[68]

The fact that the Congolese national parks institute furnished the prototype for French authorities in West Africa highlights the ever-increasing importance of cross-border cooperation in the field of colonial conservation. For wildlife protection and forestry alike, such trans-imperial links not only facilitated the sharing of knowledge, but also bolstered the scientific authority of the conservation proposals that resulted. Indeed, one of the main factors behind the late-colonial conservation boom was the growing influence of international organizations such as UNESCO and the IUPN. The Lake Success Conference of August/September 1949 was a sign of the changing times. Attended by 500 delegates representing no fewer than 49 countries, and supported by both UNESCO and the IUPN, the Conference demonstrated that conservation efforts in Europe's colonies were part of an increasingly global framework of wildlife protection.[69] Over the following years the IUPN gradually overtook the SPFE as the standard-bearer for international wildlife protection; the re-christening of the SPFE as the Fauna Preservation Society in 1950 clearly expressed the shift away from the language of colonialism. By the late 1950s, non-governmental organizations also assumed a more prominent role within the African colonies themselves, especially on the eve of independence.[70]

As colonial wildlife protection became more internationalized, it was also embedded within debates about the conservation of natural resources more generally. The Lake Success conference in 1949 already signalled a departure from wildlife protection in a narrow sense towards a broader conceptualization of sustainable management. Four years later in 1953, this trend was reinforced at the Third International Conference for the Protection of the Fauna and Flora in Africa.

---

[67] Auguste Chevalier, 'La Protection de la nature et les parcs-réserves de l'Afrique Occidentale Française', *Comptes rendus hebdomadaires des séances de l'Académie des Sciences*, no. 230 (Jan.–June 1950), 2140–2.

[68] *Décret du 4 août 1954 portant transformation en parcs nationaux de trois réserves totales de faune existant en Afrique Occidentale*, available at: <faolex.fao.org/docs/texts/sen60669.doc>. All three parks are now UNESCO World Heritage sites.

[69] The most thorough discussion is Wöbse, *Weltnaturschutz*, 301–15.

[70] Adams, *Against Extinction*, 49–51.

Held in the Congolese city of Bukavu, the explicit purpose of the conference was to review the 1933 London convention (see Chapter 7) 'in line with modern conservation concepts'. What was meant by 'modern conservation' was threefold: public campaigning as a means of mobilizing support (including financial support); the need to consider the full range of natural resources (soil, water, vegetation, etc.) instead of a narrower focus on wildlife; and, perhaps most importantly, a clearer recognition that such resources should be responsibly exploited 'in the interest of the populations of Africa'.[71]

This brief passage is worth highlighting, for in many ways it captured the overall shift of emphasis after the war. What it most certainly did not signal was any loosening of restrictions on African access to wildlife, which if anything became even tighter with the expansion of game sanctuaries and national parks. What it showed was that wildlife conservation was as much about colonial development as about the protection of threatened species.

The post-war proliferation of forest regulations, national parks, and hunting restrictions was all part of the wider colonial development campaign. However discrete the individual initiatives may appear, they were often closely interrelated. The alienation of more land for forest reserves clearly meshed with the desire to replace itinerant cultivation with settled agricultural communities, which would be capable of producing a larger marketable (and therefore taxable) surplus. The stricter segregation of human and wildlife populations and the curtailment of subsistence hunting helped to channel African labour—in many colonies the scarcest resource of all—into the cash economy.[72] Most conservation measures served more than one purpose, which helps explain why colonial governments were so eager to implement them. During the 1940s and 1950s, perhaps the lowest common denominator of all was a determination to combat soil degradation.

As we saw in Chapter 9, fears about acute soil loss reached a fever pitch in the 1930s. In the immediate post-war years, soil conservation was widely regarded as 'the most important and urgent amongst all the problems which agronomists in overseas territories were called upon to deal with'; it represented nothing less than 'the essential key to the full development of the African continent'.[73] Soon after the war, British, French, and Belgian officials busily mapped degraded areas, set aside new soil conservation zones, and established special agencies to oversee protective measures.[74] By the late 1940s their efforts were increasingly coordinated across colonial boundaries. In November 1948 the first African Soils Conference assembled around 150 officials from France, Belgium, Britain, Portugal, South

---

[71] John McCormick, *Reclaiming Paradise: The Global Environmental Movement* (Bloomington, Ind.: Indiana University Press, 1989), 43; more generally *Comptes rendus de la Conférence Internationale pour la Protection de la Faune et de la Flore en Afrique (3: 1953, Bukavu)* (Brussels, 1954).

[72] Neumann, 'Postwar Conservation', 37–40.

[73] J. Guilloteau, *Inter-African Organisations for Soil Conservation* (Paris: Bureau Interafricain d'Information sur la Conservation et l'Utilisation des Sols, undated), 3, 5.

[74] Gaudy, *Conservation*, 7; Gouvernement Générale de l'A.O.F., Inspection Générale de l'Agriculture, *Organisation et action des services de l'agriculture* (Rufisque: Imprimerie du Gouvernement Général, 1952), 6; *L'Agronomie tropicale*, vol. 2 (1947), 107.

Africa, and South Rhodesia, and in 1950 the Inter-African Bureau for Soil Conservation was set up to organize cross-border measures within different geographic and climatic zones of the continent.[75] By the early 1950s, the 'second colonial occupation' laid claim literally to vast swathes of African soil.

Most of the conservation techniques of the 1950s had been around since the inter-war period, and broadly reflected the state of the art in the United States: terracing on slopes, ridging and grass strips, hedges and bunds, contour ploughing, new crops and grazing rotations. Which specific methods were best suited to any given locality depended on topography, soil type, climate, and land-use patterns. The areas of greatest concern fell into two broad categories: those with high population densities (and a correspondingly large cultivated surface), and those with sloping terrain that was subject to heavy rainfall. Wherever both criteria were met, conservation measures were especially rigorous. A good example was Rwanda, whose intensively farmed slopes had long been prone to erosion, and where inter-war policies had severely aggravated the problem by encouraging Hutu farmers to shorten fallows and clear more land. By the 1940s erosion in Rwanda had reached such proportions that Governor Pétillon declared it 'a question of life and death for us all'. The result was one of colonial Africa's biggest soil conservation campaigns. By 1958 it was estimated that around 535,000 kilometres of hedges and ditches had been built to protect over 665,000 hectares of Rwandan farmland.[76]

In strictly technical terms, methods such as hedging, terracing, and bunding were often quite effective at maintaining fertility and holding the soil on sloping ground. But the main drawback was that they were highly labour-intensive. In Nyasaland, it was estimated that the construction of narrow contour ridges or bunds (i.e. anywhere from roughly 1 to 2.5 metres wide) required around 120 to 170 man hours per hectare, and wide ridges considerably more. In Uganda and Kenya it was reckoned that a man could build only 32 to 45 metres of bund per day.[77] Because of all the work they involved, most anti-erosion schemes relied on some form of labour conscription, whether directly organized by the state or by indigenous chiefs.

In political and economic terms such measures were therefore much more problematic. In many farmers' eyes they required far more effort than they were worth, and the element of compulsion significantly added to the sense of grievance. When agricultural officials tried to build a system of bench terraces at the Uluguru Land Usage Scheme in Tanganyika, local farmers complained that terracing was both excessively laborious and fairly useless. One problem was the thin mountain soil, which required an arduous composting system to keep the plots fertile. A more fundamental problem was that building the terraces involved the removal of large amounts of topsoil from the heel to the toe of the benches, which rendered a significant portion of the surface infertile. Because these infertile sections could support little vegetation at first, they actually exacerbated the threat of erosion,

---

[75] Guilloteau, *Inter-African Organisations*, 3–11.

[76] Quote from François Bart, *Montagnes d'Afrique, terres paysannes: le cas du Rwanda* (Bordeaux: CEGET, 1993), 23; figures from *Bulletin agricole du Congo belge*, 127.

[77] Tempany, *Practice of Soil Conservation*, 12.

at least in the short term. But despite the objections of locals, the programme of compulsory terracing continued to expand, and so did the opposition against it. By 1955 the policy even sparked riots in the region.[78]

Given the vital importance of labour in the calculus of most African farming systems, the extra work demanded by compulsory soil conservation was bound to breed antagonism. Understandably, resentments were all the more intense wherever the additional labour burden was compounded by a simultaneous deterioration of living standards. A case in point was the suppression of traditional mound and shifting cultivation methods in northern Nyasaland in favour of what were assumed to be more productive and less damaging techniques. During the 1950s colonial officials tried to transfer improved methods from the south of the colony, which involved a rotational system of grass-bunded strips, to the wetter and more sparsely populated districts in the north. But the results were so baleful, and the compulsory legislation so hard to enforce, that agricultural officers found themselves becoming 'too much involved in "police" work, unpopular with the farmer and uncomfortable for the advisory worker'.[79] The widespread hostility towards the policy culminated in an outbreak of arson in early 1959.[80]

Unlike the creation of forest reserves or wildlife sanctuaries, popular antagonism towards soil conservation was not so much about the loss of land as about the loss of control over how it was used. In the Central Province of Kenya, where compulsory terracing was introduced during the war, attempts to extend it during the late 1940s and 1950s became a major source of conflict. Antipathy towards the scheme was rife among Kikuyu farmers, and was hardly lessened by the heavy reliance on unpaid communal labour and the conscription of women, who did most of the planting, weeding, and harvesting on subsistence plots. Nor were matters helped by the colony's chief soil conservation officer, Colin Maher, who insisted on the construction of narrow terraces that local farmers (as well as many agricultural officials) deemed unlikely to withstand heavy rainfall. Although narrow terraces were easier to build than broad-based ones, their upkeep required continual labour inputs. Consequently, the chiefs responsible for maintaining the terraces demanded a *corvée* of two mornings per week, but as heavy rains repeatedly washed away the narrow benches, the countless hours that were invested in them seemed as pointless as they were endless. Before long, resentment turned into open protest. In many districts the anti-erosion measures of the 1940s played a central role in the rise of the Mau Mau, whose anger was directed as much against compliant chiefs as against the government itself, once

[78] Pamela A. Maack, ' "We Don't Want Terraces!" Protest and Identity under the Uluguru Land Usage Scheme', in Maddox, Giblin, and Kimambo (eds), *Custodians*, 152–69, esp. 158–62.

[79] The new techniques actually produced less food for more labour than existing methods. Quote from Roland Smith, who worked in the area for much of the 1950s, taken from Silk, *Post-War Food*, 14.

[80] John McCracken, 'Conservation and Resistance in Colonial Malawi: The "Dead North" Revisited', in Beinart and McGregor (eds), *Social History*, 155–74.

again highlighting the complexity of the tensions caused by late-colonial conservation policies.[81]

By contrast, where anti-erosion measures caused little extra work and brought tangible benefits, the hurdles to adoption were low. A prime example was the Kigezi district of south-western Uganda, a hilly and populous area which, as Grace Carswell has shown, became a showcase for soil conservation throughout British-ruled Africa.[82] Ever since the 1930s, agricultural officers in Kigezi encouraged farmers to construct contour-bunds along the heavily cultivated slopes at intervals of no more than 30 yards (*c*.27 metres, and no more than 20 yards on steep slopes), each separated by grass buffers and composted with crop debris. Ideally, each strip was to be furnished with ridges composed of grass or hedge plants in order to catch any soil washed downhill by the rains. Dividing the land in this way not only slowed erosion but also facilitated the use of rotation systems that would allow for significant periods of fallow under grass cover, which helped retain crumb structure and soil nutrients.[83]

In and of themselves these recommendations were nothing exceptional. What was unusual was how they built upon long-established practices and were therefore relatively easy to introduce without the need for compulsion. The similarity to local cultivation methods—which involved growing crops on strips across the slopes divided by belts of uncleared land—meant that the new anti-erosion measures had little effect on existing labour patterns. What's more, they proved quite effective when combined with more intensive manuring and intercropping practices. But the implications of the Kigezi experience went well beyond the question of conservation techniques. As a supposedly 'overpopulated' district, Kigezi should, according to the prevailing wisdom, have furnished a textbook example of overexploitation and degradation rather than sound soil husbandry. Instead, it confounded current assumptions about the relationship between demographic pressure, shorter fallows, soil exhaustion, and erosion. In fact, it turned these assumptions upside-down, for it was precisely the high population density in the area that provided the necessary labour for effective soil maintenance measures.[84]

The success of soil conservation at Kigezi, and the relatively consensual basis on which it operated, demonstrates that colonial anti-erosion measures could help protect soils that were under strain from heavy cultivation. It also shows the importance of carefully tailoring techniques to local social, economic, and environmental contexts. This was by no means lost on soil conservation officers. Within agronomic circles it was self-evident that what worked in one locality was not necessarily appropriate in another. Agriculture officials understood that the viability of anti-erosion measures crucially depended on the degree to which they could

---

[81] This paragraph is based on David W. Throup, 'The Origins of Mau Mau', *African Affairs*, vol. 84 (1985), 399–433, esp. 421–7; Mackenzie, *Land*, 161–7; Anne Thurston, *The Intensification of Smallholder Agriculture in Kenya: The Genesis and Implementation of the Swynnerton Plan* (Oxford Development Records Project Report 6, 1984), 16–19.

[82] The following discussion is largely drawn from Carswell, *Cultivating Success*, 53–77.

[83] Tempany, *Practice of Soil Conservation*, 25–6; Tothill, *Agriculture*, 107–9.

[84] Carswell, *Cultivating Success*, 152–65.

be integrated into customary work cycles and provide tangible benefits to farmers. Otherwise, as one officer later noted, they were destined to suffer from 'a costly amount of supervision and a degree of surveillance that is inevitably unpopular'.[85]

The reason why these complexities were so frequently overlooked was not that they were unknown, but rather because the prevailing discourses of population growth and environmental decline made them appear less important than they actually were. To repeat an argument made in Part II, the main reason why these narratives remained so powerful was because they served the interests of expert officials by casting them as the only responsible stewards of natural resources under threat from improvident local inhabitants. Yet the fact that such perceptions were often self-serving does not mean that soil degradation was not taking place. In some regions fallow intervals were clearly contracting; in others, cultivation was inexorably spreading onto more marginal and vulnerable land. There was, for instance, little doubt that existing rotation systems in the Teso and Buganda regions of Uganda were no longer capable of maintaining soil fertility amidst rising demographic pressures and the spread of cash-cropping.[86] In Senegal too, there were unmistakable signs of soil exhaustion from the overuse of ploughs, the shortening of older millet rotations, and the rapid expansion of groundnut cultivation.[87]

Seen in this light, the principal shortcoming of colonial soil conservation was not that it was ineffective or unnecessary, but rather its tendency to assume degradation at every turn, to blame it instinctively on the deficiencies of indigenous practices, and thus to impose expert knowledge from outside. All too often, the result was a set of interventions that diverted labour from subsistence activities, paid insufficient attention to living standards, and disrupted established land-use systems without providing a better alternative.

In all of these respects, colonial initiatives to conserve rangelands were perhaps the most contentious of all. Soil scientists were every bit as worried about the perceived deficiencies of indigenous animal husbandry as they were about crop cultivation. As the British agricultural adviser Harold Tempany put it 1949, 'It is at least probable that in Africa defective methods of livestock management, including overstocking, overgrazing, uncontrolled burning of pastures and bush, over-concentration of cattle at water sources, particularly during dry periods, and the like, are in the aggregate responsible for greater damage by erosion than defective methods of cultivation, great though the effect of the latter may be.'[88]

Throughout the 1940s and early 1950s colonial governments across Africa passed a flurry of laws and ordinances to regulate the use of rangelands. In the Maghreb, where French authorities had long tried to sedentarize transhumant pastoralists, new soil conservation services in Algeria (1941), Tunisia (1946), and Morocco (1951) prohibited grazing and burning in areas perceived to be at risk of desertification. Similar measures were introduced in the semi-arid grasslands of

85 *Bulletin Agricole du Congo belge*, 127–8.
86 Tothill, *Agriculture*, 77–84; Carswell, *Cultivating Success*, 56.
87 Gaudy, *Conservation*, 17–22.   88 Tempany, *Practice of Soil Conservation*, 38.

West Africa, though in neither region were they very effective.[89] The most ambitious plans were devised in British East Africa, where agronomists tried to implement rational animal husbandry systems as part of their broader agricultural development strategies. The basic idea was to protect soil and ground cover by ensuring that livestock concentrations did not exceed the estimated 'carrying capacity' of the land. In Kenya, the flagship Swynnerton Plan of 1954, which sought to boost agricultural productivity through the creation of consolidated holdings, included strict stock control measures.[90] In the Maasai lands straddling the border between Kenya and Tanganyika there were extensive efforts to protect rangeland, improve water supplies, and clear tsetse bush.[91] But the most systematic attempt to introduce a 'rational' grazing programme was the Sukumaland Development Scheme, the second largest development project (after the Groundnut Scheme) in colonial Tanganyika.

Launched in 1947, the Sukumaland project covered around 52,000 square kilometres of territory south of Lake Victoria. Ever since the inter-war period, officials feared that the continual rise of human and livestock numbers in the central districts of Sukumaland would lead to severe overcrowding and soil degradation.[92] The rising demographic pressure in the region was closely related to changing disease ecologies. Ever since the turn of the century, the advance of the tsetse fly had encouraged a process of settlement concentration. With the availability of Rinderpest inoculations after 1942, which promised to boost local cattle populations still further, the threat of population overshoot seemed more acute than ever.[93] The central aim of the project was to create a more 'orderly settlement of people and stock on the land at reasonable densities'.[94] This involved two main elements: the colonization of sparsely populated areas surrounding the current centres of settlement; and the restoration of overcrowded districts through livestock reductions, new crop rotations, contour ridging, and manuring. The ultimate goal was to establish a new mixed farming economy based on consolidated family plots that would be arranged according to the scientific calculation of optimal carrying capacity. The underlying formula was the so-called 'Sukumaland Equation', which determined the ideal population distribution to be 112 people and 384 livestock per square mile (*c.*2.6 km²); or, more precisely, sixteen homesteads (with an average of seven persons per household) per square mile, each comprising 40 acres of land (*c.*16 ha), 8 acres of which were used for arable crops and 32 as pasture, which could support an average of fourteen cattle and ten smaller stock per homestead.[95] On the basis of this formula, a team of senior agronomists,

---

[89] Davis, *Resurrecting the Granary*, 160–4; Gaudy, *Conservation*, 36–47, *passim*.
[90] Thurston, *Intensification*, 15–16, 22–3, *passim*.
[91] Dorothy L. Hodgson, 'Taking Stock: State Control, Ethnic Identity and Pastoralist Development in Tanganyika, 1949–58', *Journal of African History*, vol. 41 (2000), 55–78.
[92] Generally, Rohland Schuknecht, *British Colonial Development Policy after the Second World War: The Case of Sukumaland, Tanganyika* (Münster: LIT, 2010).
[93] W. M. Sykes, *The Sukumaland Development Scheme 1947–57* (Oxford Development Records Project Report 7, 1984), 4–5.
[94] Norman Rounce, an agricultural official in the region, quoted in Hodge, *Triumph*, 215.
[95] Sykes, *Sukumaland*, 51–5.

foresters, and veterinarians worked closely with the Sukuma Native Authorities to clear the appropriate area for settlement and to ensure that maximum population densities were not exceeded.

The Sukumaland Scheme was the epitome of 'high modernist' planning, and like so many projects of this ilk, its modelling did not adequately capture socio-ecological complexities on the ground. In contrast to the ill-fated Groundnut Scheme, the lack of preliminary fieldwork was not one of its main problems; feasibility studies were in fact quite extensive. Instead it fell prey to a combination of mundane difficulties (staff shortages, exaggerated targets, overlapping responsibilities, bureaucratic infighting) as well as, most importantly, acute resentment among local people. There were numerous grounds for complaint, ranging from mandated soil protection measures to restrictions on the amount of land that could be cultivated for cash crops.[96] But the main source of antipathy was the scheme's de-stocking measures, which caused grievance on multiple levels. Livestock in Sukumaland, as in much of East Africa, represented both an economic and a cultural asset. Cattle functioned not only as a security against famine but also as a form of wealth, status, and local currency. For several years after the launch of the scheme, the Federal Council of chiefs rejected even the principle of a fixed annual cull. A 1949 drought had already more than halved Sukuma cattle herds, which raised doubts about the need for de-stocking in the first place. In 1952, after stock levels had recovered, the chiefs finally accepted the case for certain limitations, but as one of the livestock officers noted, 'implementation was another matter'.[97] Over the following years, de-stocking and mandatory sales proved all but unenforceable amidst mounting opposition against the Scheme and the chiefs who complied with it. In 1955 the Sukumaland project was abandoned, though this did not put an end to livestock regulations in the region, nor to the anti-colonial sentiment that they provoked.[98] What began as a scientific attempt to protect lands and raise living standards ended up undermining colonial rule among the very people it sought to help.

All throughout East Africa, the controversies surrounding rangeland conservation stemmed in part from the ambiguity of 'overgrazing' as a concept. Although large numbers of livestock undoubtedly caused damage in certain areas, the ability of different types of rangeland to recover from the effects of foraging and drought mean that generalizations were (and still are) fraught with difficulty.[99] The reason

---

[96] Contrary to the project's anti-erosion emphasis, one of the main outcomes of clearing tsetse bush in Sukumaland was a 'capitalist land rush', especially for cotton growing in outlying districts: Iliffe, *Modern History*, 474; Sykes, *Sukumaland*, 55.

[97] John Wolstenholme, quoted in Sykes, *Sukumaland*, 58.

[98] Schuknecht, *British Colonial Development Policy*, esp. chs 3, 5; Iliffe, *Modern History*, 505–6, 523–4; Lionel Cliffe, 'Nationalism and the Reaction to Enforced Agricultural Change in Tanganyika during the Colonial Period', in Lionel Cliffe and John Saul (eds), *Socialism in Tanzania: An Interdisciplinary Reader* (Dar es Salaam: East African Publishing House, 1972), 17–24; Hodge, *Triumph*, 221–2.

[99] See K. M. Homewood, and W. A. Rodgers, 'Pastoralism and Conservation', *Human Ecology*, vol. 12 (1984), 431–41; K. M. Homewood and W. A. Rodgers, 'Pastoralism, Conservation and the Overgrazing Controversy', in Anderson and Grove (eds) *Conservation*, 111–28; on Sukumaland, Peter B. Coppolillo, 'The Landscape Ecology of Pastoral Herding: Spatial Analysis of Land Use and Livestock Production in East Africa', *Human Ecology*, vol. 28 (2000), 527–60; on Kenya, Peter D. Little, 'Pastoralism, Biodiversity, and the Shaping of Savanna Landscapes in East Africa', *Africa*, vol. 66 (1996), 37–51.

why late-colonial livestock regulations were so contentious was not merely the cultural and economic value attached to livestock. It was also because the diagnoses upon which they were based—range degradation due to poor indigenous husbandry practices—were often dubious.

A good example was the Baringo district of western Kenya. Attempts to recondition the area's pastureland began in the 1920s, and by the 1940s and 1950s the grazing and culling regulations in Baringo were widely copied in other areas. There were, however, two very different explanations for the sparse pasturage in the district. Most colonial observers were quick to pin the blame on local pastoralists for maintaining cattle herds that were almost certainly too large for the available grazing land to support. By contrast, from the perspective of local Tugen herders, the real culprit was colonial rule itself, more specifically the alienation by white settlers of highland pasture areas that had previously formed an integral part of their wider transhumant land-use patterns. Because these upland areas were no longer accessible for seasonal pasturage, any signs of 'overstocking' and land degradation in the lowlands ultimately stemmed from a shortage of available land rather than a surplus of livestock. Furthermore, colonial officials not only overlooked the root cause of range deterioration, they also overestimated its actual extent. Just like their counterparts in the Sahel or the Maghreb, officials in Baringo situated the district's meagre browsing cover into a familiar narrative of overstocking and irresponsible husbandry that had stripped the land of much of its previous vegetation. But rainfall patterns in the area were highly variable, which meant that any 'snapshot' of local conditions was deceptive. Baringo's rangeland had always been more marginal than many officials thought, and local herders knew from generations of experience that it was not suitable for more than seasonal pasturage. Since the long-term vegetation baseline was never as lush as many officials assumed, the current condition of the land was also less 'degraded'. Moreover, such deterioration as was under way probably resulted more from the effects of land alienation than from pastoralist activities per se.[100]

The problem, then, lay as much in the narrative itself as what it purported to describe, and in this respect Baringo was part of a much broader pattern. Similar misunderstandings of the interactions between population densities, land-use patterns, and environmental change affected conservation efforts throughout the drylands of Africa, perhaps most spectacularly in the Machakos district of eastern Kenya, where higher numbers of people and livestock actually reversed rather than accelerated processes of erosion and productivity decline.[101] To be sure, not all diagnoses of land deterioration were mistaken, and nor were all colonial officials entirely convinced by the degradation narrative and the assumptions that lay behind it. But dissenting voices rarely had much impact on policy, and even where rehabilitation measures brought tangible environmental benefits—as in the Kondoa Highlands of central Tanganyika, where colonial attempts to remove most

---

[100] This paragraph is based on Anderson, *Eroding the Commons*, 21–2, 140–56, 190–231.
[101] Mary Tiffen, Michael Mortimore, and Francis Gichuki, *More People, Less Erosion: Environmental Recovery in Kenya* (Chichester: Wiley, 1994); more generally, Michael Mortimore, *Roots in the African Dust: Sustaining the Sub-Saharan Drylands* (Cambridge: Cambridge University Press, 1998), esp. 124–75.

of the livestock in the 1950s were eventually brought to completion by the independent Tanzanian government[102]—they generally entailed significant costs elsewhere, whether in the form of economic losses (i.e. smaller herds) or displaced ecological damage (i.e. transferring stock pressure onto other grasslands). Perhaps most importantly, all of these policies reflected a basic understanding of conservation as something done by outside experts to protect ecosystems from reckless destruction by local people. As development efforts intensified in the 1940s–1950s, this dominant mode of intervention from above and outside increasingly turned resource conservation into one of the many aspects of colonial rule that its subjects were eager to discard.

The politics of late colonialism were in many respects a politics of ecology. From forests and fields to rivers and rangeland, the 1940s and 1950s witnessed an unprecedented surge of environmental management in the name of development. For colonial governments and state officials, the mobilization, conservation, and rehabilitation of natural resources were at the very heart of post-war attempts to modernize economies and improve living standards. For rural communities at the receiving end of these policies, however, the 'second colonial occupation' was often an unwelcome intrusion into everyday life, which only made it harder to access and control local resources. To this extent, the attempt to create a new 'climax of domestication' in Europe's tropical empire threatened to subvert the colonial order rather than stabilize it.

Yet the politics of ecology were complex, and cannot be simply reduced to a widening rift between colonial authorities and subject peoples. Within rural communities, the state-led campaign to intensify resource use and boost agricultural output often diluted the authority of indigenous elites and created new clashes of interest. Among colonial officials and technical experts, the pressure to convert more of nature's wealth into economic growth led to divergent views about the best means of achieving it. Cutting across these disputes was the question of how far existing land-use practices should be regarded as the basis of development policies rather than the problem that needed to be solved. Occasionally the different answers to these questions created areas of overlap between colonial and indigenous views.[103]

But if late-colonial development policies were never as uniform as the rhetoric would suggest, they nonetheless set the agenda for resource management throughout much of the tropical world, and largely sidelined indigenous communities from the process. All too often it was a case of 'the blind leading the dumb'.[104] While those in charge were commonly blinkered by assumptions about native

[102] Wilhelm Östberg, *The Kondoa Transformation: Coming to Grips with Soil Erosion in Central Tanzania* (Uppsala: Scandinavian Institute of African Studies, 1986), 27–31.
[103] Beinart, Brown, and Gilfoyle, 'Experts'; Hodge, 'The Hybridity'; Monica M. van Beusekom and Dorothy L. Hodgson, 'Lessons Learned? Development Experiences in the Late Colonial Period', *Journal of African History*, vol. 41 no. 1 (March 2000), 29–33; Beusekom, *Negotiating*; Bassett, *Peasant Cotton*; Sara Berry, *No Condition is Permanent: The Social Dynamics of Agrarian Change in sub-Saharan Africa* (Madison, Wis.: University of Wisconsin Press, 1993).
[104] Adams, *Green Development*, ch. 8.

profligacy, the ostensible beneficiaries were generally deprived of a voice in decision-making.

As a result, the drive to harness tropical ecosystems for the sake of economic development created two formidable obstacles for itself. First, the misjudgement of socio-ecological realities on the ground undermined the viability of colonial development and conservation initiatives, many of which collapsed outright, and nearly all of which required major readjustments along the way. Second, the lack of meaningful input by local people often corroded the perceived legitimacy of the very institutions that implemented them. It was a two-sided lesson in political ecology, and one that many governments still failed to learn after independence.

11

Beyond Colonialism
Tropical Environments and
the Legacies of Empire

The drawn-out process of decolonization was in many ways a belated reflection of Europe's loss of global pre-eminence after the Second World War. By the early 1960s, when the majority of former colonies had achieved political independence, the initiative of sculpting the global order had long since passed to the new super-powers. The decades-old project of developing what was now referred to as the 'Third World' was no longer a colonial prerogative, but was rather pursued within the new framework of international institutions such as the World Bank, FAO, and GATT. The business of protecting tropical environments and conserving natural resources had also become increasingly internationalized, led by a coalition of NGOs and framed by a series of multilateral treaties. In the ex-colonies themselves, nationalist governments were eager to modify the institutions they had inherited from the colonial era, or at least to ensure an extensive turnover of personnel. By and large their economic strategies rejected the agrarian visions of colonial development in favour of rapid industrial growth. Likewise, their approach to trade demanded a greater share of the profits from resource exports. In many respects, the post-colonial world was a very different one indeed.

But for all the changes that had taken place, there was just as much about this world that was not new. Less than a decade after leading Ghana to independence, Kwame Nkrumah was already condemning the emergence of a 'neo-colonialism' that signified 'the last stage of imperialism'.[1] Over the following years, the concept became a commonplace of academic commentary. As a host of critics argued, formal political autonomy counted little against the background of continued economic dependence and cultural subservience. And as numerous ex-colonial states became racked by corruption and clientelism, much of the early hope that had been attached to the struggle for autonomy turned into frustration and disillusionment. In practice, it seemed, independence often meant little more than a change of flags.[2]

At one level, the environmental history of Europe's former tropical colonies fits this 'neo-colonial' scenario remarkably well. Of all the many continuities spanning

---

[1] Kwame Nkrumah, *Neo-Colonialism: The Last Stage of Imperialism* (London: Nelson, 1965).

[2] For a recent discussion, see Ichiro Maekawa, 'Neo-Colonialism Reconsidered: A Case Study of East Africa in the 1960s and 1970s', *Journal of Imperial and Commonwealth History*, vol. 43 no. 2 (2015), 317–41.

the formal end of empire, its ecological legacies were as profound and persistent as any. Chief among them were a far-reaching commercialization of land and resources, a forceful extension of state power over rural hinterlands, an unprecedented rise in human numbers, and a vast expansion of export trade, all of which tended to deplete resources faster than they could recover. Decolonization did little to change the overall direction of travel, despite radically transforming the political framework.

Yet an emphasis on continuities alone fails to capture the dynamics at work, for many of these basic trends not only persisted but actually intensified after the demise of colonial rule. One reason was the further integration of tropical ecosystems into the rapidly growing global economy. The booming post-war demand for raw materials, which brightened economic prospects for a while, hardly encouraged a diversification of economic activity or a more sparing use of resources. Another factor was the unequivocally developmentalist ideology of most post-colonial governments, however weak and semi-dependent many of them remained. Their sense of urgency built on long-standing critiques of lukewarm colonial development policies, and it reflected the heightened expectations of ordinary citizens who now regarded the government as their own. In post-colonial India, government technocrats denounced the Gandhian vision of 'reverting back to the spinning wheel, the loin cloth and bullock cart' as vehemently as the ambivalent modernizing impulses of British rule.[3] The desire of nationalist governments to make up for decades of colonial rule, and thereby prove their worth to millions of recently enfranchised voters, only enhanced their partiality towards 'big push' economics and large-scale resource development projects, many of them generously funded by new multilateral lending agencies and overseen by Western (often ex-colonial) experts. All the while, rapid population growth added to the pressure, for if overall living standards were to improve, then economic growth would have to outstrip it.

All of these factors contributed to the enormous environmental changes that swept the tropical world after the end of colonialism—changes whose speed, magnitude, and implications for the planet surpassed anything that had come before. In view of the interweaving causalities at work, it makes little sense to argue over whether they were mainly the result of colonial holdovers or rather of the actions by post-colonial political and economic elites, since the two are inextricably entwined.[4] Our focus on the 'legacies of empire' is not intended to attribute primary responsibility to colonial-era precedents or the designs of powerful interests in the global North, important though they were. The purpose is rather to explore,

---

[3] Quote from the astrophysicist Maghnad Saha, cited in Deepak Kumar, 'Reconstructing India: Disunity in the Science and Technology for Development Discourse, 1900–1947', *Osiris*, vol. 15 (2000), 241–57, here 248; see also Corinna R. Unger, *Entwicklungspfade in Indien. Eine internationale Geschichte 1947–1980* (Göttingen: Wallstein, 2015); Mahesh Rangarajan, 'Environment and Ecology under British Rule', in Douglas M. Peers and Nandini Gooptu (eds), *India and the British Empire* (Oxford: Oxford University Press, 2012), 212–30, here 225–8.

[4] See the discussion in Frederick Cooper, *Africa Since 1940: The Past of the Present* (Cambridge: Cambridge University Press, 2002), 85–90; more generally, Sandra Halperin and Ronen Palan (eds), *Legacies of Empire: Imperial Roots of the Contemporary Global Order* (Cambridge: Cambridge University Press, 2015).

through several key themes and examples, how the transformation of tropical environments by various actors—Western states, multinational corporations, international institutions, as well as governments and ordinary people in the ex-colonies—continued to be shaped by relationships and ideas that were fashioned, encouraged, or reinforced by the experience of colonialism. The chapter starts by considering how attempts to modernize agriculture metamorphosed in the wake of independence, and how the closely related efforts to harness and conserve natural resources reprised many of the fundamental characteristics of colonial practice. It then examines how the international division of labour and the myriad trade linkages that were forged under colonial rule powerfully moulded intercontinental resource flows and ecological trends for decades to come.

FROM AGRARIAN DEVELOPMENT TO GREEN REVOLUTION

As we saw in Chapters 9 and 10, one of the core aims of colonial governments was to increase agricultural production. Although approaches varied greatly over the years, and although some officials grew increasingly critical of colonial policies, the central aim, especially during the post-war period, was to make farming more productive.

After independence this basic objective was retained, and if anything reinforced, by national governments and international agencies alike. In spite of—or perhaps because of—the patchy results of late-colonial intensification efforts, agricultural modernization remained a cornerstone of post-war development plans. For Western policy-makers fixated on the tactical manoeuvrings of the Cold War, material deprivation was the most powerful form of communist propaganda. During the 'development decades' after 1960, the key to solving the interrelated problems of poverty, inequality, and political unrest in the newly independent nations of the 'Third World' seemed to lie in stronger economic growth and higher living standards. At the same time, calls for a 'war on hunger' reflected mounting anxieties about rapid population growth and the potentially dire consequences that might result.[5] Throughout the tropical world, the challenge of feeding the rising number of rural poor, let alone improving their material situation, lent a new urgency to questions of agricultural productivity.

Fortunately, it seemed, technology had an answer: namely, the high-yielding strains of staple crops—especially wheat, corn, and rice—that had already helped revolutionize yields in North America, Europe, and Japan. Amidst the neo-Malthusian fears of the post-war years, the high-tech package of 'miracle seeds',

---

[5] e.g. Fairfield H. Osborn (ed.), *Our Crowded Planet: Essays on the Pressures of Population* (London: Allen & Unwin, 1962); E. John Russell, *World Population and World Food Supplies* (London: Allen & Unwin, 1954); William Vogt, *Road to Survival* (London: Gollancz, 1949); Paul R. Ehrlich and Anne H. Ehrlich, *The Population Bomb* (New York: Ballantine, 1968). For an analysis see Thomas Robertson, *The Malthusian Moment: Global Population Growth and the Birth of American Environmentalism* (New Brunswick, NJ: Rutgers University Press, 2012).

artificial fertilizers, and controlled water inputs promised finally to deliver the quantum leap in productivity that colonial policies had failed to achieve. But if the so-called 'Green Revolution' signalled a partial departure from earlier approaches, it also represented the apotheosis of the colonial emphasis on scientific knowledge, capital investment, and state-led technological modernization. Despite the leading role of American money and expertise in spreading the Green Revolution throughout the tropics, its fundamental rationale grafted directly onto the same ideas of demographic crisis, environmental decline, and technological diffusion that had long formed the basis of colonial agricultural policy.[6]

The central thrust of the Green Revolution was plant breeding, or more specifically the selection of cultivar strains that proved most responsive to high inputs of fertilizer and water. Its roots reached back to the late nineteenth century, when agricultural researchers in Japan, Europe, and North America began experimenting with a range of different crop varieties and cultivation techniques in an effort to increase land and labour productivity. Some of the earliest breeding programmes were established in Europe's colonies, most notably in India after the famines of 1876–8, and on Java with the launch of systematic rice trials in the 1900s. Yet the bulk of research was carried out in the industrialized world. By the outbreak of the First World War, agricultural research was widely recognized as a vital element of modern statecraft, and as the war dragged on, the self-sufficiency drives of the main European belligerents underscored the geopolitical significance of domestic crop-breeding programmes. In 1918 American breeders created the double-cross maize hybrid, which soon dominated the US corn-belt. In the 1920s, Japanese researchers made major breakthroughs with dwarf varieties of rice and wheat, including the renowned semi-dwarf wheat strain Norin 10, whose short stalks could support heavy heads of grain without lodging. During the 1930s, governments actively promoted the adoption of new hybrid crops in order to boost domestic food output, and by the 1940s policy-makers gained a more concrete sense of how these technologies could also be deployed abroad in pursuit of wider strategic interests.[7]

The Green Revolution was, then, not just a 'Third World' phenomenon; in fact, agricultural growth rates were highest in the industrialized countries that pioneered the technologies.[8] But it was nonetheless in the developing world that it accomplished its most celebrated feats. The first successful export of the HYV package went to Mexico in the 1940s. Financed by the Rockefeller Foundation, the Mexican Agricultural Programme was centred on extensive wheat and maize breeding trials directed by the plant pathologist Norman Borlaug, who was later

[6] Nick Cullather, *The Hungry World: America's Cold War Battle against Poverty in Asia* (Cambridge, Mass.: Harvard University Press, 2010); Perkins, *Geopolitics*.

[7] Perkins, *Geopolitics*, 76–103; Cullather, *Hungry World*, 11–42. For the USA, France, and Germany, see Jack Ralph Kloppenburg Jr, *First the Seed: The Political Economy of Plant Biotechnology*, 2nd edn (Madison, Wis.: University of Wisconsin Press, 2004); Bonneuil, Denis, and Mayaud (eds), *Sciences*; Frank Uekötter, *Die Wahrheit ist auf dem Feld. Eine Wissensgeschichte der deutschen Landwirtschaft* (Göttingen: Vandenhoeck & Ruprecht, 2010).

[8] Giovanni Federico, *Feeding the World: An Economic History of Agriculture, 1800–2000* (Princeton: Princeton University Press, 2005), 2.

awarded a Nobel Prize for his role in developing high-yield dwarf wheat varieties from crossing Norin 10 with other strains. From Mexico, the gospel of miracle crops was soon carried to other parts of the developing world by the FAO, the World Bank, and a battery of private and public agencies. In the early 1960s it reached the wheat-growing areas of India and Pakistan. Several years later it spread into the rice baskets of southern and eastern Asia, spearheaded by the famous IR-8 rice variety, which had been developed from Japanese dwarf strains at the International Rice Research Institute in the Philippines.

The initial results were striking. With the right doses of fertilizer and water, yields were up to four times higher than most traditional crop varieties.[9] Such impressive figures help explain why so many contemporaries saw the Green Revolution package as the most effective means of meeting the food needs of a rapidly expanding population. But besides the question of productivity, there was a host of other reasons why policy-makers found the HYV package so appealing. For Western governments, it represented a powerful tool for dampening revolutionary fervour and for cementing key alliances at the height of the Cold War. Aside from Mexico, efforts were overwhelmingly concentrated on southern and eastern Asia—the backyards of the Soviet Union and China—where the Green Revolution technologies promised not only to mitigate the consequences of a population explosion but also to contain the spread of communist influence. The 1960s rice improvement programmes in South Vietnam and the Philippines were explicitly paraded as 'showcases of democracy' in Southeast Asia, the focal point of US strategic concerns at the time. The attempt to prevent the spread of IR-8 seeds into North Vietnam highlights the centrality of geopolitical rather than strictly humanitarian aims.[10] By contrast, the new seed-fertilizer package made few inroads in Africa apart from moderate uptake in Egypt and on the mainly white-owned farms of Kenya and Zimbabwe.[11] Sporadic efforts to introduce it south of the Sahara were hampered by a lack of infrastructure, lukewarm interest on the part of governments, highly variable topographies, and the limited availability of irrigation water. Even where water was abundant, labour and soil problems often proved insurmountable.[12]

If the Green Revolution was a useful geopolitical device for Western governments, it was perhaps even more alluring for political elites in recipient countries. Domestic political support tended to be strongest where pressure for agrarian reform was highest, for instance in India, Pakistan, Indonesia, the Philippines, and Mexico. Wherever land was becoming scarce, the high-yield package promised to

[9] Gordon Conway, *The Doubly Green Revolution: Food for All in the 21st Century* (Harmondsworth: Penguin, 1997), 48–52.

[10] Cullather, *Hungry World*, 159–79. The attempt was singularly unsuccessful. By autumn 1969, US troops found fields of IR-8 deep in enemy territory; the communist Vietnamese government later promoted the cultivation of IR-8 as part of its rural reconstruction effort (pp. 178–9).

[11] Conway, *Doubly Green*, 55.

[12] e.g. in parts of West Africa, where agronomists sought to transfer high-yielding rice packages from Southeast Asia: Paul Richards, *Coping with Hunger: Hazard and Experiment in an African Rice-Farming System* (London: Allen & Unwin, 1986), 7–8; generally, René Dumont, *Notes sur les implications sociales de la 'révolution verte' dans quelques pays d'Afrique* (Geneva: UNRISD, 1971).

divert unwanted attention from wealthy landowners (while simultaneously boosting their incomes). In addition, rapid modernization in the agricultural sector neatly dovetailed with attempts to industrialize post-colonial economies. Higher farm productivity not only generated much-needed capital for investment (by curtailing food imports and/or increasing exports), it also released rural labour for redeployment in industry. In a word, the remarkable exportability of the Green Revolution reflected a widespread desire among post-colonial political elites, capitalist as well as communist, to achieve rapid economic growth without succumbing to the demands of foreign creditors or rural electorates at home.[13]

From the mid-1960s onwards the new crop varieties literally took root in dozens of countries throughout the tropics. Within two decades, nearly half of the developing world's rice and wheat fields were sown with modern strains. By the end of the century, high-yield rice accounted for over 70 per cent of the crop in South Asia and over 80 per cent in Southeast and East Asia (high-yield wheat accounted for 95 and 90 per cent, respectively).[14] For good reason, this massive global expansion of such a narrow range of cultivars has been regarded as one of the fundamental milestones in world agricultural history, a process of plant transfer that was arguably comparable in scope to the epoch-making 'Colombian exchange' after 1492, though accomplished in only a fraction of the time.[15] As the new breeds spread they were remarkably effective at raising productivity rates above population growth, at least for a while. From 1961 to 1991, average Asian maize yields rose from 1.2 tons per hectare to almost 3.2 tons, rice yields from 1.75 to 3.6 tons, and wheat yields from 0.6 to 3.2 tons.[16] Against this backdrop it is easy to understand why so many observers hailed the Green Revolution as a 'splendid achievement' that 'transformed agriculture and created food abundance'.[17]

But modifying agricultural practices on such a vast scale inevitably brought other changes along with it. Indeed, this was one of the deliberate aims. In many ways the Green Revolution reflected the broader shift away from 'balanced development' towards more disruptive theories of economic growth during the 1950s and 1960s. As President Kennedy proclaimed to the World Food Congress in 1963, what was needed was an agricultural revolution 'which may well rival, in its social consequences, the industrial revolution'.[18] Seen in this light, the new agricultural technologies represented the vanguard of a modernization campaign

---

[13] As emphasized by Angus Wright, *The Death of Ramón Gonzalez: The Modern Agricultural Dilemma*, 2nd edn (Austin, Tex.: University of Texas Press, 2005), 186; also Cullather, *Hungry World*, 94–107.

[14] Figures from Peter B. R. Hazell, 'The Asian Green Revolution' (International Food Policy Research Institute, 2009), 4; Derek Byerlee, *Modern Varieties, Productivity, and Sustainability* (Mexico, DF: CIMMYT, 1994), 3; FAO, *Food for All* (Rome: FAO, 1996): <http://www.fao.org/docrep/x0262e/x0262e06.htm>.

[15] McNeill, *Something*, 223. For a more sceptical view of the comparison, see Shawn William Miller, *An Environmental History of Latin America* (Cambridge: Cambridge University Press, 2007), 153. On plant transfers more generally: William Beinart and Karen Middleton, 'Plant Transfers in Historical Perspective: A Review Article', *Environment and History*, vol. 10 (2004), 3–29.

[16] Figures derived from FAO: <http://faostat.fao.org/site/567/default.aspx#ancor>.

[17] Quotes from Conway, *Doubly Green*, vii (foreword by Ismail Serageldin, chairman of CGIAR).

[18] Quoted from Cullather, *Hungry World*, 240.

that would erode existing social and economic barriers and pull other sectors along with it.[19]

At least that was how it was supposed to work. As the history of colonial agriculture showed, a sudden shift towards capital-intensive farming was bound to create losers as well as winners. Predictably, most of the benefits accrued to well-off farmers who were able to purchase the necessary fertilizer and seed inputs. By contrast, smallholders who could not afford them generally saw their incomes decline and their debts rise, often to the point of losing their land. The resulting polarization was especially acute wherever social inequalities were already stark. In some areas the ensuing tensions flared into open conflict, for instance in the irrigated wheat fields of the Punjab, where an upwelling of inter-communal violence in the 1980s was repeatedly linked to the effects of the Green Revolution.[20]

Besides its social impacts, the Green Revolution also had numerous ecological consequences. The basic aim was to transfer farming techniques that were originally developed in the soil and climatic conditions of temperate regions to a range of different tropical environments. For all the ingenuity of these techniques, many of the resulting problems recalled the colonial improvement efforts of the early 1900s. Once again, the combination of intensive cultivation, heavy rainfall, and thin tropical soils accelerated erosion and nutrient leaching. To compensate for soil losses, farmers applied heavy doses of fertilizer, much of which was washed into nearby watercourses and ended up eutrophying water bodies downstream.[21] Meanwhile, weed and pest problems were exacerbated by the standard practice of planting the new varieties in monocultures in order to economize on the purchase of specific seed and fertilizer inputs. This led to the use of more herbicides and pesticides, which were often applied indiscriminately and in excessive amounts (not least due to the lack of clear guidance) that polluted surrounding water supplies and posed a serious health risk to locals, especially the agricultural labourers who handled them.[22] Furthermore, the widespread cultivation of a small number of high-yield cultivars dramatically reduced the biodiversity of agricultural cropping systems, first by replacing the thousands of wheat and rice varieties previously planted by farmers,[23] and secondly by decreasing the proportion of land sown with other species such as pulses and oilseeds. In turn, the decline of nitrogen-fixing, protein-rich

---

[19] Perkins, *Geopolitics*, 14–15.

[20] The adverse social consequences were recognized by the early 1970s, including by the UN itself: UNRISD, *The Social and Economic Implications of Large-Scale Introduction of New Varieties of Food Grain: Summary of Conclusion of a Global Research Project* (Geneva: UNRISD, 1974). On Punjab: Marco Corsi, 'Communalism and the Green Revolution in Punjab', *Journal of Developing Societies*, vol. 22 (2006), 85–109; Vandana Shiva, *The Violence of the Green Revolution: Third World Agriculture, Ecology and Politics* (London: Zed, 1991), 23, 174–5; Trent Brown, 'Agrarian Crisis in Punjab and "Natural Farming" as a Response', *South Asia: Journal of South Asian Studies*, vol. 36 (2013), 229–42.

[21] From 1970 to 1995 fertilizer use in Asia ballooned from 24 kg/ha to 171 kg/ha: Hazell, 'Asian Green Revolution', 3; Smil, *Enriching*, 116.

[22] The best historical account of the health impacts is Wright, *Death*, on Mexico; on Asia, see Agnes C. Rola and Prabhu L. Pingali, *Pesticides, Rice Productivity, and Farmers' Health* (Manila: IRRI, 1993).

[23] It was reckoned in the 1990s that 75 per cent of India's rice fields were planted with as few as twelve rice varieties: FAO, 'Food for All': <http://www.fao.org/docrep/x0262e/x0262e06.htm>.

legumes affected the health of the soil and of the people who worked it. In India, the rise in per capita wheat consumption since the 1960s was more than offset by the decline in the consumption of lentils, peas, and beans, which fell by around one-half by the mid-1980s.[24] This was but one of the myriad ways in which the social and ecological consequences of the Green Revolution were closely linked.

In essence, the Green Revolution was an attempt to overcome the ecological restrictions that had previously limited agricultural productivity in the tropics. But like all efforts to escape nature's constraints, it ultimately exchanged old limits for new ones. A crucial measure of farming methods is their ability to maintain the conditions of productivity over the long term, and in several respects the modern seed-fertilizer package traded long-term sustainability for higher yields in the here and now. To start with the most obvious point, the fundamental reliance on fossil fuels and fossil fuel-derived fertilizers is inherently unsustainable. In fact, in energy terms it is not even remotely productive. Detailed studies in India have shown that traditional rice cultivation produces ten times more caloric energy than it consumes, whereas Green Revolution practices consume more than they produce.[25] They also depleted many other resources, above all water and soil fertility. In semi-arid regions such as the Punjab, Tamil Nadu, or Rajasthan, skyrocketing water extraction from thousands of new boreholes lowered groundwater tables at an alarming rate. Wherever the spread of irrigation got ahead of corresponding drainage works, farmers soon ran into the familiar problems of waterlogging and salinization.[26] Even where soil and water conditions were favourable, long-term fertility was often compromised by heavy nitrogen, phosphorus, and potassium inputs that depleted vital trace nutrients.

The central characteristic of the new HYVs was to raise the 'harvest index', or the ratio of edible matter to total crop phytomass. As such, they were designed to allow a greater net removal of nutrients from the soil, nutrients that subsequently had to be replenished and absorbed in the proper amounts. What distinguished the modern crop varieties from their traditional forebears was not that they were more photosynthetically efficient, but rather that they channelled a higher proportion of their photosynthate into the parts of the plants that humans eat (mainly seeds), which, in the absence of night-soil recovery, were removed from the nutrient cycle by human consumption.[27] Despite increasingly liberal doses of synthetic fertilizer, the gradual loss of trace nutrients and the creeping deterioration of soil

[24] Boudhayan Chattopadhyay, 'Growth and Fluctuation of Foodgrain Output in India since Independence', in Boudhayan Chattopadhyay and Pierre Spitz (eds), *Food Systems and Society in Eastern India* (Geneva: UNRISD, 1987), 133–54, here 137–41.

[25] Tim Bayliss-Smith, 'Energy Flows and Agrarian Change in Karnataka: The Green Revolution at Micro-scale', in Tim Bayliss-Smith and Sudhir Wanmali (eds), *Understanding Green Revolutions: Agrarian Change and Development Planning in South Asia* (Cambridge: Cambridge University Press, 1984), 153–72.

[26] In 2009 it was estimated that a quarter of all irrigated land in Pakistan was affected by salinization, and a third by waterlogging. In India, an estimated 7 million hectares had actually been abandoned due to salt build-up: Hazell, 'Asian Green Revolution', 16. More generally, see Vaclav Smil, *Feeding the World: A Challenge for the Twenty-First Century* (Cambridge, Mass.: MIT Press, 2001), 41–3.

[27] Smil, *Feeding*, 28–9.

structure eventually led to a slackening, and occasional reversal, of the yield increases that were initially achieved by the new crop breeds. The slowdown was especially marked for IR-8 rice, which also suffered from pest problems that were further aggravated by monocultural planting practices.[28]

For all these reasons it is impossible to say whether the Green Revolution was a 'success' compared to earlier improvement efforts in the tropics, since the answer largely depends on what one is measuring. On the specific question of raising yields of certain staple grains—while bracketing out other issues such as energy ratios, crop diversity, or the production of useful parts of the plant besides grain— it was clearly a major success, despite the fact that some of the promises of plenty were soon foiled by adverse environmental conditions (as in Sri Lanka) or subsequently debunked as propaganda stunts cooked up by governments to help them get re-elected (as in the Philippines).[29] On the questions of ending hunger, improving life for smallholders, or boosting agricultural resilience, it was far less successful, which is little surprise since these were not the primary objectives in the first place for many of the parties involved.

By the 1980s nearly every country that had been 'green-revolutionized' was once again a net importer of staple foods. The main reason for the reversal was the continuation of high demographic growth rates, which has prompted many observers to claim that the food situation would have been far worse without the new technologies.[30] On balance, the claim is probably true. Yet it is also probably true that at least some of this population growth was linked to the socioeconomic consequences of the Green Revolution itself. For poor smallholders and agricultural labourers, many of whom had to supplement their incomes through employment in the cash economy, a common survival tactic was to have more children who could work for wages.[31] As critics have repeatedly pointed out, the overall outcome has been a massive socio-technological lock-in based on non-renewable energy sources.

All told, the chief 'success' of the Green Revolution was to export the new high-yield but patently unsustainable agricultural systems of the industrial world throughout the tropics. When viewed against the longer backdrop of twentieth-century agricultural development, it is worth emphasizing that this was precisely the *opposite* of what some colonial agronomists had long been trying to achieve. Had the likes of Albert Howard, Herman Lovinck, or Franz Stuhlmann lived to witness the full unfolding of the Green Revolution, they surely would have despaired at much of what they saw. Howard, for one, was already scathing about the industrial model of agriculture that was taking shape in Britain before the Second

---

[28] Conway, *Doubly Green*, 123; Smil, *Feeding*, 16–17; Prabhu Pingali, Mahabub Hossain, and Roberta Gerpacio, *Asian Rice Bowls: The Returning Crisis?* (Wallingford: CAB, 1997), 4–7.

[29] Perkins, *Geopolitics*, 257–8; on comparisons between agricultural systems, Miguel Altieri, *Agroecology: The Science of Sustainable Agriculture* (Boulder, Colo.: Westview, 1995); on fraudulent production figures, Cullather, *Hungry World*, 171–2, 243–4.

[30] e.g. Conway, *Doubly Green*, 66; Federico, *Feeding*, 214.

[31] David A. Sonnenfeld, 'Mexico's "Green Revolution", 1940–1980: Towards an Environmental History', *Environmental History Review*, vol. 16 (1992), 28–52, makes this point for Mexico, though it is more widely applicable.

World War.[32] Among the swelling chorus of Green Revolution critics in the 1960s and 1970s were the voices of many ex-colonial officials who had long advocated more incremental and ecologically oriented approaches to agricultural development.[33]

How, then, did the long colonial experience with tropical agriculture help pave the way for the Green Revolution? Part of the answer is that there was no universal consensus on the best approach during the colonial period, and that mavericks such as Howard espoused controversial views. Certainly they had little direct influence on policy, which was shaped by a range of factors beyond agronomy per se. Most of the answer, however, lies in the fundamental assumptions that framed colonial development efforts, above all the idea that the apparent inability of farmers in the tropics to grow more food was because they lacked the technology to do so. As we have seen, this basic supposition underpinned a plethora of improvement initiatives stretching back to the nineteenth century. It was also closely linked to at least three other persistent assumptions: that traditional techniques posed an impediment to progress; that the key to devising better techniques was through testing in controlled field environments in order to isolate the variables that affected yields and productivity; and that the resultant yield-enhancing technologies were socially neutral, which meant that any drawbacks or failures were usually attributed to poor implementation or mismanagement rather than the shortcomings or inappropriateness of the technologies themselves.[34]

These basic ideas, deeply engrained through decades of colonial experience, formed the conceptual cornerstones of the Green Revolution, whose main innovation was to take them further than ever before through unprecedented levels of financial and technical support, largely provided by the United States. Insofar as any of this truly constituted a 'revolution', it was more a matter of degree than kind. Buoyed by the post-war faith in technological progress, and flanked by the social-scientific tenets of modernization theory, such ideas became more powerful than ever in the wake of decolonization. Together, they helped cement the notion that the new high-yield varieties were 'wholly benign' technologies whose unwanted side-effects were little more than 'teething problems'.[35] Although researchers were hardly blind to the social and ecological intricacies that were involved, the tendency to reduce complex issues into discrete problems amenable to technical solutions remained deeply embedded within the culture and practices of scientific institutions.[36] As a result, little if any thought was initially given to the numerous other reasons why food production was a problem in so many tropical countries— landholding inequalities, low domestic purchasing power, market distortions through subsidies or buying pools—which all but precluded careful consideration of the likely impact of the new production methods.

---

[32] Howard, *Agricultural Testament*, 21–4.
[33] Hodge, *Triumph*, 269–70; Dumont, *Notes*, 163–6.
[34] See, generally, Kenneth Dahlberg, *Beyond the Green Revolution: The Ecology and Politics of Global Agricultural Development* (New York: Plenum Press, 1979); Wright, *Death*, 246–51.
[35] Quotes from Norman W. Simmonds, *Principles of Crop Improvement* (1979), 38, taken from Kloppenburg, *First the Seed*, 5; Conway, *Doubly Green*, 57.
[36] Kloppenburg, *First the Seed*, 5–7; Wright, *Death*, 175; and more generally, Scott, *Seeing*.

It has been aptly argued that the Green Revolution 'offered technology as a substitute to both nature and politics', but in the end it replaced neither.[37] As the environmental and social consequences gradually came into focus, they elicited a counter-movement in the wake of *The Limits of Growth* and the 1972 Stockholm Conference on the Human Environment. As several scholars have recently pointed out, the revival of intercropping, mixed farming, soil and water conservation measures in the 1970s and 1980s unwittingly echoed the ecologically minded development maxims of the 1930s.[38] By the same token, many of the leading champions of indigenous cultivation methods and 'farmers first' approaches had started their careers in the colonial settlement schemes of the 1950s.[39]

Nonetheless, the basic seed-fertilizer package of the Green Revolution continued to spread, spurred on by the more market-based development doctrines that prevailed after the mid-1980s. By the 1990s assessments of the overall results became increasingly sanguine, at least for certain parts of the world,[40] and by the early 2000s several leading development agencies (including, once again, the Rockefeller Foundation) were calling for 'another Green Revolution' in sub-Saharan Africa, the only world region left to conquer. In the event, this most recent attempt to diffuse the presumed benefits of high-yield, high-input agriculture into new territory—often dubbed 'GR 2.0'—faced a familiar array of obstacles, not least the difficulty of adapting methods that were designed for one set of environmental conditions to quite different biophysical settings. As the UN's own expert report concluded in 2004, the diversity of African ecosystems meant that 'no single magic "technological bullet" is available for radically improving African agriculture', which instead would require 'numerous "rainbow evolutions" . . . rather than a single Green Revolution'.[41]

Such cautious assessments of new farming technologies reflect a growing appreciation of what Angus Wright has called the 'modern agricultural dilemma', or the tension between the local adaptations required for ecologically and socially sustainable agriculture, and the standardizing demands of industrial growth and international markets.[42] It is a long-standing quandary that shaped the entire

---

[37] Shiva, *Violence*, 47.

[38] Hodge, *Triumph*, 269–71; Unger, 'Agrarwissenschaftliche Expertise'; Overton, *Colonial Green Revolution?*, 198; Stephen J. Macekura, *Of Limits and Growth: The Rise of Global Sustainable Development in the Twentieth Century* (Cambridge: Cambridge University Press, 2015), 137–71.

[39] Bonneuil, 'Development as Experiment', 279.

[40] Mark W. Rosegrant and Peter Hazell, *Transforming the Rural Asian Economy: The Unfinished Revolution* (Oxford: Oxford University Press, 2000), esp. 74–5; Peter Hazell and C. Ramasamy, *The Green Revolution Reconsidered: The Impact of High-Yielding Rice Varieties in South India* (Baltimore: Johns Hopkins University Press, 1991).

[41] Inter-Academy Council, 'Realizing the Promise and Potential of African Agriculture', Amsterdam, 2004, 9: <http://www.interacademycouncil.net/24026/AfricanAgriculture/25990/26224.aspx>. For critiques, see Eric Holt-Giménez, Miguel Altieri, and Peter Rosset, 'Ten Reasons Why the Rockefeller and the Bill and Melinda Gates Foundations' Alliance for Another Green Revolution Will Not Solve the Problems of Poverty and Hunger in Sub-Saharan Africa', *Food First Policy Brief* no. 12 (2006): <https://foodfirst.org/wp-content/uploads/2013/12/PB12-Ten-Reasons-Why-AGRA-Will-not-Solve-Poverty-and-Hunger-in-Africa.pdf>; Aksel Nærstad (ed.), *Africa Can Feed Itself* (Oslo: Development Fund, 2007): <http://www.agropub.no/asset/2636/1/2636_1.pdf>.

[42] Wright, *Death*, 245.

history of colonial agricultural development. For decades, officials wrestled with the challenge of transforming tropical agriculture while trying to minimize social destabilization or land degradation.

In the end, the failure to achieve these different (many would say contradictory) objectives left an ambiguous legacy for the post-colonial world. On the one hand, it suggested that the only way to achieve substantial yield increases was through the wholesale application of the latest technologies from the industrial world. This had long been the view of many colonial officials, and it was certainly the lesson drawn by the myriad backers of the Green Revolution, insofar as they were aware of any colonial-era lessons at all. On the other hand, the litany of failed modernization projects and the multitude of unintended consequences led others to conclude that genuine and durable agricultural improvement came not through radical transformation driven by outside experts, but rather through incremental alterations adopted by farmers on the spot, whose locally tailored methods were far more appropriate and effective than many Western observers allowed (see Chapter 9). After all, practical adaptations on the ground had been the chief motor of innovation throughout the age-old history of agriculture, and the fact that the Green Revolution represented such a drastic departure from this pattern helps explain some of the problems it caused, both social and ecological.[43] It was a very different lesson to draw from the experience of colonial agriculture in the tropics, and it most likely would have brought major benefits if only more people had considered it.

CONSERVATION AND CONTROL AFTER COLONIALISM

Agriculture was by no means the only sphere of activity in which the pattern of intervention from above and afar continued long after independence. This engrained habit of modern governance shaped a wide range of efforts to manage tropical landscapes and make the most of their resources. Let us briefly consider two areas where such colonial-era linkages were particularly apparent: forestry and wildlife protection.

Colonial India was home to the largest and most sophisticated forest management system in the tropical world, and its ability to generate revenue was hardly something that Nehru's government wanted to relinquish. On the contrary, the National Forest Policy of 1952 not only affirmed state control over India's woodlands, it also paved the way for more plantations and for an increase in the production of timber, paper, pulp, and resins. Most Indian forestry officials still received their training at the Dehra Dun institute (founded in 1906), which faithfully upheld the doctrines of scientific management, maximum sustained yield, and strict rights of usage. Forest reserves remained sacrosanct, and local people had no better access to them after independence than they did before. Moreover, as contractors drove more and more roads into the hill forests, they steadily encroached on woodlands that were

---

[43] For the long view, Otto T. Solbrig and Dorothy J. Solbrig, *So Shall You Reap: Farming and Crops in Human Affairs* (Washington, DC: Island Press, 1994), 220–1.

used by farming communities, and especially onto areas used by shifting cultivators, whose land-extensive farming systems remained a target of criticism. By the 1970s, the effects of large-scale tree felling and community dispossession provoked a groundswell of grass-roots opposition. Most prominent by far was the Chipko movement and its campaign against the loss of old growth forest in the Himalaya. It not only achieved a series of local cutting bans, it also soon spread to other parts of India and gained considerable international renown in the process. In many ways such resistance echoed colonial antecedents just as much as the policies it sought to oppose. Although Chipko was more socially and politically inclusive than previous mobilizations against forest enclosures, its core motivations clearly recalled colonial-era protests over the defence of access rights and traditional woodland uses.[44]

Apart from its exceptional size, independent India's forest service was fairly typical in most other respects. Throughout the ex-colonial world, existing frameworks of state-led management were largely perpetuated as a means of capitalizing on the forests. In Burma, colonial-era policies that privileged timber extraction over subsistence farming remained broadly intact despite consecutive nationalizations of the forestry sector in 1948 and the mid-1960s.[45] In Indonesia, the huge loss of woodland during the conflicts of the 1940s (which claimed around 14 per cent of the state forests on Java by 1949, some 400,000 hectares in total) made severe access restrictions every bit as attractive to foresters after independence as they were before.[46] Throughout sub-Saharan Africa, most of the colonial forestry codes and many of the personnel remained in place long after decolonization. Even where the independence struggle brought a temporary relaxation of unpopular forest controls, as in parts of French West Africa, it was not long before the familiar alliance of bureaucratic power and scientific expertise restored the desiccationist-inspired policies of the colonial era.[47] According to Vandergeest and Peluso, it was mainly *after* the end of colonialism that the global spread of professional forestry practices through organizations such as the FAO (which many colonial foresters joined in the 1950s–1960s) created a more comprehensive and standardized 'empire of forestry' in the tropics.[48]

Sadly, such measures did little to halt the process of woodland clearance in the former colonies. Throughout the post-war period, the vast bulk of global forest loss—over half a billion hectares in less than half a century—took place in the tropics. What made this 'great onslaught'[49] so irrepressible was that it was driven

---

[44] Gadgil and Guha, *Fissured Land*, 181–214; Guha, *Unquiet Woods*, 152–84.
[45] Bryant, *Political Ecology*, 157–93.   [46] Peluso, *Rich Forests*, 101–16.
[47] As various scholars have noted, this century-old discourse thus left a remarkably durable imprint on the West African landscape by influencing where forests were protected (e.g. around headwaters) and where trees were planted (as curtains against desert encroachment): Fairhead and Leach, *Reframing Deforestation*, 173–7; Fairhead and Leach, *Misreading*, 252–4; Jeremy Swift, 'Desertification: Narratives, Winners and Losers', in Melissa Leach and Robin Mearns (eds), *The Lie of the Land: Challenging Received Wisdom on the African Environment* (Oxford: Currey, 1996), 73–90; on East Africa, Sunseri, *Wielding the Ax*, 143–63.
[48] Vandergeest and Peluso, 'Empires', Part 2.
[49] Williams, *Deforesting*, 420–93; p. 421 for the figure of half a billion hectares.

by so many factors: logging, agricultural exports, along with unprecedented demographic expansion. Although it is impossible to put precise figures on the different causes, it is highly likely that the dispersed but cumulatively gigantic clearance of tropical forest by millions of farmers and villagers did more to alter the forests than anything else.[50] The sheer ubiquity of small-scale clearance, whether for farmland, pasture, fuel-wood, or construction material, made it difficult to control, and even when states sought to regulate the process of land conversion, the effects on the forests were often devastating. As we saw in Chapter 10, Malaysia's state-backed land development schemes cleared millions of hectares after independence. Even larger expanses of woodland were lost to such projects in Indonesia. By the end of the 1980s, the attempt to relieve population pressures on Java through 'transmigration' to the outer isles—a colonial-era idea that was vigorously promoted by the Sukarno and Suharto governments, and strongly supported by the World Bank—brought some 15–20 million settlers into the jungles of Sumatra, Kalimantan, and Irian Jaya, including 5 million attached to the official programme, plus an estimated 10–15 million who migrated spontaneously. Needless to say, such policies did little to slow Indonesia's galloping deforestation rate of around 750,000 hectares per year.[51]

Timber extraction, most of it for export, merely added to the tally. The main industrial economies had a voracious appetite for lumber, wood chips, and other forest resources. Throughout the developing world, cash-strapped governments and private firms often responded by plundering the forests as a quick source of income. By the end of the twentieth century, wood was the world's third most valuable export commodity, accounting for over $135 billion in trade (and surpassed only by petroleum and natural gas).[52] Tropical hardwoods constituted a particularly lucrative slice of this trade, and found ready markets in Europe, Japan, the USA, and eventually China.

The intensity of logging, and the damage it caused, varied significantly from place to place, mainly as a result of transportation costs, labour availability, and local political circumstances. Generally speaking, commercial logging has been far less widespread in Africa than in Southeast Asia.[53] Malaysia and Indonesia (together with Brazil) have long topped the world rankings for timber exports, far surpassing the output of Africa's largest producer (Côte d'Ivoire). Both countries possessed exceptionally rich tropical woodlands. In the rush to cash in on them, loggers often cut trees faster than they could regenerate and caused extensive damage to non-target species that got in the way. Consequently, the focus of timber

---

[50] Williams, *Deforesting*, 423.

[51] P. M. Fearnside, 'Transmigration in Indonesia: Lessons from its Environmental and Social Impacts', *Environmental Management*, vol. 21 (1997), 553–70; C. Secrett, 'The Environmental Impact of Transmigration', *The Ecologist*, vol. 16 (1986), 77–88; Anthony J. Whitten, *Transmigration and the Environment in Indonesia: The Past, Present, and Future* (Gland: IUCN, 1987).

[52] Williams, *Deforesting*, 491.

[53] Yet as overexploitation has threatened Southeast Asian supplies, and as revenues from other African resources (oil, minerals) have been forecasted to dwindle, wood exports have gradually risen in some African countries: Douglas A. Yates, 'Neo-"Petro-monialism" and the Rentier State in Gabon', in Matthias Basedau and Andreas Mehler (eds), *Resource Politics in sub-Saharan Africa* (Hamburg: Institut für Afrika-Kunde, 2005), 173–90; Williams, *Deforesting*, 459.

extraction constantly shifted from one place to another. As overall tree cover contracted on Java, Sumatra, and the Malaysian Peninsula, new frontiers opened in Sabah, Sarawak, and Kalimantan.

Wherever the timber frontier moved, it set off a kind of chain reaction. The trails and clearings that loggers cut into the forest often paved the way for a subsequent influx of small-scale cultivators in search of new agricultural land. In turn, these pioneer settlements were eventually followed by commercial planters keen to cover the area with oil palm or other export crops. As a result, logged-out forests seldom returned to anything like their previous state. Even when officials tried to slow the process, they were rarely able to rein in the powerful alliance of business and political interests that profited from state-sanctioned forest stripping. And to make matters worse, illegal logging took an unknown but undoubtedly huge toll beyond what governments actually permitted, especially in remote or politically restless areas where state authority was tenuous. In parts of Cambodia, Kalimantan, and Sumatra, illegal logging networks have cleared vast areas of nominally protected forests.[54] Despite consumer unease about the provenance of tropical wood products, certification schemes have not entirely stopped importers from turning a blind eye.

In sum, colonial-era patterns of management and trade continued to shape the exploitation of tropical forests long after independence. The same was true of many other aspects of resource governance in the former colonies, nowhere more so than in the field of wildlife conservation.

By the late 1950s, there were widespread concerns about the fate of wildlife populations in territories that were soon to become independent. Such fears were not confined to colonial game departments, but were broadly shared by conservationists within the UN and other international agencies. The main focus of concern was Africa, and in particular the national parks and reserves that had recently been established there. In 1960 UNESCO and the IUCN launched an 'African Special Project' for the express purpose of gaining support for protected areas among African leaders and formally cementing their continuation after independence.

With hindsight, September 1961 was a pivotal moment for post-colonial wildlife conservation, in at least two respects. In early September, just two months before Tanzanian independence, a meeting of African leaders in Arusha (Tanzania) committed themselves to the maintenance of wildlife protection at the Pan-African Symposium on the Conservation of Nature and Natural Resources in Modern African States.[55] The so-called Arusha Conference was essentially an agreement to

---

[54] Philippe Le Billon, 'Logging in Muddy Waters: The Politics of Forest Exploitation in Cambodia', *Critical Asian Studies*, vol. 44 (2002), 563–86; J. Smith et al., 'Illegal Logging, Collusive Corruption and Fragmented Governments in Kalimantan, Indonesia', *International Forestry Review*, vol. 5 (2003), 293–302; Paul Jepson et al., 'The End for Indonesia's Lowland Forests?', *Science*, vol. 292 (2001), 859–61.

[55] Nyerere's 'Arusha Declaration on Conservation' explicitly affirmed trusteeship of Africa's wildlife, and expressed 'the earnest desire of modern African states to continue and actively expand the efforts already made in the field of wildlife management': Adams, *Against Extinction*, 53; also Holdgate, *Green Web*, 73.

retain most aspects of colonial-era wildlife conservation. Just days later, on 11 September, the launch of the World Wildlife Fund marked a whole new scale of campaigning and fund-raising activity on behalf of the international conservation movement. Unlike the IUCN, WWF had deep pockets, and the swelling flow of donations it received was soon channelled into a series of conservation initiatives stretching from the Galápagos to the savannahs of Africa to the nesting beaches of sea turtles.[56]

These two events signalled an important institutional change from the colonial period. The leadership of the global conservation movement was no longer centred on colonial game departments, park institutes, or organizations like the Fauna Preservation Society (formerly SPFE), but had largely passed to an expanding coalition of international NGOs and post-colonial leaders. Yet in practical terms, most of the ideas and practices that had long underpinned wildlife protection in the tropics remained intact. Much as before, park management in the former colonies still focused on restricting access and suppressing customary uses rather than on the needs of local communities. Conservationists' appeals for outside financial support still drew heavily on age-old notions of unspoiled wilderness and the threat of human encroachment. Well into the twenty-first century, campaigners still continued to warn about 'paradise lost' and threats to 'elephant Eden' in Africa's parks. 'Reclaiming Paradise' remained the headline slogan of the emerging global environmental movement.[57]

The remarkable persistence of these narratives was based not only on their popular allegorical appeal—as a symbol of humanity's fall from grace—but also because they pointed towards technical solutions that spoke directly to the interests of international (and often ex-colonial) conservation experts who claimed to act as the only competent custodians of the land. Since most conservationists were interested mainly in preserving ecosystems undisturbed by people, their interventions often aggravated ongoing conflicts over reserve boundaries and local resource claims. Although some, like Julian Huxley, recognized that protected areas were at one level 'relics of "colonialism" which occupy land coveted by Africans', this did not stop conservationists from lobbying for people-free parks as the best means of protecting wildlife.[58] Moreover, as the growth of air travel and tourism promised to bring in more revenues from wildlife sightseers, such 'visions of paradise' found a receptive audience among African leaders in desperate need of foreign exchange.[59]

Post-colonial wildlife conservation was, then, more than just an imperial hold-over. It also reflected the aspiration of newly independent states to bolster their control over remote hinterlands, to profit from the natural resources of their territories, and to demonstrate their credentials as 'civilized' countries. The widespread

[56] See Macekura, *Of Limits and Growth*, 54–90; William M. Adams and Martin Mulligan (eds), *Decolonizing Nature: Strategies for Conservation in a Post-Colonial Era* (London: Earthscan, 2002).
[57] Quotes from McCormick, *Reclaiming*; Richard Carroll (WWF), <http://www.livescience.com/34818-un-fights-poaching.html>. See also Adams and McShane, *The Myth of Wild Africa*.
[58] Quoted from Holdgate, *Green Web*, 72.
[59] Berhard Grzimek et al., *Visions of Paradise* (London: Hodder, 1981).

enthusiasm for 'imposing wilderness' on the land was certainly encouraged by out-side conservationists, but it could only come about with the approval and cooper-ation of the relevant government bodies. In some states, the resulting tendency towards 'fortress conservation' was essentially an amplification of colonial segrega-tion policies. In Tanzania, this even included forced removals of local residents from protected areas—for example, Ngorogoro Crater and Mkomazi Game Reserve—that uncomfortably recalled earlier mass evictions from Serengeti.[60]

The hostilities engendered by such conservation measures likewise paralleled those of the colonial period. What park authorities and wildlife organizations condemned as 'poaching' or 'illegal grazing' was often regarded by locals as the legitimate exercise of customary rights on ancestral lands. It was only towards the close of the twentieth century that more 'participatory' forms of conservation began to displace the exclusionist models inherited from the colonial era.[61] Although it is still uncertain whether such community-based management schemes can provide a long-term solution, some have undoubtedly worked to the mutual benefit of wildlife and local people, not least by attracting so-called 'eco-tourists' in search of a more socially and environmentally responsible safari experience.

In a sense, such innovations have sought to reconcile the 'environmentalism of the poor', or the legitimate demand for local access to resources, with the quite different environmentalism of conservation-minded foreigners in search of adven-ture. Yet in the competitive marketplace of African tourism, even community-based conservation projects have occasionally resorted to logos such as 'Wilderness Safaris' and 'Wildlife Paradise' to attract custom. The sad irony is that the imagery of an unspoiled and eternalized tropical nature is precisely what helped marginal-ize many of the residents of such protected areas in the first place. By obscuring the true origins of these landscapes and the human stories behind them, such images unwittingly perpetuate not only a skewed narrative of European imperial-ism, but also a 'mental colonization of Africa as a "pristine" and heterotopian wildlife paradise'.[62]

EXPORT ECOLOGIES: FROM COLONIALISM TO CONSUMERISM

For the governments of newly independent states, capitalizing on natural assets was a vital means of developing their economies and raising living standards. But how this took place was strongly influenced by the ways in which imperialism had

---

[60] Neumann, *Imposing Wilderness*, 131–48; Dan Brockington, *Fortress Conservation: The Preservation of the Mkomazi Game Reserve, Tanzania* (Oxford: James Currey, 2002).

[61] For entry points into the literature, David Hulme and Marshall Murphree (eds), *African Wildlife and Livelihoods: The Promise and Performance of Community Conservation* (Oxford: James Currey, 2001); Fred Nelson (ed.), *Community Rights, Conservation and Contested Land: The Politics of Natural Resource Governance in Africa* (London: Earthscan, 2010); Fikret Berkes, 'Rethinking Community-Based Conservation', *Conservation Biology*, vol. 18 no. 3 (June 2004), 621–30.

[62] Gißibl, *Nature*, 394–5.

previously shaped their economies and their place in the global order. For the better part of a century, and in some cases significantly longer, the basic task of tropical dependencies had been to serve the needs of their respective metropoles. As these states emerged from colonialism, most still found themselves in a subservient role as producers of raw materials. Many were heavily reliant on one or two principal exports, which made them highly dependent on overseas buyers and perilously exposed to the vagaries of international markets. Furthermore, their unfavourable position in world trade was often reinforced on the domestic front by transport infrastructures designed for the evacuation of primary goods rather than regional economic integration, as well as by the continued power of international corporations over natural resources and labour markets.

By the end of the 1960s, the resulting socio-economic distortions were increasingly regarded as a product of 'underdevelopment' rather than just the lack of development—that is, a consequence of the highly unequal terms of exchange between suppliers of raw materials and suppliers of capital and finished goods. From the viewpoint of post-colonial governments and Western *tier-mondistes* alike, this fundamental imbalance not only reflected but actively contributed to the economic disparities between the industrial powers and the rest of the world.[63]

Less often noticed, though no less significant, were the ecological ramifications of such trade structures, whose net effect was to funnel nature's wealth from poorer areas to richer ones, while simultaneously shifting the environmental burdens in the other direction.[64] Despite numerous efforts at economic diversification and import substitution in the developing world, most of the transcontinental resource flows that had powered the apparatus of European empire persisted or even accelerated after the end of colonialism. As consumer demand rose and shipping costs continued to fall, governments in most former colonies faced enormous pressure to maximize their comparative economic advantages, whether as a means of accumulating capital for investment or, by the 1980s, simply to repay mounting debts. The overall upshot was even more mining, logging, and cash-cropping, resulting in yet greater demands on tropical forests, soils, and waterways.

Some of the largest and most controversial impacts arose from mining operations. The worldwide minerals boom that had been triggered by the Second World War continued more or less unabated after the conflict was over. As war-torn economies were rebuilt, and as the Cold War quietly raged, many of the long-established colonial mining industries scaled up their operations to meet demand. Malaysia's tin industry successfully recovered from wartime damage to retain its dominant position, at

[63] e.g. Walter Rodney, *How Europe Underdeveloped Africa* (London: Bogle-L'Ouverture, 1972); André Gunder Frank, *Capitalism and Underdevelopment in Latin America* (New York: Monthly Review Press, 1969); Paul Bairoch, *Révolution industrielle et sous-développement* (Paris: Société d'édition d'enseignement supérieur, 1963); Samir Amin, *Impérialisme et sous-développement en Afrique* (Paris: Éditions Anthropos, 1976); Charles K. Wilber (ed.), *The Political Economy of Development and Underdevelopment* (New York: Random House, 1973); see also Ankie M. M. Hoogvelt, *Globalization and the Postcolonial World: The New Political Economy of Development* (Basingstoke: Macmillan, 1997), 37–42.

[64] Foster, Clark, and York, *Ecological Rift*; Hornborg, McNeill, and Martinez-Alier (eds), *Rethinking.*

least until the advent of low-cost Brazilian mines in the 1980s brought a price crash. The copper mines of Central Africa likewise flourished until the mid-1970s, buoyed by the hunger for electrical goods in Europe, North America, and Japan. Gold also continued to flow out of its historic hubs in South and West Africa, and produced more ephemeral rushes elsewhere. Nickel production on New Caledonia, the world's largest exporter before the war, increased no less than a hundredfold between 1950 and 1976.[65]

As new technologies and larger amounts of capital became available, mining firms scoured the developing world for fresh deposits. A prime example was the enormous growth of the aluminium industry. Between the First and Second World Wars, the advent of aircraft as part of the modern military arsenal turned bauxite ore into a major strategic commodity. After 1945, aluminium consumption soared with the rapid growth of the electrical, automotive, and commercial aircraft industries, along with the military requirements of the Cold War.[66] But as bauxite reserves in France and the United States were depleted, the aluminium industry became ever more dependent on supplies from other countries, most of them European colonies or ex-colonies.

The initial focal points were Guyana and Suriname, where North American mining firms had already extracted much of the Allies' wartime needs under generous concessionary and tax arrangements. Jamaica followed suit in the early 1950s, accounting for over a fifth of world production by 1960.[67] Attention then shifted to the rich bauxite deposits in the Gold Coast and especially Guinea, home to around a third of the world's known reserves. In 1958 an international consortium led by Péchiney Ugine, Europe's largest aluminium firm, opened a vast new mining and refinery complex in Guinea. By the late 1970s the mineral works at Fria, Kindia, and Sangaredi annually shipped out over 11 million tons of bauxite and 600,000 tons of alumina (aluminium oxide, which is subsequently smelted into aluminium), which covered the bulk of French and West German requirements and made Guinea the world's second largest producer.[68]

The worldwide search for bauxite exemplified the broader pattern of mineral development throughout the former colonies. Amidst spiralling post-war demand, there was certainly no shortage of examples: iron in Mauritania and Liberia, phosphates in Morocco and Senegal, platinum in South Africa. Part of the growth reflected the search for previously unused minerals. Uranium, for instance, was a critical resource during the Cold War, and much of it came from Africa. Before 1960

---

[65] Lanning and Mueller, *Africa Undermined*, 380–3; McNeill, *Something*, 34.

[66] Mimi Sheller, *Aluminum Dreams: The Making of Light Modernity* (Boston: MIT Press, 2014); Matthew Evenden, 'Aluminum, Commodity Chains, and the Environmental History of the Second World War', *Environmental History*, vol. 16 (Jan. 2011), 69–93.

[67] Ronald Graham, *The Aluminium Industry and the Third World: Multinational Corporations and Underdevelopment* (London: Zed, 1982), 80, 93–9; Carlton E. Davis, *Jamaica in the World Aluminium Industry, 1938–1973* (Kingston: Jamaica Bauxite Institute, 1989); Sheller, *Aluminum*, 147–78.

[68] Jacques Larrue, *Fria en Guinée: première usine d'alumine en terre d'Afrique* (Paris: Karthala, 1997); Bonnie K. Campbell, *Les Enjeux de la bauxite: la Guinée face aux multinationales de l'aluminium* (Montréal: Presses de l'Université de Montréal, 1983); Graham, *Aluminium*, 101–6; Sheller, *Aluminum*, 194–202.

the UMHK's Shinkolobwe mine supplied much of the United States' uranium stockpile (including the fissile material for the bombs that fell on Hiroshima and Nagasaki), but the mine was deliberately sealed off just prior to Congolese independence. Meanwhile, the French Commissariat à l'Énergie developed a cluster of uranium extraction sites in south-eastern Gabon, Madagascar, and the Agadez region of northern Niger, which soon became key suppliers for France's ambitious nuclear programme, both civilian and military.[69] But despite the demand for new minerals like uranium, most mining operations in the post-colonial world targeted metals that had been sought for millennia: copper, gold, iron, tin. Prime examples were the gigantic Melanesian mines that opened after 1970, above all the Panguna mine on Bougainville Island (one of the world's largest copper mines before its closure in 1989); the Ok Tedi copper/gold mine in Papua New Guinea; and the gargantuan Grasberg-Ertsberg (Freeport) complex in West Irian, the world's largest gold mine and third largest copper mine.[70]

The common aim of all these operations was to supply world mineral markets as efficiently and profitably as possible. But large-scale mining enterprises are fraught with risk and complexity. Most developing countries could scarcely hope to establish new mineral industries without the capital resources, technical expertise, and market access of multinational mining firms. Equally, mining firms required certain rights and guarantees from host states to ensure a stable operating environment over the long term. As a result, the development of major mining projects in former colonies typically obliged governments to surrender a measure of their 'resource sovereignty' in exchange for the necessary investment and know-how. Generally speaking, such trade-offs proved highly advantageous for mining companies, local political elites, and distant consumers. Occasionally, they also provided welcome income for nearby communities. All too often, however, they were bad news for local people and had disastrous environmental consequences.

Wherever industrial-scale mining takes place, it generates a range of environmental impacts. A certain amount of land clearance and accelerated erosion is all but inevitable, as is a degree of localized water and soil contamination. But if some of this environmental damage is unavoidable, many of the worst impacts in the developing world could (and should) have been prevented or at least substantially mitigated.

In numerous ex-colonies, the lack of effective regulation by distant or uninterested host governments gave rise to pollution levels far in excess of what would be tolerated in most developed countries. In Gabon, radioactive contamination poisoned soil, water, and human bodies for miles around the Franceville uranium mine, which by 1975 had dumped some 2 million tons of mining waste and

[69] Gabrielle Hecht, *Being Nuclear: Africans and the Global Uranium Trade* (Cambridge, Mass.: MIT Press, 2012). In 2004, the Congolese government reclosed the Shinkolobwe mine and destroyed a nearby village in an attempt to displace the approximately 6,000 small-scale *creuseurs* illegally working the site since the late 1990s: Marie Mazalto, 'Governance, Human Rights and Mining in the Democratic Republic of Congo', in Bonnie Campbell (ed.), *Mining in Africa: Regulation and Development* (New York: Pluto Press, 2009), 187–242, here 208.

[70] See n. 75.

radioactive yellowcake tailings directly into the Mitembe-Likedi river system.[71] At Kabwe, Zambia's second-largest city, the local lead and zinc mine operated almost entirely without regulation from 1902 to 1994, eventually earning the town its grim distinction as one of the world's ten most polluted places.[72] Lax controls in Guinea allowed Péchiney's Fria refinery to disgorge vast quantities of untreated 'red mud' (a caustic liquid residue from bauxite processing, laced with toxic trace metals) directly into the Konkouré River, causing extensive damage downstream before the practice was finally halted in the late 1980s.[73] 'Red mud' and bauxite dust left similar stains in Suriname and especially in Jamaica, where mine tailings polluted groundwater supplies and degraded coral reefs along the island's south coast.[74] Among the worst polluters of all were the mega-mines of New Guinea and surrounding islands. From 1972 to 1989, the Panguna copper mine dumped around half a billion tons of tailings directly into Bougainville's Kawerong-Jaba river system, destroying its once flourishing fishery. The Ok Tedi mine, whose tailings dam catastrophically failed in 1984 and was never rebuilt, has expelled around 2 billion tons of waste directly into Papua New Guinea's Fly River, raising the river bed by up to 10 metres and covering over 1,000 square kilometres of the floodplain with contaminated sludge. The Freeport complex likewise dumped billions of tons of waste material directly into the local river system, polluting West Papua's estuaries and even threatening the Lorentz National Park, a UNESCO world heritage site.[75]

Although the effects of such pollution could be felt across the lithosphere, hydrosphere, and atmosphere, it was typically the rivers and floodplains that bore the brunt of the contamination. And to make matters worse, the implications of large-scale mining for riverine ecosystems were hardly confined to pollution.

---

[71] Hecht, *Being Nuclear*, 239–48. The Franceville mine subsequently deposited its wastes in the worked-out pit and then in an open tailings pond. Meanwhile, its sibling mines in northern Niger have been criticized for causing similar environmental and health damage, as well as an alarming drop in water tables in an arid region that can ill afford it: Rasmus Kløcker Larse and Christiane Alzouma Mamosso, 'Environmental Governance of Uranium Mining in Niger', *DIIS Working Paper 2013:02* (Copenhagen: DIIS, 2013), 6–7; Hecht, *Being Nuclear*, 321–4.

[72] According to the Blacksmith Institute, lead levels in local children's blood are up to ten times the recommended maximum: <http://www.blacksmithinstitute.org/projects/display/3>.

[73] Larrue, *Fria*, 101, 301. At the other end of Fria's railway, the loading of alumina at Conakry sent out noxious dust clouds that choked much of the city, including the presidential palace.

[74] R. Williams, *Red Mud: An Annotated Bibliography* (Kingston: Jamaica Bauxite Institute, 1986); S. N. Das, R. S. Thakur, and H. S. Ray, 'Red Mud Pollution Problems: Some Observations', *Environmental and Waste Management* (1998), 11–16; Paul E. Ouboter and Bart P. D. De Dijn, 'Changes in a Polluted Swamp', in Paul E. Ouboter (ed.), *The Freshwater Ecosystems of Suriname* (Dordrecht: Kluwer Academic, 1993), 239–60.

[75] The resulting devastation eventually prompted BHP-Billiton to get out of Ok Tedi and the Norwegian government to divest itself of its shares in Freeport. See, generally, David Hyndman, *Ancestral Rain Forests and the Mountain of Gold: Indigenous Peoples and Mining in New Guinea* (Boulder, Colo.: Westview Press, 1994); Barrie Bolton (ed.), *The Fly River, Papua New Guinea: Environmental Studies in an Impacted Tropical River System* (Amsterdam: Elsevier, 2009); Stuart Kirsch, *Mining Capitalism: The Relationship between Corporations and their Critics* (Berkeley: University of California Press, 2014); Benedict Y. Imbun, *Anthropology of Mining in Papua New Guinea Greenfields* (New York: Nova Science Publishers, 2011); Nicholas A. Bainton, *The Lihir Destiny: Cultural Responses to Mining in Melanesia* (Canberra: ANU Press, 2010).

During the late 1940s and early 1950s, looming energy shortages and higher electricity costs in Europe focused attention on colonial hydroelectric potential as a means of satisfying the growing demand for energy-intensive resources, above all for aluminium. After independence, mineral exploitation remained the chief motivation behind dozens of hydroelectric projects in Europe's former colonies, nearly all of them built by foreign (mostly Western) consortia that ultimately consumed the bulk of the energy they produced. Kariba, which transmitted electricity hundreds of kilometres to the Copperbelt, was but one example of this trend. Another was the Edéa hydroelectric dam on the Sanaga River in Cameroon, built in the 1950s with FIDES funds to smelt bauxite from Péchiney's mines in France and Guinea. The same rationale lay behind the Akosombo Dam on the Volta River (completed in 1965), which sent 80 per cent of its electricity to the American-owned Volta Aluminum Company. The twin Inga dams on the Congo River (1972–82) likewise transferred power hundreds of kilometres to Katanga's mines. In Southeast Asia, the Cameron Highlands project supplied much-needed power to the Malaysian mining centres of Perak and Selangor, while across the straits in North Sumatra, the Asahan dams provided electricity for smelters producing aluminium bound mainly for Japan. In Suriname, the Afobaka Dam on the Pernambuco River, completed in 1964 to smelt aluminium for the Alcoa company, turned around 1 per cent of the entire country (nearly 1,600 km²) into a lakebed.[76] Even though such projects often included subsidiary irrigation and flood control elements, most major dams in developing countries were built primarily to tap mineral and hydropower resources for direct or indirect export to the industrialized world.

The far-reaching ecological and social consequences of such projects are well documented. Although it would be exaggerated to regard them as unvaryingly negative, the advantages for local communities rarely outweighed the disadvantages. Some of the associated costs came in the form of disease. In Ghana, the Akosombo Dam led to a sharp increase in water-borne ailments (especially malaria and bilharzia) along Lake Volta, which more than offset the parallel reduction of river blindness caused by the flooding of the black fly parasite vector's breeding grounds.[77] Other drawbacks were registered as economic losses. Fishing grounds below the dams were often severely damaged by the end of seasonal flooding. At Kariba and Cahora Bassa (built in the early 1970s in Mozambique), it was claimed that the newly created lake fisheries above the barrages would compensate

---

[76] Martin Atangana, *French Investment in Colonial Cameroon: The FIDES Era (1946–1957)* (New York: Peter Lang, 2009), 128–47; Graham, *Aluminium*, 101–6; Robert F. Kinloch, 'The Growth of Electric Power Production in Malaya', *Annals of the Association of American Geographers*, vol. 56 (June 1966), 220–35, esp. 223–5; George J. Aditjondro, 'Large Dam Victims and their Defenders: The Emergence of an Anti-Dam Movement in Indonesia', in Philip Hirsch and Carol Warren (eds), *The Politics of Environment in Southeast Asia: Resources and Resistance* (London: Routledge, 1998), 28–54; John Charles Walsh and Robert Gannon, *Time is Short and the Water Rises* (London: Thomas Nelson & Sons, 1967).

[77] By 1970 bilharzia infected around 80 per cent of the Ewe who had moved to the shores of Lake Volta to fish, necessitating a multi-million dollar spraying and weeding programme: Jobin, *Dams and Disease*, 272–83, 360–3.

for such losses, but in the event they fell far short of expectations.[78] As a general rule, the disruption of natural inundation cycles and silt supplies affected floodplains, estuaries, and mangroves many kilometres downstream, often to the detriment of flora and fauna as well as farming and fishing communities.[79] Immediately upstream, of course, the submersion of forests, fields, and grazing lands annihilated large areas of terrestrial habitat. Although conservationists repeatedly mobilized to rescue animal populations threatened by inundation (most famously 'Operation Noah' at Kariba), the results were mixed. Whereas 'Operation Gwamba' evacuated some 10,000 animals from behind the Afokaba Dam in Suriname, Portuguese rescue plans at Cahora Bassa failed to progress beyond the drawing board.[80] People were also repeatedly displaced by the tens of thousands—57,000 at Kariba, 78,000 on the Volta, 42,000 at Cahora Bassa—and almost never received adequate compensation for what they lost. In India alone, well over 10 million 'developmental refugees' had been displaced by mega-dams by the 1990s, around 40 per cent of them 'tribals' who were largely pauperized in the process (and who constitute less than 6 per cent of India's population).[81]

As a result of such experiences, mining and dam projects that were originally intended as monuments of technical and economic development often functioned instead as lightning rods for local opposition. During the 1960s and 1970s, popular protests against such schemes were mostly ignored or forcibly repressed, much as they had been in the colonial era. Since the 1980s, the growth of NGOs such as the International Rivers Network and various Mine Watch groups have helped alleviate (though not eliminate) the adverse effects of dam projects on the poor and disempowered.[82] But even so, mining ventures have remained a perennial source of conflict. Perhaps the most extreme example was on Bougainville Island, where the destruction of the Jaba River by the Panguna mine was one of the main reasons behind the islanders' revolt in the late 1980s, and for the bloody civil war that followed.[83] Pollution from the Freeport mines caused similar frictions with local

---

[78] The disappointing productivity of the new inland fisheries was largely due to the disturbance of riparian zones by periodic draw-downs and the unanticipated effects of exotic species introductions: Balon and Coche (eds), *Lake Kariba*; Allen Isaacman and Barbara Isaacman, *Dams, Displacement, and the Delusion of Development: Cahora Bassa and its Legacies in Mozambique* (Athens, Oh.: Ohio University Press, 2013), 141–4, 171–4.

[79] W. M. Adams, *Wasting the Rain: Rivers, People and Planning in Africa* (Minneapolis: University of Minnesota Press, 1992), 137–54; Isaacman and Isaacman, *Dams*, 126–35; Heather J. Hoag, *Developing the Rivers of East and West Africa: An Environmental History* (London: Bloomsbury, 2013), chs 6–7.

[80] Walsh and Gannon, *Time is Short*; Allen Isaacman and Chris Sneddon, 'Toward a Social and Environmental History of the Building of Cahora Bassa Dam', *Journal of Southern African Studies*, vol. 26 (2000), 597–632, here 623–4.

[81] Thayer Scudder, *The Future of Large Dams: Dealing with Social, Environmental, Institutional and Political Costs* (London: Earthscan, 2005), 194–5; Isaacman and Sneddon, 'Toward a Social and Environmental History', 618; Colson, *Social Consequences*; D. Hart, *The Volta River Project: A Case Study in Politics and Technology* (Edinburgh: Edinburgh University Press, 1980); R. Chambers (ed.), *The Volta Resettlement Experience* (London: Pall Mall, 1970); Rob Nixon, *Slow Violence and the Environmentalism of the Poor* (Cambridge, Mass.: Harvard University Press, 2011), 150–74.

[82] Patrick McCully, *Silenced Rivers: The Ecology and Politics of Large Dams* (London: Zed, 1996), 281–311.

[83] Due to security problems, Panguna was forced to close in 1989 and has never reopened.

Papuan communities, and eventually turned the complex into a target for attacks by the Free Papua Movement. Both of these cases were exceptional with respect to the levels of political violence they involved, but they nonetheless typified the ways in which local grievances against the environmental effects of mining were often compounded by the perception of insufficient economic benefits for nearby communities. Had the balance appeared more favourable—whether in the form of more job opportunities, or less environmental damage—things might have looked different.

But for anyone weighing up such trade-offs, it is crucial to recognize the very different time-scales at work. Whereas the ecological damage wrought by mining usually lasts for decades, the economic benefits are often cruelly ephemeral. Even in areas where mining brought relative material prosperity over a sustained period (e.g. the Copperbelt), it often took no more than a sudden hike in energy prices or the opening of a low-cost mine thousands of kilometres away to wipe out most of the gains. Worse still, wherever lax bonds and loose regulation allowed mining firms to walk away when profits evaporated, governments and local communities also ended up paying for the mess left behind. The result in some former colonies was a twofold resource curse—both economic and ecological—that distorted current growth patterns while also storing up major environmental problems for the future.[84] Such were the risks of mineral-based development.

If mining generated some of the biggest ecological impacts in the post-colonial world, the export of petroleum was, from a global perspective, the most important resource flow of all. This was especially true from the viewpoint of Western Europe. With few petroleum supplies of their own, European states were highly dependent on imports to fuel their post-war economic growth. Given that around half of their oil came from US companies at the end of the war, the post-war dollar shortage and the escalating trade imbalance prompted a systematic search for supplies elsewhere, preferably from territories under some form of European control. Even as European governments shrank their imperial ambitions in the 1950s, they redoubled efforts to secure oil supplies from their colonies, former colonies, or friendly client states.

The chief focus was the Middle East, whose enormous petroleum reserves were regarded as the 'greatest single prize in all history'.[85] Western Europe was already the main destination for Iranian and Iraqi oil, hitherto dominated by British interests, and it remained the primary market for the new oilfields of Kuwait, Saudi Arabia (managed by US-based companies), and the smaller Gulf states, most of which came on stream after the war. The completion of the 1,675-kilometre Trans-Arabian pipeline in 1950, which had a capacity equivalent to sixty tankers in constant use between the Persian Gulf and the Mediterranean, forged an important infrastructural link between the oil reservoirs of eastern Saudi Arabia and the loading docks at Sidon in Lebanon. As Middle East production swelled, it triggered a major shift

[84] Richard M. Auty, *Sustaining Development in Mineral Economies: The Resource Curse Thesis* (London: Routledge, 1993).
[85] Yergin, *Prize*, 375.

in global energy flows. In 1946, Europe imported 77 per cent of its crude from the Western hemisphere, principally from the USA, Mexico, and Venezuela. By 1951, around 80 per cent came from the Middle East. For the Italian oil magnate Enrico Mattei, the Middle East represented 'industrial Europe's Middle West', a vast hinterland of natural resources waiting to be tapped.[86]

Exploration soon expanded in Europe's African colonies as well. The French government had long sought to develop colonial oil supplies as a means of improving its payment balance and freeing itself from the corporate grip of the 'Anglo-Saxon' giants. In 1945 it established the Bureau de Recherches de Pétrole to coordinate research within the French empire, and in 1956 it made its first big strikes in Gabon and in the Algerian Sahara. The timing could hardly have been more auspicious, for just a few months later the Suez Crisis dramatically underscored the importance of diversifying supplies beyond the Middle East. Amidst rising fears about future energy shortages, the Saharan discoveries were hailed as a potential solution to 'all of Europe's energy problems'.[87] Although the Algerian war threatened to derail French development plans in the region, the de Gaulle government managed to retain its oil rights after Algerian independence in 1962, by which time the network of state-controlled oil companies produced enough crude to meet the bulk of French requirements.[88] Meanwhile, over 1,000 kilometres to the east, oil also began to pour out of the Libyan desert, whose exceptionally 'sweet' crude—ideal for making gasoline—and proximity to French and Italian refineries allowed it to capture almost a third of the European market by the end of the 1960s. South of the Sahara, strikes in the Niger Delta and Angola in the mid-1950s were brought into commercial production around a decade later.[89] In just a matter of years, oil became Africa's chief export to Europe. Whereas petroleum constituted only 0.3 per cent of Africa's trade value with future EEC states in 1955, in 1985 it accounted for nearly three-quarters.[90]

The upshot of all these finds was a flood of oil on to world markets. From 1948 to 1972, global crude production rose from 8.7 million to 42 million barrels per day, with Middle Eastern output alone soaring from 1.1 million to 18.2 million barrels. The growth of consumption was equally spectacular, especially in Europe. While daily US oil use roughly tripled from 5.8 million barrels in 1948 to 16.4 million barrels in 1972, European consumption rose fifteenfold from 970,000 to 14.1 million barrels. Coal, which still covered three-quarters of Europe's energy needs in the mid-1950s, remained a crucial source of power for industry and household electricity, but it gradually declined in relative terms as oil became cheaper and as more businesses and homeowners made the switch.[91]

[86] Yergin, *Prize*, 404–8, 487.

[87] Guy Le Rumeur, *Le Sahara avant le pétrole* (Paris: SCEMI, 1960), 313.

[88] Yergin, *Prize*, 507–9; *Le Pétrole au Gabon*, Centre de Documentation et de Diffusion des Industries Minérales et Énergétiques Outre-mer, Études et Documents (July 1957).

[89] Yergin, *Prize*, 507–11, 560; P. Steyn, 'Oil Exploration in Colonial Nigeria, c.1903-58', *Journal of Imperial and Commonwealth History*, vol. 37 (2009), 249–74.

[90] Enzo R. Grilli, *The European Community and the Developing Countries* (Cambridge: Cambridge University Press, 1993), 143.

[91] Yergin, *Prize*, 481–2, 524–6.

It scarcely needs pointing out that this torrent of petroleum fuelled an epochal set of environmental changes during the post-war period. Throughout Europe, Japan, and North America, the influx of cheap oil converted vast areas of forest and farmland into suburbs, turned city streets into expressways, fed a profusion of consumer appetites, and created mountains of plastic waste. Although the notion of an oil-driven '1950s syndrome' tends to oversimplify the timing and obscure the broad array of factors at work, there is no doubt that a pivotal change was under way and that petroleum was the key ingredient.[92]

Oil gave people in the industrialized world an unprecedented capacity to alter their physical environment. In the process, it permitted a level of resource exploitation and wastefulness unparalleled in human history. It was not long before some of the symptoms of this 'syndrome' began to appear in producer countries as well. In the Gulf region, the camel was largely replaced by the Datsun pickup in the 1970s, as 12 cent per gallon gasoline made running costs less expensive than fodder.[93] Cheap energy and generous subsidies in Saudi Arabia allowed agro-firms to turn deserts into high-input crop fields, though only by draining fossil aquifers at an alarming rate. Most of the food from these artificial oases fed the rapidly growing urban centres of the region, whose own water requirements often relied on the treatment of seawater by energy-guzzling desalination plants. These wealthy but fragile 'cities of salt', as Abd al-Rahman Munif dubbed them, epitomize the precarious social formations created by oil abundance. All of them face the threat of dissolution should people fail to prepare for the proverbial rainy day.[94]

But if the mass consumption of petroleum had enormous environmental consequences, the effects of producing it were more limited. To be sure, the immediate production areas were profoundly transformed by roads, rigs, waste facilities, housing, and miles of pipelines. Some of the largest, such as the Burgan oilfield in southern Kuwait, stretched across hundreds of square kilometres. But most oilfields were significantly smaller than this, and by the post-war period the standardization of safer drilling techniques at the wellhead greatly reduced the number of spills and blowouts compared to the early years of petroleum exploitation. Unlike hard-rock mining, drilling for oil produces relatively little waste material; indeed, much of it was so-called 'produced water' rather than solid overburden, and was relatively easy to dispose of.

Transporting such huge amounts of oil was another matter. From 1954 to 1974 the total amount of crude carried by sea rose from 250 million to 1.5 billion tons, a sixfold upsurge that greatly heightened both the risk and the scale of spills. The *Torrey Canyon* disaster of 1967, which released 130,000 tons of oil just off the Cornwall coast, may have marked a turning point in public perceptions of oil spills

[92] Christian Pfister (ed.), *Das 1950er Syndrom. Der Weg in die Konsumgesellschaft* (Bern: Verlag Paul Haupt, 1995).
[93] Yergin, *Prize*, 617.
[94] Abd al-Rahman Munif, *Cities of Salt*, trans. Peter Theroux (New York: Vintage, 1989). See also the works of Christopher M. Davidson, *Dubai: The Vulnerability of Success* (London: Hurst, 2008); *Abu Dhabi: Oil and Beyond* (London: Hurst, 2009); *The United Arab Emirates: A Study in Survival* (Boulder, Colo.: Rienner, 2005).

and the media choreography surrounding them, but in the 1980s there were still an estimated 10,000 accidental oil discharges (of greatly varying magnitude) each year. Offshore rig blowouts only added to the problem. In 1980, for instance, the Hasbah 6 spill off northern Saudi Arabia decimated seabird populations and caused untold damage to fish, crustaceans, and a host of other species all along the Saudi, Bahrain, and Qatar coastlines.[95] Although improvements in tanker design led to a gradual drop in accidental discharges, between 1960 and 1997 it is estimated that around 14,127,000 tons of oil were spilled worldwide in approximately 732,000 separate incidents. And to put this into perspective, even more oil was put into the sea by routine tank cleaning and urban-industrial run-off than by accidents.[96]

The risk of spills and blowouts was a universal feature of the global oil industry, but the ecological and social consequences of oil production nonetheless varied from place to place. The differences partly reflected the diverse ecological settings in which oil was extracted. Around the Persian Gulf, terrestrial impacts from spills and industrial sprawl were limited by the low productivity and sparse human and animal populations of the arid environment. Here, many of the biggest effects stemmed from the consumption rather than the production of oil, along with the newfound wealth that it generated. A sharp decline in game species such as gazelle and oryx was largely due to motorized hunting; likewise, swelling urban demand for dairy products and meat significantly elevated the risk of overgrazing.[97] The political context also shaped overall outcomes. Although oil production profoundly altered social structures and land use in the Persian Gulf—including the long-established migration patterns of desert pastoralists—most local communities adapted to the changes and often benefited from them in the form of jobs, mobility, and higher material living standards. Even if the bulk of the Gulf's oil rent went to local elites, who squandered much of it on obscene palaces, buying the loyalty of political allies, or suppressing domestic dissent (the anti-democratic dimensions of the so-called 'oil curse'), a sizeable portion was put towards infrastructure, education, and health facilities designed to mollify popular pressures for reform.[98]

The picture was rather different in the oilfields of sub-Saharan Africa, where the ecological drawbacks were generally higher and the social paybacks lower. In Gabon and Angola, widespread corruption and opaque payment arrangements

[95] In January 1991, the deliberate destruction of Kuwaiti oil installations by Iraqi forces dumped 813,000 tons of crude into what was already the most environmentally burdened sea in the world: see Dagmar Schmidt Etkin, 'Historical Overview of Oil Spills from all Sources (1960–1998)', Oil Spill Intelligence Report (Arlington, Mass., 1999), <http://www.environmental-research.com/site_files_base/publications/content_pdf/spill_statistics/paper1.pdf>.

[96] Olof Linden, 'Fate and Effects of Oil Pollution with Particular Reference to the Persian Gulf Region', in *Proceedings of the First International Conference on the Impact of Oil Spill in the Persian Gulf* (Tehran: Tehran University Press, 1985), 45–63; Sucaattin Kirimhan, 'Accidental Oil Spills and the Pollution of the Marine Environment', in *Proceedings of the First International Conference*, 403–15, here 406; Etkin, 'Historical Overview'; Joanna Burger, *Oil Spills* (New Brunswick, NJ: Rutgers University Press, 1997).

[97] Beinart and Hughes, *Environment*, 263–7.

[98] Michael L. Ross, *The Oil Curse: How Petroleum Wealth Shapes the Development of Nations* (Princeton: Princeton University Press, 2012); also, generally, the works of Christopher M. Davidson (n. 94).

brought huge profits for oil firms such as Elf, Shell, and Agip, while also allowing political elites to pocket a large share of the proceeds for themselves. Since much of their production took place offshore, the Gabonese and Angolan oil industries functioned as archetypal 'enclaves' with few linkages to the wider economy beyond the patronage networks controlled by oppressive regimes.[99] Cabinda, the small Angolan exclave that has been mired since the 1960s in a violent secessionist struggle, broadly epitomized the problem. Its offshore oil fields, which were first explored under Portuguese rule in the 1950s and which still number among the largest in the world, long accounted for the bulk of Angola's production. Yet Cabinda has remained one of Angola's poorest provinces, and its inhabitants have received almost none of the revenue from oil production despite watching local fish stocks plummet due to spills and drilling pollution.[100]

In Nigeria too, oil brought few benefits to ordinary citizens, and for many residents of the Niger Delta its effects were nothing short of disastrous. Shell-BP made its first big strikes in the Delta in 1956, and quickly expanded commercial production over the following decade. By 1967 the struggle over the Delta's oil wealth plunged the region into a bloody civil war, in which Biafran separatists ultimately failed in their bid to secede from the rest of the country. After the conflict, the high oil prices of the 1970s prompted a further increase in production that swelled state coffers but nearly ruined Nigeria's agricultural sector by inflating the currency. As a result, the state became almost entirely dependent on oil revenues, and in the 1980s this dependency avenged itself as oil prices declined. In the meantime, a combination of oil spills, leaks, sabotage, and neglect wreaked havoc throughout the Delta. From 1976 to 2001 around 3 million barrels were spilled in 6,817 documented incidents, including major spills at Funiwa (1980) and Jones Creek (1998), which led to the worst case of mangrove destruction ever recorded.[101] Erosion, deforestation, subsidence, dredging, fires, and air pollution merely added to the toll, resulting in severe damage to fisheries, the contamination of drinking water, and the extensive destruction of fields and animal habitat.[102] Protests among local residents were generally met with violence and intimidation, most notoriously with the occupation of Ogoniland in 1994 and the execution of the activist Ken Saro-Wiwa the following year. Since Nigeria's military rulers derived most of their revenue—and personal fortunes—from oil, they were quite willing to accept the devastation of the Delta and the suppression of its inhabitants as the cost of doing business. The gangs that siphoned crude out of pipelines or tried to extort payments from oil firms by meddling with their equipment showed equally little

---

[99] Michael C. Reed, 'Gabon: A Neo-Colonial Enclave of Enduring French Interest', *Journal of Modern African Studies*, vol. 25 (1987), 283–320; Kristin Reed, *Crude Existence: Environment and the Politics of Oil in Northern Angola* (Berkeley: University of California Press, 2009).

[100] Alban Monday Kouango, *Cabinda: un Koweit africain* (Paris: L'Harmattan, 2002); Reed, *Crude Existence*.

[101] Figures from UNDP, *Niger Delta Human Development Report* (Garki: UNDP, 2006), 76. Other estimates suggest that up to 13 million barrels have been spilled in the Delta since 1958: Gavin Bridge and Philippe Le Billon, *Oil* (Cambridge: Polity, 2013), 131.

[102] For an overview: M. A. Okoji, 'Petroleum Oil and the Niger Delta Environment', *International Journal of Environmental Studies*, vol. 57 (2000), 713–24.

concern for the local environment. Shell, however, faced awkward questions at home, and eventually had to consent to compensation negotiations and tighter regulation. All the same, the lack of adequate redress for damages has remained a bone of contention.[103]

The Niger Delta and its many inhabitants, human and non-human, are among the most unfortunate victims of the world's quest for oil. At one level, the awful scale of devastation mirrored the exceptionally rich and delicate ecosystem that was under threat. As Africa's single largest wetland and one of the world's top biodiversity hotspots, the Niger Delta had a lot to lose from oil pollution—far more, in most respects, than the deserts of the Persian Gulf. But the appalling degree of environmental damage reflected more than just the biophysical wealth of the Delta, for it was also the product of a particular set of human choices and power structures. Ultimately, the problems stemmed from decades of callous disregard on the part of government officials and their corporate partners, who knowingly profited from the Delta's destruction until the political and reputational costs of doing so prompted a change of attitude.

In this respect, the sad fate of the Niger Delta illustrates a broader problem. Throughout much of the tropical world, the consequences of resource extraction were shaped not only by the engrained imbalances of world trade, but also by a peculiar set of political continuities. Above all, they reflected the tendency of many post-colonial states to operate, like their colonial predecessors, as 'gatekeeper states'—that is, states that derived most of their strength and revenue not from their hold over domestic life, but rather from presiding over the interface between their own territories and the outside world.[104] Despite long-standing efforts to diversify production, the overwhelmingly export-oriented economies of most former colonies meant that they were poorly equipped to generate the broad-based internal prosperity that would help stabilize the new political order.

The end of colonial rule did little to alter this overall pattern. If anything, it tended to amplify rather than mitigate the worst features of this political form, for the greater vulnerability of post-colonial gatekeeper states—which, unlike their colonial forerunners, could not fall back on external force—meant that preserving control of the 'gate' and channelling the revenues to supporters was all the more important for maintaining power. On a political level, this narrow and highly manipulable method of rent collection was one of the main reasons for the widespread cronyism and corruption that characterized so many former colonies, not to mention the long series of coups and violent takeovers launched by hitherto excluded groups keen to take command of the gate for themselves. More important for our purposes here, it also helps explain some of the underlying dynamics of

---

[103] Ike Okonta and Oronto Douglas, *Where Vultures Feast: Shell, Human Rights, and Oil* (London: Verso, 2003), esp. ch. 4; UNDP, *Niger Delta*, 73–80; Phia Steyn, 'Oil, Ethnic Minority Groups and Environmental Struggles Against Multinational Oil Companies and the Federal Government in the Nigerian Niger Delta since the 1990s', in Marco Armiero and Lise Sedrez (eds), *A History of Environmentalism: Local Struggles, Global Histories* (London: Bloomsbury, 2014), 57–81.

[104] My discussion here is based on Cooper, *Africa Since 1940*, 156–90.

political ecology in the post-colonial world, for the practice of government-by-gate-keeping was, among other things, a recipe for predatory extraction, regulatory disregard, and social exclusion.

If oil-rich 'spigot states' such as Nigeria, Gabon, or Angola furnished the most extreme examples, the problems of gate-keeping applied to a whole range of natural resources coveted on world markets. In mineral-rich Zaire, the disastrous civil war that followed decolonization was driven largely by rival attempts to secure control over mining revenues. Mobutu Sese Seko, who emerged from the struggle to rule Zaire as presidential monarch from 1965 to 1997, ruthlessly pillaged the mines of Katanga for patronage and personal profit while his Western backers held their noses for the sake of a staunch anti-communist ally. In francophone West Africa, cosy relations between the French government and its former colonies facilitated a strategic trade-off of privileged access to raw materials in exchange for security guarantees and development aid from the erstwhile metropole. For many years, such arrangements helped funnel the revenue from Gabonese oil or Nigérien uranium into the pockets of kleptocratic officials or into grandiose pet building projects. Even in Guinea, the only French colony to opt for full independence instead of membership in the Communauté Française in 1958, the gears of the country's vast bauxite-alumina industry (which generated nearly 95 per cent of its export revenue) were lubricated by dubious fiscal privileges and kickbacks.[105] For government critics, the trans-continental patronage networks of '*Françafrique*' showed that the region's post-colonial elites acted more like agents of French interests than as stewards of their own countries.[106] Against this backdrop it is little wonder that the natural resources they controlled were often ransacked for export.

Along with environmental destruction, the politics of gate-keeping also led to severe social conflict. Controlling material outflows was a source of power not only for post-colonial states but also for many of their opponents. The civil war in Katanga was but the first of a long series of conflicts and insurgencies (Angola, Sierra Leone, Liberia, eastern Congo) that either revolved around or were financed by the ability to channel raw materials to international markets. Some of the worst violence was fuelled by so-called 'conflict minerals' (gold, tungsten, coltan, 'blood diamonds') that were extracted in war zones and then sold to purchase yet more arms and supplies. After passing through a series of middlemen, they eventually ended up in jewellery shops, precision instruments, and electronic gadgets throughout the world. By the turn of the millennium, the deplorable effects of unregulated mining in conflict zones, which often involved forced labour as well as the wholesale destruction of production sites and nearby watercourses, prompted far-reaching efforts to halt the illicit traffic through strict product certification systems. But even the most elaborate of these schemes, the 'Kimberley Process' for diamond certification, was partly undermined by corruptible officials who treated it as an

---

[105] On Guinea, see Campbell, *Enjeux*; on Niger, see Hecht, *Being Nuclear*, 324.
[106] François-Xavier Verschave, *La Françafrique: le plus long scandale de la République* (Paris: Stock, 1998); Frédéric Turpin, *De Gaulle, Pompidou et l'Afrique, 1958–1974: décoloniser et coopérer* (Paris: les Indes savantes, 2010).

opportunity to skim their own share of the proceeds in exchange for the necessary paperwork.[107] Many other raw materials—drugs, timber, oil, as well as various minerals and gems—have similarly figured in the 'political ecology of war' in the developing world.[108]

Not all former colonies had abundant mineral or petroleum resources, nor did they all export large quantities of timber and forest products. In many countries, agricultural goods remained the chief means of engaging with world markets. Tropical crop commodities were big business after the war. During the late 1940s and early 1950s, the relaxation of rationing and the recovery of household incomes in Europe released nearly two decades' worth of pent-up demand for exotic food-stuffs and stimulants. Over the following years, consumer appetites continued to grow as industrial economies surged and purchasing power rose.

After years of depression and wartime dislocation, this revival of previous trade flows was in many ways good news for farmers in the former colonies, at least as long as prices remained buoyant (which, since the 1970s, they increasingly have not). But seizing the opportunities of a rising market also brought new risks—not only the economic hazards of overreliance on a handful of primary goods, but also the ecological perils of forest and soil depletion.

Even amidst the booming post-war timber market, the expansion of agriculture was still the single most important driver of deforestation in the tropics. Although domestic demographic pressures were of course a critical factor behind the escalating pace of land conversion, much of it was also driven by a sharp rise in commercial cropping for international markets. In this sense, the growth of agricultural exports represented another means, alongside logging, for post-colonial states to cash in on their forest resources. Broadly speaking, this process followed three basic patterns: the extension of cultivation in established cash-cropping centres, the opening of commodity frontiers in new areas, and the emergence of new export goods.

The first pattern was exemplified by Côte d'Ivoire, whose existing cocoa and coffee industries grew rapidly after the 1950s. When the country achieved independence in 1960, it was already Africa's largest coffee exporter, shipping out 147,000 tons of *robusta* each year. By 1976, coffee exports had more than doubled to 305,000 tons, and accounted for around 1.3 million hectares of land. In the meantime, farmers were also clearing huge areas for cocoa. In the late 1970s Côte d'Ivoire overtook Ghana as the world's leading cocoa exporter, and by 2011 its output of over 1.5 million tons was roughly double that of its closest rivals

[107] W. C. Paes, '"Conflict Diamonds" to "Clean Diamonds": The Development of the Kimberley Process Certification Scheme', in Matthias Basedau and Andreas Mehler (eds), *Resource Politics in sub-Saharan Africa* (Hamburg: Institut für Afrika-Kunde, 2005), 302–24; Franziska Bieri, *From Blood Diamonds to the Kimberley Process: How NGOs Cleaned up the Global Diamond Industry* (Farnham: Ashgate, 2010).
[108] Philippe Le Billon, 'The Political Ecology of War: Natural Resources and Armed Conflicts', *Political Geography*, vol. 20 (2001), 561–84.

(Indonesia and Ghana).[109] Part of the increase came from higher crop yields as ageing cocoa and coffee stands were gradually replaced with selected varieties, but most of the growth simply reflected an expansion of acreage. Along with Côte d'Ivoire's logging industry, which accounted for a quarter of all African timber exports in 1985, the massive rise in coffee and cocoa production contributed to one of highest deforestation rates on the continent (*c.*130,000 ha/year).[110]

The second pattern—the spread of major cash crops into new areas—cleared even more forest cover than the first. A striking example was the government-backed coffee campaign in Vietnam. In the early 1980s Vietnam was no more than a marginal player in the global coffee economy, but by the turn of the century it became the world's second largest producer behind Brazil, with nearly half a million hectares under coffee. Government planners hoped that the coffee-planting drive would bring much-needed jobs and export income, which it clearly did. But the flip-side was a surge of erosion from recently deforested slopes, especially in the mountainous Dak Lak province where over half of the Vietnamese crop is grown.[111] Another example was Indonesia's cocoa industry. From humble beginnings in the late 1970s, Indonesian farmers produced nearly 850,000 tons of cocoa by 2010, much of it from smallholdings in south-western and central Sulawesi where forest land was readily available and where local elites ensured that land tenure arrangements remained favourable.[112] Most spectacular of all was the spread of oil palm across Peninsular Malaysia, Sumatra, and Borneo. Commercial palm plantations had already been established in Sumatra and Malaysia in the 1910s–1920s, but it was only after the 1950s, when Malaysian planters began to diversify out of rubber, that it really took off. By the early 1970s Malaysia surpassed Nigeria as the world's leading producer, and by the time Indonesia overtook Nigeria in 1980, Southeast Asia utterly dominated world exports. Like the region's rubber plantations, the oil palm industry was based on the propagation of an exotic species (*Elaeis guineensis*, native to West Africa) that flourished in the absence of co-evolved pests. Palm oil output grew exponentially from 1.48 million tons in 1961 to 8 million tons in 1986, to over 47 million tons in 2011, and is nowadays used for a multitude of products from soap to junk food to bio-fuels. By the early 2010s, four-fifths of global supplies came from Indonesia and Malaysia alone, claiming around 17 million hectares of forest in total. Since then, the process has continued apace in Sabah, Kalimantan, and Irian Jaya.[113]

[109] Figure from <http://faostat.fao.org/site/339/default.aspx>; Weiskel, 'Toward an Archaeology', 168–9; Chauveau and Léonard, 'Côte d'Ivoire's Pioneer Fronts'.

[110] Deforestation figure from Fairhead, Leach, *Reframing Deforestation*, 40, which is only half of FAO estimates of forest loss; logging figure from Claude Martin, *The Rainforests of West Africa: Ecology—Threats—Conservation* (Basel: Springer, 1991), 197.

[111] Frédéric Fortunel, *Le Café au Viêt Nam: de la colonisation à l'essor d'un grand producteur mondial* (Paris: L'Harmattan, 2000).

[112] François Ruf, Pierre Ehret, and Yoddang, 'Smallholder Cocoa in Indonesia: Why a Cocoa Boom in Sulawesi?', in Clarence-Smith (ed.), *Cocoa Pioneer Fronts*, 212–31; Tania Murray Li, *Land's End: Capitalist Relations on an Indigenous Frontier* (Durham, NC: Duke University Press, 2014); Tania Murray Li, *The Will to Improve: Governmentality, Development, and the Practice of Politics* (Durham, NC: Duke University Press, 2007); figures from <http://faostat.fao.org/site/339/default.aspx>.

[113] Figures from <http://faostat.fao.org/site/567/DesktopDefault.aspx?PageID=567#ancor>.

This brings us to the third pattern: the appearance of new trade commodities. By the 1980s, exports of what might be called traditional tropical crops (coffee, cocoa, tea, sugar) were increasingly accompanied by outflows of 'high value foods' (HVFs) such as fresh produce and seafood. In fact, between 1980 and 2000 the value of HVF exports rapidly outstripped that of more traditional tropical commodities, making it by far the largest sector of agricultural trade from developing countries (approximately 41 per cent in 2000–1).[114] Globally, fruit and vegetables alone accounted for over one-fifth of developing world exports at the turn of the century. Although much of this south-to-north traffic was between the Americas, countries in Africa and Southeast Asia have likewise begun to export everything from counter-seasonal green beans to pineapples, bananas, and cucumbers, mostly bound for Europe.[115]

These long-distance provisioning chains stimulated a host of environmental changes. As one might expect, the most acute effects were felt in producer areas, mainly in the form of land conversion, pesticide use, and synthetic fertilizers. But there were diffuse consequences all along the supply routes, not least the additional carbon emissions generated by the cold storage chains and rapid modes of transport required to move the perishable goods thousands of kilometres to market. Moreover, the boom in HVF exports has also raised a number of social and political concerns. The multinational supermarkets that purchase the vast bulk of HVF produce have an enormous influence on the market, and generally impose a battery of new health, work, and product standards on their suppliers. Although the underlying logic is to prevent abusive practices, critics have nonetheless shown how such external directives can function as a neo-colonial form of regulatory control over the agricultural sectors and labour regimes of exporting countries.[116]

The growth of HVF exports was not limited to agricultural goods. The fastest-growing sector of all was aquaculture, which by the turn of the century accounted for nearly one-fifth of all exports (by value) from developing countries, more than all of the conventional tropical crops combined.[117] Over the past several decades the EEC/EU has been the world's leading importer of seafood, and nothing whetted its appetite more than shrimp. From the 1970s onwards, shrimp became one of the most popular everyday delicacies among industrial-world consumers, and this was mainly thanks to the rapid expansion of aquaculture. From 1975 to 2014, global production of farmed shrimp rose from 22,292 tons to 4.58 million tons, worth a total of $23.6 billion per year.[118] Throughout this entire period, nearly all

---

[114] M. Ataman Aksoy and John C. Beghin (eds), *Global Agricultural Trade and Developing Countries* (Washington, DC: World Bank, 2005), 30.

[115] Nagatada Takayanagi, 'Global Flows of Fruit and Vegetables in the Third Food Regime', *Journal of Rural Community Studies*, vol. 102 (2006), 25–41, here, 27–8; also Ndiame Diop and Steven M. Jaffee, 'Fruits and Vegetables: Global Trade and Competition in Fresh and Processed Product Markets', in Aksoy and Beghin (eds), *Global Agricultural Trade*, 237–57.

[116] Susanne Friedberg, 'Postcolonial Paradoxes: The Cultural Economy of African Export Horticulture', in Alexander Nützenadel and Frank Trentmann (eds), *Food and Globalization: Consumption, Markets and Politics in the Modern World* (Oxford: Berg, 2008), 215–33.

[117] Aksoy and Beghin (eds), *Global Agricultural Trade*, 30.

[118] Figures from FAO:<http://www.fao.org/figis/servlet/SQServlet?file=/work/FIGIS/prod/webapps/figis/temp/hqp_7332778034432164198.xml&outtype=html>; <ftp://ftp.fao.org/FI/STAT/summary/b-1.pdf>.

of the world's cultured shrimp were produced by developing countries for consumption in developed countries. Thailand was an early pioneer, and was soon followed by India, Indonesia, Vietnam, Bangladesh, and the Philippines.

In all of these countries, multilateral lending agencies promoted the 'blue revolution' as a tool for job creation and poverty alleviation. Since the 1980s, shrimp farming has unquestionably become an important source of income and foreign exchange. But the price has been remarkably steep, for the expansion of aquaculture has also damaged littoral environments all along the coasts of Southeast Asia. By 2004, the 110,000 or so shrimp farms in the region covered approximately 1.3 million hectares, most of them carved from coastal wetlands and mangrove forests that had previously numbered among the most productive and diverse ecosystems in the entire world. In 2009 the *Ecologist* estimated that shrimp aquaculture alone was responsible for around 40 per cent of global mangrove loss.[119] The destruction of these ecosystems had effects far beyond the mangroves themselves. Because they serve as spawning grounds for a multitude of fish and crustacean species, the clearing of mangrove forests eliminates crucial habitat for marine flora and fauna, including the 'wild' shrimp whose capture and subsequent fattening in the feeding ponds forms the basis of the aquaculture industry itself. An additional problem is that the loss of mangroves deprived local communities of an important source of food, fuel, and building material. Most ominously, perhaps, it removed what was essentially a vast living bulwark against tides and storms.[120] The consequent increase in coastal erosion has not only put seaside towns and villages at risk; it has also choked coral reefs and sea grass beds that likewise serve as vital marine nurseries.

What's more, the environmental fallout from shrimp farming did not stop with the initial creation of feeding ponds. Once established, they caused a host of other problems. In the immediate surroundings, and especially in low-lying areas, the alteration of coastal hydrology threatened to salinize land and groundwater supplies. All along the affected coasts, the feeding ponds polluted nearby estuarine ecosystems through the continual efflux of organic waste, chemical additives, pesticides, and even antibiotics, which are used to control shrimp disease and maximize stock populations. Further offshore, the industry's ravenous demand for fish-meal put additional pressure on wild fish stocks that were already under strain from the loss of mangrove spawning grounds. And to make matters worse, the inexorable rise of disease and pollution levels in the shrimp ponds meant that most were abandoned after only several years of operation. Aquaculturists frequently moved around in search of fresh land to clear for new ponds, and when they relocated they often left behind a swampy and degraded wasteland.[121] Despite various initiatives to mitigate the environmental and social impacts of shrimp aquaculture (such as the

[119] <http://www.theecologist.org/investigations/politics_and_economics/368669/selling_indonesias_coast_for_cheap_prawns_and_profit.html>.
[120] See Martinez-Alier, *Environmentalism*, 79–99. It has been suggested that the shrimp industry amplified the effects of the 2004 tsunami in Indonesia: Vandana Shiva, *Stolen Harvest: The Hijacking of the Global Food Supply* (Cambridge, Mass.: South End Press, 2000), 44–52.
[121] According to the Mangrove Action Project, even highly conservative estimates suggested that abandoned shrimp ponds covered over 250,000 hectares worldwide in 2013: <http://mangroveactionproject.org/mangrove-restoration-of-abandoned-shrimp-farms/>.

WWF Shrimp Aquaculture Dialogue), it nonetheless continues to wreck coastal woodlands throughout the region.

The connection between Europe's love of shrimp and the destruction of coastal mangroves is merely one example of how the ecological burdens of a particular human behaviour are geographically displaced. Much as in the colonial era, the trade structures that facilitate this kind of exchange promote a net flow of ecological resources from the global south to north. The calculations involved in such trade-offs are not entirely straightforward. At one level, HVF exports have helped at least some rural producers in the developing world to scale up the value chains of global commerce and escape the subservient economic roles they had inherited. In other ways, however, they have perpetuated the exploitation of tropical resources for the benefit of wealthy consumers thousands of kilometres away. To this extent they still function as a form of 'ecological imperialism', especially when the influence of state and corporate power shapes markets in a way that sells off exhaustible tropical resources at discount rates that do not reflect their true value.

Not all south–north trade flows in the post-colonial world have been so damaging or uneven. Many of East Africa's indigenous-owned coffee farms, which supply a large share of the world's prized *arabica* beans, are based on a remarkably sustainable system of mixed cropping and agro-forestry that generates cash income as well as food for locals.[122] Nor have all colonial-era trade hangovers been uniformly exploitative. The protected banana trade between the EU and former colonies in Africa and the Caribbean long helped shield smallholders from the multinational mega-plantations in Central America, even if this meant higher prices for European shoppers.[123] And quite obviously, Western corporations and consumers were not the only, or even principal, actors involved. Farmers, merchants, entrepreneurs, and officials in former colonies actively tried to profit from the natural resources around them, just as many post-colonial governments promoted primary exports as a source of revenue and investment capital.

It is important that we recognize such complexities when assessing the dynamics of recent environmental change. Yet at the same time, we must also acknowledge the heavy responsibility of governments, corporations, and consumers in the global North for the ongoing transformation of tropical environments. Despite the powerful reform currents of the so-called 'era of ecology',[124] the dominant mechanisms of worldwide trade continue to encourage a spatial dissociation of production from consumption, and consumption from its ecological costs.

[122] Kenneth R. Curtis, 'Smaller is Better: A Consensus of Peasants and Bureaucrats in Colonial Tanganyika', in William Gervase Clarence-Smith and Steven Topik (eds), *The Global Coffee Economy in Africa, Asia and Latin America, 1500–1989* (Cambridge: Cambridge University Press, 2003), 312–34, esp. 315–16; Thomas Spear, 'Struggles for the Land: The Political and Moral Economies of Land on Mount Meru', in Maddox, Giblin, and Kimambo (eds), *Custodians*, 213–40, esp. 222.
[123] Gerhard Pohl and Piritta Sorsa, *European Integration and Trade with the Developing World* (Washington, DC: World Bank, 1992), 31–7; Lawrence S. Grossman, *The Political Ecology of Bananas: Contract Farming, Peasants, and Agrarian Change in the Eastern Caribbean* (Chapel Hill, NC: University of North Carolina Press, 1998); Peter Clegg, *The Caribbean Banana Trade: From Colonialism to Globalization* (Basingstoke: Palgrave, 2002), 187–8.
[124] Joachim Radkau, *Die Ära der Ökologie. Eine Weltgeschichte* (Munich: Beck, 2011).

Conclusion

This book has covered a lot of ground, and throughout its excursions it has pursued two main aims: to understand European high imperialism as a socio-ecological endeavour, and to highlight its importance to the broader transformation of the global biosphere since the late nineteenth century. As for the first point, we have examined how the biophysical environment shaped the history of empire in numerous ways, both as a motive force—for instance, how the lure of certain resources or the challenges of certain disease ecologies influenced the geography of European expansion—and as an object of imperial intervention. Efforts to govern forests, fields, soils, and rivers were critical to the extension of European authority in the tropical world, and often represented the cutting edge of colonial state-building on the ground. As for the second point, we have considered the enormous ecological implications of Europe's growing imperial power. Fuelled by fossil energy, the economies of the industrial powers consumed resources and produced goods on an unparalleled scale, and as the demand for raw materials surged, new transport and communication technologies connected producers, consumers, and ecosystems more tightly, and over greater distances, than ever before. The resulting hunger for land and other resources opened a rash of extractive frontiers across the tropical world, many of them actively encouraged by development-oriented colonial states. All throughout the colonial period, there was a seemingly relentless trend towards greater human control over the environment and a fuller mobilization of resources for the sake of economic growth.

Seen through the increasingly 'green' lenses of the twenty-first century, the history of modern imperialism appears more and more as a far-reaching eco-political campaign, one organized around the principles of enclosure, domestication, development, and trade. In view of all the damage it caused, it is tempting to read the story as one of inexorable degradation in which landscapes and peoples in the tropics were ruthlessly exploited in the service of European power. Forests that had long provided resources for rural communities and habitat for countless organisms were sequestered, standardized, and systematically harvested for the commercial production of fuel and timber. Agricultural systems that had been refined over centuries were disrupted or suppressed by the pressure to cultivate new export crops or to switch to supposedly more efficient farming methods. Land that had been communally managed for generations was confiscated for foreign-owned plantations on which the newly dispossessed were often compelled to work as wage labourers. Backwaters that had previously felt only a faint touch of human intervention were transformed into bustling centres of heavy industry that drained food and labour resources from neighbouring areas even as they polluted surrounding rivers, air, and soils. On a global scale, the net flow of resources from the colonies to the metropoles degraded tropical ecosystems, diverted wealth from subject peoples, and skewed their economies for decades to come. In the process, colonized populations themselves were induced to damage their natural surroundings, either in an attempt to profit from the changing circumstances or, in the worst cases, simply in order to survive. Looking back, many of the environmental problems in the developing world—from deforestation and soil degradation to acute water and air pollution—seem rooted, at least in part, in the transformations of the colonial era.

All in all it is a damning critique, and it has its merits. Colonial intervention and commercial penetration caused widespread destruction in many parts of the tropics, as the chapters in this book clearly attest. But if this interpretation has the virtue of simplicity, it fails to account for the multidimensionality of the changes that took place. For one thing, the colonial powers rarely if ever occupied landscapes that had not already been shaped by human hand. Most of the environments they conquered had long been the object of competing claims among indigenous groups or between locals and expansionist outsider states, all of whom altered, improved, and degraded the landscape through their various activities. In most areas, imperial conquest did not initiate a process of anthropogenic change so much as perpetuate and often magnify existing strategies of human use, not least through the ability to apply greater amounts of capital, resources, and technology to the penetration and control of spaces that local rulers had never managed to dominate. In a long-term perspective, the colonial period was not entirely distinct from what preceded it, and it differed even less from what followed.

Accordingly, many of these environmental transformations were propelled by interests and agendas besides those of the colonizers themselves. Certainly European planters, miners, concessionaires, and administrators were responsible for a disproportionate share of the changes, and certainly metropolitan consumers enjoyed the lion's share of the rewards. But many indigenous people, especially elites, also capitalized on the opportunities afforded by colonial trade and transport infrastructure to transform local ecosystems for their own benefit. The socio-ecological project of imperialism was in some respects a franchise venture, one that invited and often acquired the active participation of subject peoples: the Ashanti cocoa farmer, the Sumatran rubber smallholder, the expat-Chinese mine operator. In this sense, writing the environment into the history of empire helps us to 'provincialize' Europe not only as an epistemological framework for understanding human experience, but also as a geographical space of human activity. Doing the latter involves more than just questioning 'the generality of (European) categories'; it also requires us to compare 'on mutually more equal conceptual terms patterns of historical change found there and elsewhere'. Given that people everywhere must alter their surroundings to make a life for themselves, a focus on the biophysical dimensions of the imperial past, and especially one that recognizes the agency of colonial subjects alongside Europeans in building the ecological order of modern imperialism, is a promising way of deploying 'more equal conceptual terms' of analysis.[1]

A third complication is the multifarious nature of European environmental intervention, which included not only the plunder of tropical ecosystems but also efforts to limit or reverse the damage. Conservation was the flip-side of extraction. Over the course of the colonial period, an upwelling of concern about the reckless depletion of natural resources gave rise to an increasingly sophisticated set of regulatory arrangements. The need to place forestry and agricultural systems on a sustainable footing was widely recognized by the late 1800s, and after the turn of the century the principle of 'wise use' was complemented by initiatives to preserve 'nature' for its own sake. Although colonial conservation measures were occasionally ineffectual, and frequently undermined indigenous land-use practices and resource access, they nonetheless helped mitigate some of the worst problems caused by economic exploitation.[2]

A final issue worth noting is the role of the materials, organisms, and ecological relationships that the colonial powers sought to manage. Simply put, the matter mattered.[3] Although it is perhaps an obvious point, it is nonetheless easily obscured in historical narratives by a disciplinary bias towards human activities. To be sure, the environmental and social consequences of imperial interventions unmistakably reflected the intentions, expectations, and preferred production techniques that underlay them, but the specific nature of different crops, soils, mineral deposits, and topographies were also important factors in the equation. Cotton and rubber could be grown in a variety of ways, but their different cultivation requirements meant that the latter tended to bring more benefits and fewer drawbacks (both economic and ecological) to indigenous farmers. Irrigation systems and cultivation techniques that enhanced fertility in one area could prove worthless or even harmful on different soils or different types of terrain. Economic and social historians have long pondered why the increasingly globalized and integrated market for raw materials in the nineteenth and twentieth centuries could generate such diverse outcomes in different producer regions: coercive labour here and free labour there, peasant impoverishment in one place and rising incomes in another. To explain the differences they usually point to factors such as land tenure systems, the policies and relative strength of states, or the structure of particular commodity markets. No doubt such issues were crucial, but part of the answer also lies in how the physical and biological characteristics of the raw materials themselves shaped the manner in which they could be mass-produced—or, more precisely, how the prevailing production methods related to broader ecological processes, and how they resonated or clashed with existing socio-ecological arrangements. This is in

---

[1] See R. Bin Wong's review of Chakrabarty, *Provincializing Europe*, in *American Historical Review*, vol. 106 no. 4 (Oct. 2001), 1322–3, quotes p. 1323. My thanks to Simon Jackson for pointing me to this review.

[2] As argued also in Beinart and Hughes, *Environment*, 14–18, 124–9, 200–13.

[3] See Frank Uekötter, 'Matter Matters: Towards a More "Substantial" Global History', *World History Bulletin*, vol. 29 no. 2 (Fall 2013), 6–8.

no way to argue that such material factors determined historical outcomes, but it is to say that they influenced them.[4]

All of this makes for a much messier but also a much richer history. Of course, interpretative messiness is not to everyone's taste, and some readers may find such caveats too cautious in view of the environmental turbulences and injustices at stake. But recognizing the complex entwinement of imperial power and environmental change is not to sacrifice clarity about the enormous scale of the transformations that took place, nor about the core responsibility of European states, corporations, and individuals in bringing them about. As the preceding chapters clearly demonstrate, colonialism was based on the deliberate exploitation of faraway people and ecosystems. For all the rhetoric of imperial stewardship, structural inequality was an essential characteristic from start to finish. If anything, embracing such complexities helps us identify some of the less obvious hierarchies at work, including the ways in which environmental knowledge—even ecological modes of thinking and conservationist concerns about the productivity of natural systems—formed an important basis for imperial power.

One of the most persistent themes running throughout the book is how ecological problems and frameworks of analysis helped bolster the authority of technical experts over indigenous communities and the resources on which they relied. Time and again, Europe's colonies served as laboratories for the technocratic modes of environmental governance that became such a prevalent feature of the twentieth-century world.[5] Yet they also served as showcases for the equally prevalent sense of overconfidence in the ability of scientists and modern states to manage ecosystems on a 'rational' and sustainable basis. The history of colonial range conservation, agricultural improvement, and large-scale irrigation projects not only points to the centrality of environmental management as a source of social power; it also shows that such enterprises rarely if ever go according to plan, and that we should not expect them to. Given the sheer complexity of the biophysical world, the only sure outcome of human intervention is the need for improvisation, and as far as lessons from history go, that is perhaps the crucial point.[6]

Indeed, the entire imperial engagement with tropical ecosystems was a continual process of improvisation, one whose focus and scope changed significantly over the course of the colonial period. In the beginning, the foremost aim was to conquer supposedly 'underused' environments and boost their economic productivity. From the mid-nineteenth century to the early 1900s, the colonial powers incorporated landscapes and people into new production arrangements. Planters carved huge estates out of the jungle and brought in tens of thousands of labourers

---

[4] A suggestive, though controversial, recent study links the Neolithic rise of social hierarchies and state institutions to the specific characteristics of cereals versus root and tuber crops rather than to differences in land productivity per se (against Diamond, *Guns*): Joram Mayshar, Omer Moav, Zvika Neeman, and Luigi Pascali, 'Cereals, Appropriability and Hierarchy', *CEPR Discussion Paper* 10742 (2015), retrieved at <https://ideas.repec.org/p/cpr/ceprdp/10742.html>.

[5] Tilley, *Africa*; Omnia El Shakry, *The Great Social Laboratory: Subjects of Knowledge in Colonial and Postcolonial Egypt* (Stanford, Calif.: Stanford University Press, 2007).

[6] As emphasized by Ertsen, *Improvising*; van Beusekom, *Negotiating*.

to work them. Loggers drove inroads into the forests to extract the most valuable timber. Mining firms dug, washed, and sluiced their way across entire landscapes in a quest for mineral riches. Commercial hunters and sportsmen fanned into the bush in search of adventure and prized animal parts. Few of these people had much understanding of the ecosystems they were transforming, and nor did the officials who nominally oversaw them. In fact, colonial states generally encouraged such activities through favourable concessionary, infrastructure, and trade policies, and only intervened when the resulting damage seemed to pose an excessive risk to other economic interests or to the long-term viability of the activities themselves.

In retrospect we can discern a significant difference between this initial 'frontier' period of imperialist expansion and the more deliberate, scientifically oriented mode of environmental governance that developed after the 1910s. Although numerous continuities spanned the entire colonial period, in many ways the First World War marked a watershed. If the era of the 'new imperialism' was the heyday of the pioneering entrepreneur, the period after around 1920 saw the ascendancy of the scientific expert. In part this reflected the mounting pressure to justify colonial rule on the basis of technical progress and economic development. It also mirrored a new determination, as Albert Sarraut put it, to marshal colonial resources 'with the aid of new methods, animated by a more realistic spirit, and leading to more rapid action'.[7] The exigencies of wartime mobilization gave colonial administrations a firmer grasp over the territories under their control, but the implications of this change ran in various directions. On the one hand, it led to a more *dirigiste* mode of resource management. For rural communities, such 'scientific' colonialism was in many ways even more domineering than the frontier expansion that preceded it, especially during the interventionist crescendo of the late 1940s and early 1950s. On the other hand, it also encouraged a more nuanced approach towards colonial development. As field researchers and technical officers learned more about the lands and peoples in the colonies, they became more aware of the enormous diversity of socio-ecological relationships and correspondingly more critical of ill-conceived colonial intrusions in the past. After the phase of rapid imperial expansion, 'thinking like an empire' meant more than just amassing territory and rendering it more legible. It also involved an explicit recognition of, and attempts to deal with, bewildering complexity.[8]

Looking back, we can also see many differences between regions, colonies, and empires, which reflected the socio-ecological particularities of specific territories as well as the priorities and decisions of different colonial governments. In the field of indigenous agriculture, improvement efforts in the East Indies stood out not only for their botanical sophistication (the product of Javanese farming skill as much as the scientific standing of Buitenzorg gardens) but also for their unusual socio-ecological attentiveness during the age of 'ethical policy'. The colonies of East Africa played a central role in the development of wildlife conservation, partly because of their distinctive faunal biogeography and partly due to engrained

---

[7] Sarraut, *Mise en valeur*, 27.
[8] Cooper, *Colonialism in Question*, 154; Tilley, *Africa*, 16–23.

attitudes towards hunting among British and German officials in the region. French colonialist narratives of environmental decline in the Maghreb gave a peculiar coloration to the management of arid and semi-arid lands across large parts of West Africa. For indigenous cultivators eager to take advantage of rising commodity prices, the divergent political and labour structures in the Dutch East Indies and the Belgian Congo opened radically different sets of opportunities, just as the fusion of British 'pro-peasant' policies and indigenous entrepreneurial activities in West Africa generated an explosion of commercial cropping that for several decades dwarfed parallel developments in neighbouring French colonies. Although all of the imperial powers in Africa pressured farmers into growing certain export crops, the impact was weakest where indigenous communities maintained more control over land and markets (as in much of West Africa), and was particularly baleful in Portuguese territories where levels of coercion mirrored the repressive politics of the metropole itself after 1938. Within and between empires, diverse structures of trade, land use, 'customary' rights, labour mobilization, and scientific research had important ecological consequences.

Yet what is perhaps most striking with hindsight is not the discrepancies between colonial territories but rather the multitude of cross-border connections that helped reshape tropical environments. This was readily apparent in the realm of commerce and trade. Most colonial industries were multinational from the very beginning, supported by investors throughout the industrialized North and plugged into far-flung commercial networks. Long-distance population movements played a key role on colonial commodity frontiers, which pulled in immigrants of all sorts. Among the expatriate crowd, managers and supervisors hailed from across the (neo-)European world. In the clubs of the Sumatran plantation belt, 'frontiers, languages and customs had become blurred in this assembly. Here all were Europeans of one nationality: they were whites.'[9] Outside the sphere of white privilege, the mass recruitment of workers from China and India was critical for colonial industries throughout Southeast Asia, just as the mines of Central Africa drew in workers from British, Belgian, and Portuguese-ruled areas.

Equally important was the trans-imperial circulation of scientific knowledge and personnel. In the fields of botany, agronomy, and forestry, metropolitan institutions such as Kew Gardens and the Jardin d'Essai were closely connected to colonial hubs like Buitenzorg or India's Dehra Dun institute, along with a plethora of auxiliary gardens and experiment stations. By the turn of the century, cross-border cooperation on wildlife protection brought about a set of internationally recognized conservation norms in the 1900 London Convention. After the First World War such trans-imperial coordination became more extensive and assumed more formal institutional shape through organizations like the Anglo-French Forestry Commission and the Inter-African Bureau for Soil Conservation.[10] Of course, not

[9] Székely, *Tropic Fever*, 85.
[10] Generally: Matthew Hilton and Rana Mitter (eds), *Transnationalism and Contemporary Global History, Past & Present* Supplement 8 (Oxford: Oxford University Press, 2013); Barth and Cvetkovski (eds), *Imperial Co-operation*.

all colonial policies had a trans-imperial dimension, and there remained many differences of focus and approach. But cross-border connections were a central feature of modern imperialism, and the resulting networks of knowledge and expertise provided an important basis for the international architecture of environmental governance in the post-colonial world.

In all of these ways Europe's imperial outreach left a deep imprint on the global environment. More than half a century after the dismantling of colonial rule, the outlines remain readily discernible in the political ecology of today's world. Although drawing clear connections between past and present is always tricky, it is well worth reflecting on how the legacies of European imperialism have continued to shape human relationships with the rest of nature, and indeed show every sign of doing so for many years to come.

Chief among these imperial bequests was a more tightly interconnected world. In ecological terms, the global teleconnections that took shape under colonial rule not only augmented the inter-continental movement of organisms (both deliberate and inadvertent), they also enabled states to structure markets that drew more heavily than ever before on the resources of distant world regions. Without this heightened ability to go beyond local resource constraints, levels of affluence in the industrial world could never have risen as they did. And as consumer appetites in the industrial markets swelled, they pulled in goods faster than natural systems could replenish them. Although the historic roots of our present-day 'empire of things'[11] are chronologically longer and geographically broader than is often assumed, there can be little doubt that the spread of European power markedly expedited its growth. Moreover, it distributed the advantages and drawbacks unevenly between different groups and different parts of the world. By and large, the processes of economic globalization disproportionately benefited the so-called resource 'omnivores' (those possessing the wherewithal to draw in resources from other places) over those living off local resources, first because the omnivores could draw on a wider range of environmental assets, and secondly because the inability of the less prosperous to do so meant that they were more exposed to the problems caused by the consumption patterns of the affluent.[12] To this day, the unequal ecological flows that were channelled by imperial trade circuits remain conspicuously visible, even as they simultaneously help obscure the costs of human exactions on nature.

To a large extent these resource currents were propelled by Europe's quickening industrial metabolism, which both enabled and encouraged European states to extend their overseas reach in the first place. But as the resource-hungry tendrils of the 'new biological regime' spread around the world, they eventually began to take root elsewhere. Ever since the late colonial period, fossil fuels have driven a dramatic transformation of economic life far beyond the confines of the original

---

[11] Frank Trentmann, *Empire of Things: How We Became a World of Consumers, from the Fifteenth Century to the Twenty-First* (London: Allen Lane, 2016).
[12] The metaphor is drawn from Madhav Gadgil and Ramachandra Guha, *Ecology and Equity: The Use and Abuse of Nature in Contemporary India* (London: Routledge, 1995), 3–5.

industrial powers. In dozens of countries around the world—including many former colonies—they gradually replaced the sun as the main source of energy, thereby enabling governments to raise material living standards by transcending age-old constraints on production and consumption. Yet once again, it did not take long for this newfound productive capacity to outgrow nearby resource bases. Consequently, many of these states have themselves struck out in search of land and energy subsidies from afar, not unlike the European powers over a century ago. In the process, they have followed a formula that recalls the methods by which Europeans seized control of their own territories and resources during the age of high imperialism: defining natural assets as economically 'idle', alienating them for more efficient exploitation, and casting it all as a contribution to 'development' for everyone concerned. To what extent the planet can supply the subsidies and absorb the wastes of this ever-expanding ecological regime, and to what extent new technologies might keep the costs from catching up with us, are the key questions of the twenty-first century.

Against this backdrop, perhaps the most important environmental legacy of European imperialism was to reinforce and propagate a kind of colonial attitude towards nature, one based on the erroneous yet stubbornly persistent distinction between natural processes and an increasingly technological civilization existing above them. As we have seen, this particular understanding of the world, in which human progress was equated with a technical mastery of the biophysical environment, was an ideological cornerstone of European empire. Long after the end of Europe's global supremacy it has lived on in a tenacious determination to conquer and domesticate nature, to manage it, to maximize its performance. The inherent expansionism of the imperial enterprise still reverberates in our preoccupation with perpetual economic growth. Even as we wrestle with the colossal implications of living in the Anthropocene, such ideas still nourish a steadfast faith that technology will give us yet greater control over the environment and ultimately save the day.

It is, of course, impossible to predict how new technologies might mitigate or exacerbate our current ecological difficulties, and it is conceivable that many critics underestimate their potential, especially in the crucial realm of energy. But given the sketchy record of eco-cratic interventions in the past, and given the enormous risks associated with the new generation of 'geo-engineering' schemes, a sizeable dose of scepticism is warranted by history.[13] In this context, the warnings voiced over three-quarters of a century ago by the renowned geographer Carl Ortwin Sauer retain an almost eerie current relevance:

> The doctrine of a passing frontier of nature replaced by a permanently and sufficiently expanding frontier of technology is a contemporary and characteristic expression of occidental culture, itself a historical-geographic product. This 'frontier' attitude has the recklessness of an optimism that has become habitual, but which is residual from

---

[13] On geo-engineering, Clive Hamilton, *Earthmasters: The Dawn of the Age of Climate Engineering* (New Haven: Yale University Press, 2014).

the brave days when north-European freebooters overran the world and put it under tribute. We have not yet learned the difference between yield and loot. We do not like to be economic realists.[14]

Much has changed since these comments were made in 1938: the emergence of mass environmental movements and powerful environmental protection agencies, the growth of fair- and green-trade schemes, the advent of ecological economics as a field of academic research and political activism. But there can be no doubt that our prevailing political and economic systems still do not adequately appreciate the difference between yield and loot. Long after the global frontier has receded, we continue to expect windfalls from nature.[15] The swelling ranks of the world's 'omnivores' are, to quote again from Sauer, still 'prone to think of an ever ample world created for our benefit, by optimistic anthropocentric habits of thinking'. As a result, it still 'suits our thinking to rely on a continuing adequacy on the part of the technician to meet our demands for production of goods'.[16] At a global level, the progress that has been achieved through tighter pollution and efficiency standards has been more than offset by rising overall levels of consumption. Recent improvements in the most technologically advanced countries—cleaner air and water, declining CO_2 emissions, expanding forest cover—have as much to do with the displacement of their dirtiest activities as with a genuine reduction of ecological burdens. Unfortunately, the political determination that would be required to reverse these trends is not helped by the incremental character of the most serious environmental threats we now face. The creeping, 'unsensational' consequences of soil deterioration, global warming, the depletion of freshwater sources, and biodiversity loss receive far less media attention than they merit. Nor is the necessary resolve augmented by the fact that the people who bear the brunt of this 'slow violence' are often precisely those who lack the political and economic power to change things.[17] The expansion of consumer appetites and the pursuit of endless growth still take precedence over the logic of prudence, with the worst consequences passed on to poorer countries or future generations.

These patterns have a long history, and all of them are, in one way or another, deeply enmeshed in the fabric of the imperial past. Hopefully this book will help us realize our many connections with this past, and with the distant ecosystems that it bound together. With any luck, it may sharpen our awareness of the environmental inequalities of today's world, and the enduring structures that perpetuate them. Most importantly, perhaps, it might help us see our abiding fascination with an ever-expanding material world as the historical contingency that it is, an ideological holdover from a bygone age of conquest that is profoundly inappropriate—even

[14] Sauer, 'Theme of Plant and Animal Destruction', 154.
[15] On the long history of such ideas: Fredrik Albritton Jonsson, 'The Origins of Cornucopianism: A Preliminary Genealogy', *Critical Historical Studies*, vol. 1 no. 1 (Spring 2014), 151–68.
[16] Sauer, 'Theme of Plant and Animal Destruction', 152–3.
[17] Nixon, *Slow Violence*.

dangerous—for a post-frontier era in which resources are scarce and many of the ecological buffers that previously cushioned the impacts of human activities have already been used up. Learning how to negotiate these constraints, and creating a new way of living in Nature that does not treat it as an inexhaustible supply of resources, is our biggest collective challenge for the future.

Bibliography

SECONDARY LITERATURE

Abuzinada, A. H., et al. (eds), *Protecting the Gulf's Marine Ecosystems from Pollution* (Basel: Birkhäuser Verlag, 2008).

Acot, P., and Drouin, J.-M., 'L'Introduction en France des idées de l'écologie scientifique américaine dans l'entre-deux-guerres', *Revue d'histoire des sciences*, vol. 50 no. 4 (1997), 461–80.

Adams, J. S., and McShane, T. O., *The Myth of Wild Africa: Conservation without Illusion* (Berkeley: University of California Press, 1996).

Adams, W. M., *Wasting the Rain: Rivers, People and Planning in Africa* (Minneapolis: University of Minnesota Press, 1992).

Adams, W. M., *Against Extinction: The Story of Conservation* (London: Earthscan, 2004).

Adams, W. M., and Mulligan, M. (eds), *Decolonizing Nature: Strategies for Conservation in a Post-Colonial Era* (London: Earthscan, 2002).

Adas, M., *The Burma Delta: Economic Development and Social Change on an Asian Rice Frontier, 1852–1941* (Madison, Wis.: University of Wisconsin Press, 1974).

Adas, M., *Machines as the Measure of Men: Science, Technology, and Ideologies of Western Dominance* (Ithaca, NY: Cornell University Press, 1989).

Adelman, J., 'Mimesis and Rivalry: European Empires and Global Regimes', *Journal of Global History*, vol. 10, issue 1 (March 2015), 77–98.

Aditjondro, G. J., 'Large Dam Victims and their Defenders: The Emergence of an Anti-Dam Movement in Indonesia', in Philip Hirsch and Carol Warren (eds.), *The Politics of Environment in Southeast Asia: Resources and Resistance* (London: Routledge, 1998), 28–54.

Agnihotri, I., 'Ecology, Land Use and Colonisation: The Canal Colonies of Punjab', *Indian Economic and Social History Review*, vol. 33 no. 1 (1996), 37–58.

Aiken, S. R., et al., *Development and Environment in Peninsular Malaysia* (Singapore: McGraw-Hill International, 1982).

Ali, I., *The Punjab under Imperialism, 1885–1947* (Princeton: Princeton University Press, 1988).

Allen, R. C., *The British Industrial Revolution in Global Perspective* (Cambridge: Cambridge University Press, 2009).

Alshaebi, F. Y., 'Risk Assessment at Abandoned Tin Mine in Sungai Lembing, Pahang, Malaysia', *The Electronic Journal of Geotechnical Engineering*, vol. 14 (2009) bundle E:9, 2–3.

Altieri, M., *Agroecology: The Science of Sustainable Agriculture* (Boulder, Colo.: Westview, 1995).

Amrith, S. S., *Migration and Diaspora in Modern Asia* (Cambridge: Cambridge University Press, 2011).

Andaya, B. W., and Andaya, L. Y., *A History of Malaysia*, 2nd edn (Houndmills: Palgrave, 2001).

Anderson, D., and Grove, R. H. (eds), *Conservation in Africa: People, Policies and Practice* (Cambridge: Cambridge University Press, 1987).

Anderson, D. M., 'Depression, Dust Bowl, Demography, and Drought: The Colonial State and Soil Conservation in East Africa during the 1930s', *African Affairs*, vol. 83 no. 332 (July 1984), 321–43.

Anderson, D. M., *Eroding the Commons: The Politics of Ecology in Baringo, Kenya 1890s–1963* (Oxford: James Currey, 2002).

Anderson, R. S., Grove, R., and Hiebert, K. (eds), *Islands, Forests and Gardens in the Caribbean: Conservation and Conflict in Environmental History* (Oxford: Macmillan Caribbean, 2006).

Ang, L. H., and Ho, W. M., 'Afforestation of Tin Tailings in Malaysia', Forest Research Institute Malaysia (2002).

Anker, P., *Imperial Ecology: Environmental Order in the British Empire, 1895–1945* (Cambridge, Mass.: Harvard University Press, 2001).

Anreiter, P. (ed.), *Mining in European History and its Impact on Environment and Human Societies* (Innsbruck: Innsbruck University Press, 2010).

Arnold, D., *Famine: Social Crisis and Historical Change* (Oxford: Blackwell, 1988).

Arnold, D., *The Problem of Nature: Environment, Culture and European Expansion* (Oxford: Blackwell, 1996).

Arnold, D., *The Tropics and the Travelling Gaze: India, Landscape, and Science, 1800–1856* (Seattle: University of Washington Press, 2006).

Arnold, D., and Guha, R. (eds), *Nature, Culture, Imperialism: Essays on the Environmental History of South Asia* (Delhi: Oxford University Press, 1995).

Arsan, A., *Interlopers of Empire: The Lebanese Diaspora in Colonial French West Africa* (Oxford: Oxford University Press, 2014).

Arumugam, R. S., *State and Oil in Burma: An Introductory Survey* (Singapore: Institute of Southeast Asian Studies, 1977).

Asante, M. S., *Deforestation in Ghana: Explaining the Chronic Failure of Forest Preservation Policies in a Developing Country* (Lanham, Md: University Press of America, 2005).

Aso, M., 'Patriotic Hygiene: Tracing New Places of Knowledge Production about Malaria in Vietnam, 1919–75', *Journal of Southeast Asian Studies*, vol. 44 (2013), 423–43.

Atangana, M., *French Investment in Colonial Cameroon. The FIDES Era (1946–1957)* (New York: Peter Lang, 2009).

Austin, G., *Labour, Land and Capital in Ghana: From Slavery to Free Labour in Asante, 1807–1956* (Rochester, NY: University of Rochester Press, 2005).

Austin, G., 'Vent for Surplus or Productivity Breakthrough? The Ghanaian Cocoa Take-off, c.1890–1936', *Economic History Review*, vol. 67 no. 4 (2014), 1035–64.

Austin, G. (ed.), *Economic Development and Environmental History in the Anthropocene: Perspectives on Asia and Africa* (London: Bloomsbury, 2017).

Auty, R. M., *Sustaining Development in Mineral Economies: The Resource Curse Thesis* (London: Routledge, 1993).

Ax, C. F., Brimnes, N., Jensen, N. T., and Oslund, K. (eds), *Cultivating the Colonies: Colonial States and their Environmental Legacies* (Athens, Oh.: Ohio University Press, 2011).

Bachmann, S., *Zwischen Patriotismus und Wissenschaft. Die schweizerischen Naturschutzpioniere (1900–1938)* (Zurich: Chronos, 1999).

Badré, L., *Histoire de la forêt française* (Paris: Arthaud, 1983).

Bainton, N. A., *The Lihir Destiny: Cultural Responses to Mining in Melanesia* (Canberra: ANU Press, 2010).

Balamurugan, G., 'Tin Mining and Sediment Supply in Peninsular Malaysia with Special Reference to the Kelang River Basin', *The Environmentalist*, vol. 11 no. 4 (1991), 281–91.

Bald, D., and Bald, G., *Das Forschungsinstitut Amani. Wirtschaft und Wissenschaft in der deutschen Kolonialpolitik Ostafrika 1900–1918* (Munich: IFO, 1972).

Ballantyne, T., *Between Colonialism and Diaspora: Sikh Cultural Formations in an Imperial World* (Durham, NC: Duke University Press, 2006).

Balon, E. K., and Coche, A. G. (eds), *Lake Kariba: A Man-Made Tropical Ecosystem in Central Africa* (The Hague: Junk, 1974).

Bamberg, J. H., *The History of the British Petroleum Company*, vol. 2: *The Anglo-Iranian Years 1928–1954* (Cambridge: Cambridge University Press, 1994).

Barlow, C., *The Natural Rubber Industry: Its Development, Technology, and Economy in Malaysia* (Oxford: Oxford University Press, 1978).

Barnett, T., *The Gezira Scheme: An Illusion of Development* (London: Cass, 1977).

Barrow Jr, M. V., *Nature's Ghosts: Confronting Extinction from the Age of Jefferson to the Age of Ecology* (Chicago: University of Chicago Press, 2009).

Bart, F., *Montagnes d'Afrique, terres paysannes: le cas du Rwanda* (Bordeaux: CEGET, 1993).

Barth, B., and Osterhammel, Jürgen (eds), *Zivilisierungsmissionen. Imperiale Weltverbesserung seit dem 18. Jahrhundert* (Konstanz: UVK, 2005).

Barth, V., and Cvetkovski, R. (eds), *Imperial Co-operation and Transfer, 1870–1930: Empires and Encounters* (London: Bloomsbury, 2015).

Barton, G. A., *Empire Forestry and the Origins of Environmentalism* (Cambridge: Cambridge University Press, 2002).

Barton, G. A., 'Environmentalism, Development and British Policy in the Middle East 1945–65', *Journal of Imperial and Commonwealth History*, vol. 38 (2010), 619–39.

Bassett, T. J., *The Peasant Cotton Revolution in West Africa: Côte d'Ivoire, 1880–1995* (Cambridge: Cambridge University Press, 2001).

Bayliss-Smith, T., 'Energy Flows and Agrarian Change in Karnataka: The Green Revolution at Micro-scale', in Tim Bayliss-Smith and Sudhir Wanmali (eds), *Understanding Green Revolutions: Agrarian Change and Development Planning in South Asia* (Cambridge: Cambridge University Press, 1984), 153–72.

Bayly, C. A., and Harper, T. N., *Forgotten Armies: Britain's Asian Empire and the War with Japan* (London: Penguin, 2005).

Bayly, C. A., *Indian Society and the Making of the British Empire* (Cambridge: Cambridge University Press, 1988).

Bayly, C. A., *The Birth of the Modern World, 1780–1914: Global Connections and Comparisons* (Oxford: Blackwell, 2004).

Beattie, J., *Empire and Environmental Anxiety: Health, Science, Art and Conservation in South Asia and Australasia, 1800–1920* (Basingstoke: Palgrave, 2011).

Beattie, J., Melillo, E., and O'Gorman, E. (eds), *Eco-Cultural Networks and the British Empire: New Views on Environmental History* (London: Bloomsbury, 2015).

Beckert, S., 'Emancipation and Empire: Reconstructing the Worldwide Web of Cotton Production in the Age of the American Civil War', *American Historical Review*, vol. 109 no. 5 (Dec. 2004), 1405–38.

Beckert, S., *Empire of Cotton: A New History of Global Capitalism* (London: Allen Lane, 2014).

Beinart, W., *The Rise of Conservation in South Africa: Settlers, Livestock, and the Environment 1770–1950* (Oxford: Oxford University Press, 2003).

Beinart, W., Brown, K., and Gilfoyle, D., 'Experts and Expertise in Colonial Africa Reconsidered: Science and the Interpenetration of Knowledge', *African Affairs*, vol. 108 no. 432 (May 2009), 413–33.

Beinart, W., and Coates, P., *Environment and History: The Taming of Nature in the USA and South Africa* (London: Routledge, 1995).

Beinart, W., and Hughes, L., *Environment and Empire* (Oxford: Oxford University Press, 2007).

Beinart, W., and McGregor, J. (eds), *Social History and African Environments* (Oxford: James Currey, 2003).

Beinart, W., and Middleton, K., 'Plant Transfers in Historical Perspective: A Review Article', *Environment and History*, vol. 10 (2004).

Belich, J., *Replenishing the Earth: The Settler Revolution and the Rise of the Anglo-World, 1783–1939* (Oxford: Oxford University Press, 2009).

Benjaminsen, T. A., and Berge, G., 'Myths of Timbuktu: From African El Dorado to Desertification', *International Journal of Political Economy*, vol. 34 no. 1 (Spring 2004), 31–59.

Bennett, B., and Hodge, J. (eds), *Science and Empire: Knowledge and Networks of Science in the British Empire 1850–1970* (Houndmills: Palgrave, 2011).

Bennett, B. M., and Hodge, J. M. (eds), *Science and Empire: Knowledge and Networks of Science across the British Empire, 1800–1970* (Houndmills: Palgrave, 2011).

Bennett, T., and Joyce, P. (eds), *Material Powers: Cultural Studies, History and the Material Turn* (London: Routledge, 2010).

Benton, L., *Law and Colonial Cultures: Legal Regimes and World History, 1400–1900* (Cambridge: Cambridge University Press, 2002).

Berger, E. L., *Labour, Race, and Colonial Rule: The Copperbelt from 1924 to Independence* (Oxford: Clarendon Press, 1974).

Berkes, F., 'Rethinking Community-Based Conservation', *Conservation Biology*, vol. 18 no. 3 (June 2004), 621–30.

Berkes, F., *Sacred Ecology*, 2nd edn (London: Routledge, 2008).

Berry, S., *Cocoa, Custom, and Socio-economic Change in Rural Western Nigeria* (Oxford: Clarendon, 1975).

Berry, S., *No Condition is Permanent: The Social Dynamics of Agrarian Change in sub-Saharan Africa* (Madison, Wis.: University of Wisconsin Press, 1993).

Betts, P., and Ross, C. (eds), *Heritage in the Modern World: Historical Preservation in Global Perspective. Past & Present* supplement 10 (Oxford: Oxford University Press, 2015).

Bieri, F., *From Blood Diamonds to the Kimberley Process: How NGOs Cleaned up the Global Diamond Industry* (Farnham: Ashgate, 2010).

Biggs, D., 'Managing a Rebel Landscape: Conservation, Pioneers, and the Revolutionary Past in the U Minh Forest, Vietnam', *Environmental Histor*, vol. 10 no. 3 (July 2005), 448–76.

Biggs, D., *Quagmire: Nation-Building and Nature in the Mekong Delta* (Seattle: University of Washington Press, 2010).

Black, B., *Petrolia: The Landscape of America's First Oil Boom* (Baltimore: Johns Hopkins University Press, 2000).

Black, B., *Crude Reality: Petroleum in World History* (Lanham, Md: Rowman & Littlefield, 2012).

Black, M., 'Interior's Exterior: The State, Mining Companies, and Resource Ideologies in the Point Four Program', *Diplomatic History*, vol. 40 (2016), 81–110.

Bloembergen, M., and Raben, R. (eds), *Het koloniale beschavingsoffensief: wegen naar het nieuwe Indië, 1890–1950* (Leiden: KITLV, 2009).

Bolton, B. (ed.), *The Fly River, Papua New Guinea: Environmental Studies in an Impacted Tropical River System* (Amsterdam: Elsevier, 2009).

Bond, P., 'Sub-imperialism as Lubricant of Neoliberalism: South African "Deputy Sheriff" Duty within BRICS', *Third World Quarterly*, vol. 34 no. 2 (2013), 251–71.

Bonin, H., Hodeir, C., and Klein, J.-F. (eds), *L'Esprit économique impérial, 1830–1970: groupes de pression & réseaux du patronat colonial en France et dans l'Empire* (Paris: SFHOM, 2008).

Bonneuil, C., *Des savants pour l'Empire: la structuration des recherches scientifiques coloniales au temps de 'la mise en valeur des colonies françaises' 1917–1945* (Paris: Éditions de l'ORSTOM, 1991).

Bonneuil, C., 'Development as Experiment: Science and State Building in Late Colonial and Postcolonial Africa, 1930–1970', *Osiris*, vol. 15 (2000), 258–81.

Bonneuil, C., Denis, G., and Mayaud, J.-L. (eds), *Sciences, chercheurs et agriculture: pour une histoire de la recherche agronomique* (Paris: L'Harmattan, 2008).

Bonneuil, C., and Fressoz, J.-B., *L'Événement Anthropocène* (Paris: Seuil, 2013).

Bonneuil, C., and Kleiche, M., *Du jardin d'essais colonial à la station expérimentale, 1880–1930: éléments pour une histoire du CIRAD* (Paris: CIRAD, 1993).

Boomgaard, P., 'Forest Management and Exploitation in Colonial Java, 1677–1879', *Forest and Conservation History*, vol. 36 (1992), 4–14.

Boomgaard, P., 'Oriental Nature, its Friends and its Enemies: Conservation of Nature in Late-Colonial Indonesia, 1889–1949', *Environment and History*, vol. 5 (1999), 257–92.

Boomgaard, P., *Frontiers of Fear: Tigers and People in the Malay World, 1600–1950* (New Haven: Yale University Press, 2001).

Boomgaard, P., *Southeast Asia: An Environmental History* (Oxford: ABC-Clio, 2007).

Boomgaard, P. (ed.), *Empire and Science in the Making: Dutch Colonial Scholarship in Comparative Global Perspective, 1760–1830* (Basingstoke: Palgrave, 2013).

Boomgaard, P., and Brown, I. (eds), *Weathering the Storm: The Economies of Southeast Asia in the 1930s Depression* (Leiden: KITLV, 2000).

Boomgaard, P., Colombijn, F., and Henley, D. (eds), *Paper Landscapes: Explorations in the Environmental History of Indonesia* (Leiden: KITLV, 1997).

Booth, A., *Agricultural Development in Indonesia* (London: Allen & Unwin, 1988).

Bose, S., *A Hundred Horizons: The Indian Ocean in the Age of Global Empire* (Cambridge, Mass.: Harvard University Press, 2006).

Boserup, E., *The Conditions of Agricultural Growth: The Economics of Agrarian Change under Population Pressure* (London: Allen & Unwin, 1965).

Boulaine, J., *Histoire de l'agronomie en France* (Paris: Tec & Doc-Lavoisier, 1996).

Bowman, A., 'Ecology to Technocracy: Scientists, Surveys and Power in the Agricultural Development of Late-Colonial Zambia', *Journal of Southern African Studies*, vol. 37 no. 1 (2011), 135–53.

Bradley, K., *Copper Venture: The Discovery and Development of Roan Antelope and Mufulira* (London: Parrish, 1952).

Braudel, F., *The Structures of Everyday Life: The Limits of the Possible* (London: Collins, 1981).

Bray, F., *The Rice Economies: Technology and Development in Asian Societies* (Berkeley: University of California Press, 1986).

Bridge, G., and Le Billon, P., *Oil* (Cambridge: Polity, 2013).

Brocheux, P., *The Mekong Delta: Ecology, Economy and Evolution, 1860–1960* (Madison, Wis.: University of Wisconsin Press, 1995).

Brockington, D., *Fortress Conservation: The Preservation of the Mkomazi Game Reserve, Tanzania* (Oxford: James Currey, 2002).

Brockway, L. H., *Science and Colonial Expansion: The Role of the British Royal Botanic Gardens* (New York: Academic Press, 1979).

Brown, T., 'Agrarian Crisis in Punjab and "Natural Farming" as a Response', *South Asia: Journal of South Asian Studies*, vol. 36 (2013), 229–42.

Bryant, R., 'Shifting the Cultivator: The Politics of Teak Regeneration in Colonial Burma', *Modern Asian Studies*, vol. 27 (1994), 225–50.

Bryant, R. L., *The Political Ecology of Forestry in Burma 1824–1994* (London: Hurst & Co., 1997).

Buchy, M., 'Histoire forestière de l'Indochine (1850–1954)—Perspectives de recherche', *Revue française d'histoire d'outre-mer*, no. 299 (1993), 219–50.

Burbank, J., and Cooper, F., *Empires in World History: Power and the Politics of Difference* (Princeton: Princeton University Press, 2010).

Burger, J., *Oil Spills* (New Brunswick, NJ: Rutgers University Press, 1997).

Burke III, E., and Pomeranz, K. (eds), *The Environment and World History* (Berkeley: University of California Press, 2009).

Burr, C., 'Some Adventures of the Boys: Enniskillen Township's "Foreign Drillers", Imperialism, and Colonial Discourse, 1873–1923', *Labour/Le Travail*, vol. 51 (Spring 2003), 47–80.

Butcher, J. G., 'The Marine Animals of Southeast Asia: Towards a Demographic History, 1850–2000', in Peter Boomgaard, David Henley, and Manon Osseweijer (eds), *Muddied Waters: Historical and Contemporary Perspectives on Management of Forests and Fisheries in Island Southeast Asia* (Leiden: KITLV, 2005), 63–96.

Butler, L. J., *Copper Empire: Mining and the Colonial State in Northern Rhodesia, c.1930–1964* (Houndmills: Palgrave, 2007).

Butlin, R., *Geographies of Empire: European Empires and Colonies c.1880–1960* (Cambridge: Cambridge University Press, 2009).

Byerlee, D., *Modern Varieties, Productivity, and Sustainability* (Mexico, DF: CIMMYT, 1994).

Cadoret, A. (ed.), *Protection de la nature: histoire et idéologie* (Paris: Harmattan, 1985).

Campbell, B. K., *Les Enjeux de la bauxite: la Guinée face aux multinationales de l'aluminium* (Montréal: Presses de l'Université de Montréal, 1983).

Carruthers, J., *The Kruger National Park: A Social and Political History* (Pietermaritzburg: Natal University Press, 1995).

Carswell, G., *Cultivating Success in Uganda: Kigezi Farmers and Colonial Policies* (Oxford: James Currey, 2007).

Carter, P., *The Road to Botany Bay: An Essay in Spatial History* (London: Faber, 1987).

Chakrabarty, D., *Provincializing Europe: Postcolonial Thought and Historical Difference* (Princeton: Princeton University Press, 2000).

Chambers, R. (ed.), *The Volta Resettlement Experience* (London: Pall Mall, 1970).

Chang, J.-H., 'The Agricultural Potential of the Humid Tropics', *Geographical Review*, vol. 58 (1968), 333–61.

Chang, J.-H., 'Potential Photosynthesis and Crop Productivity', *Annals of the Association of American Geographers*, vol. 60 no. 1 (Mar. 1970), 92–101.

Charlesworth, N., 'The Myth of the Deccan Riots of 1875', *Modern Asian Studies*, vol. 6 no. 4 (1972), 401–21.

Charlesworth, N., *Peasants and Imperial Rule: Agriculture and Agrarian Society in the Bombay Presidency, 1850–1935* (Cambridge: Cambridge University Press, 1985).

Chatelin, Y., and Bonneuil, C. (eds), *Nature et environnement* (Paris: Orstom Éditions, 1995).

Chatterjee, P., *Nationalist Thought in the Colonial World: A Derivative Discourse?* (London: Zed, 1986).

Chattopadhyay, B., 'Growth and Fluctuation of Foodgrain Output in India since Independence', in Boudhayan Chattopadhyay and Pierre Spitz (eds), *Food Systems and Society in Eastern India* (Geneva: UNRISD, 1987), 133–54.

Chauveau, J.-P., 'La "Mise en valeur" coloniale en pays baule: régression économique et autonomie paysanne', *Tiers-Monde*, vol. 23 no. 90 (1982), 315–20.

Chidumayo, E. N., 'Land Use, Deforestation and Reforestation in the Zambian Copperbelt', *Land Degradation & Development*, vol. 1 no. 3 (1989), 209–16.

Chollet, R., *Planteurs en Indochine française* (Paris: pensée universelle, 1981).

Cioc, M., *The Game of Conservation: International Treaties to Protect the World's Migratory Animals* (Athens, Oh.: Ohio University Press, 2009).

Clarence-Smith, W. G., 'Plantation versus Smallholder Production of Cocoa: The Legacy of the German Period in Cameroon', in Peter Geschiere and Piet Konings (eds), *Itinéraires d'accumulation au Cameroun* (Paris: Karthala, 1993), 187–216.

Clarence-Smith, W. G. (ed.), *Cocoa Pioneer Fronts since 1800: The Role of Smallholders, Planters and Merchants* (Houndmills: Macmillan, 1996).

Clarence-Smith, W. G., *Cocoa and Chocolate, 1765–1914* (London: Routledge, 2000).

Clarence-Smith, W. G., 'The Battle for Rubber in the Second World War: Cooperation and Resistance', in Jonathan Curry-Machado (ed.), *Global Histories, Imperial Commodities, Local Interactions* (Houndslow: Palgrave, 2013), 204–23.

Clay, J., *World Agriculture and the Environment* (Washington, DC: Island Press, 2004).

Cleary, M., 'Managing the Forest in Colonial Indochina *c.*1900–1940', *Modern Asian Studies*, vol. 39 no. 2 (May 2005), 257–83.

Clegg, P., *The Caribbean Banana Trade: From Colonialism to Globalization* (Basingstoke: Palgrave, 2002).

Cliffe, L., 'Nationalism and the Reaction to Enforced Agricultural Change in Tanganyika during the Colonial Period', in Lionel Cliffe and John Saul (eds), *Socialism in Tanzania: An Interdisciplinary Reader* (Dar es Salaam: East African Publishing House, 1972), 17–24.

Cline-Cole, R., and Madge, C. (eds), *Contesting Forestry in West Africa* (Aldershot: Ashgate, 2000).

Coe, S. D., and Coe, M. D., *The True History of Chocolate* (London: Thames & Hudson, 1996).

Colson, E., *Social Organisation of the Gwembe Tonga* (Manchester: Manchester University Press, 1960).

Colson, E., *The Social Consequences of Resettlement: The Impact of the Kariba Resettlement upon the Gwembe Tonga* (Manchester: Manchester University Press, 1971).

Conklin, H. C., *Hanunóo Agriculture: A Report on an Integral System of Shifting Cultivation in the Philippines* (Rome: FAO, 1957).

Conrad, S., and Sachsenmaier, D. (eds), *Competing Visions of World Order: Global Moments and Movements, 1880s–1930s* (Houndmills: Palgrave, 2007).

Conte, C., 'Creating Wild Places from Domesticated Landscapes: The Internationalization of the American Wilderness Concept', in Michael Lewis (ed.), *American Wilderness: A New History* (Oxford: Oxford University Press, 2007), 223–42.

Conte, C. A., 'Imperial Science, Tropical Ecology, and Indigenous History: Tropical Research Stations in Northeastern German East Africa, 1896 to the Present', in Gregory Blue, Martin Bunton, and Ralph Croizier (eds), *Colonialism and the Modern World* (London: M. E. Sharpe, 2002), 246–61.

Conway, G., *The Doubly Green Revolution: Food for All in the 21st Century* (Harmondsworth: Penguin, 1997).

Cooper, F., *Decolonization and African Society* (Cambridge: Cambridge University Press, 1996).

Cooper, F., *Africa Since 1940: The Past of the Present* (Cambridge: Cambridge University Press, 2002).

Cooper, F., *Colonialism in Question: Theory, Knowledge, History* (Berkeley: University of California Press, 2005).

Cooper, F. *Africa in the World: Capitalism, Empire, Nation-State* (Cambridge, Mass.: Harvard University Press, 2014).

Cooper, F., and Packard, R. (eds), *International Development and the Social Sciences: Essays on the History and Politics of Knowledge* (Berkeley: University of California Press, 1997).

Coppolillo, P. B., 'The Landscape Ecology of Pastoral Herding: Spatial Analysis of Land Use and Livestock Production in East Africa', *Human Ecology*, vol. 28 (2000), 527–60.

Coquery-Vidrovitch, C., *Le Congo au temps des grandes compagnies concessionaires 1898–1930* (Paris: Mouton & Co., 1972).

Corley, T. A. B., *A History of the Burmah Oil Company 1886–1966*, 2 vols (London: Heinemann, 1983, 1988).

Corsi, M., 'Communalism and the Green Revolution in Punjab', *Journal of Developing Societies*, vol. 22 (2006), 85–109.

Corvol, A., *L'Homme aux bois: histoire des relations de l'homme et de la forêt (XVIIe–XXe siècle)* (Paris: Fayard, 1987).

Corvol, A., *Forêt et montagne* (Paris: Harmattan, 2015).

Cô-Trung, M. D., *La Compagnie générale des oléagineux tropicaux en Casamance: autopsie d'une opération de mise en valeur coloniale (1948–1962)* (Paris: Karthala, 1998).

Cotula, L., *The Great African Land Grab? Agricultural Investment and the Global Food System* (London: Zed, 2013).

Craig, J., 'Putting Privatisation into Practice: The Case of Zambia Consolidated Copper Mines Limited', *Journal of Modern African Studies*, vol. 39 (2001), 389–410.

Cronin, S., 'Popular Politics, the New State and the Birth of the Iranian Working Class: The 1929 Abadan Oil Refinery Strike', *Middle Eastern Studies*, vol. 46 no. 5 (2010), 699–732.

Cronon, W., *Nature's Metropolis: Chicago and the Great West* (New York: Norton, 1991).

Cronon, W., Miles, G., and Gitlin, J. (eds), *Under an Open Sky: Rethinking America's Western Past* (New York: Norton, 1992).

Crosby, A., *The Columbian Exchange: Biological and Cultural Consequences of 1492* (Westport Conn.: Greenwood, 1972).

Crosby, A., *Ecological Imperialism: The Biological Expansion of Europe, 900–1900* (Cambridge: Cambridge University Press, 1986).

Crosby, A., *Children of the Sun: A History of Humanity's Unappeasable Appetite for Energy* (New York: Norton, 2006).

Cullather, N., 'Development? It's History', *Diplomatic History*, vol. 24 (2000), 641–53.

Cullather, N., *The Hungry World: America's Cold War Battle against Poverty in Asia* (Cambridge, Mass.: Harvard University Press, 2010).

Curry-Machado, J., ' "Rich Flames and Hired Tears": Sugar, Sub-imperial Agents and the Cuban Phoenix of Empire', *Journal of Global History*, vol. 4 (2009), 33–56.

Curtin, P. D., *The Rise and Fall of the Plantation Complex: Essays in Atlantic History* (Cambridge: Cambridge University Press, 1990).

Curtis, K. R., 'Smaller is Better: A Consensus of Peasants and Bureaucrats in Colonial Tanganyika', in William G. Clarence-Smith and S. Topik (eds), *The Global Coffee Economy in Africa, Asia and Latin America, 1500–1989* (Cambridge: Cambridge University Press, 2003), 312–34.

Cushman, G. T., *Guano and the Opening of the Pacific World: A Global Ecological History* (Cambridge: Cambridge University Press, 2013).

Dahlberg, K., *Beyond the Green Revolution: The Ecology and Politics of Global Agricultural Development* (New York: Plenum Press, 1979).

Daley, B., and Griggs, P., 'Mining the Reefs and Cays: Coral, Guano and Rock Phosphate Extraction in the Great Barrier Reef, Australia, 1844–1940', *Environment and History*, vol. 12 (2006), 395–434.

Das, P., 'Hugh Cleghorn and Forest Conservancy in India', *Environment and History*, vol. 11 no. 1 (Feb. 2005), 55–82.

Das, S. N., Thakur, R. S., and Ray, H. S., 'Red Mud Pollution Problems: Some Observations', *Environmental and Waste Management* (1998), 11–16.

Davidson, C. M., *The United Arab Emirates: A Study in Survival* (Boulder, Colo.: Rienner, 2005).

Davidson, C. M., *Dubai: The Vulnerability of Success* (London: Hurst, 2008).

Davidson, C. M., *Abu Dhabi: Oil and Beyond* (London: Hurst, 2009).

Davis, C. E., *Jamaica in the World Aluminium Industry, 1938–1973* (Kingston: Jamaica Bauxite Institute, 1989).

Davis, D. K., *Resurrecting the Granary of Rome: Environmental History and French Colonial Expansion in North Africa* (Athens, Oh.: Ohio University Press, 2007).

Davis, D. K., *The Arid Lands: History, Power, Knowledge* (Cambridge, Mass.: MIT Press, 2016).

Davis, M., *Late Victorian Holocausts: El Niño Famines and the Making of the Third World* (London: Verso, 2001).

Dean, W., *Brazil and the Struggle for Rubber: A Study in Environmental History* (Cambridge: Cambridge University Press, 1987).

Dekker, J. J. H., *Curaçao zonder/met Shell: een bijdrage tot bestudering van demografische, economische en sociale processen in de periode 1900–1929* (Zubphen: Walburg, 1982).

Diamond, J., *Guns, Germs, and Steel: The Fates of Human Societies* (London: Jonathan Cape, 1997).

Diop, N., and Jaffee, S. M., 'Fruits and Vegetables: Global Trade and Competition in Fresh and Processed Product Markets', in M. Ataman Aksoy and John C. Beghin (eds), *Global Agricultural Trade and Developing Countries* (Washington, DC: World Bank, 2005), 237–57.

Domfeh, O., Dzahini-Obiatey, H., Ameyaw, G. A., Abaka-Ewusie, K., and Opoku, G., 'Cocoa Swollen Shoot Virus Disease Situation in Ghana: A Review of Current Trends', *African Journal of Agricultural Research*, vol. 6 no. 22 (Oct. 2011), 5033–9.

Dore, E., 'Environment and Society: Long-Term Trends in Latin American Mining', *Environment and History*, vol. 6 (2000), 1–29.

Doughty, R. W., *Feather Fashions and Bird Preservation* (Berkeley: University of California Press, 1975).

Dove, M. R., 'Rice-Eating Rubber and People-Eating Governments: Peasant versus State Critiques of Rubber Development in Colonial Borneo', *Ethnohistory*, vol. 43 no. 1 (1996), 33–63.

Dove, M. R., *The Banana Tree at the Gate: A History of Marginal Peoples and Global Markets in Borneo* (New Haven: Yale University Press, 2010).

Drabble, J. H., *Rubber in Malaya, 1876–1922: The Genesis of the Industry* (Oxford: Oxford University Press, 1973).

Drabble, J. H., *Malayan Rubber: The Interwar Years* (Houndmills: Macmillan, 1991).

Drabble, J. H., *An Economic History of Malaysia, c.1800–1990* (Houndmills: Macmillan, 2000).

Drayton, R., *Nature's Government: Science, Imperial Britain, and the 'Improvement' of the World* (New Haven: Yale University Press, 2000).

Driver, F., and Martins, L. (eds), *Tropical Visions in an Age of Empire* (Chicago: University of Chicago Press, 2005).

D'Souza, R., *Drowned and Dammed: Colonial Capitalism and Flood Control in Eastern India* (New Delhi: Oxford University Press, 2006).

D'Souza, R., 'Water in British India: The Making of a "Colonial Hydrology"', *History Compass*, vol. 4 no. 4 (2006), 621–8.

Dublin, H. T., 'Dynamics of the Serengeti-Mara Woodlands: An Historical Perspective', *Forest and Conservation History*, vol. 35 no. 4 (Oct. 1991), 169–78.

Dumett, R. E., 'The Rubber Trade of the Gold Coast and Asante in the Nineteenth Century: African Innovation and Market Responsiveness', *Journal of African History*, vol. 12 no. 1 (1971), 79–101.

Dumett, R. E., *El Dorado in West Africa: The Gold-Mining Frontier, African Labor, and Colonial Capitalism in the Gold Coast, 1875–1900* (Athens, Oh.: Ohio University Press, 1998).

Dumont, R., *Notes sur les implications sociales de la 'révolution verte' dans quelques pays d'Afrique* (Geneva: UNRISD, 1971).

Dunlap, T. R., *Nature and the English Diaspora: Environment and History in the United States, Canada, Australia, and New Zealand* (Cambridge: Cambridge University Press, 1999).

Dzahini-Obiatey, H., Domfeh, O., and Amoah, F. M., 'Over Seventy Years of a Viral Disease of Cocoa in Ghana: From Researchers' Perspective', *African Journal of Agricultural Research*, vol. 5 no. 7 (Apr. 2010), 476–85.

Eckart, W. U., *Medizin und Kolonialimperialismus. Deutschland 1884–1945* (Paderborn: Schöningh, 1997).

Edelman, M., Oya, C., and Borras Jr, S. M. (eds), *Global Land Grabs*, special issue of *Third World Quarterly*, vol. 34 no. 9 (2013).

Egboh, E. O., *British Forest Policy in Nigeria: A Study in Colonial Exploitation of Forest Produce (1897–1940)* (Ph.D. Dissertation, University of Birmingham, 1975).

Ehrlich, P. R., and Ehrlich, A. H., *The Population Bomb* (New York: Ballantine, 1968).

Eichholtz, D., *Deutsche Ölpolitik im Zeitalter der Weltkriege* (Leipzig: Leipziger Universitätsverlag, 2010).

Ellis, R., *Men and Whales* (New York: Knopf, 1991).

El Shakry, O., *The Great Social Laboratory: Subjects of Knowledge in Colonial and Postcolonial Egypt* (Stanford, Calif.: Stanford University Press, 2007).

Engdahl, T., *The Exchange of Cotton: Ugandan Peasants, Colonial Market Regulations and the Organisation of the International Cotton Trade, 1904–1918* (Uppsala: Acta Universitatis Upsaliensis, 1999).

Epstein, A. L., *Scenes from African Urban Life: Collected Copperbelt Papers* (Edinburgh: Edinburgh University Press, 1992).

Ertsen, M. W., *Locales of Happiness: Colonial Irrigation in the Netherlands East Indies and its Remains, 1830–1980* (Delft: VSSD, 2010).

Ertsen, M. W., *Improvising Planned Development on the Gezira Plain, Sudan, 1900–1980* (Houndmills: Palgrave, 2016).

Escobar, A., *Encountering Development: The Making and Unmaking of the Third World* (Princeton: Princeton University Press, 1995).

Etkin, D. S., 'Historical Overview of Oil Spills from all Sources (1960–1998)', Oil Spill Intelligence Report (Arlington, Mass., 1999).

Evans, D., *A History of Nature Conservation in Britain*, 2nd edn (London: Routledge, 1997).

Evans, S., *Bound in Twine: The History and Ecology of the Henequen-Wheat Complex for Mexico and the American and Canadian Plains, 1880–1950* (College Station, Tex.: Texas A&M University Press, 2007).

Evenden, M., 'Aluminum, Commodity Chains, and the Environmental History of the Second World War', *Environmental History*, vol. 16 (Jan. 2011), 69–93.

Fabian, J., *Time and the Other: How Anthropology Makes its Object* (New York: Columbia University Press, 1983).

Fairhead, J., and Leach, M., *Misreading the African Landscape: Society and Ecology in a Forest-Savanna Mosaic* (Cambridge: Cambridge University Press, 1996).

Fairhead, J., and Leach, M., *Reframing Deforestation: Global Analyses and Local Realities* (London: Routledge, 1998).

Fairhead, J., and Leach, M., 'Desiccation and Domination: Science and Struggles over Environment and Development in Colonial Guinea', *Journal of African History*, vol. 41 (2000), 35–54.

Fairhead, J., Leach, M., and Scoones, I., 'Green Grabbing: A New Appropriation of Nature?', *Journal of Peasant Studies*, vol. 39 no. 2 (2012), 237–61.

FAO, *Food for All* (Rome: FAO, 1996).

Farley, J., *Bilharzia: A History of Imperial Tropical Medicine* (Cambridge: Cambridge University Press, 1991).

Farnie, D., 'Cotton, 1780–1914', in David Jenkins (ed.), *The Cambridge History of Western Textiles* (Cambridge: Cambridge University Press, 2003), 721–60.

Fearnside, P. M., 'Transmigration in Indonesia: Lessons from its Environmental and Social Impacts', *Environmental Management*, vol. 21 (1997), 553–70.

Federico, G., *Feeding the World: An Economic History of Agriculture, 1800–2000* (Princeton: Princeton University Press, 2005).

Fenske, J., 'The Battle for Rubber in Benin', *Economic History Review*, vol. 67 no. 4 (2014), 1012–34.

Ferguson, J., *The Anti-Politics Machine: 'Development', Depoliticization, and Bureaucratic Power in Lesotho* (Cambridge: Cambridge University Press, 1990).

Ferguson, J., *Expectations of Modernity: Myths and Meanings of Urban Life on the Zambian Copperbelt* (Berkeley: University of California Press, 1999).

Fernando, M. R., 'Famine in a Land of Plenty: Plight of a Rice-Growing Community in Java, 1883–84', *Journal of Southeast Asian Studies*, vol. 41 no. 2 (2010), 291–320.

Ferrier, R. W., *The History of the British Petroleum Company*, vol. 1: *The Developing Years 1901–1932* (Cambridge: Cambridge University Press, 1982).

Fetter, B., *The Creation of Elisabethville, 1910–1940* (Stanford, Calif.: Hoover Institution Press, 1976).

Fetter, B., 'The Union Minière and its Hinterland: A Demographic Reconstruction', *African Economic History*, vol. 12 (1983), 67–81.

Filipovich, J., 'Destined to Fail: Forced Settlement at the *Office du Niger*, 1926–45', *Journal of African History*, vol. 42 (2001), 239–60.

Finlay, M. R., *Growing American Rubber: Strategic Plants and the Politics of National Security* (New Brunswick, NJ: Rutgers University Press, 2009).

Fitter, R., *The Penitent Butchers: The Fauna Preservation Society, 1903–1978* (London: FPS, 1978).

Fohlen, C., *L'Industrie textile au temps du Second Empire* (Paris: Librarie Plon, 1956).

Forbes, R. J., *Studies in Early Petroleum History* (Leiden: Brill, 1958).

Ford, C., 'Nature, Culture and Conservation in France and her Colonies 1840–1940', *Past & Present*, no. 183 (May 2004), 173–98.

Ford, J., *The Role of the Trypanosomiases in African Ecology: A Study of the Tsetse Fly Problem* (Oxford: Clarendon, 1971).

Fortunel, F., *Le Café au Viêt Nam: de la colonisation à l'essor d'un grand producteur mondial* (Paris: L'Harmattan, 2000).

Foster, J. B., and Holleman, H., 'The Theory of Unequal Ecological Exchange: A Marx–Odum Dialectic', *Journal of Peasant Studies*, vol. 41 no. 2 (2014), 199–233.

Foster, J. H., Clark, B., and York, R., *The Ecological Rift: Capitalism's War on the Earth* (New York: Monthly Review Press, 2010).

Fox, S. R., *The American Conservation Movement: John Muir and his Legacy* (Madison, Wis.: University of Wisconsin Press, 1985).

Fraser, A., and Larmer, M. (eds), *Zambia, Mining, and Neoliberalism: Boom and Bust on the Globalized Copperbelt* (New York: Palgrave, 2010), 237–68.

Fréchou, H., 'Les Plantations européennes en Côte d'Ivoire', *Les Cahiers d'outre-mer* vol. 8 no. 29 (Jan. 1955), 56–83.

Freund, B., *Capital and Labour in the Nigerian Tin Mines* (Harlow: Longman, 1981).

Friedberg, S., 'Postcolonial Paradoxes: The Cultural Economy of African Export Horticulture', in Alexander Nützenadel and Frank Trentmann (eds), *Food and Globalization: Consumption, Markets and Politics in the Modern World* (Oxford: Berg, 2008), 215–33.

Frohn, H.-W., and Schmoll, F. (eds), *Natur und Staat. Staatlicher Naturschutz in Deutschland 1906–2006* (Bonn: Bundesamt für Naturschutz, 2006).

Gadgil, M., and Guha, R., *This Fissured Land: An Ecological History of India* (Berkeley: University of California Press, 1992).

Gadgil, M., and Guha, R., *Ecology and Equity: The Use and Abuse of Nature in Contemporary India* (London: Routledge, 1995).

Gallagher, N. E., *Egypt's Other Wars: Epidemics and the Politics of Public Health* (Syracuse, NY: Syracuse University Press, 1990).

Galle, H., *La 'Famine du coton', 1861–1865: effets de la guerre de sécession sur l'industrie cotonnière gantoise* (Brussels: Université libre de Bruxelles, 1967).

Gann, L. H., *A History of Northern Rhodesia: Early Days to 1953* (London: Chatto & Windus, 1964).

Gardiner, J., 'Some Aspects of the Establishment of Towns in Zambia during the Nineteen Twenties and Thirties', *Zambian Urban Studies*, no. 3 (1970), 25–8.

Gardner, B., 'Tourism and the Politics of the Global Land Grab in Tanzania: Markets, Appropriation and Recognition', *Journal of Peasant Studies*, vol. 39 no. 2 (2012), 377–402.

Garfield, S., *In Search of the Amazon: Brazil, the United States, and the Nature of a Region* (Durham, NC: Duke University Press, 2014).

Garrier, C., *L'Exploitation coloniale des forêts de Côte d'Ivoire: une spoliation institutionnalisée* (Paris: l'Harmattan, 2006).

Geertz, C., *Agricultural Involution: The Process of Ecological Change in Indonesia* (Berkeley: University of California Press, 1963).

Gelvin, J. L., and Green, N. (eds), *Global Muslims in the Age of Steam and Print* (Berkeley: University of California Press, 2014).

Gerretson, F. C., *History of the Royal Dutch*, vol. 1 (Leiden: Brill, 1958).

Ghee, L. T., *Peasants and their Agricultural Economy in Colonial Malaya 1874–1941* (Kuala Lumpur: Oxford University Press, 1977).

Giblin, J., 'Trypanosomiasis Control in African History: An Evaded Issue?', *Journal of African History*, vol. 31 (1990), 59–80.

Giesen, J. C., *Boll Weevil Blues: Cotton, Myth, and Power in the American South* (Chicago: University of Chicago Press, 2011).

Gilmartin, D., 'Scientific Empire and Imperial Science: Colonialism and Irrigation Technology in the Indus Basin', *Journal of Asian Studies*, vol. 53 no. 4 (1994), 1127–49.

Gilmartin, D., *Blood and Water: The Indus River Basin in Modern History* (Berkeley: University of California Press, 2015).

Gißibl, B., 'Paradiesvögel: Kolonialer Naturschutz und die Mode der deutschen Frau am Anfang des 20. Jahrhunderts', in Johannes Paulmann, Daniel Leese, and Philippa Söldenwagner (eds), *Ritual-Macht-Natur. Europäisch-ozeanische Beziehungswelten in der Neuzeit* (Bremen: Überseemuseum, 2005), 131–54.

Gißibl, B., *The Nature of Colonialism: Hunting, Conservation and the Politics of Wildlife in the German Colonial Empire* (Ph.D. Dissertation, Universität Mannheim, 2009).

Gißibl, B., Höhler, S., and Kupper, P. (eds), *Civilizing Nature: National Parks in Global Historical Perspective* (New York: Berghahn, 2012).

Goldman, M., *Imperial Nature: The World Bank and Struggles for Social Justice in the Age of Globalization* (New Haven: Yale University Press, 2005).

Goodman, D., *Gold Seeking: Victoria and California in the 1850s* (Stanford, Calif.: Stanford University Press, 1994).

Gordon, D. M., *Nachituti's Gift: Economy, Society and Environment in Central Africa* (Madison, Wis.: University of Wisconsin Press, 2006).

Gorman, H. S., *Redefining Efficiency: Pollution Concerns, Regulatory Mechanisms, and Technological Change in the U.S. Petroleum Industry* (Akron, Oh.: University of Akron Press, 2001).

Graham, R., *The Aluminium Industry and the Third World: Multinational Corporations and Underdevelopment* (London: Zed, 1982).

Grandin, G., *Fordlandia: The Rise and Fall of Henry Ford's Forgotten Jungle City* (London: Icon, 2010).

Grant, K., *A Civilized Savagery: Britain and the New Slaveries in Africa, 1884–1926* (London: Routledge, 2005).

Green, R. H., and Hymer, S. H., 'Cocoa in the Gold Coast: A Study in the Relations between African Farmers and Agricultural Experts', *Journal of Economic History*, vol. 26 no. 3 (1966), 299–319.

Grévisse, F., *Le Centre extra-coutumier d'Élisabethville: quelques aspects de la politique indigène du Haut-Katanga industriel* (Brussels: Institut Royal Colonial Belge, 1951).

Griffiths, T., and Robin, L. (eds), *Ecology and Empire: Environmental History of Settler Societies* (Edinburgh: Keele University Press, 1997).

Grilli, E. R., *The European Community and the Developing Countries* (Cambridge: Cambridge University Press, 1993).

Grilli, E. R., et al., *The World Rubber Economy: Structure, Changes, and Prospects* (Baltimore: Johns Hopkins University Press, 1980).

Grischow, J. D., 'Late Colonial Development in British West Africa: The Gonja Development Project in the Northern Territories of the Gold Coast, 1948–57', *Canadian Journal of African Studies*, vol. 35 (2001), 282–312.

Groff, D. H., 'Carrots, Sticks, and Cocoa Pods: African and Administrative Initiatives in the Spread of Cocoa Cultivation in Assikasso, Ivory Coast, 1908–1920', *International Journal of African Historical Studies*, vol. 20 no. 3 (1987), 401–16.

Grossman, L. S., *The Political Ecology of Bananas: Contract Farming, Peasants, and Agrarian Change in the Eastern Caribbean* (Chapel Hill, NC: University of North Carolina Press, 1998).

Grove, R. H., *Green Imperialism: Colonial Expansion, Tropical Island Edens and the Origins of Environmentalism, 1600–1860* (Cambridge: Cambridge University Press, 1995).

Grove, R. H., Damodaran, V., and Sangwan, S. (eds), *Nature and the Orient: The Environmental History of South and Southeast Asia* (Delhi: Oxford University Press, 1998).

Grove, R. H., 'Conserving Eden: The (European) East India Companies and their Environmental Policies on St. Helena, Mauritius and in Western India, 1660 to 1854', *Comparative Studies in Society and History* vol. 36 no. 3 (1993), 318–51.

Grove, R. H., *Ecology, Climate and Empire: Colonialism and Global Environmental History* (Cambridge: White Horse Press, 1997).

Grunwald, J., and Musgrove, P., *Natural Resources in Latin American Development* (Baltimore: Johns Hopkins Press, 1970).

Grzimek, B., et al., *Visions of Paradise* (London: Hodder, 1981).

Guérin, M., *Paysans de la forêt à l'époque coloniale: la pacification des aborigènes des hautes terres du Cambodge, 1863–1940* (Caen: Association d'Histoire des Sociétés Rurales, 2008).

Guha, R., *The Unquiet Woods: Ecological Change and Peasant Resistance in the Himalaya* (Delhi: Oxford University Press, 1989).

Guha, R., 'An Early Environmental Debate: The Making of the 1878 Forest Act', *Indian Economic and Social History Review*, vol. 27 (1990), 65–84.

Guha, R., *Environmentalism: A Global History* (New York: Longman, 2000).

Guha, R., 'The Authoritarian Biologist and the Arrogance of Anti-Humanism: Wildlife Conservation in the Third World', in Vasant K. Saberwal and Mahesh Rangarajan (eds), *Battles over Nature: Science and the Politics of Conservation* (Delhi: Permanent Black, 2003), 139–57.

Guha, R., and Gadgil, M., 'State Forestry and Social Conflict in British India', *Past & Present*, no. 123 (May 1989), 141–77.

Haines, D., *Building the Empire, Building the Nation: Development, Legitimacy and Hydro-Politics in Sind, 1919–1969* (Oxford: Oxford University Press, 2013).

Halperin, S., and Palan, R. (eds), *Legacies of Empire: Imperial Roots of the Contemporary Global Order* (Cambridge: Cambridge University Press, 2015).

Hämäläinen, P., *The Comanche Empire* (New Haven: Yale University Press, 2008).

Hamilton, C., *Earthmasters: The Dawn of the Age of Climate Engineering* (New Haven: Yale University Press, 2014).

Harms, R., 'The End of Red Rubber: A Reassessment', *Journal of African History*, vol. 16 no. 1 (1975), 73–88.

Harnetty, P., 'The Cotton Improvement Program in India 1865–1875', *Agricultural History*, vol. 44 no. 4 (Oct. 1970), 379–92.

Harnetty, P., 'Cotton Exports and Indian Agriculture, 1861–1870', *Economic History Review*, vol. 24 no. 3 (Aug. 1971), 414–29.

Harnetty, P., *Imperialism and Free Trade: Lancashire and India in the Mid-Nineteenth Century* (Vancouver: University of British Columbia Press, 1972).

Harnetty, P., '"Deindustrialization" Revisited: The Handloom Weavers of the Central Provinces of India, c.1800–1947', *Modern Asian Studies*, vol. 25 no. 3 (1991), 455–510.

Harper, T. N., 'The Politics of the Forest in Colonial Malaya', *Modern Asian Studies*, vol. 31 (1997), 1–29.

Harper, T. N., *The End of Empire and the Making of Malaya* (Cambridge: Cambridge University Press, 1999).

Harrison, M., 'Science and the British Empire', *Isis*, vol. 96 no. 1 (2005), 56–63.

Hart, D., *The Volta River Project: A Case Study in Politics and Technology* (Edinburgh: Edinburgh University Press, 1980).

Havinden, M., and Meredith, D., *Colonialism and Development: Britain and its Tropical Colonies, 1850–1960* (London: Routledge, 1993).

Hays, S. P., *Conservation and the Gospel of Efficiency: The Progressive Conservation Movement, 1890–1920* (Cambridge, Mass.: Harvard University Press, 1959).

Hazareesingh, S., 'Cotton, Climate and Colonialism in Dharwar, Western India, 1840–1880', *Journal of Historical Geography*, vol. 38 no. 1 (2012), 1–17.

Hazell, P. B. R., and Ramasamy, C., *The Green Revolution Reconsidered: The Impact of High-Yielding Rice Varieties in South India* (Baltimore: Johns Hopkins University Press, 1991).

Hazell, P. B. R., 'The Asian Green Revolution' (International Food Policy Research Institute, 2009).

Headrick, D. R., *The Tools of Empire: Technology and European Imperialism in the Nineteenth Century* (Oxford: Oxford University Press, 1981).

Headrick, D. R., *The Tentacles of Progress: Technology Transfer in the Age of Imperialism, 1850–1940* (Oxford: Oxford University Press, 1988).

Headrick, D. R., *The Invisible Weapon: Telecommunications and International Politics, 1851–1945* (Oxford: Oxford University Press, 1992).

Hecht, G., *Being Nuclear: Africans and the Global Uranium Trade* (Cambridge, Mass.: MIT Press, 2012).

Hedges, E. S., *Tin in Social and Economic History* (London: Arnold, 1964).

Heidhues, M. F. S., 'Company Island: A Note on the History of Belitung', *Indonesia*, vol. 51 (Apr. 1991), 1–20.

Heidhues, M. F. S., *Bangka Tin and Muntok Pepper: Chinese Settlement on an Indonesian Island* (Singapore: Institute of Southeast Asian Studies, 1992).

Heidhues, M. F. S., 'Poor Little Rich Islands: Metals in Bangka-Belitung and West Kalimantan', in Greg Bankoff and Peter Boomgaard (eds), *A History of Natural Resources in Asia: The Wealth of Nature* (Basingstoke: Palgrave, 2007), 61–79.

Heim, S., *Plant Breeding and Agrarian Research in Kaiser-Wilhelm-Institutes 1933–1945*, trans. Sorcha O'Hagan (Dordrecht: Springer, 2008).

Herbert, E. W., *Red Gold of Africa: Copper in Precolonial History and Culture* (Madison, Wis.: University of Wisconsin Press, 1984).

Herren, M., *Hintertüren zur Macht. Internationalismus und modernisierungsorientierte Außenpolitik in Belgien, der Schweiz und den USA 1865–1914* (Munich: Oldenbourg, 2000).

Higgins, G. A., *A History of Trinidad Oil* (Port of Spain: Trinidad Express, 1996).

Higginson, J., *A Working Class in the Making: Belgian Colonial Labor Policy, Private Enterprise, and the African Mineworker, 1907–1951* (Madison, Wis.: University of Wisconsin Press, 1989).

Higgs, C., *Chocolate Islands: Cocoa, Slavery and Colonial Africa* (Athens, Oh.: Ohio University Press, 2012).

Hill, P., *The Migrant Cocoa-Farmers of Southern Ghana: A Study in Rural Capitalism*, 2nd edn (Oxford: James Currey, 1997).

Hilton, M., and Mitter, R. (eds), *Transnationalism and Contemporary Global History, Past & Present* Supplement 8 (Oxford: Oxford University Press, 2013).

Hoag, H. J., *Developing the Rivers of East and West Africa: An Environmental History* (London: Bloomsbury, 2013).

Hochschild, A., *King Leopold's Ghost: A Story of Greed, Terror, and Heroism in Colonial Africa* (London: Macmillan, 1999).

Hodge, J. M., *Triumph of the Expert: Agrarian Doctrines of Development and the Legacies of British Colonialism* (Athens, Oh.: Ohio University Press, 2007).

Hodge, J. M., 'Colonial Foresters versus Agriculturalists: The Debate over Climate Change and Cocoa Production in the Gold Coast', *Agricultural History*, vol. 83 no. 2 (Spring 2009), 201–20.

Hodge, J. M., 'Writing the History of Development', Parts 1 and 2, *Humanity*, vol. 6 no. 3 (Winter 2015), 429–63, and vol. 7 no. 1 (Spring 2016), 125–74.

Hodgson, D. L., 'Taking Stock: State Control, Ethnic Identity and Pastoralist Development in Tanganyika, 1949–58', *Journal of African History*, vol. 41 (2000), 55–78.

Holland, J. H., *Rubber Cultivation in West Africa* (London: 1901).

Holt-Giménez, E., Altieri, M., and Rosset, P., 'Ten Reasons Why the Rockefeller and the Bill and Melinda Gates Foundations' Alliance for Another Green Revolution Will Not Solve the Problems of Poverty and Hunger in Sub-Saharan Africa', *Food First Policy Brief*, no. 12 (2006).

Homburg, E., 'Operating on Several Fronts: The Trans-National Activities of Royal Dutch/ Shell, 1914–1918', in Roy M. MacLeod and Jeffrey Allan Johnson (eds), *Frontline and Factory: Comparative Perspectives on the Chemical Industry at War, 1914–1924* (Dordrecht: Springer, 2006), 123–44.

Homewood, K. M., and Rodgers, W. A., 'Pastoralism and Conservation', *Human Ecology*, vol. 12 (1984), 431–41.

Hoogvelt, A. M. M., *Globalization and the Postcolonial World: The New Political Economy of Development* (Basingstoke: Macmillan, 1997).

Hoong, Y. Y., *The Development of the Tin Mining Industry of Malaya* (Kuala Lumpur: University of Malaya Press, 1969).

Hopkins, A. G., *An Economic History of West Africa* (Harlow: Longman, 1973).

Hoppe, K., *Lords of the Fly: Sleeping Sickness Control in British East Africa, 1900–1960* (Westport, Conn.: Praeger, 2003).

Hornborg, A., 'Ecosystems and World-Systems: Accumulation as an Ecological Process', in Christopher Chase-Dunn and Salvatore J. Babones (eds), *Global Social Change: Historical and Comparative Perspectives* (Baltimore: Johns Hopkins University Press, 2006), 161–75.

Hornborg, A., McNeill, J. R., and Martinez-Alier, J. (eds), *Rethinking Environmental History: World-System History and Global Environmental Change* (Lanham, Md: AltaMira, 2007).

Howarth, S., *A Century in Oil: The 'Shell' Transport and Trading Company 1897–1997* (London: Weidenfeld & Nicolson, 1997).

Howarth, S., and Jonker, J., *A History of Royal Dutch Shell*, vol. 2: *Powering the Hydrocarbon Revolution, 1939–1973* (Oxford: Oxford University Press, 2007).

Hubbard, M., *Agricultural Exports and Economic Growth: A Study of the Botswana Beef Industry* (London: KPI, 1986).

Huber, V., *Channelling Mobilities: Migration and Globalisation in the Suez Canal Region and Beyond, 1869–1914* (Cambridge: Cambridge University Press, 2013).

Hughes, D. M., 'Whites and Water: How Euro-Africans Made Nature at Kariba Dam', *Journal of Southern African Studies*, vol. 32 no. 4 (Dec. 2006), 823–38.

Hulme, D., and Murphree, M. (eds), *African Wildlife and Livelihoods: The Promise and Performance of Community Conservation* (Oxford: James Currey, 2001).

Hyndman, D., *Ancestral Rain Forests and the Mountain of Gold: Indigenous Peoples and Mining in New Guinea* (Boulder, Colo.: Westview Press, 1994).

Iliffe, J., *A Modern History of Tanganyika* (Cambridge: Cambridge University Press, 1979).

Iliffe, J., *Africans: The History of a Continent* (Cambridge: Cambridge University Press, 1995).

Imbun, B. Y., *Anthropology of Mining in Papua New Guinea Greenfields* (New York: Nova Science Publishers, 2011).

International Maritime Organization, *Field Guide for Oil Spill Response in Tropical Waters* (London: International Maritime Organization, 1997).

Iqbal, I., *The Bengal Delta: Ecology, State and Social Change, 1840–1943* (Basingstoke: Palgrave, 2010).

Isaacman, A., *Cotton is the Mother of Poverty: Peasants, Work and Rural Struggle in Colonial Mozambique, 1938–1961* (London: James Currey, 1996).

Isaacman, A., and Roberts, R. (eds), *Cotton, Colonialism, and Social History in Sub-Saharan Africa* (London: James Currey, 1995).

Isaacman, A., and Sneddon, C., 'Toward a Social and Environmental History of the Building of Cahora Bassa Dam', *Journal of Southern African Studies*, vol. 26 (2000), 597–632.

Isaacman, A., and Isaacman, B., *Dams, Displacement, and the Delusion of Development: Cahora Bassa and its Legacies in Mozambique* (Athens, Oh.: Ohio University Press, 2013).

Isenberg, A. C., *The Destruction of the Bison: An Environmental History, 1750–1920* (Cambridge: Cambridge University Press, 2000).

Isenberg, A. C., *Mining California: An Ecological History* (New York: Hill and Wang, 2005).

Islam, M. M., *Irrigation, Agriculture and the Raj: Punjab, 1887–1947* (New Delhi: Manohar, 1997).

Iwai, Y., *Forestry and the Forest Industry in Japan* (Vancouver: UBC Press, 2002).

Jackson, J., *The Thief at the End of the World: Rubber, Power and the Seeds of Empire* (London: Duckworth, 2008).

Jacoby, K., *Crimes against Nature: Squatters, Poachers, Thieves and the Hidden History of American Conservation* (Berkeley: University of California Press, 2001).

Jeffries, C., *The Colonial Empire and its Civil Service* (Cambridge: Cambridge University Press, 1938; repr. 2014).

Jensen, W. G., 'The Importance of Energy in the First and Second World Wars', *Historical Journal*, vol. 11 (1968), 538–54.

Jepson, P., and Whittaker, R. J., 'Histories of Protected Areas: Internationalisation of Conservationist Values and their Adoption in the Netherlands Indies (Indonesia)', *Environment and History*, vol. 8 (2002), 129–72.

Jepson, P., et al., 'The End for Indonesia's Lowland Forests?', *Science*, vol. 292 (2001), 859–61.

Jerónimo, M. B., *The 'Civilising Mission' of Portuguese Colonialism, 1870–1930* (Basingstoke: Palgrave, 2015).

Jerónimo, M. B., and Pinto, A. C. (eds), *The Ends of European Colonial Empires: Cases and Comparisons* (Basingstoke: Palgrave, 2015).

Jewsiewicki, B., 'Modernisation ou destruction du village africain: l'économie politique de la "modernisation agricole" au Congo belge', *Les Cahiers du CEDAF*, no. 5 (1983) 1–79.

Jin-Bee, O., 'Mining Landscapes of Kinta', *Malayan Journal of Tropical Geography*, vol. 4 (Jan. 1955), 1–58.

Jobin, W., *Dams and Disease: Ecological Design and Health Impacts of Large Dams, Canals and Irrigation Systems* (London: E & FN Spon, 1999).

Johnson, M., and Chiu, F. Y. L. (eds), *Subimperialism*, special issue of *Positions: East Asia Cultures Critique*, vol. 8 no. 1 (Spring 2000).

Jones, E., *The European Miracle: Environments, Economies and Geopolitics in the History of Europe and Asia*, 3rd edn (Cambridge: Cambridge University Press, 2003).

Jones, P. M., *Agricultural Enlightenment: Knowledge, Technology, and Nature, 1750–1840* (Oxford: Oxford University Press, 2016).

Jonker, J., and van Zanden, J. L., *A History of Royal Dutch Shell*, vol. 1: *From Challenger to Joint Industry Leader, 1890–1939* (Oxford: Oxford University Press, 2007).

Jonsson, F. A., 'The Industrial Revolution in the Anthropocene', *Journal of Modern History*, vol. 84 no. 3 (Sept. 2012), 679–96.

Jonsson, F. A., 'The Origins of Cornucopianism: A Preliminary Genealogy', *Critical Historical Studies*, vol. 1 no. 1 (Spring 2014), 151–68.

Kaag, M., and Zoomers, A. (eds), *The Global Land Grab: Beyond the Hype* (London: Zed, 2014).

Karunaratna, N., *Forest Conservation in Sri Lanka from British Colonial Times, 1818–1912* (Colombo: Trumpet, 1987).

Kathirithamby-Wells, J., *Nature and Nation: Forests and Development in Peninsular Malaysia* (Honolulu: University of Hawaii Press, 2005).

Katzenellenbogen, S. E., *Railways and the Copper Mines of Katanga* (Oxford: Clarendon Press, 1973).

Kaur, A., 'A History of Forestry in Sarawak', *Modern Asian Studies*, vol. 32 no. 1 (1998), 117–47.

Kaur, A., and Diehl, F., 'Tin Miners and Tin Mining in Indonesia, 1850–1950', *Asian Studies Review*, vol. 20 no. 2 (Nov. 1996), 95–120.

Keeton, C. L., *King Thebaw and the Ecological Rape of Burma: The Political and Commercial Struggle between British India and French Indo-china in Burma 1878–1886* (Delhi: Manohar, 1974).

Ken, W. L., *The Malayan Tin Industry to 1914: With Special Reference to the States of Perak, Selangor, Negri Sembilan and Pahang* (Tuscon, Ariz.: University of Arizona Press, 1965).

Kent, J., *The Internationalization of Colonialism: Britain, France and Black Africa, 1939–1956* (Oxford: Clarendon Press, 1992).

Kent, M., *Oil and Empire: British Policy and Mesopotamian Oil, 1900–1920* (Houndmills: Macmillian, 1976).

Kenwood, G., *The Growth of the International Economy, 1820–2000* (London: Routledge, 1999).

Kersten, J., *Das Anthropozän-Konzept: Kontrakt, Komposition, Konflikt* (Baden-Baden: Nomos, 2014).

Khin Maung Gyi, P. U., *Memoirs of the Oil Industry in Burma* (Rangoon: Wan Sungi Sape, 1989).

Khoo, S. N., and Razzaq-Lubis, A., *Kinta Valley: Pioneering Malaysia's Modern Development* (Perak Darul Ridzuan: Perak Academy, 2005).

Kin, F., 'The Role of Waterborne Diseases in Malaysia', in Peter Boomgaard (ed.), *A World of Water: Rain, Rivers and Seas in Southeast Asian Histories* (Leiden: KITLV, 2007), 281–95.

Kirimhan, S., 'Accidental Oil Spills and the Pollution of the Marine Environment', in *Proceedings of the First International Conference on the Impact of Oil Spill in the Persian Gulf* (Tehran: Tehran University Press, 1985), 403–15.

Kirsch, S., 'History and the *Birds of Paradise*: Surprising Connections from New Guinea', *Expedition*, vol. 48 no. 1 (2008), 15–21.

Kirsch, S., *Mining Capitalism: The Relationship between Corporations and their Critics* (Berkeley: University of California Press, 2014).

Kjekshus, H., *Ecology Control and Economic Development in East African History: The Case of Tanganyika, 1850–1950* (London: Heinemann, 1977).

Kloppenburg Jr, J. R., *First the Seed: The Political Economy of Plant Biotechnology*, 2nd edn (Madison, Wis.: University of Wisconsin Press, 2004).

Koponen, J., *Development for Exploitation: German Colonial Policies in Mainland Tanzania, 1884–1914* (Helsinki: Finnish Historical Society, 1995).

Kouango, A. M., *Cabinda: un Koweit africain* (Paris: L'Harmattan, 2002).

Krajewski, P., *Kautschuk, Quarantäne, Krieg. Dhauhandel in Ostafrika 1880–1914* (Berlin: Schwarz, 2006).

Krech III, S., *The Ecological Indian: Myth and History* (New York: Norton, 1999).

Kretschmer, K., *Braunkohle und Umwelt: zur Geschichte des nordwestsächsischen Kohlenreviers (1900–1945)* (Frankfurt a. M.: Peter Lang, 1998).

Kumar, D., 'Reconstructing India: Disunity in the Science and Technology for Development Discourse, 1900–1947', *Osiris*, vol. 15 (2000), 241–57.

Kumar, D., Damodaran, V., and D'Souza, R. (eds), *The British Empire and the Natural World: Environmental Encounters in South Asia* (New Delhi: Oxford University Press, 2011).

Lagus, C., *Operation Noah* (London: William Kimber, 1959).

Landes, D. S., *Bankers and Pashas: International Finance and Economic Imperialism in Egypt* (Cambridge, Mass.: Harvard University Press, 1958).

Lanning, G., and Mueller, M., *Africa Undermined: Mining Companies and the Under-development of Africa* (Harmondsworth: Penguin, 1979).

Lanz, T. J., 'The Origins, Development and Legacy of Scientific Forestry in Cameroon', *Environment and History*, vol. 6 (2000), 99–120.

Larrue, J., *Fria en Guinée: première usine d'alumine en terre d'Afrique* (Paris: Karthala, 1997).

Larse, R. K., and Mamosso, C. A., 'Environmental Governance of Uranium Mining in Niger', DIIS Working Paper 2013:02: (Copenhagen: DIIS, 2013).

Larson, H. M., Knowlton, E. H., and Popple, C. S., *History of Standard Oil Company (New Jersey): New Horizons, 1927–1950* (New York: Harper & Row, 1971).

Latour, B., *We Have Never Been Modern*, trans. Catherine Porter (Cambridge, Mass.: Harvard University Press, 1993).

Latour, B., *Politics of Nature: How to Bring the Sciences into Democracy* (Cambridge, Mass.: Harvard University Press, 2004).

Latour, B., *Reassembling the Social: An Introduction to Actor-Network-Theory* (Oxford: Oxford University Press, 2005).

Le Billon, P., 'The Political Ecology of War: Natural Resources and Armed Conflicts', *Political Geography*, vol. 20 (2001), 561–84.

Le Billon, P., 'Logging in Muddy Waters: The Politics of Forest Exploitation in Cambodia', *Critical Asian Studies*, vol. 44 (2002), 563–86.

LeBlanc, M., and Malaisse, F., *Lubumbashi, un écosystème urbain tropical* (Lubumbashi: Université Nationale du Zaire, 1978).

LeCain, T. J., *Mass Destruction: The Men and Giant Mines that Wired America and Scarred the Planet* (New Brunswick, NJ: Rutgers Univ. Press, 2009).

LeCain, T. J., 'Against the Anthropocene. A Neo-Materialist Perspective', *International Journal for History, Culture and Modernity*, vol. 3 no. 1 (Apr. 2015), 1–28.

Le Coq, J. F., Trébuil, G., and Dufumier, M., 'History of Rice Production in the Mekong Delta', in Peter Boomgaard and David Henley (eds), *Smallholders and Stockbreeders: History of Foodcrop and Livestock Farming in Southeast Asia* (Leiden: KITLV, 2004), 163–85.

Lee, C. P., and Yeap, E. B., 'Reclamation after Tin Mining in Malaysia', in Ming H. Wong and Anthony D. Bradshaw (eds), *The Restoration and Management of Derelict Land: Modern Approaches* (Singapore: World Scientific Publishing, 2002), 211–22.

Lekan, T. M., *Imagining the Nation in Nature: Landscape Preservation and German Identity, 1885–1945* (Cambridge, Mass.: Harvard University Press, 2004).

Levine, M. J., *Pesticides: A Toxic Time Bomb in our Midst* (Westport, Conn.: Praeger, 2007).

Levrat, R., *Le Coton en Afrique Occidentale et Centrale avant 1950: un exemple de la politique coloniale de la France* (Paris: L'Harmattan, 2008).

Li, T. M., *The Will to Improve: Governmentality, Development, and the Practice of Politics* (Durham, NC: Duke University Press, 2007).

Li, T. M., *Land's End: Capitalist Relations on an Indigenous Frontier* (Durham, NC: Duke University Press, 2014).

Lieberman, V., *Strange Parallels: Southeast Asia in Global Context c.800–1830*, 2 vols (Cambridge: Cambridge University Press, 2003, 2009).

Likaka, O., *Rural Society and Cotton in Colonial Zaire* (Madison, Wis.: University of Wisconsin Press, 1997).

Lindblad, J. T., 'The Petroleum Industry in Indonesia before the Second World War', *Bulletin of Indonesian Economic Studies*, vol. 25 (1989), 53–78.

Linden, O., 'Fate and Effects of Oil Pollution with Particular Reference to the Persian Gulf Region', in *Proceedings of the First International Conference on the Impact of Oil Spill in the Persian Gulf* (Tehran: Tehran University Press, 1985), 45–63.

Little, P. D., 'Pastoralism, Biodiversity, and the Shaping of Savanna Landscapes in East Africa', *Africa*, vol. 66 (1996), 37–51.

Loadman, J., *Tears of the Tree: The Story of Rubber—A Modern Marvel* (Oxford: Oxford University Press, 2005).

Longmuir, M. V., 'Twinzayo and Twinza: Burmese "Oil Barons" and the British Administration', *Asian Studies Review*, vol. 22 no. 3 (Sept. 1998), 339–56.

Longmuir, M. V., *Oil in Burma: The Extraction of 'Earth-Oil' to 1914* (Bangkok: White Lotus, 2003).

Longrigg, S. H., *Oil in the Middle East: Its Discovery and Development* (Oxford: Oxford University Press, 1954).

Low, D., and Smith, A. (eds), *The Oxford History of East Africa* (Oxford: Oxford University Press, 1976).

Lyons, M., *The Colonial Disease: A Social History of Sleeping Sickness in Northern Zaire, 1900–1940* (Cambridge: Cambridge University Press, 1992).

Maat, H., *Science Cultivating Practice: A History of Agricultural Science in the Netherlands and its Colonies 1863–1986* (Dordrecht: Kluwer, 2001).

McAlpin, M. B., *Subject to Famine: Food Crises and Economic Change in Western India, 1860–1920* (Princeton: Princeton University Press, 1983).

McAlpin, M. B., 'Railroads, Prices, and Peasant Rationality: India, 1860–1900', *Journal of Economic History*, vol. 34 (1974), 662–84.

McBeth, B. S., and Knight, A., *Juan Vicente Gomez and the Oil Companies in Venezuela, 1908–1935* (Cambridge: Cambridge University Press, 2002).

McCook, S., *States of Nature: Science, Agriculture, and Environment in the Spanish Caribbean, 1760–1940* (Austin, TX: University of Texas Press, 2002).

McCook, S., 'Global Rust Belt: Hemileia vastatrix and the Ecological Integration of World Coffee Production since 1850', *Journal of Global History*, vol. 1 no. 2 (2006), 177–95.

McCormick, J., *Reclaiming Paradise: The Global Environmental Movement* (Bloomington, Ind.: Indiana University Press, 1989).

McCully, M., *Silenced Rivers: The Ecology and Politics of Large Dams* (London: Zed, 1996).

McDaniel, C. N., and Gowdy, J. M., *Paradise for Sale: A Parable of Nature* (Berkeley: University of California Press, 2000).

Macekura, S. J., *Of Limits and Growth: The Rise of Global Sustainable Development in the Twentieth Century* (Cambridge: Cambridge University Press, 2015).

McGregor, J., *Crossing the Zambezi: The Politics of Landscape on a Central African Frontier* (Oxford: James Currey, 2009).

Mackenzie, A. F. D., *Land, Ecology and Resistance in Kenya, 1880–1952* (Edinburgh: Edinburgh University Press, 1998).

MacKenzie, J. M. 'The Imperial Pioneer and Hunter and the British Masculine Stereotype in Late Victorian and Edwardian Times', in J. A. Mangan and James Walvin (eds), *Manliness and Morality: Middle-Class Masculinity in Britain and America, 1800–1940* (Manchester: Manchester University Press 1987), 176–98.

MacKenzie, J. M., *Empire of Nature: Hunting, Conservation and British Imperialism* (Manchester: Manchester University Press, 1988).

MacKenzie, J. M. (ed.), *Imperialism and the Natural World* (Manchester: Manchester University Press, 1990).

McLaughlin, D. H., 'Man's Selective Attack on Ores and Minerals', in William L. Thomas (ed.), *Man's Role in Changing the Face of the Earth* (Chicago: University of Chicago Press, 1956), 851–61.

MacLeod, R. (ed.) *Nature and Empire: Science and the Colonial Enterprise, Osiris*, vol. 15 (Chicago: University of Chicago Press, 2000).

McNeill, J. R., *Something New Under the Sun: An Environmental History of the Twentieth Century* (London: Penguin, 2000).

McNeill, J. R., 'Observations on the Nature and Culture of Environmental History', *History and Theory*, Theme Issue 42 (Dec. 2003), 5–43.

McNeill, J. R., *Mosquito Empires: Ecology and War in the Greater Caribbean, 1620–1914* (Cambridge: Cambridge University Press, 2010).

Maddox, G., Giblin, J., and Kimambo, I. N. (eds), *Custodians of the Land: Ecology and Culture in the History of Tanzania* (Oxford: James Currey, 1996).

Maekawa, I., 'Neo-Colonialism Reconsidered: A Case Study of East Africa in the 1960s and 1970s', *Journal of Imperial and Commonwealth History*, vol. 43 no. 2 (2015), 317–41.

Mandala, V. R., 'The Raj and the Paradoxes of Wildlife Conservation: British Attitudes and Expediencies', *Historical Journal*, vol. 58 no. 1 (Mar. 2015), 75–110.

Marini, R. M., 'Brazilian Sub-Imperialism', *Monthly Review*, vol. 23 no. 9 (1972), 14–24.

Markovits, C., *The Global World of Indian Merchants, 1750–1947: Traders of Sind from Bukhara to Panama* (Cambridge: Cambridge University Press, 2000).

Marks, R., *The Origins of the Modern World* (Lanham, Md: Rowman & Littlefield, 2007).

Marseille, J., *Empire colonial et capitalisme français: histoire d'un divorce* (Paris: Éditions Albin Michel, 1984).

Martin, C., *The Rainforests of West Africa: Ecology—Threats—Conservation* (Basel: Springer, 1991).

Martinez-Alier, J., *The Environmentalism of the Poor: A Study of Ecological Conflicts and Valuation* (Cheltenham: Edward Elgar, 2002).

Marx, L., *The Machine in the Garden: Technology and the Pastoral Ideal in America* (Oxford: Oxford University Press, 1967).

Masefield, G. B., *A Short History of Agriculture in the British Colonies* (Oxford: Clarendon, 1950).

Masefield, G. B., *A History of the Colonial Agricultural Service* (Oxford: Clarendon, 1972).

Mathis, C.-F., 'Mobiliser pour l'environnement en Europe et aux États-Unis: un état des lieux à l'aube du 20ᵉ siècle', *Vingtième Siècle: revue d'histoire*, no. 113 (Jan.–Mar. 2012), 15–27.

Matongo, A. B. K., 'Popular Culture in a Colonial Society: Another Look at Mbeni and Kalela Dances on the Copperbelt', in Samuel N. Chipungu (ed.), *Guardians in their Time: Experiences of Zambians under Colonial Rule 1890–1964* (London: Macmillan, 1992), 180–217.

Matschke, H., 'River Pollution by Mine Effluence in the Kitwe Region', in Ian D. Elgie (ed.), *Kitwe and its Hinterland* (Lusaka: Zambian Geographical Association, 1974), 125–32.

Mayshar, J., Moav, O., Neeman, Z., and Pascali, L., 'Cereals, Appropriability and Hierarchy', *CEPR Discussion Paper* 10742 (2015).

Mazalto, M., 'Environmental Liability in the Mining Sector: Prospects for Sustainable Development in the Democratic Republic of the Congo', in Jeremy Richards (ed.), *Mining, Society, and a Sustainable World* (Berlin: Springer, 2009), 289–317.

Mazalto, M., 'Governance, Human Rights and Mining in the Democratic Republic of Congo', in Bonnie Campbell (ed.), *Mining in Africa: Regulation and Development* (New York: Pluto Press, 2009), 187–242.

Melillo, E., *Strangers on Familiar Soil: Rediscovering the Chile–California Connection* (New Haven: Yale University Press, 2015).

Metcalf, T. R., *Imperial Connections: India in the Indian Ocean Arena, 1860–1920* (Berkeley: University of California Press, 2007).

Michel, M., *Les Africains et la Grande Guerre: l'appel à l'Afrique (1914–1918)* (Paris: Éditions Karthala, 2003).

Mikhail, A., *Nature and Empire in Ottoman Egypt: An Environmental History* (Cambridge: Cambridge University Press, 2011).

Miller, S. W., *An Environmental History of Latin America* (Cambridge: Cambridge University Press, 2007).

Milner II, C. A. (ed.), *A New Significance: Re-Envisioning the History of the American West* (Oxford: Oxford University Press, 1996).

Ming, H. T., *Ipoh: When Tin was King* (Ipoh: Perak Academy, 2009).

Mitchell, J. C., 'A Note on the Urbanization of Africans on the Copperbelt', *Rhodes-Livingstone Journal*, no. 12 (1951), 20–7.

Mitchell, J. C., *The Kalela Dance: Aspects of Social Relationships among Urban Africans in Northern Rhodesia*, Rhodes-Livingstone Papers no. 27 (Manchester: Manchester University Press, 1956).

Mitchell, T., *Colonising Egypt* (Cambridge: Cambridge University Press, 1988).

Mitchell, T., *Rule of Experts: Egypt, Techno-politics, Modernity* (Berkeley: University of California Press, 2002).

Mitchell, T., 'Carbon Democracy', *Economy and Society*, vol. 38 no. 3 (Aug. 2009), 399–432.

Mitchell, T., *Carbon Democracy: Political Power in the Age of Oil* (London: Verso, 2011).

Moon, S., *Technology and Ethical Idealism: A History of Development in the Netherlands East Indies* (Leiden: CNWS, 2007).

Moore, H. L., and Vaughan, M., *Cutting Down Trees: Gender, Nutrition and Agricultural Change in the Northern Province of Zambia, 1890–1990* (London: James Currey, 1994).

Moore, J. W., 'Environmental Crises and the Metabolic Rift in World-Historical Perspective', *Organization & Environment*, vol. 13 (2000), 123–57.

Moore, J. W., 'Sugar and the Expansion of the Early Modern World-Economy: Commodity Frontiers, Ecological Transformation, and Industrialization', *Review*, vol. 23 (2000), 409–33.

Moore, J. W., ' "Amsterdam is Standing on Norway" Part II: The Global North Atlantic in the Ecological Revolution of the Long Seventeenth Century', *Journal of Agrarian Change*, vol. 10 (2010), 188–227.

Morse, K., *The Nature of Gold: An Environmental History of the Klondike Gold Rush* (Seattle: University of Washington Press, 2003).

Mortimore, M., *Adapting to Drought: Farmers, Famines and Desertification in West Africa* (Cambridge: Cambridge University Press, 1989).

Mortimore, M., *Roots in the African Dust: Sustaining the Sub-Saharan Drylands* (Cambridge: Cambridge University Press, 1998).

Mosse, D., *The Rule of Water: Statecraft, Ecology, and Collective Action in South India* (New Delhi: Oxford University Press, 2003).

Munro, J. F., 'Monopolists and Speculators: British Investment in West African Rubber, 1905–1914', *Journal of African History*, vol. 22 no. 2 (1981), 263–78.

Murray, M. J., *The Development of Capitalism in Colonial Indochina (1870–1940)* (Berkeley: University of California Press, 1980).

Musambachime, M. C., 'Rural Political Protest: The 1953 Disturbances in Mweru-Luapula', *International Journal of African Historical Studies*, vol. 20 no. 3 (1987), 437–53.

Myint-U, T., *The Making of Modern Burma* (Cambridge: Cambridge University Press, 2001).

Nærstad, A. (ed.), *Africa Can Feed Itself* (Oslo: Development Fund, 2007).

Nash, R., *Wilderness and the American Mind* (New Haven: Yale University Press, 2001, orig. 1967).

Naylor, S., 'Spacing the Can: Empire, Modernity, and the Globalisation of Food', *Environment and Planning A*, vol. 32 (2000), 1625–39.

Nelson, F. (ed.), *Community Rights, Conservation and Contested Land: The Politics of Natural Resource Governance in Africa* (London: Earthscan, 2010).

Neumann, R. P., *Imposing Wilderness: Struggles over Livelihood and Nature Preservation in Africa* (Berkeley: University of California Press, 1998).

Neumann, R. P., 'The Postwar Conservation Boom in British Colonial Africa', *Environmental History*, vol. 7 (2002), 22–47.

Nicholson, S. E., 'The West African Sahel: A Review of Recent Studies on the Rainfall Regime and Its Interannual Variability', *ISRN Meteorology*, vol. 2013 (2013), Article ID 453521, 32 pages, doi:10.1155/2013/453521.

Nixon, R., *Slow Violence and the Environmentalism of the Poor* (Cambridge, Mass.: Harvard University Press, 2011).

Nkrumah, K., *Neo-Colonialism: The Last Stage of Imperialism* (London: Nelson, 1965).

Oba, G., *Climate Change Adaptation in Africa: An Historical Ecology* (London: Routledge, 2014).

Oelschlaeger, M., *The Idea of Wilderness: From Prehistory to the Age of Ecology* (New Haven: Yale University Press, 1991).

Okoji, M. A., 'Petroleum Oil and the Niger Delta Environment', *International Journal of Environmental Studies*, vol. 57 (2000), 713–24.

Okonta, I., and Douglas, O., *Where Vultures Feast: Shell, Human Rights, and Oil* (London: Verso, 2003).

Olmstead, A. L., and Rhode, P. W., *Creating Abundance: Biological Innovation and American Agricultural Development* (Cambridge: Cambridge University Press, 2008).

Olstein, D. A., *Thinking History Globally* (Basingstoke: Palgrave, 2015).

Onyeiwu, S., 'Deceived by African Cotton: The British Cotton Growing Association and the Demise of the Lancashire Textile Industry', *African Economic History*, no. 28 (2000), 89–121.

Osborn, F. H. (ed.), *Our Crowded Planet: Essays on the Pressures of Population* (London: Allen & Unwin, 1962).

Östberg, W., *The Kondoa Transformation: Coming to Grips with Soil Erosion in Central Tanzania* (Uppsala: Scandinavian Institute of African Studies, 1986).

Osterhammel, J., *Geschichte der Globalisierung. Dimensionen, Prozesse, Epochen* (Munich: Beck, 2003).

Osterhammel, J., *Die Verwandlung der Welt. Eine Geschichte des 19. Jahrhunderts* (Munich: Beck, 2009).

Ouboter, P. E., and De Dijn, B. P. D., 'Changes in a Polluted Swamp', in Paul E. Ouboter (ed.), *The Freshwater Ecosystems of Suriname* (Dordrecht: Kluwer Academic, 1993), 239–60.

Overton, J., *Colonial Green Revolution? Food, Irrigation and the State in Colonial Malaya* (Wallingford: CAB International, 1994).

Owen, R., *Cotton and the Egyptian Economy, 1820–1914: A Study in Trade and Development* (Oxford: Clarendon, 1969).

Paes, W. C., '"Conflict Diamonds" to "Clean Diamonds": The Development of the Kimberley Process Certification Scheme', in Matthias Basedau and Andreas Mehler (eds), *Resource Politics in sub-Saharan Africa* (Hamburg: Institut für Afrika-Kunde, 2005).

Palaniappan, V. M., 'Ecology of Tin Tailings Areas: Plant Communities and their Succession', *Journal of Applied Ecology*, vol. 11 no. 1 (Apr. 1974), 133–50.

Paris, M., 'Air Power and Imperial Defence, 1880–1919', *Journal of Contemporary History*, vol. 24 no. 2 (Apr. 1989), 209–25.

Paris, M., 'The First Air Wars: North Africa and the Balkans, 1911–13', *Journal of Contemporary History*, vol. 26 no. 1 (Jan. 1991), 97–109.

Parpart, J. L., *Labor and Capital on the African Copperbelt* (Philadelphia: Temple University Press, 1983).

Parthasarathi, P., *Why Europe Grew Rich and Asia Did Not: Global Economic Divergence, 1600–1850* (Cambridge: Cambridge University Press, 2011).

Peet, R., Robbins, P., and Watts, M. (eds), *Global Political Ecology* (London: Routledge, 2011).

Peluso, N. L., *Rich Forests, Poor People: Resource Control and Resistance in Java* (Berkeley: University of California Press, 1992).

Peluso, N. L., and Vandergeest, P., 'Genealogies of the Political Forest and Customary Rights in Indonesia, Malaysia, and Thailand', *Journal of Asian Studies*, vol. 60 no. 3 (Aug. 2001), 761–812.

Pelzer, K., *Pioneer Settlement in the Asiatic Tropics: Studies in Land Utilization and Agricultural Colonization in Southeastern Asia* (New York: American Geographical Society, 1948).

Pelzer, K., *Planter and Peasant: Colonial Policy and the Agrarian Struggle in East Sumatra 1863–1947* (The Hague: Nijhoff, 1978).

Penot, E., 'From Shifting Cultivation to Sustainable Jungle Rubber: A History of Innovations in Indonesia', in Malcolm Cairns (ed.), *Voices from the Forest: Integrating Indigenous Knowledge into Sustainable Upland Farming* (Washington, DC: RFF, 2007), 583–605.

Penot, E., and Budiman, A. F. S., 'Environmental Aspects of Smallholder Rubber Agroforestry in Indonesia: Reconcile Production and Environment', International Rubber Conference (1998).

Perera, N. P., 'Mining and Spoiled Land in Zambia: An Example of Conflicting Land Use in the Third World', *Geojournal,* Supplement 2 (1981), 95–103.

Perkins, J. H., *Geopolitics and the Green Revolution: Wheat, Genes and the Cold War* (New York: Oxford University Press, 1997).

Perrings, C., *Black Mineworkers in Central Africa: Industrial Strategies and the Evolution of an African Proletariat in the Copperbelt, 1911–1941* (New York: Africana Pub. Co., 1979).

Pfister, C. (ed.), *Das 1950er Syndrom. Der Weg in die Konsumgesellschaft* (Bern: Verlag Paul Haupt, 1995).

Phillips, J., 'Alfred Chester Beatty: Mining Engineer, Financier, and Entrepreneur, 1898–1950', in Raymond E. Dumett (ed.), *Mining Tycoons in the Age of Empire, 1870–1945: Entrepreneurship, High Finance, Politics and Territorial Expansion* (Farnham: Ashgate, 2009), 215–38.

Phimister, I., *Wangi Kolia: Coal, Capital and Labour in Colonial Zimbabwe, 1894–1954* (Johannesburg: Witwatersrand University Press, 1994).

Phimister, I., 'Foreign Devils, Finance and Informal Empire: Britain and China *c.*1900–1912', *Modern Asian Studies*, vol. 40 no. 3 (2006), 737–59.

Pingali, P., Hossain, M., and Gerpacio, R., *Asian Rice Bowls: The Returning Crisis?* (Wallingford: CAB, 1997).

Pitcher, M. A., 'Sowing the Seeds of Failure: Early Portuguese Cotton Cultivation in Angola and Mozambique, 1820–1926', *Journal of Southern African Studies*, vol. 17 no. 1 (Mar. 1991), 43–70.

Podobnik, B., *Global Energy Shifts: Fostering Sustainability in a Turbulent Age* (Philadelphia: Temple University Press, 2006).

Pohl, G., and Sorsa, P., *European Integration and Trade with the Developing World* (Washington, DC: World Bank, 1992).

Poley, J. P., *Eroïca: The Quest for Oil in Indonesia (1850–1898)* (Dordrecht: Kluwer Academic Publishers, 2000).

Pomeranz, K., *The Great Divergence: China, Europe, and the Making of the Modern World Economy* (Princeton: Princeton University Press, 2000).

Poncelet, M., *L'Invention des sciences coloniales belges* (Paris: Éditions Karthala, 2008).

Powdermaker, H., *Copper Town: Changing Africa. The Human Situation on the Rhodesian Copperbelt* (New York: Harper & Row, 1962).

Prain, Sir R., *Copper: Anatomy of an Industry* (London: Mining Journal Books, 1975).

Pratap, A., *The Hoe and the Axe: An Ethnohistory of Shifting Cultivation in Eastern India* (Delhi: Oxford University Press, 2000).

Purwanto, B., *From Dusun to the Market: Native Rubber Cultivation in Southern Sumatra, 1890–1940* (Ph.D. Dissertation, SOAS, 1992).

Radkau, J., 'Holzverknappung und Krisenbewusstsein im 18. Jahrhundert', *Geschichte und Gesellschaft,* vol. 9 (1983), 513–43.

Radkau, J., 'Das hölzerne Zeitalter und der deutsche Sonderweg in der Forsttechnik', in Ulrich Troitzsch (ed.), *Nützliche Künste. Kultur- und Sozialgeschichte der Technik im 18. Jahrhundert* (Münster: Waxmann, 1999), 97–118.

Radkau, J., *Die Ära der Ökologie. Eine Weltgeschichte* (Munich: Beck, 2011).

al-Rahman Munif, A., *Cities of Salt*, trans. Peter Theroux (New York: Vintage, 1989).

Rajan, S. R., *Modernizing Nature: Forestry and Imperial Eco-development 1800–1950* (Oxford: Clarendon, 2006).

Rangarajan, M., 'Imperial Agendas and India's Forests: The Early History of Indian Forests, 1800–1878', *Indian Economic and Social History Review*, vol. 21 (1994), 147–67.

Rangarajan, M., *Fencing the Forest: Conservation and Ecological Change in India's Central Provinces, 1860–1914* (New Delhi: Oxford University Press, 1996).

Rangarajan, M., *India's Wildlife History* (Delhi: Permanent Black, 2001).

Rangarajan, M., 'The Raj and the Natural World: The War against "Dangerous Beasts" in Colonial India', in John Knight (ed.), *Wildlife in Asia: Cultural Perspectives* (London: Routledge, 2004), 207–32.

Rangarajan, M., 'Environment and Ecology under British Rule', in Douglas M. Peers and Nandini Gooptu (eds), *India and the British Empire* (Oxford: Oxford University Press, 2012), 212–30.

Ranger, T. M., *Voices from the Rocks: Nature, Culture and History in the Matopos Hills of Zimbabwe* (Oxford: James Currrey, 1999).

Ravesteijn, W., *De zegenrijke heeren der wateren: irrigatie en staat op Java, 1832–1942* (Delft: Delft University Press, 1997).

Ravestijn, W., 'Controlling Water, Controlling People: Irrigation Engineering and State Formation in the Dutch East Indies', *Itinerario*, vol. 31 (2007), 89–118.

Reed, K., *Crude Existence: Environment and the Politics of Oil in Northern Angola* (Berkeley: University of California Press, 2009).

Reed, M. C., 'Gabon: A Neo-Colonial Enclave of Enduring French Interest', *Journal of Modern African Studies*, vol. 25 (1987), 283–320.

Reid, A., 'Humans and Forests in Pre-colonial Southeast Asia', *Environment and History*, vol. 1 no. 1 (Feb. 1995), 93–110.

Réseau Ressources Naturelles, *L'Impact de l'exploitation minière sur l'environnement du Katanga: table ronde* (Lubumbashi: Réseau Ressources Naturelles, 2007).

Richards, A., *Egypt's Agricultural Development, 1800–1980: Technical and Social Change* (Boulder, Colo.: Westview, 1982).

Richards, J. F., *The Mughal Empire* (Cambridge: Cambridge University Press, 1993).

Richards, J. F., *The Unending Frontier: An Environmental History of the Early Modern World* (Berkeley: University of California Press, 2003).

Richards, J. F., and Flint, E. P., 'A Century of Land-Use Change in South and Southeast Asia', in Virginia H. Dale (ed.), *Effects of Land-Use Change on Atmospheric CO_2 Concentrations: South and Southeast Asia as a Case Study* (New York: Springer, 1994), 15–63.

Richards, J. F., Haynes, E. S., and Hagen, J. R., 'Changes in the Land and Human Productivity in Northern India, 1870–1970', *Agricultural History*, vol. 59 no. 4 (Oct. 1985), 523–48.

Richards, J. F., and Tucker, R. P. (eds), *World Deforestation in the Twentieth Century* (Durham, NC: Duke University Press, 1988).

Richards, P., *Indigenous Agricultural Revolution: Ecology and Food Production in West Africa* (Boulder, Colo.: Westview, 1985).

Richards, P., *Coping with Hunger: Hazard and Experiment in an African Rice-Farming System* (London: Allen & Unwin, 1986).

Ricklefs, M. C., *A History of Modern Indonesia* (London: Macmillan, 1981).

Riello, G., *Cotton: The Fabric that Made the Modern World* (Cambridge: Cambridge University Press, 2013).

Riello, G., and Roy, T. (eds), *How India Clothed the World: The World of South Asian Textiles, 1500–1850* (Leiden: Brill, 2009).

Rizzo, M., 'What Was Left of the Groundnut Scheme? Development Disaster and Labour Market in Southern Tanganyika, 1946–1952', *Journal of Agrarian Change*, vol. 6 no. 2 (Apr. 2006), 205–38.

Robbins, P., *Political Ecology: A Critical Introduction* (Chichester: Wiley, 2012).

Roberts, A., *The Colonial Moment in Africa: Essays on the Movement of Minds and Materials, 1900–1940* (Cambridge: Cambridge University Press, 1990).

Roberts, R. L., *Two Worlds of Cotton: Colonialism and the Regional Economy in the French Soudan, 1800–1946* (Stanford, Calif.: Stanford University Press, 1996).

Robertson, E., *Chocolate, Women and Empire: A Social and Cultural History* (Manchester: Manchester University Press, 2009).

Robertson, T., *The Malthusian Moment: Global Population Growth and the Birth of American Environmentalism* (New Brunswick, NJ: Rutgers University Press, 2012).

Robertson, W., *Tin: Its Production and Marketing* (London: Croom Helm, 1982).

Robins, E., and Legge, R., *Animal Dunkirk: The Story of Lake Kariba and 'Operation Noah', the Greatest Animal Rescue since the Ark* (London: Herbert Jenkins, 1959).

Robins, J., '"The Black Man's Crop": Cotton, Imperialism and Public–Private Development in Britain's African Colonies, 1900–1918', *Commodities of Empire Working Paper* no. 11 (2009).

Robins, J., 'Lancashire and the "Undeveloped Estates": The British Cotton Growing Association Fund-Raising Campaign, 1902–1914', *Journal of British Studies*, vol. 54 no. 4 (2015), 869–97.

Roe, E., '"Development Narratives" or Making the Best of Blueprint Development', *World Development*, vol. 19 (1991), 287–300.

Rola, A. C., and Pingali, P. L., *Pesticides, Rice Productivity, and Farmers' Health* (Manila: IRRI, 1993).

Rolff, A., *Erdöl in Südostasien und seine volkswirtschaftliche Bedeutung für Westeuropa* (Berlin: Duncker & Humblot, 1978).

Rollins, W. H., 'Imperial Shades of Green: Conservation and Environmental Chauvinism in the German Colonial Project', *German Studies Review*, vol. 22 (1999), 187–213.

Rome, A., 'What Really Matters in History: Environmental Perspectives on Modern America', *Environmental History*, vol. 7 no. 2 (Apr. 2002), 303–18.

Rosegrant, M. W., and Hazell, P., *Transforming the Rural Asian Economy: The Unfinished Revolution* (Oxford: Oxford University Press, 2000).

Rosenberg, E. S. (ed.), *A World Connecting, 1870–1945* (Cambridge, Mass.: Belknap, 2012).

Ross, A. R. (ed.), *Grabbing Back: Essays Against the Global Land Grab* (Oakland, Calif.: AK Press, 2013).

Ross, C., 'The Plantation Paradigm: Colonial Agronomy, African Farmers and the Global Cocoa Boom, 1870s–1940s', *Journal of Global History*, vol. 9 no. 1 (Mar. 2014), 49–71.

Ross, C., 'The Tin Frontier: Mining, Empire and Environment in Southeast Asia, 1870s–1930s', *Environmental History*, vol. 19 (2014), 454–79.

Ross, M. L., *The Oil Curse: How Petroleum Wealth Shapes the Development of Nations* (Princeton: Princeton University Press, 2012).

Rotberg, R. I., *Joseph Thomson and the Exploration of Africa* (London: Chatto & Windus, 1971).

Ruddiman, W. F., *Plows, Plagues, and Petroleum: How Humans Took Control of Climate* (Princeton: Princeton University Press, 2005).

Ruf, F., *Booms et crises du cacao: les vertiges de l'or brun* (Paris: Karthala, 1995).

Ruf, F., 'The Myth of Complex Agroforests: The Case of Ghana', *Human Ecology*, vol. 39 (2011), 373–88.

Ruppenthal, J., *Kolonialismus als 'Wissenschaft und Technik'. Das Hamburger Kolonialinstitut 1908 bis 1919* (Stuttgart: Steiner, 2007).

Russell, E., 'Introduction: The Garden in the Machine: Toward an Evolutionary History of Technology', in Susan R. Schrepfer and Philip Scranton (eds), *Industrializing Organisms: Introducing Evolutionary History* (New York: Routledge, 2004), 1–16.

Russell, E., *Evolutionary History: Uniting History and Biology to Understand Life on Earth* (Cambridge: Cambridge University Press, 2011).

Russell, E., et al., 'The Nature of Power: Synthesizing the History of Technology and Environmental History', *Technology and Culture*, vol. 52 no. 2 (Apr. 2011), 246–59.

Saha, M., 'The State, Scientists, and Staple Crops: Agricultural "Modernization" in Pre-Green Revolution India', *Agricultural History*, vol. 87 no. 2 (Spring 2013), 201–23.

Sahlins, P. M., *Forest Rites: The War of the Demoiselles in Nineteenth-Century France* (Cambridge, Mass.: Harvard University Press, 1994).

Sanchez, P. A., 'Science in Agroforestry', in Fergus L. Sinclair (ed.), *Agroforestry: Science, Policy and Practice* (Dordrecht: Kluwer, 1995), 5–55.

Sand, J., 'Subaltern Imperialists: The New Historiography of the Japanese Empire', *Past & Present*, vol. 225, issue 1 (2014), 273–88.

Santiago, M. I., *The Ecology of Oil: Environment, Labor, and the Mexican Revolution, 1900–1938* (Cambridge: Cambridge University Press, 2006).

Satre, L. J., *Chocolate on Trial: Slavery, Politics, and the Ethics of Business* (Athens, Oh.: Ohio University Press, 2005).

Satya, L. D., *Cotton and Famine in Berar 1850–1900* (New Delhi: Manohar, 1997).

Schabel, H. G., 'Tanganyika Forestry under German Colonial Administration, 1891–1919', *Forest and Conservation History*, vol. 34 no. 3 (July 1990), 130–43.

Schmoll, F., *Erinnerung an die Natur. Die Geschichte des Naturschutzes im deutschen Kaiserreich* (Frankfurt a. Main: Campus, 2004).

Schnurr, M. A., 'Breeding for Insect-Resistant Cotton across Imperial Networks, 1924–1950', *Journal of Historical Geography*, vol. 37 no. 2 (2011), 223–31.

Schouwenberg, H., 'Back to the Future? History, Material Culture and New Materialism', *International Journal for History, Culture and Modernity*, vol. 3 no. 1 (Apr. 2015), 59–72.

Schreyger, E., *L'Office du Niger au Mali 1932 à 1982: la problématique d'une grande entreprise agricole dans la zone du Sahel* (Wiesbaden: Steiner, 1984).

Schuknecht, R., *British Colonial Development Policy after the Second World War: The Case of Sukumaland, Tanganyika* (Münster: LIT, 2010).

Schumacher, E. F., *Small is Beautiful: A Study of Economics as if People Mattered* (London: Abacus, 1974).

Schumaker, L., 'Slimes and Death-Dealing Dambos: Water, Industry and the Garden City on Zambia's Copperbelt', *Journal of Southern African Studies*, vol. 34 no. 4 (Dec. 2008), 823–40.

Scott, J. C., *Seeing Like a State: How Certain Schemes to Improve the Human Condition Have Failed* (New Haven: Yale University Press, 1998).

Scott, J. C., *The Art of Not Being Governed: An Anarchist History of Upland Southeast Asia* (New Haven: Yale University Press, 2009).

Scudder, T., *The Ecology of the Gwembe Tonga* (Manchester: Manchester University Press, 1962).

Scudder, T., *The Future of Large Dams: Dealing with Social, Environmental, Institutional and Political Costs* (London: Earthscan, 2005).

Secrett, C., 'The Environmental Impact of Transmigration', *The Ecologist*, vol. 16 (1986), 77–88.

Sen, A., *Poverty and Famines: An Essay on Entitlement and Deprivation* (Oxford: Clarendon, 1981).

Shamololo, T.-O. E., *Le Kasai à la péripherie du Haut-Katanga industriel* (Brussels: Les Cahiers du CEDAF, 1984).

Sheller, M., *Aluminum Dreams: The Making of Light Modernity* (Boston: MIT Press, 2014).

Shermer, M., *In Darwin's Shadow: The Life and Science of Alfred Russel Wallace* (Oxford: Oxford University Press, 2002).

Shiva, V., *The Violence of the Green Revolution: Third World Agriculture, Ecology and Politics* (London: Zed, 1991).

Shiva, V., *Stolen Harvest: The Hijacking of the Global Food Supply* (Cambridge, Mass.: South End Press, 2000).

Showers, K. B., 'Electrifying Africa: An Environmental History with Policy Implications', *Geografiska Annaler: Series B, Human Geography*, vol. 93 no. 3 (2011), 193–221.

Sieferle, R. P., *The Subterranean Forest: Energy Systems and the Industrial Revolution* (Cambridge: White Horse Press, 2001).

Silk, B., *Post-War Food and Cash Crop Production in Former Colonial Territories* (Oxford Development Records Project, 1985).

Singaravélou, P., *Professer l'empire: les 'sciences coloniales' en France sous la IIIe République* (Paris: Publications de la Sorbonne, 2011).

Singaravélou, P. (ed.), *Les Empires coloniaux xixᵉ–xxᵉ siècle* (Paris: éditions Points, 2013).

Singh, N. T., *Irrigation and Soil Salinity in the Indian Subcontinent: Past and Present* (Bethlehem, Pa: Lehigh University Press, 2005).

Sinha, S. P., *Conflict and Tension in Tribal Society* (New Delhi: Concept, 1993).

Sivaramakrishnan, K., *Modern Forests: Statemaking and Environmental Change in Colonial Eastern India* (Stanford, Calif.: Stanford University Press, 1999).

Sivaramakrishnan, K., 'Histories of Colonialism and Forestry in India', in Paolo Squatriti (ed.), *Nature's Past: The Environment and Human History* (Ann Arbor: University of Michigan Press, 2007), 103–44.

Smil, V., *Energy in World History* (Boulder, Colo.: Westview, 1994).

Smil, V., *Enriching the Earth: Fritz Haber, Carl Bosch, and the Transformation of World Food Production* (Cambridge, Mass.: MIT Press, 2001).

Smil, V., *Feeding the World: A Challenge for the Twenty-First Century* (Cambridge, Mass.: MIT Press, 2001).

Smith, D. A., *Mining America: The Industry and the Environment, 1800–1980* (Lawrence, Kan.: University of Kansas Press, 1987).

Smith, J., et al., 'Illegal Logging, Collusive Corruption and Fragmented Governments in Kalimantan, Indonesia', *International Forestry Review*, vol. 5 (2003), 293–302.

SNC-Lavalin International, *Étude sur la restauration des mines de cuivre et de cobalt, République Démocratique du Congo* (April 2003).

Solbrig, O. T., and Solbrig, D. J., *So Shall You Reap: Farming and Crops in Human Affairs* (Washington, DC: Island Press, 1994).

Soluri, J., *Banana Cultures: Agriculture, Consumption and Environmental Change in Honduras and the United States* (Austin, Tex.: University of Texas Press, 2005).

Sonnenfeld, D. A., 'Mexico's "Green Revolution", 1940–1980: Towards an Environmental History', *Environmental History Review*, vol. 16 (1992), 28–52.

Southall, R. J., *Cadbury on the Gold Coast, 1907–1938: The Dilemma of the 'Model Firm' in a Colonial Economy* (Ph.D. dissertation, University of Birmingham, 1975).

Spence, M. D., *Dispossessing the Wilderness: Indian Removal, National Parks, and the Preservationist Ideal* (Oxford: Oxford University Press, 1999).

Spinage, C., *Rinderpest: A History* (New York: Kluwer Academic, 2003).

Stanfield, M. E., *Red Rubber, Bleeding Trees: Violence, Slavery, and Empire in Northwest Amazonia* (Albuquerque, N. Mex.: University of New Mexico Press, 1998).

Stanley, D. J., 'Degradation of the Nile Delta', *Environmental Review*, vol. 4 (1997), 1–7.

Stanley, D. J., and Warne, A. G., 'Nile Delta in its Destruction Phase', *Journal of Coastal Research*, vol. 14 no. 3 (Summer 1998), 794–825.

Staubli, M., *Reich und arm mit Baumwolle. Exportorientierte Landwirtschaft und soziale Stratifikation am Beispiel des Baumwollanbaus im indischen Distrikt Khandesh (Dekkan) 1850–1914* (Stuttgart: Steiner, 1994).

Steffen, W., Broadgate, W., Deutsch, L., Gaffney, O., and Ludwig, C., 'The Trajectory of the Anthropocene: The Great Acceleration', *Anthropocene Review*, vol. 2 no. 1 (Apr. 2015), 81–98.

Steffen, W., Grinevald, J., Crutzen, P., and McNeill, J., 'The Anthropocene: Conceptual and Historical Perspectives', *Philosophical Transactions of the Royal Society A*, vol. 369 no. 1938 (Mar. 2011), 842–67.

Steinhart, E., *Conflict and Collaboration: The Kingdoms of Western Uganda, 1890–1907* (Princeton: Princeton University Press, 1977).

Stepan, N. L., *Picturing Tropical Nature* (Ithaca, NY: Cornell University Press, 2001).

Steyn, P., 'Oil Exploration in Colonial Nigeria, c.1903–58', *Journal of Imperial and Commonwealth History*, vol. 37 (2009), 249–74.

Steyn, P., 'Oil, Ethnic Minority Groups and Environmental Struggles Against Multinational Oil Companies and the Federal Government in the Nigerian Niger Delta since the 1990s', in Marco Armiero and Lise Sedrez (eds), *A History of Environmentalism: Local Struggles, Global Histories* (London: Bloomsbury, 2014), 57–81.

Stoler, A. L., *Capitalism and Confrontation in Sumatra's Plantation Belt, 1870–1979*, 2nd edn (Ann Arbor: University of Michigan Press, 1995).

Stone, I., *Canal Irrigation in British India: Perspectives on Technological Change in a Peasant Economy* (Cambridge: Cambridge University Press, 1985).

Stott, P., and Sullivan, S. (eds), *Political Ecology: Science, Myth and Power* (London: Arnold, 2000).

Streets-Salter, H., and Getz, T., *Empires and Colonies in the Modern World: A Global Perspective* (Oxford: Oxford University Press, 2016).

Striffler, S., *In the Shadows of State and Capital: The United Fruit Company, Popular Struggle, and Agrarian Restructuring in Ecuador, 1900–1995* (Durham, NC: Duke University Press, 2002).

Stuchtey, B. (ed.), *Science across the European Empires, 1800–1950* (Oxford: Oxford University Press, 2005).

Stürzinger, U., *Der Baumwollanbau im Tschad* (Zurich: Atlantis, 1980).

Stürzinger, U., 'The Introduction of Cotton Cultivation in Chad: The Role of the Administration, 1920–1936', *African Economic History*, no. 12 (1983), 213–25.

Sunseri, T., 'The *Baumwollfrage*: Cotton Colonialism in German East Africa', *Central European History*, vol. 34 no. 1 (Mar. 2001), 31–51.

Sunseri, T., *Vilimani: Labor Migration and Rural Change in Early Colonial Tanzania* (Oxford: Currey, 2002).

Sunseri, T., *Wielding the Ax: State Forestry and Social Conflict in Tanzania, 1820–2000* (Athens, Oh.: Ohio University Press, 2009).

Sutter, P. S., 'What Gullies Mean: Georgia's "Little Grand Canyon" and Southern Environmental History', *Journal of Southern History*, vol. 76 no. 3 (Aug. 2010), 579–616.

Sutter, P. S., 'Nature's Agents or Agents of Empire? Entomological Workers and Environmental Change during the Construction of the Panama Canal', *Isis*, vol. 98 no. 4 (Dec. 2007), 724–54.

Sutter, P. S., 'The World with Us: The State of American Environmental History', *Journal of American History*, vol. 100 no. 1 (June 2013), 94–119.

Sutter, P. S., 'The Tropics: A Brief History of an Environmental Imaginary', in Andrew C. Isenberg (ed.), *The Oxford Handbook of Environmental History* (Oxford: Oxford University Press, 2014), 178–204.

Swadling, P., *Plumes from Paradise: Trade Cycles in Outer Southeast Asia and their Impact on New Guinea and Nearby Islands until 1920* (Boroko: Papua New Guinea National Museum, 1996).

Swenson, A., *The Rise of Heritage: Preserving the Past in France, Germany and England, 1789–1914* (Cambridge: Cambridge University Press, 2013).

Swenson, A., and Mandler, P. (eds), *From Plunder to Preservation: Britain and the Heritage of Empire, c.1800–1940* (Oxford: Oxford University Press, 2013).

Swift, J., 'Desertification: Narratives, Winners and Losers', in Melissa Leach and Robin Mearns (eds), *The Lie of the Land: Challenging Received Wisdom on the African Environment* (Oxford: Currey, 1996), 73–90.

Sykes, W. M., *The Sukumaland Development Scheme 1947–57* (Oxford Development Records Project Report 7, 1984).

Takayanagi, N., 'Global Flows of Fruit and Vegetables in the Third Food Regime', *Journal of Rural Community Studies*, vol. 102 (2006), 25–41.

Tate, D. J. M., *The RGA History of the Plantation Industry in the Malay Peninsula* (Kuala Lumpur: Oxford University Press, 1996).

Tetzlaff, R., *Koloniale Entwicklung und Ausbeutung: Wirtschafts- und Sozialgeschichte Deutsch-Ostafrikas, 1890–1914* (Berlin: Duncker & Humblot, 1970).

Thomas, F., *Histoire du régime et des services forestiers français en Indochine de 1862 à 1945* (Hanoi: Thé Giói, 1999).

Thompsell, A., *Hunting Africa: British Sport, African Knowledge and the Nature of Empire* (Basingstoke: Palgrave Macmillan, 2015).

Throup, D. W., 'The Origins of Mau Mau', *African Affairs*, vol. 84 (1985), 399–433.

Thurston, A., *The Intensification of Smallholder Agriculture in Kenya: The Genesis and Implementation of the Swynnerton Plan* (Oxford Development Records Project Report 6, 1984).

Tiffen, M., Mortimore, M., and Gichuki, F., *More People, Less Erosion: Environmental Recovery in Kenya* (Chichester: Wiley, 1994).

Tilley, H., *Africa as a Living Laboratory: Empire, Development, and the Problem of Scientific Knowledge, 1870–1950* (Chicago: University of Chicago Press, 2011).

Tischler, J., *Light and Power for a Multiracial Nation: The Kariba Dam Scheme in the Central African Federation* (Houndmills: Palgrave, 2013).

Tischler, J., 'Cementing Uneven Development: The Central African Federation and the Kariba Dam Scheme', *Journal of Southern African Studies*, vol. 40 no. 5 (2014), 1047–64.

Tooze, A., *The Wages of Destruction: The Making and Breaking of the Nazi Economy* (London: Allen Lane, 2006).

Topik, S., 'Historicizing Commodity Chains: Five Hundred Years of the Global Coffee Commodity Chain', in Jennifer Bair (ed.), *Frontiers of Commodity Chain Research* (Palo Alto, Calif.: Stanford University Press, 2009), 37–62.

Tosh, J., 'The Cash-Crop Revolution in Tropical Africa: An Agricultural Reappraisal', *African Affairs*, vol. 79 no. 314 (1980), 79–94.

Tregonning, K. G., *Straits Tin: A Brief Account of the First Seventy-Five Years of The Straits Trading Company, Limited. 1887–1962* (Singapore: Straits Times Press, 1962).

Trentmann, F., *Empire of Things: How We Became a World of Consumers, from the Fifteenth Century to the Twenty-First* (London: Allen Lane, 2016).

Tsutsui, W. M., 'Landscapes in the Dark Valley: Toward an Environmental History of Wartime Japan', in R. P. Tucker and E. Russell (eds), *Natural Enemy, Natural Ally: Toward an Environmental History of Warfare* (Corvallis, Ore.: Oregon State University Press, 2004), 195–216.

Tucker, R., *Insatiable Appetite: The United States and the Ecological Degradation of the Tropical World* (Berkeley: University of California Press, 2000).

Tucker, R. P., and Richards, J. F. (eds), *Global Deforestation and the Nineteenth-Century World Economy* (Durham, NC: Duke University Press, 1983).

Turpin, F., *De Gaulle, Pompidou et l'Afrique, 1958–1974: décoloniser et coopérer* (Paris: les Indes savantes, 2010).

Turrell, R. V., *Capital and Labour on the Kimberley Diamond Fields 1871–1890* (Cambridge: Cambridge University Press, 1987).

Tvedt, T., *The River Nile in the Age of the British: Political Ecology and the Quest for Economic Power* (London: Tauris, 2004).

Twagira, L. A., '"Robot Farmers" and Cosmopolitan Workers: Technological Masculinity and Agricultural Development in the French Soudan (Mali), 1945–68', *Gender & History*, vol. 26 no. 3 (November 2014), 459–77.

Uekötter, F., *Die Wahrheit ist auf dem Feld. Eine Wissensgeschichte der deutschen Landwirtschaft* (Göttingen: Vandenhoeck & Ruprecht, 2010).

Uekötter, F., 'Matter Matters: Towards a More "Substantial" Global History', *World History Bulletin*, vol. 29 no. 2 (Fall 2013), 6–8.

Uekötter, F. (ed.), *Comparing Apples, Oranges, and Cotton: Environmental Histories of the Global Plantation* (Frankfurt a. Main: Campus, 2014).

Uekötter, F. (ed.), *Ökologische Erinnerungsorte* (Göttingen: Vandenhoeck & Ruprecht, 2014).

Uekötter, F., 'Why Panaceas Work: Recasting Science, Knowledge and Fertilizer Interests in German Agriculture', *Agricultural History*, vol. 88 no. 1 (2014), 68–86.

UNCTAD, *Prospects for the World Cocoa Market Until the Year 2005* (New York: UN, 1991).

UNDP, *Niger Delta Human Development Report* (Garki: UNDP, 2006).

Unger, C. R., 'Agrarwissenschaftliche Expertise und ländliche Modernisierungsstrategien in der internationalen Entwicklungspolitik, 1920er bis 1980er Jahre', *Geschichte und Gesellschaft*, vol. 41 (2015), 552–79.

Unger, C. R., *Entwicklungspfade in Indien. Eine internationale Geschichte 1947–1980* (Göttingen: Wallstein, 2015).

UNRISD, *The Social and Economic Implications of Large-scale Introduction of New Varieties of Food Grain: Summary of Conclusion of a Global Research Project* (Geneva: UNRISD, 1974).

van Beusekom, M. M., *Negotiating Development: African Farmers and Colonial Experts at the Office du Niger, 1920–1960* (Oxford: Currey, 2002).

van Beusekom, M. M., and Hodgson, D. L., 'Lessons Learned? Development Experiences in the Late Colonial Period', *Journal of African History*, vol. 41 no. 1 (Mar. 2000).

van de Weghe, J.-P., et al., *Profil Environnemental—République Démocratique du Congo—Rapport provisoire* (European Commission, EURATA, Jan. 2006).

van Zanden, J. L., 'The First Green Revolution: The Growth of Production and Productivity in European Agriculture, 1870–1914', *Economic History Review*, vol. 44 (1991), 215–39.

Vandergeest, P., and Peluso, N. L., 'Empires of Forestry: Professional Forestry and State Power in Southeast Asia', Parts 1 and 2, *Environment and History*, vol. 12 (2006), 31–64, 359–93.

Vellut, J.-L., 'Hégémonies en construction: articulations entre état et entreprises dans le bloc colonial Belge (1908–1960)', *Canadian Journal of African Studies/Revue canadienne des études africaines*, vol. 16 no. 2 (1982), 313–30.

Vellut, J.-L., 'Mining in the Belgian Congo', in David Birmingham and Phyllis M. Martin (eds), *History of Central Africa*, vol. 2 (London: Longman, 1983), 126–62.

Venn, F., *Oil Diplomacy in the Twentieth Century* (Houndmills: Macmillan, 1986).

Venn, F., 'Oleaginous Diplomacy: Oil, Anglo-American Relations and the Lausanne Conference, 1922–23', *Diplomacy & Statecraft*, vol. 20 no. 3 (2009), 414–33.

Verschave, F.-X., *La Françafrique: le plus long scandale de la République* (Paris: Stock, 1998).

Verst, E. M., *Karl Mauch als Forschungsreisender: Wissenschaft und Karriere zwischen Deutschland und Südafrika* (St Ingbert: Röhrig, 2012).

Vickers, A., *A History of Modern Indonesia*, 2nd edn (Cambridge: Cambridge University Press, 2013).

von der Heyden, C. J., and New, M. G., 'Groundwater Pollution on the Zambian Copperbelt: Deciphering the Source and the Risk', *Science of the Total Environment* vol. 327 (2004), 17–30.

von der Heyden, C. J., and New, M. G., 'Sediment Chemistry: A History of Mine Contaminant Remediation and an Assessment of Processes and Pollution Potential', *Journal of Geochemical Exploration*, vol. 82 (2004), 35–57.

Wächter, H. J., *Naturschutz in den deutschen Kolonien in Afrika (1884–1918)* (Münster: LIT, 2008).

Wadley, R. (ed.), *Histories of the Borneo Environment* (Leiden: KITLV, 1995).

Wah, F. L. K., *Beyond the Tin Mines: Coolies, Squatters and New Villagers in the Kinta Valley, Malaysia, c.1880–1980* (Singapore: Oxford University Press, 1988).

Walsh, J. C., and Gannon, R., *Time is Short and the Water Rises* (London: Thomas Nelson & Sons, 1967).

Warde, P., *Energy Consumption in England and Wales, 1560–2000* (Rome: Instituto di Studio sulle Società del Mediterraneo, 2007).

Watts, M., *Silent Violence: Food, Famine and Peasantry in Northern Nigeria* (Berkeley: University of California Press, 1983).

Webb, W. P., *The Great Frontier* (London: Secker & Warburg, 1953).

Weinstein, B., *The Amazon Rubber Boom, 1850–1920* (Stanford, Calif.: Stanford University Press, 1983).

Weiskel, T. C., 'Toward an Archaeology of Colonialism: Elements in the Ecological Transformation of the Ivory Coast', in Donald Worster (ed.), *The Ends of the Earth: Perspectives on Modern Environmental History* (Cambridge: Cambridge University Press, 1998), 141–71.

Wesseling, H. L., *Indië verloren, rampspoed geboren: en andere opstellen over de geschiedenis van de Europese expansie* (Amsterdam: Bakker, 1988).

Whitcombe, E., *Agrarian Conditions in Northern India: The United Provinces under British Rule, 1860–1900* (Berkeley: University of California Press, 1972).

Whitcombe, E., 'Irrigation', in Dharma Kumar and Meghnad Desai (eds), *The Cambridge Economic History of India*, vol. 2 (Cambridge: Cambridge University Press, 1983), 677–736.

White, N. J., 'Reconstructing Europe through Rejuvenating Empire: The British, French, and Dutch Experiences Compared', in Mark Mazower, Jessica Reinisch, and David Feldman (eds), *Post-War Reconstruction in Europe: International Perspectives, 1945–1949, Past & Present* Supplement 6 (Oxford: Oxford University Press, 2011), 211–36.

White, R., *The Organic Machine: The Re-Making of the Columbia River* (New York: Hill & Wang, 1995).

Whited, T. L., *Forests and Peasant Politics in Modern France* (New Haven: Yale University Press, 2000).

Whitten, A. J., *Transmigration and the Environment in Indonesia: The Past, Present, and Future* (Gland: IUCN, 1987).

Wickizer, V. D., *Coffee, Tea and Cocoa: An Economic and Political Analysis* (London: Stanford University Press, 1951).

Williams, M., *Deforesting the Earth: From Prehistory to Global Crisis* (Chicago: University of Chicago Press, 2003).

Williams, R., *Red Mud: An Annotated Bibliography* (Kingston: Jamaica Bauxite Institute, 1986).

Wittfogel, K., *Oriental Despotism: A Comparative Study of Total Power* (New Haven: Yale University Press, 1957).

Wöbse, A.-K., 'Der Schutz der Natur im Völkerbund—Anfänge einer Weltumweltpolitik', *Archiv für Sozialgeschichte*, vol. 43 (2003), 177–90.

Wöbse, A.-K., 'Paul Sarasins "anthropologischer Naturschutz": Zur "Größe" Mensch im frühen internationalen Naturschutz. Ein Werkstattbericht', in Gert Gröning, and Joachim Wolschke-Bulmann (eds), *Naturschutz und Demokratie?!* (Munich: Martin Meidenbauer, 2006), 207–13.

Wöbse, A.-K., *Weltnaturschutz. Umweltdiplomatie in Völkerbund und Vereinten Nationen 1920–1950* (Frankfurt a. M.: Campus, 2012).

Wolford, W., Borras Jr, S. M., Hall, R., Scoones, I., and White, B. (eds), *Governing Global Land Deals: The Role of the State in the Rush for Land* (Chichester: Wiley, 2013).

World Bank, *Copperbelt Environment Project*, Rep. No. 25347-ZA (2003).

Worster, D., *Nature's Economy: A History of Ecological Ideas*, 2nd edn (Cambridge: Cambridge University Press, 1994).

Wright, A., *The Death of Ramón Gonzalez: The Modern Agricultural Dilemma*, 2nd edn (Austin, Tex.: University of Texas Press, 2005).

Wrigley, E. A., *Continuity, Chance, and Change: The Character of the Industrial Revolution in England* (Cambridge: Cambridge University Press, 1988).

Wrigley, E. A., *Energy and the English Industrial Revolution* (Cambridge: Cambridge University Press, 2010).

Yates, D. A., 'Neo-"Petro-monialism" and the Rentier State in Gabon', in Matthias Basedau and Andreas Mehler (eds), *Resource Politics in sub-Saharan Africa* (Hamburg: Institut für Afrika-Kunde, 2005).

Yergin, D., *The Prize: The Epic Quest for Oil, Money and Power* (New York: Free Press, 2009).

Young, A., *The Chocolate Tree: A Natural History of Cacao* (Washington, DC: Smithsonian, 1994).

Zimmermann, A., *Anthropology and Antihumanism in Imperial Germany* (Chicago: University of Chicago Press, 2001).

Zimmerman, A., 'A German Alabama in Africa: The Tuskegee Expedition to German Togo and the Transnational Origins of West African Cotton Growers', *American Historical Review*, vol. 110 (2005), 1362–98.

Zimmerman, A., *Alabama in Africa: Booker T. Washington, The German Empire, and the Globalization of the New South* (Princeton: Princeton University Press, 2010).

PUBLISHED PRIMARY MATERIAL

Adam, J., *De l'écologie agricole à l'écologie coloniale* (Paris: Imprimerie Nationale, 1937).

Allan, W., *Studies in African Land Usage in Northern Rhodesia*, Rhodes-Livingstone papers no. 15 (Cape Town: Oxford University Press, 1949).

Allan, W., et al., *Land Holding and Land Usage among the Plateau Tonga of Mazabuka District: A Reconnaissance Survey, 1945* (Oxford: Oxford University Press, 1945).

Arnold, R. A., *The History of the Cotton Famine, from the Fall of Sumter to the Passing of the Public Works Act (1864)* (London: Saunders, Otley & Co., 1865).

Attenborough, L. G., 'Tin Mining in Malaya', in *Empire Mining and Metallurgical Congress, Proceedings. Part II. Mining* (London: Congress, 1925), 490–514.

Aubert, G., *Les Sols des régions tropicales de la France d'outre-mer: leur nature, leur conservation, leur prospection, leur étude* (Paris, 1944).

Aubert, G., *Les Sols et l'aménagement agricole de l'Afrique Occidentale Française* (Paris, 1951).

Aubréville, A., *La Forêt coloniale: les forêts de l'Afrique Occidentale Française* (Paris: Société d'Éditions Géographique, Maritimes et Coloniales, 1938).

Aubréville, A., *Climats, forêts et désertification de l'Afrique tropicale* (Paris: Société d'Éditions Géographique, Maritimes et Coloniales, 1949).

Aubréville, A., et al., *Contribution à l'étude des réserves naturelles et des parcs nationaux* (Paris: Lechevalier, 1937).

Azzi, G., *Ecologia agraria* (Turin, 1925).

Baldwin, K. D. S., *The Niger Agricultural Project: An Experiment in African Development* (Oxford: Blackwell, 1957).

Balls, W. L., *The Cotton Plant in Egypt: Studies in Physiology and Genetics* (London: Macmillan, 1919).

Bartelink, E. J., *Handleiding voor kakao-planters* (Amsterdam: de Bussy, 1885).

Bauer, P. T., *Report on a Visit to the Rubber Growing Smallholdings of Malaya, July–September 1946* (London: HMSO, 1948).

Bauer, P. T., *The Rubber Industry: A Study in Competition and Monopoly* (London: Longmans, 1948).

Baumann, O., *Eine Afrikanische Tropen-Insel. Fernando Póo und die Bube* (Vienna: Hölzel, 1888).

Baumann, O., *Durch Massailand zur Nilquelle. Reisen und Forschungen der Massai-Expedition des deutschen Antisklaverei-Komité in den Jahren 1891–1893* (Berlin: Reimer, 1894).

Beckett, W. H., *Koransang 1904–1970* (Legon: University of Ghana Institute of Statistical, Social and Economic Research, 1972).

Beeby-Thompson, A., *Oil Pioneer: Selected Experiences and Incidents Associated with Sixty Years of World-Wide Petroleum Exploration and Oilfield Development* (London: Sidgwick & Jackson, 1961).

Bentley, C. A., *Malaria and Agriculture in Bengal: How to Reduce Malaria in Bengal by Irrigation* (Calcutta: Bengal Secretariat Book Depot, 1925).

Birchard, R. E., 'Copper in the Katanga Region of the Belgian Congo', *Economic Geography*, vol. 16 (1940), 429–36.

Birkinshaw, F., 'Reclaiming Old Mining Land for Agriculture', *Malayan Agricultural Journal*, vol. 19 (1931), 470–6.

Blache, J., 'La Campagne en pays noir: essai sur les caractères du paysages rural en Afrique occidentale', *Revue de géographie alpine*, vol. 28 no. 3 (1940), 346–88.

Bloud, H., *Le Problème cotonnier et l'Afrique Occidentale Française: une solution nationale* (Paris: Émile Larose, 1925).

Boeke, J. H., *Ontwikkelingsgang en toekomst van bevolkings- en ondernemingslandbouw in Nederlandsch-Indië* (Leiden: Brill, 1948).

Brandis, D., *Suggestions Regarding Forest Administration in the Madras Presidency* (Madras: Government Press, 1883).

Brelsford, W. V., *Copperbelt Markets: A Social and Economic Study* (Lusaka: Government Printer, 1947).

Brouwer, G. A., *De Organisatie van de Natuurbescherming in de verschillende Landen* (Amsterdam: De Spieghel, 1931).

Brown, R. H., *History of the Barrage at the Head of the Delta of Egypt* (Cairo: E. Diemer, 1896).

Buttgenbach, M. H., *Les Mines du Katanga* (Brussels: A. Lesigne, 1908).

Büttikofer, J., *Report on the Conference for the International Protection of Nature* (Basel: Swiss League for the Protection of Nature, 1946).

Cardot, J., *Note sur la production du caoutchouc en Indochine* (Paris: Agence Économique de l'Indochine, 1929).

Carle, E., *Le Riz en Cochinchine: étude agricole, commerciale, industrielle, avec diverses notes concernant cette culture dans le monde* (Cantho: Imprimerie de l'Ouest, 1933).

Carruthers, J. B., 'Report of the Director of Agriculture of F.M.S. for 1907', *Agricultural Bulletin of the Straits and Federated Malay States*, vol. 8 (Singapore: GPO, 1908), 523–48.

Cassels, W. R., *Cotton: An Account of its Culture in the Bombay Presidency* (Bombay, 1862).

Charles-Roux, F., *La Production du coton en Égypte* (Paris: A. Colin, 1908).

Chevalier, A., 'Les Zones et les provinces botanique de l'Afrique–Occidentale française', *Comptes rendus des séances de l'Académie des Sciences*, vol. 130 no. 18 (1900), 1202–8.

Chevalier, A., *La Situation agricole de l'ouest africain enquête* (Domfront: Senen, 1906).

Chevalier, A., *Le Cacaoyer dans l'ouest africain* (Paris: Challamel, 1908).

Chevalier, A., *Première Étude sur les bois de la Côte d'Ivoire* (Paris: Challamel, 1909).

Chevalier, A., *Exploration botanique de l'Afrique Occidentale Française* (Paris: Lechevallier, 1920).

Chevalier, A., *L'Agriculture coloniale: origines et évolution* (Paris: Presses Universitaires de France, 1942).

Chevalier, A., *Révolution en agriculture* (Paris: Presses Universitaires de France, 1946).

Chevalier, A., 'Amélioration et extension de la culture des arachides au Sénégal', *Revue de botanique appliquée* (May 1947), 173–92.

Chevalier, A., 'La Protection de la nature et les parcs-réserves de l'Afrique Occidentale Française', *Comptes rendus hebdomadaires des séances de l'Académie des Sciences*, no. 230 (Jan.–June 1950), 2140–2.

Christy, D., *Cotton is King: Or, The Culture of Cotton, and its Relation to Agriculture, Manufactures and Commerce* (Cincinnati: Moore, Wilstach, Keys, 1855).

Cleghorn, H., *The Forests and Gardens of South India* (London: W. H. Allen, 1861).

Commission de Coopération Technique en Afrique au Sud du Sahara, *1ère Conférence forestière interafricaine: Abidjan, 4–12 décembre 1951* (Paris: de Jouve, 1952).

Conwentz, H., *Die Gefährdung der Naturdenkmäler und Vorschläge zu ihrer Erhaltung* (Berlin: Borntraeger, 1904).

Conwentz, H., *The Care of Natural Monuments with Special Reference to Great Britain and Germany* (Cambridge: Cambridge University Press, 1909).

Dacosta, J., *Facts and Fallacies Regarding Irrigation as a Prevention of Famine in India* (London: W. H. Allen & Co., 1878).

Davis, J. M. (ed.), *Modern Industry and the African: An Enquiry into the Effect of the Copper Mines of Central Africa upon Native Society and the Work of Christian Missions made under the auspices of the Department of Social and Industrial Research of the International Missionary Council* (London: Macmillan, 1933).

de Bauw, J. A., *Le Katanga: notes sur le pays, ses ressources et l'avenir de la colonisation belge* (Brussels: Larcier, 1920).

Deeken, R., *Die Landwirtschaft in den deutschen Kolonien* (Berlin: Süsserott, 1914).

de Groof, G., 'Conservation des sols congolais et politique agricole', *Bulletin agricole du Congo belge*, vol. 35 (1944), 118–36.

de Keyser, P. A., and Villiers, A., 'Recherche scientifique et protection de la nature', *Institut Français d'Afrique Noire*, no. 2 (undated, *c.*1950), 1–3.

de Keyser, P. A., and Villiers, A., 'Protection des animaux', *Institut Français d'Afrique Noire*, no. 4. (Jan. 1951).

DeMille, J. B., *Strategic Minerals: A Summary of Uses, World Output, Stockpiles, Procurement* (New York: McGraw-Hill, 1947).

Denys, O., *Du rôle de l'agriculture indigène dans les colonies d'exploitation* (Paris: Jouve, 1917).

Dernburg, B., *Zielpunkte des deutschen Kolonialwesens* (Berlin: Mittler, 1907).

Derscheid, J.-M., 'La Protection de la nature au Congo belge', *La Protection de la nature et l'Union Internationale des Sciences Biologiques: communications présentées aus assemblées générales de 1925, 1926, 1927 et 1928* (Brussels, 1929), 39–46.

Deutsche Kolonial-Gesellschaft, *Bericht über die Arbeiten der Wildschutz-Kommission der Deutschen Kolonial-Gesellschaft* (Berlin: Süsserott, 1912).

de Wildeman, E., *Contribution à l'étude de la flore du Katanga* (Brussels: D. Reynaert, 1921).

Dumont, R., *La Culture du riz dans le delta du Tonkin: étude et propositions d'amélioration des techniques traditionnelles de riziculture tropicale* (Paris: Société d'Éditions Géographiques, Maritimes et Coloniales, 1935).

Dumont, R., *False Start in Africa*, trans. Phyllis Nauts Ott (London: Andre Deutsch, 1966).

Durand, Sir M., *Life of the Right Hon. Sir Alfred Comyn Lyall* (Edinburgh: Blackwood, 1913).

Duval, C., *Question cotonnière: la France peut s'emparer du monopole du coton par l'Afrique; elle peut rendre l'Angleterre, l'Europe, ses tributaires; l'Afrique est le vrai pays du coton* (Paris: Cosson, 1864).

du Vivier de Streel, M., *La Culture en Afrique Équatoriale Française* (Coulommiers: Dessaint, 1917).

Edelman, C. H., *Studiën over de Bodemkunde van Nederlandsch-Indië* (Wageningen: Veenman, 1947).

Everwyn, G., 'Which Way in Katanga?', *African Affairs*, vol. 61 no. 243 (Apr. 1962), 149–57.

Fabri, F., *Bedarf Deutschland der Colonien? Eine politisch-ökonomische Betrachtung* (Gotha: Perthes, 1879).

Fabricius, J., *East Indies Episode: An Account of the Demolitions Carried out and of Some Experiences of the Staff in the East Indies Oil Areas of the Royal Dutch-Shell Group during 1941 and 1942* (London: Shell, 1949).

Fauck, R., *Érosion et mécanisation agricole* (Bureau des Sols en AOF, Sept. 1956).

Fauconnier, H., *The Soul of Malaya*, trans. Eric Sutton (Singapore: Oxford University Press, 1990).

Faulkner, O. T., and Mackie, J. R., *West African Agriculture* (Cambridge: Cambridge University Press, 1933).

Federated Malay States, *Report on the Administration of the Mines Department and on the Mining Industry* (Singapore: GPO, 1914, 1920).

Ferguson, H. (Ministry of Agriculture, Sudan Government), *Notes on Cotton Growing from the Research Division* (Khartoum: Agricultural Publications Committee, 1954).

Fermor, Sir L. L., *Report upon the Mining Industry of Malaya*, 3rd printing (Kuala Lumpur: Government Press, 1943).

Ferrar, H. T., *Preliminary Note on the Subsoil Water in Lower Egypt and its Bearing on the Reported Deterioration of the Cotton Crop* (Cairo: National Printing Dept, 1910).

Forbes, H., *A Naturalist's Wanderings in the Eastern Archipelago: A Narrative of Travel and Exploration from 1878 to 1883* (London: Low, Marston, Searle & Rivington, 1883).

Forthomme, P., *La Véritable Signification du Katanga pour la Belgique: des moyens de l'accentuer* (Brussels: Hayez, 1911).

Fowler, T. K., *Report on the Cultivation of Cotton in Egypt: Its Origin, Progress, and Extent at the Present Day; The Obstacles which Prevent its Extension; Suggestions for Effectually Removing them, etc.* (Manchester, 1861).

Gaitskell, A., *Gezira: A Story of Development in the Sudan* (London: Faber & Faber, 1959).

Gaudy, M., *La Conservation des sols en A.O.F.* (Gouvernement Générale de l'AOF, 1953).

Gedenkboek Billiton 1852–1927 (The Hague: Nijhoff, 1927).

Girard, E., *Notes sur la culture de l'Hévea en Cochinchine* (Saigon: Ardin, 1918).

Gourou, P., *L'Utilisation du sol en Indochine française* (Paris: Hartmann, 1940).

Gourou, P., 'Les Plantations de cacaoyers en pays Yoruba: un exemple d'expansion économique spontanée', *Annales: économies, sociétés, civilisations*, vol. 15 no. 1 (1960), 60–82.

Gourou, P., *The Tropical World: Its Social and Economic Conditions and its Future Status*, 4th edn (London: Longmans, 1966).

Gouvernement Générale de l'AOF, Inspection Générale de l'Agriculture, *Organisation et action des services de l'agriculture* (Rufisque: Imprimerie du Gouvernement Général, 1952).

Greaves, I. C., *Modern Production among Backward Peoples* (London: Allen & Unwin, 1935).

Grijns, G., and Kiewiet de Jonge, G. W., *Plantage-Hygiene* (Batavia: Javasche Boekhandel, 1914).

Grist, D. H., *Nationality of Ownership and Nature of Constitution of Rubber Estates in Malaya* (Kuala Lumpur: Caxton Press, 1933).

Grove, A. T., *Land Use and Soil Conservation in Parts of Onitsha and Owerri Province* (Kaduna: Nigerian Government, 1951).

Grove, A. T., *Land Use and Soil Conservation on the Jos Plateau* (Kaduna: Nigerian Government, 1952).

Guilloteau, J., *Inter-African Organisations for Soil Conservation* (Paris: Bureau Interafricain d'Information sur la Conservation et l'Utilisation des Sols, undated).

Haines, W. B., *The Uses and Control of Natural Undergrowth on Rubber Estates* (Kuala Lumpur: Rubber Research Institute, 1934).

Harris, H. G., and Willbourn, E. S., *Mining in Malaya* (London: Malayan Information Agency, 1940).

Harroy, J.-P., *Afrique: terre qui meurt. La Dégradation des sols africaines sous l'influence de la colonisation* (Brussels: Académie Royale de Belgique, 1944).

Haushofer, M., *Der Schutz der Natur* (Munich, 1906).

Helbig, K., 'Die Insel Bangka. Beispiel des Landschafts- und Bedeutungswandels auf Grund einer geographischen "Zufallsform"', *Deutsche Geographische Blätter*, vol. 43 nos 3/4 (1940), 137–209.

Henderson, W. O., *The Lancashire Cotton Famine, 1861–1865* (Manchester: Manchester University Press, 1934).

Henry, Y., *La Question cotonnière en Afrique Occidentale Française* (Melun: Imprimerie Administrative, 1906).

Henry, Y., *Le Coton dans l'Afrique Occidentale Française* (Paris: Challamel, 1906).

Henry, Y., *Terres rouges et terres noires basaltiques d'Indochine: leur mise en culture* (Hanoi: Gouvernement Général de l'Indochine, 1931).

Higgs, J. W. Y., et al., *Report of a Survey of Problems in the Mechanization of Native Agriculture in Tropical African Colonies* (London: HMSO, 1950).

Hollings, M. A. (ed.), *The Life of Sir Colin C. Scott-Moncrieff* (London: John Murray, 1917).

Honig, P., and Verdoorn, F. (eds), *Science and Scientists in the Netherlands Indies* (New York: Board for the Netherlands Indies, Surinam and Curaçao, 1945).

Hornaday, W. T., *Our Vanishing Wildlife: Its Extermination and Preservation* (New York: New York Zoological Society, 1913).

Hornaday, W. T., *The Extermination of the American Bison* (Washington, DC: Smithsonian Institution Press, 2002; originally 1889).

Howard, A., *Crop Production in India: A Critical Survey of its Problems* (Oxford: Oxford University Press, 1924).

Howard, A., *An Agricultural Testament* (orig. 1940) (Oxford: Oxford City Press, 2010).

Hubert, H., 'Le Desséchement progressif en Afrique Occidentale', *Bulletin du Comité d'Études Historiques et Scientifiques d'AOF* (1920), 401–67.

Humbert, H., *La Protection de la nature dans les territoires d'outre-mer pendant la guerre* (Paris: Société d'Éditions Géographiques, Maritimes et Coloniales, 1940).

Hume, A. O., *Agricultural Reform in India* (London: W. H. Allen, 1879).

Hutchins, D. E., *East Africa Protectorate: Report on the Forests of Kenia* (London: HMSO, 1907).

Hutchins, D. E., *Report on the Forests of British East Africa* (London: HMSO, 1909).

Imperial Mineral Resources Bureau, *The Mineral Industry of the British Empire and Foreign Countries. War Period. Copper (1913–1919)* (London: HMSO, 1922).

Imperial Mineral Resources Bureau, *The Mineral Industry of the British Empire and Foreign Countries. War Period. Tin (1913–1919)* (London: HMSO, 1922).

Jacks, G. V., and Whyte, R. O., *The Rape of the Earth: A World Survey of Soil Erosion* (London: Faber & Faber, 1939).

Jentsch, F., 'Die Entwicklung des Forstwesens in den deutschen Kolonien', *Mitteilungen des deutschen Forstvereins*, vol. 25 (1914), 71–81.

Jezler, H., *Das Ölfeld Sanga Sanga in Koetei* (Berlin: Scholem, 1916).

Joleaud, L., *Le Pétrole dans l'Afrique du Nord* (Paris: Revue Pétrolifère, 1926).

Jolyet, A., *Le Transport des bois dans les forêts coloniales* (Paris: Challamel, 1912).

Jones, G. H., *The Earth Goddess: A Study of Native Farming on the West African Coast* (London: Longmans, 1936).

Joralemon, I. B., *Copper: The Encompassing Story of Mankind's First Metal* (Berkeley: Howell-North, 1973), first published as *Romantic Copper: Its Lure and Lore* (London: D. Appleton-Century Co., 1934).

Jumelle, H., *Les Plantes à caoutchouc et à gutta dans les colonies françaises* (Paris: Challamel, 1898).

Jumelle, H., *Le Cacaoyer: sa culture et son exploitation dans tous les pays de production* (Paris: Challamel, 1900).

Kelly, R. T., *Burma* (London: Black, 1908).

Keynes, J. M., 'National Self-Sufficiency', *The Yale Review*, vol. 22 no. 4 (June 1933), 755–69.

Kidd, B., *Social Evolution* (London: Macmillan, 1894).

Kidd, B., *The Control of the Tropics* (London: Macmillan, 1898).

Kies, C., *Nature Protection in the Netherlands Indies* (Cambridge, Mass.: American Committee for International Wild Life Protection, 1936).

King, A. W., 'Plantation and Agriculture in Malaya, with Notes on the Trade of Singapore', *Geographical Journal*, vol. 93 no. 2 (Feb. 1939), 136–48.

Klopstock, F., *Kakao. Wandlungen in der Erzeugung und der Verwendung des Kakaos nach dem Weltkrieg* (Leipzig: Bibliographisches Institut, 1937).

Knapp, A. W., *Cocoa and Chocolate: Their History from Plantation to Consumer* (London: Chapman & Hall, 1920).

Kolonial-Wirtschaftliches Komitee, *Kupfer und die deutschen Kolonien* (Berlin: KWK, 1917).

Kolonial-Wirtschaftliches Komitee, *Kautschuk und die deutschen Kolonien* (Berlin: KWK, c.1917).

Lahache, M. J., 'Le Desséchement de l'Afrique française est-il demontré', *Bulletin de la Société de Géographie et d'Études Coloniales de Marseilles*, vol. 31 (1907), 149–85.

Lambert, G., *India, the Horror-Stricken Empire: Containing a Full Account of the Famine, Plague, and Earthquake of 1896–7, including a Complete Narration of the Relief Work through the Home and Foreign Relief Commission* (Elkhart, Ind.: Mennonite Publishing Company, 1898).

Lamminga, A. G., *Beschouwingen over den tegenwoordigen stand van het irrigatiewezen in Nederlandsch-Indië* (The Hague: van Langenhuysen, 1910).

Lange, H. M., *Het eiland Banka en zijne aangelegenheden* (Gebr. Muller, 1850).

Legraye, M., 'La Production minière du Congo belge et son rôle dans le relèvement économique de la Belgique', *Annales de la Société Géologique de Belgique*, vol. 68 (1945), 157–74.

Leplae, E., *La Crise agricole coloniale et les phases du développement de l'agriculture dans le Congo central* (Brussels: Hayez, 1932).

Leroy-Beaulieu, P., *De la colonisation chez les peuples modernes* (Paris: Guillaumin, 1874).

Le Rumeur, G., *Le Sahara avant le pétrole* (Paris: SCEMI, 1960).

Less, H. M. N., *Organisation for the Production of a Working Plan for the Forests Supplying the Copperbelt of Northern Rhodesia* (Lusaka: Government Printer, 1962).

Letcher, O., *South Central Africa* (Johannesburg: African Publications, 1932).

Lulofs, M., *Rubber* (orig. 1931), trans. G. J. Renier and Irene Clephane (Singapore: Oxford University Press, 1987).

Macfayden, E., *Rubber Planting in Malaya* (London: Malay States Information Agency, 1924).

McLeod, N. C., *Address on Forestry in Connection with the Cocoa Industry of the Gold Coast* (Accra: Government Press, 1920).

Malengreau, G., *Vers un paysannat indigène: les lotissements agricoles au Congo belge* (Brussels: Institut Royal du Congo Belge, 1949).

Martin, F., *Principes d'agriculture et d'économie rurale appliqués aux pays tropicaux* (Paris, 1935).

Maxwell, Sir G., *In Malay Forests* (Edinburgh: Blackwood, 1907).

Meads, H. D., *Bark Consumption and Bark Reserves on Small Rubber Holdings in Malaya* (Kuala Lumpur: Kyle, Palmer & Co., 1934).

Michaux, P., *L'Hévéaculture en Indochine: son évolution* (Paris: Exposition Internationale, 1937).

Milne, G., *A Provisional Soil Map of East Africa* (Southampton: Ordnance Survey, 1936).

Milstead, H. P., 'Cacao Industry of Grenada', *Economic Geography*, vol. 16 no. 2 (Apr. 1940), 195–203.

Mingot, R., and Canet, J., *L'Heveaculture en Indochine* (Paris: Exposition Internationale, 1937).

Ministère des Colonies, *Manuel pratique de la culture du caféier et du cacaoyer au Congo belge* (Brussels: Van Campenhout, 1908).

Mohnike, O., *Banka und Palembang nebst Mittheilungen über Sumatra im Allgemeinen* (Münster: Aschendorfss'chen Buchhandlung, 1874).

Moll, E. R., *Cacao in Trinidad and Tobago* (1960).

Mollema, J. C., *De Ontwikkeling van het Eiland Billiton en van de Billiton-Maatschappij* (The Hague: Martinus Nijhoff, 1918).

Moore, R. J. B., *These African Copper Miners: A Study of the Industrial Revolution in Northern Rhodesia, with Principal Reference to the Copper Mining Industry* (London: Livingstone, 1948).

Morel, E. D., *Red Rubber: The Story of the Rubber Slave Trade Flourishing on the Congo in the Year of Grace 1906* (London: T. F. Unwin, 1906).

Northern Rhodesia, *Annual Report of the Mines Department for the Year 1963* (Lusaka: Government Printer, 1964).

Northern Rhodesia Chamber of Mines, *Yearbook* (1962).

Northern Rhodesia, Mines Department, *Annual Report for the Year 1952* (Lusaka: Government Printer, 1953).

Northern Rhodesia, Ministry of Local Government and Social Welfare, *Report on the Preliminary Investigation into the Complaints as to the Conduct and Management of the Affairs of the Municipal Council of Luanshya* (Lusaka, 20 Nov. 1959).

Nowell, W., *The Agricultural Research Station at Amani* (Dar es Salaam, 1933).

Ormsby-Gore, W. G. A., *Report by the Hon. W. G. A. Ormsby-Gore, M.P. (Parliamentary Under-Secretary of State for the Colonies) on his Visit to West Africa during the Year 1926* (London: HMSO, 1926).

Ormsby-Gore, W. G. A., *Report by the Right Honourable W. G. A. Ormsby-Gore on his Visit to Malaya, Ceylon, and Java during the Year 1928* (London: HMSO, 1928).

Osborn, H. F., and Anthony, H. E., 'Close of the Age of Mammals', *Journal of Mammalogy*, vol. 3 no. 4 (Nov. 1922), 219–31.

Pascoe, E. H., *The Oil-Fields of Burma* (Calcutta: Geological Survey of India, 1912).

Paulin, H., *Le Pétrole: recherches et indices de gisements de pétrole dans les colonies françaises et pays de protectorat* (Paris: Librairie d'Enseignement Technique, 1924).

Penzer, N. M., *Cotton in British West Africa Including Togoland and the Cameroons* (London: Murby, 1920).

Posewitz, T., *Die Zinninseln im Indischen Ozean II. Das Zinnzvorkommen und die Zinngewinnung in Bangka* (Budapest: Franklin-Verein, 1886).

Prades, J., *Déboisement—incendies—rays: préservation et reconstitution de la forêt* (Hanoi: Imprimerie Tonkinoise, 1921).

Preuss, P., *Expedition nach Central- und Südamerika* (Berlin: KWK, 1901).

Rabichon, A., *Le Pétrole en Algérie* (Paris: Lafayette, 1921).

Reichskolonialamt, *Jagd und Wildschutz in den deutschen Kolonien* (Jena: Fischer, 1913).

Report of a Soil and Land-Use Survey of the Copperbelt, Northern Rhodesia (Lusaka: Government Printer, 1956).

Ribbentrop, B., *Forestry in British India* (Calcutta: GPO, 1900).

Richards, A. I., *Land, Labour and Diet in Northern Rhodesia: An Economic Study of the Bemba Tribe* (London: Oxford University Press, 1939).

Ridley, H. N., 'Reclaiming Abandoned Mining Lands', *Agricultural Bulletin of the Straits and Federated Malay States*, Second Series, no. 2 (1903), 63–4.

Robequain, C., *The Economic Development of French Indo-China*, trans. Isabel A. Ward (London: Oxford University Press, 1944).

Robert, L., *La Culture du coton en Afrique Occidentale Française* (Paris: Domat-Montchrestien, 1931).

Robert, M., *Le Centre Africain: le domaine minier et la cuvette congolaise* (Brussels: Lamertin, 1932).

Royle, J. F., *On the Culture and Commerce of Cotton in India and Elsewhere: With an Account of the Experiments Made by the Hon. East India Company up to the Present Time* (London: Smith, Elder & Co., 1851).

Russell, E. J., *World Population and World Food Supplies* (London: Allen & Unwin, 1954).

Sampson, H. C., and Crowther, E. M., *The West African Commission 1938–1939: Technical Reports* (London: Waterlow, 1943).

Sarasin, P., *Weltnaturschutz: Global Protection of Nature* (Basel, 1911).

Sarasin, P., *Ueber die Aufgaben des Weltnaturschutzes* (Basel: Helbig & Lichtenhahn, 1914).

Sarraut, A., *La Mise en valeur des colonies françaises* (Paris: Payot, 1923).

Sarraut, A., *Grandeur et servitude coloniales* (Paris: Éditions du Sagittaire, 1931).

Sauer, C. O., 'Destructive Exploitation in Modern Colonial Expansion', in *Comptes rendus du Congrès International de Géographie Amsterdam 1938*, vol. 2, IIIc (Leiden: Brill, 1938), 494–9.

Sauer, C. O., 'Theme of Plant and Animal Destruction in Economic History' (1938), repr. in John Leighley (ed.), *Land and Life: A Selection from the Writings of Carl Ortwin Sauer* (Berkeley: University of California Press, 1963), 145–54.

Scaëtta, H., *Les Famines périodiques dans le Ruanda* (Brussels: Hayes, 1932).

Schanz, M., *Cotton in Egypt and the Anglo-Egyptian Sudan* (Manchester: Taylor, Garnett, Evans, 1913).

Scherer, J. A. B., *Cotton as a World Power: A Study in the Economic Interpretation of History* (New York: Stokes, 1916).

Schwarz, L. J., *Cocoa in West Africa* (Washington, DC: Government Printing Office, 1928).

Schwarz, L. J., *Cocoa in the Ivory Coast* (Washington, DC: Government Printing Office, 1931).

Schwarz, L. J., *Cocoa in the Cameroons under French Mandate and in Fernando Po* (Washington, DC: Government Printing Office, 1933).

Shantz, H. L., and Marbut, C. F., *The Vegetation and Soils of Africa* (New York: NRC and AGS, 1923).

Shephard, C. Y., *Report on the Economics of Peasant Agriculture in the Gold Coast* (Accra: Government Printer, 1936).

Shephard, C. Y., *The Cacao Industry of Trinidad: Some Economic Aspects. Series III–IV* (Port-of-Spain: Government Printer, 1937).

Sherlock, R. L., *Man as a Geological Agent: An Account of his Action on Inanimate Nature* (London: Witherby, 1922).

Smith, H. H., *Notes on Soil and Plant Sanitation on Cacao and Rubber Estates* (London: Bale, 1911).

Spire, C., and Spire, A., *Le Caoutchouc en Indo-Chine: étude botanique industrielle et commerciale* (Paris: Challamel, 1906).

Stamp, L. D., 'Land Utilization and Soil Erosion in Nigeria', *Geographical Review*, vol. 28 (1938), 32–45.

Stamp, L. D., 'The Southern Margin of the Sahara: Comments on Some Recent Studies on the Question of Desiccation in West Africa', *Geographical Review*, vol. 30 no. 2 (Apr. 1940), 297–300.

Stebbing, E. P., *The Forests of India*, 2 vols (London: Bodley Head, 1922–3).

Stebbing, E. P., 'The Encroaching Sahara: The Threat to the West African Colonies', *Geographical Journal*, vol. 85 (1935), 506–19.

Stebbing, E. P., *The Forests of West Africa and the Sahara* (London: Chambers, 1937).

Stockdale, F. A., *Report by Mr. F. A. Stockdale on his Visit to Nigeria, Gold Coast and Sierra Leone, October 1935–February 1936* (London: Colonial Office, 1936).

Stockdale, F. A., *Report by Sir Frank Stockdale on his Visit to East Africa, January–March 1937* (London: Colonial Office, 1937).

Stockdale, F. A., *Report by Sir Frank Stockdale on a Visit to Malaya, Java, Sumatra and Ceylon 1938* (London: Colonial Office, 1939).

Stokes, R., *Malay Tin-Fields: Mining Position Broadly Reviewed* (Singapore: Straits Times Press, 1906).

Swart, N. L., and Rutgers, A. A. L. (eds), *Handboek voor de Rubbercultuur in Nederlandsch-Indië* (Amsterdam: de Bussy, 1921).

Swettenham, F. A., *About Perak* (Singapore: Straits Times Press, 1893).

Swettenham, F. A., *British Malaya: An Account of the Origins and Progress of British Influence in Malaya* (London: Allen & Unwin, 1907).

Székely, L., *Tropic Fever: The Adventures of a Planter in Sumatra* (orig. 1937), trans. Marion Saunders (Singapore: Oxford University Press, 1979).

Tayler, V. A., and Stephens, J., *Native Rubber in the Dutch East Indies* (London: Rubber Growers' Association, 1929).

Tempany, Sir H. A., *The Practice of Soil Conservation in the British Colonial Empire* (Harpenden: Commonwealth Bureau of Soil Science, 1949).

ter Braake, A. L., *Mining in the Netherlands East Indies* (Bulletins of the Netherlands and Netherlands Indies Council, 1944).

Todd, J. A., *The World's Cotton Crops* (London: Black, 1915).

Tondeur, G., and Bergeroo-Campagne, B., *L'Agriculture nomade*, vol. 1: *Congo belge, Côte d'Ivoire* (Rome: FAO, 1956).

Tothill, J. D. (ed.), *Agriculture in Uganda* (London: Oxford University Press, 1940).

Trapnell, C. G., and Clothier, J. N., *The Soils, Vegetation and Agricultural Systems of North Western Rhodesia: Report of the Ecological Survey* (Lusaka: Government Printer, 1937).

Troup, R. S., *The Work of the Forest Department in India* (Calcutta: Superintendent Government Printing, 1917).

Troup, R. S., *Report on Forestry in Kenya Colony* (London: Waterlow, 1922).

Troup, R. S., *Colonial Forest Administration* (Oxford: Oxford University Press, 1940).

United States Geological Survey, Minerals Yearbook 1932/3–1960 (Washington, DC: Government Printing Office, 1933–61).

Unwin, A. H., West African Forests and Forestry (London: T. Fisher Unwin Ltd, 1920).

Vageler, P., Über die Düngungsfrage in den deutschen Kolonien (Berlin: Süsserott, 1911).

Vageler, P., An Introduction to Tropical Soils, trans. H. Greene (London: Macmillan, 1933).

Vageler, P., Koloniale Bodenkunde und Wirtschaftsplanung (Berlin: Parey, 1941).

van de Leemkolk, W. J., De Rubber-Cultuur en de Rubber-Handel van Nederlandsch-Indië (Batavia: Ruygrok, 1914).

van Gelder, A., 'Bevolkingsrubbercultuur', in C. J. J. van Hall, and C. van de Koppel (eds), De Landbouw in de Indische Archipel, vol. 3 (The Hague: van Hoeve, 1950), 427–75.

van Steenis, C., Album van Natuurmonumenten in Nederlandsch-Indië (Batavia: Nederl.-Indische Vereenig. tot Natuurbescherming, 1937).

van Straelen, V., 'La Protection de la nature: sa nécessité et ses avantages', in Les Parcs nationaux et la protection de la nature (Brussels: Institut des Parcs Nationaux du Congo Belge, 1937), 41–87.

Vaxelaire, J., Le Caoutchouc en Indochine (Hanoi: Imprimerie d'Extrême-Orient, 1939).

Vayssière, P., and Mimeur, J., Les Insectes nuisibles au cotonnier en Afrique Occidentale Française (Paris: Émile Larose, 1926).

Viton, A., Cacao: tendances actuelles de la production, des prix et de la consommation (Rome: FAO, 1957).

Voelcker, J. A., Report on the Improvement of Indian Agriculture (London: Eyre & Spottiswoode, 1893).

Vogt, W., Road to Survival (London: Gollancz, 1949).

Volker, T., Van Oerbosch tot Cultuurgebied: een Schets van de Beteekenis van de Tabak, de andere Cultures en de Industrie ter Oostkust van Sumatra (Medan: Deli Planters Vereeniging, 1928).

von Schellendorf, F. B., Internationaler Wildschutz in Afrika (Munich, 1900).

Vuillet, F., Henry, Y., and Lavergne, H., Les Irrigations au Niger et la culture du cotonnier (Paris: Émile Larose, 1922).

Wallace, A. R., The Malay Archipelago: The Land of the Orang-utan, and the Bird of Paradise. A Narrative of Travel, with Studies of Man and Nature (New York: Harper, 1869).

Warburg, O., Die Kautschukpflanzen und ihre Kultur (Berlin: KWK, 1900).

Warnford-Lock, C. G., Mining in Malaya for Gold and Tin (London: Crowther & Goodman, 1907).

Watson, Sir M., The Prevention of Malaria in the Federated Malay States, 2nd revised edn (London: Murray, 1921).

Watson, Sir M., African Highway: The Battle for Health in Central Africa (London: Murray, 1953).

Watt, Sir G., The Wild and Cultivated Cotton Plants of the World: A Revision of the Genus Gossypium (London: Longmans, Green, 1907).

Willcocks, Sir W., The Assuan Reservoir and Lake Moeris (London: Spon, 1904).

Willcocks, Sir W., The Restoration of the Ancient Irrigation of Bengal (Lecture to the British India Association, 6 Mar. 1928) (Calcutta: Calcutta General Printing Co., 1928).

Willcocks, Sir W., and Craig, J. I., Egyptian Irrigation, vol. 1, 3rd edn (London: Spon, 1913).

Williamson, J. W., In a Persian Oil-Field: A Study in Scientific and Industrial Development (London: Ernest Benn, 1927).

Willis, J. C., A Report upon Agriculture in the Federated Malay States (Kuala Lumpur: FMS Government Printing Press, 1904).

Wilson, G., *An Essay on the Economics of Detribalization in Northern Rhodesia*, Parts 1 and 2 (Livingstone: Rhodes-Livingstone Institute, 1941–2).

Wood, A., *The Groundnut Affair* (London: Bodley Head, 1950).

Worthington, E. B., *Science in Africa: A Review of Scientific Research Relating to Tropical and Southern Africa* (London: Oxford University Press, 1938).

Wray, L., 'Some Account of the Tin Mines and the Mining Industries of Perak', *Perak Museum Notes*, vol. 2 part 2 (1898), 83–4.

Wright, A., and Cartwright, H. A., *20th-Century Impressions of British Malaya: Its History, People, Commerce, Industries, and Resources* (London: Lloyds, 1908).

Wright, H., *My Tour in Eastern Rubber Lands* (London: McLaren, 1908).

Zacher, F., *Die wichtigsten Krankheiten und Schädlinge der tropischen Kulturpflanzen und ihre Bekämpfung* (Hamburg: Thaden, 1914).

Zimmermann, A., *Anleitung für die Baumwollkultur in den deutschen Kolonien*, 2nd edn (Berlin: KWK, 1910).

Zischka, A., *La Guerre secrète pour le pétrole* (Paris: Payot, 1933).

Zondervan, H., *Bangka en zijne bewoners* (Amsterdam: J. H. de Bussy, 1895).

FURTHER PRIMARY MATERIAL

Annales de géographie, 1891– (vol. 1–).

Annual Report of the Drainage and Irrigation Department of the Malay States and the Straits Settlements for the Year 1937 (Kuala Lumpur: FMS, 1938).

Bulletin agricole du Congo belge et du Ruanda-Urundi: volume jubilaire (Brussels: Place Royale, 1960).

Comptes rendus de la Conférence Internationale pour la Protection de la Faune et de la Flore en Afrique (3: 1953, Bukavu) (Brussels, 1954).

Congrès du Perfectionnement de l'Agriculture Indigène (Quinzaine Nationale de la Production Agricole d'Outre-mer, 1931).

Congrès International pour la Protection de la Nature (Paris, 1925).

Der Pflanzer. Zeitschrift für Land- und Forstwirtschaft in Deutsch-Ostafrika, 1904–14 (vols 1–10).

Der Tropenpflanzer. Zeitschrift für tropische Landwirtschaft, 1897–1944 (vols 1–47).

Deuxième Congrès International pour la Protection de la Nature (Paris, 1932).

First Report on a Regional Survey of the Copperbelt 1959 (Lusaka: Government Printer, 1960).

L'Agronomie coloniale: bulletin mensuel du Jardin colonial (subsequently de l'Institut National d'Agronomie Coloniale; de l'Institut National d'Agronomie de la France d'Outre-Mer), 1913–39 (vols 1–28).

L'Agronomie tropicale: publication mensuelle du Ministère des colonies, 1946–61 (vols 1–16).

L'Exploitation des richesses minières du Congo belge et du Ruanda-Urundi (Brussels: Centre d'Information et de Documentation du Congo Belge et du Ruanda-Urundi, 1955).

La Protection de la nature et l'Union Internationale des Sciences Biologiques: communications présentées aux assemblées générales de 1925, 1926, 1927 et 1928 (Brussels, 1929).

Le Pétrole au Gabon, Centre de Documentation et de Diffusion des Industries Minérales et Énergétiques Outre-mer, Études et Documents (July 1957).

Le Plan quadriennal d'equipement et de modernisation de l'A.O.F. (1953–1957).

Les 'Amis de l'Éléphant', société fondée à Paris, le 6 décembre 1905 (Paris, 1907).

Malayan Forester, 1931–72 (vols 1–35) (continued after 1935 as *The Malayan Forester*).

Memorandum by the Anti-Slavery and Aborigines Protection Society on the Report of the Commission Appointed to Enquire into the 1940 Disturbances in the Copperbelt of Northern Rhodesia (London: ASAPS, 1941).

Northern Rhodesia Government Gazette, Ordinances, 1959 (Lusaka: Government Printer, 1960).

Notes on Perak, With a Sketch of its Vegetable, Animal and Mineral Products (London: William Clowes, 1886).

Planteurs d'hévéas en Indochine, 1939–1954 (Amicale des Planteurs d'Hévéas, 1996).

Recueil des Procès-Verbaux de la Conférence Internationale pour la Protection de la Nature: Berne, 17–19 Novembre 1913 (Bern: Wyss, 1914).

Report and Proceedings of the Mining Conference Held at Ipoh, Perak, Federated Malay States, September 23rd to October 6th, 1901 (Taiping: Perak Government Printing Office, 1902).

Report of the Anglo-French Forestry Commission 1936–37 (Lagos: Government Printer, 1937).

Report of the Commission Appointed to Enquire into the Disturbances in the Copperbelt of Northern Rhodesia (London: HMSO, 1935).

Report of the Commission Appointed to Enquire into the Disturbances in the Copperbelt of Northern Rhodesia (Lusaka: Government Printer, 1940).

Report of the Commission Appointed to Inquire into and Report upon Certain Matters Regarding the Rivers in the Federated Malay States (Kuala Lumpur: Government Printing Office, 1928).

Resettlement and the Development of New Villages in the Federation of Malaya, 1952 (Kuala Lumpur: Government Press, 1952).

Rubber in the Netherlands East Indies (Weltevreden: Landsdrukkerij, 1925).

The Royal Dutch Petroleum Company, Diamond Jubilee Book (The Hague: Royal Dutch, 1950).

Union Minière du Haut-Katanga: 1906–1956 (Brussels: Cuypers, 1956).

Union Minière du Haut-Katanga: Évolution des Techniques et des Activités Sociales (Brussels: Cuypers, 1957).

Verhandlungen des deutschen Kolonialkongresses, 4 vols (1902, 1905, 1910, 1924) (Berlin: Reimer, 1903–25).

VIe Congrès International d'Agriculture Tropicale et Subtropicale, Paris 15–19 Juillet 1931, vol. 2 (Abbeville: Paillart, 1932).

VIIe Congrès International d'Agriculture Tropicale et Subtropicale: comptes-rendus et rapports (Paris, 1937).

Index

Printed in the USA/Agawam, MA
February 5, 2019

696921.002